Frommer's®

W9-BEH-945

7th EDITION

EXPLORING AMERICA by RV

by Shirley Slater & Harry Basch

WILEY

John Wiley & Sons, Inc.

To Joanna Senn, who found RVing a joy for the disabled.

Published by:

John Wiley & Sons, Inc.
111 River St.
Hoboken, NJ 07030-5774

ISBN 978-1-118-08602-5 (paper); 978-1-118-22325-3 (ebk); 978-1-118-23669-7 (ebk); 978-1-118-26163-7 (ebk)

Editor: Kathleen Warnock
Production Editor: Michael Brumitt
Cartographer: Guy Ruggiero
Production by Wiley Indianapolis Composition Services

Author photo by Donna Carroll

Front cover photo: RV in Alaska winding its way up to Thompson Pass; © Alan Majchrowicz/Alamy

Back cover photo: Glen Canyon National Recreation Area, Arizona: Mushroom Rock in fore-ground; © Heeb Christian/Prisma/AGE Fotostock, Inc.

For information on our other products and services or to obtain technical support, please contact our Customer Care Department within the U.S. at 877/762-2974, outside the U.S. at 317/572-3993 or fax 317/572-4002.

Wiley also publishes its books in a variety of electronic formats. Some content that appears in print may not be available in electronic formats.

Manufactured in the United States of America

5 4 3 2 1

CONTENTS

Introduction: The RV Life & Reasons to Hit the Road xi
You Set the Lifestyle xii
RVing for Travelers with Disabilities xiv

PART 1:
GETTING READY TO HIT THE ROAD 1

1 Life on the Road: A Personal & Public History of RVing 3
Excerpts from a Road Diary; or, If We Can Do This, Anyone Can 3
How to Give Backing-Up Directions Without Destroying
　　Your Marriage 7
RV History: The Tin Can Tourists 8
13 Notable Dates in RV History 9
Six Common Misperceptions About RVs & Their Owners 11

2 Getting Prepared: RVing Tips & Hints 13
Driving Schools 13
Learning Your Vital Statistics 13
Making a List, Checking It Twice . . . 14
The Things You Carry: Useful Items to Bring Along 14
What Kind of Wardrobe Is Right? 16
Stocking the Larder 16
Don't Drink the Water 24
Trimming Costs: Eight Money-Saving Tips for the Road 25
Safety, Sanity & Insurance 26
Ain't Misbehavin': Road Etiquette 27
The Community of Man: Getting Together with Other RVers 31

3 Where to Sleep: Campgrounds & RV Parks 35
Campground Glossary 35
Should You Sleep by the Side of the Road? 36
Campsites: The Good, the Bad & the Ugly 37
Revealing the Secrets of the Seasons 38

Using the Directories to Find a Campground 39
10 Ways to Save Money on Campgrounds 41
Membership Campgrounds 43
Special Camping Situations 44
Ain't Misbehavin': Campground Etiquette 46
10 Tips for Cozy Winter Camping 47
Becoming Campground Hosts 48
Plugging in Your Rig 49
Keeping a Clean Machine 50

PART 2:
RV ADVENTURES 53

4 The California Desert & Las Vegas 55
RVing in the California Desert & Las Vegas 55
Travel Essentials 59
The Best Desert Sights, Tastes & Experiences 61
On the Road 67
Fairways & Five-Irons, Desert Style 72
10 Scenic Side Trips 86

5 Utah's Parks & Canyons 91
RVing Utah's National Park Country 95
Travel Essentials 97
The Best Utah Sights, Tastes & Experiences 99
Talkin' Utah: A Glossary 107
On the Road 108
How Nature Painted Zion's Landscape 109
Showtime . . . and a Tasty Dinner, Too! 114
Late-Summer Bonanza: The Cedar Breaks Wildflowers 119
About Edward Abbey 126
11 Scenic Side Trips 130

6 Driving the Alaska Highway 135
RVing Along the Alaska Highway 138
Travel Essentials 140
The Best Alaska Highway Sights, Tastes & Experiences 144
Native Art: Finding the Real Thing 146
A Crash Course in Speaking Alaskan 148

On the Road 150
Seven Tough Side Trips & Three Easy Ones 162

7 **The Dakotas: Black Hills & Buffalo Burgers 165**
RVing the Dakotas 165
Travel Essentials 168
The Best Dakotas Sights, Tastes & Experiences 170
On the Road: South Dakota 182
The Custer Connection 186
South Dakota Nightlife 190
On the Road: North Dakota 192
A Dozen Terrific Side Trips in the Dakotas 198

8 **The Rio Grande Valley & the Wilds of West Texas 201**
RVing Along the Rio Grande 201
Travel Essentials 204
The Best Sights, Tastes & Experiences of the Rio Grande 206
I See by Your Outfit That You Are a Cowboy . . . 208
On the Road 215
Texas Talk 217
The Comanche Moon 220
The Sounds of the Rio Grande 222
Big Bend Wildlife, or How to Avoid an Unpleasant Encounter 224
Five Ways to Enter Terlingua's International Chili Cook-Off 230
Six Special Side Trips 232

9 **In the Heart of the Heartland: Iowa, Illinois & Indiana 235**
RVing in the Heartland 236
Travel Essentials 240
The Best Heartland Sights, Tastes & Experiences 242
On the Road 249
Moonlight Serenade 252
Classic Americana 257
Tender Tenderloins 275
A Box of Popcorn 280

10 **The Florida Keys (with Side Trips to the Everglades & Orlando) 285**
RVing the Keys 285
Travel Essentials 286

The Best Sights, Tastes & Experiences of the Keys 289
Talkin' Conch: A Keys Glossary 293
On the Road 297
And Then I Wrote . . . 306
Two Great Side Trips 308

11 **The Blue Ridge Parkway & Skyline Drive 313**
RVing the Blue Ridge Parkway & Skyline Drive 316
Travel Essentials 316
The Best Blue Ridge Sights, Tastes & Experiences 318
Southern Accents: A Glossary 328
On the Road 329
Celebrating Patsy Cline 330
Country Music's Crooked Road 335
Literary Lights 336
Great Smoky Mountains RV Safety Tips 342

12 **The Lobster Coast: New England &
the Canadian Maritimes 345**
RVing in New England & the Maritimes 346
Travel Essentials 348
Best Sights, Tastes & Experiences of the Lobster Coast (& Inland) 351
Lobster Trivia Quiz 363
The Story Behind PEI's Lobster Suppers 364
On the Road 369
Investing with the Mashantucket Pequots & Mohegans 372
The Museum of Family Camping 374
The Beans of Freeport, Maine (& More) 376
A Dollar Is a Dollar 378
The Loyalists & the Acadians 381
Anne of Green Gables Sites 383
Five Side Trips 384

**PART 3:
HARRY & SHIRLEY'S RV BUYING & RENTING
GUIDE 387**

13 **RV Types & Terms 389**
The ABCs of RVs: A Glossary of Common RV Terms 389
Types of RVs 392

14 **To Rent or Buy? 409**
Two Ways to Check Out Campground Life Without an RV 409
Renting 410
Buying 414
Useful RV Websites 417

Index 419

LIST OF MAPS

California Desert Highlights 56
California/Nevada Desert
  Campgrounds 70
Palm Springs 73
Las Vegas 81
Utah Highlights 92
Southern Utah Campgrounds 111
Zion National Park 112
Bryce Canyon National Park 117
Capitol Reef National Park 123
Canyonlands National Park 125
Northern Utah Campgrounds 131
Alaska Highlights 136
Western Canada Highlights &
  Campgrounds 151
Alaska Campgrounds 155
Denali National Park 159
North Dakota Highlights 167
South Dakota Highlights 169
Little Bighorn Battlefield National
  Monument 185
Black Hills 187
South Dakota Campgrounds 189
Theodore Roosevelt National Park 193
North Dakota Campgrounds 197
South Texas Highlights 202

South Texas Campgrounds 218
Big Bend National Park 225
Iowa Highlights 237
Illinois Highlights 239
Indiana Highlights 241
Iowa Campgrounds 253
Northern Illinois Campgrounds 261
Lincolnland Campgrounds 263
Southern Illinois Campgrounds 267
Southern Indiana Campgrounds 273
Northern/Central Indiana
  Campgrounds 281
Florida Keys Highlights 287
Florida Keys Campgrounds 301
Key West Highlights 303
Everglades National Park
  Campgrounds 309
Orlando/Disney Area Campgrounds 311
Virginia Highlights 315
Blue Ridge Highlights &
  Campgrounds 321
Virginia Campgrounds 333
Highlights of the New England Coast 347
Canadian Maritimes Highlights 350
New England Coast Campgrounds 371
Canadian Maritimes Campgrounds 379

Major Interstate Highways

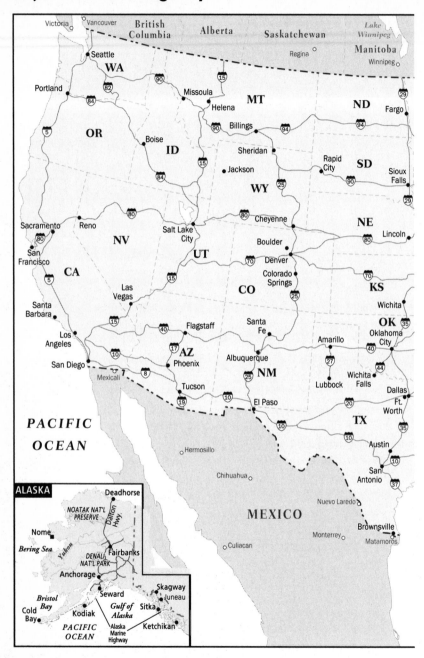

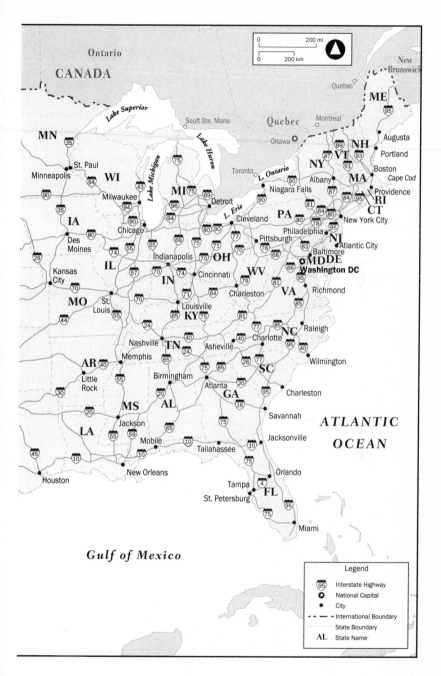

ABOUT THE AUTHORS

Shirley Slater and **Harry Basch** are a husband-and-wife travel writing team whose books, articles, and photographs have been published internationally for more than 30 years. Former stage, film, and television actors, they have written their syndicated column "Cruise Views" for the *Los Angeles Times* and other major newspapers for more than 20 years, produced six annual editions of *The North American Ski Guide* for Prodigy Computer Services, and written *Shirley and Harry's RV Adventures* (a monthly newsletter), plus four books on worldwide cruising.

In 1990, at the 60th World Travel Congress in Hamburg, Germany, the authors were only the third writers (and the first freelancers) to receive the prestigious Melva C. Pederson Award from the American Society of Travel Agents for "extraordinary journalistic achievement in the field of travel."

On assignment for publications as diverse as *Bon Appétit* and *Travel Weekly,* they have covered 188 countries by barge, elephant back, hot-air balloon, luxury cruise ship, cross-country skis, paddle-wheel steamer, and supersonic aircraft, but their favorite method of transportation is by RV. In their first motor home, a 27-foot Winnebago Brave, and their subsequent 36-foot Itasca Sunflyer, they have logged more than 100,000 miles traveling all over the United States, Canada, and Mexico. Aboard other RVs—from mini-motor homes to 36-foot wide-bodies with slide-outs—they have traveled an additional 60,000 miles exploring the back roads and campgrounds of America. The journeys in this book are all based on the authors' personal experiences.

Shirley Slater and Harry Basch inside their RV.

Introduction: The RV Life & Reasons to Hit the Road

THERE'S SOMETHING QUINTESSENTIALLY AMERICAN ABOUT HIT-
ting the road. You can almost hum along as the wheels eat up the highway—"King of
the Road," "Hit the Road, Jack," "On the Road Again," "I've traveled each and every
highway . . . I did it my way."

In an RV (recreational vehicle), you're free of airports, timetables, shuttles, and
public transport. RVers can go anywhere without any advance reservations or preparations and have a good time discovering something new, interesting, or weird about the
world around us.

"On the road" is shorthand for freedom, independence, discovery, self-reliance—
but only if you search out routes that are off the beaten track, with an occasional jaunt
via an interstate to speed through less interesting terrain. As TV's "On the Road"
guru, the late Charles Kuralt, warned, "Thanks to the interstate highway system, it is
now possible to travel from coast to coast without seeing anything." Leave the free-
ways to the truckers, the information highway to the computers, and virtual reality to
the almost alive. With a folding camping trailer, van, travel trailer, truck camper, or
motor home, an RVer can explore firsthand the famous, infamous, and off-the-wall
attractions scattered all over North America, from the legendary Alaska Highway to
Key West, the southernmost point in the United States.

This guidebook picks and chooses overnight oases, from private RV parks with
heated swimming pools and golf courses to quiet, forested campgrounds in state and
national parks. You'll also find offbeat places to eat or pick up tasty treats, including
picking your own farm-fresh fruits and vegetables.

Big cities and famous attractions do not fit our travel style—anyone can find them
(though we do swing by Las Vegas and Orlando with advice tailored specifically for
RVers). Instead, we may opt to retrace the route of the Klondike Gold Rush, trying
our hand at gold-panning; shuffle off to see the buffalo in Custer State Park; or place
a bet at Diamond Tooth Gertie's Casino in the Yukon's Dawson City.

In winter, RVers can learn rock climbing at Joshua Tree National Park or take in the sizzling Terlingua Chili Cook-off in West Texas. In the spring, we set out to catch the dogwoods in bloom in the Blue Ridge Mountains. Late summer is the time to watch an Alaskan grizzly bear as it fishes for spawning salmon, or go rafting on the Colorado River. RVers can hang around New Hampshire in the autumn to sample fresh lobster or see the dazzling display of red and gold leaves, or head south for stone crab season in the Florida Keys.

For some of us, discovering America may happen only after we've had a chance to explore Europe, Asia, Africa, or South America, and that makes the discoveries even richer. Though we'd like to think this book is so riveting you'll read it from cover to cover at one sitting like a mystery novel, we know you'll dip in and out of chapters at random.

And if we seem partial to KOA-member campgrounds, it's because we've learned through our years of travel that we can rely on a certain standard of excellence, toll-free reservations numbers, and a membership card discount.

The important thing, as Robert Louis Stevenson said, is "to travel for travel's sake. The great affair is to move."

John Lennon said, "Life is what happens to you / While you're busy making other plans."

You Set the Lifestyle

Our introduction to RVs was during our many years as actors in film and television programs shot in Hollywood and on location, where the self-contained vehicles are used as dressing rooms. So when we leased a Winnebago motor home in 1992 to research an online ski guide we were producing, it was the first time we had been in an RV that actually moved, let alone under our own nervous control.

But what made us even more nervous than operating the machine itself was what we had always heard termed "the RV lifestyle." The suggestion was that by acquiring a recreational vehicle, you bought into a lifestyle—we pictured communal campfire visits, campground pancake breakfasts, and tours of each other's "rigs," culminating in an annual group caravan tour to some scenic area.

Instead, we quickly learned that while you can participate in group and club activities if you're so inclined, you can also use your recreational vehicle to continue whatever lifestyle you most enjoy.

Because of our intense, high-pressure work as travel writers and performers, constantly on the move and in social situations, when on vacation, we prefer what we call "the Garbo Gourmet Lifestyle." We "want to be alone" with the best food and wine and scenery, to read, go bird-watching or hiking, or listen to music. This doesn't mean we don't enjoy exchanging views with fellow RVers, only that we don't want to feel we *have* to.

It came as a tremendous relief to learn that we were free to do as we pleased. In our first RV journey, 6 weeks on the road all across the United States, nobody came over to urge us to join a club or otherwise identify with some larger group. We did, however, meet some very hospitable individuals, from a campground manager in Independence, Missouri, who taught us, with a flashlight after dark, how to dump the

RV TRIVIA

RV campers drive an average of 4,585 miles a year, spend 28 to 35 nights on the road, and, on a 13-day vacation, spend an average of $250 a day, including meals, gas, and campground fees.

holding tanks we'd been trying to ignore for 3 days, to an exuberant group of hockey fans who shared a keg of beer with us at a campground in LaCrosse, Wisconsin.

The truth is, there's not one RV lifestyle; there are as many lifestyles as there are people who travel in RVs.

Here are a few:

12 PERSONALITIES IDEAL FOR RVS

1. **Garbo Gourmets.** They like to be alone together luxuriating in the best life can offer. They dislike tiptoeing through creaky B&Bs or suffering second-rate food and service at expensive hotels and resorts, preferring to carry their own wine and food, sleep in their own beds, and select their own surroundings by serendipity.

2. **Sportsmen.** Skiers, fishermen, surfers, golfers, and mountain bikers among others want to be in the heart of the action with all the comforts of home, including heating, air-conditioning, and hot showers, plus plenty of storage space to carry fishing rods, skis, golf clubs, and bikes.

3. **Weekenders.** These stressed-out folks want to get out of the rat race and into the countryside to delete the pressures of the workweek from their hard drives. Their RV is always packed for a quick getaway, with only a shopping stop to load up on perishables on the way out of town. TGIF!

4. **Families on Vacation.** They offset a visit to a pricey theme park by traveling with their own budget hotel, with a self-serve restaurant at hand. A comfortable journey for the kids means no more "Are we there yet?" or "I have to go potty!" or "I'm hungry!" Everything they need is in the vehicle. They'll even sit still for an educational journey.

5. **Ecotourists.** They go back to nature the easy way, with dawn bird-watching, twilight wildlife-spotting, photography, and hiking. It places less of a burden on Mother Earth than staying at hotels and resorts with heavy infrastructures.

6. **The Ultimate Shoppers.** They hit all the antiques shops, estate sales, and the biggest swap meets in comfort and style, with room in their vehicle to take their treasures back home.

7. **Relatives, Retirees, and Empty Nesters.** An RV is ideal for family visits, because you bring your own bedroom and bathroom and can even entertain your hosts in your own home on wheels. Conversely, when parked at home, the RV doubles nicely as a guest room and bathroom.

8. **Pet Lovers.** Take Fifi and Fido along for the ride, enjoy their company, and avoid facing rebellious and destructive pets after a spell of boarding them out. Many (but not all) campgrounds welcome pets.

9. **Travelers with Disabilities.** For those who get impatient with the well meaning, but often bungled, accommodations in hotels (from shelves hung out of reach to bathroom doors too narrow to navigate), a customized RV can open up the world with familiar and accessible surroundings. (For more information, see "RVing for Travelers with Disabilities," below.)

10. **Special Events Attendees.** Day or overnight RV trips to jazz festivals, weekend art shows, outdoor dramas, garlic festivals, tailgate parties, jumping frog jubilees, and Civil War reenactments let you sidestep overbooked hotels and restaurants. RVers can take off, even on the spur of the moment, and have bed, bathroom, and breakfast and lunch facilities on the spot.

11. **Snowbirds.** For escaping from −10°F in Minnesota to the balmy Rio Grande Valley of Texas or heading for the high country to get out of summer's heat, an RV makes you a man (or woman) for all seasons.

12. **Full-Timers.** Whether you're quitting the rat race for a season or forever, chasing a dream, or discovering America, an RV is the only way to go.

RVS FOR EVERYONE

Of course, besides these dozen travel styles, there are hundreds more that can be beautifully accommodated by one of the types of available RVs. We've heard about RVers who follow a clothing-optional campground itinerary (yes, Virginia, there are nudist campers); travel newsletter editors who use their RVs as a combination home, office,

RVing for Travelers with Disabilities

RVing makes an enjoyable and easy vacation for travelers with disabilities, particularly those who use a wheelchair, as long as the camping units are configured to take care of the chair's width and turning radius and are free of steps or level differences inside. A few manufacturers providing equipment for RVers with disabilities are Foretravel, Play-Mor, and Winnebago; some dealers also rent RVs which are equipped for travelers with disabilities. For more information, you can write **GO RVing**, 1896 Preston White Dr., Reston, VA 20191, or visit their website (**www.gorving.org/pubs/rvs_for_ the_disabl_1.cfm**).

Clubs for RVers with disabilities include **Handicapped Travel Club,** 604 Twilight St., Placentia, CA 92870 (www.handicappedtravelclub.com), and **SATH,** formerly the **Society for the Advancement of Travel for the Handicapped,** 347 Fifth Ave., Ste. 605, New York, NY 10016 (✆ **212/447-7284;** www.sath.org).

and research vehicle; spa-goers who tootle from one hot spring to another; singles of both sexes who opt for the wandering life of a loner without a look back; and leaf peepers who live from one fall foliage tour to the next.

The vehicle adjusts to you and becomes an extension of your own life and travel style. It is simply a means to an end, a very well-designed and comfortable way to access the wilderness, nature, sightseeing, going to the sun, heading for the beach, the mountains, the woods—whatever will make you happy and enhance your life. It's your dream; you call the shots.

Campers have always found a sense of accomplishment in day-to-day survival: cooking food over a fire, finding a comfortable place to sleep, protecting oneself from the sun, rain, heat, or cold. With RVs, everything is less work-intensive, without taking away the sense of self-reliance, by having along everything you need for survival. Celebrities from Loretta Lynn to Danny DeVito, Michael Douglas to Matthew McConaughey, John Madden to Bruce Willis are RV owners who use their vehicles for both business and pleasure. More than one film megastar has had a contract sweetened with the perk of a big-bucks motor home, used as a private location dressing room during the shoot and given as a gift at the end of filming.

Many pro golfers have taken to the RV for the tour because it allows them to travel with their families and not have to deal with the hassles of hotels, airports, or lost clubs. Rory Sabbatini says, "Now my wife and son come with me on tour. That has allowed me to relax and play more events without getting fatigued or stressed out."

But much as we love RVing, something we had never really anticipated before we tried it, we also will admit that perhaps not everyone is an ideal candidate for life on the road. If your idea of the perfect vacation is to check into a luxury resort and phone for room service, you may not be ready for an RV—that is, unless you have a mate who loves to wait on you.

A QUICK DO-IT-YOURSELF QUIZ TO TEST YOUR RVC (RECREATIONAL VEHICLE COMPATIBILITY)

1. Do you ever sing along with "My Way," "On the Road Again," or "King of the Road"?

2. Have you ever considered getting a second vacation home, but can't decide between the mountains or the seashore?

3. Do you like to putter around the house or spend an entire Saturday morning browsing the shelves of a hardware store?

4. Did you ever envy Jack Kerouac, William Least Heat Moon, or Charles Kuralt, even a little bit?

5. Do you dislike timetables and schedules, the hurry-up-and-wait routine of catching a flight, and bumper-to-bumper commutes?

6. Are you tired of dress codes in restaurants that want men to wear a jacket and tie and women to wear a skirt?

7. Do you dislike using public toilets and showers, or wonder who slept in that motel bed the night before you?

8. Could you find paradise with "a loaf of bread, a jug of wine and thou / Beside me in the wilderness"?

9. Does the smoky smell of a campfire, a charred hot dog, or a burned marshmallow turn you on?

10. Are you susceptible to serendipity and doing things on a whim, like turning down a side road that seems to call to you, buying something offbeat that instantly becomes a favorite possession, or striking up a conversation with an interesting looking stranger who turns out to be a friend forever after?

If you answered "yes" to any 1 of the 10 questions, you might consider trying out an RV by rental. See chapter 14, "To Rent or Buy?" for details.

If you answered "yes" to 5 or more of the 10 questions, check out chapter 13, "RV Types & Terms."

If you answered "yes" to all 10 questions, what are you waiting for? Hit the road, Jack!

If you answered "no" to all 10 questions, you still haven't wasted your money. Thumb to one of the following chapters, grab your car keys and a lodging guide, or settle down in an easy chair, and set out on one of our roving RV adventures for a fast and funny look at weird, wonderful America.

Getting Ready to Hit the Road

Words of Wisdom on Preparing for Life on the Road and in the Campgrounds

1. Life on the Road: A Personal & Public History of RVing

2. Getting Prepared: RVing Tips & Hints

3. Where to Sleep: Campgrounds & RV Parks

Life on the Road: A Personal & Public History of RVing

AMERICANS ARE A RESTLESS PEOPLE, CONSTANTLY ON THE MOVE, always expecting greener grass and greater opportunities over the next hill, beyond the horizon. For our predecessors, the covered wagon served as a traveling home, despite its lack of luxury. Tent camping provided a little more comfort for exploring America, but still slowed down the footloose wanderers.

Once the automobile came into everyday use, pioneering RVers didn't wait for specialty camping vehicles to be invented—they began to create their own motor homes just after the turn of the 20th century, in 1901. We discovered RVing in the early 1990s and, after an initial shakedown period, learned to love our life on the road. Our only regret now is that we didn't start earlier.

Excerpts from a Road Diary; or, If We Can Do This, Anyone Can

After more than 25 years on the road as travel writers, we've taken just about every mode of transportation known to man, including hot-air balloons, elephants, and dugout canoes. But our lives changed when we set out for the first time in an RV, a leased 27-foot Winnebago Brave motor home, on a 6-week trip. We visited more than 100 remote ski areas all over the United States in order to research a guidebook.

In an earlier life, as film and television actors, we spent many long days in RVs changing clothes and studying scripts—they are used as dressing rooms on film locations and studio sound stages—but we had never been in one that actually *moved*. In selecting an RV, we took into account what we could deal with in terms of the size of both the inside and outside spaces; then we compromised. Here are some notes from that first time, written in the passion of the moment.

AUGUST 12

At the California dealer from which we are leasing the motor home, a young man named Daryll, with sun-bleached, shoulder-length hair and a (first) Persian Gulf War T-shirt, walks us through the RV, noting how easy everything is and how nothing can go wrong. We nod wisely and make frantic scribbled notes like "circuit breaker and fuses in bedroom" and "generator runs off gas tanks" and "water pump—switch off while moving." When he leaves us alone for a while, we go into a frenzy of measuring and drawing diagrams.

AUGUST 14

The day before we are scheduled to leave, we lay out newspaper sections on the floor of our apartment, folded to fit the measurements of the RV's cupboards. Then we set out the items we intend to put in each cupboard and pack only those items in a box labeled for it.

AUGUST 15

Unfortunately, life isn't that rational and orderly. On packing day, we are forced to double-park in our crowded urban neighborhood and carry boxes of books, cartons of pots and pans, and hangers of clothes back and forth from our apartment to the street. One of us keeps a constant eye on everything so nothing is stolen, dumping things wherever there is space in the RV, most of it on the plastic-wrapped mattress and in the bathroom shower.

When Daryll saw us off at the dealer's, he turned on the generator so the rooftop air-conditioner could cool down the interior and chill the refrigerator and freezer, but neglected to tell us whether to keep it on while driving, or turn it off. At some point, we remember him saying it's capable of running 16 hours straight with no problem, so we leave it on.

The soothing noise from the air-conditioner drowns out many of the small crashes and thuds from the back as our possessions settle in on their own, with only an occasional loud *thunk* causing us to glance furtively backward.

AUGUST 15 (FROM THE DRIVER'S SEAT)

The first impression is that you're way above the traffic and at the same time divorced from the road itself. Suddenly, you realize you're looking down at the middle of your lane and half your vehicle is in the next lane. To keep from slipping over into an adjacent lane, you have to hug the left-lane line. The back of the vehicle seems to have a mind of its own and wants to turn at a shorter distance than does the front end. We soon learn to make wide turns, particularly to the right. Another problem is that at any bump or rut, the vehicle leans to the right or left, then rolls back to the other side. Our fingers and arms are stiff from white-knuckling the wheel after several hours.

AUGUST 15 (NIGHTFALL)

It is after dark when we stop for gas in Kingman, Arizona, and Harry goes into a state of shock as he watches the numbers on the tank turn and turn and turn, as gallon after gallon flows in. The pump turns off automatically at $50 and the tank still isn't full. (Obviously, this was some time ago!)

Exhausted, we agree it's time to stop. In front of us, between the gas station and the freeway, is an RV campground—we can see the sign—but we can't figure out how to get to it since a used-car lot and a mall are in the way. (About now, we give up the fantasy of waking to birdsong and the breeze wafting through the pine trees.)

Not far away, we find a second campground and something better than bird-song—a space called a "pull-through," which means we can drive the motor home in one side, plug it in, and then drive out the other side the next morning without backing up—something we haven't learned how to do yet. We begin to speed-read the instruction manual and learn that it is necessary to turn off the generator before plugging in the electricity. That part is a snap—our plug fits into the campground's receptacle.

We make a long, fruitless search by flashlight through the outdoor storage bins for a hose so we can hook up the water connection. (Harry is positive Daryll pointed one out, but Shirley thinks Harry has located the sewage hose instead. Harry thinks that maybe we should get a divorce or at least go check into a motel with running water. As it turns out, we have plenty of water in the storage tanks without having to use the external hookup.)

We studiously ignore the sewage hookup. The refrigerator has been turned down to the coldest setting—obviously, Daryll wanted it to get chilled quickly—and we find frozen romaine lettuce, eggs, and chicken breasts inside. Instead of a gourmet dinner, we settle for soup warmed in the microwave.

Stunned, almost stupid with exhaustion, we wash the dishes, close the blinds and curtains, and move back to the bedroom to make up the bed. Clearing it is easier than we expect, since most of the gear piled on the bed has already fallen onto the floor.

We raise the mattress to remove its plastic cover, and the hinged supports lock into the open position, leaving the bed set at a rakish 45-degree angle. By this time we're so tired that we probably could sleep in it anyhow, but we get out the toolbox and unscrew the supports so we can flatten the mattress. Somehow we manage to simultaneously make up the bed and fall asleep in it!

AUGUST 16

The skies have opened up in the high desert of western New Mexico, dumping so much water in the streets of Socorro that the intersections are flooded ankle-deep. Although our campground guidebook promises there is an RV park in town, we spot the flickering light of a Motel 6 just ahead and, with no discussion, pull in behind a battered truck camper from Texas. If the veterans can't weather the storm, we amateurs can't be expected to either.

AUGUST 17

The sun comes out. We stop at a hardware store and buy a water hose, which we hook up, but for some reason it never fills the tank. Later, we realize we hooked the water hose to the outside connection that feeds water directly into the system. While we're still not able to make the TV work, we've gotten very good at plugging in the electric cord, once we realize our large three-prong plug has to fit into a three-prong 30-amp receptacle.

We studiously ignore the sewage hookup.

AUGUST 18

While checking out the ski resort at Crested Butte, we make a left turn uphill into the parking garage of the Grande Butte Hotel, which causes the tow-bar connection at the rear of the motor home to drag and stick fast in the asphalt. The concierge arrives and says a Greyhound bus got stuck there only last week, and then asks if she should call the tow truck again. Harry congratulates himself on taking out Auto Club emergency insurance, and the tow truck duly frees us. We vow never again to turn into a hotel driveway that heads uphill.

AUGUST 19

In the ski town of Breckenridge, we spot a locksmith standing beside his truck talking to a pretty blonde, and ask if he could help us get into our outdoor storage area because either the lock is broken or the key doesn't fit. The locksmith takes one look at the key and says we're using it upside down. At Dillon Reservoir, we settle down to lunch beside the lake, opening a couple of the roof vents for air, when a sudden gust of wind tears across the roof of the motor home and takes off one of the white plastic roof vents. Harry chases it down and climbs on the roof to replace it, just as the rain begins. At a nearby gas station, we buy a roll of duct tape and batten down the vent. We vow never again to open the roof vents on a windy day.

AUGUST 20

We get lost in Kansas City looking for Arthur Bryant's famous barbecue restaurant, so it is once again after dark when we check into a small RV campground in Independence. A kindly campground manager with a flashlight loans us a sewage hose (ours is too short for the hookup) and talks us step-by-step through the dumping procedure for the holding tanks, which have reached their capacity. The same helpful manager shows us where to push a black button that activates the TV set.

Harry, I don't think we're in Kansas anymore.

AUGUST 27

It is almost with a sense of relief that we return to Winnie (for some reason, we have begun calling the vehicle that lately) after staying overnight in the lavish West Virginia country cottage of some friends. Their gardens are lovely and their hospitality warm, but Winnie has become home.

AUGUST 29

It has taken us 2 weeks to discover why the bedroom in the back of the motor home gets so hot while we're traveling, then cools down once we stop for the night. It turns out Harry thought that a control switch was turned off, only it wasn't! It was actually the "low" setting for the bedroom heater.

SEPTEMBER 1

There is great comfort in riding along and listening to the sounds inside the motor home behind us. We recognize the sharp clatter of the cutlery drawer suddenly swinging open, the more subdued sounds of the mug of wooden utensils spilling onto the stove top, and the rolling thud of the canned foods swaying back and forth in their bin. Then there's the rattle when the bedroom blinds come unhooked from their pins and are swaying, the bump when a camera forgotten and left on a chair falls onto the floor and breaks its wide-angle lens, and the swishing sound of the cardboard box containing water jugs sliding on the plastic floor covering. (We did not remove the plastic over the carpeting, figuring that was one way to keep it cleaner inside.)

After we have the bed supports repaired, the bed develops a mind of its own and pops up occasionally, as if to have a look around.

SEPTEMBER 15

We drive into Yellowstone Park, suddenly aware of how special it is to travel in a motor home with wide scenic views through the big windows, as if we're looking down from a high bus seat. Herds of bison shamble around in the roadway, in no hurry, and our vantage point is ideal for photographing them. We stop for lunch by the Yellowstone River in a grove of trees, their leaves turned golden, and for the first time, discuss buying a motor home of our own.

SEPTEMBER 27

Partly because we despair of ever having to unpack Winnie, we buy her from the dealer. That was well over 100,000 miles ago. Winnie served us well for a number of years, and then was replaced by an Itasca Sunflyer.

How to Give Backing-Up Directions Without Destroying Your Marriage

Whenever possible, request a pull-through campsite and postpone the agony of a back-in site as long as possible.

When no pull-throughs are available, we prefer to start with a quick chat about the broad general aims of the driver, particularly in regard to where the RV will end up, along with some general observations about the presence of boulders, picnic tables, and low-hanging tree limbs. Unfortunately, if the vehicle is blocking campground traffic, this prologue step has to be eliminated.

It is critical to establish a mutual signal that means "Stop immediately before you back into that _____" (fill in as applicable: truck, tree, utility post, fence, fire grate, and so on).

The first step is for the signaler to learn to stand where the driver can see him or her in the side mirror. The same rule applies here as for cameras: If you can see the mirror, the driver can see you.

Next, the signals should be clear and decisive. The fewer signals used, the simpler it usually becomes. We use a two-hand beckoning signal for "keep coming back," a right-hand signal to move toward the right, a left-hand signal to move toward the left, and a dramatic thrust of hand up and palm open toward the driver that means "For God's sake, stop!"

If all else fails, you still have a couple of options: Invest in a closed-circuit TV backup system (which are now standard on some higher end RVs) that shows the driver exactly what is behind the RV as he or she backs—expensive, but effective (although these, too, have their limitations)—or a walkie-talkie system, with one unit in the cockpit and the second hand-held. If you do this, get one with more than a single channel. It seems like everybody and his brother have the same one-channel system, and you'll wind up having overlapping conversations with your neighbors.

RV History: The Tin Can Tourists

They called themselves "Tin Can Tourists." They braved the dust and mud to drive their tin lizzies across the United States before transcontinental roads were paved, camping by the side of the road, heating tin cans of food on a gasoline stove, and bathing in cold water.

They dressed in their Sunday clothes in the days before jogging suits and running shoes. A photograph of one 1920s camping club reveals owners in front of their Weidman Camp Body vehicles, the men in fedoras, suits, and ties, and the women in dresses, cloche hats, stockings, and high-heeled shoes.

It took ingenuity to travel across the country in those days before the first motel, which opened in 1925 in California. In 1921, for instance, Lee Scoles of Fort Wayne, Indiana, converted his 1916 Federal truck to "a house on wheels" and drove it on an 8-month, round-trip journey to San Francisco with 11 relatives aboard. Such additions as solid rubber tires, a canvas awning, cots, a stove, and washtubs added to their comfort, according to his granddaughter Alice Worman, herself a motor home owner, who chronicled the story in *Lifestyles,* one of many such publications dedicated to RVing.

According to a story in *RV West* magazine, the family of Charles Ulrich set out for California in 1929 in a General Motors truck body mounted on a Ford chassis, with built-in bunks, overhead wardrobe storage areas, and a dining table with six folding chairs. The interior was polished mahogany and on the rear was a caboose-type open platform with iron railings. After their "once-in-a-lifetime" trip, which continued on to Hawaii aboard a Matson Line cruise ship, the Ulrichs stored the camper until the 1960s, when it was purchased by a group of hunters to serve as a forest base camp.

A fire-engine-red 1929 Ford Model A converted to a mini–motor home camper complete with pop-up top still carries the Ray Glenn family on trips around the Seattle area, according to *MotorHome* magazine.

Originally, auto camping was regarded as a rich man's hobby. The well-publicized outings of auto manufacturer Henry Ford, inventor Thomas Edison, naturalist John Burroughs, and tire manufacturer Harvey Firestone, who called themselves "the four vagabonds" as they camped in America's parks, had paved the way. Interestingly, the affordability and popularity of Henry Ford's Model T, which debuted in 1909, helped to bring auto camping to the average American.

Nobody knows more about the early history of recreational vehicles than David Woodworth of Tehachapi, California, who owns the largest collection of antique camping equipment, photography, and literature known to exist. Much of his material appeared in the Smithsonian Institution's 1986 show "At Home on the Road," which he helped to produce.

Alaska-born Woodworth attributes his fascination with RVs to his childhood memories, when his family traveled around the country in a Detroiter travel trailer, following his carpenter father from job to job.

At RV shows and state fairs, he exhibits vehicles like his Art Deco–style 1937 Hunt House Car, designed and manufactured by a Hollywood cinematographer and inventor named J. Roy Hunt. (Among Hunt's many credits was the classic 1929 film *The Virginian,* starring Gary Cooper.)

13 Notable Dates in RV History

1901 (or so): The first motor homes are built as special-order units by auto-body builders.

1907: Henry Ford introduces the first mass-produced Model T Fords, automobiles with a 2.9-liter, four-cylinder engine, which make auto camping affordable for most Americans for the first time.

1910–15: The first manufactured, mass-produced RVs—folding camping trailers—start coming off the line from Los Angeles Trailer Works, Auto-Kamp Trailers in Saginaw, Michigan, and other pioneers.

1917: The first fifth-wheel trailer is built by airplane manufacturer Curtiss-Wright; its name probably originated from the trailer hitch, which is located in the center of the towing truck's bed and could be considered a "fifth" wheel after the four on the bottom of the trailer unit.

1919: The Tin Can Tourists gather for their first rally, in a Florida campground near Tampa called DeSoto Park, with 20 members present, most of them Model T owners; by the mid-1930s, the club numbers 150,000.

1922: Fifteen million auto campers hit the road, according to the *New York Times,* most of them sleeping on cots, in tents, or in "newfangled houses on wheels."

1923: There are 7,000 free campgrounds in the United States, including Denver's Overland Park, with 800 campsites, piped water, a garage, restaurant, beauty shop, billiards hall, soda fountain, and eight electric washing machines.

1926: Fords equipped with Weidman Camp Bodies are first produced in Tonawanda, New York; the 1929 model sells for $1,900.

1962: John Steinbeck publishes *Travels with Charley,* a book about his RV journey around America with his elderly poodle.

1966: Winnebago becomes the first mass-production motor home assembly line, turning out its early models (with moldings above the windshield that resembled eyebrows) in lengths of 17, 19, and 22 feet.

1966: David Garvin begins selling RV parts and camping accessories at his family's campground in Bowling Green, Kentucky; by 1993, his chain of Camping World stores (which he calls "Toys 'R' Us for grown-ups") has become the world's largest retailer of camping supplies, with 29 stores, 10 million mail-order catalogs distributed annually, and a sales base of $150 million.

1967: Charles Kuralt rents a Dodge motor home to begin broadcasting "On the Road," his famous CBS-TV series of news features that bring small-town Americans and their stories into the living rooms of people everywhere. During his 27 years on the road, Kuralt uses six different motor homes; the last, a 29-foot FMC motor coach, is in the Henry Ford Museum near Detroit.

1976: Winnebago Industries introduces the Heli-Home, a helicopter camper for off-road exploration, which can sleep six; we note that it's no longer included in their published brochures.

The sleek, 19-foot, teardrop-shaped motor home, crafted on a Ford truck chassis and powered by a Ford flathead V-8 engine, includes a bathroom with hand-pumped shower, lavatory, and toilet (which must be manually removed to empty); a stove with two burners; an icebox; a sofa and a dinette (both of which convert to beds); and even a kitchen sink.

Woodworth proudly claims membership in the Tin Can Tourists, whose last surviving affiliates have appointed him "Grand Can Opener."

Among the 30 or so antique camping vehicles in Woodworth's collection are 1928 and 1931 Covered Wagon Travel Trailers, manufactured in Detroit; a 1935 York Rambler built in York, Pennsylvania; a Hays from Grand Rapids, Michigan; and a Harley Bowless, created by the builder who oversaw the construction of Charles Lindbergh's historic transatlantic aircraft, the *Spirit of St. Louis.* Airstream later used the Harley Bowless as an inspiration for its famous aerodynamic travel trailer back in 1936, according to Woodworth.

Woodworth can also spout nonstop historical information about auto camping and the early campers. Here are some of his revelations:

- The first campgrounds were free, built and maintained by cities and towns hoping to attract affluent travelers with disposable income. In the days before World War I, only the wealthy had the time and money to go auto camping. When Ford's Model T made auto camping affordable for everyone, campgrounds started charging fees to discourage some of the overflow crowds.

- One early pair of auto campers was a couple who were afraid their new travel trailer might pull the rear end off their car, so the husband drove the car and the wife sat in the trailer for the entire journey, watching the car's rear end to make sure nothing happened to it.

- Highways were notoriously bad in the early days. Woodworth quotes from the memoirs of some 1924 auto campers who termed themselves "Modern Gypsies" and wrote about a local resident telling them, "That's a good road; somebody just

INSIDER TIP

The **Museum of Family Camping** in Bear Brook State Park (exit Rte. 28, then turn right on the road after the toll booth), 157 Deerfield Rd., Allenstown, NH (© **603/485-3782;** www. ucampnh.com/museum/Welcome.html), includes "typical campsites" from each decade of camping, as well as photographs and taped reminiscences of old-timers. Its Hall of Fame commemorates such pioneers as Airstream's Wally Byam, who organized and led camping caravans all over the world. Memorial Day to Labor Day, daily 10am to 4pm. Free admission; donations accepted.

made it through there yesterday." Later, he says, the travelers commented, "When we left New York for Chicago, we were motorists. When we left Chicago for California, we were pioneers."

Six Common Misperceptions About RVs & Their Owners

As Gary Cooper said in the movie *The Virginian,* "When you call me that, smile!" Because we enjoy our freewheeling life on the road so much, we shudder at every false stereotype perpetuated by some uninformed person. Here, then, are a few common misperceptions, followed by the reality.

• **Misperception No. 1:** We find misperceptions particularly hard to take when the perpetrator is a fellow travel writer who should know his nomenclature. A writer in a popular travel magazine, who described driving in Utah, noted that Arches National Park "makes even the most remote rock formations visible to wheezing geezers willing to take a short walk from motor home to overlook." (The same writer spent much of his article bragging about the speed of his $40,000 Nissan Infiniti on the empty highways and complaining about the dearth of gas stations and fast-food outlets in southern Utah.) **Reality:** *Puh-leeze,* wheeze, us no geezers! A Recreation Vehicle Industry Association (RVIA) study states that the average RV owner is 49 years old, married with children, owns his own home, and has a household income of around $68,000 a year. At present, 1 of every 12 motor-vehicle-owning families in the United States has an RV. In the 35-to-54-year age group, it's 1 out of every 9. In fact, the RVers between ages 35 and 54 outnumber those older than 55. During the next decade, the highest RV ownership category by age will be college-educated baby boomers between ages 55 and 64. At present, there are 8.2 million RVs on the road in the U.S.

• **Misperception No. 2:** Another writer, describing a lonely highway he drove, says he met "only a few Winnebagos" along the way. **Reality:** While he might have met a series of RVs that were produced by Iowa-based Winnebago Industries, he probably used the term Winnebago to mean recreational vehicles. While all Winnebagos are RVs, not all RVs are Winnebagos. Out of today's 64 million campers, nearly half use a recreational vehicle.

• **Misperception No. 3:** A real-estate developer friend inquiring politely about our RV passion asked about our "mobile home" and was startled to be so instantly and vehemently corrected. **Reality:** Our motor home is not a "mobile home." The latter is not a recreational vehicle, but manufactured residential housing that is infrequently moved after initially being set in place.

• **Misperception No. 4:** Well-meaning environmentalists like to say that, unlike backpacking and tent camping, RVing pollutes the environment and guzzles gas and water resources. **Reality:** Having graduated from the ranks of backpackers and tent campers, we're acutely aware of this "purist" attitude. A Recreation Vehicle Industry Association (RVIA) poll shows that 98% of all RVers practice one or more forms of "green" RVing. In our case, our low-water toilet and quick showers use much less water than public facilities in the parks. We put all waste-water into holding tanks and then properly empty them at dump stations, rather than pouring anything on the ground or into streams. We never build a campfire that leaves layers of pollution hanging in the atmosphere, never dig up the ground or tie anything to trees and bushes, and recycle everything possible. RVing is probably very "green" when compared to other travel, such as flying by plane or staying in hotels (all that water to wash linens and take showers).

- **Misperception No. 5:** According to a University of Michigan study, some 14% of all potential RVers believe their state requires a special license to drive an RV. **Reality:** No state requires a special license to operate an RV; your normal driver's license is all you need.

- **Misperception No. 6:** When city officials of the former naval base town of Port Hueneme in Southern California proposed to bolster the town's sagging econ-omy by building an oceanfront luxury RV resort, the proposal passed. It hap-pened despite a handful of residents at a town meeting, who claimed "typical" RVers are "homeless, jobless, use drugs, commit crimes, belong to gangs, and desecrate any area they happen to park in," according to a journalist on the scene. **Reality:** Wow! And we thought our neighbors in the next campsite were just toasting marshmallows!

2 Getting Prepared: RVing Tips & Hints

THE FIRST TIME WE SET OUT IN AN RV, WE DEVOTED AS MUCH attention to it as the Allies planning D-day, and had about as much success as Napoleon at Waterloo. Now, we can decide on the spur of the moment to go away for a few days, pick up the RV keys, and set out. In this chapter, we'll discuss some of the nuts and bolts of life on the road so that you, too, can overcome disorganization and have the courage to just hit the road.

Driving Schools

While most confident (or overconfident) drivers pick up RV-wrangling fairly quickly, if you want to acquire some certifiable, professional RV-driving skills, contact Dennis Hill at **RV Driving School: 119 Rainbow Dr., Livingston, TX 77399 (✆ 530/878-0111;** www.rvschool.com). Dennis is a longtime RVer and instructor who recently took over the school from founder Dick Reed. The classes cover the use of mirrors, driving defensively, courtesy, backing into campsites, safety checks, and braking and control. Students may learn on their own rigs or on those belonging to the school. Driving seminars are also given at the Los Angeles RV Show each October at the Fairplex in Pomona. Classes are taught at training locations in southern and northern California, Arizona, Texas, and Florida. One private lesson is 2 days long. Each day consists of 4 hours of training, and the total lesson costs $475; 1 day (3½ hr.) is $295. Discounts are available to members of certain organizations (such as Good Sam, Escapees, FMCA, AAA, AARP, and SMART).

Your local RV dealer may also provide such instruction or be aware of an RV driving school in your area.

Learning Your Vital Statistics

As beginners, our lack of technical knowledge was most frightening the first time we encountered a narrow, rickety, one-lane bridge near New Harmony, Indiana, with a small sign noting its weight limit was 5 tons. But how much did our RV weigh? We didn't know. Finally, since there was no way to turn around and go back, and the traffic was beginning to build up behind us, we gingerly inched our way across, holding our breath until we made it.

Making a List, Checking It Twice . . .

It's a good idea for beginning RVers to make up a checklist to follow when packing for a trip, preparing the vehicle, or when setting up and breaking up camp. Some veterans laminate the list, then check off the items in grease pencil or erasable marker so it can be wiped clean to use again. 🚐

Later, we studied the brochure that detailed our floor plan and learned that our maximum weight fully loaded and with passengers could be just over 12,000 pounds, or 6 tons.

The moral: Memorize your height, weight, and width before getting behind the wheel.

Before August 2000, the following terms were used on the weight information sheets provided with new vehicles:

- **GVW (Gross Vehicle Weight):** Total weight of a fully equipped and loaded RV with passengers, gas, oil, water, and baggage; must not be greater than the vehicle's GVWR.

- **GVWR (Gross Vehicle Weight Rating):** The amount of total loaded weight a vehicle can support; determined by the manufacturer, this amount must not be exceeded.

- **Dry Weight:** The weight of the RV without fluids such as gas, oil, and water added.

Beginning in August 2000, new terms were added:

- **UVW (Unloaded Vehicle Weight):** The weight with full fuel, water, propane, driver, and passengers.

- **CCC (Cargo Carrying Capacity):** The maximum permissible weight of all pets, belongings, food, tools, and other supplies you can carry in your motor home. This is the GVWR minus the UVW.

- **GAWR (Gross Axle Weight Rating):** The maximum permissible weight that can be carried by each axle with weight evenly distributed throughout the vehicle.

- **GCWR (Gross Combination Weight Rating):** The maximum allowable loaded weight of the motor home with towables.

The Things You Carry: Useful Items to Bring Along

A big difference exists between what you *have* to carry and what you *want* to carry, but some so-called optional items have become essentials to us:

- **Binoculars** are important for helping you see a great distance ahead on the road to determine whether you need to be in the right or left lane for a turn or to access or exit the interstate, to figure out which service station on the exit road has the lowest gas prices, and to read the highway signs ahead when you're look-ing for an address.

- A folding, artificial-grass **cloth or mat** large enough to go under the picnic table and around the entrance to the RV helps keep sand and dirt from being tracked in. It also makes a dirt or sand campsite seem more hospitable.

- **Folding outdoor chairs** are a must, because some campgrounds provide no outside table or furniture. We also carry small folding tables, so we can have snacks, drinks, or lunch outside even without a picnic table.

- We always take some sort of **grill** along for outdoor cooking. Although some campgrounds and many public parks provide grills, they're often so rusty and dirty that you won't want to put food directly on them. You can, however, carry a wire grill that looks like a popcorn popper with a sliding wire top to keep the food inside. We find that carrying a portable grill is easier. We started with one of the cheap charcoal grills that you can buy in most supermarkets or hardware stores and then graduated to a propane-fired portable grill with a lid that sits atop a folding base. Neither the charcoal grill nor the propane-fired grill requires an electric hookup. Now we also carry a new electric grill (which uses the same base) with a lid, because the grill cook thinks it's easier to clean up afterward.

- In the kitchen, a **burner igniter**, which sparks to light the propane stove burners, is easier and cleaner to use than matches. You may not need one, however, if your RV has an igniting device built into the cooktop.

- Because picnic tables provided in most campgrounds have seen plenty of wear and tear and may be dusty and pocked with bird droppings, we carry a small **whisk broom** to brush the table and seats, a plastic **tablecloth** held down with clamps, and plastic **bench covers** with tie-ons to secure them. These items are sold in camping supply stores.

- Because we work on the road, our **office supplies** are always packed in the draw-ers near the bedroom desk and in small plastic stacking bins that fit under the kneehole of the desk. We always make sure to have Post-it notes, envelopes in several sizes, pens, pencils, staples, highlighters, and paper—everything we have in our home office but in smaller quantities.

- We like to take **games and puzzles** along for lazy days in camp. Our chess set and Scrabble board are travel editions—they're smaller and easier to store than the standard issue. The Scrabble game even has little indentations to hold each letter on the board so that bumping or jarring doesn't upset the game. With the chess set, however, we bought a travel set with a durable folding wooden board that stores the pieces inside, but then we exchanged the lightweight pieces that came with the game for heavier-than-normal pieces so they stay in place if we're playing outdoors on a windy day.

  Jigsaw puzzles are a favorite pastime, and after we finish one, we usually donate it to the game room of whatever campground we're occupying at the time. Occa-sionally, the time to move on comes before a puzzle is finished or we start putting it together outside on the picnic table but don't finish before dark. That's when puzzle caddies or felt cloths come in handy; you can fold up the puzzle carefully with all the pieces inside, store it, and unfold it somewhere else later on.

• When traveling with children and/or pets, be sure to pack all their favorite **play-things** and **security blankets**.

What Kind of Wardrobe Is Right?

Like most RVers, we have a wardrobe stowed in our motor home to cover any situation we may encounter on the road, from an impromptu dinner in a fine restaurant to cold-weather camping or white-water rafting.

Since wardrobe and drawer space is fairly limited, except in the largest motor homes and fifth-wheels, you'll want to confine your carry-along wardrobe to a few carefully selected basics, adding seasonal or special apparel when the journey requires it.

We concentrate on basic clothing that is machine washable, stretchable with elastic waists, and a comfortable fit, in styles and colors that will harmonize with other items in the closet. For cold-weather camping, even in parts of the California desert in winter, a set of silk long underwear is invaluable under sweatshirts and pants. A loose cotton gauze or linen shirt and a pair of shorts are always on hand for unusually hot weather, like the heat wave we encountered in New England one summer.

A spare pair of hiking or jogging shoes is handy, along with a comfortable pair of slippers for the evenings after outside chores are finished. We each take one pair of slightly worn but acceptable dress-up shoes, along with one business or evening outfit, in case of an important appointment en route. Anyone planning to use the public showers in the campground should also take a pair of shower shoes.

Several changes of underwear, socks, and pajamas, along with a bathrobe, are folded and tucked into nightstand drawers beside the bed. We even carry spare bottles of prescription medication and a full supply of toiletries so we can slip away on the spur of the moment, yet still have everything we need. (If you do this, check regularly to make sure your medications haven't expired.)

Knit clothes that can be folded and stacked rather than put on a hanger take up less room and don't need ironing. We often take travel- or sample-size toiletries, stowing them at home in a special RV box that's ready to be taken along on the next trip.

On our initial 6-week journey, we took far too many clothes, forgetting that a lot of campgrounds have Laundromats and that items of clothing can be worn more than once. The other thing to remember is that in a campground, nobody pays much attention to what anyone wears anyway.

Stocking the Larder

Because we use our RV all year, we keep it stocked with nonperishables that are always ready to go and need only be supplemented with fresh food, ice, and water before we set off for a weekend. But since even canned goods should not be stored for a long period of time, we mark the date of purchase on top of each can with an indelible marker and use them in order of age.

A cook's kitchen on the road may have fresh herbs and a food processor.

Particularly in warm weather, we avoid leaving open cardboard packages of crackers, flour, or cornmeal in the RV. We store small amounts of dried beans, rice, and grains in screw-top jars or resealable plastic bags, along with coffee beans and sugar. Open bottles of olive oil, mustard, or mayonnaise are brought back home at the end of each outing, to be replaced by other small, unopened containers on the next trip. All bottles of wine are returned home at the end of every trip, but liquors can usually be stored in the vehicle between trips.

Because we both enjoy cooking for ourselves, we include among our permanent equipment a food processor, spice rack, and pots of fresh herbs (which go back home btw. journeys).

A large, French enameled cast-iron soup pot, which doubles as a spaghetti pot, is the biggest item in our cookware collection. It is accompanied by several smaller, nonstick-enameled, cast-iron skillets and pans, a small whistling tea kettle, an earthenware teapot that travels in an old-fashioned, padded tea cozy, and several microwaveable measuring cups and dishes. We've also added a pressure cooker, which cuts down on cooking time, thereby saving propane. In hot summer weather, or to keep cooking odors outside, when we have a hookup at the campground we plug a single electric burner hot plate into the outlet by the counter of the outdoor entertainment center if we're cooking something like Southern fried chicken or a long-simmering stew, again saving on propane consumption.

For dishware, we have a set of sturdy French bistro plates, soup bowls, and wine glasses, plus two oversize ceramic mugs that fit nicely into the beverage carrier on the cockpit dashboard. New dish towels double as place mats and/or napkins, then become dish towels after a few uses. We try to avoid using disposable paper products, preferring to recycle.

A large wooden cutting board, padded with a rubberized mat on the bottom, doubles as a cooktop cover when we're traveling; it keeps the burners from rattling and has a slide-out drawer that stores four sharp knives safely. In overhead cabinets or drawers under the cooktop, we store a food processor; electric can opener; utensils that include tongs, a funnel, and a long-handled cooking fork; and measuring cups. On nonskid matting the same color as our countertop, we put a spice rack, a jar of coarse salt, paper towels on a wooden spindle, and vacuum-topped canisters to keep dry items like cereals, chips, and snacks crisp.

Optional appliances we've taken along include a toaster oven (indispensable if you don't have a regular oven), a sorbet maker (you need a freezer that can be set extra-low), and a bread maker (as easy to use on the road as at home).

AN ODE TO BUBBLE WRAP

Mel Brooks, in the classic comic routine "The 2,000-Year-Old Man," lauded plastic wrap as the greatest invention of the past 2 millennia, but we'd say bubble wrap is a close second in the wonderful world of RV cupboards.

It's not realistic to expect to stack dishes and glasses in an RV cupboard without some protection to keep them from chipping or breaking if you hit a rough stretch of highway. The cylinder-shaped bubble wrap containers that come around bottles in airport duty-free shops make great sleeves for mugs and glasses, while the flat sheets that come in packing boxes are easy to slide between plates or pots and pans to protect them. You can also buy plastic foam sleeves for glasses and pan and plate protectors in camping supply stores such as the Camping World chain.

Alternately nesting baskets and metal bowls keeps down the clatter from the cup-boards as well. And lining the bottoms of drawers and cupboards with waffle-pat-terned rubber matting, available by the yard at RV dealers and camping stores, makes a nonskid surface for dishes.

We store fragile items like champagne flutes in their original boxes and use other boxes or shaped Styrofoam packing protectors that come around appliances to wedge them firmly in the cupboard. Whenever possible, we use real dishes and utensils and cloth napkins instead of disposable paper and plastic products. If we're having guests for dinner, we like to surprise them with a dinner party comparable to one we'd have at home, including china, crystal, linens, and candles, when they're probably expect-ing paper plates and hot dogs on a stick.

DELICIOUS, QUICK & EASY ONE-POT MEALS

The following are some of our favorite meals which can be quickly assembled after a day of driving or hiking, made with ingredients that are easy to keep on hand. Each involves one pot and a few simple preparatory steps. For some, there are vegetarian and/or low-fat adaptations of the original recipe.

Quick Tortilla Soup

The cook controls the spiciness in this dish with the ratio of enchilada sauce to chicken broth. Makes 2 to 4 servings.

1 8-ounce can of mild enchilada sauce

1 to 2 14-ounce cans of low-sodium, low-fat chicken broth (for milder flavor, use more broth)

1 15-ounce can of beans, drained and rinsed (black, red, or pinto beans)

2 seeded and chopped fresh tomatoes

Cut kernels from 2 ears shucked and washed fresh corn

Tortilla chips

Combine enchilada sauce, chicken broth, beans, and tomatoes in a saucepan. Heat thoroughly; then stir in the corn kernels. Stir and let warm through briefly. Remove from heat, garnish with tortilla chips, and serve with any or all of these toppings: grated cheese, sliced green onions, fresh cilantro, cooked chicken breast slivers, or wedges of fresh lime to squeeze over the soup.

Easy Fried Rice

With leftover cooked rice, this is a tasty hot main dish that takes less than 15 minutes. Makes 2 main servings or 4 side-dish portions.

4 slices bacon chopped in 1-inch pieces

1 green pepper, seeded and chopped

2 green onions, washed, trimmed, and chopped

2 tbsp. fresh Italian parsley, washed and chopped (optional)

2 cups cold cooked rice

2 beaten whole eggs

2 tbsp. bottled soy sauce

Arrange bacon in large, nonstick frying pan. Cook over medium heat until the bacon browns, then remove to drain on paper towels, leaving the fat in the pan. Still over medium heat, in the same pan, sauté green pepper, green onions, and parsley until tender but not browned. Stir in rice. Continue stirring until heated through. Blend eggs with soy sauce, then pour evenly over the top of the mixture. Cook over medium heat, stirring constantly, until eggs are no longer runny. Sprinkle the cooked bacon on top and serve at once.

Variation: Low-Fat Fried Rice

Omit the bacon from the recipe above. Instead, lightly spray the pan with no-stick cooking oil or heat ¼ cup vegetable or chicken broth in the pan. Sauté the vegetables and follow the recipe above until the addition of the eggs. Instead of two whole eggs, add one whole egg and two egg whites beaten with the soy sauce.

Three-Bean Tuna Salad

For lunch on a warm day after a hike, this is ideal. Makes 4 to 6 servings.

> 1 15-ounce can kidney beans or white cannellini beans
>
> 1 15-ounce can black beans
>
> 1 15-ounce can garbanzo beans
>
> 1 6-ounce can of solid tuna in water, well drained
>
> ¼ cup finely chopped red or green onions
>
> 2 tbsp. minced parsley, basil, oregano, or other fresh herb (optional)
>
> Juice of 1 large lemon or lime
>
> 1 to 2 tbsp. olive oil
>
> Lettuce leaves

Drain and rinse beans in cold water. Combine beans in a mixing bowl. Add tuna, onions, parsley or other herb(s), lemon or lime juice, and olive oil. Toss gently and serve on lettuce leaves. Can be prepared as much as a day ahead and refrigerated, tightly covered, until serving time.

Easy Low-Fat Oven-Fried Chicken

This is good hot or cold or in sandwiches. We sometimes make a double recipe and refrigerate part of it for another meal. Makes 4 servings.

> 4 boneless, skinless chicken breasts (about 1 lb.)
>
> ½ cup vermouth, dry white wine, or chicken broth
>
> 1 minced clove of garlic
>
> ½ cup bread crumbs
>
> 2 tbsp. cornmeal
>
> ½ tsp. each cumin, ground cayenne pepper, and crumbled dry sage or thyme

Rinse chicken and pat dry. Marinate for 30 minutes in a mixture of vermouth (or wine or chicken broth) and garlic.

Remove from marinade and dip each piece in a mixture of bread crumbs, cornmeal, and a mixture of cumin, cayenne, and sage or thyme. Arrange in a baking pan that has been sprayed lightly with no-stick cooking spray, and bake at 450°F for about 20 minutes or until no longer pink inside.

Microwave Fish Dinner

We like this when we're driving along the coast and spot a fish market. Makes 2 main-dish servings.

2 boneless, skinless fresh fish filets or steaks

1 cup diced, unpeeled red potatoes, parboiled until almost tender, then drained

1 cup thin spears of fresh asparagus or zucchini

Salt

White pepper

Juice of ½ to 1 fresh lemon

1 to 2 tbsp. olive oil

Arrange fish filets side by side in the center of an ovenproof pie plate. Arrange potatoes around the edges of the dish. On top of the fish, place asparagus or zucchini. Sprinkle lightly with salt and pepper and lemon juice, to taste. Drizzle olive oil across the top. Cover tightly with plastic wrap and microwave on high for 11 minutes. Serve with slices or chunks of fresh sourdough bread (optional) to mop up the delicious juices.

Rest Area Huevos Rancheros

On a driving day, we like to start early in the morning with only some fruit or juice and a cup of tea, then stop later at a highway rest area for something more substantial. This dish takes less than 30 minutes from the start of cooking through cleanup after the meal. Makes 2 servings.

2 to 4 corn tortillas

½ tbsp. butter

2 to 4 eggs

¼ to ½ cup prepared salsa or canned enchilada sauce

Sauté tortillas in a skillet sprayed with no-stick cooking spray. When hot, remove to serving plates. Melt butter in the same pan. Fry eggs over easy or as preferred. Put the cooked eggs on top of the tortillas. Then add salsa or canned enchilada sauce to the same pan. Heat through and spoon on top of eggs.

Variation: Low-Fat Huevos Rancheros

Warm the tortillas without oil in a nonstick skillet, at the same time poaching the eggs in water with a tablespoon of vinegar in a second pan. Remove tortillas; put drained poached eggs on top, and spoon over the heated salsa as directed above.

Quick Pozole

This is a low-fat version of a full-meal, traditional winter soup from Mexico and New Mexico, easy to put together and good enough for guests. It's even better reheated the next day. Makes 4 to 6 servings.

> 2 pounds of boneless, skinless chicken thighs, cut into 1-inch pieces
>
> 2 quarts of chicken broth (canned or made using bouillon cubes or powder with water)
>
> 3 cloves minced garlic (optional)
>
> 1 yellow onion, peeled and chopped
>
> 1 tbsp. ground New Mexico chili or commercial chili powder
>
> 1 sprig fresh or 1 tsp. dried thyme or oregano
>
> 2 14-ounce cans of white or yellow hominy, drained and rinsed

Mix chicken, chicken broth, garlic, onion, chili, and thyme or oregano in a large soup pot. Simmer for an hour or so; then add hominy. Simmer until heated through. Serve in soup bowls with any or all of the following toppings: thinly sliced raw radishes, thinly sliced green cabbage, diced avocado, prepared corn chips, lime wedges, chopped red or green onions, sprigs of fresh cilantro.

Eggplant Parmesan

This dish can be prepared in a regular oven or a 650-watt microwave. Makes 2 to 3 main-dish servings or 4 to 6 side-dish portions.

> 1 medium eggplant cut into ½-inch slices, then diced
>
> 2 seeded, diced fresh tomatoes
>
> 1 to 2 cloves minced garlic
>
> 2 tbsp. chopped fresh basil or parsley (optional)
>
> 1 tbsp. olive oil
>
> ½ cup grated mozzarella cheese
>
> 2 tbsp. freshly grated Parmesan cheese

Combine eggplant, tomatoes, garlic, basil or parsley, and olive oil in a baking dish. Cover tightly with foil and bake in a 400°F oven for 1 hour.

Uncover and sprinkle with mozzarella and Parmesan. Return, uncovered, to oven and bake 5 minutes or until cheese has melted.

To prepare in a microwave oven, put the cheeses on top of the eggplant/tomato mixture, cover tightly with plastic wrap, and microwave on high for 5 minutes.

One-Pot Garlic Spaghetti

This vegetarian dish contains heart-healthy olive oil and garlic. Spraying the cooking pot before adding the water keeps the spaghetti from sticking to the bottom, making the pan much easier to wash. Makes 2 to 4 servings.

1 to 2 tbsp. salt

¼ pound dry spaghetti for each serving

¼ cup olive oil for 2 servings, ½ cup for 4 servings

4 to 6 cloves minced garlic

Minced fresh parsley, basil, and/or oregano

Freshly grated Parmesan cheese

Spray a very large cooking pot with no-stick cooking spray, fill with water, and add salt. When water is boiling rapidly, add spaghetti. Cook until al dente (just soft enough to bite through easily, but not soft and flabby); then drain and rinse with hot water. Wipe out the spaghetti pot with a paper towel and return to the heat. Put in olive oil and garlic. Cook until garlic begins to sizzle, and then stir in minced fresh parsley, basil, and/or oregano to taste. Return spaghetti to the pot and toss over heat until warmed through. Serve at once with freshly grated Parmesan cheese. A big green salad goes well with this, along with fruit and cheese for dessert.

French Vegetable Soup

This soup from the south of France is incredibly delicious, although it is simple and easy to make. It is even better with a spoonful of pesto stirred in just before serving. Makes 6 to 8 servings.

2 quarts water or chicken broth

2 cups unpeeled red or new white potatoes chopped into ½-inch cubes

2 cups fresh green beans, cut into 2-inch pieces

2 to 3 zucchini, washed and sliced

2 cups fresh tomatoes, preferably plum, seeded and chopped into small pieces

4 ounces dry spaghetti, broken into short pieces

1 15-ounce can garbanzo beans or cannellini beans, drained and rinsed

Salt and pepper

Freshly grated Parmesan cheese or pesto sauce (optional)

In a large soup pot, combine water or chicken broth, potatoes, green beans, zucchini, and tomatoes. Bring to a boil, lower heat, cover and simmer for 1 hour, then add spaghetti and beans. Cook until spaghetti is tender, season to taste with salt and pepper, then serve in wide soup bowls. Top each portion with grated Parmesan cheese or pesto sauce (optional).

Pesto Sauce

3 cloves peeled garlic

1 cup fresh basil leaves (can use a blend of basil and fresh parsley)

2 tbsp. olive oil

Finely chop the garlic and basil together, using a blender or food processor for convenience, or a knife or mortar and pestle for authenticity, then drizzle in olive oil, beating with a fork or mixing with the blender until combined.

Microwave Polenta with Mushrooms

This rustic Italian dish technically takes two pots, one for the microwave and one for the stove top. We like this recipe when we find fresh wild mushrooms in farmers' markets or supermarkets. The microwave eliminates the stirring from the traditional recipe, as well as cutting down the preparation time considerably. Any leftovers can be put in a dish or small loaf pan and refrigerated to slice and sauté later for a side dish. Makes 2 to 4 servings.

4 cups water

1 cup yellow cornmeal

1 tsp. salt

1 pound wild or cultivated mushrooms (preferably a mix of several, such as oyster, portobello, chanterelle, or shiitake)

1 tbsp. unsalted butter or margarine

1 tbsp. olive or other cooking oil

1 clove garlic, peeled and minced

2 to 3 tbsp. fresh sage leaves, chopped, or 1 tsp. dry sage

To make the polenta, mix water, cornmeal, and salt in a large microwavable bowl. Microwave uncovered for 12 minutes, stirring once about halfway through. Remove from microwave and let stand 3 minutes; then spoon onto serving plates.

While the polenta is cooking, prepare the mushroom sauce. Clean, trim, and slice the mushrooms. In a large nonstick skillet, melt butter with olive or cooking oil. Over medium heat, sauté the mushrooms until tender and lightly browned, about 5 to 8 minutes. Remove and keep warm. Sauté the garlic and sage in the same pan.

Spoon polenta on warm serving plates, and top with mushroom sauce and herbs.

Don't Drink the Water

When there's no bottled water available in the fishing villages of Fiji or the mountain-side inns of the Himalayas, we brush our teeth with whiskey. We veto street food vendors in Madras, Mazatlán, or Manhattan, and always skip summer shellfish salads, rare hamburgers, and anything with custard in it.

As veteran world travelers, we're cautious—some of our friends say overly cautious—but with a schedule that requires us to be on the road 60% of the time, we can't risk getting sick, even for a day.

So we decided long ago that whenever we're on the road, we'd stick with, and recommend, using **bottled water** for drinking and cooking, and always use **bags of commercial ice** if your RV does not have a built-in icemaker. We use the campground water supply and the surplus stored in our tank only for washing and flushing. While most of the city water in North America is safe to drink, a constantly changing mineral content when you're making 1-night stands can throw off your system. Pick up 2 or 3 gallons at a time at a supermarket, convenience store, or campground store; put one in the galley and the others below in outside storage; and store a plastic bag of ice cubes in the freezer.

People who have a restricted sodium intake would also be wise to use **sodium-free bottled water,** available in most supermarkets, since the sodium content of water varies widely from one campground area to the next.

A solution for RVers who don't want to buy ice and water is to use a **water filter**—either one that's permanently installed in the RV's kitchen sink or one you hook up to the hose system when filling the tank initially.

Even more thorough is **a water purifier** that not only removes sediment from the water like a filter does, but also takes out bacteria and delivers clean, good-tasting drinking water. When we bought our Itasca Sunflyer, one of the options we ordered was a water filter for the sink and an icemaker for the refrigerator. If you don't have an RV with these, you can simply stay with bagged ice and bottled water for daily use.

We also saw, at the Los Angeles RV Show, a Rexhall motor home that was equipped with an optional water exchange, with which you could separate your own freshwater source for drinking and cooking and use the campground plug-in source for washing and flushing only.

It's wise to use **biodegradable toilet paper** and **holding-tank chemicals,** both available from camping stores and many campground stores. Follow the RV instruction booklet or the directions on the chemical container.

When you're driving every day, you rarely need to use your **water heater,** since the engine keeps the water hot. If you have an electric water heater, you may want to operate it only when necessary or during the night, since it draws a lot of power that you may need for the air conditioner, TV, or microwave.

Trimming Costs: Eight Money-Saving Tips for the Road

1. **Buy local produce.** Shopping at roadside fruit stands or farmers' markets will usually net the freshest and the cheapest local produce and give you a chance to chat with the locals.

2. **Watch for "pick-your-own" farms and orchards in season,** where a few minutes of work can save a lot of money on luxuries like fresh raspberries and cherries. One national park campground in Utah is set in the midst of fruit orchards where campers pick their own. (See chapter 5, "Utah's Parks & Canyons.")

3. **Clip coupons locally.** Pick up local newspapers or free circulars in towns where you stay overnight and use the ads and supermarket discount coupons to save grocery money.

4. **Take advantage of capitalism.** If you see a gas station having a price war with a neighboring station, go back and fill up your tank. While price wars are uncommon during these days of high gas prices, every penny counts when you have a 75-gallon gas tank on a vehicle that gets fewer than 10 miles to the gallon. (And check out the apps on computers/smartphones that allow you to look for the lowest gas price in the area where you're traveling.)

5. **Cash or charge?** Some gas stations charge more when you use a credit card than when you pay cash. Keep your eye out for stations that list the same price for credit or cash. If there's no sign that says so, ask before filling the tank.

6. **Don't skimp on service.** Spend that extra money for regular engine and vehicle upkeep on a long haul. This saves a lot of money in the end.

7. **Be rational about your campground needs.** When staying overnight in campgrounds that charge based on hookups and facilities used, opt for the most basic, since RVs are designed to be self-contained. Instead of paying extra for a sewer connection, use the free (for registered campers) dumpsite at a campground as you're pulling in for the night or out in the morning. Opting for water and electric only may save as much as $5 a night. (For more campground money-savers, see chapter 3, "Where to Sleep: Campgrounds & RV Parks.")

8. **Buy out of season (antifreeze, for instance, in summer) and in quantity.** When canned or paper goods are on sale in bulk, buy two or three for the house and two or three for the RV.

Safety, Sanity & Insurance

DRIVING TIPS

To combat glare, fog, snow, or oncoming headlights when driving after dark, slip on a pair of yellow glasses (sold in ski shops as ski goggles) or clip a pair over your regular glasses.

Binoculars for the navigator solve that ever-present problem of changing lanes with a large vehicle when approaching an on-ramp to an interstate. It's easy to look ahead to see if the entrance is from the left lane or the right lane, or to read the street names at intersections.

Defensive driving is always important. Many drivers who pause at an intersection while our RV has the right of way don't seem to realize that motor homes are like big tractor-trailer rigs; they can't stop on a dime. Many other drivers also make the

Ain't Misbehavin': Road Etiquette

1. **Don't hog the highway;** pull over at turnouts or into slow-moving lanes to let vehicles behind you have a chance to pass. In some states, it's against the law for a slow-moving vehicle not to allow following vehicles to pass at the first opportunity when five or more are trailing.

2. **Keep in the right lane except when passing a car,** and when you do pass, make sure you have the speed and space to do it quickly and easily. Some motor homes don't have the power to easily overtake vehicles on an uphill route, especially if the driver speeds up as you attempt to pass.

3. **As with your car, dimming your RV headlights for an approaching car is a must.** It is also a good idea to do the same when driving into a campground after dark.

4. **It is customary to make a friendly wave to an oncoming RV as you meet,** particularly if it's a make and model similar to your own.

5. **Always signal your intention to turn or change lanes well ahead of time** so the driver in back of you has plenty of warning. Your vehicle is not as agile as those around you.

6. **The person in the passenger seat should use binoculars to check out the road signs ahead to make it easier for the driver to change lanes in traffic.** They are especially useful when trying to determine whether the on-ramp will require being in the right or left lane, since changing lanes in a big vehicle takes additional time and distance. 🚌

erroneous assumption that RV drivers are elderly slowpokes, when most of us drive at the prevailing speed limit with the rest of the traffic. So we're always half-expecting a driver to pull out of a side road in front of us, and we're rarely disappointed. One rule of thumb: If you see a pickup truck waiting at a side road to pull into traffic, you can count on him to pull out in front of your RV.

SAVING MONEY ON FUEL

Fuel conservation is important for all RVers. Cutting down on the amount of gas you use not only helps your budget, but also the environment. The following are tips for conserving gas and finding the best fuel prices:

- Consider **staying longer** in one location. Because we're so happy and comfortable in our newer, larger motorhome, we find ourselves staying longer in each place than we used to. Doing so cuts fuel costs by reducing the average number of miles we drive per day. Interestingly enough, we get almost the same gas mileage in our 36-foot motorhome as we did in our old 27-footer.

- **Forget the tow-along** and walk or bike. We still don't tow a car: another fuel savings. Instead, we enjoy a walk of a mile or two to the market, a museum, or a restaurant. Other RVers carry bicycles for short trips from and around the campground.

- **Mind and maintain the speed limit**. Experts say that observing the speed limit saves fuel because the fuel economy of your vehicle decreases at higher speeds. Cruise control, for those vehicles that have this feature, also contributes to fuel savings, because you maintain a constant speed. Being light-footed with the gas pedal, rather than applying too much throttle, also saves gas.

- **Keep your air filter clean.** Make sure your air filter is checked and replaced often. U.S. Department of Energy studies say that a dirty air filter can raise the consumption of fuel as much as 10 percent. Keeping your engine tuned and not carrying any extraneous weight also help, the study points out.

- Take advantage of **gas price wars**. We carry binoculars to check out posted gas prices along an interstate exit or on the outskirts of a town. Always go for the cheaper price, even when doing so requires turning around. Even in the same area, the prices can vary a lot; a helpful website to find the lowest prices in any area is **www.gasbuddy.com**.

- **Pay cash for gas when you can.** Sometimes the cash price for gas is lower than the price if you pay by credit card. If you prefer using a credit card, watch for stations where prices are the same. If nothing is posted, ask before filling your tank.

SPEEDERS BEWARE & OTHER GOOD ADVICE

While exceeding the speed limit is never laudable, it can also be extremely inconvenient for residents of California, Alaska, Montana, Michigan, and Wisconsin—states that are not signatories to the Non-Resident Violators Compact, which is used to process traffic citations across state borders.

What it means is that drivers with license plates from these five states are subject to having their driver's license confiscated for out-of-state moving violations, such as speeding, and being required to go to the nearest office of a judge, sheriff, or justice of the peace to appear before an officer, post bond, and/or pay a fine. If said officer is not available, the individual may be jailed until a court appearance can be arranged, which may be several hours later.

Keep your headlights on. More and more states are requiring the use of headlights in the daytime. We think it should be mandatory throughout the country. It's amazing how some cars can blend into the roadway and suddenly appear headed your way, particularly when you're planning to pass another car. Having headlights on during daytime can be a lifesaving factor.

We also try to avoid driving at night, preferring to get an early morning start and stopping for the day by midafternoon.

GENERAL RV SAFETY & SECURITY TIPS

Remember that you are driving a vehicle with a propane tank that, while it simplifies your daily life by allowing for heating and refrigeration when your RV is not hooked up to shore power (a campground's electrical hookup), it also complicates things by being flammable. Modern RVs also have propane gas leak detectors to warn you with a sound signal if there is a propane leak. If you hear the signal, get out of the RV, turn off the propane valve at the tank (reached from an outside door), and leave the RV open to let the gas escape. Some experts recommend that it is safest to drive with the propane tank turned off. Many long highway bridges and tunnels require that the tank be turned off before entering.

Occasionally, your gas leak detector will signal when you're cooking garlic in an open pan, because the odor is similar to the odor added to propane to make it easy to detect a leak. If this happens, turn off the burner and remove the pan of garlic to see if it is the source of the alarm. If the alarm stops, open the windows and roof vents, turn off the detector, turn the burner back on, and finish cooking the dish, but be sure to reactivate the detector.

Always check the gas leak detector and smoke detectors installed in your RV to make sure the batteries are fresh.

Carbon monoxide detectors are also mandatory in RVs. You want to inspect your unit regularly to make sure the floor, sidewalls, doors, and windows have no holes or openings that would allow the gas to come into the vehicle while you're driving; if you find any, seal them up with silicone adhesive or have repairs made before driving again.

Never run your generator while you're sleeping, and *always* open one of the roof vents when the generator is operating. And don't stay long when you're parking in a roadside rest area in the vicinity of a tractor-trailer running its motor to keep the refrigeration operating.

When packing an RV, or adding more items to a motor home that's already outfitted, be aware of the vehicle's load limit and the necessity to balance the weight equally. You can check the weight at a public scale, sometimes found at big truck-stop complexes. Get a reading for each wheel and, for a trailer, the tongue weight, which is the weight the trailer coupler puts on the tow hitch. Check that against the net carrying capacity listed on the weight information label installed somewhere inside the RV.

SHOULD YOU CARRY A GUN IN YOUR RV?

If you want to start a lively argument around a campground, try this as an opener. We personally would never carry a firearm in our motor home, but then we would never have one at home, either. While many frequent and full-time RVers agree, there are just as many who disagree, sometimes vociferously.

Entering Mexico with a firearm of any sort can land an RV owner in jail—and did, in a case in 1993. A veteran RVer had bought a semiautomatic rifle at an Arizona gun show and stowed it, along with 500 rounds of ammunition, in his travel trailer. Mexican police found the AK-47 in the trailer and a pistol in his truck, and confiscated the vehicle, firearms, and ammunition, and put him in jail. He spent months incarcerated with no bedding or regular meal service, both optional luxuries for which the prisoner's family members are expected to pay, before his attorney could bring the case to trial. Canada also prohibits entering the country with guns.

Despite our feelings that our motor home is indeed our home, the law in many states considers the RV a motor vehicle when moving and a home only when parked in camp. Therefore, any firearms carried must be unloaded and the bullets kept separately from the weapon when in transit.

Firearms are also prohibited in many state parks.

If we did choose to carry a firearm, we would make it a point to keep abreast of the regulations in every state, which can differ radically the minute you cross a state line. Check each state's website.

SHOULD YOU CARRY A CELLPHONE IN YOUR RV?

They're ubiquitous these days, but a cellphone can provide almost as much frustration as assistance. The places we like to drive and camp are frequently, if not always, in a borderline or "no service" area, even though we have (and are willing to pay a sizable sum for) a Follow Me Roaming system that theoretically can forward our calls to almost anywhere in the United States and Canada. Our editors have been able to reach us in the wilds of British Columbia or when we're driving down an interstate in West Texas, but can't seem to get through to us when we're on a 2-day outing in a national park in San Diego or Santa Barbara, only a hoot and a holler from our Los Angeles base.

We find cellphones most helpful for dialing ahead for a campground reservation or for returning business calls from our voice mail when there's no available landline or campground or highway pay phone (and there are fewer of them than ever these days). And we're certainly happy to have one in case of an emergency, which we've had to deal with on occasion.

Still you might find that your calls drop more frequently and the quality of the sound may not be the greatest when you're in a fringe reception area. Some pricing plans include long-distance and roaming charges throughout the United States with a flat fee for a certain number of minutes; check with the cellphone provider.

SIX OFF-THE-WALL TIPS FOR RV AILMENTS

1. **To remember to lower your TV antenna before pulling out of the campground,** put some sort of label or tag—one RVer suggests a spring-loaded clothespin—on the antenna crank in the travel position. When the antenna is up, put the same tag or device on the gearshift or steering wheel. Then, as you prepare to move out, the item will remind you the antenna is still raised.

2. **To get unstuck when mired in snow, mud, or sand,** one Canadian RVer suggests using two strips of metal plasterer's lath, available in hardware stores, approximately 10 by 30 inches each, either in front of or behind the drive axle

wheels to extricate the vehicle. The lath can be hosed off and stored flat to be reused as many times as needed.

3. **To get rid of mice,** tuck sheets of Downy fabric softener around the sofa, under the sinks, and near the furnace.

4. **When lights or turn signals on a tow vehicle fail to work,** spray white vinegar on the electrical connectors.

5. **When sensors on holding tanks for gray and black water do not read properly,** an online bulletin board posting suggests filling the problem tank half full of water and adding a half cup of Dawn liquid dish detergent before leaving home, then emptying the tank on arrival at the campground. Try repeating the technique if the first effort doesn't fix it.

6. **To do the wash,** a Nevada man reminds us of the hero in Anne Tyler's novel, *The Accidental Tourist* (1988) with his suggestion: Put hot water, dirty clothes, soap, and a (clean) tennis shoe (to act as an agitator) in a large cooler and strap the whole thing to the rear bumper of the motor home. At lunchtime, empty the soapy water in an appropriate spot, refill the cooler with clean water, and drive on. In camp, set up a clothesline and hang the clean laundry out to dry.

RV INSURANCE

We were pleasantly surprised to find that our RV insurance was affordable, even in costly Southern California. Safe driving records, a shorter use period during the year, and slightly older drivers on the average mean less risk for the insurer. Before buying, check your own automobile insurance carrier as well as specialized RV insurance carriers, such as **Good Sam Club's National General** (✆ **800/234-3450;** www.goodsamclub.com), **Foremost Insurance Company** (✆ **800/237-2060;** www. foremost.com), **AARP Insurance** (✆ **888/687-2277;** www.aarp.com), **PoliSeek RV Insurance** (✆ **800/521-2942;** www.poliseek.com/rv), and for Mexican insurance, **Sanborn's** (✆ **800/222-0158;** www.sanborninsurance.com) or **Oscar Padilla** (✆ **800/466-7227;** www.mexicaninsurance.com). Towing insurance in case of a breakdown is a good idea; in many cases, **AAA** members can extend that company's towing coverage to their RV.

The Community of Man: Getting Together with Other RVers

CARAVANS & RALLIES

RVers who would prefer to travel or camp with a group can join up with any number of like-minded people for a paid vacation tour in their own rig instead of a tour bus, or a friendly get-together with other owners of the same brand of RV. Caravans are the RV equivalent of a group tour with structured itineraries, sightseeing, communal meals, and many group social functions.

Popular caravan destinations include Mexico, Alaska, and New England at autumn foliage time. To find out about caravan and club tours, read general RV publications such as *Trailer Life* (**www.trailerlife.com**, available in both hard copy and digital subscriptions) and *MotorHome* (**www.motorhomemagazine.com**), also available by subscription or from many newsstands and bookstores; *Family Motor Coaching Magazine* (for FMCA members); *Highways* (for Good Sam Club members); or other club or RV manufacturing company publications.

RV CLUBS

Escapees RV Club. Founded in 1978 by veteran RV writers Joe and Kay Peterson, Escapees is a support system for full-timers. Membership numbers more than 33,000. Members have pooled resources to build their own nonprofit RV parks across the country, as well as create a new CARE (Continuing Assistance for Retired Escapees) program that provides parking facilities and support services for temporarily or permanently incapacitated full-timers. Costs are $70 first year, $60 a year thereafter. 100 Rainbow Dr., Livingston, TX 77351 (✆ **888/757-2582;** www. escapees.com).

Family Motor Coach Association. For owners of self-propelled, self-contained vehicles with cooking, sleeping, and sanitary facilities in which the living quarters can be accessed directly from the driver's seat. Members number around 170,000 families, each with its own ID number. The group provides a monthly magazine and other benefits, including insurance. Costs are $50 for a family, including initiation fee and first-year dues, $40 thereafter. 8291 Clough Pike, Cincinnati, OH 45244 (✆ **800/543-3622** or 513/474-3622; www.fmca.com).

Flying J Real Value Club. A free membership provides fuel (gasoline or diesel) discounts of 3¢ a gallon for diesel, 2¢ a gallon for regular gas, and 10¢ a gallon for propane. Additional credit can be gained from non-fuel purchases in their restaurants and convenience stores. Insurance, roadside assistance, and prepaid calling card programs are also available. 5508 Lonas Dr., Knoxville, TN 37909 (✆ **800/562-6210;** www. pilotflyingj.com).

Good Sam Club. A broad-range club with insurance, campground affiliates, financing, and other services. Members number nearly a million, and the club also has special-interest chapters for hobbyists, computer aficionados, singles, hearing-impaired, and others. Cost is $20 a year. Write to PO Box 6888, Englewood, CO 80155-6888 (✆ **800/234-3450;** www.goodsamclub.com).

Handicapped Travel Club. For individuals with disabilities who enjoy traveling and camping; club also welcomes those without disabilities. Cost is $12 first year, $8 a year thereafter. For membership requirements, send SASE with first-class postage to Bill Gratze, 2660 SE 7th Pl., Homestead, FL 33033 (✆ **305/230-0687;** www. handicappedtravelclub.com).

Loners on Wheels. Now 25 years old, Loners on Wheels is a club for single RVers, numbering around 3,000 widowed, divorced, or never-married members. While members who subsequently give up traveling alone turn into nonmembers, they are welcomed back at special anniversaries and rallies. Call for a sample newsletter. Cost is $45 a year. 1795 O'Kelly Rd., Deming, NM 88030 (✆ **866/569-2582;** www. lonersonwheels.com).

Passport America. A $44 yearly membership provides 50% discounts at more than 1,400 campgrounds throughout the U.S., Canada, and Mexico. Some restrictions apply, depending on the individual campground, the time of year, and the length of stay. 21263 Tucker Rd., Long Beach, MS 39560 (✆ **800/283-7183** or 228/452-9972; www.passport-america.com).

Road Scholar (formerly Elderhostel). Offers educational trips and courses all over the U.S. (and internationally). RV owners who "bring their own" accommodations, so to speak, are often eligible for steep discounts in the price of the programs. No dues, fee for courses (varies). 11 Ave. de Lafayette, Boston, MA 02111 (✆ **800/454-5768** or 617/426-7788; www.roadscholar.org).

Vagabundos del Mar. A club of RV travelers who spend a lot of time in Mexico. Also provides Mexican auto insurance and information on RV parks south of the border. Cost is $35 a year. 190 Main St., Rio Vista, CA 94571 (✆ **800/474-BAJA** [2252] or 707/374-5511; www.vagabundos.com).

ONLINE RV RESOURCES

Online groups and bulletin boards give RV enthusiasts or wannabe RVers from all over a virtual meeting place to exchange dialogue, give helpful hints, and discuss the pros and cons of the various vehicle brands. There are several dozen RV groups on "Yahoo Groups" (**http://groups.yahoo.com**) with topics ranging from general RV discussion to classic RVs, RV communications, and many others. Many special-interest RV groups like the ones mentioned above offer message boards or live chat capabilities on their websites.

It's easier than ever to check your e-mail on the road. Even if you don't have a smartphone (and reception!), more and more campgrounds provide Internet access, some for free, some for a modest charge. Some upscale campgrounds now have phone connections at the site for those newer motor homes with phone lines built into the wiring system, and many more campgrounds now have wireless Internet service, or Wi-Fi (some free, some for a fee).

FREEWHEELING FULL-TIMING

So you're thinking of selling the farm, giving the furniture to the kids, and taking off in the RV for a full-timing adventure—STOP! Take a minute and think about it. Full-timing isn't for everybody. Give it a trial—take your RV out for a 3- or 4-month trip, traveling several days in a row and then sitting still in a pleasant campground for a week or so. See if you get cabin fever or start longing for that outsize bedroom and bath.

If not, and you pass the test, start planning. Join a club like Escapees (see above) or the Good Sam Club. Go on the Internet and search out "Full-timing," "Mail Forwarding," and, if interested, "Homeschooling." You'll find more than you ever wanted to know about the subjects. Check out some of the following websites: **www. familiesontheroad.com**; **www.forwardnevada.com** (for mail, and for convenience, you should find a service in your hometown, if possible, to save on double forwarding); and **www.texashomebase.com**.

After that: Happy traveling!

Where to Sleep: Campgrounds & RV Parks

THE ANSWER TO THE QUESTION OF WHERE TO SLEEP IN YOUR RV is "almost anywhere." There are more than 16,000 campgrounds in the United States that can accommodate RVs. Some provide hookups, while others are for self-contained or "dry" camping.

A few campgrounds are free, but many more are lavish resorts that may cost $50 a night and up for full hookups, cable TV, phone service, spas, swimming pools, tennis courts, playgrounds, and miniature or par-3 golf courses.

If you prefer ranger hikes and scenery to horseshoe pits and pancake breakfasts, head for one of the 29,000 campsites at our national parks and monuments. The U.S. Forest Service has 4,000 developed campgrounds in 155 forests, and the Bureau of Land Management (BLM) oversees 270 million acres of scenic outdoor sites, many with free camping.

For watery wonderlands, check out the U.S. Army Corps of Engineers projects, with 53,000 campsites near oceans, rivers, and lakes, and opportunities for fishing, boating, swimming, and water-skiing.

Bird-watchers can stay overnight in many of the nation's wildlife refuges to get the drop on feathery friends, and game-watchers can take advantage of the optimum spotting times of dawn and dusk. (See "The Best Campground Directories," below, for obtaining full listings of wildlife-refuge campgrounds, as well as guides for all the other campgrounds.)

Campground Glossary

Black water: Wastewater from the toilet.
Boondock: To camp without electrical or other hookups.
Dual electrical system: An RV system in which lights and other electrical systems can run on 12-volt battery power, a 110 AC electrical hookup, or a gas generator.
Dump station: Also called sanitary dump, disposal station, and so on; this is where an RV dumps the "gray water" and "black water" from its holding tanks.
Gray water: Wastewater from the sinks and shower.
Hookups: Umbilical cords that connect your RV with electrical power, water, and sewer service. (Full hookups are sites furnished with all three connections. Partial hookups are sites furnished with one or two of the three connections.)
Propane or LPG: Liquefied petroleum gas used for heating, cooking, and refrigeration in RVs.

Mini–motor home in a tree-shaded campsite near Anacortes, Washington.

Pull-through: A campsite that allows the driver to pull into the site to park and then pull out the other side when leaving, without ever having to back up—a boon for beginners.

Spirit level: A device for determining true horizontal or vertical directions by the centering of a bubble in a slightly curved glass tube or tubes filled with alcohol or ether. Some RVs come with built-in levels. If yours does not, small spirit levels can be purchased in hardware stores or RV supply centers.

Three-way refrigerator: An RV refrigerator/freezer that can operate on LPG, an electrical hookup, or a gas generator.

Should You Sleep by the Side of the Road?

More than half the states in the U.S. permit some overnight parking in highway rest areas, except where posted. However, we have heard of too many incidents of violence in these areas and would not consider parking our RV overnight in a rest area, mall parking lot, truck stop, or by the side of the road. Some of our friends do, though, and consider us money-wasting wimps for staying overnight at a secure private or public campground.

The thing that amazes us is how many owners of expensive motor homes take the risk of sleeping for free in a parking lot or by the side of the road when their pricey vehicle advertises how much in cash, credit cards, and expensive electronics might be inside. All this to save a few dollars? Campground fees are a modest enough investment in security and peace of mind. Besides, unlike RVers, the truckers with whom you share the road have few other options when they need to rest. Why take up their space?

INSIDER TIP: A RESOURCE FOR THE RV CURIOUS

A good way to begin to learn about RVs and RVing is to spend some time exploring the website and watching the online videos at **GoRVing.com.** You can also sign up for an e-newsletter, and connect with the group on Facebook. The GO-RVing Coalition is a group of RV manufacturers, retailers, campground owners, and parts manufacturers.

Campsites: The Good, the Bad & the Ugly

As former backpackers, we would set up camp at any clearing that didn't have too many rocks and spread out the ground cloth and sleeping bags.

As tent campers, we looked for scenery, shelter, and seclusion, but not too far away from the water source and facilities.

Now, as RV campers, we have a long list of "Ls":

- **Location:** We want to be away from the highway and campground entrance and not too near the swimming pool, bathroom facilities, garbage dumpster, playground, or dog-walking area.

- **Large:** It must be big enough to back our 36-foot motor home in and park it, open two slide-outs, and still have space for chairs, a table, and a charcoal grill.

- **Level:** We used to do a lot of running back and forth to check spirit levels inside and outside the vehicle; sometimes we would have to wedge wooden blocks under the tires until that pesky little bubble hit the center. Hydraulic jacks on our new motor home make this procedure much easier. (What happens if it's not level? Something dire and expensive befalls the refrigerator.)

- **Length:** The umbilical cords from the vehicle to the electric, water, and sewer connections (where applicable) must reach comfortably.

- **Look out:** Watch for any low-hanging branches or wires that could damage the roof air conditioner or TV antenna. Also, look out for a potentially noisy neighbor, and for wet or marshy ground that could mire you down if it should rain all night.

- **Width:** It's not an "L," but it's important: With most newer vehicles containing one or more slide-outs (a portion of the living room and/or bedroom that slides out to expand the interior area), the width of the site becomes more important. Some older campgrounds can't handle a slide-out and will say so. Others may have room for the slide, but there won't be space left to use as a recreation area. Any campsite width less than 15 feet will limit comfortable use of the site, unless you're just stopping overnight.

Revealing the Secrets of the Seasons

Summer is the most popular vacation time for families because the kids are out of school. But for RVers looking for more solitude and milder weather, spring and fall may be preferable. In the southernmost parts of the United States, winter is best for its mild, sunny weather, but in resort areas, prices can climb with popularity, peaking between Christmastime and the weekend of Presidents' Day.

In RV parlance, retirees from northern regions fleeing winter weather are known as "snowbirds," and they're warmly welcomed in the south, particularly southern Texas along the Rio Grande, along the Gulf of Mexico from Florida to Louisiana, in southern Arizona and New Mexico, and in the California deserts. Snowbirds usually flee the Northeast, Midwest, or Northwest when the first cold weather hits, spend the winter months in the sun, and then head back north in the spring.

Summer is prime time almost everywhere in the North, but it's too hot for optimum comfort in the snowbird winter retreats of the South.

Off season means smaller crowds and lower prices, but it also can mean that some campgrounds, restaurants, and shops are closed. In each destination chapter, we list opening and closing dates for seasonal campgrounds and attractions, so pay close attention if your trip is scheduled during transitional months, such as April or October.

Traffic almost always is heavy on the interstate highways, no matter what the season. On the first and last days of a holiday weekend, the highways—and even some back roads—are more crowded than usual. Smart RVers often opt to stay over an extra night at the campground to avoid the rush and drive home after most people have already returned to work. 🚐

A campsite may or may not contain a picnic table, grill, or fire ring. What is critical for tent campers becomes an added luxury for an RVer, who already has a table, chairs, and stove. While we all want to stay overnight in the best campgrounds, we find that campground ratings—for example, those in the popular annual *Trailer Life Campground/RV Park & Services Directory* (which is available at **www.trailerlifedirectory. com**) do not always seem to relate to us. The guide, issued annually, rates campgrounds according to a detailed form that scores in three areas: facilities, cleanliness (particularly of toilets and showers), and visual or environmental appeal.

Since we always use our own toilet and shower facilities, we're not concerned with those at the campgrounds, and we rarely, if ever, take advantage of a TV lounge, swimming pool, Saturday night dance, or children's playground.

Therefore, for us, a highly rated campground may have less appeal than a remote area in a national forest, or a simpler family-run park in the country. However, in recent years, *Trailer Life* has added some new elements to its ratings, listing amenities like Internet access and Wi-Fi availability at the campsites. (They've even added a free RV Park Finder app for smartphone users, downloadable from iTunes.)

Occasionally, in both private and state park campgrounds, you may encounter what we call a "parking lot" design, with rows of paved spaces fairly close together. The upside is that you're usually level and don't have to spend time checking spirit-level bubbles. The downside is that your dining room window may be 2 feet away from your neighbor. The saving grace is that with an RV, you can close your curtains or blinds, turn on some soft music, and be alone in the universe.

On the other hand, we are always thrilled to find those enlightened campground owners who have spent extra time and money to create terraced areas with landscaping that give a sense of space, light, and privacy.

Using the Directories to Find a Campground

While we frequently are at odds with campground ratings, we find the directories, especially the one from *Trailer Life,* invaluable when traveling, particularly when we're making 1-night stands and need to find a place to stay overnight. Being able to call ahead for reservations is also helpful; you won't have to drive 5 miles off the route only to find there are no campsites left. This is where a cellphone comes in handy (see discussion in chapter 2, "Getting Prepared: RVing Tips & Hints").

Careful reading of an entry can also tell you the site width (important if you have an awning or slide-out), if there are pull-throughs, if you can expect any shade trees, if the campground is open year-round or only seasonally, and if there's a dump station on the premises.

THE BEST CAMPGROUND DIRECTORIES

Bureau of Land Management (BLM), 270 million acres of public land. Ask for free camping information from BLM, U.S. Department of the Interior, 1849 C St. NW, Ste. 5665, Washington, DC 20240 (✆ **202/208-3801;** www.blm.gov).

The authors' Itasca Sunflyer in the Jamestown, North Dakota, KOA campground.

A private RV park in Bend, Oregon.

KOA, 460 campgrounds in the United States, Canada, and Mexico. You can receive a guide free, or send $5 for an annual guide from Kampgrounds of America Executive Offices, P.O. Box 30558, Billings, MT 59114-0558 (✆ **888/562-0000** or 406/255-7402; www.koa.com).

National Association of RV Parks and Campgrounds has a directory with listings of more than 3,000 RV parks and campgrounds. National ARVC, 113 Park Ave., Falls Church, VA 22046 (✆ **800/395-2267** or 703/241-8801; www.gocamping america.com).

National Wildlife Refuges, 488 refuges. For free publications, write to U.S. Fish and Wildlife Services, Public Affairs Office, 1849 C St. NW, MS-5600/MIB, Washington, DC 20240 (✆ **800/344-9453** or 202/452-5125; www.fws.gov/refuges).

Trailer Life Campground, RV Park and Services Directory, published annually, covers 12,500 campgrounds in the United States, Canada, and Mexico. Available for $25 at bookstores and camping stores (with deep discounts for Good Sam members and when ordered from the website); P.O. Box 6888 Englewood, CO 80155-6888 (✆ **877/209-6655;** www.trailerlifedirectory.com).

U.S. Army Corps of Engineers, 53,000 campsites near oceans, rivers, and lakes. For free publications, write to U.S. Army Corps of Engineers, U.S. ACE Publications Depot, Attn: CEHEC-IM-PD, 2803 52nd Ave., Hyattsville, MD 20781-1102 (✆ **301/394-0081;** www.usace.army.mil).

U.S. Forest Service, 4,000 campgrounds. For a free guide, write to U.S. Department of Agriculture Forest Service, Public Affairs Office, 1400 Independence Ave., Mailstop 1111, Washington, DC 20250-0003 (✆ **800/832-1355;** www.fs.fed.us).

Wheelers RV Resort & Campground Directory, 3116 S. Mill Ave., Ste. 610, Tempe, AZ 85282 (✆ **480/784-4771;** www.wheelersguides.com); a searchable online database (and CD) of properties in North America.

Woodall's Campground Directory. Order the guide (which comes with a searchable CD), or purchase online for $29.95 (there's usually a deep discount for pre-ordering the next year's guide) by writing to 2575 Vista del Mar Dr., Ventura, CA 93001 (✆ **877/680-6155;** www.woodalls.com).

Yogi Bear's Jellystone Park Campground Directory is available free online or by contacting Leisure Systems, Inc., 50 W. Techne Center Dr., Ste. G, Milford, OH 45150 (✆ **800/558-2954;** www.campjellystone.com).

10 Ways to Save Money on Campgrounds

1. **Never pay for more park than you'll use.** Posh playgrounds with swimming pools, spas, tennis courts, and miniature golf are usually pricier than simple, clean, mom-and-pop campgrounds. The latter are adequate for an overnight stay. If there is a charge per hookup, take the electric and water and forgo the sewer unless you really need it.

2. **Remember, you can camp without hookups comfortably for several nights** as long as you don't insist on using the TV, air conditioner, or microwave. Read a book or listen to music, and cook on your gas cooktop or outdoors on a grill. You'll still have running water, lights, refrigeration, heat, and hot water for dishes and the shower.

3. **If you're on a tight budget, watch out for campground surcharges** such as extra fees for running your air conditioner or hooking up to cable TV, a surcharge for 50-amp electricity, or "extra person" charges for more than two people when you're traveling with your kids. Some of the campgrounds that accept pets may also levy a fee on Fido's head.

CAMPGROUND COSTS

A family of four can vacation in a family campground for less than $275 a week, and a snowbird can spend the entire winter in a full-service, warm-climate resort for less than $2,750, according to the **National Association of RV Parks and Campgrounds.**

4. **Join membership clubs that offer a discount to member campgrounds,** such as KOA (Kampgrounds of America) and Good Sam, which usually discount 10%. KOA promises the discount whether you pay by cash or credit card. In most cases, you can join up right at the campground when you register.

5. **Take advantage of age.** If one of you is older than 62, purchase a $10 National Parks and Federal Recreational Lands **Senior Pass** (this is a lifetime pass); if you are permanantly disabled you can apply for a free **Access Pass.** You can get this pass at any national park visitor center, national monument, recreation area, or wildlife refuge. In addition to free admission from then on, you then get a 50% discount on overnight camping areas administered by the federal government. (This replaces the former **Golden Age Passport,** which is still valid for a lifetime if you have one of those). For more information on these passes, visit: **www.nps.gov/meve/plan yourvisit/passprogram.htm**. Seniors should also check for any special discounts such as those offered to AARP members. Always ask at check-in.

6. **Look for free campgrounds,** such as those in the southwestern desert, administered by the Bureau of Land Management (**www.blm.gov**).

7. **Invest in a current campground guide to scout out the best value campgrounds,** or request a list of free campgrounds from a state tourism office. County, city, and national forest campgrounds range from free to much less expensive than most privately owned campgrounds, though they don't usually provide the luxury of hookups.

8. **If you arrive late at a campground, ask about staying overnight self-contained** in an overflow area at a reduced price. Some owners are amenable; some are not.

9. **Stay longer than a week and you can negotiate discounts,** usually from 10% to 20% or more, depending on the season and length of stay.

10. **Consider volunteering as a campground host** if you're interested in staying a long time in one area. You can camp free and may pick up a bit of pocket change for performing specified duties on the premises. (See "Becoming Campground Hosts," later in this chapter.)

SCAM ALERT!

A recurring scam preys on people who want to sell their memberships in campgrounds or resorts: An individual contacts the seller and says he has a buyer; if the seller sends him a check for an amount to cover expenses, he then sends an official-looking contract with the buyer's name and purchase price by Federal Express. All the eager seller has to do is send back a certified check for $500 or so via FedEx. You can guess what happens next—nothing.

INSIDER TIP: GATHERING INFORMATION

Always stop at the **tourist information offices** or welcome centers when you enter a new state on an interstate highway. You can pick up everything from maps to campground booklets to individual flyers for private RV parks that may offer a discount for visitors—all of it free.

Membership Campgrounds

Membership campgrounds and resorts are sort of like timeshare condos; once an RVer is a member, he can stay at any of the areas participating with the group. Joining something of this sort has to be weighed carefully against the initial cost, the amount of time you'll stay in the various resorts (note the locations and your access to them), and the amenities they offer.

For example, we checked out two upscale membership RV resorts affiliated with Outdoor Resorts of America in the Palm Springs area (see chapter 4, "The California Desert & Las Vegas," for details), the older of which is owner-operated and mostly owner-occupied. We were quite impressed with the cleanliness and security, as well as the landscaping. A great many expensive motor homes and fifth-wheels, as well as a few more modest travel trailers and mini–motor homes, are parked seasonally or permanently on the sites, many of them owned by Southern Californians who use them as weekend homes in the desert.

While a few owners make their sites available for overnighters or transient RVers, most seem to keep their vehicles based there. The base lot price in the newer park limited to motor homes is $50,000 to $200,000 for a 35x69-foot site, plus a monthly fee of $305.

There are about 450 membership resorts nationwide for RV travelers who want a range of indoor and outdoor activities. Most sell memberships for a one-time fee, much like a country club, plus an annual or monthly fee. One company, **Thousand Trails** (© **800/205-0606;** www.thousandtrails.com), has more than 80 member resorts nationwide; members may stay in any of their campgrounds for up to 30 days each year after paying an enrollment fee (which is sometimes waived) and an annual zone fee. If you spend more than 30 days per year at their resorts, a daily fee of $3 is charged. In general, you can stay at one campground for up to 14 consecutive days at a time.

In general, the spokesman said, the cost of joining a membership campground has dropped considerably from a peak of $10,000 a few years ago. Thousand Trails members pay an enrollment fee ranging from nothing (for one "camping zone") to $1,995 (for access to all resorts), and an annual fee of $499.

At all membership campgrounds, memberships can be sold after a specified period of time, but it appears to be a buyer's market with a lot of members opting to sell.

INSIDER TIP: CALIFORNIA CAMPING

California state parks have instituted something called **Enroute Camping** (http://parks.ca.gov/?page_id=21687), in which self-contained RVs may stay overnight in the day parking lot, from sunset until 9 or 10am the next morning, for the park's basic camping fee. These parks are located primarily along the coast and designated with RV profile signs.

Because some membership resorts in the past have been plagued by bankruptcies and undelivered promises, potential buyers should check with the local Better Business Bureau, the state attorney general's office, and members of the prospective resort before signing up or making a payment.

Avoid resorts that use high-pressure sales tactics and promise big prizes for buyers who sign up right away. And be wary of resorts that seem reluctant to provide information unless you make a personal visit. If you're interested in buying someone's membership, check the classified ads each month in RV magazines (and their online sites) such as *Trailer Life* and *MotorHome.*

Special Camping Situations

CAMPING WITH KIDS

Children make great campers. Veterans of family camping suggest involving children in the preliminary planning, assigning them regular duties at the campsite, and assigning them seats in the car or RV en route to the campsite. Curfew and campfire times should be established, taking into consideration any special evening events, from ranger talks to movies and dances at the campground. Older children might also be assigned a last-minute duty at home before leaving, whether locking doors and windows or removing perishable food from the refrigerator.

Even infants can happily go camping. Experts recommend taking along a backpack for a toddler or a chest pack for an infant for use on hikes, as well as a folding stroller and playpen, mosquito netting, and a baby bed guardrail to use in camp. A baby seat that clamps to a picnic table will also allow the child to participate with the rest of the family at meals or game time.

Sunscreen to protect a baby's delicate skin is essential, along with a gentle insect repellent like Avon's Skin-So-Soft lotion. (That works for adults as well; we've used it in buggy places like the jungles of Honduras.)

CAMPING WITH PETS

About 6% of all traveling dog owners take their pets with them on vacation, but only 1% of cat owners do, according to the Travel Industry Association of America. Here are 10 tips that will keep you and your campground neighbors from wishing that figure were lower.

- **Keep the cat's litter box in the shower or tub, encased inside a 30-gallon plastic trash bag.** Put the bottom of the box in the trash bag, dump a 10-pound bag of kitty litter inside, and snap on the litter box cover. The same cat owner who suggested this to us carries a folding cat cage so her pets can enjoy the outdoors.

- **Put a throw rug or two on top of the carpeting** in a motor home to protect it from cat (or dog) feet. It can be taken out and shaken when necessary, and washed and dried in the campground laundry.

- **Decide whether or not to use a kennel crate.** Owners get into debates about whether to keep dogs and cats in airline-type kennel crates when the RV is in motion, or let them lie on the floor, furniture, or dashboard. The lie-about school suggests the pet could protect itself better from possible injury in an accident if it's free, while the kennel crowd (many of them professional dog handlers) assert just as doggedly that the pet and driver are both safer when a crate is used.

- **Always carry resealable plastic bags to pick up after your pet,** even in camping and hiking areas (or should we say *especially* in camping and hiking areas?).

- **Never leave your pet alone in the RV for more than 10 minutes in any weather,** and less than that in summer when heat can cause great discomfort or even death.

- **Feed pets at night only** (especially if they're susceptible to motion sickness), so they will have digested the food before the next day's drive. Give only water during the day, preferably bottled water that you have introduced at home several days before leaving.

- **Check in a campground guide to ascertain whether the campground will accept pets.** While many do, some assess a surcharge, and all require that dogs be kept on a leash. When in doubt, call ahead. (See "The Best Campground Directories," earlier in this chapter, for a list of campgrounds.)

- **Bring familiar bedding and toys for the pet.** For about a week ahead of setting off on your pet's first trip, spend some time just sitting with it in the RV to help it become accustomed to the new space.

- **Bring along your pet's vaccination records and extra leashes and collars,** as well as flea treatment products that will kill not only live fleas, but eggs and larvae as well.

- **Good Sam Club members can take advantage of the club's Lost Pet Service.** They provide a tag imprinted with a toll-free number to call so your pet can be returned during, rather than after, the trip.

WINTER CAMPING

Some of our best RVing adventures have been in winter in snow-covered campgrounds in national parks such as the Grand Canyon and Bryce Canyon, as well as at various ski resorts. Skiers on a budget will find that many good ski areas permit free, or low-cost, self-contained RV parking overnight in their parking lots—Killington and Aspen

Ain't Misbehavin': Campground Etiquette

1. **No claim jumping.** Anything marking a campsite, from a jug of water on a picnic table to a folding chair in the parking space, means the site is occupied and the campers are temporarily away in their car or RV. You may not set it aside and move into the site.

2. **Mind your fellow campers' personal space.** Teach your kids never to take a shortcut across an occupied campsite, but to use the road or established pathways to get where they're going.

3. **Keep your pets from roaming.** Never let your dog roam free in a campground. It should be walked on a leash and exercised in a designated pet area.

4. **Avoid using your generator whenever possible,** even within designated generator-use hours, to keep from disturbing other campers with the noise and fumes. If using electrical appliances such as microwaves and TV sets is that important, go camping in a private campground with hookups.

5. **Avoid loud and prolonged engine revving** in the early morning and late evening hours.

6. **Don't play stereos, TVs, or boom boxes loudly at any time in a campground.** Many of your fellow campers are there to enjoy the peace and quiet.

7. **Never, ever dump wastewater from holding tanks, even gray water, on the ground.** While some claim it's good for the grass, it can also contain virulent salmonella bacteria, if raw chicken has been rinsed in the sink, or bits of fecal matter from diapers. This matter can be transferred to anyone touching or stepping on contaminated ground. Gray water, like black water, belongs *only* in a dump station.

8. **Do not cut trees for firewood.** Most campgrounds sell firewood at special stands or the camp store. Even picking up or chopping dead wood is forbidden in many parks.

9. **Watch what you throw in the fire.** Never leave aluminum foil, aluminum cans, bottles, or filter-tipped cigarette butts in a campground fire ring or grill. They do not burn, but remain as litter. And never crush out cigarettes on the ground without picking up the butts and putting them in the garbage.

10. **Don't leave porch or entry lights on all night in camp;** they may shine in someone else's bedroom window.

Highlands, for example—while other resorts such as Breckenridge, Deer Valley, and New York's Holiday Valley have RV hookups or year-round RV campgrounds at or near the site. California's Sierra Summit has free RV hookups for skiers.

Many RVers enjoy snowmobiling, sledding, cross-country skiing, skating, and ice-fishing in winter. Besides being able to stay toasty warm with a propane heater that does not require a hookup, winter RVers can enjoy hot meals, hot showers, and a snug, cozy feeling despite ice and snow all around.

We've found winter a good time to visit and photograph national parks, particularly in the Southwest, where a light dusting of snow highlights the vivid red canyons and green pines. Another bonus is the wildlife, especially deer and elk, that retreats to lower elevations in winter for better feeding. (See chapter 5, "Utah's Parks & Canyons.")

10 Tips for Cozy Winter Camping

1. **Don't connect your water hose to an outdoor faucet overnight** unless you want to create a 25-foot Popsicle. Use water from the RV's supply and refill when necessary.

2. **Add antifreeze to holding tanks** to keep drains from freezing.

3. **Don't park under trees** where branches heavily weighted with snow and ice could break off and fall on your RV.

4. **Watch battery strength;** the colder it gets, the faster it will discharge.

5. **Open one window slightly for fresh air when using a propane heater;** we use the window above the kitchen sink.

6. **Leave the bathroom door open at night** so the heat from the main living area can circulate inside this normally unheated room.

7. **Keep a pair of après-ski boots handy** for good traction on even short walks through the snow, especially to a photo opportunity.

8. **Carry chains or have snow tires** for your tow vehicle and RV.

9. **Don't let snow accumulate** on the refrigerator roof vent or exhaust ports.

10. **Drive with extreme care.** Even an experienced driver will find handling a motor home or pulling a towable trickier in snow and ice. A heavy motor home can be difficult to stop on an icy surface.

MAKING RESERVATIONS AT FEDERAL CAMPSITES

You can call for campsite reservations in many national parks, forests, and U.S. Army Corps of Engineers Campgrounds—although the line is usually busy and you'll probably wait on hold for a long time. It's easier to book your reservation on the Internet. The phone line is answered daily from 7am to midnight Eastern Standard Time (℃ **877/444-6777;** www.recreation.gov).

Becoming Campground Hosts

Energetic retirees or full-timers on a budget can camp free and sometimes pick up a little extra income as well by volunteering as campground hosts or work campers. In theory, it's a great idea—living in your RV in a lovely campground with free hookups, maybe even with your pick of sites.

In practice, however, veterans of a season's work seem to either love it or hate it. Some mutter darkly of being treated like migrant labor, while others describe it as a highlight of their lives. A lot depends on how thoroughly you check out the campground and its management ahead of time and how realistic you are about doing hard and sometimes unpleasant chores, like cleaning toilets and showers or telling a noisy camper to turn off his generator at curfew.

If campground-hosting sounds like something you may want to do, here's how to get started:

- **Apply well ahead of time.** Veterans of the program suggest a year in advance is not too early.

- **Learn about job openings in RV publications/online bulletin boards** under "Help Wanted," or from the online newsletter/community/website called Workamper News. Point your browser to **www.workamper.com**, where you can check out some general information for free, or join the community/have access to more specific information for a membership fee, which ranges from $42 to $198. To speak to a live person, call ✆ **800/446-5627,** weekdays between 9am and 4pm, Central Standard Time, or write 709 W. Searcy St., Heber Springs, AR 72543.

- **Volunteer at federal and state campgrounds.** If you'd like to be a campground host at a federal campsite, start your search at **www.nps.gov/getinvolved/volunteer.htm**, which has a searchable list of positions available at parks across the nation, and a downloadable application. You can also e-mail or write for information to: volunteer@nps.gov; or National Park Service, 1849 C St. NW, Washington, DC 20240. For state campgrounds, start with a call or visit the website of the individual state's department of recreation or official tourism website.

You should apply to several campgrounds, using a résumé that includes both personal and business references. Some ads ask for a recent photograph, which many applicants think shows possible discrimination because of age, physical appearance, or condition. Many campgrounds prefer a couple to a single person, or require a single person to work 30 to 40 hours a week rather than the 15 or 20 a couple would work.

If you get a positive response, ask for references from the campground managers so you can interview people who have worked previously for them. Check privately owned campgrounds with the local chamber of commerce or Better Business Bureau.

One cautionary note: Out-of-state workers who volunteer for California campgrounds are required to register their motor vehicles, including RVs, in California, since live-in volunteers are considered to be gainfully employed.

Plugging in Your Rig

ELECTRICAL HOOKUPS

Many older campgrounds, especially in state parks, may have 15- or 20-amp electric, for which modern RVs with a three-prong plug will need an adapter. When we first encountered this, we were at a Texas state park that loaned out adapters, but we soon got one of our own. You can use the lower amperage as long as you remember not to run the air conditioner, microwave, and TV set at the same time. Otherwise, you'll blow a fuse.

Each manufacturer issues a list of the amperage used by the various appliances, such as TV, refrigerator, microwave, and air conditioners. The total amperage of those units in use should not exceed your campground hookup amperage limitation, which is 15, 20, 30, or 50 amps. If you do exceed it, the power goes off, which is not so much a problem if you are in a campground with circuit breakers. But older campgrounds still using fuses will make resetting more difficult. Learn when to turn off one appliance before turning on another to keep from going over the limit.

Cable TV

Many private RV parks offer cable TV connections as an option, sometimes with an added dollar or two on the nightly fee. If you don't have a built-in exterior cable connection, you can use a length of coaxial cable hooked to the campground connection at one end, then routed through a window to your RV's TV set. You can also use an alternative outdoor entertainment area hookup as the connector. It's best if you carry your own cable, since the campground often does not provide it. Don't forget to turn off the switch to your roof antenna. (It usually has a little red light beside it.) It is also wise to have a male and female connector since campground cable connections vary.

Satellite TV

Many newer RVs have satellite dishes on the roof with internal wiring to the control box, usually installed near the TV set. The software for whatever system you use is usually included with the package. (The two major systems are DISH and DirecTV.) One disadvantage of the mounted dish is that in many campgrounds, there always seems to be a tree in the direct path of the satellite signal, requiring you to move the vehicle. If you have a dish, mention it when checking in so the registrar can assign you a site that is tree-free.

We carry a portable dish on a tripod using a secondary control box from our home, which means we don't have to have a separate account for the RV. We've found that it is a simple matter to make a connection to the satellite by moving the dish to an open viewing area. Satellite dishes are particularly advantageous when you travel in rural areas with little or no local TV reception, or when you plan to stay in one area for several days.

Remember, your dish programming is set on your home time, so as you move to other time zones, programs are still based on your home time.

Keeping a Clean Machine

We find that keeping the RV as clean as possible day by day while we're on the road is easier than going through the equivalent of spring cleaning every week or two. Here's how you should spend some of your downtime at the campsite or RV park when you're on the road.

OUTSIDE THE VEHICLE

Although car owners are accustomed to wielding a hose around in the driveway or in one of the little wash-it-yourself bays at a carwash, cleaning the outside of a motor home by yourself is akin to bathing an elephant; you can't do it in your driveway or the average carwash even if you wanted to. Even a coin-operated carwash with an extra-large bay is far from satisfactory for us. We run out of quarters or patience long before the job is done. And most campgrounds don't allow you to wash the vehicle at the campsite.

Washing

For a big-time RV wash, which you'll want to do after it's been in storage or slogged through some dusty terrain, look for a truck wash. You're most likely to find them along interstate highways adjacent to truck stops. Simply get in line behind the trucks (if you're lucky, two or three bays may be available on a busy day) and ease your way into the wash bay where an energetic team armed with hoses cleans your RV—soaping, rinsing, wiping, and waxing (which is optional) until your home on wheels is sparkling. For this service, which takes 15 to 30 minutes after you get into the bay, expect to pay $30 to $45. You'll want to be sure that all the windows and roof vents are closed tightly before you pull into the washing bay. While the truck wash cleans the outside, you can also put some of your own elbow grease into cleaning the inside—washing mirrors or polishing the woodwork and cabinetry.

Dusting & Debugging

To cut down on costly full-vehicle wash jobs, we've found that using a dry dusting mop cuts down on the number of washings. Each evening after hooking up and settling in, do a quick once-over on the exterior with the dry mop and get the day's dust and grime off before overnight dew cakes it. And don't forget the windshield and the vehicle's front end, which need a scrubbing with a wet brush or windshield scrubber to remove the bugs that have accumulated during the day's drive. Putting the job off until morning lets them solidify into something like cement and doubles your job of cleaning.

Waxing

Regardless of whether it's a motor home, travel trailer, or fifth-wheel, waxing an RV is a major job and costly if done professionally. Many campground and RV supply stores, such as Camping World, offer a number of waxes and protective materials. The work is up to you. We try to spread the joy around so we're not physically wrecked—doing the front of the vehicle one day, half the driver's side a few days later, the rest of the driver's side a few days after that, and so on, until after a couple of weeks the vehicle has been completely covered. But no matter how you approach the job, it's one that needs to be done regularly to save the finish of your exterior. Waxing is much cheaper than a new paint job.

INSIDE THE VEHICLE

Keeping the interior clean is a matter of tidying up daily. Regular tasks, such as cleaning the windows and mirrors, can be done when you stop for gas; a 50-plus-gallon tank takes 10 or 15 minutes to fill.

- **Woodwork:** Spray-and-polish wood cleaner repels dust and does a good job of keeping the cabinets and wood furniture looking and smelling clean.

- **Upholstery:** Even with modern fabrics that appear comparable to home interiors, RV upholstery is usually tough and hard to stain. We find spot-cleaning using a spray rug-and-upholstery cleaner that comes with a brush attachment accomplishes the job well.

- **Glass:** Windows and mirrors simply need a spray-and-wipe glass cleaner and a paper towel to be spotless and shiny in no time.

- **Floors:** A small, portable vacuum cleaner that can run on rechargeable batteries is handy for quick cleaning or even heavy-duty cleaning in an area as compact as an RV. Spot-cleaning spills on the carpet rarely is a problem, because most carpets in motor homes are stain resistant. We put a washable rug over high-traffic areas, such as the residential entrance, in front of the sink, beside the bed, and between the sofa and easy chair when the slideout is open.

- **Kitchen:** Wiping up kitchen spills when they happen helps keep the galley clean. We usually clean out the refrigerator when we bring the RV back home from a week or weekend away, or we clean it once a week when we're on the road. We give the sink a quick wipeover every evening after doing the dinner dishes.

HOLDING TANKS

Most RVs have two holding tanks—one for gray water (the water from the kitchen and bathroom sinks and shower) and one for black water (the waste from the toilet). Ongoing maintenance of these tanks requires the use of a liquid or powder, made especially for RV tanks, that deodorizes and dissolves solids. RV manufacturers recommend using biodegradable toilet paper, which breaks up more readily in the tank.

When hooked up to the sewage drain in a campground, keep the black water outlet closed; the gray water outlet can remain open. When the time comes to empty the tanks, close the gray water outlet to allow water to build up in the tank, and empty the black water tank first. Flush it out at the end with water poured in the toilet. (We store an empty 1-gallon plastic water jug for this job.) When you're finished, close off the black water valve. Next, run about a gallon of fresh water into the gray-water tank from the kitchen or bathroom faucets and then open the gray-water valve. This flushes out the hose as the gray-water tank empties. Close the valve, unhook the hose, and flush out the hose again before storing. Wear disposable rubber gloves when handling the sewage hoses and draining the tanks.

Part
2 RV Adventures

Hitting the Road on Nine Great RV Excursions

4. The California Desert & Las Vegas

5. Utah's Parks & Canyons

6. Driving the Alaska Highway

7. The Dakotas: Black Hills & Buffalo Burgers

8. The Rio Grande Valley & the Wilds of West Texas

9. In the Heart of the Heartland: Iowa, Illinois & Indiana

10. The Florida Keys (with Side Trips to the Everglades & Orlando)

11. The Blue Ridge Parkway & Skyline Drive

12. The Lobster Coast: New England & the Canadian Maritimes

The California Desert & Las Vegas

ACTUALLY, THERE'S NOT ONE DESERT IN CALIFORNIA, BUT MANY: Death Valley's low desert with its sizzling heat records, the **Mojave**'s high desert with its ghost towns and mines, and vast **Anza Borrego**, the biggest state park in California with 600,000 acres of cactus and canyons. Death Valley and Joshua Tree, previously designated national monuments, have been turned into national parks by Congress.

And then there's *The Desert:* **Palm Springs** and vicinity, where Beverly Hills residents go to desiccate. It's safe once again after its own Desert Storm action, when the late celebrity-mayor Sonny Bono outlawed teen Spring Break frivolities and put Palm Canyon Drive back in the hands of the Waxworks (the area's senior celebrity residents). It's where 10,000 swimming pools and countless lawn sprinklers, water slides, and misting outdoor air conditioners turn bone-dry air damp; and where cows are allotted 1,000 acres of feeding area apiece to browse on vitamin-rich desert spinach.

The California deserts gave us trail mix and date milkshakes, the state's first nudist bed-and-breakfasts, the world's first broken sound barrier, 20-Mule-Team Borax, and the Twentynine Palms Outhouse Race.

It's where Wyatt Earp retired; where Al Capone took the waters; where Lawrence of Arabia rode his camel across the dunes; where General Patton left his tank tracks; and where Paul Newman, Steve McQueen, and James Garner learned how to drive race cars.

It's where Elvis and Priscilla Presley honeymooned; where Frank Sinatra lived on Frank Sinatra Drive; and where old-time radio favorites Jack Benny, Amos and Andy, and Fibber McGee and Molly beamed their shows out to a simpler nation.

RVers can find the Hullabaloo World Tobacco Spitting Championships in Calico every Palm Sunday, visit an endangered desert pupfish in Anza Borrego State Park, attend camel and ostrich races in Indio during the National Date Festival in mid-February, and go sand-sailing on a dry lake at speeds up to 70 mph—with no brakes.

RVing in the California Desert & Las Vegas

A lazy loop around California's deserts can be made in one long haul or on a series of shorter drives from a central base. From the Palm Springs area, the route fans south and east as far as the Arizona and Mexico borders. From San Bernardino, it radiates east to the Colorado River, northeast to Las Vegas, and northwest to Death Valley. From Lancaster/Palmdale, it runs north into the Owens Valley east of the Sierra Nevada. The whole circuit is about 1,000 miles, plus side trips, but can be divided into a number of shorter trips.

California Desert Highlights

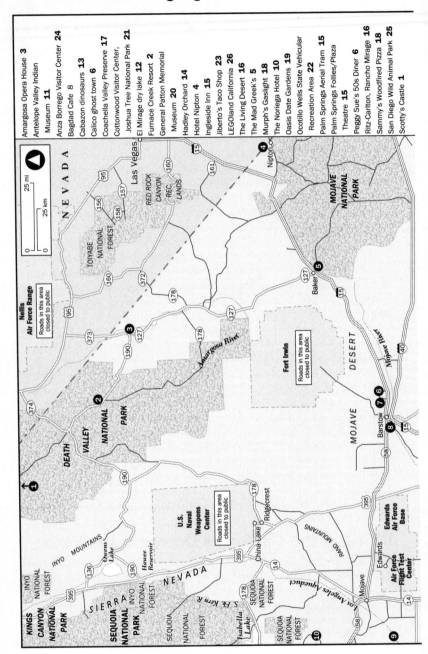

Amargosa Opera House **3**
Antelope Valley Indian
Museum **11**
Anza Borrego Visitor Center **24**
Bagdad Cafe **8**
Cabazon dinosaurs **13**
Calico ghost town **6**
Coachella Valley Preserve **17**
Cottonwood Visitor Center,
Joshua Tree National Park **21**
El Mirage dry lake **12**
Furnace Creek Resort **2**
General Patton Memorial
Museum **20**
Hadley Orchard **14**
Hotel Nipton **4**
Ingleside Inn **15**
Jiberto's Taco Shop **23**
LEGOland California **26**
The Living Desert **16**
The Mad Greek's **5**
Murph's Gaslight **18**
The Noriega Hotel **10**
Oasis Date Gardens **19**
Ocotillo Wells State Vehicular
Recreation Area **22**
Palm Springs Aerial Tram **15**
Palm Springs Follies/Plaza
Theatre **15**
Peggy Sue's 50s Diner **6**
Ritz-Carlton, Rancho Mirage **16**
Sammy's Woodfired Pizza **18**
San Diego Wild Animal Park **25**
Scotty's Castle **1**

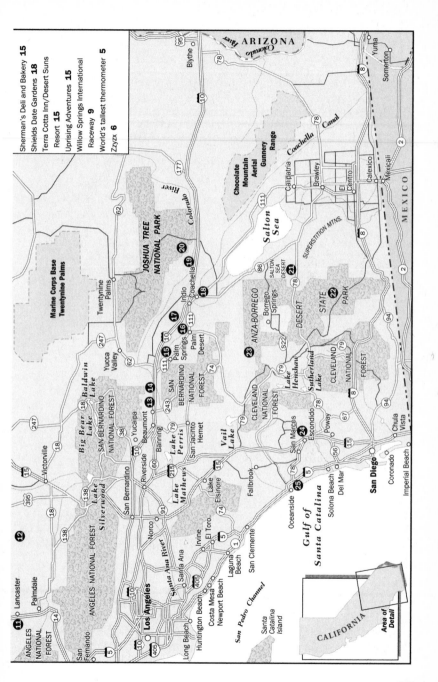

Sherman's Deli and Bakery **15**
Shields Date Gardens **18**
Terra Cotta Inn/Desert Suns Resort **15**
Uprising Adventures **15**
Willow Springs International Raceway **9**
World's tallest thermometer **5**
Zzyzx **6**

Calico's bottle house.

Stay on roads and trails at all times, whether driving or walking. The desert terrain is fragile and slow growing, and one careless off-road driver can destroy decades-old vegetation.

HITTING THE HIGHLIGHTS

If you divide your time between Death Valley, the Palm Springs area, Joshua Tree National Park, and Anza Borrego State Park, you should get to know the California desert fairly well. Allow 4 days in Death Valley, and then drive south through Baker, Barstow, and Calico, or detour into Nevada for a fling at the gaudy casinos of Las Vegas or Laughlin. Allow 2 or 3 days in Joshua Tree, longer if you want to make day trips over into nearby Palm Springs. Anza Borrego State Park is south from Indio and Coachella, then west on Route 78 through Ocotillo Wells.

If you're flying in and renting an RV, either Los Angeles or San Diego makes a good base.

GOING FOR THE LONG HAUL

If you want to spend a winter among the snowbirds in the California desert, you could explore all three major desert areas, take leisurely side trips, then settle in around Palm Springs if you're affluent or on the Bureau of Land Management (BLM) areas (see "Trimming Costs: Eight Money-Saving Tips for the Road," in chapter 2) if you're strapped.

Most recreation areas, state parks, and U.S. Forest Service campgrounds have posted camping limits, often around 14 days, but you can check out and then check in again at a later date. Or you could become a VIP (Volunteer in Parks) and camp free all season long as a campground host (see "Becoming Campground Hosts," in chapter 3).

Travel Essentials

WHEN TO GO

Winter is ideal in California's desert country: balmy and warm days with cool nights. Early spring and late autumn are also good seasons. Summer in the low desert is only for mad dogs and Englishmen, as well as Germans, Swiss, and Japanese, who dote on traveling in Death Valley during August when the temperature can top 115°F.

WHAT TO TAKE

Bring binoculars, a camera (and batteries), and a tripod if you plan to shoot photos of cactus, wildflowers, or dazzling sunsets. Carry a strong sunscreen and a canteen or water carrier for hikes.

WHAT TO WEAR

In the desert, lightweight and light-colored natural-fiber fabrics are best. Stout-soled hiking shoes and tough-fabric pants are essential to repel cactus spikes if you're hiking in cactus country. Winter evenings cool quickly once the sun sets, so be prepared with a down vest or jacket, windbreaker, or heavy sweatshirt. A wide-brimmed hat, preferably one that can be tied down, is best in the strong desert sun.

TRIMMING COSTS ON THE ROAD

Ask any snowbird–turned–desert rat how to live off the land—or rather, the Bureau of Land Management—and he'll tell you about "the Slabs" or one of the other Long-Term Visitor Areas (LTVAs) in the southern desert.

Here's how it works: You can buy an **Annual Pass** to the parks for $80 from any participating federal recreation site or office, which gives you a camping discount good for 1 year. If you're a senior citizen (62 or over) you can get a lifetime **Senior Pass** for $10 or a free **Access Pass** if you are a U.S. citizen or permanent resident with disabilities. Prices and discounts vary depending on the season, state, and camping area. To make an advance purchase, call one of the district offices listed below and they'll supply a permit by mail. If you want to spend only a few days, you can buy a short-term permit from campground hosts in each camp area.

Don't expect hookups, paved parking (except at "the Slabs," which were once cement pads for military buildings), water, or sanitary dumpsites. What you get is plenty of desert, some solitude if you wish, and all the warm sunshine you can handle.

The sites are generally located off I-8 west of Yuma, off I-10, and in Arizona at Quartzsite on U.S. 95 off I-10. The most established areas are Hot Spring, off I-8 east of El Centro at Hwy. 115; Imperial Dam, off I-8 at Winterhaven, then west on

Senator Wash Road; Pilot Knob, off I-8 at Sidewinder Road, 5 miles west of Yuma; Dunes Vista, off I-8 at Ogilby Road, 10 miles west of Yuma; La Posa at Quartzsite, Arizona, on both sides of Route 95; Midland, off I-10 at Lovekin Boulevard; and Mule Mountain, off I-10 at Wiley's Well Road, then north 9 miles. To get more information and desert maps, call the **Bureau of Land Management,** California State Office, 2800 Cottage Way, Ste. W-1623, Sacramento, CA 95825-1886 (℗ **916/978-4400;** www.blm.gov).

WHERE TO GET TRAVEL INFORMATION

The following organizations can supply you with any visitor information you need for your desert trek.

- **The Borrego Springs Chamber of Commerce,** 786 Palm Canyon Dr., Borrego Springs, CA 92004 (℗ **800/559-5524** or 760/767-5555; www.borregosprings chamber.com).

- **California Travel and Tourism,** P.O. Box 1499, Sacramento, CA 94812 (℗ **877/225-4367;** www.visitcalifornia.com).

- **Inland Empire Tourism Council** (providing information for Riverside and San Bernardino counties), 1201 Research Park Dr., Ste. 100, Riverside, CA 92507 (℗ **951/779-6700;** www.discoverie.com).

- **Las Vegas Convention and Visitors Authority,** 3150 Paradise Rd., Las Vegas, NV 89109 (℗ **877/847-4858** or 702/892-0711; www.lvcva.com).

- **Palm Springs Desert Resorts,** 70-100 Hwy. 111, Rancho Mirage, CA 92270 (℗ **800/967-3767** or 760/770-9000; www.palmspringsusa.com).

- **Palm Springs Visitors Information Center,** 777 North Palm Canyon Dr., Palm Springs, CA 92262 (℗ **800/34-SPRINGS** [347-7746] or 760/778-8418; www.visitpalmsprings.com).

DRIVING & CAMPING TIPS

- **Leave an itinerary with friends.** Never head out on back roads in the desert without telling someone where you're going and when you expect to return.

- **Carry water**—at least 1 gallon per person per day.

- **Carry good, detailed local maps.** Desert access guides are available for $4 and up, each from the Bureau of Land Management, 2800 Cottage Way, Ste. W-1623, Sacramento, CA 95825-1886 (℗ **916/978-4400;** www.blm.gov). There are 22 desert area maps, so be specific about what area map you'd like.

- **Never trespass on private desert land**—some of the "desert rats" don't take kindly to strangers.

- **Be aware of where you set up camp.** Set up at least 200 yards away from a man-made water source for wildlife and no more than 300 yards from the road. Don't set up camp in a wash where flash floods could literally wash you away.

The Best Desert Sights, Tastes & Experiences

OFF-THE-WALL ATTRACTIONS

Amargosa Opera House. The ballerina used to dance for an audience of painted figures if there was no live audience at the Amargosa, at the intersection of highways 127 and 190. Here, dancer Marta Becket has painted in 250 spectators for her dances and pantomimes scheduled on winter weekends. Marta now does "The Sitting Down Show" from Nov–May, and the Opera House hosts other live performances. Tickets $15 adults, $12 children. Call for reservations (© **760/852-4441;** www.amargosa-opera-house.com).

Antelope Valley Indian Museum, Lancaster. Hand-built by a romantic, self-taught artist in 1928, this whimsical and eclectic place, built in the style of a Swiss chalet, is filled with giant kachina dolls, bird-claw fishhooks, grass skirts, and some unlikely illustrated Indian legends; a second-story cave is open on weekends only. The museum is open Sat and Sun from 11am–4pm. Admission $3 adults, free for children 14 and under. 15701 E. Ave. M, btw. E. 150th and 170th sts., in Lancaster (© **661/946-3055;** www.avim.av.org).

The Bagdad Cafe is nowhere near Iraq, although the terrain is not that different. This unassuming road cafe was the location of a 1988 movie, *Bagdad Cafe,* which was later made into a television series starring Whoopi Goldberg. The movie was a minor success in the U.S., but was very big in Europe, and today French and German tourists drive up to visit the cafe and have a Jack Palance burger (with bacon) or a Bagdad omelet. The regulars look on with a bemused attitude. The Bagdad Café is on Route 66 in Newberry Springs, about 18 miles east of Barstow (© **760/257-3101**).

Barstow Station. East of Barstow on East Main Street (off I-15), the station looks like several railway cars parked beside a railway station, but it is really one big building. Inside is a huge, rambling shop with an astonishing collection of great tacky souvenirs, from life-size plaster-of-Paris howling coyotes to plastic cacti and personalized mugs for every Tom, Dick, and Lupe that happens by. Things dangle from the ceilings and are stacked precariously on random shelves and counters around the premises. A tour-bus rest stop, the station also has a McDonald's and takeout food counters. We were fascinated with the 42 jelly-bean flavors, not to mention the life-size plaster American eagles and the Marilyn Monroe cookie jars. Barstow/California Welcome Center (© **760/253-4782;** www.barstowstation.net).

Coachella Valley Preserve covered-wagon tours. If you've always yearned for the rugged pioneer life, hop into a genuine bone-crusher of a prairie schooner, drawn by draft mules, with campfire and barbecue also on the agenda. Cost $60 adults, $30 children, for a 2-hr. tour. Located north of I-10 and about 6 miles east of Thousand Palms at the north end of Washington St. on the Coachella Valley Preserve. Call ahead for reservations (© **800/367-2161** or 760/347-2161; www.coveredwagon tours.com).

Death Valley may look deserted, but you'll find lots of interest to discover there.

Long-eared owls and short-eared owls. If you've ever wondered what the difference is (besides the obvious), take a winter's day drive on the dry side to Harper Lake, 25 miles east of Barstow via Hwy. 58, then 5 miles north to the dry lake. The long-eared owls hang out in woodland thickets, while the short-eared owls stay close to the marsh. One veteran birder reports seeing 300 short-eared owls feeding in a single field. Bureau of Land Management (© **916/978-4400;** www.blm.gov/ca/st/en/fo/barstow/harper.html).

The moving rocks of Death Valley. They skitter along the desert floor at Racetrack Playa, leaving behind a trail of their route. Scientists suspect rain-slick clay allows the wind to push the rocks back and forth at speeds of up to 2 mph, but no one has ever seen them in motion. Death Valley National Park, at state highways 127 and 190 (© **760/786-3200;** www.nps.gov/deva).

Nudist bed-and-breakfasts, Palm Springs. We haven't run across many of these anywhere, but Palm Springs has a selection. The **Terra Cotta Inn** is a clothing-optional, 17-room resort for couples, open year-round. Rates $149–$189 double. 2388 E. Racquet Club Rd. (© **800/SUNNY-FUN** [786-6938] or 760/322-6059; www.sunnyfun.com).

Desert Sun Resort also welcomes naturists with 74 year-round units, at $150–$495. 1533 Chaparral Rd. (© **800/960-4SUN** [4786]; www.desertsunresort.com). Other small, clothing-optional boutique hotels in Palm Springs cater to gay male or female clientele. For a full hotel list, contact Palm Springs Visitors Information Center (© **800/347-7746;** www.visitpalmsprings.com).

The Palm Springs Aerial Tram has a new Peaks Restaurant with breathtaking views of the desert, along with fine dining. The cuisine is California Modern. Appetizers begin at $10, entrees at $21. Daily noon–3pm and 4–8pm. Reservations recommended (© **760/325-4537**; www.pstramway.com). Take the tram after 3pm for reduced ticket prices.

The Palm Springs Follies. Retired chorus girls, ages 50–80 with great gams, still kick 'em high at the city's nostalgic Plaza Theatre. Daily matinees at 1:30pm, nightly performances at 7pm, Nov–May. Tickets $50–$95. 128 S. Palm Canyon Dr. (© **760/327-0225** for tickets; www.psfollies.com).

The roadside dinosaurs at Cabazon. About 13 miles west of Palm Springs on I-10 (Main St. exit), the dinosaurs appeared in the film *Pee-wee's Big Adventure* and serve to promote a chow stop at the Wheel Inn. Here, no less a gourmet authority than Gault-Millau praised the huge helpings of homemade desserts, from strawberry shortcake to bread pudding. The original owners of the complex sold out to a group that now uses them to promote a "creationist" view of evolution. All is best seen from the roadway. 50770 Seminole Dr., Cabazon (© **951/922-0076**; www.cabazondinosaurs.com).

Scotty's Castle, Death Valley. A $2-million Moorish mansion built by Albert Johnson, a Chicago insurance executive, and his radio evangelist wife (but named for a performer in Buffalo Bill's Wild West Show who also lived there), the castle has an unfinished 270-foot swimming pool, 25 rooms with tapestries and fireplaces, and a 26-ft. clock tower. Johnson and his friend Walter Scott (Scotty) rejected designs submitted by Frank Lloyd Wright in favor of an unknown architect who didn't go on to fame and fortune. Scotty died in 1954, and his estate consisted of one well-worn cowboy hat. Guided 1-hr. tours led by costumed docents are so popular that you can expect a wait of an hour or two in season; arrive early for the first available spots. Advance tickets may be purchased at www.recreation.gov or © **877/444-6777**. (Tickets must be purchased at least 1 day in advance). Daily 9am–5pm. Admission $11 adult, $9 seniors, $6 children. The castle is on Scotty's Castle Road in Death Valley National Park. You can get there from Hwy. 190. Look for a sign. You can also take Hwy. 95 to 267 S. and take the Scotty's Castle exit (© **760/786-2392**; www.nps.gov/deva/historyculture/scottys-castle.htm).

The world's tallest thermometer, Baker. It soars above the Bun Boy restaurant in the Mojave Desert town of Baker, showing 1 foot for each degree of temperature, up to the hottest recorded day in history at Death Valley (July 10, 1913, when it hit 134°F/57°C). You can see it as you drive along I-15, with the current temperature recorded day and night. The restaurant dates from 1926, and has a mini-museum about Death Valley in the entrance. The intriguingly named Bun Boy Motel and Country Store is next door (© **760/733-4252**).

PUTTING YOURSELF IN PERIL, AT SPEED

Daytime in the desert allows for plenty of extremes besides the heat. Here are four of the better extreme sports for the adventurous:

Willow Springs International Raceway. Willow Springs Raceway is an appointment in the fast lane, a chance to watch or take part in fast-track racing. You can watch a race, take a lesson on handling your own car from an expert at any of several schools, or book a formula-car racing session, just as many movie-star drivers like Paul Newman and James Garner have done in the past. 3500 75th St. W., in Rosamond. From Hwy. 14 N., exit west on Rosamond Blvd. Continue for 6 miles to the track (*©* **661/256-6666;** Fast Lane Racing School *©* **888/948-4888;** www.willowsprings raceway.com).

El Mirage dry lake. El Mirage, in the eastern Mojave, is a haven for sand sailors on windy weekend afternoons. With the right wind, their sand-sail crafts—T-shaped, tubular 6x10-ft. frames, with a triangular sail on a 17-ft. mast—reach speeds of up to 70 mph—but there are no brakes. Get there via Ave. P in Lancaster, which turns into El Mirage Rd.; then drive north on El Medio Rd. (unpaved) 5 miles to the lake. You need a permit to drive into the Off-Highway Vehicle Recreation area, which costs $15 for one day, $30 for a week, and $90 for an annual permit. For more information, call *©* **760/252-6000;** www.blm.gov/ca/st/en/fo/barstow/mirage.html.

Vegas Extreme Skydiving in Las Vegas has classes for first-timers as well as experienced jumpers. Dive from the highest elevation for the longest freefall. It's $224 per jump, plus $99 for first-time instruction. And to really remember the experience, get a video of the whole event. If you think you need it, book a skydiving wedding starting at $1,299. 23600 S. Las Vegas Blvd. (*©* **866/398-5867** or 702/303-3914; www. vegasextremeskydiving.com).

Uprising Adventures, Joshua Tree, offers rock-climbing packages at Idyllwild, Joshua Tree, Mission Gorge, and Stoney Point for various stages of ability. Minimum of three people to a class, $150 per person per day. There are also introductory classes emphasizing equipment, knots, rope handling, belaying, and more. Private guiding is also available. P.O. Box 129, Joshua Tree, CA 92252 (*©* **888/254-6266;** www.uprising.com).

THREE DESERT SPLURGES

1. **The Inn at Furnace Creek and the Ranch at Furnace Creek.** Furnace Creek, Hwy. 190 in Death Valley National Park, has a dazzling, cerulean swimming pool and a palm garden that looks like a mirage from the 1930s. Stone arches frame distant views of snow-capped mountains beside a lush oasis shaded by palms. $126–$213 standard double at the Ranch, $320–$365 at the Inn (*©* **800/236-7916** or 760/786-2345; www.furnacecreekresort.com).

2. **Desert Adventures of Palm Springs.** A bouncy jeep ride along private dirt roads with this outfit lends insight into everything from the lifestyles and rituals of the local Cahuilla tribes to fascinating facts about desert flora and fauna. Try to catch a ride with Morgan Wind-in-Her-Hair Levine, a mile-a-minute talker and one of the company's co-owners. Jeep eco-tours last 3 hr. and cost $99–$150 for adults. Reservations required (*©* **888/440-5337** or 760/340-2345; www.red-jeep.com).

3. **Ingleside Inn in Palm Springs.** Sit under the shade trees on a lawn by the pool at the inn, built around 1935, on the corner of Hwy. 111 and Ramon, where Howard Hughes used to check in under the name "Earl Martyn," along with Ava Gardner as "Mrs. Clark." In Melvyn's Restaurant, you can still dine on

1950s-style martinis, shrimp cocktails, and steak while overhearing remarks like, "Sheila, you look wonderful—not even in the light can you tell!" $150–$425 double. 200 Ramon Rd. (© **800/772-6655** or 760/325-0046; www.ingleside inn.com).

GREAT TAKEOUT (OR EAT-IN) TREATS

Murph's Gaslight, Bermuda Dunes. The pan-fried chicken with all the trimmings— black-eyed peas, mashed potatoes, cornbread, hot biscuits, country gravy, and fruit cobbler—can be ordered as takeout if you call ahead. You can also feast family-style at a table inside on a first-come, first-served basis; the platters of chicken keep on coming. Tues–Sat 11am–3pm and 5–9pm; Sun 3–9pm. Early bird special at $10 starts at 5pm. 79-860 Ave. 42, by the airport in Bermuda Dunes (© **760/345-6242;** www. murphsgaslight.com).

The Mad Greek's, Baker. The hummus and homemade pita bread and falafel sandwich with tahini are good choices to go at the Mad Greek's. A photo of Zsa Zsa Gabor hangs over the door. Truckers like the $10 ham-and-three-egg breakfast pictured on the wall. Daily 24 hr. Take Hwy. 127 to the Baker exit. 72112 Baker Blvd. (© **760/733-4354**).

Hadley Orchard, Cabazon. The original recipe for trail mix, concocted many years ago by an employee of Hadley Orchard, is still for sale at the freeway farmstand, along with dried fruit and nuts and what appears to be the world's largest assortment of fruit-and-nut gift packs. Take the Apache Trail exit from I-10 near Palm Springs. Daily 9am–5pm. (© **800/854-5655** or 951/849-5255; www.hadleyfruitorchards. com).

Sammy's Woodfired Pizza, Palm Desert. In a mall complex on El Paseo at Larkspur Avenue is a great inexpensive restaurant for families. Fronting a misted outdoor patio is a large room with booths and tables. Choose from 21 wood-fired pizzas drizzled with chili oil, such as the New York pizza, a concoction of homemade tomato sauce, sautéed mushrooms, pepperoni, salami, and Italian sausage, all for $13. The menu also has a variety of salads and pastas. Daily 11am–9pm. 73595 El Paseo, Palm Desert (© **760/836-0500;** www.sammyspizza.com).

Sherman's Deli and Bakery, Palm Springs. At this indoor and outdoor-patio restaurant, join the locals eating 2-inch-thick deli sandwiches or lox and bagels. The bakery has rich, delicious cakes and pastries that would put any calorie-conscious dieter into trauma if it weren't for the Lite Lunch Special: mushroom barley soup or matzo ball soup with half of any regular deli-variety sandwich. Daily 7am–9pm. Early bird dinner at $12 is from 4–7pm. 73-161 Country Club Dr., Palm Springs (© **760/ 325-1199;** www.shermansdeli.com).

Fresh dates, Indio. Dates are harvested btw. Sept and mid-Dec around Indio; check **Shields Date Gardens,** here since 1924, for Royal Medjool-Super Jumbo dates, the world's biggest. Daily 9am–5pm. 80-225 Hwy. 111 (© **760/347-7768;**

www.shieldsdategarden.com). The **Oasis Date Gardens** in Thermal on Hwy. 111 shows a free enlightening video on the sex life of the date (© **800/827-8017;** www.oasisdate.com).

Peggy Sue's 50's Diner, Yermo. This great roadside eatery brightens the night with salads, pizzas, malts, and burgers, plus kitschy souvenirs, old movie-star photos (what is it about the desert that brings out old movie-star photos?), and souvenir dolls. In Yermo, it's off I-15 at the Ghost Town Rd. exit at 35654 Yermo Rd. (© **760/254-3370;** www.peggysuesdiner.com).

The Noriega Hotel, Bakersfield. A family-style Basque restaurant, the Noriega Hotel is always worth a detour. Founded in 1893 by Faustino Noriega, it has been operated since 1931 by the Elizalde family. Breakfast ($10), tailored to the appetites of the Basque sheepherders who've always eaten here, includes fried eggs or omelets, Basque sausage, bacon or ham, California jack cheese, sheepherder bread, salsa, coffee, and wine. At lunch ($14) and dinner ($20), the long tables are set with tureens of hot soup, platters of salad, beans, meats (chicken, lamb, pork chops, liver and onions, corned beef and cabbage), vegetables, bottles of house red wine, loaves of sheepherder's bread with butter, and dishes of bleu cheese. Tues–Sun 7–9am; noon seating; 7pm seating. The hotel has a medium-size parking lot; large RVs will also find adequate street parking within a block or two. Reservations recommended, even if only a few minutes ahead of arrival time. The hotel is at 525 Sumner St., near the intersection of Golden State and Union avenues (© **661/322-8419;** www.noriegahotel.com).

Jiberto's Taco Shop, Borrego Springs. Ensenada-style fish tacos, *carne asada* (roasted meat) burritos, or Sonoran chimichangas can be found at Jiberto's in Borrego Springs. Call ahead for takeout. Daily 7am–10pm. 655 Palm Canyon Dr. (© **760/767-1008**).

WILDLIFE-WATCHING

Dusk and dawn are the best wildlife-watching times in the desert, especially where there's a water source. Stay downwind so the animals can't smell you.

Besides the bandit **coyotes** that lurk around all day, you might spot the elegant little **desert kit fox** or the malevolent **sidewinder** in the sand dunes around Stovepipe Wells in Death Valley at dawn or dusk. **Roadrunners** are everywhere, looking exactly like the cartoon version.

California's endangered state reptile, the **desert tortoise,** can often be seen in its Mojave Desert sanctuary near California City. Chances of sighting one are best from mid-March to mid-June, but if you spot one moving slowly across the highway, don't touch him or pick him up. He'll panic and pee, losing the precious water he's been hoarding from those rare winter showers.

One of the best places to see **desert bighorn sheep** is on the manicured lawns of the posh Ritz-Carlton Hotel in Rancho Mirage. They hoof down from their adjacent hilltop wildlife sanctuary to feast on the foliage, and don't seem to mind tourists and cameras.

Another good spot to look for bighorns, especially rams, is in Anza Borrego State Park on road S22 between markers 12.5 and 13.5. The best time is in the morning; pull your vehicle off the road and do not disturb them.

In Death Valley, you can spot the endangered **desert pupfish** from a boardwalk at Salt Creek Interpretive Trail off 190 south of Stovepipe Wells.

Both the pupfish and the rare **fringe-toed lizard,** which can shut off all its body orifices and "swim" through sand dunes, can be found in the Coachella Valley Preserve (**http://coachellavalleypreserve.org**) and may be glimpsed on one of several easy walking trails radiating out from the visitor center. Take Thousand Palms Canyon Road off Ramon Road north of I-10 near Palm Springs. The preserve is open year-round, but the visitor center is only staffed September to April.

The **Living Desert** is a 1,200-acre wildlife and botanical park located off Haystack Road in Palm Desert, showcasing captive and wild-roaming desert species year-round. Look for roadrunners, quail, desert tortoises, desert pupfish, rattlesnakes, desert kangaroo rats, Peninsular bighorn sheep, coyotes, golden eagles, Mexican wolves, bobcats, mountain lions, javelinas, and rare naked mole-rats. It's open daily 9am to 5pm. Admission is $13 adults, $11 seniors, $7.50 children ages 3 to 12. 47-900 Portola Ave. (© **760/346-5694;** www.livingdesert.org).

On the Road

ACTIVE ADVENTURES IN ANZA BORREGO

In the 600,000 acres of California's largest state park, tent campers can set up almost anywhere as long as they follow the park's guidelines, spelled out in a free publication at the visitor center in Borrego Springs. Campers will have to carry their own water in and all trash and garbage back out.

The earth-covered "underground" **visitor center** (© **760/767-4205;** www.parks. ca.gov/?page_id=638), on S22 (aka Palm Canyon Dr.) 2 miles west of the town of Borrego Springs, provides an introduction to the park, including the endangered desert pupfish. The visitor center is open daily from November through April, and on weekends May through October.

More organized camping is available at **Borrego Palm Canyon Campground,** part of the state park system, with full hookups and 30-amp electrical capacity, $35 (maximum camper length 35 ft.). Sites are unshaded and not particularly attractive, but the surroundings are pretty. Hot showers and flush toilets are on-site, and a self-guided nature trail sets out from the campground area. It's located on S22, just 2 miles west of Borrego Springs (© **760/767-5311,** reservations can also be made online at www.reserveamerica.com).

The best time to visit is during the winter months. With good January rains, expect to see blossoms in February when the flowering Mojave yucca breaks out in cream-colored bursts from spiny stalks, ocotillos take on sprays of tiny red flowers, and beavertail cactuses are topped with big jaunty pink blooms. And don't be surprised to see 10,000 other like-minded visitors. Check on conditions in advance by calling the visitor center.

You can get a recorded message about **wildflower viewing** at © **760/767-4684** and if you send a stamped, self-addressed postcard to Wildflower Notification, Anza-Borrego Desert SP, 200 Palm Canyon Dr., Borrego Springs, CA 92004, they'll notify you of the best time for wildflower viewing.

East of Anza Borrego on the north side of Hwy. 78, just west of the San Diego County border with Imperial County, is the **Ocotillo Wells State Vehicular Recreation Area** (http://ohv.parks.ca.gov/?page_id=1217), where owners of 125s with "knobbies" (tires with knobby tread) can play "pretend-moto" (or motocross) and new owners of 4X4s can check out the equipment without offending the neighbors.

CAMPGROUND OASES AROUND ANZA BORREGO

Fountain of Youth Spa Campground. This campground has 400 RV sites with full hookups; flush toilets; showers; artesian steam rooms; hydrojet pools; a masseur; a Laundromat; a barber shop; a salon; propane; a grocery store; and church services for Catholics, Protestants, Mormons, and Adventists. Huge and almost mind-boggling, Fountain of Youth says it's for those over 55. Sites $39 a day, $235 a week, $595 a month. On Coachella Canal Rd. near Salton Sea, 15 miles north of **Niland** off Hwy. 111 (℃ **760/354-1558** information or ℃ 888/8000-SPA [772] reservations; www. foyspa.com).

Palm Canyon Resort and RV Park. Palm Canyon Resort in Borrego Springs makes a good family getaway, except on major winter holiday weekends when many RVs are so close together that it looks like gridlock. With 130 full hookups (30-amp), cable TV, modem hookups, a heated pool and spa, and an Old West–style resort hotel adjoining it, the park is appealing despite its fairly narrow, 20-ft. sites. Sites $36. Located at 221 Palm Canyon Dr., Borrego Springs. From Hwy. 86, take S22, then make a right on Palm Canyon Dr. (℃ **800/242-0044** or 760/767-5341; www.palm canyonresort.com/rvpark.htm).

ELSEWHERE IN SAN DIEGO COUNTY

Kids and their parents adore the **LEGOland California** theme park off I-5 in Carlsbad, 1 hour south of Disneyland, 30 minutes north of San Diego. Created by the Danish company that makes the brightly colored interlocking plastic building blocks called LEGO, the 128-acre family theme park has 40 interactive rides and attractions. Most attendees make a day of it and enjoy the low-key, relaxed sense of fun and creativity. It's particularly good for smaller children who are sometimes intimidated by bigger, noisier theme parks; open at 10am daily in summer. Admission is $69 for adults, $59 for seniors and children 3 to 16 (℃ **760/918-5346**; www.legoland.com).

San Diego Zoo Safari Park makes another good family getaway for a day. Located in Escondido just off Route 78 from I-15, the park is an offshoot of the famous San Diego Zoo, with safari trails through the forest, savanna, and wetlands to see more than 200 exotic animals in their natural habitats. Open daily 9am to 5pm or later. Admission is $40 adults, $30 children. 15500 San Pasqual Valley Rd. (℃ **619/231-1515**; www.wildanimalpark.org).

PALM SPRINGS

Every other one of Palm Springs' checkerboard lots belongs to the Agua Caliente band of Cahuilla Indians, who control 42% of the land in the Coachella Valley and are the richest tribe in North America. The **Spa Resort Casino,** at 401 E. Amado Rd. (℃ **888/999-1995**; www.sparesortcasino.com), is one of the tribal ventures, offering

24-hour poker, slot machines, and Spa-21, which we interpret as a healthy version of blackjack.

While many of Palm Springs' senior celebrity residents are irreverently referred to as "the Waxworks," there's nothing sedentary about the area. You can splish-splash in California's largest wave-action pool or ride an inner tube down a 600-foot white-water river at the **Knotts Soak City water park,** at 1300 S. Gene Autry Trail between Ramon Road and East Palm Canyon Drive in Palm Springs (© **760/327-0499;** www.knotts.com/public/park/soakcity/palm_springs/index.cfm); float above the cactus with **Balloon Above the Desert** (© **760/347-0410;** www.balloonabovethedesert.com); or ride the **Aerial Tramway** from the desert floor to the cool crest of 8,516 feet in 15 minutes. Take I-10 west to the Indian Avenue exit, turn left at the exit, then make a right on San Rafael (© **888/515-TRAM** [8726] or 760/325-1391; www.pstramway.com).

For couch potatoes, we'd recommend more sedentary amusements. Watching Nutcorns being made at the **Palm Springs Candy Company** is riveting. It's closed in summer. 68-845 Perez Rd. Cathedral City. (© **760/321-1231;** www.palmsprings candy.com). **Ruddy's 1930s General Store Museum,** at 221 S. Palm Dr. on the Village Green, makes nostalgic browsing for anyone who remembers Uneeda Biscuits, Rinso, sarsaparilla, and silk stockings. It's open Saturday and Sunday only in summer, Thursday through Sunday in winter, 10am to 4pm (© **760/327-2156**). Admission is 95¢ for adults, free for children under 12.

Wind Farm Tours, 62-950 20th Ave., west of the Indian Avenue exit on the north side of I-10, North Palm Springs, gives tours in electric vehicles powered by the wind. Visitors can see the forest of giant windmills that dominates the desert landscape

In Palm Springs, you'll find lush greens and fairways in the desert.

California/Nevada Desert Campgrounds

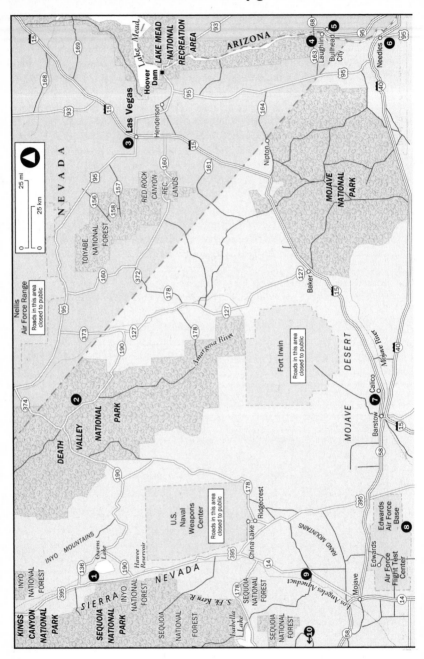

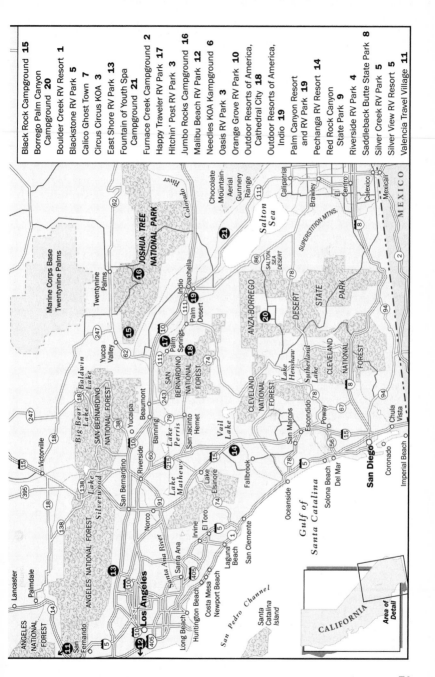

Black Rock Campground	**15**
Borrego Palm Canyon Campground	**20**
Boulder Creek RV Resort	**1**
Blackstone RV Park	**5**
Calico Ghost Town	**7**
Circus Circus KOA	**3**
East Shore RV Park	**13**
Fountain of Youth Spa Campground	**21**
Furnace Creek Campground	**2**
Happy Traveler RV Park	**17**
Hitchin' Post RV Park	**3**
Jumbo Rocks Campground	**16**
Malibu Beach RV Park	**12**
Needles KOA Kampground	**6**
Oasis RV Park	**3**
Orange Grove RV Park	**10**
Outdoor Resorts of America, Cathedral City	**18**
Outdoor Resorts of America, Indio	**19**
Palm Canyon Resort and RV Park	**19**
Pechanga RV Resort	**14**
Red Rock Canyon State Park	**9**
Riverside RV Park	**4**
Saddleback Butte State Park	**8**
Silver Creek RV Park	**5**
Silver View RV Resort	**5**
Valencia Travel Village	**11**

Fairways & Five-Irons, Desert Style

This all-season golfer's paradise boasts more than 100 courses, their lush fairways and velvety greens carved from the arid desert scruff. Both public and resort/semiprivate courses range in difficulty to accommodate low-handicappers and weekend duffers alike, and every imaginable service is available nearby.

In case you'd like to sharpen your game, all the principal clubs have resident pros, and several schools and clinics are available, including the **Indian Wells Golf School** at Indian Wells Resort (✆ 760/346-4653) or the **1st Tee in Palm Desert** (✆ 760/779-1877). If you're looking to pick up new equipment or golf attire, try **Lumpy's Discount Golf**, 67–625 Hwy. 111 in Cathedral City (✆ 800/553-2117 or 760/321-2437) and 46630 Washington St. in La Quinta (✆ 760/904-4911); and **Lady Golf** at 42–412 Bob Hope Dr., Rancho Mirage (✆ 760/773-4949).

Many resorts offer generous golf packages (if you'd like to spend a night or two away from the RV or enjoy a spa treatment), among them **Marriott's Desert Springs Spa & Resort** in Palm Desert (✆ 760/341-2211), **Marriott's Rancho Las Palmas Resort & Spa** in Rancho Mirage (✆ 760/568-2727), the **Hyatt Grand Champions** in Indian Wells (✆ 760/341-1000), and **La Quinta Resort & Club** in La Quinta (✆ 760/564-4111).

Tee times at many courses cannot be booked more than a few days in advance for nonguests, but **Golf à la Carte** (✆ 877/887-6900 or 760/397-7670; www.palmspringsgolf.com) will make arrangements several months earlier or construct a package with accommodations, golf, meals, and other extras. A valuable service for the budget traveler, **Stand-By Golf** (✆ 866/224-BOOK [2665] or 760/321-2665; www.stand-bygolf.com) helps more than 40 area courses—including semiprivate and resort courses—fill their bookings by offering players a last-minute discount of 40% to 60%. You can book some courses in advance, but many tee times are for the same or next day; call between 7am and 9pm daily. 🚐

around Palm Springs. The 1½-hour tours leave three times a day in winter—9 and 11:30am and 2:30pm—and sometimes less frequently in summer. Reservations are encouraged, although walk-ins are accepted, provided there is space. Admission is $25 adults, $23 seniors, $10 children (✆ 760/320-1365).

"How could you travel to California and not see the San Andreas Fault?" your neighbors back home might well ask. Two different companies hawk tours of it in Palm Springs. **Desert Adventures,** (✆ 888/440-JEEP (5337); http://red-jeep.com), has tours 3 to 5 hours from $99 to $150. **Jurassic Expeditions** (✆ 760/862-5540) offers a 3-hour "Indiana Jones" motorcoach eco-adventure tour.

RVing golfers who carry along their clubs (and even their carts, in some cases) can book a round at one of the nearly two dozen golf courses in the Palm Springs area.

Palm Springs

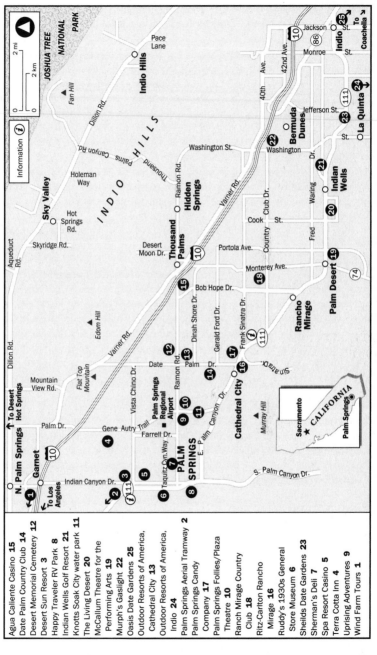

Agua Caliente Casino **15**
Date Palm Country Club **14**
Desert Memorial Cemetery **12**
Desert Sun Resort **3**
Happy Traveler RV Park **8**
Indian Wells Golf Resort **21**
Knotts Soak City water park **11**
The Living Desert **20**
McCallum Theatre for the Performing Arts **19**
Murph's Gaslight **22**
Oasis Date Gardens **25**
Outdoor Resorts of America, Cathedral City **13**
Outdoor Resorts of America, Indio **24**
Palm Springs Aerial Tramway **2**
Palm Springs Candy Company **17**
Palm Springs Follies/Plaza Theatre **10**
Ranch Mirage Country Club **18**
Ritz-Carlton Rancho Mirage **16**
Ruddy's 1930s General Store Museum **6**
Sheilds Date Gardens **23**
Sherman's Deli **7**
Spa Resort Casino **5**
Terra Cotta Inn **4**
Uprising Adventures **9**
Wind Farm Tours **1**

Tee times are obviously easier to come by in summer than in the winter high season, and as long as you get on the course by 6am to play 18 holes, you'll survive before the worst of the dry heat hits.

Most private golf courses require that you play with a member; however, the following do not: **Rancho Mirage Country Club,** 38-500 Bob Hope Dr. (✆ **760/324-4711;** www.ranchomiragegolf.com); the **Golf Center at Palm Desert,** 74-945 Sheryl Ave. (✆ **760/779-1877**); **Date Palm Country Club,** 16-200 Date Palm, Cathedral City (✆ **760/328-1315;** www.datepalmcountryclub.net); and **Indian Wells Golf Resort,** 44-500 Indian Wells (✆ **760/346-4653;** www.indianwellsgolfresort.com).

A **Celebrity Tour** (✆ **760/770-2700;** www.thecelebritytour.com) drives past 30 to 40 homes where the rich and famous once lived; the 2½-hour Grand Tour also includes the Eisenhower Medical Center, the Sinatra and Annenberg Estates, and the Springs and Rancho Mirage Country Clubs, plus a rest-and-refreshment stop at Edwards Date Shoppe. Reservations are required. Admission for the 2½-hour tour is $44 adults, $40 seniors, and $25 children 14 and under.

Elite Land Tours (✆ **800/514-4866** or 760/318-1200; www.elitelandtours.com) gives tours of the desert in an air-conditioned Hummer. Rates are $119 to $149 per person for a party of four.

To see stars in a different light, the **Desert Memorial Cemetery** has a free guide to their graves. It lists locations and birth and death dates for such big names as Frank Sinatra, Sonny Bono, songwriters Jimmy van Heusen and Frederick Lowe, director Busby Berkeley, actors William Powell *(The Thin Man)* and Cameron Mitchell *(How to Marry a Millionaire),* and actor/bon vivant Charlie Farrell, who founded the Palm Springs Racquet Club. The cemetery is open daily 7am to 7pm; ask in the office for the guide or refer to a copy posted outside when the office is closed. It's at 69-920 Ramon Rd. at Da Vall Road; enter from Da Vall (✆ **760/328-3316;** www.pscemetery.com).

Special events in the desert for which it's worth planning ahead include the **Indio Date Festival camel and ostrich races** in mid-February (✆ **760/863-8247;** www.datefest.org); the **Nude Recreation Week** in early July at various clothing-optional couples resorts (✆ **800/TRY-NUDES** [879-6833]); the **Bob Hope Golf Classic** in La Quinta, mid-January (✆ **888/672-4673;** www.bhcc.com); as well as the famous **Coachella Music Festival** in Indio (**www.coachella.com**) in mid-April.

Palm Springs Nightlife

Every month, a different club is the hot spot in the Springs, and the best way to tap into the trend is by consulting the *Desert Guide,* the *Bottom Line,* or one of many other free newsletters available from area hotels and merchants. **VillageFest** turns Palm Canyon Drive into an outdoor party every Thursday night. Here are a couple of the enduring arts-and-entertainment attractions around the desert resorts.

The **Fabulous Palm Springs Follies,** at the Plaza Theatre, 128 S. Palm Canyon Dr., Palm Springs (✆ **760/327-0225;** www.psfollies.com), a vaudeville-style show filled with elaborate costumed production numbers, is a long-running hit in the historic Plaza Theatre in the heart of town. With a cast of retired showgirls, singers, dancers, and comedians plus guest stars, the revue is hugely popular. The season runs from November through May; call for the exact schedule. Tickets range from $50 to $95. Matinees are at 1:30pm, evening shows at 7pm.

The **McCallum Theatre for the Performing Arts,** 73000 Fred Waring Dr., Palm Desert (© **866/889-ARTS** [2787]; www.mccallumtheatre.com), provides the only cultural high road around. Frequent symphony performances with visiting virtuosos such as conductor Seiji Ozawa or violinist Itzhak Perlman; musicals like *Hairspray, Chicago,* and *Riverdance;* and pop performers like Jack Jones or Patti Lupone have been among the theater's offerings. Call or visit the website for upcoming event information.

In addition, small restaurants and clubs feature local musicians and entertainers who are desert favorites.

CASINOS

Native American gaming has been around in the desert for years now, but now the industry seems to have joined the major leagues, with a professionalism and polish that create a "virtual Vegas."

The best known and most centrally located casino is the **Spa Resort Casino** (© **866/923-7244;** www.sparesortcasino.com) in the heart of Palm Springs. The gaming rooms that used to be almost an afterthought now share the spotlight with the hot springs. Attendees at the hotel's conference center can often be found playing hooky from business at one or both of the casinos!

You can't help but be impressed by the brilliant neon fireballs of the **Agua Caliente Casino,** 32-250 Bob Hope Dr., Rancho Mirage (© **888/999-1995** or 760/321-2000; www.hotwatercasino.com), down the street from the Westin Mission Hills. The complex boasts a full house of dining spots, plus musical entertainers and boxing matches; it will also eventually include an on-site hotel of its own.

And it was only a matter of time before Donald Trump came to mine gold in the California desert (and went!): The casino formerly called **Trump 29** is now operated by the Twentynine Palms Band of Mission Indians, and is now called **Spotlight 29,** 46-200 Harrison Place, Coachella (© **866/377-6829;** www.spotlight29.com), about a half-hour from Palm Springs. This sophisticated complex is Vegas all the way, from the big-name shows and a high-roller players' club to 24-hour fine dining and even an all-you-can-eat prime-rib buffet.

Other tribal casino/resorts flank the valley with the **Morongo Casino, Resort and Spa** in the north at 49500 Seminole Dr., Cabazon (© **888-MORONGO** [667-6646]; www.morongocasinoresort.com), with 310 rooms, 32 suites, and six casitas by the pool. Four restaurants, a food court, and a full-service salon and spa augment the three nightclubs that keep you entertained when not at the gaming tables. At the southern end of the valley is the **Hotel Fantasy Springs Resort Casino,** 84-245 Indio Springs Pkwy. (© **800/827-2946;** www.fantasyspringsresort.com). The hotel has 250 rooms and suites; guests are entertained with 2,000 slot machines, four restaurants, a 3-acre pool, and an outdoor entertainment complex.

Campground Oases in & Around Palm Springs

Happy Traveler RV Park is the closest campground to downtown Palm Springs (walking distance). Here are 130 full hookups with 30- and 50-amp electric. Sites are paved, but narrow, with a maximum length of 40 ft. There's a pool, Wi-Fi, a TV, and a Laundromat. Sites $40. From Hwy. 111, turn onto S. Palm Canyon Dr., then turn right onto W. Mesquite Ave. (✆ **760/325-8518;** www.happytravelerrv.com).

Outdoor Resorts of America. Outdoor Resorts of America has two Palm Springs–area RV parks, one for motor homes only. The nicely landscaped, individually owned sites are available to travelers when space is open. Both parks have lavish spa facilities, swimming pools, and par-3 golf courses. The **Cathedral City** property, 69411 Ramon Rd. (use the Date Palm Dr. exit south from I-10), is open to both motor-driven and towable RVs (✆ **800/843-3131** or 760/328-3834). Rates are $45–$91 for full hook-ups. The **Indio** location is off Jefferson St. on Ave. 48 (reached from the Jefferson St. exit south 3⅓ miles from I-10). It's open only to type A and type C motor homes (✆ **800/892-2992** or 760/775-7255). Rates are $40–$80 for deluxe full hookups.

Pechanga RV Resort has 168 full-service sites with 25 pull-throughs, cable TV, and free Internet hookup. The resort is adjacent to a 24-hour casino and restaurant. Rates are $42–$52. 45000 Pachenga Pkwy., in **Temecula** (✆ **877/99-RVFUN** [997-8386] or 951/587-0484; www.pechangarv.com).

THE MOJAVE DESERT & JOSHUA TREE NATIONAL PARK

The Mojave is dotted with twisted green Joshua trees that explorer John C. Fremont, never a happy camper, considered "the most repulsive trees in the vegetable kingdom."

Explorers, immigrants, and miners alike endured rather than adored the high desert, but latter-day desert rats get rapturous about such ersatz doings as chili cook-offs, tobacco-spitting contests, and burro-biscuit tossings.

Cynics forget that **Calico,** for example, was a real ghost town before it became an artificial ghost town re-created by Walter Knott of Knott's Berry Farm. Silver was mined there in the late 1880s, and a dog named Dorsey used to carry the mail from Calico to Bismarck, a half-mile away. Take the Calico exit off I-15 between Barstow and Yermo (**www.calicotown.com**).

JOSHUA TREE CAMPSITE TIP

If you visit Joshua Tree in early to midwinter or on a weekday, you'll be able to choose a great campsite on a first-come, first-served basis, but if you arrive on weekends or during the prime rock-climbing season in early spring, you'll have to take any vacancy you can find. See "Campground Oases in the Mojave Desert," below, for campground listings.

Calico is a ghost town you can still visit.

You may notice the exit markers from I-15 for **Zzyzx,** where Dr. Curtis Howe Springer, a radio evangelist and health-food vendor, developed a health resort for refugees from Los Angeles' Skid Row. After 30 years of tending the urban ill free of charge, the Springers were suddenly evicted by the Bureau of Land Management in the 1970s for trespassing. The site, which was nearly destroyed by vandals over the years, was rescued and restored not long ago by the **Desert Studies Center (http://biology. fullerton.edu/dsc).**

At nearby **Nipton** (pop. 26), the four-room **Hotel Nipton,** 107-355 Nipton Rd. (© **760/856-2335;** rooms start at $79), recalls the days when silent film star Clara Bow and cowboy-actor husband Rex Bell had a ranch nearby. An outdoor hot tub lets you soak under the stars while listening to the whistle of a passing freight train. Nipton is about 70 miles from Las Vegas near the California-Nevada border. Take I-15 east to Nipton Road. Continue for just over 10 miles to the railroad tracks, then make a right to the hotel.

Joshua Tree National Park (www.nps.gov/jotr) is a wonderland of bizarre boulders and glorious gardens of cactus, ideally visited by RVers who can tent or stay overnight in a self-contained recreational vehicle; there are no hookups or water available. At all but two of the park's campgrounds (Cottonwood and Black Rock Canyon), campers must bring in all the water and firewood they plan to use, and toilet facilities are primitive. Jumbo Rocks, our favorite campground, is also a top draw for rock climbers. (See "Campground Oases in the Mojave Desert," below, for details.) Joshua Tree is one of the world's most popular climbing areas, with more than 3,500 climbing spots for all degrees of ability.

Cottonwood Visitor Center is 7 miles north of the Joshua Tree National Park exit from I-10 (© **760/367-5500;** www.nps.gov/jotr).

While vehicles of all sorts can negotiate the main roads in the park, four-wheel-drive vehicles, motorcycles, and bicycles are best for exploring unpaved roads. Rules require all bicycles and motor vehicles to stay on established roadways. Good **back-country roads** include Pinkham Canyon Road, 20 miles from Cottonwood Visitor Center to an I-10 service road; Covington Flats, which accesses some of the best Joshua tree stands, 4 miles from Covington Flats picnic area to Eureka Peak; Geology Tour Road, 5¾ miles from Jumbo Rocks to Squaw Tank; and Black Eagle Mine Road, up through the canyons in the Eagle Mountains. Alert freewheelers may spot roadrunners, coyotes, kangaroo rats, golden eagles, and sidewinders.

Birders will find good watching at Cottonwood Spring, while photographers and wildflower enthusiasts will want to walk Lost Palms Oasis Trail in early spring to find dozens of native desert wildflowers.

The **General Patton Memorial Museum** at 2 Chiriaco Rd. in Chiriaco Summit, a marked exit just off I-10 about 50 miles east of Palm Springs, is built on the site of Camp Young, the World War II desert training center. Here, you can see Patton memorabilia, boots, and saddles, and plenty of tanks and war film footage. Open daily 9am to 5pm; admission is $5 adults, $4.50 seniors, $1 for children 7–12. Open 9:30am to 4:30pm (℃ **760/227-3483;** www.generalpattonmuseum.com).

Campground Oases in the Mojave Desert

Black Rock Campground. Located at the northern end of Joshua Tree National Park, this campground has 100 sites with piped water and flush toilets; 15 are pull-throughs. Sanitary dump available. Good hiking. Oct–May. Sites $15. Take I-10 east to Hwy. 62 E. to Yucca Valley. Turn right on Joshua Lane. Follow signs 5 miles to the campground. Sites may be reserved from Oct 1–May 31 by calling ℃ **877/444-6777** up to 6 months in advance of the date you want to reserve, or you may make reservations online at www.recreation.gov.

Jumbo Rocks Campground. In the middle of Joshua Tree National Park near Twentynine Palms, this campground has 124 sites, 20 pull-throughs, pit toilets, and evening ranger programs. Rock-climbing is allowed at sites surrounded by huge boulders. No hookups, no water, no slide-outs. There are no reservations; it's first-come, first-served. It's easiest to find space in winter when nights are nippy; early spring weekends are chockablock with rock climbers and desert-flower photographers. Sites $10. Take Hwy. 62 to the Park Blvd. exit. Enter at west entrance. Continue for 23 miles to campground. Call this campground (℃ **760/367-7511**) to contact the Joshua Tree National Park Association, an educational support group.

Calico Ghost Town. This San Bernardino County campground in **Yermo,** located in the canyons just steps from the commercialized, but genuine, silver mining town of Calico, near Baker, has 104 sites, 46 with full hookups (30 and 50-amp), some grills, picnic tables, showers, flush toilets, and a sanitary dump. There are restaurants, shops, and attractions in Calico, and groceries, propane, and a Laundromat nearby. Families with children, ghost-town collectors, and rock hounds will especially like the area. Up to $22 a night with hookups. Reservations essential on weekends. Take Calico exit off I-15 btw. Barstow and Yermo (℃ **760/254-2122;** www.calicotown.com).

Saddleback Butte State Park. Once called Joshua Tree State Park, it has well-preserved stands of Joshua trees, rocky buttes, and excellent hiking trails. The 50 sites accommodate self-contained RVs up to 30 feet and have piped water, flush toilets, and a sanitary dump, but no hookups. No reservations, except for groups. Sites $22. Located off Hwy. 14, 17 miles east of Lancaster; use the Ave. J turnoff (✆ **661/942-0662;** www.parks.ca.gov/?page_id=618).

Red Rock Canyon State Park. This state park has 50 primitive sites with no hookups. Water and a sanitary dump are available. No reservations. There are ranger campfire programs in summer and fall, hiking trails, dramatic geological formations, and archaeological displays at the visitor center. Expect occasional winter snowfalls; cool to cold nights; and nesting falcons, hawks, and owls in spring. Sites $12. Take Hwy. 14 northeast from Mohave for 25 miles. The turnoff to the campground is well marked (✆ **661/942-0662;** www.parks.ca.gov/?page_id=631).

CAMPGROUND OASES AROUND LOS ANGELES & ELSEWHERE

If you're on the way to or from the desert in the Los Angeles area, here are a few RV parks where you can stay in and around the huge city.

East Shore RV Park. This RV park in **San Dimas** has 160 full-hookup paved sites, perched atop a hill overlooking Pomona's Fairplex, site of the Los Angeles County Fair. You enjoy cool breezes even on the hottest days. Large, grassy sites, mature shade trees, and some lakefront locations make East Shore a reliable getaway year-round. Sites $46–$54. 1440 Camper View Rd. Exit I-10 via Fairplex Dr. and follow the signs. Reserve ahead, especially on weekends or holidays (✆ **800/809-3778;** www.eastshorervpark.com).

Malibu Beach RV Park. On Pacific Coast Highway in Malibu, this RV park overlooks the sea, and the beach is only a short walk downhill and across the road from your campsite. In winter, you may see whales migrating along the coast. Sites are small, but the views are great. Sites $31–$124. 25801 Pacific Coast Hwy. (✆ **800/622-6052** reservations; www.maliburv.com).

Valencia Travel Village. On Route 126 off I-5 north of Los Angeles near Magic Mountain, this place has 385 sites, 73 full hookups, with cable and satellite TV. It has shade trees, swimming pools, a large convenience store, and a quiet, convenient location less than an hour from Los Angeles. Sites $55–$59. 27946 Henry Mayo Dr. (✆ **888/588-8678** or 661/257-3333 reservations; www.valenciatravelvillagellc.com).

Orange Grove RV Park. Off Hwy. 58 east of **Bakersfield** at Edison Rd., 177 full hookup sites are nestled in an orange grove. Visitors enjoy pick-your-own privileges, a pool, a recreation room with big-screen TV, a playground, a country store, hot showers, air-conditioned restrooms, cable TV, a Laundromat, and propane. Bakersfield's famous Basque restaurants are nearby. Sites $27–$39. 1452 S. Edison Rd. (✆ **661/366-4662;** www.orangegrovervpark.com).

COYOTE TIP

Keep an eye out for the **bandit coyotes of Stovepipe Wells,** a trio (when we last visited) of brazen animals that come out at midday alongside the highway to stop traffic in hopes of scrounging food. Don't encourage them by giving them food or the rangers will banish them to the far-off regions of the park.

DEATH VALLEY NATIONAL PARK

If publicists had been around during wagon train days, Death Valley would have been named Golden Sands or Shimmering Haze. Instead, it took nearly a century to shake off the bad-mouthing from pioneers. It wasn't until stalwart, sincere Ronald Reagan brought TV's *Death Valley Days* into our living rooms that it became a tourist destination.

Now, as a national park with an additional 1.3 million acres, it's busy even in summer, when European tourists flock here to experience the hottest, driest, lowest, loneliest, and so on.

Tent campers and self-contained RVs (no hookups available) will find comfortable spots to spend a winter weekend at **Furnace Creek Campground,** which has shade trees and some privacy, flush toilets, hot showers, and a dump station. (See "Campground Oases in & Around Death Valley National Park," below.) Bigger, less attractive camping areas include **Stovepipe Wells** (which has RV hookups) and **Sunset Campground,** near the **Furnace Creek Visitors Area,** Hwy. 190, 30 miles east of Death Valley Junction on S.R. 127 at Hwy. 190 (🕿 **760/786-2331;** www.nps.gov/deva). Furnace Creek is the only campsite that requires reservations, the rest are first-come, first-served.

Bicyclists can tour the mostly flat terrain of Death Valley quite comfortably in winter. Rain is rare, but winds can hinder your progress. Use touring bikes on paved roads, mountain bikes on sandy or rocky routes. The 13-mile, paved **Artists Palette Road** is particularly scenic—a winding, narrow one-way with a lot of up and down. This is definitely not for trailers or large RVs. A 9-mile paved route from Furnace Creek to Zabriskie Point is best at daybreak, but a 7-mile loop to the sand dunes from Stovepipe Wells is easy any time of day.

Campground Oases in & Around Death Valley National Park

Furnace Creek Campground. Located in the community of Furnace Creek in Death Valley, the grounds have 136 back-in sites, most large enough for an RV. Spacious campsites look across open desert terrain. No hookups, but flush toilets, hot showers, fire grates, drinking water, a sanitary disposal station, a general store, a restaurant, and propane are nearby. Get there early on winter weekends or holidays or you'll be banished to the overflow campground across the road, which has much less ambience.

Las Vegas

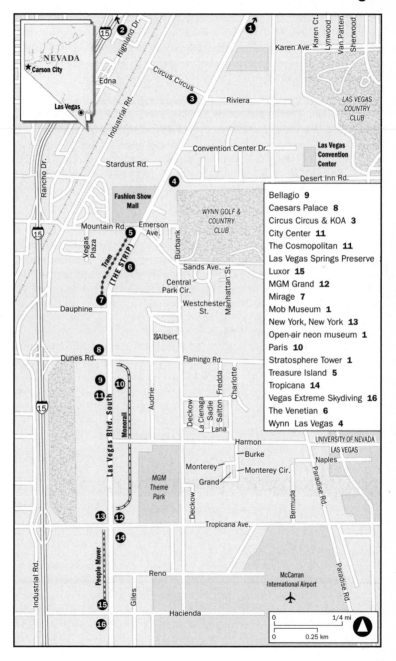

NEVADA

★ Carson City

Las Vegas

Karen Ave.

Karen Ct.
Lynwood
Van Patten
Sherwood

Circus Circus

Riviera

LAS VEGAS
COUNTRY
CLUB

Edna

Highland Dr.

Industrial Rd.

Convention Center Dr.

Las Vegas
Convention
Center

Stardust Rd.

Desert Inn Rd.

Rancho Dr.

Fashion Show
Mall

WYNN GOLF &
COUNTRY
CLUB

Mountain Rd.

Emerson
Ave.

Burbank

Sands Ave.

Vegas
Plaza

Tram
(THE STRIP)

Central
Park Cir.

Manhattan St.

Dauphine

Westchester
St.

Albert

Dunes Rd.

Flamingo Rd.

Audrie

Monorail

Deckow
La Cienaga
Sadie
Salton
Fredda
Lana
Charlotte

Harmon

Burke

Las Vegas Blvd. South

MGM
Theme
Park

Monterey

Monterey Cir.

Grand

Naples

UNIVERSITY OF NEVADA
LAS VEGAS

Bermuda

Paradise Rd.

Deckow

Tropicana Ave.

People Mover

Reno

Giles

McCarran
International Airport

Paradise Rd.

Industrial Rd.

Hacienda

Bellagio **9**
Caesars Palace **8**
Circus Circus & KOA **3**
City Center **11**
The Cosmopolitan **11**
Las Vegas Springs Preserve
Luxor **15**
MGM Grand **12**
Mirage **7**
Mob Museum **1**
New York, New York **13**
Open-air neon museum **1**
Paris **10**
Stratosphere Tower **1**
Treasure Island **5**
Tropicana **14**
Vegas Extreme Skydiving **16**
The Venetian **6**
Wynn Las Vegas **4**

0   1/4 mi

0   0.25 km

Sites $18 from mid-Oct to mid-Apr. The campground becomes first-come, first-served and costs $12 per night from mid-Apr to mid-Oct. Take Hwy. 190 to Furnace Creek Visitors Center; the campgrounds are less than a mile north of the center. Reservations are now available by calling ✆ **877/444-6777** or online at www.recreation.gov.

Boulder Creek RV Resort. A few miles south of Lone Pine, this handsome, modern campground has 103 full hookup campsites with views toward Mount Whitney and makes a great year-round stop for travelers driving to Death Valley or Yosemite. Buffet breakfasts and dinners are occasionally available. It's the RV headquarters for the Lone Pine Film Festival every Oct, saluting the Western films shot in Lone Pine's scenic Alabama Hills. Sites $35. 2550 S. Hwy. 395 (✆ **800/648-8965** reservations; www.bouldercreekresort.com).

LAS VEGAS

We've driven up I-15 to Las Vegas many times over the years. Now, as we approach the skyline of resort high-rises, move along the clogged expressways around the metropolis, wonder at the expanding communities of tract houses that make this the most expansive city in Nevada, we think back to vintage Las Vegas. It was a time when Sinatra ruled the entertainment world of the "Strip" (he got miffed when a new owner of the Sands resort cut off his credit, so he drove a golf cart through a plate-glass window, later moving his show to Caesars Palace). It was a time when Elvis married Priscilla at the Aladdin Hotel, while Mickey Rooney made the altar trip eight times beginning with Ava Gardner in 1942. A longer union involved Paul Newman and Joanne Woodward, who wed at the El Rancho in 1958, and stayed married for half a century. It was a time when Liberace dazzled his audiences as much with his wardrobe as his music. You can see a bit of this at the Golden Gate Casino (1906) at 1 Fremont St.; or the El Cortez (1941), once owned by Bugsy Siegel at the east end of downtown; or the Little Church of the West (1942), 4617 Las Vegas Blvd., which has been the site of celebrity weddings among the 100,000 celebrated at this landmark.

Las Vegas traffic is heavy on I-15—always under reconstruction—as well as downtown and on the often-gridlocked Strip. RVers will probably want to leave their rigs on hookup IVs in the campground and commute by city bus, casino shuttle, towed car, or rental car (some campgrounds have car rentals available on the premises). Shuttle buses are provided by the campgrounds and/or casinos. Hours vary, but some run all night. Inquire locally.

Las Vegas Hotel Casinos

Since you're in your RV and don't need a hotel room, you're free to wander along the Strip and enjoy the fantasy venues, in addition to those we've listed below:

- **Bellagio** is lush and lavish, with an art gallery with millions of dollars worth of masterpieces by such artists as Monet, van Gogh, and Picasso; a glassed-in garden conservatory; a stunning blown-glass chandelier centerpiece by Dale Chihuly; and 1,200 fountains splashing to synchronized classical music. 3600 Las Vegas Blvd. S. (✆ **888/987-6667;** www.bellagio.com).

Visitors stroll through the lush Wynn conservatory.

- **Caesars Palace** has expanded its Roman extravaganza with a 26-story all-suite tower. Celebrity chefs Bradley Ogden and Guy Savoy enhance the dining, and Bette Midler and Cher are typical of the stars performing at the Colosseum. 3570 Las Vegas Blvd. S. (② **866/227-5938;** www.caesars.com).

- **Circus Circus** is roller-coaster heaven, with the world's only indoor, double-loop, double-corkscrew coaster and an unlimited-rides wristband admission. 2880 Las Vegas Blvd. S. (② **800/634-3450;** www.circuscircus.com).

- **City Center** is the new kid on the block and actually is the whole block itself. The 18-million square foot city includes casinos, 4 hotels, residences, high-end shops, restaurants, and sculpture-filled public areas. 3700 Las Vegas Blvd. S. (Resort and Casino: ② **866/359-7111;** www.citycenter.com.)

- **The Cosmopolitan** entered the upscale hotel scene during a downturn in visitors to the city, but it has been able to hold its own with a vast casino, a dozen restaurants, and a unique day and nightclub area. 3708 Las Vegas Blvd. S. (② **702/698-7000;** www.cosmopolitanlasvegas.com.)

- **Luxor** features the Sphinx, a glass pyramid, and King Tut's tomb, just like Howard Carter found it in 1922. When not at the tables, you can be entertained in the Luxor Theatre or the Pharaoh's Theatre. 3900 Las Vegas Blvd. S. (② **877/396-4658;** www.luxor.com).

- **Mirage** has an erupting volcano that spews nightly every 15 minutes from 6pm to midnight. Feel the blast when the volcano erupts, with flames leaping into the air. Cool off in the lush foliage of the Atrium beside the 20,000-gal. aquarium. 3400 Las Vegas Blvd. S. (② **800/374-9000;** www.themirage.com).

You can take a gondola through Las Vegas at the Venetian.

- **MGM Grand** has added a new wing, but has retained its extravagant casino, and Centrifuge, a 77-seat bar with live entertainment that supplements the large production shows in the Grand Theater. 3799 Las Vegas Blvd. S. (© **877/880-0880;** www.mgmgrand.com).

- **New York, New York** has the Manhattan Express roller coaster that zips you around past the Statue of Liberty and the city skyline. 3790 Las Vegas Blvd. S. (© **866/815-4365;** www.nynyhotelcasino.com).

- **Paris** presents the Eiffel Tower, L'Opera, the back streets of old Paree, and a variety of music and comedy shows. 3655 Las Vegas Blvd. S. (© **877/374-7469;** www.paris-lv.com).

- **Stratosphere Tower,** the tallest free-standing observation tower in the United States at 1,149 ft., offers three thrill rides at the top. In daytime, you get a panoramic view of the desert, at night the bright lights of Vegas. 2000 Las Vegas Blvd. S. (© **800/99-TOWER** [999-6937]; www.stratospherehotel.com).

- **Treasure Island** has a free Sirens of TI pirate show with sailing ships, dancing, and special effects every 90 min. from 7–10pm, later on weekends. 3300 Las Vegas Blvd. S. (© **800/288-7206;** www.treasureisland.com).

- The **Venetian** offers gondola rides along a canal in a Venice replica, complete with singing gondolier. 3355 Las Vegas Blvd. S. (© **877/883-6423;** www.venetian.com).

- **Wynn** is a creation of Steve Wynn and it's a Strip hotel without a theme. Wynn is merely a 50-story tower with 2,700 luxury rooms, 22 food and beverage outlets, the only 18-hole golf course on the strip, and, of course, a dazzling casino. 3131 Las Vegas Blvd. S. (© **877/321-9966;** www.wynnlasvegas.com).

Off-the-Wall Las Vegas

The Mob is back! Las Vegas crime history is depicted in two new arenas with two different views. The city has opened the **Las Vegas Museum of Organized Crime and Law Enforcement** at 300 Stewart Ave. The site, a former courthouse, once held Kefauver Committee hearings on organized crime. Open Sun–Thu 10am to 7pm; Fri–Sun 10am to 8pm. Admission $19; $14 seniors, military, law enforcement, and teachers; $12 children/students 23 and under (© **702/229-6581;** www.themobmuseum.org). Back on the Strip, on a lighter side, the Tropicana Hotel presents a hands-on show with actors posing as mobsters and others from the era. Open 10am to 10pm. $40 adults, $30 seniors and children (© **702/739-2662;** www.troplv.com/entertainment/las-vegas-mob-experience).

Ethel M Chocolates, in nearby Henderson, fulfills that childhood fantasy of touring a chocolate factory, then getting to pick out a free sample. The tour is self-guided and free, both in the chocolate factory and in the adjacent cactus gardens. The factory is open daily from 8:30am to 6pm and has spacious parking lots that can easily handle RVs. Take exit 64 at Sunset Road to the junction with Mountain Vista Street and follow the signs to 2 Cactus Dr. (© **888/627-0990** or 702/435-2608; www.ethelm.com).

The open-air **neon museum,** best seen at night, preserves the vintage signs that no longer have a hotel to cling to—Chief Hotel Court from 1940, the Flame from 1961, Aladdin's Lamp from 1966, the Hacienda horse and rider of 1967, and dairy mascot Andy Anderson from 1956. Other signs are in the process of being restored; look for them near the Fremont Street Experience between 4th Street and Las Vegas Boulevard (© **702/387-6366;** www.neonmuseum.org).

The **Clark County Heritage Museum** shelters indoor and outdoor collections of railway cars, vintage furnished bungalows from the 1930s and 1940s, ranching displays, and a ghost town. Open daily from 9am to 4:30pm. Admission is $2 adults, $1 seniors and children. It's at 1830 S. Boulder Hwy., in Henderson, just north of where Hwy. 582 meets routes 93/95; there's plenty of RV parking space. Open 9am–4:30pm (© **702/455-7955;** www.clarkcountynv.gov/Depts/parks/Pages/clark-county-museum.aspx).

The **Las Vegas Springs Preserve.** This wouldn't be off-the-wall anywhere else but Vegas. This 180-acre tract about 4 miles northwest of the Strip aspires to be the Central Park of Las Vegas. It features 8 acres of botanical gardens, 2.5 miles of walking trails, and a cafeteria operated by Wolfgang Puck enterprises. You'll find a garbage truck made from recycled materials, buildings made from recycled wood beams and straw bale, and gardens lined with several species of indigenous cacti, palms, and other desert-friendly flora. Open daily 10am to 6pm. Admission is $19 adults, $17 seniors and students 18 and over, $11 children 5 to 17. 333 S. Valley View Blvd., Las Vegas (© **702/822-7700;** www.springspreserve.org).

Campground Oases in & Around Las Vegas

Circus Circus KOA. Behind Circus Circus Casino, Circus Circus KOA is the only RV park on the Strip. The 368 spaces are served with 30- and 50-amp electric (you'll need it in summer for the air-conditioning) and there's a pool, sauna, and hot tub. Sites $40–$107. 500 Circus Circus Dr. (© **800/562-7270** or 702/733-9707 reservations; www.circuscircus.com).

Hitchin' Post RV Park. This RV park has cable TV, a pool, 107 wide pull-throughs, 30- and 50-amp electric, a central modem hookup, and a gated secured entrance. Sites $29. 3640 Las Vegas Blvd. N. (℃ **888/433-8402;** www.hprvp.com).

Oasis RV Park. At 2711 Windmill Pkwy. just off Las Vegas Blvd., this luxury park has 701 full hookups, with 282 pull-throughs. There's an on-site restaurant, a pool and spa, an 18-hole putting course, and a daily shuttle to the Strip. Sites $38–$70 (℃ **800/566-4707;** www.oasislasvegasrvresort.com).

Campground Oases in Laughlin, Needles & Bullhead City

Bullhead City, Arizona, has a number of RV parks across the river from Laughlin, with a little less flash and noise and a lovely distant view of the bright lights from the casinos. There are three good choices: **Blackstone RV Park,** 3299 Boundary Cone Rd., off Hwy. 95 toward Oatman, where sites are $25 (℃ **928/768-3303**); **Silver Creek RV Park,** 1515 Gold Rush Dr., off Rte. 95, where sites are $23 (℃ **928/763-2444**); and **Silver View RV Resort,** 1501 Gold Rush Rd., off Hwy. 95, where sites are $35 (℃ **928/763-5500;** www.silverviewrvresort.com).

Needles KOA Kampground. This park bills itself as the closest KOA to Laughlin, Nevada. Some 85 of the sites are pull-throughs, and 67 are 50-amp full hookups, so it's definitely a big-rig-friendly campground. In winter, the Cactus Kafe serves meals for those times when you don't feel like cooking. Sites $28–$38. It's at I-40 and the W. Broadway River Rd. exit, then north 1 mile to Old Trails Hwy., then left and drive 1 mile (℃ **800/562-3407** reservations; www.koa.com).

Riverside Resort RV Park. Riverside RV Park in Laughlin is another huge parking-lot place with 732 full hookup sites (30-amp electric). There's a 24-hr. shuttle to the Riverside Resort Casino, but advance reservations are required. Sites $23–$28. 1650 Casino Dr. (℃ **800/227-3849;** www.riversideresort.com/rv-reservations.aspx).

10 Scenic Side Trips

1. **The California poppy trail** (about 50 miles). When the winter has the right amount of rain, early spring looks like Dorothy's dream in *The Wizard of Oz,* except the poppies are orange instead of red. There's a parking fee ($10), so you may, as we did one year, see more poppies in bloom along the roadsides than in the reserve itself. Call ahead to determine bloom time, usually best from March through May. Drive along California 138 between Gorman and Lancaster, turning south on Avenue I to the **Antelope Valley California Poppy Reserve** (Poppy information: ℃ **661/724-1180;** www.parks.ca.gov/?page_id=627).

2. **The Alabama Hills Loop, Lone Pine** (about 10 miles, unpaved). Make a circle through this wacky terrain where countless good guys in white hats have headed off bad guys at endless passes, not to mention where Cary Grant's 1939 classic *Gunga Din,* Humphrey Bogart's *High Sierra* (1941), and James Stewart's (et al.) *How the West Was Won* (1962) were shot. The rounded, sculpted outcroppings that resemble animals, castles, temples, and skyscrapers are best viewed in early

morning or late afternoon. If you leave the signposted movie road, pay attention to your route or you could get lost forever in this weird place. North of Lone Pine off Hwy. 395. Contact **Lone Pine Chamber of Commerce** (© **760/876-4444;** www.lonepinechamber.org).

3. **The road to Bodie** (13 miles, some of it unpaved). Bodie was one of the most rip-roaring gold towns in California, with some 12,000 residents in its heyday between 1876 and 1880. Today, the remaining houses, school, and mines exist in a state of arrested decay preserved by the state park system. Schoolbooks lie open on wooden desks and rusting tins of food line the grocery store shelves. It's best not to attempt the road in bad weather, since the last 3 miles become a dirt washboard road. The best time to go is summer or early fall. Take Hwy. 270 east off U.S. 395, 7 miles south of Bridgeport to **Bodie State Historic Park** (© **760/647-6445;** http://parks.ca.gov/?page_id=509). Daily 8am to 4pm in winter, 8am to 7pm in summer; admission is $7 for adults, $5 for children 6–16.

4. **The bristlecone pine forest.** From late June through October, a narrow, winding road is often (but not always) open to an enclave of the world's oldest living creatures, the oldest more than 4,300 years old. The tough, twisted trees have only a few limbs, but sturdy trunks that grow about an inch a century. From U.S. 395 at Big Pine, turn east on Route 168; a sign will be posted within a half-mile that will tell you whether the 25-mile road to the trees is open. If you're in a motor home or towing a travel trailer, you should go no farther than Schulman Grove, where the pavement ends. From here, a ranger station offers maps and self-guided walking trails leading into the pines. Call **Inyo National Forest** in Bishop (© **760/873-2500;** http://fs.usda.gov/inyo).

5. **Along the Salton Sea** (41 miles plus side trips). From Niland to the evocatively named Mecca, Route 111 skirts the Sonny Bono Salton Sea National Wildlife Refuge, great for spotting Canada geese, snowy egrets, snow geese, and pelicans, with an occasional glimpse of the endangered Yuma clapper rail. Thousands of migratory birds winter here, filling the air with noise as they chatter or argue back and forth. You'll have to leave the main road at marked intervals and proceed on short, sometimes rough, unpaved stretches to the observation areas. **Sonny Bono Salton Sea National Wildlife Refuge** (© **760/348-5278;** www. fws.gov/saltonsea).

6. **The desert rat's road to Randsburg.** This offbeat mining town never quite became a ghost town, and today it still has a small but hardy population, a museum, and some antiques shops. The Hard Rock Cafe is a piker compared to the Hard Rock Dinner in the town's Desert Museum at 161 Butte Ave.—eggs, pie, sausage, cauliflower, potatoes, even (yes!) hamburgers—all of it actually natural rocks and minerals that just look like food (**www.randsburg.com**). You can then swing 5 miles northeast of California City (itself about 10 miles from Hwy. 14 at the California City exit), following Randsburg Mojave Road to the marked entrance, 5½ miles from town, to the **Desert Tortoise Natural Area** (© **951/683-3872;** www.tortoise-tracks.org/dtna.html), a 38-square-mile sanctuary. The best time for sightings is mid-March to mid-June.

A loop of roughly 100 miles from the Lancaster area on Route 14 could include **Red Rock Canyon State Park** (www.parks.ca.gov/?page_id=631) and **Mojave Airport** (www.mojaveairport.com), with its huge grounded fleet of resting or retired jets near the junction of highways 14 and 58. There are tours offered Mon–Sat at 2pm; admission is $5. The town of Mojave was the terminus of the 20-mule-team borax wagons from Death Valley.

7. **Along the lower Colorado River.** A 150-mile loop from Needles can snare you a camping, gaming, and watersports excursion. First go north on U.S. 95 and Route 163 to bustling Laughlin, Nevada, where every casino welcomes RVers. Then head south on State Road 95 via Oatman, Arizona, on old Route 66, where wild burros roam the colorful main street. Farther south is Lake Havasu City, Arizona, where London Bridge spans the Colorado. Go west again on Parker Dam Road to Route 62 into Earp, a minuscule California desert town where the famous marshal retired to try his hand at mining instead of shooting.

8. **The Barstow Triangle.** Despite certain similarities to the more infamous Bermuda Triangle, you won't have to worry about dropping out of sight here so long as you stay off the desert's back roads. Start in the town of Barstow and its **Chamber of Commerce,** on Barstow Road between Virginia Way and Kelly Drive (✆ **760/256-8617;** www.barstowchamber.com), for a quick read of the Mojave Desert, then check out the **Barstow Station,** the ultimate curiosity shop built in and around a 1900s railway station. Head east on I-15 to Yermo and the thriving ghost town of Calico (see "Campground Oases in the Mojave Desert," earlier in this chapter), where mining lore shares the spotlight with archaeology and the Early Man site excavated by Dr. Louis Leakey. A few miles east of Barstow on I-40 is the 1860s town of Daggett, where you can take a self-guided walking tour. Another few miles east, you'll find Newberry Springs with its Bagdad Café. Then back to Barstow and head west on Route 58 into the triangle, brushing Edwards Air Force Base (where space shuttles often land—and some say UFOs as well) at Four Corners before dropping south to Victorville. (For more about Barstow Station and the Bagdad Café, see "Off-the-Wall Attractions," earlier in this chapter.) For more information, contact the **California Welcome Center** (✆ **760/253-4782**).

9. **The I-8 to Yuma.** The 171 miles between San Diego and the California-Arizona border could whiz by in a blur, but not if you take these detours: **Desert View Tower** at the In-Ko-Pah Park Road exit near Jacumba gives you a great view of what's ahead, plus some eccentric carved stone animals lining the trail; Calexico, separated by a fence from its Mexican neighbor Mexicali, is mysteriously chockablock with Chinese restaurants; and the **Imperial Sand Dunes Recreation Area** (www.blm.gov/ca/st/en/fo/elcentro/recreation/ohvs/isdra.html), where retakes of the film *Lawrence of Arabia* (1962) were shot, draws off-road-vehicle types between October and May. Allow some sightseeing time for the Yuma Territorial Prison, now a state park, but once "the hellhole of Arizona." Imperial Sand Dunes, **Yuma County Chamber of Commerce,** 180 W. First St., Ste. A, Yuma (✆ **928/782-2567;** www.yumachamber.org).

10. **East Mojave National Scenic Area.** This "wannabe" failed to get full national park honors in the recently passed California Desert Protection Act; instead, it ended up with a "preserve" status, a designation for which the National Rifle Association lobbied, because it will allow hunting to continue in this 1.2-million-acre high-desert reserve. Cattle grazing, as well, will go on. In Kelso, visit the singing dunes—the sand you dislodge when you walk on a dune makes moaning and humming sounds as it slides. Head north from Kelso on Kelbaker Road to see the cinder cones and lava beds where astronauts trained for the 1969 moon landing. When you join I-40, drive east to the Essex Road exit, then north 16 miles to Mitchell Caverns in Providence Mountain State Recreation Area, where rangers lead tours into the caves and self-contained camping is allowed. North on Black Canyon Road, the Mid Hills and Hole-in-the-Wall campgrounds have a total of 63 sites and are connected by 11-mile Wild Horse Canyon Road, a scenic, unpaved, backcountry byway. **Mojave National Preserve,** Barstow (℃ **760/252-6100;** www.nps.gov/moja).

Utah's Parks & Canyons

UTAH CONTAINS FIVE NATIONAL PARKS, SEVEN NATIONAL MONU-
ments, seven national forests, two national recreational areas, one national historic site,
and 45 state parks.

Utah is where Butch Cassidy and Etta Place rode a bicycle in *Butch Cassidy and the
Sundance Kid* (1969), where the heroines of *Thelma & Louise* (1991) drove off the cliff
into the canyon, and where Max von Sydow delivered the Sermon on the Mount in
The Greatest Story Ever Told (1965).

It's where the California gull is the state bird, the world's most famous automobile
commercial was filmed, and Brigham Young took his 27th wife.

America's first department store was unveiled in Salt Lake City in 1868, Philo T.
Farnsworth (the inventor of television) was born in Beaver in 1906, and the first
licensed franchise for Kentucky Fried Chicken—still serving up finger-lickin' chicken
today—is located on State Street in Salt Lake City.

Mountain man Jim Bridger tasted the waters of the Great Salt Lake and thought
he'd reached the Pacific; mountain man Robert Redford, shooting the film *Jeremiah
Johnson* (1972), sniffed the clear, clean air of the Wasatch Mountains and thought
he'd reached Nirvana, so he bought a mountain; and countless wandering hobos
dreamed of licking the Big Rock Candy Mountain.

Early tourists flocked to take the waters at Schneitter's Hot Pots, later turned into
the Homestead Resort, and to gawk at the wild man of Borneo, a pair of Siamese
twins, and an alligator pit at the fantasy towers of Saltair, the Coney Island of Salt
Lake, whose ghost pavilion still lurks off I-80 some 17 miles west of Salt Lake City.

This is where dinosaurs roamed 500 million years ago, where the Anasazi,
or Ancient Ones, planted corn 2,000 years ago, and where Chinese miners at
Silver Reef put food on family graves a century ago (giving local Paiutes a taste
for Chinese cuisine).

Utah has the highest literacy rate, largest average household size, second-highest
birth rate, and second-lowest death rate
in the 50 states. More than 70% of the
state's residents are members of the Church
of Jesus Christ of Latter-day Saints, also
known as Mormons.

> *"This is the most
> beautiful place
> on earth."*
> —Edward Abbey,
> *Desert Solitaire*, 1968

Utah Highlights

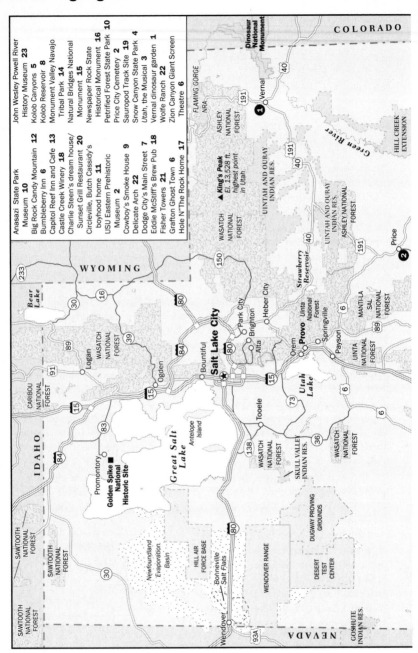

Anasazi State Park Museum **10**
Big Rock Candy Mountain **12**
Bumbleberry Inn **6**
Capitol Reef Inn and Cafe **13**
Castle Creek Winery **18**
Charlie Steen's dream house/Sunset Grill Restaurant **20**
Circleville, Butch Cassidy's boyhood home **11**
USU Eastern Prehistoric Museum **2**
Cowboy's Smoke House **9**
Delicate Arch **22**
Dodge City's Main Street **7**
Eddie McStiff's Brew Pub **18**
Fisher Towers **21**
Grafton Ghost Town **6**
Hole N"The Rock Home **17**

John Wesley Powell River History Museum **23**
Kolob Canyons **5**
Kolob Reservoir **8**
Monument Valley Navajo Tribal Park **14**
Natural Bridges National Monument **15**
Newspaper Rock State Historical Monument **16**
Petrified Forest State Park **10**
Price City Cemetery **2**
Sauropod Track Site **19**
Snow Canyon State Park **4**
Utah, the Musical **3**
Vernal dinosaur garden **1**
Wolfe Ranch **22**
Zion Canyon Giant Screen Theatre **6**

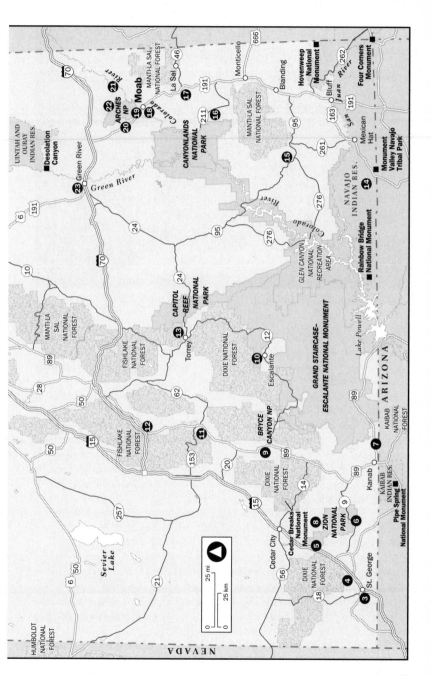

Countryside around Zion National Park.

THE MORMONS

In the spring of 1830, Joseph Smith, a devout young man in Fayette, New York, published the *Book of Mormon* and founded the Church of Jesus Christ of Latter-day Saints, a charismatic religion claiming to be a restoration of the original church. Among its tenets were polygamy and an active program of proselytism, neither of which were favorably received in the neighborhood.

Chased from New York and then Ohio and Missouri, Smith and his followers settled in Nauvoo, Illinois, where they developed a city of 20,000. But the new neighbors were no more hospitable than the old ones, burning and killing until Smith decided in 1844 that it was time to move again. In the meantime, however, he declared himself a candidate for president of the United States and said that, if elected, he would not move west.

When members of the church smashed a printing press which they believed was publishing libels against them, Smith and his brother were jailed, then taken from prison by a mob and killed.

The man who succeeded Smith as church leader was Brigham Young. At the end of 1845, when the state of Illinois repealed the city charter for Nauvoo, he organized an advance party to go west looking for a new settlement. Beginning in early 1846, church members loaded their goods onto covered wagons, hitched up their horses, and led them down to ferries on the Mississippi River. The great Mormon exodus had begun.

That year, they got as far as Iowa. Then, on July 24, 1847, Brigham Young and his pioneers entered the Salt Lake Valley. The migration continued, with thousands of the devout literally walking and pulling their possessions in handcarts, until by 1900 the

Mormons had established 500 settlements in and around Utah, many of them in arid, inhospitable desert.

Certainly the most dramatic moment was at Hole-in-the-Rock in 1879, when 230 Mormons blasted a hole through a 50-foot cliff at Glen Canyon and lowered their 80 wagons by chains and ropes to the river 1,800 feet below, where homemade rafts waited. They went on to found the town of Bluff, which today claims a population of 320, just 90 more people than when it was founded. Today, boaters and travelers in four-wheel-drive vehicles can see the spot where the hole was blasted in the rock.

"This is the right place!"
—Brigham Young in 1847, on first seeing Salt Lake Valley

The Mormon cause was severely set back in 1857 when some xenophobic members became fearful of federal interference and anxious to keep out both miners and eager new settlers. This triggered the infamous Mountain Meadows Massacre, when Mormon militia members and local American Indians slaughtered 120 of the 137-member Fancher wagon-train party bound for California. The only survivors were 17 children under the age of 7. A marker off Route 18 near the town of Central in southwestern Utah identifies the massacre site.

It took almost 50 years and the church outlawing polygamy before Utah achieved statehood in 1896.

RVing Utah's National Park Country

Early on an October morning, the snowcapped Henry Mountains glisten against a blue sky. Down every wash, a stalwart line of cottonwoods has turned a glowing gold. Flocks of tiny Berwick's wrens, exuberant after the rain, flutter up past our windshield and across the Bicentennial Highway. Water shines from holes and grooves in slickrock, and snow dusts the red mesas and buttes and throws twisted black junipers into sharp relief. As we begin to climb toward Natural Bridges National Monument, the whole desert forest of piñon pines and sagebrush is covered with puffy white clumps of snow. Everything is breathtakingly beautiful.

Because so much of Utah is public land, it makes an ideal getaway for RVers, especially those who enjoy self-contained camping in parklands and the wilderness. Driving through the state, we always imagine the pioneers and early Mormon settlers moving through the eerie terrain with plenty of time on their hands and a little creative daydreaming. It's the only way some of the geological landmarks could have been named. We stare at spots like Capitol Reef's Capitol Dome or Zion's Great White Throne and wonder who could have thought that particular rock really looked like a dome or a throne.

The state tourism people have divided southern Utah into four different areas— **Color Country** in the south-central and southwest region, including Zion and Bryce Canyon national parks; **Canyonlands** to the southeast, including Canyonlands and Arches national parks; **Panoramaland** in the west-central region, including Capitol Reef National Park; and **Castle Country** in the east-central sector, the terrain where Butch Cassidy used to ride.

RV TRAVEL ADVICE

It was 4pm, and the Canyonlands park ranger, standing by a sign saying campground full, suggested we might drive around anyhow and check for space. We discovered a couple packing up to check out and nabbed the last free space in the park. Moral: Don't give up without a try.

Northern Utah is divided into **Golden Spike Empire,** the extreme northwest corner reaching from the Nevada border east to Ogden, named for the spot where the first transcontinental railroad was finished in 1869; **Bridgerland,** the northeastern corner surrounding Logan, named for mountain man Jim Bridger; **Great Salt Lake Country,** which includes Great Salt Lake, the Bonneville Salt Flats, and Salt Lake City; **Mountainland,** with Utah's best ski country and Robert Redford's Sundance Resort; and **Dinosaurland,** notable for dinosaur digs, Green River rafting, and dude ranches. You'll need to remember the divisions when using the state travel guides.

One of the newest recreation areas in Utah is **Grand Staircase–Escalante National Monument,** the first to be administered by the Bureau of Land Management instead of the National Park Service. Gateways to the new national monument are Escalante and Boulder on Route 12 and Kanab on Route 89, in the south-central area of Utah. With world-class paleontological sites and a panoramic geologic sampler, Escalante attracts adventuresome hikers and four-wheel-drive explorers. Few services and facilities are yet available inside the monument.

I-70 is the only paved road accessing the spectacular scenery of the **San Rafael Swell,** Utah's most inaccessible wilderness area. We've done the drive in both directions, and strongly urge you to go from west to east for the most dramatic impact. There are numerous scenic turnouts on the 100-mile route between Salina and Green River, but no services, so be sure to top off your gas tank before crossing the reefs.

Utah **state parks** accept advance reservations by phone and online. Call weekdays between 8am and 5pm, Mountain Standard Time (© **800/322-3770** or 801/322-3770; http://stateparks.utah.gov/reservations). Also call for reservations in Utah **national forests** (© **877/444-6777;** www.reserveusa.com).

HITTING THE HIGHLIGHTS

The roads are generally very good in Utah, so you'll be able to move along as briskly as necessary, except when the first snow begins to fall in late October or early November. The highlights could be covered in as little as 7 days, but you'd have very little time to hike and explore.

Zion and **Bryce Canyon national parks** require a minimum of a full day each, or 2 days each to allow time to hike a bit as well.

RVers who choose not to take the tunnel route from Zion to Bryce can return to I-15, and make the short detour into Kolob Canyons from the interstate. Then exit at Cedar City to drive through Cedar Breaks and along Route 143 past Panguitch Lake, a very scenic route, before turning south on U.S. 89 to connect with Route 12 to Bryce.

Although geology buffs will enjoy the dead-end scenic drive that delves more deeply into **Capitol Reef National Park,** travelers pressed for time can skip it. But everyone should take the time to drive into the orchards and campground area at **Fruita,** as well as make roadside stops along the way at the old schoolhouse and the cliff petroglyphs.

If time permits, swing south from the junction at Hanksville to drive **Bicentennial Highway,** which allows you a good look at **Glen Canyon National Recreation Area** at Hites Crossing and a visit to **Natural Bridges National Monument.** Otherwise, head north to I-70 and take U.S. 191 south at exit 180 to drop down in Moab, Arches, and Canyonlands.

Allow a full day each for **Arches,** the **Needles,** and **Islands in the Sky,** adding to the latter a side detour into **Dead Horse Point State Park.**

GOING FOR THE LONG HAUL

We ran across quite a few people in Utah who came out on a vacation and never went home, so consider yourself warned. One could certainly spend a long, happy season RVing, hiking, and biking in and around the public lands with an occasional hop into town to restock the larder, fill up with gas, top off the water, and dump the holding tanks.

Two weeks in each park or national monument, taking into consideration the 14-day camping limit, would allow plenty of time to explore, and a week or two on a houseboat on **Lake Powell** would provide pure pleasure. Add another 2 weeks at particularly scenic BLM areas, such as the **Colorado River** outside Moab, and you'll have an entire season filled with things to do.

The temporary employment scene in Moab is usually active, so full-timers can find seasonal shops looking for clerks and restaurants hiring waiters. In winter, ski areas are good sources for seasonal employment.

Travel Essentials

WHEN TO GO

At any time of year, some part of Utah is in its prime. In winter, skiers flock to "the greatest snow on earth," Utah's champagne powder. Most of the dozen major ski areas are clustered to the east of Salt Lake City, but Brian Head ski resort, at nearly 10,000 feet elevation with a long snow season, is 12 miles off I-15 at Parowan, near Cedar City. St. George in the southwest's Dixie area is mild in winter. Fall and spring are the ideal times for RVers to visit Utah's national parks; summer is hot in the lower elevations, but cooler at Brian Head, Cedar Breaks, and Bryce Canyon. All the national parks, however, are jam-packed in summer with Americans and Europeans.

WHAT TO TAKE

Take along sunblock, a sun hat, good walking or hiking shoes, an adequate supply of water, and a camera. If you're still using film, take at least twice as much as you'd expect to use, or make sure you have enough memory for your digital camera (it's that photogenic!).

WHAT TO WEAR

Wear layered clothing for all of Utah's parks. In late fall and winter, you'll want heavy parkas and boots or shoes with snow-safe treads. We encountered considerable snow in mid-October at Bryce Canyon and Cedar Breaks, while Zion, Canyonlands, Arches, and Capitol Reef still had sunny, shirt-sleeve weather. In summer's heat, natural fibers help absorb perspiration.

TRIMMING COSTS ON THE ROAD

As a state, Utah is much less expensive than many, although sparsely settled southern Utah does not have frequent or varied shopping opportunities. Keep your larder well stocked and your gas and water tanks topped off when venturing into less-traveled territory.

With so much of southern Utah's most scenic terrain under **Bureau of Land Management (BLM)** administration, RVers will find some no-fee undeveloped campsites where camping is permitted under the following conditions: Camping in one site is limited to 14 days, campers must pack out all trash, campfires may not be left unattended, and camping is not permitted within 300 feet of springs or ponds so that water is accessible to wildlife. Self-contained RVs meet with BLM's regulations as long as dumping of gray or black water takes place only in designated sanitary dump stations and never on the ground. Call the **BLM** in Salt Lake City for information (© **801/539-4001;** www.blm.gov).

WHERE TO GET TRAVEL INFORMATION

All of the following park offices will be able to provide you with travel information and entrance fees are per vehicle:

- **Arches National Park:** © 435/719/2299; www.nps.gov/arch. $10
- **Bryce Canyon National Park:** © 435/834-5322; www.nps.gov/brca. $25
- **Canyonlands National Park:** © 435/719-2313; www.nps.gov/cany. $10
- **Capitol Reef National Park:** © 435/425-4111; www.nps.gov/care. $5
- **Cedar Breaks National Monument:** © 435/586-9451; www.nps.gov/cebr. $4
- **Dead Horse Point State Park:** © 435/259-2614; www.go-utah.com. $7
- **Glen Canyon National Recreation Area:** © 928/608-6200; www.nps.gov/glca. $15
- **Grand Staircase of the Escalante National Monument:** © 435/644-4300; www.ut.blm.gov/monument. $12
- **Natural Bridges National Monument:** © 435/692-1234; www.nps.gov/nabr. $6

• **Utah Office of Tourism:** ✆ **800/200-1160;** www.utah.com.

• **Zion National Park:** ✆ **435/772-3256;** www.nps.gov/zion. $25

DRIVING & CAMPING TIPS

• **Use the plat system.** Brigham Young directed Utah's early Mormons to lay out street plats with streets running true north and south and true east and west from a central point. If an address is 500 S. 700 E., for instance, you drive 5 blocks south from the center and then 7 blocks east. Blocks are laid out in increments of 100. Whether you're in Salt Lake City or Moab, the plan holds true. The Mormons were also instructed to make streets "wide enough for a team of four oxen and a covered wagon to turn around."

• **Bring along your own music or subscribe to satellite radio.** Otherwise you'll have to listen to the car radio, and in Utah you can get only three sounds day or night: the Mormon Tabernacle Choir, country music, and Rush Limbaugh.

• **Be aware of Utah's mysterious liquor laws.** Utah's liquor laws allow purchases of wine and spirits by the bottle in state liquor stores and some hotels in many areas, except on Sundays and holidays. Beer with 3.2% alcohol can be purchased in grocery and convenience stores 7 days a week. Licensed restaurants may serve alcohol by the drink, but neither drinks nor a wine list can be offered by the server; the patron must request them. Lounges and taverns serve only beer. "Brown-bagging," bringing your own alcohol for consumption in a location, is no longer permitted.

• **Don't break the cryptobiotic crust.** The most dire thing you can do in southern Utah is to walk, bike, drive on, or otherwise break the cryptobiotic crust, a fragile and ancient covering on the ground that looks dark brown and crumbly and nurtures virtually all desert life, both flora and fauna. One careless step can destroy crust that will take 50 to 100 years to recover. Always stay on the trail or roadway. As locals say, "tiptoe through the crypto."

The Best Utah Sights, Tastes & Experiences

OFF-THE-WALL ATTRACTIONS

The Big Rock Candy Mountain. Located on Hwy. 89 south of Richfield, off I-70, exit 23 to Sevier, it really does look a little like a mound of caramel. Neither folk singer Burl Ives nor songwriter Harry McClintock ever saw it, but that didn't stop them from making money from a hit song about it. Folk experts John Lomax and Charles Seeger said the original version, with its "lemonade springs" and "lakes of stew," was sung by old-time hobos to lure young farm boys into a life on the road.

The dinosaur garden in Vernal. Sculpted by Elbert Porter at the Utah Field House of Natural History State Park in Vernal, the garden displays 13 critters, from woolly mammoths to triceratops. Daily 9am–6pm. The park is at 235 E. Main St. in Vernal

(© **435/789-3799**). Utah is also home to the largest dinosaur egg found, discovered at the Cleveland-Lloyd Dinosaur Quarry south of Price and exhibited in the **Prehistoric Museum of the College of Eastern Utah,** 155 E. Main St., in Price. Admission $5 adults, $4 senior, $2 children ages 2–12 (© **435/613-5060;** http://museum.ceu.edu).

Hole N" The Rock Home, South of Moab. Not to be confused with where the Mormons crossed Glen Canyon, the Hole N" The Rock Home in Moab is a 5,000-square-foot drilled-out cavern that was home to Albert and Gladys Christensen beginning in 1952. It has 14 rooms, a 65-foot chimney, and a bathtub carved from a rock. During the 12 years Albert spent creating it, he also painted a Sermon on the Mount and carved the head of Franklin D. Roosevelt in the rock above the house. After Albert died, Gladys continued to run their cafe and gift shop until her death in 1974. Now their family operates it as a museum and memorial, and the gift shop sells souvenirs. Daily 9am–5pm. Admission $5 adults, $3.50 children 5–10, free for children 4 and under. 11037 S. Hwy. 191, south of Moab (© **435/686-2250;** www.theholeintherock.com).

The Zion Canyon Giant Screen Theatre. It's hard to believe, but near the entrance to Zion National Park is a giant screen theater purporting to show "the Zion you came to see—the real Zion." Since we didn't succumb to the come-on and pay the ticket price for a 37-minute film—$10 adults, $8 children—we're not sure what it showed that we missed by driving into the park itself. Located at 145 Zion Park Blvd., in Springdale. Call for showtimes (© **888/256-3456;** www.zioncanyontheatre.com).

The John Wesley Powell River History Museum, Green River. This has to be the only museum in America dedicated to river-rapids runners, with some 15 Hall of Fame members to date. The handsome new museum commemorates Powell, the one-armed Civil War veteran who first mapped the Grand Canyon and navigated the Colorado River seated in a chair lashed atop a pine rowboat. Daily 8am–7pm. Admission $6 adults and children 13 and over, $2 children 3–12, free for children 2 and under, family $10. Located at 1765 E. Main St., in Green River (© **435/564-3427;** www.johnwesleypowell.com).

Circleville, boyhood home of Butch Cassidy. Circleville, on U.S. 89 about 25 miles south of I-70, was the boyhood home of Butch Cassidy, and where he came upon his return from Bolivia (if, indeed, he ever went there), to meet with his mother for the last time in 1925. The family shared a blueberry pie, according to Butch's sister, Lula Parker Betenson, who wrote a book about her brother. The outlaw's real name was Robert LeRoy Parker. What remains of their two-room log cabin is still standing south of town on U.S. 89.

Charlie Steen's dream house, Moab. Now the Sunset Grill Restaurant, the dream house sits atop the tallest hill in Moab, north of town on Hwy. 191. (Locals opine that the view surpasses the food, mostly steaks, pasta, and seafood.) Charlie was, you may remember, the Texan who became a millionaire in the uranium market during the Cold War days of the 1950s. He struck pay dirt in 1952, and the rush of miners that

Indian petroglyphs at Newspaper Rock State Historical Park.

followed quadrupled the population of Moab. His mine, named Mi Vida, brought him $60 million in a few short years. The house became a restaurant in 1974 when Charlie ran into bad luck in taxes and mining. Mon–Sat 5–9:30pm. 900 N. Main St. (© **435/259-7146;** www.sunsetgrillmoab.com).

Newspaper Rock State Historic Park. Located 12 miles off Hwy. 191 via Route 211 W., Newspaper Rock is an Indian-era billboard made up of petroglyphs (prehistoric rock carvings). Most of the drawings date back 1,000 years, attributed to prehistoric Indians and early Utes, with additions by white pioneer settlers and, unfortunately, a few contemporary vandals. The area is 24 miles northwest of Monticello on the main road into the Needles section of Canyonlands National Park. Open daily. Free admission. Call the BLM for camping information (© **435/587-1500;** www.utah.com/ schmerker/2000/newsrock.htm).

Price City Cemetery. The Price City Cemetery is the final resting place for a body shot by a posse in 1898, identified as Butch Cassidy, and laid out with great fanfare before burial. One of the many visitors couldn't stop laughing when viewing the corpse. Later, when a Wyoming lawman made a positive identification of the body as another outlaw, people realized that the visitor had been Cassidy himself. The whole story is carved on his tombstone. Price is at the junction of U.S. 6 and Hwy. 191 in the center of the state. For more information, visit **www.pricecityutah.com.**

The Sauropod Track Site. Eight miles south of I-15 on U.S. 191 and north of the Arches National Park entrance, then 2 miles down a dirt road, is where four dinosaurs

HOT ROCKS IN UTAH

Moab's bounty of **uranium** was first noted by France's Madame Curie when she used ore from Moab to develop radium in 1896 (some say she traveled to Utah and conducted experiments on-site). The supply finally bottomed out in the late 1960s.

tramped through a damp river channel some 150 million years ago, leaving only footprints (but probably not taking pictures). Discovered in 1989, the footprints of the single brontosaurus are 2 feet wide, and one of the carnivores, probably an allosaurus, left evidence of having a limp. Don't attempt the trip in an RV during or after a rainstorm or you also may end up as a sightseeing attraction for some future tourists.

Wolfe Ranch, in Arches National Park. Civil War veteran John Wesley Wolfe came here with his son Fred searching for a place to raise cattle. His wife and three younger children remained in Etna, Ohio. Eventually, in 1906, his daughter Flora and her family came to stay, and they talked her father into gentrifying the ranch. For her sake, he built a new cabin with a wood floor (the one you see today), ordered a 100-piece set of china dishes from the Sears Roebuck catalog because she disliked tin plates, and bought her a camera and film-developing kit, with which she made one of the earliest known photographs of Delicate Arch. To get there, turn east off the main road onto Wolfe Ranch Road and continue to the parking area. A short walk leads to what's left of the ranch. Farther up the trail, you'll see some Ute petroglyphs (**www.nps.gov/arch/historyculture/index.htm**).

SEVEN SITES OFFERING *DÉJÀ VU* ALL OVER AGAIN

1. **Grafton.** This picturesque ghost town, set against the towering rock walls of Zion National Park, is where Paul Newman and Katharine Ross rode a bicycle to the music of "Raindrops Keep Fallin' on My Head" in the film *Butch Cassidy and the Sundance Kid* (1969). Take State Rte. 9 to Rockville, then turn south on Bridge Lane (near the entrance to Zion National Park), cross the river on an old iron bridge, and follow a 4-mile dirt road to the old cemetery and town. Larger motor homes and trailers might find it a tight squeeze in some spots, so we'd recommend pulling off at the tunnel information/scenic view turnout on Rte. 9 west of Rockville for an overview of the area.

2. **Fisher Towers.** History's most famous TV car commercials were shot outside Moab at a pair of 1,500-foot looming spires called Fisher Towers (**www.discovermoab.com/pdf/fishertowers.pdf**). A Chevrolet, lowered by helicopter, was shown sitting all alone atop a tall, narrow pinnacle, surrounded only by desert and craggy red rocks in all directions. The first commercial was such a big hit in

1964 that a second one was shot in 1974. The towers are on Scenic Route 128 east from Moab at Mile 21, with a road sign identifying them. A hiking trail to the towers and a picnic table are also at the site.

3. **Delicate Arch, Arches National Park.** All the book covers and posters that you've ever seen about Utah leap to life at Delicate Arch (**www.utah.com/ nationalparks/arches/delicatearch.htm**). Early cowboys called the much-photographed 45-foot-high red sandstone arch "the Schoolmarm's Drawers," but for us it most closely resembles the bottom half of a bowlegged cowboy wearing chaps. The hike, the park's most popular walk, is a strenuous 480-foot ascent over a huge rock mountain similar to Australia's Uluru/Ayers Rock; it seems much longer than the 3-mile round-trip claimed by the park literature, especially on the uphill part. Once there, many visitors sit and stare in awe at the arch (trying, perhaps, to catch their breath) while photographers clamber over precarious rocks for an ever-better angle. Late afternoon is the best time to photograph the golden light against the stone. The walk sets out from the Wolfe Ranch parking lot off the park's main road.

4. **Movie location in Moab.** Pick up a free "Moab Movie Locations" brochure in the Moab Information Center, Center and Main streets, and you can head to all your favorite movie locations in the area (**www.discovermoab.com/movie. htm**). See where scenes for *Indiana Jones and the Last Crusade* (1989) were shot in Arches National Park. At Canyonlands' Island in the Sky, Max von Sydow as Christ delivered the Sermon on the Mount in *The Greatest Story Ever Told* (1965); he stood facing the Green River at the Green River Overlook on a rock to the left of the fence. Just 2,000 years later in cinema time, the two heroines of *Thelma & Louise* (1991) drove off the cliff under Dead Horse Point 10 miles down the Shafer Trail (also called Potash Rd.), an unpaved road off Rte. 279, 19 miles south of Moab. Earlier in the film, at Arches' Courthouse Towers, they locked a pursuing police officer in his patrol car trunk, and several chase scenes were filmed in the La Sal Mountains outside the town of La Sal off Rte. 46. More recently, *Star Trek, 127 Hours, Austin Powers 3*, and *Guns, Girls and Gambling* have found locations in the area.

   For Western movie fans, in *Rio Grande* (1950), John Wayne rescued kidnapped cavalry children from a pueblo just off Utah Scenic Byway 128, a half-mile up a dirt road from Milepost 19, and located the hideout in *The Comancheros* (1961), 1 mile east of Milepost 21. In *Cheyenne Autumn* (1964), cavalryman Richard Widmark chased the Cheyenne across a flat area south of the Arches' South Park Avenue. And Devils Garden in Arches served as the site where an Indian ambush trapped the U.S. Cavalry in the truly terrible *Taza, Son of Cochise* (1954), starring Rock Hudson and Barbara Rush.

5. **Monument Valley Navajo Tribal Park.** In southeastern Utah on the Arizona border, Monument Valley Park is bisected by Hwy. 163. Famous for its appearances in a host of John Ford films, Monument Valley stood in for Texas in *The*

Searchers (1956), Arizona in *My Darling Clementine* (1946), and New Mexico in *Stagecoach* (1939). Stop by the **Visitor Center,** east on Monument Valley Road off Rte. 163 (✆ **435/727-5874;** www.navajonationparks.org/htm/monument valley.htm), for a self-guided driving map and information; daily 9am–5pm. The **Navajo Tourism Department** offers a guide for tours lasting anywhere from 2 hours to a full day.

Goulding's Monument Valley Campground & RV Park has nightly shuttle service to the company's historic lodge and trading post for a sound-and-light show. The park's 66 RV sites have satellite TV and full hookups with 30- and 50-amp electric, and there's a heated indoor pool. Sites $29–$44. Mid-Mar–Oct. Take Rte. 163 south to Monument Valley west; go 2 miles (✆ **435/727-3235** reservations; www.gouldings.com).

6. **Snow Canyon State Park.** Northwest of St. George, Snow Canyon State Park (**http://stateparks.utah.gov/parks/snow-canyon**) is where Robert Redford in *The Electric Horseman* (1979) freed his stallion at the end of the film; Jane Fonda and Willie Nelson costarred in the contemporary Western set in Las Vegas.

7. **The Main Street of Dodge City.** The very main street where Marshall Dillon in TV's long-running series *Gunsmoke* faced weekly gun battles still stands in Johnson Canyon, 9 miles east of Kanab off Hwy. 89 on Johnson Canyon Road. Sometimes the set is open to visitors for a fee; otherwise, you can see it from the roadway with binoculars.

MACHO THINGS TO DO IN UTAH

1. **Go mountain biking.** The tiny town of Brian Head, reached via Rte. 143 from exit 78 on I-15, has 12 different routes rated "easy" to "advanced." Because the area is at 10,000 feet, it's cool enough in summer to enjoy biking, but snow-covered from November through May. Expect a rich variety of flora and fauna in the four life zones: alpine, subalpine, Canadian, and transitional. You can get essential detailed maps locally. There are bike-rental shops in town: **Brian Head Sports,** 269 S. Village (✆ **435/677-2014;** www.brianhead.com); and **Georg's,** 612 S. Hwy. 143, (✆ **435/677-2013**). Information: **Cedar City Brian Head Tourism Bureau,** 581 N. Main St./ Ste. A (✆ **800/354-4849;** www.scenic southernutah.com). Reservations: **Brian Head Resort,** 329 S. Hwy. 143 (✆ **866/930-1010;** www.brianhead.com).

   Local shuttle services or chairlifts can take you to the top of the hill, and you can ride down. The nearest camping is in Cedar Breaks.

2. **Go white-water rafting and four-wheeling.** One-day expeditions that combine white-water river rafting and four-wheel-drive land tours are offered by **Navtec Expeditions of Moab,** 321 N. Main St. in Moab (✆ **800/833-1278;** www.navtec.com). A morning sports boat ride goes along the Colorado River gorge just underneath Dead Horse Point State Park, stopping to see dinosaur tracks, petrified wood, and Indian rock art. A buffet picnic lunch is served, then

a transfer to 4X4s for a tour up White Rim and Shafer Trail in Canyonlands National Park. Cost: $120 adults, $100 children 16 and under.

3. **Go cross-country skiing or snowshoeing at Bryce Canyon.** Bryce Canyon (© 435/834-5322; www.nps.gov/brca) in winter has extraordinary views of bright red Navajo sandstone sprinkled with snow and sparkling in the sunlight against a clear blue sky. Cross-country skiing and snowshoeing are two excellent ways to see it. Self-contained RVs can stay in the park's North Campground near the visitor center during winter, although water is cut off and the sanitary dump closed down. There are no hookups. The 11-mile Rim Trail with its level terrain and sensational views down into the canyon is a good place to start. Snowshoer wannabes who take the twice-weekly snowshoe hikes led by a ranger can borrow a pair free from the visitor center (at the north end as you enter the park), leaving a credit card or driver's license as a deposit, and set off in the snow.

4. **Go mountain biking on the Slickrock Trail.** From Moab, the North American capital of the sport, you can start on the 10-mile Slickrock Trail, tackled by 100,000 eager sprocket-heads a year. Beginners are advised to start with Gemini Bridges or Hurrah Pass, each 14 miles long. In town, six bike shops, each with its obligatory espresso machine, rent or sell anything you might need, from maps to machines: **Chile Pepper Bike Shop,** 702 S. Main St. (© **888/677-4688** or 435/259-4688; www.chilebikes.com); **Dreamrides,** 96 E. Center St. (© **888/662-2882** or 435/259-6419; www.dreamride.com); **Escape Adventures Bike Tours,** 391 S. Main St. (© **800/559-1978;** www.escapeadventures.com); **Nichols Expeditions,** 497 N. Main St. (© **800/648-8488** or 435/259-7423; www.nichols expeditions.com); **Poison Spider Bicycles,** 497 N. Main St. (© **800/635-1792** or 435/259-7882; www.poisonspiderbicycles.com); and **Rim Tours,** 1233 S. U.S. 191 (© **800/626-7335** or 435/259-5223; www.rimtours.com).

5. **Take a 1-day river run through Gray Canyon.** A run on the Green River with **Moki Mac River Expeditions in Salt Lake City** is a quick, easy option for beginners. They'll pick you up at your campground in the Green River area off I-70 and take you through six or so splashy rapids and some rugged scenery on an oar-powered expedition. Cost: $69 adults, $55 children 15 and under (© **800/284-7280;** www.mokimac.com).

6. **Run the Green in Desolation Canyon.** Desolation Canyon, with its calm waters and peaceful put-in point, is a favorite for first-timers and families. But with more than 60 rapids and an ultimate Class III rating, the river challenges experienced river rafters and kayakers as well. Contact **Adrift Adventures in Canyonlands** (© **800/824-0150;** www.adrift.com), **Adventure Bound Trips** (© **800/423-4668;** www.raft-utah.com), **Moab River and Canoe Company** (© **800/746-6622;** www.moab-rafting.com, www.redrivercanoe.com), or **Western River** (© **866/904-1160;** www.westernriver.com).

7. **Rent a houseboat and go exploring on Lake Powell.** Explore ancient Anasazi caves, photograph remote Rainbow Bridge, and swim and picnic at a deserted

Lake Powell at sunset.

beach—all from the comfort of home. Houseboating on Lake Powell, second-largest man-made lake in North America, is something akin to having your RV walk on water. Houseboats ranging from 36 to 59 feet are available for rent year-round from four perimeter marinas in Glen Canyon National Recreation Area—Bullfrog, Hite Marina, Wahweap, and Halls Crossing. Between October and May, houseboats can be reserved for trips as short as 1 or 2 days. The rest of the year, minimum-rental requirements are longer. Call **ARAMARK** well ahead of time in summer for reservations (© **888/896-3829;** www.lakepowell. com).

8. **Go horseback riding along the scenic rim of Bryce Canyon.** Head through the Butch Cassidy country or a 1,600-year-old bristlecone pine forest. Any of these can be booked through the office in **Ruby's Inn** at the entrance to Bryce Canyon (© **800/679-5859** or 435/834-5358; www.rubysinn.com). All rides are guided and range from an hour to all day. There is no age or weight limit on Bryce Canyon rides. Big-game hunting is also available in season.

TAKEOUT (OR EAT-IN) TREATS

Castle Creek Winery, Moab. Red Cliffs Lodge's Winery is Utah's oldest winery, and offers tastings of its red and white table and dessert wines. Daily noon–6:30pm. It's at Mile 14 on Hwy. 128 (© **435/259-2002;** www.redcliffslodge.com/winery).

Bear Lake raspberries. Dark-red Bear Lake raspberries that grow in the tiny north-eastern Utah town of Bear Lake are the world's most delicious. Aficionados arrive in

Talkin' Utah: A Glossary

Butte: An isolated hill or mountain rising suddenly out of flat land.

Cairn: A heap of stones serving as a memorial or a landmark.

Desert varnish: A dark, glossy finish on rock created by heat-loving bacteria that draw iron and manganese from airborne dust.

Gentile: In Latter-day Saints usage, any non-Mormon.

Hoodoo: An eroded pillar of sandstone topped with a hard rock cap and sculpted into eerie shapes.

LDS: Church of Jesus Christ of Latter-day Saints, also called Saints or Mormons.

Mesa: A flat-topped, steep-walled land area; a table mountain.

Natural arches: Water-cut rock formations that stand on the skyline.

Natural bridges: Water-cut (including snow melting and refreezing) rock formations in the bottoms of canyons.

Petroglyphs: Carvings incised on rock surfaces.

Pictographs: Pictures drawn on rock surfaces.

Slickrock: A smooth, slippery rock formation burnished by "desert varnish."

Wash: The dry bed of a sometimes stream; never camp in these areas, and avoid them during rainstorms.

the last week of July and the first week or two of August to eat them fresh from the vine at **Hildt's Famous Bear Lake Raspberry Stand,** or have them whirled into milkshakes at **Le Beau's** or **Raspberry and Yummy Things Bakery.** The climate limits the vines to one instead of the usual two annual crops, and locals believe that results in more flavor intensity. If you can't make it to Bear Lake, taste the fresh Bear Lake raspberry ice cream at **Dreyer's,** a local chain of ice-cream stores in Salt Lake City.

Bumbleberry Inn, Springdale. Bumbleberry pie is the house specialty at the Bumbleberry Inn, gateway town to Zion National Park. The management provides a whimsical description of its fruit—"burple and binkel berries that grow on giggle bushes"— and the black-red loganberries or boysenberries in sauce are served in a pie with a fairly thick crust. A wedge-to-go costs $3.25; it's $13 for a whole pie. 97 Bumbleberry Lane in Springdale (© **800/828-1534** or 435/772-3224 inn and restaurant; www.bumbleberry.com).

Capitol Reef Inn & Cafe, Torrey. The Capitol Reef Inn & Cafe, west of Capitol Reef National Park, may or may not be the only restaurant in southern Utah serving fresh vegetables, but it's the best bet in the area for vegetarians, as well as carnivores. The former can feast on 10-vegetable salad and stir-fry vegetables atop steamed brown rice, while the latter can tuck into fresh local rainbow trout, grilled rib-eye steak, or charbroiled lemon hickory chicken. Beer and wine are available. Breakfast-eaters get hearty omelets with optional bacon or smoked trout, or an order of French toast or pancakes.

It's a good idea to call ahead. Daily 7am–9pm. 360 W. Main St. in Torrey (✆ **435/425-3271;** www.capitolreefinn.com).

The Cowboy's Smoke House, Panguitch. It's closed during the winter, but otherwise open from early morning for breakfast (we got the sausage biscuit, a huge biscuit with a spicy patty inside) until the last of the barbecued beef, chicken, and ribs are gone and the last customer leaves in the evening. Some of the mounted animal heads around the room were bagged by Smokehouse employees, like the elk "shot down by Panguitch Lake" by one of the waitresses. Located at 95 N. Main St. in Panguitch (✆ **435/676-8030;** www.cowboyssmokehousecafe.com).

Eddie McStiff's, Moab. This place serves several unique boutique brews, including a jalapeño beer, a spruce beer with the forestry tang of spruce needles and bark, light blueberry and raspberry wheat beers, cream ale, amber ale, chestnut brown beer, and full-bodied stout. All food and beer are available to go. Daily 11:30am–11pm. You'll find it at 57 S. Main St. (✆ **435/259-BEER** [2337]; www.eddiemcstiffs.com).

Green River melons. The town of Green River is famous for its melons, which reach their peak in late summer and early fall. We tried Dunham's fruit stand on the east end of town and their honeydew, Crenshaw, and cantaloupe melons were all delicious. They grow watermelons, too.

WILDLIFE-WATCHING

Mule deer are almost everywhere in southern Utah, especially in Bryce Canyon, Capitol Reef around the Fruita campground, Dead Horse Point State Park, and Natural Bridges National Monument.

Unexpected glimpses of **Shiras moose,** as well as **elk** and **Great Basin mule deer** are possible in the Hogan Pass area along Route 72 between I-70 at Fremont and the town of Loa 32 miles to the south, with the best possibility between the pass and Loa.

Buffaloes have been reestablished in the Henry Mountains around Hanksville. A resident herd of buffaloes, some of them in enclosures and thereby guaranteed to be seen, can be visited on Antelope Island, reached by the Route 127 causeway off I-15 at Syracuse, north of Salt Lake City.

We saw lots of inquisitive Utah **prairie dogs,** a threatened species of this ubiquitous Western rodent, popping up from holes beside the road on Route 211 into the Needles area of Canyonlands.

Along the Colorado River, keep a lookout for **river otters, beavers,** and birds. **Bald eagles** winter in the area around Fremont Indian State Park, and Canyonlands allows glimpses of **peregrine falcons** and other birds of prey.

On the Road

ZION NATIONAL PARK

The national park, which began its official life as Mukuntuweap National Monument in 1909, dates from 1917 with the name Zion, given to it by Mormon settlers who did not like the Paiute name. Its early description as an "extraordinary example of

How Nature Painted Zion's Landscape

Zion National Park is many things to many people: a day hike down a narrow canyon, a rough climb up the face of a massive stone monument, a moment of quiet appreciation as the sun sets with a red glow over majestic peaks. At least to some degree, each of these experiences is possible only because of rocks—their formation, uplifting, shifting, breaking, and eroding. Of Zion's nine rock layers, the most important in creating the park's colorful formations is Navajo sandstone—at up to 2,200 feet, the thickest rock layer in the park. This formation was created some 200 million years ago during the Jurassic period when North America was hot and dry. Movements in the earth's crust caused a shallow sea to rise up and cover sand dunes. Minerals from the water, including lime from the shells of sea creatures, glued sand particles together, eventually forming sandstone. Later crust movements caused the land to lift, draining away the sea but leaving rivers that gradually carved the relatively soft sandstone into the spectacular shapes seen today.

So where do the colors come from? Essentially, from plain old rust. Most of the rocks at Zion are stained by iron or hematite (iron oxide), either contained in the original stone or carried into the rocks by groundwater. Although iron often creates red and pink hues, seen on many of Zion's sandstone faces, it can also result in shades of brown, yellow, black, and even green. Sometimes the iron seeps into the rock, coloring it through, but it can also stain just the surface, often in vertical streaks. Deposits of salt left by evaporating water frequently cause white streaks, and rocks are also colored by bacteria that live on their surfaces. These bacteria ingest dust and expel iron, manganese, and other minerals that stick to the rock and produce a shiny black, brown, or reddish surface called desert varnish.

canyon erosion" fails to do justice to the rich palette of colors in the canyon, which range from creamy white to burnished copper and dark rose.

Dramatic, accessible, and beautiful, Zion is Utah's most popular national park, with more than 2½ million visitors a year. Some 800 species of wildflowers bloom here, and 75 species of mammals, 271 birds, 32 reptiles and amphibians, and 8 varieties of fish are native to the park, including the unique (and endangered) Zion snail. More than 100 varieties of plants, introduced after European settlement began in the mid-1800s, are presently being eliminated. The wide-ranging elevations and temperatures, as well as water and sunlight, create microenvironments that showcase diverse flora and fauna, from hanging gardens with "weeping" rocks and cascading ferns to forested canyons and arid mesas.

Despite its hot summers, Zion's mild springs, autumns, and winters make the park a year-round destination. There may be some snow in winter, but the roads are plowed, and one campground is open at the south entrance.

ZION RV RESTRICTIONS

RVs entering Zion National Park are subject to parking and tunnel restrictions that do not cause any major inconveniences, but you must adhere to them. A fee of $15 is required for any RV wider than 7 feet, 10 inches (including side mirrors) or taller than 11 feet, 4 inches to drive through the 1-mile tunnel on the Zion–Mount Carmel Road. This is because the vehicle has to proceed through the middle of the tunnel without oncoming traffic, which is controlled by park rangers posted at either end. The tunnel is open to RVs under 13 feet high from March to October, from 8am to 8pm. To pass through any other time, call to make advance arrangements (✆ **435/772-3256**). The fee is collected at the park's entrance, where drivers are issued a receipt to display on the windshield. Decide before you enter if you are going to exit via the tunnel. It is not essential to go through the tunnel; simply arrive and leave the park by the same Springdale gate.

Zion National Park's top attraction is the 7-mile **Zion Canyon Drive,** which has been notoriously traffic-clogged during the past decade and so is now served by a propane-fueled shuttle-bus system, meaning no private vehicles are allowed in the canyon between April and November. Hikers and bicyclists are still permitted, as are visitors with confirmed reservations at Zion Lodge. But anyone else arriving between March and October will be expected to board buses into Zion Canyon. Motor vehicles, including RVs, are still permitted on the park's eastern side and in the campground area at the south entrance from Springdale. Parking is available at various areas in the town of Springdale and at the new visitor center, just inside the south park entrance at Springdale. The park entry fee is $25, which includes shuttle fees. If you want to visit Kolob Canyons, off I-15 in the northwestern part of the park, the fee is $10. Call the **Zion Canyon Visitors Bureau** for park information (✆ **435/772-3256;** www.nps.gov/zion) or **shuttle information** (✆ 435/772-0312).

Based on our experience, RVs, particularly trailers and large motor homes, never had adequate turnaround or parking space at popular points along the canyon road anyway, so we've always supported the shuttle-system concept.

There are four **driving entrances** into Zion, only two of which connect—the Route 9 south entrance at Springdale and the east entrance on Zion–Mount Carmel Highway. The 25-mile dead-end drive along Kolob Terrace Road from the town of Virgin to the Kolob Reservoir winds in and out of the park's western boundaries through varying terrain, and the not-to-be-missed Kolob Canyons Road enters the northernmost part of the park from I-15 south of Cedar City. For more about both, see "11 Scenic Side Trips," later in this chapter.

Southern Utah Campgrounds

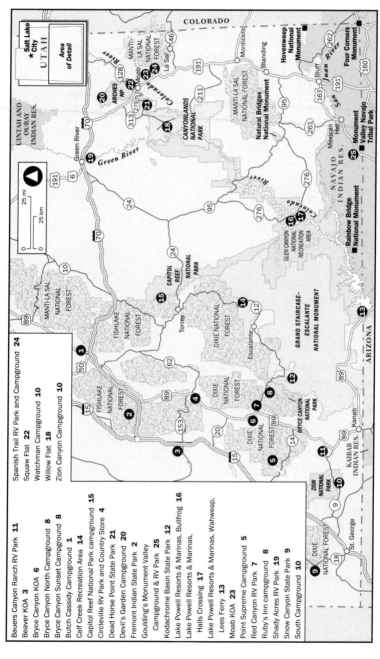

Bauers Canyon Ranch RV Park **11**

Beaver KOA **3**

Bryce Canyon KOA **6**

Bryce Canyon North Campground **8**

Bryce Canyon Sunset Campground **8**

Butch Cassidy Campground **1**

Calf Creek Recreation Area **14**

Capitol Reef National Park campground **15**

Circleville RV Park and Country Store **4**

Dead Horse Point State Park **21**

Devil's Garden Campground **20**

Fremont Indian State Park **2**

Goulding's Monument Valley Campground & RV Park **25**

Kodachrome Basin State Park **12**

Lake Powell Resorts & Marinas, Bullfrog **16**

Lake Powell Resorts & Marinas, Halls Crossing **17**

Lake Powell Resorts & Marinas, Wahweap, Lees Ferry **13**

Moab KOA **23**

Point Supreme Campground **5**

Red Canyon RV Park **7**

Ruby's Inn campground **8**

Shady Acres RV Park **19**

Snow Canyon State Park **9**

South Campground **10**

Spanish Trail RV Park and Campground **24**

Squaw Flat **22**

Watchman Campground **10**

Willow Flat **18**

Zion Canyon Campground **10**

Zion National Park

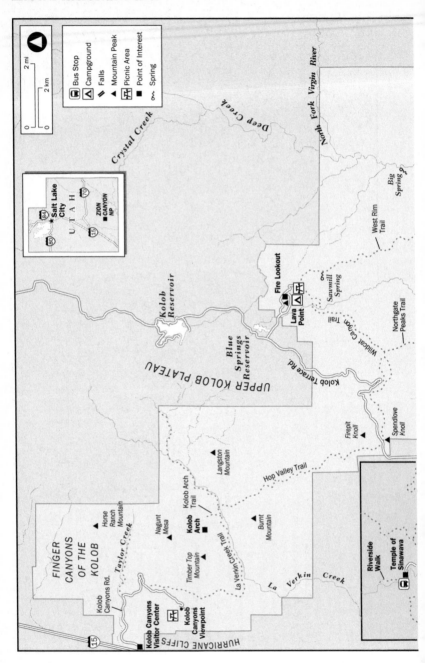

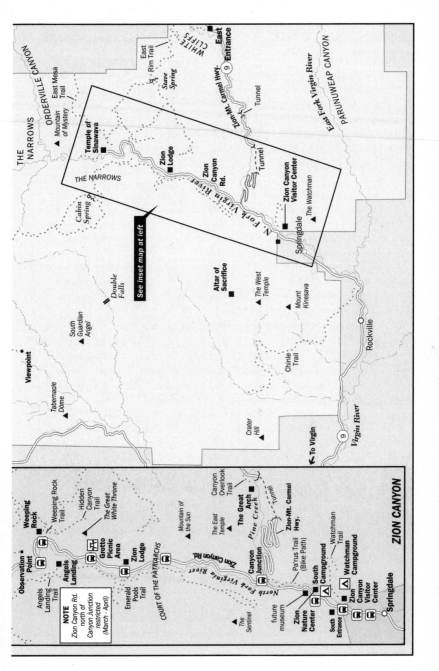

Showtime . . . and a Tasty Dinner, Too!

Down in St. George, southwest of Zion off I-15, the **Tuacahn Amphithe-atre** (www.tuacahn.org) is open on summer nights between June and September, offering productions of such hit musicals as *Aladdin* and *Hairspray*. Admission is $29 to $59 adults, $23 to $59 children 12 and under. Call for reservations (© **800/746-9882**). An optional Western Dutch-oven dinner or "family feast" is served ($13 adults, $9.50 children), but must be reserved when tickets are booked. The theater is 10 miles from St. George at Tuacahn, off Route 300 near Snow Canyon State Park.

The best way to see the canyon is to use **hiking trails.** Hikers should arrive early in the morning since most parking areas fill by midday. Permits are required for overnight hikes; you can get one at the visitor center after 8am the day before the hike begins. Permits require a fee of $12 per person.

Among the park's most popular hiking trails are several that are short and/or easy. **Weeping Rocks trail** is a steep .3-mile climb leading to an enormous rocky ledge covered with mosses and plants with a stream of "tears" dripping from it. It's also a cool place to linger on a hot summer day.

The 2-mile **Emerald Pools trail** loop is not too demanding if you go uphill via the right-hand trail after crossing the footbridge by the parking lot, climb to the Middle Pool, and then take the other trail, somewhat rougher and steeper, back downhill.

The **Lower Emerald Pool trail** and the **Gateway to the Narrows trail** at the Temple of Sinawava are wheelchair-accessible if a companion is along to help with the rough spots along the cement paving. The latter trail is a fairly level 2-mile loop that goes through the hanging gardens area, bright with wildflowers in spring and early summer.

Dedicated hikers like to strike out along the 10-mile **West Rim trail** between the canyon and Lava Point, but those starting from the canyon are cautioned not to try to make it uphill to Lava Point on a 1-day hike. The **Zion Narrows trail,** which splashes through the icy waters of the Virgin River, requires a free hiking permit for the 2-day, 32-mile round-trip. (Permits can be obtained from a ranger station in the park, and you have to apply in person.) Fall is best, when water levels in the river are lowest; take along a dry change of clothing in a sealed plastic bag.

Bicyclists are limited to paved roads in the park, and are not permitted to ride through the Mount Carmel tunnel. Rangers will transport your bicycle through the tunnel free of charge, however.

Photographers should try to visit the canyon in early morning and again in late afternoon to take advantage of the dramatic light that models the contours of the rocks.

Campground Oases in & Around Zion National Park
Bauers Canyon Ranch RV Park, in Glendale, is about halfway between Zion and Bryce Canyon. This Good Sam park has 20 full hookups (30 and 50-amp) with 14 pull-throughs. There is a central modem hookup and Wi-Fi. It's also a working ranch

with a fishing stream. If you're there in August, you can get apples fresh from the tree. Sites $26. 10 miles north on U.S. 89 from the junction of Hwy. 9 (© **888/648-2564** or 435/648-2564; www.bauersrv.com).

Beaver KOA. This KOA in Beaver is convenient to both Zion and Bryce Canyon and makes a handy stopover for travelers between Salt Lake City and Las Vegas. It has 75 pull-through sites with water and 30- and 50-amp electrical, and 35 full hookups. Mar–Nov. Sites $29–$35. It's reached from I-15, exit 112 (© **800/KOA-2912** [562-2912] or 435/438-2924 reservations; www.koa.com).

Snow Canyon State Park. Snow Canyon, in **Ivins** near St. George in Utah's Dixie district, has 14 sites with water and electrical hookups, and picnic shelters lined up in a row, plus 22 non-hookup sites that are more spacious and tree-shaded. No slide-outs. The park has flush toilets, showers, a sanitary dump station, and hiking trails with spectacular scenery. It's open year-round, and the weather is mild, although summer can be hot; the canyon was named after a pioneer family's surname, not the falling white stuff, which rarely falls here. The .8-mile hike to Johnson's Arch is the park's most popular hike, although some visitors take flashlights and explore the lava caves near the north end of the park. Sites $20. Take exit 6 (Bluff St.) from I-15 and drive northwest of St. George on Rte. 18 for 10 miles, then 2 miles southwest on Rte. 8 (© **800/322-3770** or 435/628-2255 reservations; http://stateparks.utah.gov/reservations).

Watchman & South Campgrounds. The two campgrounds in Zion suitable for RVs can be found just beyond the park's Springdale entrance: Watchman

Bryce Canyon seen through one of its arches.

Campground with Loops A, B, and C (79 sites), and adjacent South Campground (127 sites). The sites, without hookups except for 63 electrical connections in Watchman, are generally widely spaced with some shade trees. All have metal picnic tables and cooking grills; some of the nicest are along the Virgin River at the edge of Loop A. Campgrounds have flush toilets, but no showers, and a 14-day limit on a first-come, first-served basis, except for some sites at Watchman. Many sites are handicapped-accessible. All spaces fill before noon in summer. One of the two sites is open in winter. A sanitary dump station and water are located at the entrance to Watchman. Reservations are available for Watchman in summer. Sites $16–$20 (© **877/444-6777** or 435/772-3256; www.recreation.gov).

Zion Canyon Campground. There are 105 full sites with 30- and 50-amp electric, pull-throughs and back-ins, dataports for e-mail, along with cable TV and wheelchair accessibility—all available just a half-mile from the entrance to the national park in the town of Springdale. You can walk to the shuttle or the town's restaurants. Sites $30–$39. 479 Zion Park Blvd. (© **435/772-3237** reservations; www.zioncamp.com).

BRYCE CANYON NATIONAL PARK

Bryce Canyon (**www.nps.gov/brca**)—"a hell of a place to lose a cow," in the words of one early rancher—is a collection of needlelike red limestone hoodoos (see "Talkin' Utah: A Glossary," earlier in this chapter), jewel-like eroded spires seen at their best in early morning or late day light. The best time of all is after a snowfall, when white puffs dust the bright red rocks. Local Paiute legend has it that the rocks are men turned into stones by an angry god.

Winter can be a rewarding time to visit if you enjoy cross-country skiing or snowshoeing; the park lends snowshoes free of charge at the visitor center for the ranger-guided treks (at the north end as you enter the park) if you leave a credit card or driver's license for deposit.

Mule deer are plentiful and easily spotted. **Elk** are also present, but more rarely seen. With **172 species of birds** identified in the park, you'll have a good chance of spotting some; a checklist is available at the visitor center.

BRYCE CANYON RV RESTRICTIONS

RV restrictions abound in Bryce Canyon National Park, but they should not inhibit RVers from sampling some of the park's best scenery. Vehicles towing trailers are not permitted beyond Sunset Point turnoff, but after a winter snowfall, the road is usually closed off at this point anyway. Travel trailers may be left in designated parking areas at the visitor center or Sunset Campground. RVs longer than 25 feet are not allowed at Bryce Point or Paria Point because of extremely limited turnaround space.

Bryce Canyon National Park

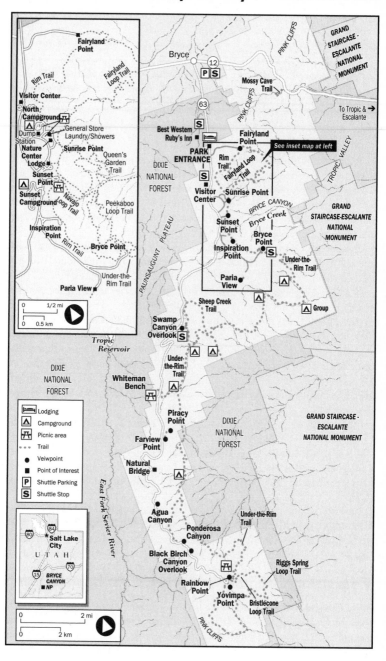

Inset map (upper left):

Fairland Point

Rim Trail

Fairyland Loop Trail

Visitor Center

North Campground

Dump Station

General Store Laundry/Showers

Nature Center

Sunrise Point

Queen's Garden Trail

Lodge

Sunset Point

Sunset Campground

Navajo Loop Trail

Peekaboo Loop Trail

Inspiration Point

Rim Trail

Bryce Point

Under-the-Rim Trail

Paria View

0   1/2 mi
0   0.5 km

Main map:

GRAND STAIRCASE - ESCALANTE NATIONAL MONUMENT

Fairyland Point

Bryce

P S

12

Mossy Cave Trail

PINK CLIFFS

63

S

TROPIC VALLEY

To Tropic & Escalante

Best Western Ruby's Inn

PARK ENTRANCE

Fairyland Point

See inset map at left

Rim Trail

Fairyland Loop Trail

S

Visitor Center

Sunrise Point

DIXIE NATIONAL FOREST

BRYCE CANYON

Bryce Creek

GRAND STAIRCASE-ESCALANTE NATIONAL MONUMENT

Sunset Point

Inspiration Point

Bryce Point

S

Under-the-Rim Trail

Paria View

PAUNSAUGUNT PLATEAU

Sheep Creek Trail

Group

Swamp Canyon Overlook

S

Under-the-Rim Trail

Tropic Reservoir

DIXIE NATIONAL FOREST

Whiteman Bench

Piracy Point

Farview Point

Natural Bridge

East Fork Sevier River

GRAND STAIRCASE - ESCALANTE NATIONAL MONUMENT

DIXIE NATIONAL FOREST

Agua Canyon

Ponderosa Canyon

Under-the-Rim Trail

Black Birch Canyon Overlook

Rainbow Point

Yovimpa Point

Riggs Spring Loop Trail

Bristlecone Loop Trail

PINK CLIFFS

Legend:

Lodging
Campground
Picnic area
Trail
Veiwpoint
Point of Interest
P Shuttle Parking
S Shuttle Stop

Utah inset:

84
80
Salt Lake City
UTAH
70
15
BRYCE CANYON NP

0   2 mi
0   2 km

SAFETY TIPS

Be careful to allow a day or two to acclimatize to the area's elevation—in Bryce, 6,500 to 9,100 feet—before setting out on a major hike. And if a lightning storm comes up, stay away from the canyon rims, particularly the iron railings.

A number of **hiking trails,** a total of 61 miles, wend their way into the canyons among the hoodoos. The most popular half-day trek is a combination of the **Queens Garden** and **Navajo Loop** trails, a 3-mile round-trip jaunt through the most dramatic part of the amphitheater. Just remember that every trail that goes down in the early part of the hike when you're fresh comes back up later when you may be tired; don't overestimate your ability.

Bristlecone Loop trail from Rainbow Point takes a 1.5-mile circuit through a forest. If a level walk sounds ideal, the Rim trail follows an 11-mile route, with paved walking areas accessible for wheelchairs between Sunrise and Sunset Points. Naturalists lead morning walks daily in summer, and moonlight hikes on the 3 nights a month preceding a full moon.

The reconstructed **Bryce Canyon Lodge** (℃ **877/386-4383** or 435/834-8700; http://foreverlodging.com/brycecanyon), a National Historic Landmark, echoes some of the 1920s feeling of the original. It's closed in winter. Ruby's Inn, north of the park entrance on State Hwy. 63, dates from 1919, but has suffered so many fires over the years that its period look is gone. There is a private campground at **Ruby's Inn** with 113 full hookups; closed in winter. Sites $33–$41 (℃ **435/834-5301;** www.rubysinn.com).

The most direct connection to Bryce Canyon is from Zion National Park north on U.S. 89, then east on Route 12—one argument in favor of paying the $15 RV tunnel fee on the Zion–Mount Carmel Road. Otherwise, you can access U.S. 89 from the west via routes 14 or 20 from I-15, or from the north via I-70. Red Canyon on Route 12 is a particularly scenic approach, with rock tunnels and bridges framing the road ahead.

Campground Oases in Bryce Canyon National Park

Bryce Canyon KOA. This RV park, in the town of Panguitch, is about 25 miles from Bruce Canyon. It has big, level sites, 59 with water and 30- or 50-amp hookups, 48 full hookups, Wi-Fi, and lots of camping cabins. Sites $28–$38. 555 S. Main St. (℃ **800/KOA-1625** [562-1625] or 435/679-8988 reservations; www.koa.com).

Bryce Canyon National Park. Bryce has two campgrounds, both near the entrance, open from late spring to early fall, with some limited winter camping. **North Campground** has 107 sites, and **Sunset** has 96, none with hookups. A sanitary dump station (fee), showers (fee) at Sunset Campground, and flush toilets are available, along with picnic tables, fireplaces, and piped water. Bring your own firewood. There's a 14-day camping limit; pets are permitted on a leash. Sites $15. North Campground has 13 RV sites available by reservation and 86 sites available first-come, first-served, the RV sites at Sunset are all first-come, first-served. To reserve, call © **877/444-6777;** www. recreation.gov.

Kodachrome Basin State Park. Named by the National Geographic Society for its colorful, phallic rock formations called chimneys, Kodachrome Basin has trails for hiking and horseback riding. A campground has 27 concrete pad sites, tables, grills, piped water, flush toilets, and showers. You'll find a sanitary dump station and camper supply store, but no hookups. Sites $16. It's off Rte. 12 on an unnamed road 7⅓ miles south of the junction of Hwy. 12 and Main St. in **Cannonville**—look for the sign for Kodachrome Basin (© **435/679-8562** reservations; www.utah.com/stateparks/kodachrome.htm).

Red Canyon RV Park. Red Canyon, a Good Sam member in **Panguitch,** has 30 sites, all full hookups and many suitable for big rigs. Mid-Apr to Oct. Sites $25–$28. Located 15 miles from Bryce Canyon on Hwy. 12, 1 mile east of the junction with Rte. 89 (© **435/676-2690** reservations; www.redcanyon.net).

CEDAR BREAKS NATIONAL MONUMENT & CEDAR CITY

The "breaks" in the park name comes from early settlers in the region, who called any terrain too steep for wagon travel "breaks" or "badlands." The same folks thought the junipers and ancient bristlecone pine trees growing on the rim of the red-rock amphitheater were cedars.

Similar to Bryce Canyon but even more vivid in color, Cedar Breaks (**www.nps.gov/cebr**) is less visited, despite its location only 23 miles from I-15 via Route 14.

A huge rock **amphitheater** with trails leading 3,400 feet down into the gorge, it presents a special challenge to hikers in good shape. Two special 2-mile walks for those already acclimated to the elevation are the **Alpine Pond Trail,** a fairly easy jaunt to a

Late-Summer Bonanza: The Cedar Breaks Wildflowers

During its brief summer season, Cedar Breaks makes the most of the warmth and moisture in the air with a spectacular wildflower show. The rim comes alive in a blaze of color—truly a sight to behold. The dazzling display begins practically as soon as the snow melts and reaches its peak in mid-July. The annual 2-week **Wildflower Festival,** which celebrates the colorful display, starts the weekend closest to Independence Day. Watch for mountain bluebells, spring beauty, beard tongue, and fleabane early in the season. Those beauties then make way for columbine, larkspur, Indian paintbrush, wild roses, and other flowers. For more information, visit **www.nps.gov/cebr/wildflower-festival.htm**.

A panorama of the natural beauty of Cedar Breaks National Monument.

pond and forest glade, and the **Spectra Point Trail,** a good place to see bristlecone pines. There are also ranger-led nature walks, geology talks, and campfire programs in summer. Information on these activities is listed in the free newspaper you get upon entering the park.

Although roads are closed by snow in winter, visitors can come into the park by cross-country skis or snowmobile, entering via Brian Head ski resort. A campground is open from June through September only. The Rim Drive along Scenic Byway 148 goes through the monument when weather permits.

The **Utah Shakespearean Festival** in nearby Cedar City, going strong for more than 30 years, presents three classic plays in repertory every summer in the outdoor Shakespearean theater, as well as three contemporary plays in a smaller indoor theater. The season runs from early July through August, and theatergoers come early to enjoy the evening's Greenshow of jugglers, puppeteers, and vendors dressed in Elizabethan costume. At 351 W. Center St., Cedar City. Call for information on the festival and reservations (© **800/PLAY-TIX** [752-9849] or 435/586-7878; www.bard.org).

Campground Oases in the Cedar Breaks/Cedar City Area & North off Interstate 15

Butch Cassidy Campground. A Good Sam member, **Salina's** Butch Cassidy Campground has 50 tent sites and 40 RV sites, all full hookups with 20-, 30-, and 50-amp electric, and a heated swimming pool. Open year-round. Sites $23–$25. Reached by taking exit 54 from I-70 and driving north ¾ of a mile on Rte. 89 (© **800/551-6842** or 435/529-7400 reservations; www.butchcassidycampground.com).

Circleville RV Park and Country Store. The park is in the heart of Butch Cassidy country and has 33 sites, some pull-throughs, and 25 full hookups with 30- and 50-amp electric. Sites $28–$35. Located a half-mile south of Circleville on Rte. 89 (© **888/978-7275** or 435/577-2437 reservations; www.circlevillervpark.com).

Fremont Indian State Park. Near **Loa/Richfield,** this former Fishlake National Forest campground, previously called Castle Rock, was shifted over to state-park status to supplement the park, where part of a large Fremont River Indian village has been excavated. The little-known Fremont River Indians, who preceded the Anasazi, vanished before the first Spanish arrived. We found the campground quiet and uncrowded (we shared its 15 sites with one other RV on a moonlit Oct night). The $13 camping fee also includes admission to the museum. Sites are well spaced out, many shaded by aspens, all with tables; there are flush toilets, but no hookups or dump station. Open year-round to RVs 30 ft. and under. Sites $13. Located a couple of miles off I-70 near the junction of I-15 (© **435/527-4631;** www.utah.com/stateparks/fremont.htm).

Point Supreme Campground. Point Supreme Campground provides 30 sites suitable for RVs, with picnic tables, piped water, and flush toilets. Because the elevation is above 10,000 feet, the campground is open mid-June through mid-Sept only. No reservations are taken, and there are no hookups. Sites $14. Located in the **Cedar Breaks National Monument** 1 mile north of the visitor center on Hwy. 148 (© **435/586-0787;** www.nps.gov/cebr).

CAPITOL REEF NATIONAL PARK

Little-known and little-visited Capitol Reef (**www.nps.gov/care**) lies about halfway between Bryce Canyon and Canyonlands on Route 24. The park is notable primarily for its unique **Waterpocket Fold,** a 100-mile wrinkle in the earth's crust formed by enormous pressures deep inside the earth that caused ancient rock beds to buckle. After a rain, pockets in the fold hold water and serve as residence and nursery for the unique **spadefoot toad** that lays eggs in the water as soon as it rains so they can hatch into tadpoles, perhaps even make it to adulthood, before the puddles dry up.

Early settlers thought a white sandstone formation in the park resembled the Capitol Dome in Washington and that the Waterpocket Fold looked like a coral reef (although few settlers had ever seen either one). Ergo, the park is named Capitol Reef.

A 10-mile, one-way **scenic drive** is accessible to small- to medium-size RVs; pick up a self-guided trail map at the beginning of the drive to follow the layers of rock that tilted, folded, and eroded to create today's dramatic formations. While we confess to a certain shortsightedness in recognizing every Egyptian Temple, Golden Throne, Castle, and Chimney dotted on the map, we admire the structure of them. Let's face it—the old-timers had more leisure time than we do to sit and contemplate what the formations resemble.

Fifteen hiking trails, from .1 mile to 4.5 miles, are designated as very easy, easy, moderate, and strenuous. A trail to **Hickman Bridge,** a natural bridge, is 1 mile each way and termed moderate, while a strenuous climb to Cassidy Arch is 1.8 miles each way.

Petroglyphs on the canyon walls on the main drive near the visitor center are only a few short steps from the turnout.

TRAVEL TIP

Always take drinking water with you, especially in summer, when hiking or exploring in Capitol Reef National Park. There's no reliable source of water outside the Fruita settlement.

In 1900, 8 to 10 Mormon families lived here, planting orchards, operating a blacksmith shop, and teaching in a one-room log schoolhouse. The last of the community's residents moved away in 1960, and now the park maintains the village as a restored historic site known as the **Fruita settlement.** The park campgrounds are built in and around the orchards, which are open for visitors to pick their own fruit—you pay by weight at a scale and honor cash box. Browsing mule deer are common in the campgrounds, especially at dawn and dusk.

Butch Cassidy and his gang used to hang out in the neighborhood. Cassidy Arch, on the Grand Wash road off the Scenic Drive, was named for the famous outlaw.

Even more fascinating is the **Behunin Cabin,** a tiny one-room rock cabin where an early Mormon settler raised 10 children. The historical plaque says they ate their meals outdoors, which is only logical, since it would be hard for them all to be inside at the same time. We can't imagine where they all slept.

Campground Oases in & Around Capitol Reef National Park

Capitol Reef National Park campground. The only RV campground in the park is among the orchards at the Fruita settlement, less than a mile from the visitor center. The 71 sites are mostly level, grassy, and tree-shaded, with gorgeous red-rock cliffs on all sides and grazing mule deer at dawn and dusk. It's open year-round. There are no hookups and no reservations, and there's a 14-day limit. Flush toilets and a sanitary dump station are on-site. One wheelchair-accessible campsite in Loop B is held until 6pm nightly. Sites $10 (© 435/425-3791; www.nps.gov/care).

Calf Creek Recreation Area. This campsite, near **Escalante,** lies in a river-bottom canyon surrounded by red-cliff walls and has 11 well-spaced sites, some of them adequate for RVs limited to 25 feet. Trout fishing is nearby. There are no hookups and there's a 14-day camping limit and primitive toilets. A 5-mile trail leads to Calf Creek Falls. Mid-Mar to late Nov. Sites $7. Operated by the Bureau of Land Management, the park is 15 miles northeast of Escalante off Rte. 12 (© **435/826-5499;** www.ut.blm.gov/monument).

CANYONLANDS NATIONAL PARK

The pristine serenity of Canyonlands has been protected for more than a century, largely because early white settlers deemed the land totally worthless. The **Anasazi** had lived and farmed the region until A.D.1200, when they mysteriously left, perhaps because of drought, tribal warfare, or the arrival of hostile strangers.

Capitol Reef National Park

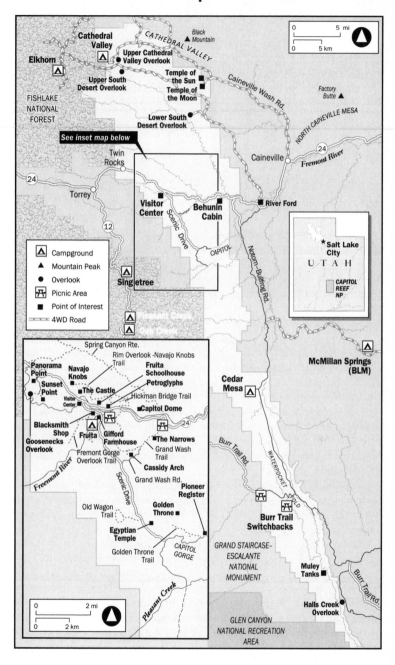

Cathedral
Valley

Black
Mountain

CATHEDRAL VALLEY

Elkhorn

Upper Cathedral
Valley Overlook

Upper South
Desert Overlook

Temple of
the Sun

Temple of
the Moon

Caineville Wash Rd.

FISHLAKE
NATIONAL
FOREST

Lower South
Desert Overlook

Factory
Butte

NORTH CAINEVILLE MESA

0   5 mi

0   5 km

See inset map below

Twin
Rocks

Caineville

24

Fremont River

24

Torrey

12

Visitor
Center

Behunin
Cabin

River Ford

★ Salt Lake
City

U T A H

CAPITOL
REEF
NP

CAPITOL

Naom–Bullfrog Rd.

Campground
Mountain Peak
Overlook
Picnic Area
Point of Interest
4WD Road

Singletree

Spring Canyon Rte.

Rim Overlook -Navajo Knobs
Trail

Panorama
Point

Navajo
Knobs

Sunset
Point

The Castle

Visitor
Center

Fruita
Schoolhouse

Petroglyphs

Hickman Bridge Trail

Capitol Dome

McMillan Springs
(BLM)

Cedar
Mesa

24

Blacksmith
Shop

Fruita

Gifford
Farmhouse

The Narrows

Grand Wash
Trail

Burr Trail Rd.

WATERPOCKET

OLD

Goosenecks
Overlook

Fremont Gorge
Overlook Trail

Fremont River

Cassidy Arch

Grand Wash Rd.

Old Wagon
Trail

Scenic Drive

Pioneer
Register

Golden
Throne

Burr Trail
Switchbacks

Egyptian
Temple

Golden Throne
Trail

CAPITOL
GORGE

GRAND STAIRCASE-
ESCALANTE
NATIONAL
MONUMENT

Muley
Tanks

Burr Trail Rd.

0   2 mi

0   2 km

Pleasant Creek

Halls Creek
Overlook

GLEN CANYON
NATIONAL RECREATION
AREA

CAMPING AT GLEN CANYON

If you're heading into the Glen Canyon National Recreation Area, Lake Powell Resorts & Marinas provides RV camping with full hookups at **Wahweap, Bullfrog,** and **Halls Crossing** in Glen Canyon. Call for reservations (© **888/896-3829;** www.lakepowell. com). A national park campground at Lees Ferry has no hookups, but does have a dump station, showers, and a coin Laundromat, with sites available on a first-come, first-served basis. Wahweap, Bullfrog, and Halls Crossing campgrounds each have a Laundromat and showers, and Halls Crossing also has a dump station.

Canyonlands National Park (**www.nps.gov/cany**) is divided into three separate areas, each self-contained and reached only by exiting one area of the park and re-entering elsewhere. The **Maze,** a dense, impenetrable mass of convoluted rock described as "a 30-square-mile puzzle in sandstone," lies southwest of the confluence of the Green and Colorado rivers. The **Needles** is southeast of it, and **Island in the Sky** is north of it. A trail leads to the confluence of the rivers from the road's end at **Big Spring Canyon Overlook** in the Needles.

Only experienced hikers with good topographic maps and compasses should venture into the Maze, the most remote and forbidding part of Canyonlands, a dense and complex system of chasms and ravines. Two roads suitable only for four-wheel-drive vehicles enter it from the west, but after a long and rough journey from Route 24 near Goblin Valley State Park.

Spired sandstone walls, some as high as 400 feet, characterize the **Needles** in the southern part of Canyonlands, 75 miles from Moab, 49 miles from Monticello, and 31 miles off U.S. 191 via Route 211. Less visited than its northern counterpart, the Needles has a particularly scenic drive outside the park perimeters as an introduction to its wonders.

Island in the Sky, the mesa that comprises much of the northern part of Canyonlands, is outlined in a V-shape as the Colorado and the Green rivers meet at the park's bellybutton. This area is reached by Route 313 off U.S. 191 north of Moab (**www. nps.gov/cany**).

Views are memorable, especially in early morning or late afternoon when the landscape is gilded with red and gold. **Upheaval Dome,** a short walk from the parking lot at the end of the road at Holman Spring Canyon Overlook, may have been formed when struck by a meteorite—at least that's the explanation we prefer of the two possibilities provided by the information sign at the overlook. The other, much less sexy reason is the underground salt buildup that eroded until a crater appeared.

Here at the edge of Canyonlands' Island in the Sky, not at what most viewers assumed was the Grand Canyon, is where the heroines of *Thelma & Louise* (1991) drove their Thunderbird convertible off the cliff.

Canyonlands National Park

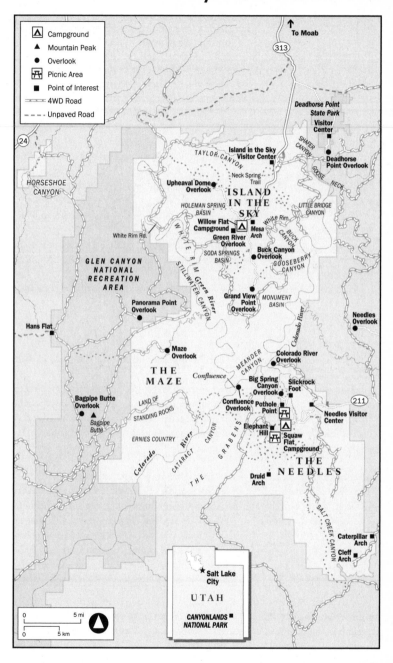

About Edward Abbey

You won't travel far in southeastern Utah without running across the ghost of the late Edward Abbey, a tough-minded, combative outdoor writer and environmentalist who spent several seasons as a park ranger in Arches.

He was best known for comments like, "You can't see anything from a car; you've got to get out of the goddamned contraption and walk, better yet crawl, on hands and knees, over the sandstone and through the thornbush and cactus. When traces of blood begin to mark your trail, you'll see something, maybe. Probably not." Nevertheless, he wasn't above poking fun at himself as he railed against overuse of his beloved Utah desert. On an early trip into the Maze, the most remote part of Canyonlands, he and a friend stopped to look at an almost-new hiker register.

"Keep the tourists out," a tourist from Salt Lake City had written, to which Abbey added, "As fellow tourists we heartily agree."

Later, still at the Maze, he wrote in the log, "For God's sake, leave this country alone—Abbey," to which his friend added, "For Abbey's sake, leave this country alone—God."

Pick up a copy of his book, *Desert Solitaire,* at any of the park visitor centers. It makes a good companion on the journey. 🚐

Both bobcats and mountain lions are occasionally seen in the park, as well as mountain sheep in the White Rim area.

Four-wheel-drive vehicles and backpackers can get much deeper into the park than RVs and family cars, and there are primitive campsites at intervals along the routes. Throughout Canyonlands, campers are expected to carry their own water and firewood. The only water supply in the park is at the Squaw Flat campground in the Needles, and it is not operative in winter.

Campground Oases in Canyonlands National Park

Squaw Flat. Squaw Flat, in the **Needles section of Canyonlands,** has 26 well-separated sites, many snuggled into rock-surrounded coves with trees; some, but not all, are adequate for RVs limited to 28 feet. Each site has fire grates and a table, and there are pit toilets and water available by the bucketful from a water wagon. If you need to top off your RV tank, follow signs to a water hose connection on Cave Spring Road near Wooden Shoe Arch. Sites $15, no reservations taken. 2282 S. W. Resource Blvd. in Moab. From U.S. 191 take Utah 211 W. to the Needles (© **435/719-2313;** www.nps.gov/cany).

Willow Flat. The only campground in the **Island in the Sky area of Canyonlands** accessible to most RVs is Willow Flat, down a rough washboard dirt road off Route 313. It has 12 primitive sites for smaller RVs only (under 28 ft.). Unfortunately, gnats are a problem much of the summer. There are pit toilets and fire grates, but no water. Sites $10 (© **435/719-2313**), no reservations taken.

MOAB, THE MOUNTAIN BIKE CAPITAL OF THE WORLD (AND MORE!)

Suddenly, this faded uranium-prospecting town, best known as a Western-movie location area, has become the mountain bike capital of the world, attracting as many European yuppies as American outdoorsmen to its gentrified streets. The **Moab Slickrock Bicycle Trail,** which begins on Sand Flats Road, 2.3 miles from the intersection of the Sand Flats Road and Millcreek Drive in Moab, and follows a 12.6-mile loop through orange Navajo sandstone, is for experienced bikers with only a little time to spare. The big deal, though, is the 142-mile **Kokopelli's Trail,** between Moab and Loma, Colorado. The trails around Moab are overseen by the Bureau of Land Management, and for information about them, visit www.blm.gov/ut/st/en/fo/moab/recreation/mountain_bike_trails.html.

The mid-October **Fat Tire Festival** brings hundreds of bikers to join both fun and semi-competitive events. Leading manufacturers of bikes and equipment are there to show off their products and host parties. The weekend before the Festival, Granny Gear Productions organizes an endurance race for four-person teams called **"24 Hours of Moab"** (© 304/259-5533; www.grannygear.com). For more information, contact **Moab Area Travel Council** at 25 E. Center St., at Main Street in Moab (© **435/635-6622;** www.discovermoab.com).

A detailed list of activities in the Moab area, described in the town's visitor guide, includes aerial tours, backpacking, campouts and cookouts, dirt biking, hiking, horse and llama pack rides, hot-air balloon rides, helicopter rides, boating, cross-country skiing, and four-wheel-drive and all-terrain tours. You can also watch the local sound-and-light show called "Canyonlands by Night."

The uranium miners wouldn't recognize the town with its trendy business names, everything from **Poison Spider Bicycles,** 497 N. Main St. (© **800/635-1792;** http://poisonspiderbicycles.com), with its espresso bar, to the **Moab Brewery,** a boutique brewery with a dozen beers on tap at 686 S. Main St., next door to an art gallery promising "an eclectic mix of fun, folk art, and funk" (© **435/259-6333;** www.themoabbrewery.com).

Campgrounds in & Around Moab

Dead Horse Point State Park. This park makes an excellent alternative to the campgrounds at Canyonlands or Arches when they are full, which is most of the time. There are 21 campsites with 20-amp electrical hookups, covered cooking/eating areas and windbreaks, metal picnic tables, and concrete pads for RVs. A sanitary dump station is available. A family of mule deer is often seen grazing in the area. The $20 camping fee includes park admission. The campground is open year-round. The park is off Rte. 313 northwest of Moab (© **800/322-3770** or 435/259-2614 reservations; www.utah.com/stateparks/dead_horse.htm).

Moab KOA. This has 49 full hookups with 30- and 50-amp electric, city water, sewer and cable, and 78 hookups with water and electricity, as well as an innovative miniature golf course. Sites $33–$73. South on U.S. 191 (© **800/KOA-0372** [562-0372] or 435/259-6682 reservations; www.moabkoa.com).

Spanish Trail RV Park and Campground. This Good Sam park has 60 full hookups with 20-, 30-, and 50-amp electric, cable TV, Wi-Fi, and city water. Sites $36–$47. South of Moab on U.S. 191 (✆ **800/787-2751** or 435/259-2411 reservations; www.spanishtrailrvpark.com).

ARCHES NATIONAL PARK

Arches National Park (**www.nps.gov/arch**) boasts the world's largest concentration of stone arches, perhaps as many as 2,000 by the most recent tally. To qualify as an arch, the formation has to pass light through an opening at least 3 feet wide.

Some are visible from the paved roadway; others are reached by short or medium hikes from .1 to 7 miles long. Daily ranger-guided hikes are also led; check schedules at the visitor center, located just inside the entrance gate. The **Fiery Furnace,** for instance, in a labyrinth of red sandstone cliffs and narrow passageways, can be visited only with a ranger; hikes are scheduled twice a day in season and must be reserved in person ahead of time at the visitor center.

See "Seven Sites Offering *Déjà Vu* All Over Again," earlier in this chapter, for the park's most popular long hike, a half-day trip to Delicate Arch.

Rock climbers also love Arches for its cliffs, walls, towers, and cracks in the rock, coupled with incredible views. Modern techniques in rock-climbing often avoid the old system of pounding pitons into the rock, then ascending by nylon ladders. Today, the goal is to do "free" climbing; either face climbing, in which the climber grasps or steps on natural holds in the rock; or crack climbing, by wedging part of the body into cracks in the rocks. Women can often outdo men with dexterity in rock climbing.

If you're hiking or camping here, be sure your gas tank is adequately full, and take along your own water, food, and firewood, since nothing is available in the park.

Campground Oases in & Around Arches National Park

Devil's Garden Campground. Devil's Garden is situated amid red rocks and green pines near the end of an 18-mile road, with 52 first-come, first-served sites. We suggest that if campground space is still available when you enter the park, no matter what time of day, you should drive straight to the campground, pick out a spot and register, and then go out for your sightseeing. Sites have tables and grills, with flush toilets and piped water. While all the pads are paved, RV owners will need to check their levels, since many are uneven. No slide-outs. There is no camping fee when the water is turned off, usually from the end of Oct until mid-Mar. Park entrance fee $20. Located in Arches National Park (✆ **435/259-8161**).

Shady Acres RV Park. In the town of Green River, it's a favorite of river rafters, fishers, and melon aficionados (for the festival in late Sept). This place is popular with big rigs, with its 86 paved pull-throughs, 71 full hookups, an RV car wash, cable TV, Wi-Fi, and 30- and 50-amp electric. Sites $20–$35. It's at 360 E. Main St., also known as Business Rte. 70 (✆ **800/537-8674** or 435/564-8290 reservations; www.shadyacresrv.com).

SALT LAKE CITY

In the early 19th century, itinerant fur traders trapped beavers along the waterways of the Wasatch Mountains. But by midcentury, Mormon colonists, following the commands of Brigham Young, had established farms and settlements in the "vast desert" of the Great Salt Lake Valley, through irrigation and a lot of hard work. Many of the colonists who walked to Utah, pulling handcarts filled with their possessions, were immigrants recruited in Europe by Mormon missionaries. Settlers fought off hostile Indians, bad weather that destroyed the crops, and clouds of locusts. A flock of seagulls flew in and devoured the locusts, and to this day you'll see large numbers of California gulls, the state bird of Utah, all around the Great Salt Lake.

In **This Is the Place State Park** in Emigration Canyon, east of Salt Lake City on Sunnyside Avenue, a monument marks the spot where Brigham Young stopped on July 24, 1847. He proclaimed he'd found the haven that would shelter his 148 weary followers from persecution, because no outsider would covet this barren basin with its saltwater lake.

RVers will enjoy Salt Lake City's wide streets and easy layout. Primary tourist goals are **Temple Square,** where the Mormon Tabernacle Choir's Thursday night rehearsals and Sunday broadcasts are open to the public, as well as daily organ recitals. Two visitor centers are on the square, with tours of the Temple Square area starting by the flagpole every few minutes.

You can even search out your family roots at the **Family Search Center** in the famous genealogy files of the Church of Jesus Christ of Latter-day Saints. Call for more information on tours and events (© **800/537-9703**).

Winter visitors to Salt Lake City, site of the Winter Olympics in 2002, can take advantage of Utah's champagne-powder snow at smaller ski resorts like **Brighton** (© **800/873-5512;** www.brightonresort.com) and **Solitude** (© **800/748-4754;** www.skisolitude.com), both in Big Cottonwood Canyon, 30 miles east of town by exit 7 from I-215.

Taste-bud treats abound in this legendary sweet-tooth town: **Dreyer's** ice cream at locations all over town; **Cumming's Studio Chocolates** at 679 E. 900 S. (© **801/328-4858**); **Peppermint Place** at 188 N. Main St. (© **801/756-7400**); and **Deli Lama Tony Caputo's** downtown at 308 W. 300 S. (© **801/531-8669**).

Campground Oases in Northern Utah

Antelope Island State Park. Antelope Island has several parking-lot RV "campsites" by the beach and at White Rock Bay. No hookups. Fees are $9 for day use and $13 for overnight stays. In the Great Salt Lake, accessible by the Rte. 127 causeway (© **801/773-2941** reservations; www.utah.com/stateparks).

Bear Lake KOA. This KOA is in Utah's northeast corner, en route to Yellowstone and adjacent to Bear Lake, home of the world's most delicious raspberries. Only a mile north of town, the campground is open year-round, but book well ahead for the end-of-July raspberry season. There are 100 pull-through sites and 44 with 30-amp electric and water hookups; 56 are full hookups. Sites $39–$91. U.S. 89 in **Garden City** (© **800/KOA-3442** [562-3442] or 435/946-3454 reservations; www.koa.com).

Salt Lake City KOA. Within walking distance of Temple Square in downtown Salt Lake City, the campground is open year-round and has 190 full hookups with 30- and 50-amp electric, Wi-Fi, an RV wash, and a heated spa. Only a half-hour from many of the ski areas, this park attracts long-term visitors and big rigs. Sites $38–$56. 1400 W. N. Temple (*©* **800/226-7752** or 801/328-0224 reservations; www.slckoa.com).

Century Mobile Home & RV Park. Near three local ski areas, it's open year-round and has pull-throughs, big-rig sites, and 70 full-hookup sites with 30- and 50-amp electric, cable TV, and Wi-Fi. Sites $28–$34. Located off I-15 at exit 346 in **Ogden**. 1399 W. 2100 S. (*©* **801/731-3800** reservations; http://centuryparkrv.com).

Cherry Hill. Cherry Hill provides splashy summer fun for the family between early Apr and early Nov with its water park, miniature golf, hamster haven, aeroball, and batting cages. There are 124 RV campsites with 30- and 50-amp electrical hookups, and 112 full hookups. Note, however, that the amusements are closed on Sun. From the junction of I-15 and U.S. 89, take exit 324 and drive 2 miles north on 89. The campground is on the left. Sites $38. 1325 S. Main. It's 20 min. north of Salt Lake City in **Kaysville** (*©* **888/4-GO-CAMP** [446-2267] or 801/451-5379 reservations; www.cherry-hill.com).

11 Scenic Side Trips

1. **Kolob Terrace Road to Kolob Reservoir.** Kolob Terrace Road strikes out to the north for 25 miles from the town of Virgin (like the river) on Route 9 west of Zion National Park. From farms with lush grass and trees, it climbs up through ranchland terrain amid red rocks, into groves of aspen and oaks, and into the high country. If the dirt road to Lava Rock looks passable, take the short detour out to an overlook down into Zion Canyon. The lightly traveled Kolob Terrace Road, paved for most of its length, is not recommended for long travel trailers and RVs over 32 feet because there are few pullouts and no good turnarounds along the way. Allow 1½ to 2 hours for the round-trip.

2. **Kolob Canyons.** The northern end of Zion National Park, Kolob Canyons is only 5 minutes away from I-15 at exit 42, and cannot be reached by vehicle from the rest of the park. The beautiful 5-mile drive winds its way between the red Navajo sandstone Finger Canyons to a forested overlook among groves of piñon pine and aspen. Several hiking trails set out from the overlook area, including a moderately strenuous 5-mile trek along Taylor Creek and a strenuous 14-mile hike to Kolob Arch, believed to be the world's largest freestanding arch.

3. **Scenic Byway Route 12.** Running between Escalante and Boulder, Scenic Byway Route 12 climbs a narrow hogback ridge near Calf Creek Recreation Area, amid breathtaking views and sheer drop-offs. The Civilian Conservation Corps built the road here in the early 1940s; until then, the mail was delivered by mule into Boulder. Mountain bikers and four-wheel-drive vehicles can take the original Hell's Backbone dirt road into Dixie National Forest and Box Death Hollow Road, scourge of the mule-riding mailmen.

Northern Utah Campgrounds

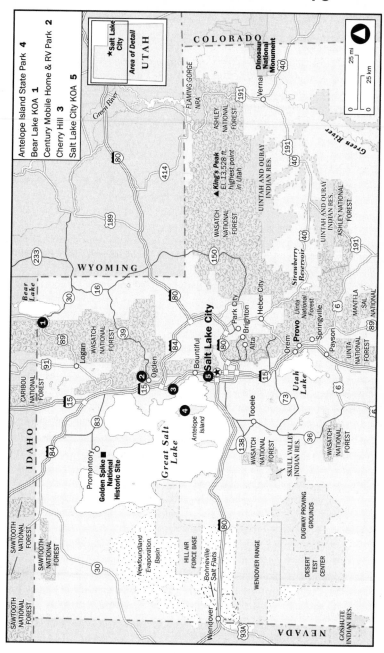

Antelope Island State Park **4**
Bear Lake KOA **1**
Century Mobile Home & RV Park **2**
Cherry Hill **3**
Salt Lake City KOA **5**

131

4. The **Petrified Forest State Park** at **Escalante** displays colorful specimens of petrified wood (© **435/826-4466;** http://stateparks.utah.gov/parks/escalante). **Anasazi State Park Museum** at Boulder (© **435/335-7308;** http://stateparks.utah.gov/parks/anasazi) exhibits a reconstructed pueblo where you can try your hand at grinding corn. The former also has a campground, but a more attractive spot, if there's space, is **Calf Creek Recreation Area** (see listing under "Campground Oases in & Around Capitol Reef National Park," earlier in this chapter). The 32-mile road between Boulder and Grover, the last of it not paved until 1985, passes through elegant groves of aspen, past several forest service campgrounds, and over a 9,600-foot pass. Call the **Escalante Visitors Center** for information (© **435/826-4466**).

5. **Bicentennial Highway.** So named because it was built in 1976, the Bicentennial Highway opens up one of the most sensational stretches of countryside in the West. From Hanksville south on Route 95 to Blanding in the Four Corners country, the terrain unfolds with one spectacular vista after another. The Henry Mountains, snowcapped and framed with red-rock buttes and golden fields of hay, stand out against a vast blue sky. Washes are delineated with narrow stripes of cottonwood, leaves bright green in summer and gold in autumn. After a rain birds flock to the water, shining from holes and grooves in the rock. At Hites Crossing on Lake Powell, a delicate arched bridge crosses the Colorado River, while houseboats bob at anchor all around the nooks and crannies of the lake.

6. **Natural Bridges National Monument.** For RVers in a hurry, there are three natural bridges easily seen from roadside viewpoints along the Route 275 circle loop through the monument; they're accessible by hiking trails for travelers who want to explore. A small visitor center provides a description of the difference between natural bridges and arches. The campground here, though it has trees and is very attractive, is too small for any RVs longer than 26 feet. Don't even attempt to drive a big rig into it (© **435/692-1234;** www.nps.gov/nabr).

7. **The 50-mile loop around Brian Head and Cedar Breaks National Monument.** It's beautiful anytime of year, but especially in winter, when snow sets off the bright red-rock formations of the huge natural amphitheater. Many photographers feel it's even more dramatic than Bryce Canyon. The roads are usually clear into Brian Head, but might sometimes be closed in winter into Cedar Breaks. Exit 78 at Parowan from I-15 leads to Route 143 and Brian Head; from there, take Route 148 through Cedar Breaks and Route 14 back downhill into Cedar City. Call **Cedar Breaks** for information (© **435/586-9451;** www.nps.gov/cebr).

8. **Kodachrome Basin State Park.** The aptly named Kodachrome Basin State Park, 7 miles off Hwy. 12 at Cannonville, makes a dramatic detour by paved road into more stunning rock formations. The National Geographic Society, by the way, is the group that named this colorful basin (© **435/679-8562;** www.utah.com/stateparks/kodachrome.htm).

9. **The Bullfrog Basin loop, Glen Canyon National Recreation Area.** Some 75 miles long, the Bullfrog Basin loop ventures more deeply into Glen Canyon than Route 95. Take the Route 276 cutoff north of Hite Crossing and rejoin Route 95 just before Natural Bridges National Monument. The Bullfrog Marina provides rentals for powerboats and houseboats, as well as an 86-unit campground and some beach areas for swimmers. To complete the loop, you'll have to take the toll ferry called the *John Atlantic Burr* that goes to Halls Crossing; it can handle all sizes of RVs. You could also take a houseboat out for a few days, towing a small powerboat behind, and explore Anasazi caves, discover remote rock arches, and go hiking. Call © **928/608-6200;** www.nps.gov/glca).

10. **The Riverway (Rte. 128).** North of Moab, Route 128, also called the Riverway, strikes east along the Colorado River for 45 miles. It follows a winding, scenic drive into Negro Bill Canyon, named for William Granstaff, a prospector who ventured through in 1877 and is rumored to have sold whiskey to the Indians. Along the route, you can go camping; river running by raft, kayak, or canoe; mountain biking; hiking; or riding off-road vehicles on designated trails. The **Bureau of Land Management** suggests wearing a life jacket when swimming or boating in the river. Big Bend Recreation Site has attractive non-hookup campsites by the river, which are big enough for RVs and have tables and grills—a good alternative when Arches is full (© **801/539-4001;** www.ut.blm.gov).

11. **Dead Horse Point State Park.** Dead Horse Point takes your breath away as you peer over the edge of a sheer 2,000-foot cliff into the double gooseneck loops of the muddy Colorado River as it cuts its way through red earth and green vegetation. Because of exposed cliff edges and a paucity of railings, we heard a local guide caution his group of chattering Japanese schoolgirls to "Be careful." They chorused back cheerfully in unison, "Be careful!" Wild mustangs were herded and broken here in the old days, because a simple brush fence could close the narrow neck to the point. After taking the best of the horses, cowboys would leave the fence open to let the "broomtails" (culls) from the herd pick their way back to the open range. Unfortunately, one group of broomtails got confused and wandered in circles until they died of thirst, ironically while looking at the waters of the Colorado River far below. To get to the park, take U.S. 191 to Route 313 south, which ends at the park (© **435/259-2614;** www.utah.com/stateparks/dead_horse.htm).

Driving the Alaska Highway

ALASKA IS WHERE PEOPLE RELISH SPAM AND LINE UP ON ROADKILL lists for a chance at the next moose struck down by a car. It's where Warren G. Harding drove a golden spike to mark the completion of the Alaska Railroad in 1923, and where the most powerful earthquake ever to hit the North American continent struck on Good Friday in 1964—a 9.2 on the Richter scale, which lasted an incredible 5 minutes.

It's where you can stand in mud up to your knees and have dust blow in your face, where mosquitoes are as big as hummingbirds, and where you won't be considered a real Alaskan until—to paraphrase the locals in more polite terms—you've wrestled a grizzly, urinated in the Yukon, and had an amorous encounter with a bear.

It's where Arco tapped a $10-billion oil reserve at Prudhoe Bay in 1968 and Exxon spilled 11 million gallons of oil off Valdez in 1989. Russia established an outpost here in the 19th century, where Sarah Palin (or Tina Fey) said she could see Russia from her front porch, and a historical marker at a creek-side bordello describes the area as a place where the salmon and the fishermen both came upstream to spawn.

It's where wannabe gold miners once headed for the Klondike by any means possible, crammed into any boats that could float and some that couldn't. Here, salesmen brought their inventory, gamblers their cards and dice, and women their bodies for sale or their scrub boards and sadirons for labor. All of them intended to get rich.

Finally, Alaska is home to the Alaska Highway, the road that helped prevent the Japanese from invading the North American mainland during World War II and aided Alaska in achieving statehood in 1959. More recently, it set off a flourishing bumper-sticker and T-shirt industry with lurid illustrations around the theme "I drove the Alaska Highway."

BUILDING THE HIGHWAY

When Japan bombed Pearl Harbor in December 1941, it didn't take long for the U.S. government to look at a map and see that the narrow Bering Strait separating the westernmost spot of North America—in Alaska—from the easternmost spot of Asia—in Siberia—was only 36 miles across. With the Japanese navy lurking close to North American shores (and even invading the Aleutians) and Russia an ally that desperately needed supplies, the United States decided its Corps of Engineers should construct an inland road to Alaska. Because timing was important, trainloads of U.S. soldiers and equipment began arriving in tiny, remote Dawson Creek before any agreement was

Alaska Highlights

MILEAGE CHART Approximate driving distances in miles between cities.	Anchorage	Circle	Dawson City	Eagle	Fairbanks	Haines	Homer	Prudhoe Bay	Seattle	Seward	Skagway	Tok	Valdez
Anchorage		520	494	501	358	775	226	847	2234	126	832	328	304
Circle	520		530	541	162	815	746	1972	2271	646	872	368	526
Dawson City	494	530		131	379	548	713	868	1843	619	430	189	428
Eagle	501	541	131		379	620	727	868	1974	627	579	173	427
Fairbanks	358	162	379	379		653	584	489	2121	484	710	206	364
Haines	775	815	548	620	653		1001	1142	1774	901	359	447	701
Homer	226	746	713	727	584	1001		1073	2455	173	1058	554	530
Prudhoe Bay	847	1972	868	868	489	1142	1073		2610	973	1199	695	853
Seattle	2243	2271	1843	1974	2121	1774	2455	2610		1361	1577	1931	2169
Seward	126	646	619	627	484	901	173	973	1361		958	454	430
Skagway	832	872	430	579	710	359	1058	1199	1577	958		504	758
Tok	328	368	189	173	206	447	554	695	1931	454	504		254
Valdez	304	526	428	427	364	701	530	853	2169	430	758	254	

Chukchi Sea

Little Diomede Island

Nome

Norton Sound

YUKON DELTA NWR

Bethel

YUKON DELTA NWR

Attu Island

Bering Sea

Pribilof Islands

Bristol Bay

Cape St. Stephen   Rat Islands

Aleutian Islands

Adak

Adak Island   Atka

Atka Island

Fort Glen

Unimak Island   Cold Bay

Dutch Harbor

Unalaska

ALASKA PENINSULA

Action Jackson's Bar 7	Denali State Park 5	Midnight Sun 8
The Bird House 9	Diamond Tooth	Nenana tripod 2
Braeburn Lodge 11	Gertie's 8	Pioneer Park 1
Dawson Peaks Resorts 11	Frantic Follies 10	Pump House Restaurant 3
Denali National Park	Hyder Ghost Town 15	Taku Smokeries Market
Visitor Access Center 4	Kantishna Roadhouse 13	Place 13

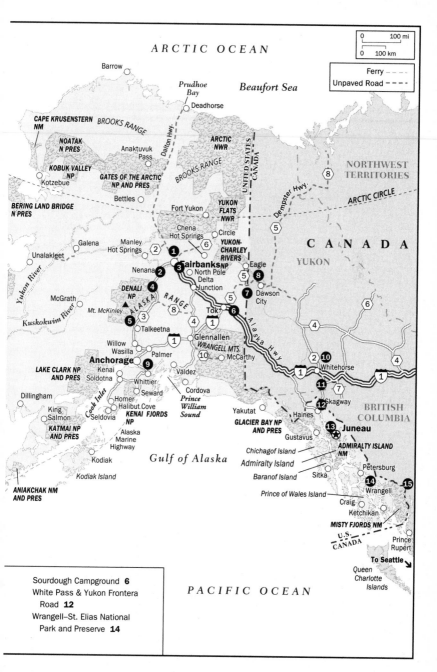

ARCTIC OCEAN

Barrow

Prudhoe
Bay

Beaufort Sea

Deadhorse

CAPE KRUSENSTERN
NM

BROOKS RANGE

NOATAK
N PRES

Anaktuvuk
Pass

ARCTIC
NWR

KOBUK VALLEY
NP

GATES OF THE ARCTIC
NP AND PRES

BROOKS RANGE

NORTHWEST
TERRITORIES

Kotzebue

BERING LAND
BRIDGE
N PRES

Bettles

Fort Yukon

YUKON
FLATS
NWR

Dempster Hwy.

ARCTIC CIRCLE

Dalton Hwy.

UNITED STATES
CANADA

Galena

Unalakleet

Manley
Hot Springs

Nenana

Chena
Hot Springs

Circle

YUKON-
CHARLEY
RIVERS
NP

CANADA

YUKON

Fairbanks

North Pole

Eagle

Yukon River

DENALI
NP

Delta
Junction

Dawson
City

McGrath

Mt. McKinley

ALASKA RANGE

Tok

Alaska Hwy.

Kuskokwim River

Talkeetna

Glennallen

WRANGELL MTS.

Willow
Wasilla

Palmer

McCarthy

Whitehorse

Anchorage

LAKE CLARK NP
AND PRES

Kenai
Soldotna

Valdez

Cordova

Whittier

Seward

Prince
William
Sound

Skagway

BRITISH
COLUMBIA

Dillingham

Homer
Halibut Cove

KENAI FJORDS
NP

Yakutat

Haines

King
Salmon

Seldovia

Cook Inlet

Alaska
Marine
Highway

GLACIER BAY NP
AND PRES

Gustavus

Juneau

KATMAI NP
AND PRES

Kodiak

Gulf of Alaska

Chichagof Island

Admiralty Island

ADMIRALTY ISLAND
NM

Kodiak Island

Baranof Island

Sitka

Petersburg

ANIAKCHAK NM
AND PRES

Prince of Wales Island

Wrangell

Craig

Ketchikan

MISTY FJORDS NM

U.S.
CANADA

Prince
Rupert

Sourdough Campground **6**
White Pass & Yukon Frontera
    Road **12**
Wrangell–St. Elias National
    Park and Preserve **14**

PACIFIC OCEAN

To Seattle

Queen
Charlotte
Islands

0   100 mi
0   100 km

Ferry · · · · · ·
Unpaved Road - - - -

You can still count on a Mountie on the Canadian part of the highway!

signed with Canada. All told, 33,000 men would work on the road that year, 11,000 of them U.S. Army troops, and some 200 would die in the sub-zero temperatures and hazardous working conditions.

The surveyors were just steps ahead of the bulldozers in the winter of 1942, sinking into the mud and the permafrost below. Not much attention was paid to grades or curves. As the surveyors pointed to what they perceived as the horizon, the bulldozers followed in their footsteps. The original 1,422-mile road was built in just over 8 months.

Canadian construction crews cleaned up and straightened out the roadway for the next several years, but the Japanese threat in Alaskan waters had subsided. By 1949, the road was open to traffic, and paving continued sporadically until the last stretch was more or less covered by macadam in 1992. Drivers today still encounter rough stretches undergoing construction.

> *"They didn't build a city here; they found gold. That's the whole story of Alaska."*
> —Ruth Allman,
> Alaska pioneer

RVing Along the Alaska Highway

While the mighty Alaska Highway still strikes fear into the hearts of travelers, it's become tamer over the past years. The main attraction to the RVer is a combination of end-of-the-world roadways peeling off at intervals and all the incredible scenery and wildlife waiting to be discovered along the way. There are craggy peaks capped with perpetual snow, hanging and calving glaciers, golden midnight sunsets, and swirling acid-green northern lights, along with grizzly bears, moose, caribou, bald eagles, and sometimes wolves.

The **eastern access route** goes from Great Falls to Calgary, across Alberta to Edmonton and northwest to Dawson Creek. The **western access route** sets out from Seattle, north on I-5 to the Trans-Canada 1, east to Hope and north via either the new Coquihalla Highway or the slower Route 97 to Cache Creek, Quesnel, Prince George, and Dawson Creek.

The first challenge in driving the Alaska Highway is to get to the starting point, the famous **Mile 0,** located in Dawson Creek, British Columbia (BC), 817 miles north of Seattle on the western access route (or 867 miles northwest of Great Falls, Montana, on the eastern access route).

About 80% of the Alaska Highway is in Canada, which is why some people still call it by its nickname, "the Alcan." While it sounds appropriate, even hip, to some citizens from the Lower 48, the very word *"Alcan"* makes Alaskans and Canadians of a certain age bristle. That's because it was an acronym for the Alaska-Canada Military Highway, which did not permit civilian travel during the war years. Locals equate it to calling San Francisco "Frisco."

Despite losing their box office billing in the highway's official name, the Canadians got a good deal. In 1946, after the war that inspired the highway's construction, they bought their share at half of what it cost to build.

The precise length of the Alaska Highway keeps changing as engineers straighten out its notorious curves. The original, or historic, mileposts are still used as addresses

Rocky Crest Lake, near Muncho Lake on the Alaska Highway.

by the businesses and residents along the highway. Contemporary mileposts reflect the present distances, while in Canada, kilometer posts are also in service.

Another point of contention is where the highway actually starts and stops. Historic Mile 0 is in **Dawson Creek, British Columbia,** and the true terminus is in **Delta Junction, Alaska,** because a road connecting Delta Junction and Fairbanks already existed. Most Alaska Highway travelers, however, consider **Fairbanks** the real end of the highway, after which they usually head south via **Denali National Park and Preserve** to **Anchorage.**

HITTING THE HIGHLIGHTS

With only a 2-week vacation, you can still see a lot of Alaska, especially if you fly in (say, to Anchorage) and pick up an RV there (see "Bring Your Own RV or Rent?" below, for rental information). From Anchorage, take Route 3 north to Fairbanks; Route 2 east to Delta Junction, where you pick up the official Alaska Highway; and continue southeast on Route 2, which becomes Hwy. 1 when you cross the Canadian border. Through the Yukon, continue southeast on Hwy. 1 to Whitehorse. From here, you could follow Route 2 north to Dawson City or continue along the Alaska Highway, Route 1, to Watson Lake. If time permits, follow the Alaska Highway, now Route 97 in British Columbia, to Dawson Creek, the beginning of the Alaska Highway. If you want to vary your return route once you're back in Alaska, take Route 1 (the Glenn Hwy.) southwest from Tok to Anchorage.

GOING FOR THE LONG HAUL

If you want to stretch out your Alaska RV adventure for a full summer, follow as many of the 10 side trips listed at the end of this chapter as you can squeeze in and weather permits. In spring and fall, check ahead on weather conditions since there could be a late thaw and some roads still closed by snowpack in spring. We were snowed in one August day in Dawson City when a storm dumped so much of the white stuff that the roads were closed.

Travel Essentials

WHEN TO GO

While the highway is open and maintained year-round, RV visitors will find the best times for visiting are mid-May to late September. The "season," according to the locals we met on our mid-May trip, had not yet begun, which meant we could find empty campsites late in the day. But a few lodges and service stations had not yet opened for the summer. Try to avoid July and August, when RVs are almost bumper-to-bumper along some stretches of the highway.

BRING YOUR OWN RV OR RENT?

To bring your own RV to Alaska without amassing a lot of overland miles or doubling back over the same territory, consider taking it aboard one of the **Alaska ferries** from Bellingham, Washington, to Skagway, which connects by road with Whitehorse or Watson Lake. Call or check the website for reservations as soon as possible after

Ferries in Alaska carry RVs as well as cars.

January 1 of the year you want to travel—and be patient, the line is often busy (© **800/382-9229;** www.akms.com/ferry).

Alternatively, you can rent, starting out from Seattle, Skagway, or Anchorage. To rent an RV in British Columbia or Alaska, reserve as early as possible and determine whether you can pick up at one point and drop off at another. In Alaska, Anchorage is the center of RV rentals, with a number of companies such as these:

- **ABC Motorhome Rentals:** © **800/421-7456;** www.abcmotorhome.com.

- **Alaska Motorhome Rentals:** © **800/323-5757;** www.alaskarv.com. Provides one-way rentals between Skagway and Seattle.

- **Clippership Motorhome Rentals:** © **800/421-3456;** www.clippershiprv.com.

- **Cruise America:** © **800/671-8042;** www.cruiseamerica.com.

- **Great Alaskan Holidays, Inc.:** © **888/225-2752;** www.greatalaskanholidays. com.

- **Murphy's RV:** © **888/562-0661;** www.alaskaone.com/murphyrv.

Rental prices can vary sharply, so shop around. Look for a rental with unlimited mileage included. In Alaska, the miles pile up quickly and expensively at 15¢ a mile. Daily rates will be around $250 a day. If you do the Anchorage-to-Seattle run, there will be a drop-off fee of about $500. Also, there may be a preparation fee and utensils and linens fee, each about $40.

A Seattle-based company called **Alaska Highway Cruises** (© **800/323-5757;** www.alaskahighwaycruises.com), a division of Alaska Travel Adventures, offers a combination package with one of several customized overland itineraries in a type C motor home, paid reserved campsites nightly, and an Alaska cruise aboard a Holland America Line luxury ship. On the 15-day "Northern Highlights" itinerary, you board your ship in Vancouver, then take a 7-night cruise to Ketchikan, Juneau, and Skagway, along with Glacier Bay National Park and College Fjord. After disembarking in Seward, you take a motorcoach to Anchorage, where you pick up an RV. Your 7-night motor home tour starts with a drive to Denali National Park for 2 nights, then continues along the Alaska Highway to Glennallen, before returning to Anchorage for your flight home. The whole package starts at around $2,600 per person, double occupancy, and includes the cruise with all meals and entertainment, a fully furnished rental RV, campground reservations, and fees. You buy the gas and food, as well as your round-trip flight between your home city and Vancouver. (Also, check out **www. bestofalaskatravel.com**.)

Our 21-foot Fleetwood Jamboree rented from Alaska Highway Cruises averaged 6 to 7 miles per gallon on the Alaska Highway. We drove a total of 3,100 miles, spending approximately $600 on gas and about $500 on food and beverages for two. That was several years ago. These days (early 2012), gas is running about $3.67 a gallon in Anchorage, and $4.12 for diesel.

WHAT TO TAKE

Bring your **passport** (required for any border crossing to and from Canada), binoculars, cameras, batteries, a world-class mosquito repellent, sunscreen, and good maps. Anglers will want to carry fishing gear for lake trout, northern pike, Dolly Varden, arctic grayling, and five species of Pacific salmon. Spin or bait-cast fishing and/or fly-fishing rods and tackle capable of handling fish up to 30 pounds are recommended by the experts. Some RV rental companies will also rent fishing gear.

For the RV, take spare parts such as a fan belt, oil filter, air filter, radiator hose, and heater hose. Mud flaps or "eyelashes" for the back are a good idea to keep gravel and mud from splashing all over the rear window. We took a basic tool kit and an emergency medical kit.

WHAT TO WEAR

Although we took along heavyweight down parkas and heavy-soled hiking boots, we never donned either one. Walking or jogging shoes were adequate on the short trails we hiked, but dedicated hikers and climbers should carry specialized equipment. A raincoat and umbrella are a good idea, since it can rain or snow, but don't be surprised to find Fairbanks sunny and hot. Dress is casual everywhere in Alaska, so typical RV outfits will always pass muster (except on a cruise ship, if you take the Alaska Highway Cruises package).

TRIMMING COSTS ON THE ROAD

The type of RV you choose to drive can make a big difference in expenses on the road. The best gas mileage and greatest route flexibility come from a four-wheel-drive truck camper with a cab-over sleeping and cooking unit, but you'll sacrifice some of the comforts provided by a type C or type A motor home. (This quandary inspired a popular bumper sticker: "Sure it gets lousy gas mileage for a car, but it gets great mileage for a house.")

Staying in **government campgrounds** without facilities is much cheaper than private campgrounds with hookups. Parking by the side of the road is cheapest of all, if you're in an area where you feel safe. However, after noting how many RV parks list security as a plus, we don't recommend it. (See "Should You Sleep by the Side of the Road?" in chapter 3, "Where to Sleep: Campgrounds & RV Parks.")

Food is expensive in the north, so stock as many provisions as you can in the gateway cities to the south.

Note: At press time, the U.S. and Canadian dollars were trading at about 1 to 1, although that exchange rate may change. Go to **www.oanda.com** for currency updates.

WHERE TO GET TRAVEL INFORMATION

Contact the **Alaska Travel Industry Association,** 2600 Cordova St., Anchorage, AK 99503. Call for a free booklet, "Alaska State Vacation Planner" (© **907/929-2200;** www.travelalaska.com).

Tourism British Columbia, Parliament Buildings, Victoria, BC, Canada V8V 1X4 (© **800/435-5622;** www.hellobc.com), provides a lot of free material about the province, including maps, campground guides, and other specialized information.

Tourism Yukon, P.O. Box 2703-VG, Whitehorse, YT, Canada Y1A 2C6 (© **800/661-0494;** www.travelyukon.com), can also provide material, including maps and campground guides.

Finally, don't set out on the Alaska Highway drive without the road bible called *The MILEPOST* ($34, including shipping), published annually (© **800/243-0495;** www.themilepost.com). It includes mile-by-mile logs of all the North Country highways, as well as updated road conditions, the best places to spot wildlife, and every hiccup of life along the highway.

Remember, U.S. citizens need a passport to get into Canada (and come back!). See **http://travel.state.gov/passport** for details.

DRIVING & CAMPING TIPS

- **Expect to drive with your headlights on.** In this part of Canada, the law requires it, and when dust is billowing, you'll be glad the oncoming traffic is visible to you through the clouds.

- **Don't try to "make time" on the road;** it can make you crazy. We saw too many RVers limping into camp exhausted at 9pm—they'd kept driving because the sun was still high, either not knowing or ignoring the fact that in summer, it almost never sets this far north. If you drive your RV hell-for-leather, ignoring loose gravel, buckled roadways, and potholes, you'll miss a lot of the scenery and wildlife, two of the most important reasons for being there.

- **Always top off your gas tank when you pass an open station.** Sometimes a station ahead may be closed for the day or has gone out of business. Our closest call came on the Klondike Highway when we had to drive 269 miles between open stations and finally rolled into Dempster Corner on fumes. Another time, we turned around and drove back 20 miles to buy gas at a station we had passed, because the one to which we were headed was closed.

- **Watch for frost heaves.** These are the biggest enemies of your vehicle: irregular bumps where the pavement has buckled or sunk because of permafrost melting and refreezing. Spots may be marked with red flags by the roadside, but sometimes the wind takes them away. If the white center or side lines look squiggly, slow down.

- **Don't drink the water.** We make it a habit never to assume that any piped campground water is potable, but instead use it only for the kitchen and bathroom. We drink bottled water and use prepackaged ice, which is available almost everywhere along the route in Alaska and northern Canada, where tap water sometimes comes out in shades of brown. If your rig has a water filter and an ice maker with a filter, you'll do fine. Also, never drink water from a stream or lake. The parasite *giardia,* which can cause extreme intestinal upset and is impervious to antibiotics, is present in northern Canada and Alaska waterways.

- **Come prepared.** Stock up your RV with any necessary personal items before you get into the woods. You'll be able to find basic groceries, towing services, RV repairs, and telephones along the road; but if you want to prepare a bouillabaisse with your freshly caught fish, be sure to take along your own saffron and sauvignon blanc.

The Best Alaska Highway Sights, Tastes & Experiences

OFF-THE-WALL ATTRACTIONS

A collection of **3,600 billed caps.** They're stapled to the ceiling at **Toad River Lodge,** Mile 422, making an intricately textured soundproofing. The lodge also has a full-service campground (© **250/232-5401;** www.toadriverlodge.com).

The Sign Post Forest, Watson Lake. Located at Mile 612, the Sign Post Forest started in 1942 when a homesick GI from Illinois who was working on the highway put up a road sign to his hometown. It has since grown to some 42,000 signs from all over the world (**www.yukoninfo.com/watson/signpostforest.htm**).

The "Teslin taxi." Photographer George Johnston had a 1928 Chevrolet shipped up to the little Tlingit town of Teslin by barge, despite the fact there were no roads. He built a 3-mile road for summer use, then put chains on the "taxi" and drove it across the frozen lake in winter. See the restored vehicle in the George Johnston Museum, on the left of the highway as you head north. Daily May 15–Sept 1 9am–6pm. Admission $5 adults, $4 seniors/students, $2.50 children, $15 family (© **867/390-2550;** www.gjmuseum.yk.net).

Action Jackson's Bar, Boundary. At the Top of the World Highway on the Alaska side of the Alaska/Canada border, Yukon Hwy. 9, Action Jackson's was one of Alaska's first roadhouses, manned by its eponymous owner who kept a six-shooter strapped to each hip. Restless citizens used to drive the 70 miles from Dawson City on a Fri or Sat night for the action. Today, it has no liquor license, but you can get gas, as a rule.

The Bird House Bar, Indian. Located in Indian, 27 miles southeast of Anchorage on the Seward Highway, the Bird House collapsed during the 1964 earthquake and is half buried, with a giant blue bird head facing the highway and everything inside on a slant.

Chetwynd, the chainsaw-carving capital of the world. With its distinctive three bears, heroic loggers, and other rustic road sculptures, this district sits on BC's Hwy. 97 at the junction with Route 29 (**www.gochetwynd.com**).

North Pole. This town, at Mile 349 on the Richardson Highway, 13 miles south of Fairbanks, is where letters to Santa Claus are delivered by the U.S. Postal Service. See **Mr. and Mrs. Claus at Santa Claus House,** 101 St. Nicholas Dr., North Pole, AK 99705 (© **800/588-4078** or 907/488-2200; www.santaclaushouse.com).

The big black-and-white tripod in Nenana. It's put out on the Nenana River ice in winter, connected to a clock. When the ice breaks up enough in the river to drag the tripod cable and stop the clock, lottery ticket holders who guessed the closest date and time share a prize that can run over $300,000. A hint to would-be winners: The ice usually breaks up sometime between mid-Apr and mid-May. Nenana is an hour's drive south of Fairbanks on the Parks Highway. Purchase lottery tickets in person only at Nenana Visitor Center, at the intersection of the highway and A St., P.O. Box 272, Nenana, AK 99760 (© **907/832-5446;** www.nenanaakiceclassic.com).

Hyder, "the friendliest ghost town in Alaska." Off the Cassier Highway straddling the Canadian border at Stewart, Hyder is where people traditionally pin a dollar to the wall in the Glacier Inn. That's in case they pass through again in the future, broke and in need of a drink. The bars here are open 23 hours a day. Contact the Hyder Chamber of Commerce (© **888/366-5999;** www.stewart-hyder.com/hyder.html).

EIGHT GREAT SPLURGES

1. **An evening of gaming at Diamond Tooth Gertie's.** Named for Gertie Lovejoy, who had a diamond wedged between her two front teeth, Gertie's is located at the corner of Queen Street and 4th Avenue in Dawson City. It gets especially rambunctious at the end of the season when all the locals are trying to win enough money to head south for the winter. (No one under 19 admitted.) Contact the **Klondike Visitors Association** for information (© **867/993-5575;** www.dawsoncity.org).

2. **An overnight or two at the Kantishna Roadhouse.** The Roadhouse is an appealing, if archly rustic, place at the end of the road inside Denali National Park. From here, you can go on guided hikes deep into the park. A special

Native Art: Finding the Real Thing

If you'd like a piece of authentic Native art as a keepsake from your trip, follow the tips below, and you'll have a much better chance at coming home with a unique item crafted in Alaska by a real artisan.

Estimates of the amount of counterfeit Alaska Native art sold annually don't exist, but authorities have put it close to $100 million. That's money taken from Alaska Bush economies where jobs in the cash economy are virtually nonexistent and prices for essentials such as fuel and housing are astronomical. Buying fake Native art is cultural and financial theft from subsistence hunters and fishermen who can least afford it.

You can avoid being scammed if you pay attention. Ask questions before you buy. Any reputable art dealer will provide you with a biography of the artist who created an expensive work. Ask specifically if that artist actually carved the piece: Some Native artists have sold their names and designs to wholesalers who produce knockoffs. Price is a tip-off. An elaborate mask is more likely to cost $1,000 than $100. Another indicator is the choice of materials; most soapstone carvings are not made in Alaska. Even relatively inexpensive craftwork should bear the name of the person who made it, and the shop owner should be able to tell you how he or she acquired the item.

Another caution for international visitors: Do not buy products made from marine mammals, such as walrus ivory, whale bone, or seal skin. Except for antiques, export of these materials is illegal.

The **Alaska State Council on the Arts** (© **907/269-6610**) authenticates Native arts and crafts with a **silver hand** label, which assures you it was made by the hands of an Alaska Native with Alaskan materials. But the program isn't universally used, so the absence of the label doesn't mean the work definitely isn't authentic. Other labels aren't worth much: An item could say ALASKA MADE even if only insignificant assembly work happened there. Of course, in Bush Alaska and in some urban shops, you can buy authentic work directly from craftspeople. Buying in Native-owned co-ops is also safe.

Another program covers any item made within the state, both Native and non-Native. The logo of a mother bear and cub (**www.madeinalaska.org**) indicates that a state contractor has determined that the product was made in Alaska, when possible with Alaskan materials. Non-Natives produce Alaskan crafts of ceramics, wood, or fabric, but not plastic—if it's plastic, it probably wasn't made there.

You can learn about and buy authentic work from the **Alaska Native Arts Foundation,** a nonprofit with online shopping at **www.alaskanative arts.org** and a brick-and-mortar gallery in Anchorage. **Sealaska Heritage Foundation** offers a nonprofit website selling work by Southeast Alaska Natives at **www.alaskanativeartists.com**.

permit is necessary to drive in, but there's the park shuttle bus or, if you're in a hurry, a resort airstrip for a Denali air shuttle. Reserve well in advance (© **800/942-7420;** www.kantishnaroadhouse.com).

3. **A performance of the Frantic Follies.** Performances are in the Westmark Hotel in Whitehorse nightly at 8:30pm. The show is a wild mixture of Gay Nineties, barroom madcaps, and audience participation. Admission is $26. The hotel is at 201 Wood St. in Whitehorse (© **867/393-9700;** www.franticfollies.com).

4. **A 3-hour excursion aboard the White Pass and Yukon Route Railroad.** It takes you along the famous Trail of '98 from Skagway to the White Pass Summit and back. There's also daily afternoon service from Skagway to Whitehorse (via train to Fraser, BC, then motorcoach to Whitehorse) with a morning return. Built in 1899, the narrow-gauge train has one of the steepest railroad grades in North America. Summers only. $112 adults, $56 for children (© **800/ 343-7373;** www.wpyr.com).

5. **A dinner of rare white King salmon at Simon & Seafort's Saloon & Grill.** It's all the rage in **Anchorage** during its brief season. Start with fresh King crab and follow the salmon with the house's brandy ice, a concoction of vanilla ice cream, brandy, Kahlúa, and crème de cacao. 420 L St. (© **907/274-3502;** www.simonandseaforts.com).

6. **Shopping for *qiviut.*** In northern craft shops, look for rare and costly qiviut, the soft underwool of the musk ox, gathered when it's shed each spring and woven into warm, feather-light gloves, scarves, caps, and sweaters. Alternatively, seek carved soapstone pieces, ceremonial wooden masks, or last season's trendy *ulus* (fan-shaped chopping knives with wood handles).

7. **Flying over Mount McKinley.** On a clear day, you can fly over Mount McKinley and the Susitna Valley, where you might catch a glimpse of moose, bear, foxes, and eagles, then land in Talkeetna, the staging area for climbers who tackle the high peaks of the Alaska Range. For details, call **K2 Aviation** (© **800/764-2291;** www.flyk2.com), or **Sheldon Air Service** (© **800/478-2321** or 907/733-2321; www.sheldonairservice.com). Rates $190 to $795 per person depending on the tour.

8. **Dinner at the Pump House Restaurant.** The colorful Pump House, on the banks of the Chena River, 2 miles southwest of Fairbanks on Chena Pump Road, is now a national historic site crammed with gold rush–era artifacts (© **907/479-8452;** www.pumphouse.com).

TAKEOUT (OR EAT-IN) FAR NORTH TREATS

Alaska Wild Berry chocolates. Get some chocolate and check out the flowing 20-ft. chocolate waterfall at the company's Anchorage outlet. Filling options include wild rosehip, elderberry, salmonberry, high bush cranberry, and lingonberry. 5225 Juneau St. (© **800/280-2927** or 970/562-8858; www.alaskawildberryproducts.com).

Alaskan Brewing Company. This Juneau-based company has been around only since 1986, but its Alaskan Amber has already been twice voted the most popular brew at the Great American Beer Festival in Colorado. Tours leave every half-hour. May–Sept Tues–Sat 11am–5pm; Oct–Apr Thurs–Sat 11am–5pm. The brewery is at 5429 Shaune Dr., outside Juneau. To get there, turn right from Egan Dr. onto Vanderbilt Hill Rd., which becomes the Glacier Hwy., and then right on Anka St. and right again on Shaune Dr. (✆ **907/780-5866;** www.alaskanbeer.com).

Bonanza Meat Company, Dawson City. At Bonanza Meat, you can design your own sandwich. Mon–Sat 8:30am–7pm. The company is located on 2nd Ave. in Dawson City (✆ **867/993-6567**).

The Braeburn Lodge. Try the Braeburn's superburgers—one is big enough for two. They also serve what they call "gianormous" cinnamon buns. Big, yes, but not particularly tasty. At Mile 55, Klondike Hwy. (radio phone ✆ **2M-3987, Fox Channel;** www.karo-ent.com/braeburn).

Dawson Peaks Resort & RV Park, southeast of Teslin. Try the grilled Teslin lake trout and prizewinning rhubarb pie. The resort and RV campground is 7 miles southeast of Teslin on the lake, at Mile 769 (✆ **866/402-2244** or 867/390-2244; www.dawsonpeaks.ca).

The Double Musky Inn Restaurant, Girdwood. It serves classic New Orleans and Cajun dishes with Alaska seafood. Try the Double Musky cake and savor the layers of pecan meringue, brownielike chocolate, chocolate mousse, and cocoa cream frosting. Tues–Sat 5–10pm. At 3 Crow Creek Rd. in Girdwood, south of Anchorage (✆ **907/ 783-2822;** www.doublemuskyinn.com).

Goldfields Bakery, Barkerville. Grab some whole wheat or sourdough bread from Goldfields, in the historic gold-rush town of Barkerville, near Quesnel, BC. Call the bakery for information (✆ **250/994-3241;** www.barkerville.ca).

A Crash Course in Speaking Alaskan

The Bush: Any place reached by plane instead of road or Alaska ferry.
Cheechako: A newcomer.
Native: Not just anyone born in Alaska; only those belonging to one of the **Native American peoples of Alaska:** the Athabascan, Yup'ik, Cup'ik, Inupiaq, St. Lawrence Island Yupik, Aleut, Alutiiq, Eyak, Tlingit, Haida, or Tsimshian peoples.
Outside: Anywhere that isn't Alaska; generally the lower 48 states.
Permafrost: The permanently frozen subsoil that covers much of the state.
Sourdough: Anyone who's been in Alaska longer than one season, as in "Sour on Alaska without enough dough to get out."

Encounter a caribou, like these in Denali National Park.

Lung Duck Tong Restaurant, Barkerville. Chinese dim sum in a gold-rush town? Why not? Call for reservations (© **888/994-3332**). For information, call the **Barkerville Reception Centre** (© **250/994-3458**).

Sourdough pancakes. You'll find sourdough pancakes almost anywhere up here, but they're especially good in **Dawson City's Midnight Sun,** at Third and Queen sts. (© **867/993-5495** or 604/291-2652; www.midnightsunhotel.com). In Juneau's **Westmark Baranof Hotel,** 127 N. Franklin St. (© **907/463-6208;** www.westmark hotels.com), they're the size of Frisbees and accompanied by reindeer sausages, and in **Tok** you can camp next door to a pancake house at the **Sourdough Campground** (see "Campground Oases: Dawson to Fairbanks," later in this chapter).

Taku Smokeries Market Place, Juneau. The smoked salmon is packaged to go at Taku Smokeries Market Place in Juneau, but it can also be ordered by mail. 550 S. Franklin Ave. (© **800/582-5122;** www.takusmokeries.com).

WILDLIFE-WATCHING

We were never sated with **moose sightings** on our May trip, perhaps because spring is calving time. In early fall, however, plenty of them come down into the lower meadows in Denali. Pulling over to cook breakfast at a rest stop on the road between Denali and Anchorage, we saw a moose cow browsing at the edge of the trees and managed to snap a couple of shots before she gave us an aggrieved look and ambled back into the woods.

INSIDER TIP: BEAR NECESSITIES

One expert says that if you encounter a bear while out on a hike, don't turn and run because it may give chase. Instead, walk backward to get away, facing the bear and continue to talk in a normal tone ("Nice bear, nice bear"?). Above all, "do not imitate bear sounds or positions, even if they seem funny to you."

A close sighting of a **porcupine** in the wild, waddling up a bank with his silver-tipped quills aquiver, or a **bald eagle** in the roadway snacking on roadkill, is as exciting as seeing the bigger animals. Unless you're very quick or patient, or the animal is slow, your memory will be clearer than your photo.

Our first good day of wildlife-spotting was on an early morning transit of the Crooked River Nature Corridor south of McLeod Lake in British Columbia, with a **wolf, deer,** and **great blue herons** spotted. We were too late in the season to catch the **trumpeter swans** that spend the winter here.

Hummingbird-size mosquitoes—aka "Alaska's state bird"—in a campground at Fort Nelson were the next creatures we spotted. Fortunately, they were too large to get through the window screens of the RV.

An early morning roadside sighting of a **black bear** a few miles north of Fort Nelson did not result in any photographs. He spotted us first, so all we saw was his backside disappearing into the woods.

One of the best places to spot **caribou** is by the side of the road, oddly enough. They stand around morosely by signs and at road junctions, as if waiting for a bus. They are, incidentally, the only type of deer in which both sexes grow horns. At Stone Mountain Park, there have been great caribou sightings right past a huge sign warning caribou in the roadway. **Mountain sheep,** too, like the roadsides. The indigenous stone sheep in Stone Mountain Park, colored cream and brown and bigger than Dall or Rocky Mountain sheep, can be glimpsed as they look down from craggy rock cliffs, or photographed as they gather by the roadside to lick salt deposits.

On the Road

NORTHERN BRITISH COLUMBIA

Once past Calgary on the eastern access road or Kamloops on the western access road, urbanites need to make an important mental adjustment. There are no more cities until Whitehorse, Yukon Territory, just small towns separated by almost 8 hours of driving past gorgeous, uninhabited scenery. Those places on the map with serious names and major crossroads might not be what you expect by the time you arrive; however, the inhabitants are generally friendly and helpful.

Western Canada Highlights & Campgrounds

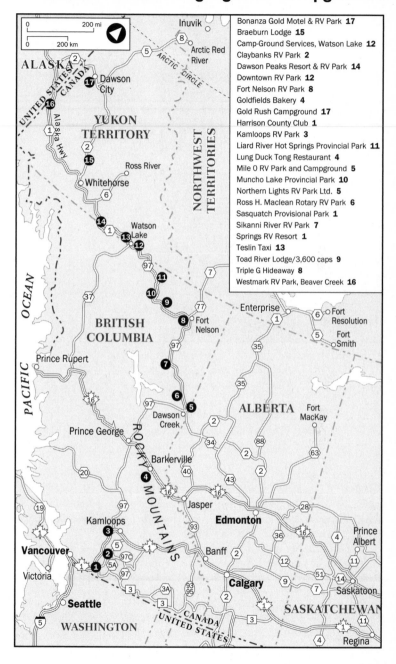

Bonanza Gold Motel & RV Park **17**
Braeburn Lodge **15**
Camp-Ground Services, Watson Lake **12**
Claybanks RV Park **2**
Dawson Peaks Resort & RV Park **14**
Downtown RV Park **12**
Fort Nelson RV Park **8**
Goldfields Bakery **4**
Gold Rush Campground **17**
Harrison County Club **1**
Kamloops RV Park **3**
Liard River Hot Springs Provincial Park **11**
Lung Duck Tong Restaurant **4**
Mile 0 RV Park and Campground **5**
Muncho Lake Provincial Park **10**
Northern Lights RV Park Ltd. **5**
Ross H. Maclean Rotary RV Park **6**
Sasquatch Provisional Park **1**
Sikanni River RV Park **7**
Springs RV Resort **1**
Teslin Taxi **13**
Toad River Lodge/3,600 caps **9**
Triple G Hideaway **8**
Westmark RV Park, Beaver Creek **16**

The world-famous Sign Post Forest has some 20,000 signs from all over the world.

Dawson Creek is where most of the Alaska Highway drivers stop both coming and going to trade war stories, especially at service stations, car washes, RV parks, and the town's major drinking and dining spot, the venerable **Alaska Hotel Café & Dew Drop Inn (www.alaskahotel.com)**. This is where you photograph your RV in front of the Mile 0 Alaska Highway sign, take a look at one of the three competing pioneer villages, and admire the big red grain elevator that doubles as art gallery and tourist information office.

In **Fort Nelson,** as we were running out of reading and cocktail materials, we found an office supply store with a treasure-trove of secondhand paperback books for half the cover price, and a liquor store with a sparse and pricey inventory. Less exciting was a highly advertised "European deli" with a meager supply of meats and cheese, but doing a land-office business in microwaved burritos.

Watson Lake, on the Yukon border, has a sign forest (see "Off-the-Wall Attractions," earlier in this chapter) and a modest supermarket. **Campground Services RV Park** has 140 sites, full and partial hookups, and a coin-operated car/RV wash for getting rid of the top layer of road dust. Don't worry about street addresses—the whole town is laid out in a strip along the highway.

The "lodges" grandly promoted by road signs before you get there usually turn out to be basic roadside cafes with a straggle of cabins in back and a gas tank out front, and a cashier/waitress who also sells fishing licenses, pumps the gas, makes beds, and does the home cooking in her spare time.

CAMPGROUND OASES: HARRISON HOT SPRINGS TO TESLIN

Springs RV Resort. Harrison Hot Springs makes a good stopover for anyone interested in the legend of Bigfoot, who apparently hangs around this area a great deal. Perhaps it's too obvious to look for him at this campground, where the logo is a silhouette of the 12-foot hairy humanoid. Of the 142 RV sites, all have 30- or 50-amp electric. Enjoy the 18-hole minigolf and stay in touch with home through the Internet connection. Sites C$45–C$59. 670 Hot Springs Rd. It's on Hwy. 9, 2 miles north of the junction with Hwy. 7 (✆ **800/294-9907** or 604/796-9767; www.springsrv.com).

Harrison Country Club (formerly Sasquatch Springs RV Resort). Sasquatch, the Indian name for Bigfoot, shows up in place names around Harrison Hot Springs, so of course it's in campground names as well . . . or it was. We think they should have kept it. This seasonal campground is 4 miles north of the junction of highways 7 and 9 on Harrison Hot Springs Road, where 70 full hookups provide 15- and 30-amp electric, plus cable TV. Sites C$30–C$40. 400 Hot Springs Rd. (✆ **604/796-9228**).

Sasquatch Provincial Park. Located 4 miles north of Harrison Hot Springs on Rockwell Dr., this place has 177 campsites, but no hookups. Sites C$10–C$24 (✆ **604/795-6169;** www.discovercamping.ca).

Claybanks RV Park. Claybanks is a pleasant, family-run campground at the edge of the historic little town of Merritt and near enough for an easy stroll into town. Take exit 290 from Hwy. 5 and follow the Sani-Dump signs along Voight Street to the campground, which has 36 full-hookup sites with 15- and 30-amp electric. Open year-round. Sites C$25–C$30. 1300 Voight St. (✆ **250/378-6441;** www.claybanks rv.com).

Kamloops RV Park. Kamloops is a good major stop for stocking up on groceries and supplies, and a convenient place to stay overnight. The Kamloops RV Park has plenty of holiday diversions for the whole family, including two 18-hole golf courses only 5 minutes away. 83 sites have water and 30-amp electric and sewer connections. Sites C$35–C$40. 9225 Dallas Dr., 12 miles east of town on Hwy. 1 (✆ **250/573-3789;** www.kamloopsrvpark.ca).

Mile 0 RV Park and Campground. Dawson Creek marks Mile 0, the beginning of the Alaska Highway, with a half-dozen public and private RV parks and two pioneer villages. We like the Good Sam Mile 0 RV Park and Campground, which has 41 tree-shaded sites with water and 20- and 30-amp electrical hookups, 26 full hookups, restrooms, showers, a sanitary dump station, a Laundromat, and e-mail service. It's an easy stroll away from the Walter Wright Pioneer Village. You'll need reservations, because it seems as though everyone overnights in Dawson Creek to swap war stories. Sites C$22–C$41. Located at Mile 1.5. Call for reservations (✆ **250/782-2590**).

Northern Lights RV Park Ltd. Located in Dawson Creek, Northern Lights has an almost intimidating list of vehicle preparations before you set out on the Alaska Highway: lube and oil changes, windshield repairs, bug-screen installation, headlight protectors, tow-car protectors, and do-it-yourself RV wash for $5. Why you'd want to wash your RV on the way north is a mystery, but you'll certainly want to take care of it on the way back. The place also has 70 full hookups with 20- and 30-amp electric. Sites C$35–C$42. On Rte. 97 S., 1½ miles before Mile 0 (✆ **250/782-9433;** www. nlrv.com).

Ross H. Maclean Rotary RV Park. If everything in Dawson Creek is already spoken for, drive another 52 miles to this Good Sam RV Park in **Fort St. John.** There are 68 gravel sites, with 28 pull-throughs and 10 full hookups. Bring out your rod and reel for the boat ramp and lake fishing. Sites C$19–C$38 (✆ **250/785-1700;** http:// rotaryrvparkfsj.com/).

Sikanni River RV Park. Sikanni River RV Park, in the British Columbia community of Sikanni Chief, has 38 sites, 24 of them with 20-amp electric, along with 14 full hookups, restrooms and showers, security, LP gas, and firewood. Sites C$25–C$30. Mile 162, Alaska Hwy. (✆ **250/772-5400;** www.sikannirivercampground.ca).

Triple G Hideaway. The former Westend RV Park has 170 sites with water and 30-amp electric, and 128 full hookups. Sites C$20–C$30. Also in Fort Nelson on the west side of town (✆ **250/774-2340;** www.tripleghideaway.com).

Muncho Lake Provincial Park. The lake's icy waters are a gorgeous blue and turquoise from a combination of copper in the rocks and glacial runoff. There are 30 sites, 15 in each location (**Strawberry Flats Campground** and **MacDonald Campground**), with piped water, firewood, a boat launch, fishing, and hiking. Caribou, moose, and sheep are sometimes seen here, and bears may frequent the area. No hookups, no reservations. Sites C$15. Between miles 437 and 442 on the Alaska Hwy. in British Columbia (✆ **250/776-7000;** www.env.gov.bc.ca/bcparks/explore/ parkpgs/muncho_lk).

Liard River Hot Springs Provincial Park. This is the most popular park along the route, and its 53 sites fill up by noon (no reservations). Besides handsome, tree-shaded spots spaced well apart, campers will find free firewood and hot springs for soaking away travel aches, but no RV hookups. There are playgrounds, heated restrooms, and a wheelchair-accessible toilet. Bears sometimes prowl the area. Sites C$14–C$19. Mile 496 (✆ **250/776-7000;** www.env.gov.bc.ca/bcparks/explore/parkpgs/liard_rv_hs). There are RV hookups at the lodge across from the park.

Downtown RV Park. By the time you get to **Watson Lake** in the Yukon Territory, you and your RV will both be ready for a good bath. The Downtown RV Park throws in a free RV wash (it supplies the water; you supply the labor) when you stay overnight in one of the 78 full-hookup sites with 30-amp electric. Sites C$32. Mile 635, Alaska Hwy. (✆ **867/536-2646**).

Campground Services, Watson Lake. It has 100 sites with water and 30- and 50-amp electrical hookups, 64 full hookups, showers, a Laundromat, a grocery store,

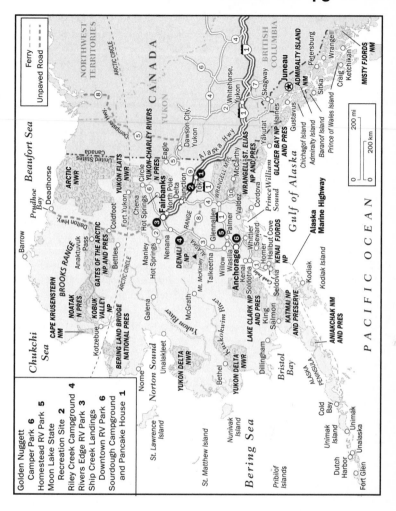

free Wi-Fi, LP gas, a dump station, an RV wash, and an adjacent service station. Sites C$10–C$30. Mile 632.5, Alaska Hwy. (© **867/536-7448**).

Dawson Peaks Resort & RV Park. Dawson Peaks Resort is famous along the route for its grilled Teslin lake trout and rhubarb pie. RVers will find 17 sites, with water and 15- and 30-amp electric, south of Teslin at Mile 769. Sites C$16–C$27 (© **866/402-2244;** www.dawsonpeaks.ca).

Whitehorse

Whitehorse marks a dividing point in the road. From here, you'll head north to Dawson City if you want to drive the Klondike Highway, then rejoin the Alaska Highway at Tok, Alaska.

THE YUKON

This is a destination for North Americans with a yen to wander, nagged by restlessness and an insatiable desire to see what lies at the end of the road. It is written in the faces of men wearing rumpled plaid shirts and blue jeans as they climb out of dirty, mud-streaked RVs and 4X4s with license plates from Florida, New Brunswick, Texas, California, and Ontario. They have made it to the place where the Yukon and the Klondike rivers meet, to the fabled city of gold and the end of the infamous Trail of '98.

Coming to Dawson City is like meeting a childhood idol or your favorite movie star 3 or 4 decades after the fact and being surprised to find the old dear is still alive, let alone lively enough to dance a fandango and tell a couple of salty tales.

Far from being some saccharine gold-rush theme park or horsehair-stuffed historical monument, Dawson is alive and kicking. Under the aegis of Parks Canada, where "money is always iffy," the town is slowly being renovated. Some buildings—like the splendid Palace Grand Theatre, the old post office, the Arctic Brotherhood Hall (now Diamond Tooth Gertie's Casino), and Madame Tremblay's store—have been restored. Others, sagging and unpainted, lean wearily against each other, waiting their turn and looking as though they won't last much longer.

Some of the wilder goings-on from earlier years are not in evidence lately. The "Miss Nude Yukon" contest has faded into obscurity, and the Eldorado's famous Sourtoe Cocktail—a pickled human toe (frostbitten and amputated) tossed into a beer mug of champagne—has moved over to the Downtown Hotel. But the annual Great International Outhouse Race and Bathroom Wall Limerick Contest are still on the Labor Day weekend agenda.

Today Dawson's biggest gold mine is **Diamond Tooth Gertie's Casino,** the first legal gambling casino in the Yukon.

Campground Oases: Dawson to Fairbanks

Gold Rush Campground. This is the best bet in downtown Dawson City, although the main appeal is its location within walking distance of the sights. There are 15- and 30-amp electrical connections, 49 of them full hookups, a sanitary dump station, and narrow parking lot–type sites. Reserve well ahead if you want a spot in midsummer. Sites $20–$40. 5th Ave. and York St. (© **867/993-5247;** www.goldrushcampground. com).

The Bonanza Gold Motel and RV Park. Located at the south end of Dawson City, this Good Sam Park has 73 full hookup sites with water and 30- and 50-amp electrical hookups, cable TV, and a Laundromat. Visitors can also try their hand at gold-panning or buy gold nuggets in a jewelry shop. Sites $20–$40. Bonanza Creek Rd. at the Klondike Hwy. junction (© **888/993-6789;** www.bonanzagold.com).

Westmark RV Park, Beaver Creek. The Westmark park has 67 sites with 20- and 30-amp electrical hookups and water. It's adjacent to the Westmark Inn if you want to treat yourself to a meal or two out. There's a lounge, a Laundromat, cable TV, a gift shop, showers, a wildlife display, and a sanitary dump. Sites $20–$27. Located at Mile 1202 (✆ **867/862-7501**).

Sourdough Campground. The RV park has 43 sites with 20- and 30-amp electrical hookups and water, and 23 full hookups. It's been voted "Alaska's Funnest" by Good Sam. There's a sanitary dump station, a Laundromat, showers, flush toilets, a cafe, a gift shop, a walk-through museum of Alaskan artifacts, and a car wash. The cafe specializes in sourdough pancakes. In season, there's evening entertainment and a "pancake toss." Sites $30–$45. Located in Tok, Alaska, 2 miles south on the Anchorage Hwy. (✆ **907/883-5543**).

Moon Lake State Recreation Site. Moon Lake has 15 campsites amid the trees by a beautiful lake. There are toilets, piped water, and a boat launch, but no hookups or reservations. Sites $15. On the Alaska Hwy. at Mile 1332, west of Tok (✆ **907/883-3686;** dnr.alaska.gov/parks/aspunits/northern/moonlksrs.htm).

FAIRBANKS

In 1902, when the Klondike excitement had quieted down a little, a prospector named Felix Pedro discovered gold in the Tanana Valley near present-day Fairbanks, and a new rush was on. The prospectors and gamblers from Dawson hurried west to the new boomtown, rode the crest of the wave, and then crashed in the depression that followed.

Vestiges of those days can still be seen in **Pioneer Park** (formerly Alaskaland)—located at Airport Way and Peger Road (✆ **907/459-1087;** www.co.fairbanks.ak.us/pioneerpark), and not as commercial as it sounds—where the history of the gold mining days is re-created. Original cabins, a replica Indian village, the Crooked Creek & Whiskey Island railroad with its little steam engine, and the stern-wheeler *Nenana,* one-time star of the Yukon riverboats, are all on display. There is no admission fee to the park, but some of the museums charge a nominal fee. You can park your RV in their parking lot up to 4 days for $12 per night, but there are no hookups.

From Fairbanks, you can take a paddle-wheeler day cruise along the Chena and Tanana rivers with **Alaska Riverboat *Discovery.*** The boat sails at 8:45am and 2pm, and tickets cost $55 adults, $38 children 3 to 12 (✆ **866/479-6673** or 907/479-6673; http://riverboatdiscovery.com). Take a multiday motorcoach excursion along the Dalton Highway, following the Trans-Alaska Oil Pipeline farther into Prudhoe Bay than private vehicles can go, through the **Northern Alaska Tour Company.** It offers a wide variety of 1-day and fly/drive tours. Check the website for availability (✆ **800/474-1986** or 907/474-8600; www.northernalaska.com).

When in Alaska, do as the tourists do and take in a salmon bake: the **Alaska Salmon Bake** at Pioneer Park ($31). Follow it up with an after-dinner musical about life in Fairbanks, held at 8:15pm in summer at the Palace Theatre and Saloon ($18). Call for information about the salmon bake and musical (✆ **800/354-7274;** www.akvisit.com/salmonbake.htm).

Pioneer Park is one of the sights to see in Fairbanks.

Campground Oasis: Fairbanks

Rivers Edge RV Park. Rivers Edge has 170 sites with 30-amp electrical hookups, 115 full hookups, a sanitary dump station, a Laundromat, showers, and free shuttle service to attractions such as the stern-wheeler *Discovery* and the Alaska Salmon Bake. Located on the Chena River, it allows fishing and has a boat ramp. Sites $24–$32. Off the Parks Hwy. in Fairbanks. There is a shuttle to local attractions. Call for reservations (© **800/770-3343** or 907/474-0286; www.riversedge.net).

DENALI NATIONAL PARK

Denali means "the high one" in the language of the local Athabascan people, and it's the official designation for the former Mount McKinley National Park. It's also the original Native designation for 20,320-foot Mount McKinley itself, renamed in 1917 for an assassinated president who never saw it. (The mountain is still called Denali by most Alaskans, Native and non-Native alike, although repeated attempts to change it back officially have been unsuccessful.) The 4-million-acre Denali Park, slightly bigger than the state of Massachusetts, includes a **wilderness area** and a **national preserve;** sport hunting, fishing, and trapping are allowed in the latter by state permit.

Denali State Park (**http://dnr.alaska.gov/parks/units/denali1.htm**), southeast of the national park area, is bisected by Parks Highway, which is named for George Parks (a territorial governor in the 1920s), not for the two major parks that lie along it.

Denali National Park

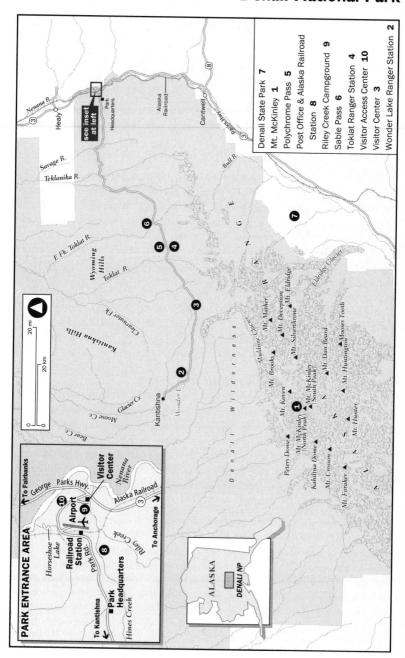

Denali State Park **7**
Mt. McKinley **1**
Polychrome Pass **5**
Post Office & Alaska Railroad Station **8**
Riley Creek Campground **9**
Sable Pass **6**
Toklat Ranger Station **4**
Visitor Access Center **10**
Visitor Center **3**
Wonder Lake Ranger Station **2**

see inset at left

Nenana R.

Healy

Park Headquarters

Alaska Railroad

Cantwell

Parks Hwy.

Savage R.

Teklanika R.

E. Fk. Toklat R.

Wyoming Hills

Toklat R.

Clearwater Fk.

Kantishna Hills

Glacier Cr.

Moose Cr.

Bear Cr.

Kantishna

Wonder L.

Denali Wilderness

Mt. Mather

Muldrow Glacier

Mt. Deception

Mt. Eldridge

Mt. Silverthrone

Eldridge Glacier

Mt. Brooks

Mt. Dan Beard

Moose's Tooth

Mt. Koven

Mt. McKinley (South Peak)

Mt. Huntington

Peters Dome

Mt. McKinley (North Peak)

Kahiltna Dome

Mt. Crosson

Mt. Hunter

Mt. Foraker

A L A S K A   R A N G E

Bull R.

20 mi

20 km

PARK ENTRANCE AREA

To Fairbanks

George Parks Hwy.

Visitor Center

Nenana River

Alaska Railroad

To Anchorage

Horseshoe Lake

Airport

Riley Creek

To Kantishna

Railroad Station

Park Rd.

Park Headquarters

Hines Creek

ALASKA

DENALI NP

DENALI TIP

If you don't have a day or two to wait for space on the free park shuttles, advance tickets for the Wildlife Tours into Denali National Park can be obtained by calling **Denali Park Resorts** (✆ **800/276-7234**; www.denaliparkresorts.com). Tours cost $150 adults, $75 children.

With rare exceptions, you cannot drive through Denali, but must park near the visitor center and take one of the shuttle buses run by **Denali Park Resorts** (✆ **800/276-7234** reservations or 907/272-7275; www.denaliresorts.com). The bus takes you into the park and allows you to hop on and off at various stops to explore on foot (shuttles come by every half-hour or so). The park entrance fee is $20 per family, $10 per person, and is good for 7 days. Walk-in reservations for the shuttles begin 2 days out. If it's a busy time, desirable shuttle reservations are snapped up early, and you may have to wait until the next day. On the other hand, you could get lucky, as the flow of visitors rises and falls unpredictably.

The information desk at the **Denali National Park Visitor Access Center,** Denali Park Road, a half-mile from the park entrance (✆ **907/683-2294**; www.nps.gov/dena), is the easiest place to get Park Service information. Stop here for the park map. For advance shuttle reservations, contact the number above.

Campground Oases: Denali to Anchorage

Riley Creek Campground. Riley Creek, at **Denali,** has 147 well-separated and tree-shaded sites not far from the railway station. Sites have flush toilets and piped water in summer, and there's a sanitary dump station, but no hookups or slide-outs. An overnight or two at Denali will allow time to get a spot on the park service shuttle bus. There's a 14-day maximum stay. After mid-June, any empty sites are usually filled as soon as the previous tenant pulls out. Sites $22–$28. Follow the signs in the park for directions to campground (✆ **907/683-2294**; reservations: ✆ 800/622-7275; www.reservedenali.com).

The Homestead RV Park. In **Palmer,** Alaska, the Homestead is handily located in the Matanuska Valley near the junction of the Parks Highway between Denali and Anchorage and the Glenn Highway between Tok and Anchorage. With the long hours of summer, you can commute to Anchorage for dinner and get home before dark, as well as walk to a trout fishing stream, go hiking, and take in a square dance on Thurs nights. There's Wi-Fi, and some 63 sites have water and 20- and 30-amp electrical hookups. Sites $30–$34. Mile 36.2, Glenn Hwy. (✆ **907/745-6005**; www.homesteadrvpark.com).

ANCHORAGE

In the bush country, they like to say, "The nicest thing about Los Anchorage is that it's only 30 miles from Alaska."

People who don't know Alaska usually visualize Anchorage as being an icy outpost in the wilderness populated by moose, grizzly bears, and bush pilots. True, you will find moose and bears—most often in the Anchorage Zoo—and plenty of bush pilots taking off and landing at Lake Hood. But the first time we arrived there, on a July day, it was warmer and sunnier than Los Angeles and bright with summer flowers. On our most recent May visit, however, it was cold and windy and socked in with fog.

Earthquake Park, on the west end of Northern Lights Boulevard, still shows graphically the results of the 9.2 earthquake on Good Friday in 1964, when two huge chunks of earth fissured and dropped 20 feet in an instant. "It looked like chocolate pudding somebody had been dragging their fingers through," one eyewitness said.

A statue of Captain James Cook looks out on **Turnagain Arm,** so named when the captain told his first mate William Bligh to turn the ship around when it was discovered the place was not the Northwest Passage he was seeking.

The fine **Anchorage Museum of History and Art,** in a stylish building with a frieze of Alaskan designs across the top, displays an excellent collection of contemporary Alaskan and Native arts and crafts. Admission is $12 adults, $9 seniors, $7 children. 121 W. Seventh Ave. (© **907/929/9201;** www.anchoragemuseum.org).

Chilkoot Charlie's Rustic Alaskan Bar says it all, and notes in its ad: "We cheat the other guy and pass the savings on to you!" It's open 7 nights a week with live entertainment, burgers, and brews. 2435 Spenard Rd. (© **907/272-1010;** www. koots.com).

Campground Oases in Anchorage

Golden Nugget Camper Park. Just outside of town, from the junction of Glenn Hwy. and Bragaw St., go south ¾ mile to 4100 De Barr Rd. There are 215 sites, including 190 full hookups with 30-amp electric, along with picnic tables, Wi-Fi, and TV. Sites $40–$45 (© **800/449-2012** or 907/333-2012; www.goldennuggetcamper park.com).

Ship Creek Landings Downtown RV Park. Close to Anchorage's downtown area, Ship Creek Landing faces the railroad tracks and Ship Creek. The 150 full hookups provide city water, 20- and 30-amp electric, and Wi-Fi. You can walk to shopping,

---

INSIDER TIP: ALASKAN TRAFFIC JAMS

Don't attempt to drive down to the Kenai Peninsula on a summer weekend; it's bumper-to-bumper traffic heading south from Anchorage on Friday afternoons and heading north back to town on Sunday nights and Monday mornings.

fishing areas, the farmers' market, and also to rail, boat, and bus excursions. Sites $26–$47. 150 N. Ingra St. at E. 1st Ave. Call for reservations (℃ **888/778-7700** or 907/277-0877).

Seven Tough Side Trips & Three Easy Ones

TOUGH TRIPS

1. **The Top of the World Highway (Yukon Rte. 9).** The Top of the World, from Dawson City to Eagle, is 146 miles of unpaved, white-knuckling terror. You'll talk about it for years, especially if you go early in the season when half the roadway is still covered with ice and snow. There are no guardrails and few markers to indicate whether you're still on the roadway or have ventured off onto a side road that peters out in the tundra. Eagle, where author John McPhee set much of his classic *Coming into the Country* (Farrar, Straus and Giroux, 1991), is an optional destination at the end of the rough, narrow road. There's been a trading post here for gold miners since the 1880s, and today Eagle is populated by some 150 pioneers, curmudgeons, and refugees from urban life.

2. **The Taylor Highway.** From Eagle to Tetlin Junction are 161 miles of rough road, with the biggest metropolis en route being the town of Chicken, population 37. There's a saloon, a cafe, a gas station, and two gift shops where you can buy T-shirts with slogans like I GOT LAID IN CHICKEN, ALASKA. The old mining town is off the main road and closed to visitors, except on a daily guided walking tour or gold-panning venture in summer. The original settlers wanted to name it after the ptarmigan, the plump little edible grouse that was a dietary mainstay, but since they couldn't spell it, they called the town Chicken instead.

3. **The Dalton Highway.** This road to Prudhoe Bay takes you across the Arctic Circle, the Brooks Range, and the Continental Divide, but you might have to stop a few miles short of Prudhoe Bay itself; the oil companies sometimes limit access. The 414-mile road was constructed to build and service the Alaska pipeline, and there are very few services available along it. Before setting out, call the **Alaska Department of Transportation** (℃ **800/437-7021;** www.dot.state.ak.us) for a recording that will give you road conditions and an update on how far you'll be able to drive. In some years, it's open only to Dietrich Camp, about halfway down the highway.

4. **Canada's 456-mile Dempster Highway.** The Dempster Highway crosses the Arctic Circle at Mile 252 after striking north from Dawson City and Klondike Hwy. 2. Its final destination is the Northwest Territories' Inuit village of Inuvik, with 57 days of midnight sun beginning on May 24 each year. The gravel road, with some slippery clay surface sections, also requires two ferry crossings; the most feasible time to go is between mid-June and the end of August. Black flies and mosquitoes are also a problem, so take plenty of repellent. You may spot wolves, caribou, grizzly bears, moose, eagles, and gyrfalcons.

Allow 2 days in each direction to drive this tough tundra route. Government campgrounds are spotted along the road, but few services are available. Stop for gas whenever you see an open station. Experts recommend carrying at least two spare tires.

5. **Atlin Road (Yukon/BC 7).** From Jake's Corner, Mile 836, turn south for a 58-mile scenic route to Canada's Little Switzerland, with its snowcapped mountains and lakes with prime fishing. You have a good chance of spotting moose or grizzly bears. The all-weather gravel road is fairly good, although winding and slippery in wet weather. The **Atlin Visitors Association** (© **250/651-7522**) can provide updated road information for you.

6. **The Cassiar Highway (BC 37).** The Cassiar drops south from Mile 726 west of Watson Lake down to the Yellowhead Hwy. 16. It's also possible to use the Cassiar as an alternative to the Alaska Highway between Prince George and Watson Lake. A lot of adventuresome drivers prefer this route, which they liken to driving the Alaska Highway in the '50s and '60s. There are some stretches of gravel instead of road, and services are few and far between, but the scenery, from hanging glaciers to snowcapped mountains, is stunning. Watch out for the logging trucks. Call for **road conditions** (© **800/550-4997;** www.drivebc.com).

7. **Wrangell–St. Elias National Park and Preserve.** Chitina, the gateway to this 13-million-acre park, is reachable by the paved, 33-mile Edgerton Highway, running from the Richardson Highway, which is the route between Tok and Valdez. Only small RVs or four-wheel-drive vehicles without trailers should attempt the next 58 miles of unpaved, steep, and sometimes slippery road into McCarthy, but the effort is worth it. The privately owned copper company town of Kennicott, now a ghost town, can be visited by hikers crossing the Kennicott River via a hand-operated cable tram (wear thick gloves). Guided glacier walks, Kennicott tours, backcountry hikes, and horseback riding are available in McCarthy. Ask for road conditions in Chitina at the **National Park Service Ranger Station** (© **907/823-5234;** www.nps.gov/wrst).

EASY TRIPS

1. **Visiting Barkerville, BC.** From Quesnel, BC, take Route 26 over to the Cariboo gold rush town of Barkerville, in its heyday the largest city north of San Francisco and west of Chicago. More than 125 original and restored buildings, many of them occupied by costumed docents, are open, including **Lung Duck Tong Chinese Restaurant, Eldorado Gold Panning,** the **Wake-Up-Jake Restaurant,** and **McPherson's Watchmakers Shop.** A historic stage stop called **Cottonwood House** is also on the route; the round-trip from Hwy. 97 is 100 miles. The best time to visit is between June 1 and Labor Day. Call the **Barkerville Reception Centre** (© **888/994-3332** or 250/994-3332; www.barkerville.ca).

2. **Klondike Hwy. 2.** The Klondike, between Whitehorse and Skagway (99 miles south), via Carcross (short for Caribou Crossing), looks nothing like the precipitous trail, lake, and river route followed by the prospectors of '98. Most of them were ill-equipped cheechakos who were required by the Northwest Mounted Police to carry a ton of supplies to the gold fields. A few had horses and some had "sled dogs" that were usually poodles or terriers stolen from Seattle backyards. But most had to carry the stuff on their backs, caching it along the trail, then doubling back for more supplies. Skagway, at the end of the road, is the town where sharpies like gambler Soapy Smith and his cronies fleeced the innocent. The two-lane paved asphalt road is fairly wide.

3. **Turnagain Arm, Alyeska & Portage Glacier.** From Anchorage, drive south along the Arm, keeping an eye out for whales. Stop at Alyeska, Alaska's top ski resort (the lifts take you sightseeing in summer) and the Portage Glacier with its self-guided nature trail to the ice worms. If time permits, keep going south to the town of Seward or take the Sterling Highway to Homer and the Kenai Peninsula.

The Dakotas: Black Hills & Buffalo Burgers

NORTH DAKOTA IS WHERE TEDDY ROOSEVELT SHOT A BUFFALO, where Peggy Lee learned to sing, and Lawrence Welk learned to talk (he spoke only German until he was 21), where Cream of Wheat was invented, and thin Norwegian pancakes called *lefse* are the state dish.

It's where native son Louis L'Amour learned his ABCs, and Roger Maris got to first base playing for the Fargo American Legion team as a kid. Here, Angie Dickinson was born, rodeo great Casey Tibbs first saddled a horse, and Sitting Bull surrendered. The Space Aliens Grill & Bar is next door to the Kmart in Bismarck, and New York–style bagels are explained to the locals as "like bread with an attitude."

North Dakota is where the film *Fargo* (1996) didn't take place (you betcha!), and although it's the least-visited state in the union, tourism is its third-largest industry. It could also be called the golf capital of America, since it boasts more golf links per capita than any other state.

South Dakota is where Kevin Costner danced with wolves, where the buffaloes roam, and where cows outnumber people five to one. It's where Wild Bill Hickok was gunned down, and where the Black Hills Motorcycle Classic in Sturgis draws as many as 300,000 bikers every August. The town also boasts the National Motorcycle Museum and Hall of Fame.

You can tour North America's largest gold mine or watch the world's biggest mountain carving under construction. Reminisce at the Amateur Baseball Hall of Fame in Lake Norden, or slurp a soda at a 115-year-old marble fountain in a grocery store where Hickok's killer sought refuge.

Both states cover two time zones. South Dakota hosts the annual Lewis & Clark Cribbage Classic in July, the Sitting Bull Sailboard Regatta in August, and the Jesse James Bicycle Stampede in September. North Dakota gets a little more down-to-earth with Irrigation Days in Oakes in June, Coteau Hill's Annual Beef Barbecue and Cow Penning in Forbes in July, and Sauerkraut Day in Wishek in October.

RVing the Dakotas

The West happens suddenly when you arrive at the Missouri River on highways paved with the rose-colored, local rock. Tumbleweeds roll across the road, and the grasslands sway in a persistent wind.

If you pull off South Dakota's I-90 at exit 263, you can walk over to a bluff and look down at the Missouri River, which, together with the Mississippi, makes up the longest stretch of river on earth. In North Dakota, you get a similar sensation on I-94 crossing the Missouri between Bismarck and Mandan.

Lewis and Clark and their 40-man expedition traveled through these waters in their search for a waterway to the Pacific. They were paid $2,500 for their 8,000-mile, 862-day journey, and spent almost one-third of their time traversing the Dakotas.

HITTING THE HIGHLIGHTS

If you've got 2 weeks for your holiday and live on one of the coasts, you might consider flying to the Dakotas and renting an RV there (see chapter 14, "To Rent or Buy?" for a list of nationwide rental outfits). That way, you can take your time sightseeing, hiking, fishing, learning to pan gold, or watching a mountain being carved.

Mount Rushmore itself doesn't take that long; you can drive by, take a snapshot from the parking lot, and move on. But the **Black Hills** and **Badlands** deserve more time, especially if you're interested in outdoor activities and seeing wildlife, and the two units of **Theodore Roosevelt National Park** should be seen.

If you have an RV-load of kids or your taste is jejune, you'll find more than enough gee-whiz commercial attractions around **Rapid City:** Bear Country USA, a drive-through wildlife park; Reptile Gardens; Evans Plunge water complex; the Flintstones Bedrock City Theme Park and Campground; the Wild West Wax Museum; Rushmore Water Slide Park; Pioneer Auto Museum; Mountain Music Show; Ghosts of Deadwood Gulch Wax Museum; Cosmos Mystery Area; Wonderland Cave; and Big Thunder Gold Mine.

GOING FOR THE LONG HAUL

If you want to spend more than 2 or 3 weeks on your Dakotas visit, aim for fall and try to avoid the peak summer months. Spring is also a possibility, but the weather can be cold and rainy.

Depending on where you begin, it might take awhile to get to and from the Dakotas. The side trips described in this chapter are spread out around both states.

Although there's a tremendous summer demand for campsites in the Black Hills, you might be able to arrange a seasonal stay in a commercial RV park or work as a campground volunteer in one of the state or national parks or national forests. (See "Become Campground Hosts" in chapter 3, "Where to Sleep: Campgrounds & RV Parks.")

If time and money are no problem, you might consider adding on a trail ride with a pack horse or hiking the 111-mile Centennial Trail. (See "Five Active Adventures," later in this chapter.)

Winter camping in the area, while not for everyone, could include plenty of cross-country or downhill skiing. Terry Peak near Lead is South Dakota's primary ski area, while North Dakota's Turtle River State Park is open in winter for sledding and cross-country skiing.

North Dakota Highlights

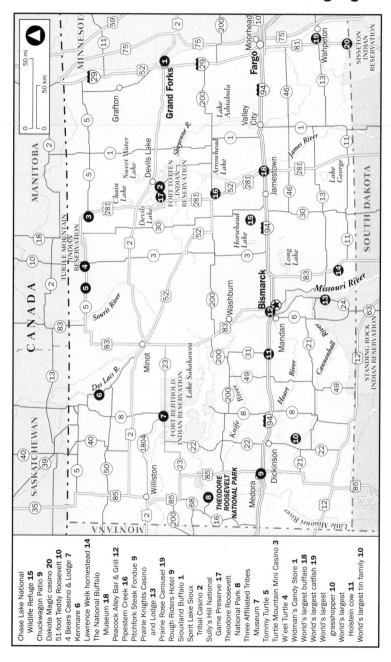

Chase Lake National
Wildlife Refuge **15**
Chuckwagon Patio **9**
Dakota Magic casino **20**
51-foot Teddy Roosevelt **10**
4 Bears Casino & Lodge **7**
Kenmare **6**
Lawrence Welk homestead **14**
The National Buffalo
Museum **18**
Peacock Alley Bar & Grill **12**
Pipestem Creek **16**
Pitchfork Steak Fondue **9**
Prairie Knights Casino
and Lodge **13**
Prairie Rose Carousel **19**
Rough Riders Hotel **9**
Siouxland Buffalo **1**
Spirit Lake Sioux
Tribal Casino **2**
Sully's Hill National
Game Preserve **17**
Theodore Roosevelt
National Park **8**
Three Affiliated Tribes
Museum **7**
Tommy Turtle **5**
Turtle Mountain Mini Casino **3**
W'eel Turtle **4**
Widman's Candy Store **1**
World's largest buffalo **18**
World's largest catfish **19**
World's largest
grasshopper **10**
World's largest
Holstein cow **11**
World's largest tin family **10**

Travel Essentials

WHEN TO GO

The ideal time is late August or September, when the trees are changing color, but the sun still warms the air. However, some attractions and campgrounds start closing down in September. Early August is when motorcyclists head for Sturgis, and all summer the South Dakota campgrounds and attractions are crowded with tourists. On the other hand, North Dakota isn't crowded even on the Fourth of July. Late spring and early summer can be almost as good as late summer, but sometimes cool and rainy.

WHAT TO TAKE

Bring hiking boots, cameras and enough memory cards so you can take lots of photos, binoculars, a gold pan if you're planning to camp in the Black Hills National Forest, and fishing tackle for dry-fly trout fishing or lake-bass fishing.

WHAT TO WEAR

Summers can be very hot, but in spring and fall the temperature is cool in early morning and at night, so dress in layers. Nowhere, including Deadwood's casinos, is the attire very dressy, so camping and RV clothing will fit in anywhere.

TRIMMING COSTS ON THE ROAD

Once you get to the admittedly remote Dakotas, you'll find prices modest. And if hearty Midwestern home cooking is to your taste, restaurant fare is inexpensive all over both states.

If you can visit the casinos and avoid gambling, meals are especially cheap there. If you're traveling with children, beware of commercial attractions no matter how "educational" they purport to be, because you'll end up spending more than you'd like.

In heavily touristy **Rapid City,** skip the big commercial attractions, and instead ask for the city-tour brochure listing 10 free family attractions. Start at the **Rushmore Plaza Civic Center** (© 605/394-4115; www.gotmine.com), 444 Mount Rushmore Rd. N., where the Visitor Information Center has directions for following the city circle tour, marked by buffalo head signs. The **Dahl Fine Arts Center** at 7th and Quincy (© 605/394-4101; www.thedahl.org) features work by local Indian artists and a cyclorama of American history with lighted highlights and taped narration. The **Museum of Geology,** on the campus of the South Dakota School of Mines at 501 E. St. Joseph (© 605/394-2467; http://museum.sdsmt.edu), shows the dinosaurs that once roamed the Badlands; after the museum, head for the **Dinosaur Park** on Skyline Drive, where the kids can climb aboard the outdoor dinosaurs. Adults might enjoy that too, since the park is open until 10pm and the city lights make a great view. Take Quincy west from its junction with West Boulevard, an extension of I-190. Quincy Street turns into Skyline Drive. The park is about 1 mile west of the intersection of Quincy and West (© 605/343-8687).

Staying in campgrounds without hookups when possible always saves money, but in summer they may be hard to find. Check at the city park in many South Dakota towns, where camping is often free.

South Dakota Highlights

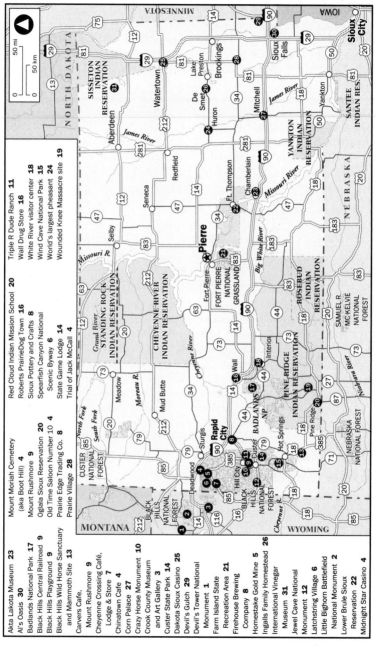

Akta Lakota Museum **23**
Al's Oasis **30**
Badlands National Park **17**
Black Hills Central Railroad **9**
Black Hills Playground **9**
Black Hills Wild Horse Sanctuary
  and Mammoth Site **13**
Carvers Cafe,
  Mount Rushmore **9**
Cheyenne Crossing Café,
  Lodge & Store **7**
Chinatown Cafe **4**
Corn Palace **27**
Crazy Horse Monument **10**
Crook County Museum
  and Art Gallery **3**
Custer State Park **14**
Dakota Sioux Casino **29**
Devil's Gulch **9**
Devil's Tower National
  Monument **1**
Farm Island State
  Recreation Area **21**
Firehouse Brewing
  Company **8**
Homestake Gold Mine **5**
Ingalls Family Homestead **26**
International Vinegar
  Museum **31**
Jewel Cave National
  Monument **12**
Latchstring Village **6**
Little Bighorn Battlefield
  National Monument **2**
Lower Brule Sioux
  Reservation **22**
Midnight Star Casino **4**

Mount Moriah Cemetery
  (aka Boot Hill) **4**
Mount Rushmore **9**
Oglala Sioux Reservation **20**
Old Time Saloon Number 10 **4**
Prairie Edge Trading Co. **8**
Prairie Village **28**

Red Cloud Indian Mission School **20**
Roberts PrairieDog Town **16**
Sioux Pottery and Crafts **8**
Spearfish Canyon National
  Scenic Byway **6**
State Game Lodge **14**
Trial of Jack McCall **4**

Triple R Dude Ranch **11**
Wall Drug Store **16**
White River visitor center **18**
Wind Cave National Park **15**
World's largest pheasant **24**
Wounded Knee Massacre site **19**

WHERE TO GET TRAVEL INFORMATION

The **South Dakota Department of Tourism,** 711 E. Wells Ave., Pierre, SD 57501, will send you a handsome free vacation guide on request; and its nine welcome centers at major highway entrances to the state are stocked with all kinds of information helpful to an RVer (© **800/SDAKOTA** [732-5682]; www.state.sd.us or www.travelsd. com).

You can also contact the **Black Hills Badlands & Lakes Association,** 900 Jackson Blvd., Rapid City, SD 57702 (© **605/355-3760;** www.blackhillsbadlands.com), and **North Dakota Tourism,** 1600 E. Century Ave., Ste. 2, Bismarck, ND 58505 (© **800/HELLO-ND** [435-5663] or 701/328-2525; www.ndtourism.com).

Another resource is the **Rapid City Convention and Visitors Bureau,** 444 Mount Rushmore Rd. N. (© **800/487-3223** or 605/718-8484; www.visitrapidcity. com).

DRIVING & CAMPING TIPS

- **Rent a recorded narration.** Drivers entering South Dakota can rent an audio CD, "South Dakota Stories" about the state from the tourist information offices at the border for $20; $15 is refunded when you turn it back in, or you can mail it back. In exchange, you get a series of anecdotes, songs, and historical narratives about the state, and they're timed for each stretch of the roadway.

- **Watch for low and narrow passes.** The narrow roads and tunnels in the Black Hills might present problems for extra-wide or long RVs. The maximum RV size that can safely negotiate Iron Mountain Road, Route 16A, is 12 feet, 6 inches high and 8 feet, 6 inches wide. On State Hwy. 87 around Sylvan Lake, anything larger than 10 feet, 8 inches high or 8 feet, 7 inches wide can't make it through the tunnels; on Needles Highway, the limit is 11 feet, 5 inches high and 8 feet, 7 inches wide. When checking your width, be sure to include the side mirrors; when checking height, don't forget the antennae and air-conditioning units on the roof.

The Best Dakotas Sights, Tastes & Experiences

OFF-THE-WALL ATTRACTIONS

Wall Drug Store. Only the most travel-hardened curmudgeon could refuse to turn off I-90 into **Wall,** South Dakota, to see the richly advertised wonders of Wall Drug Store at 510 Main St. It started small back in 1931 with road signs promising free ice water for hot, thirsty travelers, and has grown into a monumental Western-themed mall of shops, restaurants, museums, and entertainment, which draws 20,000 visitors a day in summer. The ice water is still free, and a cup of coffee costs a nickel. Daily 7am–10pm (© **605/279-2175;** www.walldrug.com).

The Corn Palace, Mitchell, South Dakota. Located at 604 N. Main St. in Mitchell, the Corn Palace is unique. It's a Taj Mahal of chicken feed: its walls, domes, and

The Corn Palace graces Mitchell, SD.

turrets newly covered every year with elaborate murals made of corn—bushel after bushel of red, calico, and white corn—augmented with oats and prairie grass. The decoration is replaced with a new theme every September, when Corn Palace Week carries out the corn motif with concerts by performers like Myron Floren and the Stars of Lawrence Welk and a 3-day polka festival. One version or another of the Corn Palace has been here for more than 100 years. Admission is free, except during the Corn Palace festival. Dec–Mar Mon–Sat 8am–5pm; Apr to Memorial Day and Labor Day to Nov daily 8am–5pm; Memorial Day to Labor Day daily 8am–9pm. Contact the **box office** (✆ **605/995-8430;** www.cornpalace.org) and the **Convention & Visitors Bureau,** 601 N. Main St. (✆ **605/996-6223;** www.visitmitchell.com).

Crazy Horse Memorial, North of Custer, South Dakota. The world's largest mountain carving is so big that all four heads on Mount Rushmore would fit inside the chief's head. Begun in 1947 by the late Polish-American sculptor Korczak Ziolkowski in response to a request from Lakota chief Henry Standing Bear, the monument is being carried on by Korczak's wife and large family with donations and private funding. The finished sculpture will be 641 feet long and 563 feet high when completed sometime this millennium. A multimedia laser light show is held at 9pm in summer. Memorial Day to early Oct daily 7am–9:30pm; visitor complex year-round daily 8am–5pm. Admission $10 adults, $27 carload. The memorial is north of Custer on U.S. 385 (✆ **605/673-4681;** www.crazyhorse.org).

The Crazy Horse Memorial remains a (huge) work in progress.

Mount Moriah Cemetery (aka Boot Hill), Deadwood, South Dakota. This ceme- tery is where Calamity Jane and Wild Bill Hickok ended up side by side with match- ing rock mounds and white granite tombstones. Wild Bill was shot in 1876 by Crooked Nose Jack McCall; Jane died in 1903, so it looks like she called the shots for who was buried with whom. Midnight is a popular time to visit the graves. Contact the **Deadwood Visitors Bureau** (✆ **800/999-1876;** www.deadwood.org).

Old Time Saloon Number 10, Deadwood, South Dakota. Catch a reenactment of the shooting of Wild Bill Hickok, presented at 1, 3, 5, and 7pm, as Hickok plays out the famous Deadman's Hand at the poker table: a pair of aces, a pair of eights, and the nine of diamonds (✆ **800/952-9398;** www.saloon10.com).

The Trial of Jack McCall, Deadwood, South Dakota. This 60-year-old audience- participation performance recruits onlookers as jurors when it depicts the capture and trial of the man who shot Wild Bill Hickok. A clue: McCall most often gets off, just as he did at the original trial. Tues–Sun 8pm. Free admission, but reservations are required. In the Masonic Temple at the top of Main St. Contact the **Visitors Bureau** (✆ **800/999-1876;** www.deadwood.com).

The Carvers Cafe at Mount Rushmore. This cafeteria has a great close-up view of the carved presidents' heads and the memory of Cary Grant running amok through the tourists in Alfred Hitchcock's film *North by Northwest* (1959). On the buffet line, you'll find a Monumental Breakfast consisting of cereals, eggs and bacon, pancakes, and so on, as well as Jeffersonian Gourmet Salads, Americana Stew, or Teddy's Bison Chili. Daily 7am–9pm. 13000 Hwy. 244, in Keystone (✆ **605/574-2515;** www. mountrushmorenationalmemorial.com/carverscafe/1882).

Devil's Gulch. This is where Jesse James and his horse, hotly pursued after the failed bank robbery in Northfield, Minnesota, jumped across a 20-foot-wide chasm to clear the 50-foot-deep gulch, leaving the dumbfounded posse behind. It's located near Garrotson, 10 miles north of I-90 at the first exit past the Minnesota/South Dakota border.

The world's largest pheasant. At 40 feet high and 22 tons, it stands by U.S. 14 in Huron, about 50 miles north of Mitchell. It proclaims Huron as the "Pheasant Capital of the World."

The International Vinegar Museum, Roslyn, South Dakota, provides the chance to see vinegar in the making, observe vinegar art, taste and sniff, and learn more about vinegar than you could possibly imagine. 502 Main St. June–Oct Thurs–Sat 10am–6pm. Admission $2 adults, $1 children (✆ **605/486-0075;** www.vinegarman.com).

The Crook County Museum and Art Gallery, Sundance, Wyoming. Located just across the border from the Black Hills in Sundance, Wyoming, the jumping-off town for Devil's Tower, this museum displays the courtroom where Harry Longabaugh was sentenced to 18 months in jail for stealing horses. His nickname, "Sundance Kid," came from his time in this jail; the town's name came from the sun dance ceremony performed in summer by the Sioux on the mountain back of town. Free admission. Mon–Fri 8am–5pm. Located in lower level of Crook County Courthouse (✆ **307/283-3666;** www.crookcountymuseum.com).

The buffalo is commemorated in this statue in Deadwood.

Giant men and giant animals. In a burst of civic pride, North Dakota gives drivers along the interstates a gee-whiz respite from turnpike tedium: the **world's largest buffalo,** 26 feet high, 46 feet long, and 60 tons, but strangely androgynous when you take a closer look (at exit 258 off I-94 in Jamestown); the **world's largest Holstein cow,** 38 feet high and 50 feet long (at exit 124 off I-94 in Salem); the **world's largest catfish,** the Wahpeton Wahpper (off I-29 at exit 23), the **world's largest pheasant,** 20 feet tall, 40 feet long, atop the Huron liquor store, Huron; and the **world's largest tin family,** the **world's largest grasshopper,** and a **51-foot Teddy Roosevelt** made from livestock watering tanks, sickles, barbed wire, and other discarded scrap metal (off I-94 at exit 72 along the Enchanted Hwy. btw. Gladstone and Regent).

The National Buffalo Museum. Sitting in the shadow of the world's biggest buffalo (see above), this museum protects the world's most sought-after buffalo, the rare (one birth in a billion) female albino White Cloud. Considered sacred by ancient North American tribes, the white buffalo is thought to be a sign of great things to come. The resident herd, which includes White Cloud, can sometimes be seen from the museum's deck on the hillside above the pastures. The parking lot is big enough for RVs to turn around; museum admission is $5 adults, $4 seniors, $1 students, $10 families. The adjacent Frontier Village (free) has historical buildings moved here, along with a general store that sells souvenirs and North Dakota food products and a leather goods store selling locally made hats, belts, and moccasins. Daily May–Sept 9am–5pm. Located at the junction of I-94 and U.S. 281, exit 258, at 500 17th St. SE. (© 800/802-1511 or 701/252-8648; www.buffalomuseum.com).

Giant turtles. Turtles, too, are big in North Dakota. Tommy Turtle is a 33-foot-high turtle riding a snowmobile on Route 5, near the junction of Route 14 in Bottineau, in the north central area of the state. W'eel Turtle is a giant crawling turtle made of 2,000 discarded tire rims at the junction of U.S. 281 and Route 3 in Dunseith. Both towns are in the Turtle Mountains near the International Peace Garden. Call the **Bottineau Chamber of Commerce** (© 701/228-3849; www.bottineau.com/chamber.htm).

Prairie Rose Carousel, Wahpeton. This restored 1926 Spillman with 29 handcrafted wooden horses and two chariots is one of only 150 operating carousels in the United States. It's located in Chahinkapa Park on Route 13, off I-29 at exit 23 in Wahpeton, North Dakota, in the southeast corner of the state. Memorial Day to Labor Day daily 10am–6pm. For information, call the **Wahpeton Visitors Center** at 118 N. 6th St. (© 800/892-6673; www.wahpetonbreckenridgechamber.com).

The Lawrence Welk homestead, Strasburg. This is a pilgrimage site for the Welk faithful, although the maestro left here the day he turned 21, carrying his accordion, a train ticket, and $3 in cash. The wood-sided sod house of the Welk family is typical of those occupied by Germans from Russia, who settled North Dakota around the turn of the 20th century, after fleeing first from Alsace to the Ukraine and then to America. Take exit 182 off I-94 and drive south on U.S. 83 to Strasburg, then west on a marked but unpaved road. Mid-May to mid-Sept Thurs–Sun 10am–5pm. Admission $5 adults, $3 children. Call for appointment (© 701/336-7103).

THE DAKOTAS GAMBLING SCENE
Deadwood, South Dakota

Thanks to its 80 licensed casinos, the once-dormant town of Deadwood looks as bustling as it must have in 1876, when 25,000 miners came looking for gold, and Calamity Jane and Wild Bill Hickok were an item. Today, at least that many tourists are still looking for gold, an early lunch, or a T-shirt that reads MY GRANDMA WENT TO DEADWOOD AND ALL I GOT WAS THIS LOUSY T-SHIRT.

The casino was put in place on the premise that gambling would generate funds to restore the deteriorating town, a National Historic Landmark. (Old-timers have some lively ongoing discussions about what is and isn't historic.) Gambling originally went on in Deadwood until 1947, its proponents pointed out, and brothels did discreet business until 1980. Gambling was restored in 1989, and now summer visitors gamble as much as $1 million a day, which should be enough to gold-plate the historic buildings in a few years. A lot of restoration has already been completed. Day and evening variety shows with cowboys and dance-hall girls are plentiful, along with live music for dancing, dinner theater suitable for the whole family, and the nightly reenactment of "the Trial of Jack McCall," about the man who shot Wild Bill Hickok.

RVers will find bright green trolleys to shuttle them from the edge-of-town RV parking lots to the casinos along the main street.

The old Western town of Deadwood draws visitors to its many casinos.

Elsewhere in South Dakota

The **Lower Brule Sioux reservation** allows card games and coin slots, and herds of buffalo and elk roam in the vicinity. Take exit 248 at Reliance and drive north 15 minutes to Lower Brule. For information, call the **Alliance of Tribal Tourism Advocates** at 522 7th St., Rm. 210, in Rapid City (© **605/791-1058;** www.attatribal.com).

The **Dakota Sioux Casino** in **Watertown** runs blackjack, poker, poker machines, and progressive slots, and it has a bar and restaurant. Watertown is 100 miles north of Sioux Falls on I-29 (© **800/658-4717;** www.dakotanationgaming.com).

North Dakota

North Dakota has five tribal casinos: **4 Bears Casino & Lodge** located 4 miles west of New Town, in northwest North Dakota, at the junction of routes 8 and 23 (© **800/294-5454;** www.4bearscasino.com); **Dakota Magic** off I-29, exit 2, south of Hankinson (© **800/325-6825;** www.dakotanationgaming.com); **Spirit Lake Sioux Tribal Casino,** 6 miles south of Devils Lake on Route 57 (© **800/946-8238;** www.spiritlakecasino.com); **Turtle Mountain Mini Casino,** at U.S. 281 and Route 5 in Belcourt (© **701/477-6438;** www.500nations.com/casinos/ndTurtleMountainMini.asp); and **Prairie Knights Casino and Lodge,** 44 miles south of Mandan on Route 1806 (© **800/425-8277;** www.prairieknights.com). All of these casinos feature Las Vegas–style gambling and headliner entertainment.

A HALF-DOZEN SPLURGES IN THE DAKOTAS

1. **Take a helicopter tour around Mount Rushmore's faces.** You'll get good close-up photos to wow the neighbors back home. The choppers cover only side and distant views; you won't fly into George Washington's nostril. **Black Hills Aerial Adventures,** $49 to $189 (© **605/673-2163;** www.coptertours.com).

2. **Take a couple of days at the Triple R Dude Ranch in Keystone, South Dakota,** especially if you have kids age 7 or older who can go with you on trail rides into the Black Elk Wilderness Area. Fishing, swimming, easy game-spotting, and cookouts supplement the daily wilderness and breakfast rides. Call for details (© **605/666-4605;** www.guestranches.com/tripler).

3. **Hop aboard the 1880 steam-engine Black Hills Central Railroad.** It's a 20-mile chug through the Black Hills along some of the steepest grades in North America. You can get aboard in Hill City or Keystone. Tickets $24 adults, $12 children 3 to 14. Call for the schedule and reservations (© **605/574-2222;** www.1880train.com).

4. **Invest in museum-quality reproductions of Sioux artifacts,** such as the distinctive hand-thrown pottery with Western motifs available at **Sioux Pottery and Crafts,** 1441 E. St. Joseph St., Rapid City (© **800/657-4366;** www.siouxpottery.com).

5. **Head to Prairie Edge Trading Co. & Galleries** at Sixth and Main streets in Rapid City, for reproductions of Plains Indian beadwork and beadwork supplies, quilts, blankets, and other Native American items (© **800/541-2388;** www.prairieedge.com).

6. **Visit Pipestem Creek.** One of our favorite offbeat shops, Pipestem Creek creates dried floral wreaths and bird feeders from grasses and flowers grown on the family ranch. SunFeeders and SunFlorals are two of the products built around giant dried sunflower heads. Birds love them! On Route 9 south of **Carrington** in the center of North Dakota. Weekdays 8am–4pm. Call for a catalog (© **701/ 652-2623;** www.pipestemcreek.com).

TAKEOUT (OR EAT-IN) TREATS

Cheyenne Crossing Café, Lodge & Store, Cheyenne Crossing. Breakfasts at Cheyenne, at U.S. 85 and the Spearfish Canyon Rte. 14A, feature sourdough pancakes, homemade sausage and gravy, eggs and buttermilk biscuits; lunch brings buffalo burgers and Indian tacos. Daily 7:30am–4pm, 8pm on weekends. 21415 U.S. Hwy. 14A (© **605/584-3510;** www.cheyennecrossing.org).

Chinatown Cafe, Deadwood. Funny, we don't remember ever seeing *Gunsmoke*'s Amanda Blake dishing up chop suey. Daily 11:30am–2pm and 5–10pm. Located in Miss Kitty's Gaming Saloon, 649 Main St., in Deadwood (© **605/578-7778;** www. deadwood.com).

The Chuckwagon Patio, downtown Medora. The Chuckwagon, at 3rd Ave. near 3rd St., serves barbecued chicken and ribs of beef brisket for less than $6 (Sat only 4:30–7:30pm). Eat inside in the air-conditioning or outside at the open-air picnic tables (© **701/623-4444;** www.medora.com).

The Firehouse Brewing Company, Rapid City. Firehouse Brewing Company makes boutique beers while you watch, and serves homemade pub food to go with them. Mon–Thurs 11am–10pm; Fri 11am–11pm; Sun 3–9pm. 610 Main St. (© **605/348-1915;** www.firehousebrewing.com).

Visit the Big Spud in Grand Forks. In September, join the party to celebrate Potato Bowl USA, with french fry day, a potato queen, pancake breakfast, and football game. Contact the **Grand Forks Convention and Visitors Center** (© **701/746-0444;** www.visitgrandforks.com).

Peacock Alley Bar & Grill, Bismarck. Despite its prestige and romantic 19th-century ambience, Bismarck's Peacock Alley Bar & Grill serves homemade dishes. Daily 11am–2pm and 4:30–10pm. Located at 422 E. Main St. (© **701/255-7917;** www. peacock-alley.com).

The Pitchfork Steak Fondue, Medora. Imagine Grant Wood's painting *American Gothic,* but with rib-eye steaks impaled on the tines of the farmer's pitchfork. That's the general idea of Pitchfork Fondue, a pre-theater dinner buffet served at the outdoor theater before the *Medora Musical* (performed from June to Sept) in an open-air pavilion with a great view on all sides. The 12-ounce rib-eye steaks are impaled on each tine and immersed in vats of boiling oil. The buffet also includes raw vegetables with dip, fruit salad, coleslaw, rolls, butter, baked potatoes, and baked beans. It's served at 6:30pm sharp; $21 and $26 adults, with a $6 hot dog meal for kids 12 and under.

Show tickets $36–$55. Advance reservations required. It all takes place at the Burning Hills Amphitheatre on the marked drive off the west end of Pacific Ave. in Medora (© **800/633-6721** or 701/623-4444; www.medora.org).

Widman's Candy Store, Grand Forks. The Red River flooded disastrously in 1997, and Widman's was one of the first downtown businesses to reopen after the waters receded. The store was more fortunate during the 2011 flooding. This charming candy box of a store is famous for its Widman's Chippers: Red River potatoes cut and cooked into ruffled chips, then hand-dipped in chocolate. Thicker, less salty, and more like a candy bar than the chocolate-dipped Maui potato chips from Hawaii, the Widman's Chippers are cheaper, too, at $12 a pound. Midwestern chocolate humor dictates novelty candies such as Moo Pies, Moose Muffins, and such. The Widman family has other shops in **Fargo** and in **Crookston, Minnesota,** across the river from Grand Forks. Grand Forks store: Mon–Sat 8:30am–5:30pm. Located at 106 S. Third St. (© **701/775-3490;** main store in Fargo, **800/688-8351** or 701/281-8644).

BRING ON THE BUFFALO

According to the U.S. Department of Agriculture, **buffalo meat** is lower in fat, calories, and cholesterol than either beef sirloin or chicken breast, with more protein per gram than beef and no growth hormones, stimulants, or antibiotics. Typical Dakota recipes for buffalo include steaks, roasts, salami, sausage, hamburger, and jerky. Here are some places to sample it or see it running around the prairie, preprocessed:

1. **The Rough Riders Hotel, Medora, North Dakota.** The hotel's Theodore Roosevelt dining room offers a full menu. Located at 3rd St. and 3rd Ave. in Medora. Call for reservations (© **701/623-4444;** www.medora.com).

2. **Siouxland Buffalo, Grand Forks, North Dakota.** Chuckwagon buffalo burgers and a gen-u-wine Buffalo Gift Shop are found at the Earl Buffalo Farm, Route 2 in Grand Forks. Daily 8am–5pm (© **701/772-1594**).

3. **Al's Oasis, outside Sioux Falls, South Dakota.** Buffalo burgers South Dakota–style are the big seller at Al's. Al's is also famous for homemade pie and 5¢ coffee. Located about halfway between Sioux Falls and the Black Hills, off exit 260 on I-90. Daily 6:30am–10pm (© **605/234-6051;** www.alsoasis.com).

4. **Wall Drug Store, Wall, South Dakota.** Wall stars buffalo burgers at the top of its tourist menu, along with hot beef sandwiches, homemade doughnuts, pies, cinnamon rolls, 5¢ coffee, and free ice water. Daily 7am–6pm. Take exit 109 or 110 from I-90 (© **605/279-2175;** www.walldrug.com).

5. **State Game Lodge, Custer State Park Resort, South Dakota.** Spicy buffalo-sausage and biscuits make a great breakfast or midmorning snack at the lodge's **Dining Room.** It's on U.S. 16, east of the junction with Rte. 87 in southwestern South Dakota. Daily 7am–9pm (© **605/255-4541;** www.custer resorts.com).

6. **Custer State Park buffalo safari, South Dakota.** Take a buffalo safari ride, which leaves from the State Game Lodge and goes into the backcountry to see some of the park's 1,400 bison. Admission: $40 adults, $30 children. Located

on U.S. 16 east of the junction with Rte. 87 in southwestern South Dakota (℃ **605/255-4541;** www.sdgfp.info/parks/directory/custer/index.htm).

7. **Custer State Park buffalo roundup, South Dakota.** In late Sept or early Oct, the bison are rounded up, branded, vaccinated, and sorted to separate the culls for a Nov auction. Entrance fee: $6 per person or $15 per carload (℃ **605/255-4515;** www.gfp.sd.gov/state-parks/directory/custer/events/buffalo-roundup.aspx).

DANCES WITH NATIVE AMERICANS

The success of Kevin Costner's Oscar-winning film *Dances with Wolves* (1990) brought a lot of attention to South Dakota. Ever since then, visitors have wanted to learn more about the Lakota people and the achingly beautiful film locations. The film was shot in South Dakota, much of it at a private ranch near Pierre called Roy Houck's Triple U Ranch, home of the world's largest privately owned herd of 3,500 bison. From the Sioux community came 150 extras, along with consultants on the Lakota language and tribal customs. At the end of the shoot, many props and costumes were auctioned to local buyers, so if you run across someone claiming to have original artifacts from the film, you can probably believe him. Props can be seen at the Akta Lakota Museum in Chamberlain (see below). Costumes are on display at the Midnight Star Casino in Deadwood.

Guided van tours into this area are provided by **Affordable Adventures of Rapid City** ($40–$115; ℃ 605/342-7691; www.affordableadventuresbh.com).

You can go on your own to the winter camp location in **Little Spearfish Canyon.** Ask for directions at **Cheyenne Crossing Store,** at the junction of highways 14A and 385, open daily 7:30am to 4pm (℃ **605/584-3510;** www.cheyennecrossing.org); or at **Latchstring Village,** on Hwy. 14A in Spearfish Canyon (℃ **605/584-3333;** www.spfcanyon.com), 20 minutes from Deadwood or Spearfish, and famous for fresh trout and buttermilk pancakes. It's open daily 7am to 9pm in summer only.

The **Akta Lakota Museum** is a fine Lakota Sioux cultural and heritage museum; take the Chamberlain exit 263 off I-90 and drive 2 miles north into town. The museum is free and open daily 8am to 6pm in summer, closed November to April. Besides arts and artifacts, you'll find Lakota-made crafts for sale in the gift shop (℃ **605/234-3300;** www.stjo.org). **St. Joseph Indian School** in Chamberlain also welcomes visitors (℃ **800/798-3452;** www.aktalakota.org). For information, call the **Chamberlain Area Chamber of Commerce** (℃ **605/234-4416;** www.chamberlainsd.org).

Other central and western South Dakota reservations welcome visitors, including the **Cheyenne River Sioux Tribe,** in the center of the state. It celebrates with various powwows in the summer and gives tours of its 100-head bison herd, along with hunting and fishing opportunities.

The **Crow Creek Sioux Tribe,** in the middle of the state, allows for walleye fishing and has a powwow and fair during the third week of August. For information, call the **Chamberlain Area Chamber of Commerce** (℃ **605/234-4416;** www.chamberlainsd.org) or the **Alliance of Tribal Tourism Advocates** (℃ **605/545-3351;** www.atta tribal.com).

The Pine Ridge reservation for the **Oglala Sioux Tribe** in southwest South Dakota is the second largest in the United States and adjoins Badlands National Park. For Sioux tourism, call **Tribal Tourism** (© **605/791-1058;** www.attatribal.com). The **White River visitor center at Badlands** is south of the South Unit of Badlands National Park, Route 27, about 20 miles north of the Wounded Knee battlegrounds; tribal crafts are sold, and the **Cuny Table Cafe** sells Indian tacos. The **Red Cloud Indian Mission School** on Route 18 near Pine Ridge presents an art show representing 30 different tribes, and there's a gift shop, open on weekdays. The **Oglala Fair, Rodeo, and Powwow** is held during the first weekend in August. The **Wounded Knee memorial** is also on the reservation.

In North Dakota, where the various Native American tribes are, as a group, commonly referred to as Sioux, visitors are welcome to help celebrate powwows throughout the spring and summer. You can join tribal members in dancing when the powwow announcer calls for an "intertribal" dance. One of the biggest is the **United Tribes International Powwow in Bismarck** just after Labor Day (© **701/255-3285,** ext. 1234; www.unitedtribespowwow.com). Ask the **North Dakota Tourism Department** (© **800/435-5663;** www.ndtourism.com) for a full list, or contact individual tribal groups for their own special events: Mandan, Hidatsa, and Arikara, the **Three Affiliated Tribes in New Town** (© **701/627-4781;** www.mhanation.com); **Spirit Lake Sioux Tribe in Fort Totten** (© **701/766-4221;** www.spiritlakenation. com); or **Standing Rock Sioux Tribe in Fort Yates** (© **701/854-8500;** www.standing rock.org).

Powwow Protocol

- **Take along your folding chairs** from the RV since seats are at a premium.

- **Stand for the grand entry,** when the flags are brought in; there may be two grand entries a day. Remain standing during the opening prayer. When in doubt, do as the people around you.

- The program generally begins with a grand entry, then come honor songs, followed by men's traditional dancing in several categories, then women's traditional dancing, then children's dancing. **You're not permitted to film some parts of the ceremony;** the announcer will tell you when cameras are prohibited. Otherwise, you may photograph the groups of dancers in performance, but be sure to ask permission before photographing an individual not in performance.

- **It is also a Native American tradition to give money or other gifts** when a performance has stirred you; you may follow this example if you want, but should not feel compelled to do so.

FIVE ACTIVE ADVENTURES

1. **Fishing the Black Hills.** Head for one of the 14 lakes or 1,300 miles of streams in the Black Hills in pursuit of rainbow, brook, or brown trout. Fishermen at Lake Pactola have set state records with a 22-pound brown trout and a 15-pound lake trout. Deerfield is best for catching brook trout. Try fly-fishing

in Rapid Creek, Spearfish Creek, Castle Creek, and French Creek in Custer State Park. Lakes in the park are stocked, but you may catch some wild trout as well. You can also snag walleyes, bass, bluegills, perch, crappies, and bullheads. Buy a license first: You can purchase one online at **http://gfp.sd.gov/licenses/general-hunt-fish/default.aspx**, or in person at a local office.

2. **Dakota golfing.** Golf courses may include hazards like deer grazing on the fairways or beaver dams by the water holes. You'll find 12 courses around the Black Hills with various degrees of difficulty. Meadowbrook Municipal in Rapid City and Boulder Canyon Country Club near Sturgis are considered the toughest. For more information on golfing, call the **Rapid City visitor bureau** (© **800/487-3223** or 605/718-8484; www.visitrapidcity.com) and the **Sturgis Chamber of Commerce** (© **605/347-2556;** www.sturgis-sd.org).

3. **Horseback riding.** Riders can find more than a dozen outfitters with everything from hour-long rides to a 10-day pack trip on the Centennial Trail in the Black Hills. If you bring your own horse along, you'll find "horse camps" with corrals, water wells, feed bunks, picket posts, and stock-trailer parking, with room for your RV as well. **Dakota Badland Outfitters** lead full- and half-day trail rides into the Badlands (© **605/574-3412;** www.ridesouthdakota.com). **Gunsel Horse Adventures** in Rapid City runs 4-, 7-, and 10-day adventure treks into the Badlands and Black Hills, for about $325 a day, with everything included (© **605/343-7608;** www.gunselhorseadventures.com).

4. **Canoeing the Missouri and Sheyenne rivers.** You'll be saying proudly, "I can canoe" after a beginner's river-paddling trip. Rentals and shuttle services for the Missouri River in North Dakota can be arranged at the **Lewis and Clark Café** in Washburn (© **701/462-3668**), or at **Cross Ranch State Park,** in nearby Hensler (© **701/794-3731;** www.ndparks.com). Along the shyer Sheyenne, also in North Dakota, you can go canoeing while camped at **Fort Ransom State Park;** rentals are available (© **701/973-4331;** www.ndparks.com). Always call ahead and ask about river conditions. (See "Campground Oases in North Dakota," later in this chapter, for directions to the park.)

5. **Fishing for paddlefish.** The prehistoric paddlefish, a 75- to 100-pound freshwater billfish, runs in North Dakota's Yellowstone and Missouri rivers from early May to late June. Locals promise that once you hook one of these fighting fish, you're hooked forever. Contact the **North Dakota Game and Fish Department,** 100 N. Bismarck Expwy., Bismarck, ND 58501 (© **701/328-6300;** www.gf.nd.gov).

WILDLIFE-WATCHING

The Great Plains were once dark with 60 or 70 million **buffaloes,** and while not many remain, you'll still see a surprising number of small herds, particularly in Custer State Park, where they like to graze around the State Game Lodge. Between 400 and 500 bison calves are born each spring in the park.

Also in Custer State Park, you might see bighorn sheep, mountain goats, coyotes, pronghorn antelope, white-tailed deer, mule deer, and, rarely, elk.

As president of the United States, Theodore Roosevelt originally set aside **Sully's Hill National Game Preserve** near North Dakota's Devils Lake for a national park in 1904, but it was turned into a game reserve to save the endangered American bison. Now, at 2½ square miles, it's the biggest "zoo" in the Midwest, with not only bison and elk, but also **prairie dogs, white-tailed deer, foxes, swans, ducks,** and **geese,** and sometimes **bald** and **golden eagles.** A 4-mile Big Game Auto Tour route is best in early morning and early evening. Admission is free. It's open May 1 to October 31, and it's 12 miles south of Devils Lake on Hwy. 57. Call for information (© **701/766-4272;** www.fws.gov/sullyshill).

The largest breeding colony of **white pelicans** in the United States can be seen at **Chase Lake National Wildlife Refuge,** 23 miles northwest of Medina; take exit 230 off I-94. To see snow geese, visit **Kenmare** on U.S. 52 in northwestern North Dakota, host to hundreds of thousands of migrating **snow** and **blue geese** in the fall (© **701/752-4218;** www.fws.gov/arrowwood/chaselake-nwr).

On the Road: South Dakota

THE BADLANDS

Geologists and Great Plains aficionados will claim this national park got a bad rap when the first men to record their impressions, French-Canadian trappers, called the area *les mauvaises terres à traverser* ("bad lands to travel across"). But if you stand alone listening to the wind, singing a solitary song and imagining yourself tracking your way across it, you'll understand their observations.

The Badlands of South Dakota.

Dakota prairie dog (and friend).

Wind and water wreaked havoc with erosion, delivering an endless landscape of folds and crags and gullies, canyons, spires, and pinnacles. The austerity of this landscape is relieved only faintly in spring with a fuzzy green outline of fresh grass, which is burned down to the bone again in the summer heat.

This region was once lush grassland in the Oligocene epoch 35 million years ago, and the plains now hold the fossilized bones of prehistoric animals. About 10 million years later, volcanoes erupted to the west in what is now Yellowstone National Park, and the rich lands were covered with layers of white ash. Rains lessened, and dry winds from the north continued the sculpting. But over millions of years, life forms adapted and the bison and Rocky Mountain bighorn sheep were reintroduced somewhat recently.

If the loneliness begins to get you down, forge ahead on the **Badlands Loop Road** and take the **Creek Rim Road** northwest for 5 miles toward **Roberts Prairie Dog Town,** which is 5 miles beyond the State Route 240 turnoff to Wall. The social, short-tailed prairie dogs seem tremendously busy as they go about their daily chores, ignoring the occasional hungry coyote or badger that stands by waiting to pounce. They pop up from a hole, stand on their hind legs, and look around, emitting a sharp barking cry as if to signal their friends below.

LITTLE BIGHORN & WOUNDED KNEE

The **Little Bighorn Battlefield National Monument (www.nps.gov/libi)**, just off I-90 and 286 miles from Rapid City at the town of Crow Agency, Wyoming, commemorates the battle that lasted less than an hour on a hot June day in 1876. A force of 1,500 Sioux and Cheyenne warriors led by Sitting Bull wiped out Custer's troops

The gravestones
at Little Bighorn.

while two other battalions of the regiment were on a distant ridge. Custer, underestimating the Plains Indian forces, had decided to divide his 600 troops into thirds to create a pincers action, then attacked without waiting for the others.

The battlefield is a riveting spot, still haunted, still mysterious. From a visitor center, you walk uphill to a fenced cemetery with tombstones naming the soldiers where they were believed to have fallen, insofar as the names were known. A mass grave under a hilltop monument contains the remains that have not been removed by relatives. It is debated whether the bones exhumed in 1877 and reburied at West Point are actually those of Custer.

Although eyewitness accounts vary widely, it is thought that perhaps 150 braves died in the battle.

Signs at the site caution visitors to watch out for rattlesnakes; one wonders if the snakes were there on the day of the battle. The monument is open from June to September only.

The **Wounded Knee Massacre site** is south of the Black Hills on Route 27, a few miles north of the Nebraska border on the Pine Ridge reservation, headquarters for the Oglala Sioux. In 1889, Native Americans experienced growing pressure from occupying military forces, which had banned their traditional sun dance ceremony. So they turned to other spiritual pursuits, including the use of peyote cactus tips to induce visions. The Ghost Dance ritual, introduced by a Paiute mystic, was done under the premise that whites would be eliminated in a flood, the vanished game and all the Indians' dead kin would come back, and Indians would return to the old ways.

Little Bighorn Battlefield National Monument

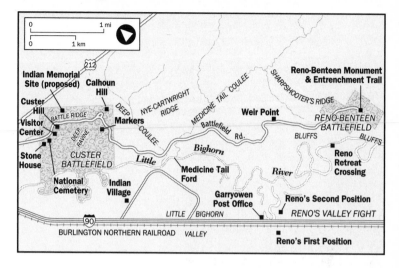

Troops were ordered in to stop the ritual dances, and on December 15, 1890, Chief Sitting Bull was shot while troops attempted to arrest him. A total of 350 Sioux, under the command of Big Foot, were among the last groups to be caught by the 500 cavalrymen; they were led to a military camp at Wounded Knee Creek. A medicine man called for the young warriors to resist being disarmed; fighting broke out and cannons and carbines tore apart the camp. More than 150 of the Sioux, many of them women and children, were killed on the spot, and 44 others did not recover from their wounds.

The battlefield at Wounded Knee was the scene of demonstrations in the 1970s, when 200 Indian militants fought off law-enforcement officers and occupied the village for 70 days.

MOUNT RUSHMORE & THE CRAZY HORSE MEMORIAL

The best time to see **Mount Rushmore** (**www.nps.gov/moru**) is in early morning, and the best vantage points are the carved rock tunnels that frame the mountain from Alternate U.S. 16 heading north, also called Iron Mountain Road. The 17-mile route is narrow with pigtail bridges and one-way tunnels, some of them a tight fit for big RVs. If you're early enough, you may glimpse deer, bighorn sheep, raccoons, and some buffaloes on the drive through Custer State Park.

The mountain itself got its name by accident, when a gold miner in a claim litigation was riding past with his recently arrived eastern lawyer, who was named Rushmore. The lawyer asked the name of that mountain, and the miner, as a joke, said, "It's Mount Rushmore." And so it became.

Sculptor Gutzon Borglum, who started work on Mount Rushmore in 1927 when he was 60, was a man of boundless energy, a prolific sculptor (175 of his works are in

Mount Rushmore is a favorite destination for RVers.

the Cathedral of St. John the Divine in New York City), and a controversial and argumentative character. He charmed President Calvin Coolidge and his wife, who stayed in the State Game Lodge on their 1927 visit to dedicate the sculpture, by hiring a small plane, flying over the lodge, and swooping down to drop a bouquet of wild-flowers to the First Lady.

The Custer Connection

The last big gold rush in the contiguous United States was set off by the discovery of gold in French Creek by a civilian prospector tagging along with Lt. Colonel George Armstrong Custer in 1874. (A major general during the Civil War, Custer was reappointed a lieutenant colonel after the war.) The flamboyant Custer, dressed in buckskins, rode at the head of a 1,000-man company of soldiers, scientists, newspaper correspondents, and miners, ostensibly surveying for a railroad, but actually checking out the possibility of gold in the Black Hills. The area had been designated part of the Great Sioux Reservation only 6 years earlier by the Treaty of Laramie, presumably before rumors of gold in the area had reached Washington.

There was also one woman in the group, Sally Campbell, the cook for sutler John Smith. She stayed in the Black Hills, staking a gold claim and, in her later years, enjoyed telling stories about her adventures. As a non–Native American, she has gone down in history as "the first white woman in South Dakota," despite her African roots.

Black Hills

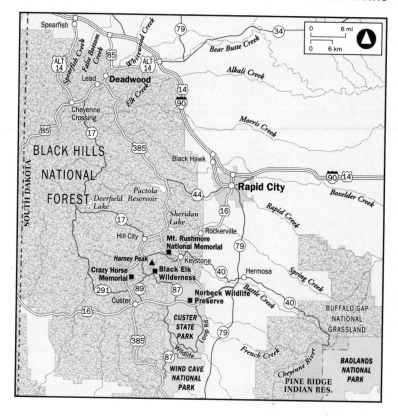

Borglum wanted to add a Hall of Records on the mountainside so that future archaeologists wouldn't think Americans of the mid–20th century worshiped giant stone figures. He even persuaded Coolidge to write a text for a Hall of Records dedication, but then sat down and rewrote it to his own taste and released it to the newspapers as the president's work, infuriating the taciturn Coolidge.

It was also on his agenda to finish the figures as busts, carved down to the waist, and to remove the stone rubble and build an amphitheater; however, shortly after he died in 1941, work ceased on the project.

Korczak Zielkowski, the sculptor of the nearby **Crazy Horse Memorial,** worked for a while with Borglum at Rushmore, but the two men did not always get along. Zielkowski began his work in 1947, and since his death in 1982, his wife and 10 children have continued the project, working from private donations and monies from admission to the site with its museum, shop, and restaurant. It's located on U.S. 385 north of Custer at the Avenue of the Chiefs (© 605/673-4681; www.crazyhorse memorial.org).

GOLD-PANNING COURTESY

Don't pan for gold anywhere except in the streams of the Black Hills National Forest or at commercial attractions that promote it. Otherwise, you run the risk of trespassing or claim-jumping—"there's still gold in them thar hills."

CAMPGROUND OASES IN SOUTH DAKOTA

Mount Rushmore/Hill City KOA. The closest campground to Mount Rushmore provides free shuttle service to the evening lighting ceremonies at Mount Rushmore and the Crazy Horse Memorial. Some 184 RV sites have full hookups, flush toilets, showers, and fire grates. There's a swimming pool, a sanitary dump, a restaurant, a playground, and a pond for trout fishing. Sites are close together in parking-lot style, although some have trees and/or grass. The place is modem-friendly and has cable TV, along with horses and cars for rent, a water slide (fee), hayrides, movies, and Indian dances. Sites $43–$72. The campground is on Rte. 244 btw. Hill City and the Four Faces, reached from U.S. 16 at S.R. 244, then 3 miles east (✆ **800/KOA-8503** [562-8503] or 605/574-2525; www.koa.com).

Mystery Mountain Resort. Next to Bear Country USA on the road to Mount Rushmore Road, Mystery Mountain should please families looking for lots to do. It has a playground, a heated 50-ft. pool, a hot tub, shade trees, and hiking trails. There are 42 tree-shaded, full-hookup sites with 30- and 50-amp electric, and a modem-friendly office. Sites $39–$38. 13752 Hwy. 16 out of **Rapid City** (✆ **800/658-CAMP** [2267] or 605/342-5368 reservations; www.blackhillsresorts.com).

Lazy J RV Park and Campground. The Lazy J in **Rapid City** has campsites with views and terraces, daily bus tours of the region, car rentals on the premises, and a big heated pool and spa. There are 126 sites with water and 30- and 50-amp electrical hookups, and sewer hookups at 66 sites. There's plenty of room for big rigs. Sites $25–$43. It's at 4110 S. Hwy. 16, off exit 57 of Rte. 90, followed by a 4-mile drive south (✆ **605/342-2751** reservations; www.lazyjrvpark.com).

Cedar Pass Campground. Cedar Pass has 100 sites with flush toilets, piped water (in summer), and a sewage disposal station. A fee is charged in summer, but not in winter when the water is off. No hookups, no reservations. Sites $10. Located near the Ben Rifel Visitor Center in the **Badlands National Park** on Rte. 240 (✆ **605/433-5361**; www.nps.gov/badl, reservations: www.reserveusa.com).

The Black Hills National Forest Campgrounds. Six campgrounds at **Hill City and Keystone** have a total of 321 sites suitable for RVs, most with piped water, picnic tables, fire grates, and pit or flush toilets, but no hookups or disposal stations. Closest to Mount Rushmore and most popular is **Horsethief Lake** at **Keystone** with 36 sites.

South Dakota Campgrounds

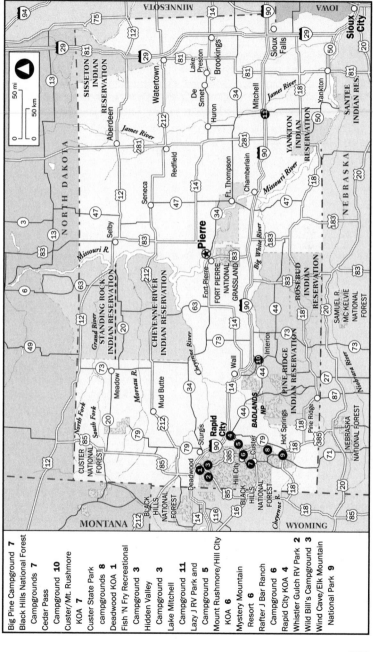

Big Pine Campground **7**
Black Hills National Forest
    Campgrounds **7**
Cedar Pass
    Campground **10**
Custer/Mt. Rushmore
    KOA **7**
Custer State Park
    campgrounds **8**
Deadwood KOA **1**
Fish 'N Fry Recreational
    Campground **3**
Hidden Valley
    Campground **3**
Lake Mitchell
    Campground **11**
Lazy J RV Park and
    Campground **5**
Mount Rushmore/Hill City
    KOA **6**
Mystery Mountain
    Resort **6**
Rafter J Bar Ranch
    Campground **6**
Rapid City KOA **4**
Whistler Gulch RV Park **2**
Wild Bill's Campground **3**
Wind Cave/Elk Mountain
    National Park **9**

South Dakota Nightlife

If the ruckus in Deadwood doesn't appeal to you, you can go to Mount Rushmore to sing the national anthem and watch the lights around the presidents' heads (it doesn't take long, and it doesn't cost anything). Hit a campfire program at one of the parks, attend a free Thursday night band concert in Rapid City (© **800/487-3223;** www.visitrapidcity.com), or catch the **Black Hills Playhouse** productions of vintage Broadway shows—showtime 8pm, $37 adults, $15 children. Call for reservations (© **605/255-4141;** www.blackhills playhouse.com). 🚐

Sites $21–$23. From Rapid City, take Hwy. 16 south to Hill City. Take Hwy. 16/385 south to Custer (© **877/444-6777** or 605/574-4402).

Big Pine Campground, Custer. Big Pine has 74 sites with 30-amp electric and water, and 42 sites with full hookups, all of them pine-shaded and fairly well spaced. It also has flush toilets, showers, a sanitary dump, a Laundromat, a playground, and limited groceries. Sites $32–$39. It's 2 miles west of Custer on Rte. 16 W. (© **800/235-3981** or 605/673-4054 reservations; www.bigpinecampground.com).

Rafter J Bar Ranch Campground. Located in **Hill City,** the grounds have 156 sites, 130 with full hookups, in 160 acres of ponderosa pines. You can choose a campsite near the pool and playground or a more secluded spot back in the trees. There are supervised pony rides for kids, flush toilets, showers, a sanitary dump, a Laundromat, and satellite TV, along with a grocery store and RV supplies—and a trout stream runs through it. Sites $31–$48. Take Rte. 16 south to Hill City; go 3 miles and follow the signs (© **888/RAFTER-J** [723-8375] or 605/574-2527 reservations; www.rafterj. com).

Custer State Park. Custer Park has some first-come, first-served spaces in each of its seven campgrounds. The areas most accessible to larger RVs are **Game Lodge Campground** with 59 sites, **Legion Lake** with 26 sites, and **Stockade Lake** with 66 sites. Paved camping pads, fire grates, and picnic tables are supplied, and there's a dump station at Game Lodge. None of the campgrounds have hookups. The park accepts some campsite reservations. Sites $18. From Rapid City, take Hwy. 79 to Hwy. 36; Hwy. 36 turns into Rte. 16A in Custer Park (© **605/255-4515;** www.custerstatepark. info).

Custer/Mount Rushmore KOA. This KOA has 43 sites, most of them shaded by pine trees, all with electricity and water, and 41 with sewer facilities. The place has flush toilets, showers, a sanitary dump, a Laundromat, a grocery store, a heated swimming pool, optional chuckwagon breakfasts and buffalo barbecue dinners, and car rentals. Sites $35–$54. It's 3 miles west of Custer on Rte. 16 (© **800/KOA-5828** [562-5828] or 605/673-4304; www.koa.com).

Rapid City KOA. This campground is a bit closer to Rapid City: Take exit 61 off I-90, then go 2½ miles south to Hwy. 44, and go left at the stoplight to the campground. You'll find 139 sites with 30-amp electric, 89 of them with full hookups. Deluxe patio sites have 50-amp electric and can cost up to $66. A large, 50-ft. pool is heated and a mini–golf course is nearby. There's also Wi-Fi and two Laundromats. Mid-Apr to mid-Oct. Sites $36–$66 (© **800/562-8504** or 605/348-2111; www. rapidcitykoa.com).

Wind Cave/Elk Mountain National Park. Located in **Hot Springs,** south of Custer State Park, Wind Cave Park has a year-round campground with no hookups and no reservations. Flush toilets and piped water are available in summer. Hiking, wildlife viewing, and guided tours of the caves are among the attractions, as well as a popular ranger-led "night prowl" every evening after the campfire programs. Tents and RVs with slide-outs are not permitted, and there are pet restrictions. Sites $15. From Rapid City, take Rte. 79 south to Hot Springs. Take Hwy. 385 north directly into the park (© **605/745-4600;** www.nps.gov/wica).

Deadwood KOA. At the closest campground to the gambling casinos, you'll enjoy a free shuttle bus to town and gold-panning in Deadwood Creek, if you want to kill two urges with one stop. The terraced campground is on the side of a hill, but the entrance road has been improved and shouldn't hamper a big rig, although sites large enough for them are limited. The KOA has 56 sites with 30-amp electric and water, 39 with full hookups, plus a heated pool, a playground, a grocery store, a Laundromat, and a dump station. Sites $34–$44. From the junction of U.S. 85 and U.S. 14A (in Deadwood), head west 1 mile on 14A (© **800/KOA-0846** [562-0846] or 605/578-3830; www.koa.com).

Lake Mitchell Campground. Located in **Mitchell,** only a mile or so from the Corn Palace (see "Off-the-Wall Attractions," earlier in this chapter), this campground has

---

BEGGING BURROS

Depending on your point of view, the **begging burros** along Iron Mountain Road are a road hazard or an irresistible attraction. They'll poke their heads inside your car windows looking for something to eat. Originally brought to carry tourists to the top of Harney Peak during the 1950s, they now roam freely and panhandle. They'll accept and eat almost anything, but bread, cookies, and crackers are their favorites. These are the only animals in the park that visitors are permitted to feed. Don't think you can feed the buffaloes! They are large, dangerous animals and should not be approached, even in a vehicle.

61 shaded sites, 45 full hookups (some pull-throughs), 20- and 30-amp electric, and cable TV. It makes a convenient stopover in the eastern part of South Dakota. Sites $15–$25. From Rapid City, take I-90 to exit 330. Turn left at the ramp to the Hwy. 37 bypass, then left at Main St. It's less than a mile to the campground (© **605/995-8457** reservations).

Other Deadwood campgrounds: Other campgrounds in the Deadwood area include **Fish 'N Fry Recreational Campground** ($32–$38), 6 miles south of Deadwood on U.S. 385 (© **605/578-2150**); **Hidden Valley Campground** ($26–$30), 7 miles south on U.S. 385 (© **866/578-1342**); **Whistler Gulch RV Park** ($39), 3 miles south of the U.S. 85/U.S. 14A junction on U.S. 85 (© **800/704-7139**); and **Wild Bill's Campground** ($20–$32), 5¼ miles south on U.S. 385 (© **605/578-2800**).

On the Road: North Dakota

THEODORE ROOSEVELT NATIONAL PARK

"I would not have been president if it had not been for my experience in North Dakota," Theodore Roosevelt often said and wrote.

Remembered as the preserver of our natural resources, a founder of our national parks, and the namesake of the teddy bear, Roosevelt as a young man was dedicated to big-game hunting. He had read of the threatened extinction of the American bison and first came to North Dakota's Badlands in 1883 on a hunting trip, afraid that some other hunter would shoot the last buffalo before he could get there. He had married 5 years earlier, and took the trip west when his wife Alice was pregnant with their first child.

He and his guide struggled through more than a week of cold, rainy days, not finding any buffaloes until the 10th day. Roosevelt killed the buffalo, then thrust a $100 bill into the hands of his astonished guide.

Smitten with the frontier countryside, he invested in a cattle-ranching plan with two other partners at the Maltese Cross Ranch in the Badlands, then returned to New York. But on February 14, 1884, both his mother and his wife died within hours of each other, his mother from typhoid, his wife from complications of childbirth. Brokenhearted, he returned to throw himself into his ranch business, buying a second spread, the Elkhorn. He changed almost overnight from a hunter to a conservationist protecting the land and wildlife. In 1901, after being elected president, he established the U.S. Forest Service and proclaimed 18 national monuments. He also got permission from Congress to establish five national parks and 51 wildlife refuges.

The park that honors Roosevelt was dedicated in 1978. One of the most fascinating and least visited of the national parks, it is divided into two units; a **North Unit,** 52 miles north of I-94, and a **South Unit,** 70 miles to the south at Medora. A 7-day pass is $10 per vehicle. Both have scenic loop drives; a mile-by-mile "Road Log Guide" for the drives is sold at the visitor centers in the park for $1.50. The **Elkhorn Ranch Unit,** 35 miles north of Medora, is also part of the park, but difficult to reach

Theodore Roosevelt National Park

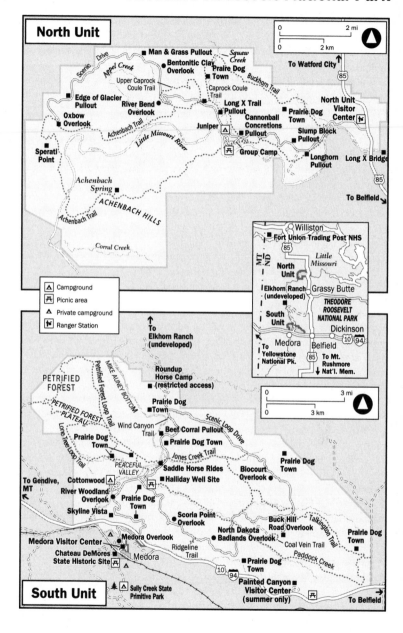

North Unit

0   2 mi
0   2 km

Scenic Drive
Appel Creek
Man & Grass Pullout
Squaw Creek
Bentonitic Clay Overlook
Prairie Dog Town
Buckhorn Trail
To Watford City
85
Upper Caprock Coule Trail
Caprock Coule Trail
Edge of Glacier Pullout
River Bend Overlook
Long X Trail Pullout
Cannonball Concretions Pullout
Prairie Dog Town
North Unit Visitor Center
Oxbow Overlook
Achenbach Trail
Little Missouri River
Juniper
Slump Block Pullout
Sperati Point
Group Camp
Longhorn Pullout
Long X Bridge
85
Achenbach Spring
ACHENBACH HILLS
To Belfield
Achenbach Trail
Corral Creek

- △ Campground
- 🛆 Picnic area
- ▲ Private campground
- 🛈 Ranger Station

Williston
Fort Union Trading Post NHS
85
Little Missouri
MT / ND
North Unit
Grassy Butte
Elkhorn Ranch (undeveloped)
THEODORE ROOSEVELT NATIONAL PARK
South Unit
Dickinson
Medora
Belfield
10   94
To Yellowstone National Pk.
85
To Mt. Rushmore Nat'l. Mem.

To Elkhorn Ranch (undeveloped)

PETRIFIED FOREST
Petrified Forest Loop Trail
Mike Auney Bottom
Roundup Horse Camp (restricted access)
Prairie Dog Town
PETRIFIED FOREST PLATEAU
Wind Canyon Trail
Scenic Loop Drive
Beef Corral Pullout
Prairie Dog Town
Prairie Dog Town
Long Tree Loop Trail
Jones Creek Trail
Prairie Dog Town
PEACEFUL VALLEY
Saddle Horse Rides
Biocourt Overlook
Prairie Dog Town
To Gendive, MT
Cottonwood
Halliday Well Site
River Woodland Overlook
Prairie Dog Town
Skyline Vista
Scoria Point Overlook
North Dakota Badlands Overlook
Buck Hill Road Overlook
Talkington Trail
Prairie Dog Town
Medora Visitor Center
Medora Overlook
Coal Vein Trail
Chateau DeMores State Historic Site
Ridgeline Trail
Medora
Paddock Creek
10   94
Prairie Dog Town
Sully Creek State Primitive Park
Painted Canyon Visitor Center (summer only)
To Belfield

South Unit

0   3 mi
0   3 km

unless you ford the streams. The **South Unit visitor center** is in Medora at the west end of Pacific Avenue (© **701/623-4730,** ext. 3417); the **North Unit visitor center** is on U.S. 85, 15 miles south of Watford City (© **701/842-2333;** www.nps.gov/thro).

The **North Unit 30-mile scenic drive** goes past herds of buffaloes and longhorns; geological formations like slump rock, caprock, and lignite coal seams; and steeply eroded canyons in what were once grassland prairies. Seen less often are herds of wild horses and pronghorns, elk, deer, and mountain lions.

On the **South Unit 36-mile loop,** look for the **Prairie Dog Town** at Milepost 3.3, with adequate RV parking space; petrified tree stumps and ribbons of lignite coal in the cliffs; the **Buck Hill Road overlook** with a good view across the Badlands; and, of course, the buffaloes, part of a herd of 400.

Don't miss the photogenic **Painted Canyon** turnout on I-94 and the scenery behind the visitor center. Tourists have been coming here since 1883, and the canyon was a popular tourist rest stop in the 1930s, with curio shops, caged animals on display, and a restaurant and gas station.

For more information, contact the **park headquarters** at P.O. Box 7, Medora, ND 58645 (© **701/623-4730 3417;** www.nps.gov/thro).

MEDORA

In this rustic little town of rough-sawn wood buildings, a young Theodore Roosevelt sipped iced champagne with the town's founder, the Marquis de Mores—a French business tycoon who built a meatpacking plant in 1883 and named the town for his American-born wife. The couple lived in their private railway car while building a lavish 26-room château on a hilltop outside town, which is now owned by the state and open for tours.

The meat plant ran for only 3 years; then de Mores and his wife went back to France, and the plant gradually fell into ruin. Today, the site is marked only by one towering brick chimney and some random foundation stones.

The Marquis went on to try to build a railway between China and what is now Vietnam, and also ran for office in France. He attempted to forge a Franco-Islamic alliance to drive the British from Africa, until he was killed by Tuareg natives in the Sahara.

History buff Harold Shafer, owner of Gold Seal Floor Wax and Mr. Bubble, was instrumental in restoring the town of Medora in the mid-1960s. Roosevelt's Maltese Cross cabin has been moved into the national park headquarters here and is open for visitors, with guided tours only. An annual **Cowboy Poetry Gathering** happens in Medora every spring in late May.

The **Medora Musical,** running nightly in a 2,900-seat amphitheater from mid-June through Labor Day, salutes Roosevelt with a song-and-dance revue that climaxes with his Rough Riders at the Battle of San Juan Hill. You'll find signs directing you up the hill to the amphitheater at the west end of Pacific Avenue in Medora. Call for reservations (© **800/MEDORA-1** [633-6721]; www.medora.com). While you're at it, reserve a spot at the Pitchfork Fondue—listed in "Takeout (or Eat-In) Treats," earlier in this chapter—for dinner before the show.

CAMPGROUND OASES IN NORTH DAKOTA

Fort Ransom State Park. One of the quietest, prettiest spots for camping in the state is at Fort Ransom Park in the tiny Norwegian town of Fort Ransom by the Sheyenne River. Canoes are for rent, and you'll find 15 sites with electrical hookups, a sanitary dump, toilet facilities, and spacious pull-throughs. You'll have trouble finding the park if you want to get there on paved roads. Sites $20. From I-94, take exit 288 and follow Rte. 1 south to Rte. 27, turn east for about 5 miles, and follow the Fort Ransom turnoff north. Call for more information (or the cavalry if you get lost; © **701/973-4331;** www.ndparks.com).

Turtle River State Park. Turtle River has large pull-throughs and 70 20- and 30-amp electrical connections. It's open year-round for self-contained camping (the utilities are turned off in winter), along with sledding, snowshoeing, skating, and cross-country skiing in cold months. Sites $20. It's near **Grand Forks** in Arvilla, 22 miles west of Grand Forks on Hwy. 2 (© **701/594-4445;** www.ndparks.com).

Minot KOA. Our site at the KOA in Minot had its own resident prairie dog, something that delighted us, but made our North Dakota neighbors turn up their noses at "that rodent." Some of the sites are shaded and grassy, and 49 sites have 30-amp electric. There are 15 full hookups and some big-rig sites with 50-amp electric. The office is modem-friendly, and there's Wi-Fi. Sites $22–$33. The campground is a little more than 2½ miles southeast of Minot at 5261 Hwy. 52 E. (© **800/KOA-7421** [562-7421] or 701/839-7400; www.koa.com).

Buffalo frolic in Custer State Park.

4 Bears RV Park. The campground is, like the casino, operated by the Three Affiliated Tribes: the Mandan, Hidatsu, and Arikara. While the 85 full-service hookup sites with 20- and 30-amp electric are free-form rather than rigidly outlined, you can usually figure out a way to park to best access the connection. Rates are modest, and you can walk to the tables or to the fishing lake. Sites $13–$26. Located behind the 4 Bears Casino in **New Town,** on Dakota 23 on the Fort Berthold Reservation (© **800/294-5454** or 701/627-7500; www.4bearscasino.com).

Cottonwood Campground. In the south unit of **Theodore Roosevelt National Park,** Cottonwood has 76 sites accessible for RVs. Some are pull-throughs large enough for big rigs, but with no hookups and no reservations. Sites $20. Mile 5.6 on the Little Missouri River, 14 miles west of U.S. 85 (© **701/623-4730,** ext. 3417; www.nps.gov/thro).

Juniper Campground (formerly Squaw Creek Campground). Juniper Campground has 50 paved and shaded sites, none with hookups, plus a dump station and toilets. Sites are available on a first-come, first-served basis. Sites $20. In the north unit of Theodore Roosevelt National Park, 4⅔ miles off U.S. 85, north of **Watford City,** opposite the Cannonball Concretions pullout (© **701/842-2333;** www.nps. gov).

Jamestown Campground. This Good Sam campground cooks up light meals between mid-June and mid-Aug, a boon for travelers who don't want to heat up the galley. The 48 gravel sites are shady, some adequate for big rigs, and 50-amp hookups are available. You'll also find cable TV and a modem-friendly office. Sites $30–$35. It's located on the frontage road south of I-94 at exit 256 (© **701/252-6262**).

Red Trail Campground. The town of **Medora** has so many diversions that an RVer could spend a week there. Unfortunately, its two campgrounds with hookups are not so appealing at peak season when the crowds are there, though each place has its pros and cons. **Red Trail Campground,** where we stayed, allows an easy walk into town and is owned and operated by a friendly family, but the campground is behind a motel and the 100 sites are fairly close together. It has live entertainment some nights, cable TV, city water, and 30- and 50-amp electrical hookups, with a surcharge for cable and 50-amp electric. Sites $26–$45 (© **800/621-4317** or 701/623-4317 reservations).

Medora Campground is operated by the nonprofit Theodore Roosevelt Medora Foundation, with 106 sites closer together than those at Red Trail. It's on the edge of town, across from the road to the Medora Musical and Pitchfork Fondue Dinner (but not within walking distance, unless you want to walk uphill ¾ mile). Sites provide 20- and 30-amp electric. Sites $29–$35. Call for reservations (© **800/MEDORA-1** [633-6721]); it's the same number to call for tickets for the Pitchfork Fondue Dinner (see "Takeout [or Eat-In] Treats," earlier in this chapter).

North Dakota Campgrounds

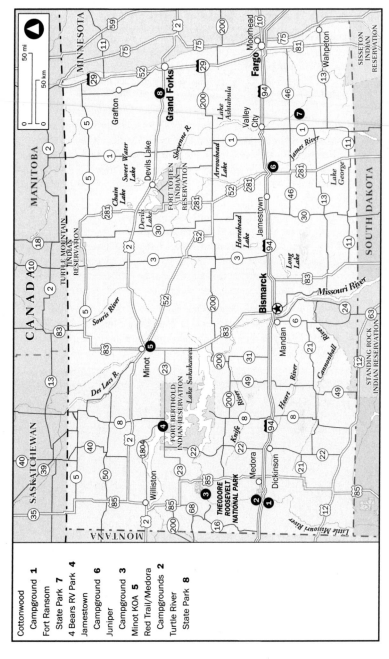

Cottonwood
Campground **1**
Fort Ransom
State Park **7**
4 Bears RV Park **4**
Jamestown
Campground **6**
Juniper
Campground **3**
Minot KOA **5**
Red Trail/Medora
Campgrounds **2**
Turtle River
State Park **8**

A Dozen Terrific Side Trips in the Dakotas

1. **Devil's Tower National Monument.** Remember Richard Dreyfus sculpting his mashed potatoes into a flat-topped mountain in *Close Encounters of the Third Kind* (1977)? You can take a detour to that **Wyoming** mountain, Devil's Tower National Monument, 20 miles west on I-90, then 27 miles north via exit 185 (℃ **307/467-5283;** www.nps.gov/deto). The 867-foot core of an ancient volcano is surrounded by the pine trees of the Black Hills, and near its base is one of the few protected prairie dog towns in the west. Inside the park, there are 51 campsites without hookups (closed in winter). Outside the park, there are 50 hookups with 30- and 50-amp electric at the **Devil's Tower KOA,** on the location site for the film, with a fantastic view of the tower. Sites $27 to $90 (℃ **800/562-5785** or 307/467-5395; www.koa.com). The monument is open year-round.

2. **The trail of Lewis and Clark, South Dakota.** From I-90, take exit 212 to U.S. 83 north for about 30 miles to **Pierre;** then drive 4 miles east on Hwy. 34 to visit the **Farm Island Recreation Area.** Here, a monument and interpretive center describes the expedition of those two intrepid explorers. Most of the buffaloes in the fields around here were extras in the 1990 film *Dances with Wolves* (℃ **605/773-2885;** www.sdgfp.info/parks/regions/oahesharpe/farmisland.htm).

3. **Badlands National Park, South Dakota.** Access is from I-90 via exit 131 from the east or exit 110 from the west (at **Wall Drug Store**). A 40-mile loop on Route 240 leads you through this eroded but majestic landscape in watercolor brushstrokes of pink, soft gray, and green—except at sunrise or sunset, when it

Devil's Tower National Monument.

takes on a warm, burnished glow. To visit the **Prairie Dog Town,** continue on Route 590 along a gravel road for about 5 miles, then turn north again to Wall (*C* **605/433-5361;** www.nps.gov/badl).

4. **Spearfish Canyon National Scenic Byway, South Dakota.** It's a dramatically beautiful, 20-mile route at any time of year, but especially in early fall, when the trees lining the riverbanks change color. Take U.S. 85 southwest from **Dead-wood,** then U.S. 14A north along the canyon. The views are better if you set out from Lead and drive north.

5. **Wildlife Loop Road in Custer State Park, South Dakota.** This 18-mile loop provides a chance to see antelopes, bison, white-tail and mule deer, elk, coyotes, prairie dogs, eagles, and hawks. Try to drive the loop in early morning or late afternoon for the best sightings (*C* **605/255-4515;** www.custerstatepark.info).

6. **Ingalls Family Homestead, South Dakota.** In tiny **DeSmet,** northeast of Mitchell on U.S. 14, is the Ingalls Family Homestead, the childhood home of Laura Ingalls Wilder, who wrote *Little House on the Prairie.* Her books inspired the long-running TV series. A do-it-yourself tour of 18 sites related to her stories begins at the Surveyors' House at Silver Lake. Fans of the show will enjoy a 3-week pageant ($10 adults, free for children 4 and under) that takes place in early July, with wagon rides, home-cooked meals, and an all-volunteer cast in an outdoor stage production. The homestead is marked off U.S. 14, east of town on the south side of the highway, on an unpaved road (*C* **800/776-3594** information on the memorial in town; www.ingallshomestead.com).

7. **Wind Cave National Park, South Dakota.** South of Custer State Park, via Route 87, Wind Cave has 28,000 acres of wildlife habitat for buffaloes, antelopes, elk, deer, and prairie dogs; and a 53-mile maze of tunnels underground, with unusual boxwork, frostwork, and popcorn formations (*C* **605/745-4600;** www.nps.gov/wica).

8. **Black Hills Wild Horse Sanctuary and Mammoth Site, South Dakota.** The Hot Springs area south of the Black Hills on U.S. 18/385 has two outstanding attractions: the **Black Hills Wild Horse Sanctuary** (*C* **605/745-5955;** www.wildmustangs.com), where hundreds of wild American mustangs are protected; and the **Mammoth Site,** where the dig goes on to excavate as many as 100 mammoths who died in a sinkhole at the springs 26,000 years ago. Bones are displayed where they were found. Admission: $8 adults, $7.50 seniors, $6 children (*C* **645/745-6017;** www.hotsprings-sd.com). For additional information, call the **Hot Springs Chamber of Commerce** (*C* **800/325-6991;** www.mammothsite.com).

9. **Homestake Gold Mine, South Dakota.** If you drive over to Deadwood, add a short detour to Lead (pronounced *Leed,* which means "lode") to tour the surface workings of the Homestake Gold Mine on one of its daily tours (closed in winter). The largest underground gold mine still operating in the Western Hemisphere was financed by George Hearst, father of William Randolph Hearst, and

two California partners. From Deadwood, take Route 14A and continue on to Lead. Admission: $7 adults, $6.75 seniors, $6.50 children. Call the **visitor center** for information (© **605/584-3110;** www.homestakevisitorcenter.com).

10. **Jewel Cave National Monument, South Dakota.** Just 1⅓ miles west of Custer on U.S. 16, Jewel Cave is the fourth-largest cave in the world, with 80 miles of passageways explored and charted. Sparkling calcite crystals and bizarre drapery, balloon, and column formations make this a favorite of cavers, who can take special tours by advance reservation. Open 8am to 7:30pm. Guided tours for the general public are provided on a regular schedule in summer, intermittently the rest of the year, with evening lantern tours. Tours: $8 adults, $4 seniors and children 6 to 16, free for children 5 and under (© **605/673-8300;** www.nps. gov/jeca).

11. **Prairie Village, South Dakota.** Located in **Madison,** Prairie Village offers considerably more than its name suggests, from an 1893 steam-driven Hershel-Spillman **carousel** to a Barney and Smith railway "chapel car." **Chapel Car Emanuel,** equipped with pews, an organ, a pulpit, and a room in the back for the minister to change vestments, is one of seven chapel cars built under the auspices of the Reverend Boston Smith. As a Baptist minister, it was his idea to send out the clergy by rail to serve frontier settlements without churches. This chapel car is one of only two that remain. The **Social Hall,** now named the Lawrence Welk Opera House, originally graced the town of Oldham, South Dakota, where Welk used to play in his early days. The church in the village is still used for Sunday morning services, and some 40 buildings are spread out over 140 acres, evoking a sense of time and place. In August, the village holds a threshing jamboree with steam-driven farm machinery, and three coal-fired steam locomotives are fired up on occasion to give rail excursions. Prairie Village is 2 miles west of **Madison** on Hwy. 34. Mon–Sat 10am–5pm, Sun 11am–5pm. Admission: $5 adults, $4.50 seniors, $2 children (© **800/693-3644** or 695/ 256-3644; www.prairievillage.org).

12. **Take a zigzag route from Minot to Medora, North Dakota.** For a good overview of the state's farm and ranch land, drive along Route 83 south from Minot, then west along Route 23. Both the 4 Bears Bridge across the Missouri and the 4 Bears Casino were named for a great Mandan chief; while Lake Sakakawea, a few miles north, is named for the Shoshone woman called Sacajawea, who was instrumental in the Lewis and Clark expedition. The **Three Affiliated Tribes Museum,** operated by the Mandan, Hidatsu, and Arikara people, is on Route 23, 4 miles west of New Town on the Fort Berthold Indian Reservation; it's open daily year-round. Continue south along U.S. 85 from Watford City, detouring to drive the loops through the North and South Units of **Theodore Roosevelt National Park.** For information, contact the **Tribes Museum** (© **701/627-4781;** www.mhanation.com).

8

The Rio Grande Valley & the Wilds of West Texas

ONCE INHABITED BY GIANT FLYING REPTILES WITH 50-FOOT WING-spans, Texas has more miles of inland lake and stream water than Minnesota; a million road signs and markers on its highways; and, as its tourism publications point out, a ranch, a military base, and two counties bigger than some New England states.

The bottom half of Texas is where rock 'n' roll was sent out all over the universe by Wolfman Jack in the 1950s, broadcasting from a Del Rio radio station's 500,000-watt "pirate" transmitter located across the river in Mexico. The Del Rio station was built in the 1930s by "Doctor" John R. Brinkley to promote his famous goat gland surgery to restore virility.

It's where Pancho Villa and Zsa Zsa Gabor once slept (not at the same time) in El Paso's Paso del Norte Hotel, where nachos were invented by Ignacio "Nacho" Anaya at the Victory Club in Piedras Negras, and where fajitas were first served at Ninfa's restaurant in Houston on July 13, 1973.

John Dillinger and his gang vacationed in the sleepy little West Texas town of Balmorhea in 1934, pretending to be "Oklahoma oil men." Locals were mystified by their pastimes, things like jumping on and off the running boards of moving cars, shooting at tin cans tossed in the air, and lobbing an occasional hand grenade. Only after the gunning down of Public Enemy Number One outside a Chicago movie house a few months later did the good citizens of Balmorhea realize who their big-spending visitors really were.

Southwest Texas is where camels were trained for combat, where Mexican revolutionary Antonio Zapata was beheaded, and where beauty-queen makers Rex Holt and Richard Guy of GuyRex Associates in El Paso became famous for grooming a string of beauty-contest winners.

RVing Along the Rio Grande

The road that follows the Rio Grande twists and turns 940 miles from the Gulf of Mexico to El Paso, laying out the border between Texas and Mexico.

It was originally a good idea to use the Rio Grande as the border, except that the river kept changing its course. A 600-acre piece of land called the Chamizal in El Paso/Juarez was wrangled over for 100 years until President John F. Kennedy and Mexico's Adolfo Lopes Mateos worked out a compromise. And one mission church, Nuestra

South Texas Highlights

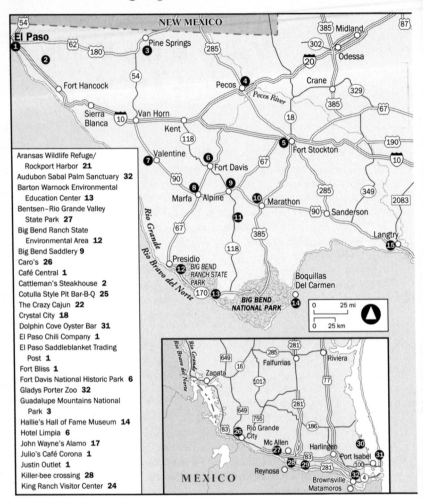

Aransas Wildlife Refuge/
   Rockport Harbor **21**
Audubon Sabal Palm Sanctuary **32**
Barton Warnock Environmental
   Education Center **13**
Bentsen–Rio Grande Valley
   State Park **27**
Big Bend Ranch State
   Environmental Area **12**
Big Bend Saddlery **9**
Caro's **26**
Café Central **1**
Cattleman's Steakhouse **2**
Cotulla Style Pit Bar-B-Q **25**
The Crazy Cajun **22**
Crystal City **18**
Dolphin Cove Oyster Bar **31**
El Paso Chili Company **1**
El Paso Saddleblanket Trading
   Post **1**
Fort Bliss **1**
Fort Davis National Historic Park **6**
Gladys Porter Zoo **32**
Guadalupe Mountains National
   Park **3**
Hallie's Hall of Fame Museum **14**
Hotel Limpia **6**
John Wayne's Alamo **17**
Julio's Café Corona **1**
Justin Outlet **1**
Killer-bee crossing **28**
King Ranch Visitor Center **24**

Señora del Socorro, was moved back and forth between Mexico and Texas as a result of flooding several times, though it never shifted from its foundation.

In West Texas, you can whiz through more territory in an hour in your RV than stagecoaches and wagon trains could travel in 3 days. It's an easy and interesting journey, so long as you avoid the broiling hot days of summer.

Texas likes RVers a lot. Not only do many of its state parks provide hookups, but at the information centers when you drive across the border, you can usually find free booklets with lists of RV campgrounds, state parks, sanitary dump locations, and

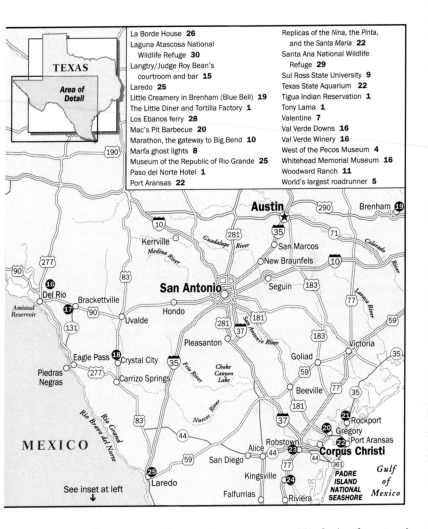

La Borde House **26**
Laguna Atascosa National
    Wildlife Refuge **30**
Langtry/Judge Roy Bean's
    courtroom and bar **15**
Laredo **25**
Little Creamery in Brenham (Blue Bell) **19**
The Little Diner and Tortilla Factory **1**
Los Ebanos ferry **28**
Mac's Pit Barbecue **20**
Marathon, the gateway to Big Bend **10**
Marfa ghost lights **8**
Museum of the Republic of Rio Grande **25**
Paso del Norte Hotel **1**
Port Aransas **22**

Replicas of the *Nina*, the *Pinta*,
    and the *Santa Maria* **22**
Santa Ana National Wildlife
    Refuge **29**
Sul Ross State University **9**
Texas State Aquarium **22**
Tigua Indian Reservation **1**
Tony Lama **1**
Valentine **7**
Val Verde Downs **16**
Val Verde Winery **16**
West of the Pecos Museum **4**
Whitehead Memorial Museum **16**
Woodward Ranch **11**
World's largest roadrunner **5**

places that sell propane gas. The state also puts out a wealth of other free printed materials at all visitor information centers.

HITTING THE HIGHLIGHTS

Spend 1 night in the Corpus Christi area, visiting Padre Island National Seashore, but skipping South Padre Island. Take the back road, Route 281, through the Rio Grande Valley, allowing time to visit at least one bird sanctuary if you're there in winter.

If you have kids along, detour up to Brackettville for the Alamo Village theme park, then drive fairly briskly along the border, stopping in Langtry to see Judge Roy Bean's Jersey Lilly Saloon.

Spend as much time as you can spare in Big Bend and the Davis Mountains, then finish up with a day or two in El Paso.

GOING FOR THE LONG HAUL

If you want to spend the winter in the Rio Grande Valley, you'll be welcomed with open arms by the dozens of RV parks, some of them quite lavish, in the area between Brownsville and McAllen. The climate is semitropical, with a wide range of fresh fruit and vegetables locally grown, and prices are moderate based on the national average.

There's plenty to do, with golf courses, nearby beaches, extraordinary bird-watching, shopping in Mexican border towns, and organized activities in every community. Want to dance? You can learn and practice tap, jazz, square-dancing, clogging, and line-dancing. Some RV parks have their own dance halls and square- or line-dance programs on a regular basis.

Adult education classes in Spanish, art, music, local ecology, and other subjects are offered through colleges in Harlingen, McAllen, and Brownsville. Contact the **Harlingen Chamber of Commerce,** 311 E. Tyler St. (© **800/531-7346** or 956/423-5440; www.harlingen.com); the **Brownsville Visitor Information Center,** at the exit to Farm Road 802 from U.S. 77/83 in North Brownsville (© **800/626-2639** or 956/546-3721; www.brownsville.org); and the **McAllen Visitors Information Center,** 1200 Ash Ave. (© **956/682-2871;** www.mcallenchamber.com).

About 3 months is the average stay for "winter Texans," and the RV parks will give discounted rates for long stays. The state parks in the area usually limit your stay to 14 consecutive days.

Travel Essentials

WHEN TO GO

Winter is best, with mild and sunny days that cool down to crisp nights. Late fall and early spring are also comfortable. Summer is extremely hot, humid in the east and bone dry in the west, except for a few cool spots in the upper reaches of Big Bend, where roads are not suitable for large RVs or trailers, and in the Davis Mountains, where big rigs are able to maneuver.

WHAT TO TAKE

Bring a camera and batteries/charger, binoculars, strong sunblock and a sun hat, insect repellent, stout high-topped hiking boots if you plan to hike the Big Bend and other desert terrain, and an antacid if you intend to follow the chili trail.

WHAT TO WEAR

Casual and comfortable clothing is correct all over Texas, except in its biggest Eastern-oriented cities, which this tour excludes. If you plan to dine in one of the splurge restaurants (see "Five Special Splurges," later in this chapter), you might take along a slightly dressier outfit, but it's not essential.

TRIMMING COSTS ON THE ROAD

Fortunately, this part of Texas is relatively inexpensive for the RV traveler, even if you eat out more often than in. Year-round, roadside produce stands sell regional food products at low prices.

Winter Texans get rates by the month or season in most of the commercial RV parks in the Rio Grande Valley, lowering the cost somewhat.

The state of Texas permits RVers who sleep inside their vehicles to park for rest periods up to 24 hours at any of the 1,000-plus highway rest areas. Pitching a tent is forbidden. While we have some personal reservations about staying overnight in a roadside rest area (see "Should You Sleep by the Side of the Road?" in chapter 3, "Where to Sleep: Campgrounds & RV Parks"), many RVers don't worry about it. You would be able to save a lot of campground fees.

Gas is less expensive in this oil-producing state, but not much. It tends to get cheaper as you travel eastward.

WHERE TO GET INFORMATION

The **Texas Department of Commerce, Tourist Division,** has a free Texas travel guide (© 800/888-8-TEX [839], ext. 728; www.traveltex.com). The **Texas Travel Information Centers** (© 800/452-9292; www.texas.worldweb.com) also can provide information. Call the latter for free booklets on public and private RV parks and campgrounds and road conditions.

DRIVING & CAMPING TIPS

- **Stock up on gas.** Particularly in West Texas, where stretches between gas stations may be long, top off your tank whenever convenient. Never let the gas gauge needle drop below half.

- **Winter in the tropics.** Winter Texans head for the Texas Tropics when snow starts blowing around in the Midwest. For new RVers and wannabe snowbirds, these tropics can be found in the Rio Grande Valley between Brownsville and Mission, which is thick with RV parks offering rates by the week, month, or season.

- **Camp in state park campgrounds.** Many Texas state park campgrounds have RV hookups and take reservations. Seniors, too, get free park entrance and a price break on camping if they apply for a special state park windshield sticker at any Texas state park.

- **Beware of spring break.** Avoid Padre Island, Corpus Christi, and Port Aransas during "spring break" days in late March and early April unless you like to be inundated with rowdy crowds of party-hearty college students.

- **BYOB?** Each of Texas's 254 counties rules individually on the if, when, what, and how of alcohol sales. Liquor stores are closed on Sundays and holidays throughout the state.

• *¡Habla español?* If you drive U.S. 281 along the Rio Grande between Browns-ville and Hidalgo, be careful not to cross any bridges unless you want to find yourself in Mexico. You can also walk across. (See "Six Special Side Trips," later in this chapter, for some border-crossing tips—applicable whether you go on purpose or by accident.)

The Best Sights, Tastes & Experiences of the Rio Grande

OFF-THE-WALL ATTRACTIONS

Hallie's Hall of Fame Museum, Boquillas. The late Hallie Stillwell was a genuine pioneer who arrived here at the age of 12, ran a ranch, taught school, and carried a gun. Her ranch near Boquillas now contains a museum in tribute to her. Daily 8am–9pm. Free admission. Located 46 miles southeast of Marathon. Call ahead for directions (© **432/376-2244;** www.stillwellstore.com).

Replicas of the *Niña,* the *Pinta,* and the *Santa María,* Corpus Christi. You'll find them moored in town, along with the authentic World War II aircraft carrier *Lexington,* which is now a naval museum. Daily 9am–5pm. Admission $13 adults, $11 seniors, $8 children 4–12. 2914 N. Shoreline Blvd., Corpus Christi. Call the Lexington Museum (© **800/LADY-LEX** [523-9539] or 361/888-4873; www.uss lexington.com).

The killer-bee crossing, Hidalgo. On the border just west of Brownsville, a fre-quently photographed, 20-foot fiberglass-and-steel bee that cost $20,000 stands by the city offices at 704 E. Texano. It commemorates the first crossing of the Africanized honeybees into the United States at this point in 1990.

The town of Valentine. Valentine gets very busy every February postmarking heart-shaped cards for romantics everywhere. You can drop off your cards anytime in person at the town's only post office, or mail them in before Feb 14 to Postmaster, Valentine, TX 79854.

The world's largest roadrunner, Fort Stockton. It's Paisano Pete, 11 ft. tall and 22 ft. long. Find him on U.S. 290 at Main St.

Crystal City, former U.S. spinach capital. Don't tell any of the Texans they're passé; they still have their Popeye statue in place on the main street. The town is on U.S. 83, 11 miles north of the junction of U.S. 277 and U.S. 83.

Laredo, capital of the Republic of the Rio Grande. Adding to the usual Six Flags over Texas (Spain, France, Mexico, the Republic of Texas, the Confederacy, and the United States), Laredo can claim one more: It was the capital of the short-lived Republic of the Rio Grande. See the flags at the **Republic of the Rio Grande Museum.** Tues–Sun 9am–4pm. Admission $2. 1000 Zaragoza St. (© **956/727-3480;**

The world's largest roadrunner, Paisano Pete.

www.webbheritage.org). And Fredonia didn't start with the Marx Brothers; the Republic of Fredonia was founded in East Texas by disgruntled settlers in the 1820s.

Val Verde Winery, Del Rio. Val Verde, the oldest licensed winery in Texas, founded by Italian immigrants, offers free tours and tastings. Its tawny port is a local favorite; it also produces a so-so cabernet sauvignon, a Muscat Canelli, and a Texas Rosé. Mon–Sat 10am–5pm. 100 Qualia Dr. (© **830/775-9714;** www.valverdewinery.com).

The Marfa ghost lights, Marfa. The mysterious lights have been seen almost nightly since 1883. After it gets dark, drive west of town on Route 90/87 for 8 miles, and you'll see the sign for the "official viewing area." Look southwest toward the mountains, and you may or may not see a series of shimmering white balls of light. No one has been able to determine what causes them, but our favorite attempt was the expert who said they are bats with radioactive dust on their wings. Marfa is at the junction of U.S. 67 and U.S. 90, northwest of Big Bend. For more information, contact the **Marfa Chamber of Commerce** in the Paisano Hotel at 207 N. Highland Ave. (© **432/729-4942;** www.marfacc.com).

10 TERRIBLY TEXAS THINGS TO DO

1. **Pick up fresh shrimp in Aransas Pass.** Aransas Pass is the shrimp capital of Texas. The seafood shacks around the ferry landing sometimes sell 5 pounds of shrimp for $15 or $20. Another place to shop is Peoples Street T-Head at the marina in Corpus Christi. Also here: a nationwide chain, **Landry's Seafood,**

I See by Your Outfit That You Are a Cowboy . . .

Care to do some shopping? Here are a few places to gear up.

Saddles
Get King Ranch Running W saddles from the ranch's own **saddle shop** at the Ragland Building, 6th and Kleberg, in Kingsville (© 800/282-KING [5464]; www.king-ranch.com). Visitor center, Hwy. 141 W. (© 361/592-8055).

Saddle Blankets
El Paso Saddleblanket Trading Post has hand-woven saddle blankets and rugs in southwestern designs. 6926 Gateway E., El Paso (© 800/351-7847 or 915/544-1000; www.elpasosaddleblanket.com).

Boots
When trying on a ready-made Western boot, be sure the heel slips a bit when you walk. When the sole gets more flexible, the slippage will stop. If it doesn't slip, it's too tight and will give you blisters. The instep should be snug, the boot shank long enough to cover your arch fully, and the ball of the foot should fit into the widest part of the boot, not sit forward or back of it.

You can get boots in El Paso at the **Justin Outlet,** 7100 Gateway E., I-10 at Hawkins (© 915/779-5465), or **Cowtown Boots,** 11451 Gateway Blvd. W. just off I-10 (© 915/593-2565; http://store.cowtownboots.com).

Wrangler Cowboy-Cut Jeans
The **VF Factory Outlet,** the best place to buy bargain jeans of the brand worn by most working cowboys, has branches in Corsicana, Grapevine, Hempstead, Livingston, Mineral Wells, La Marque, San Marcos, and Sulphur Springs (www.vffo.com).

Custom-Crafted, Working-Cowboy Leather Accessories
Bandannas, hats, belts, belt buckles, and everything else for the well-turned-out cowboy can be had in **Alpine** at the **Big Bend Saddlery,** E. Hwy. 90 (© 800/634-4502; www.bigbendsaddlery.com).

600 N. Shoreline (© **361/882-6666;** www.landrysseafoodhouse.com), which sells early-bird special shrimp and oysters at happy hour, starting at 4:30pm.

2. **Stare down a shark at the Texas State Aquarium, Corpus Christi.** You'll also see sting rays, barracudas, giant grouper, and tropical fish swimming around an artificial reef created from an oil derrick. Daily 9am–5pm (closed Christmas). $16 adults, $15 seniors, $11 children 4–12. 2710 N. Shoreline Blvd. (© **800/477-GULF** [4853]; www.texasstateaquarium.org).

3. **Join a jalapeño-eating contest.** Enter the one at the Brownsville-Matamoros Charro Days during Mardi Gras, when parades, carnivals, and costume balls highlight the festivities. Check out **Brownsville Visitor Information**

(© **800/626-2639;** www.brownsville.org). Or hit the streets of Laredo, where the jalapeño-downing derby happens every Feb at George Washington's birthday party celebration. (Don't ask what chilies have to do with George's birthday; the town combined two festivals into one.) The winner is crowned King Chile and may even get a spicy kiss from Miss Jalapeño.

4. **Go fishing.** Try dam fishing, for instance, at Amistad Lake near Del Rio, or saltwater sport fishing at Corpus Christi, or join in the big daddy of them all, the **Texas International Fishing Tournament (TIFT),** in Port Isabel in early Aug. Call for details (© **956/943-8438;** www.tift.org).

5. **Go river rafting along the Rio Grande.** Various companies lead 1-day trips into Santa Elena and Colorado canyons in Big Bend National Park year-round, water flow permitting. No previous experience is necessary, but reservations are required. Contact **Far Flung Adventures** in Terlingua (© **800/839-7238;** www.farflungoutdoorcenter.com) or **Big Bend River Tours** in Terlingua (© **800/545-4240;** www.bigbendrivertours.com).

6. **See the stars at family "star parties," Fort Davis.** The McDonald Observatory in the Davis Mountains hosts 2-hour stargazing parties on Tues, Fri, and Sat nights, with no reservations required. Dress warmly and bring binoculars. Located on Route 118 northwest of the town of Fort Davis. Tours are conducted daily, for $12 adults, $10 seniors, $8 children 6–12, $40 family. Call for times and any other information (© **432/426-3640;** http://mcdonaldobservatory.org).

7. **Go prospecting outside Alpine.** At Woodward Ranch, 16 miles south of Alpine on Route 118, you can find red plume agate, precious opal, and other minerals and gemstones, and they'll help you identify what you've got (and charge per pound for the rocks you keep). There is an RV campground with 30- and 50-amp electrical hookups. Sites $30. Call the **Woodward Ranch** for information (© **432/364-2271;** www.woodwardranch.net).

8. **Catch a game of cowboy polo.** It's sometimes featured at professional rodeos or at arenas in towns with National Cowboy Polo Association teams. The season runs from Mar through Aug, and players are required to wear jeans and Western shirts and ride Western saddles, never English ones. Headgear is optional; many riders play in cowboy hats. The cowboy polo field is smaller than in English polo, and the ball is made of rubber rather than wood. The audience is a bit rowdier, too. Top Texas teams are from San Angelo in West Texas and San Jacinto, near Houston. Most matches during the season are held in rodeo arenas. **San Angelo's Visitor Information Center** can supply current events information (© **800/375-1206;** www.visitsanangelo.org).

9. **Check out the rodeo classes at Sul Ross State University, Alpine.** It's considered the best school for wannabe professional saddle bronco riders, ropers, rodeo clowns, barrel racers, and steer wrestlers. Call the school for a visit and tour (© **432/837-8011;** www.sulross.edu).

A cowboy surveys the scene at Indian Cliffs ranch.

10. **Walk over the river and climb the mountain.** Actually it's Trilingual Creek at Big Bend National Park, which much of the year is merely a trickle, making it an easy, dry crossing. On the other side, a sheer cliff rises, seemingly impenetrable, but a series of switchbacks on the Santa Elena Canyon Trail take you up and around and along the Rio Grande Valley. To get there, take the Castolon/Santa Elena junction road, which is the Ross Maxwell Drive, to the Castolon Visitor Center. Then bear right and follow the Ross Maxwell Drive 8 miles to the end, which is the beginning of the Santa Elena Trail. Be sure to carry a water bottle and wear sturdy shoes. For information, call the visitor center (© **432/477-2251;** www.nps.gov/bibe).

FIVE SPECIAL SPLURGES

1. **Visit Marathon, the gateway to Big Bend.** Allow some time and/or money for the little town of Marathon, whose antiques shops have cornered the market on Georgia O'Keeffe–type cow skulls. The vintage **Gage Hotel** from 1927, 102 NW 1st St. (© **800/884-GAGE** [4243] or 432/386-4205; www.gagehotel. com), has been gentrified only to the extent that it had to be (if you ignore the motel-like annex with pool next door). In early Mar, the town hosts the **Texas Cowboy Poetry Gathering.** Marathon was named by a retired sea

captain who said it reminded him of Marathon, Greece. (Funny, it doesn't remind us of Marathon, Greece.) Contact the **Marathon Chamber of Commerce** (© **482/386-4516;** www.marathontexas.com).

2. **Drop into the old Paso del Norte Hotel for a drink.** The **Dome Bar** at El Paso's former Paso del Norte Hotel (now the Camino Real) is the original lobby of the hotel, with its Tiffany stained-glass dome ceiling and marble walls and floor. At 101 S. El Paso St. (© **800/769-4300** or 915/534-3000; www.camino real.com/elpaso).

3. **Chow down on a steak at Cattleman's Steakhouse at Indian Cliffs Ranch.** The restaurant serves huge steaks that *People* magazine called the best in the country, plus side orders from ranch beans to homemade bread. Your dinner reservation also gives free admission to the ranch's Western-style attractions, which kids particularly enjoy. Mon–Fri 5–10pm; Sat–Sun 12:30–9pm. Drive 33 miles southeast of El Paso to the I-10 Fabens exit, then north 5 miles on Rte. 793 (© **915/544-3200;** www.cattlemanssteakhouse.com).

4. **Go cowboy.** Grab yourself some cowboy garb, a Stetson, some hand-tooled boots, or a saddle. See "I See by Your Outfit That You Are a Cowboy . . ." (p. 208) for suggested shops and outlets.

5. **Check out the beautifully restored La Borde House in Rio Grande City.** Designed in France and built by a turn-of-the-20th-century French merchant, the New Orleans–style mansion is now a sedate hotel and restaurant with a modern annex at the back. 601 E. Main St., west of McAllen on U.S. 83. Call for reservations (© **956/487-5101;** www.labordehouse.com).

TAKEOUT (OR EAT-IN) TREATS

Blue Bell ice cream, Brenham. Some ice-cream aficionados swear by Texas's Blue Bell brand, once not available outside Texas. *Time* magazine went on record saying it was the best in the United States. The old-fashioned "Little Creamery in Brenham" keeps its small-town image and its logo, a girl and a cow, but you can find the brand now in seven states. The top flavor is vanilla, but strawberry, rocky road, pistachio almond, and chocolate chip also scoop up compliments. If you want to tour the plant, you'll get a free sample at the end. Tours are held weekdays and cost $5 adults, $3 seniors, free for children 13 and under. Rte. 290, about halfway btw. Austin and Houston (© **800/327-8135;** www.bluebell.com).

Café Central, El Paso. El Paso's most romantic restaurant—meaning it does not have saddles and horseshoes—the Café Central is elegant, with piano music during cocktails and dinner. The menu changes daily, but is a combination of Continental and contemporary cuisine. Mon–Thurs 11am–10:30pm; Fri–Sat 11am–11:30pm. It's across from the Camino Real Hotel at 109 N. Oregon St. (© **915/545-2233;** www. cafecentral.com).

You can visit the Blue Bell Creamery in Brenham, Texas.

Caro's, Rio Grande City. Caro's is a small, traditional Northern Mexico/Tex-Mex cafe that's famous around these parts for freshly ground corn tortillas and freshly ground seasonings, as well as its puffed taco, stuffed with cooked ground beef, fresh tomato, and lettuce, and then fried. The combination plate for hearty eaters includes an enchilada, rice and beans, guacamole, a 4-ounce rib-eye steak, and a grilled chicken breast. For dessert, pick up one of the homemade candies heaped by the cash register. Opens daily at 11am for lunch and dinner, lunch only on Sun. Located at 607 W. 2nd St. (© **956/487-2255**).

Cotulla Style Pit Bar-B-Q, Laredo. In the streets of Laredo, feast on Cotulla pit-style barbecue meat (like Mexico's *carne asada*) and side dishes. There's a separate takeout area to the right of the restaurant. We noticed that locals call in their orders ahead of time on weekends, and the takeout is ready when they get there. Otherwise, lines can be long. You might also want to try two unique Laredo dishes: the *mariachi*, a fiery version of a breakfast taco; and *panchos*, which are nachos with beef in layers alongside the cheese and jalapeños. Daily 6am–3pm. 4502 McPherson (© **956/724-5747**).

The Crazy Cajun, Port Aransas. Try a shrimp and crawfish boil at the Crazy Cajun restaurant in Port Aransas on Mustang Island; take the free 24-hour ferry over from the end of Hwy. 361 in Aransas Pass. Sort of a southern clambake, the boil includes shrimp, crawfish, stone-crab claws, smoked sausage, potatoes, and corn on the cob, all served on butcher paper. Mon–Fri 5–10pm; Sat–Sun noon–10pm. On Alister St. Square (© **361/749-5069;** www.thecrazycajun.com).

Dolphin Cove Oyster Bar, South Padre Island. Dolphin Cove Oyster Bar serves up fresh oysters, and you-peel-'em shrimp from a grass shack in Isla Blanca Park. Tues–Sun noon–9pm (© **956/761-2850**).

El Paso Chili Company, El Paso. Stop by the El Paso Chili Company for terrific cactus salsa, *chile con queso* (chili with cheese dip), chile beans, or fajita marinade, all in jars to take away with you. Daily 10am–5pm. 100 Ruhlin Court in downtown El Paso next to the river (© **888/4-SALSAS** [472-5727] or 915/544-3434; www.elpaso chile.com).

Grapefruit and onions. The ruby red grapefruit of the Lower Rio Grande Valley is justifiably famous. Hit the late-Jan to early-Feb Citrus Fiesta in Mission and buy a bagful, or find an orchard that lets you pick your own. Don't forget the mild Super-sweet 1015 onions you can bite into like an apple. Both are on sale at **Bell's Farm to Market** in **McAllen** at 116 S. Ware Rd. and Business 83. Closed in summer (© **800/ 798-0424**).

Hotel Limpia, Fort Davis. On the town square in Fort Davis, the pink limestone Hotel Limpia has a restaurant with dishes you would have expected to find in 1912, the year it was built, including buttermilk pies, chicken-fried steak, fried chicken, and fresh catfish. It also serves the only alcohol in town, but you have to join a club to get it, $3 for 4 people. Tues–Sun 5:30–9pm; Sun 11am–2pm (© **800/662-5517** or 432/426-3237; www.hotellimpia.com).

Julio's Café Corona, El Paso. Julio's originated in Juarez, but also has a branch on the south side of El Paso. The house specialty is a dish from Zacatecas, Mexico, called *salpicón,* a cold shredded beef brisket with cubes of white cheese and chili chipotle served with sliced tomatoes, chopped lettuce, and sliced avocados—sort of a Mexican version of a Thai beef salad. Hot flour tortillas are served on the side. Daily 11am– 9pm. 8050 Gateway E., just off I-10 at the Yarborough exit (© **915/591-7676;** www. julioscafecorona.com).

The Little Diner and Tortilla Factory, Canutillo. Try the *gorditas*—deep-fried masa patties filled with chunks of pork in a red chili sauce, or, as some prefer, ground beef with chopped lettuce and tomatoes. They're about $1 apiece. Homemade thick corn tortillas are $1 a dozen and thin corn tortillas, $1. For a salad, order avocado *tapatía* (chopped lettuce and guacamole on a crisply fried tortilla) and sample the chiles rel-lenos if you're still not full. Mon–Tues and Thurs–Sun 11am–8pm. Closed Wed. Canutillo is just north of El Paso. Take exit 6 off I-10 and follow the signs in Canutillo to 7209 7th St. (© **915/877-2176;** www.littlediner.com).

Mac's Pit Barbecue, Gregory. In tiny Gregory, north of Corpus Christi at 219 Hwy. 35, just north of 181, Mac's Pit Barbecue serves old-fashioned Texas barbecue cooked over mesquite wood. Feast on beef brisket, beef finger ribs, pork ribs, ham, chicken, or Polish sausage. Mon–Sat 11am–8pm (© **361/643-5589**).

Tigua Indian Reservation, El Paso. The green chili at El Paso's Tigua Indian Reser-vation is fiery enough to sear your tongue, and the red chili is only slightly less incendi-ary. "White-eyes don't know how to make chili," one of the Tigua told us. The casual cafeteria is open at lunchtime; the prettier, more formal restaurant is Wyngs (Wed– Sun 11am–3pm and 5–10pm). Both will serve up takeout portions if you bring your own dishes. Homemade bread baked in an outdoor adobe oven is sold in the cafe and gift shop area as well. Take the Ave. of the Americas exit off I-10 south to Ysleta. For information, call **Wyngs** (© **915/859-3916**) or the **Tigua Cultural Center** (Wed–Sun 9am–3pm; © **915/859-7700;** www.ysletadelsurpueblo.org).

WILDLIFE-WATCHING

Birds are a primary reason to travel the Rio Grande Valley, especially in winter. The **Santa Ana National Wildlife Refuge** near the town of **Alamo** claims the national record for the most bird sightings in a single day, and famed naturalist Roger Tory Peterson ranks it in the top 12 birding areas of the United States. To date, 390 species have been recorded on the 2,088 acres. Between Thanksgiving and Easter, a tram travels through the refuge from Thursday through Monday at 9:30am, noon, and 2pm, making birding easy. You can catch the tram from the visitor center when you first enter the refuge. Admission $2 adults, $1 children, $3 per car (© **956/784-7500;** www.fws.gov/refuges/santana).

A diligent searcher in the refuge may even glimpse endangered **wildcats.** Four of the only five remaining wildcat species in the United States still live in the valley—cougars, bobcats, ocelots, and jaguarundi. Two other species, the jaguar and the margay cat, have disappeared during the past half-century.

Laguna Atascosa National Wildlife Refuge, east of Harlingen on the lagoon inside Padre Island, hosts as many as 394 bird species, notably in fall and winter when **Canada geese, snow geese,** and **sandhill cranes** can be seen, along with **great blue herons.** On the mammal side, inhabitants include **bats, armadillos, coyotes, foxes, mountain lions, ocelots, jaguarundis, bobcats, javelinas,** and **white-tailed deer.** Both driving and walking tours can be taken. Open sunup to sundown. Admission $3 adults. Call for information (© **956/784-3607;** www.fws.gov/refuges/profiles/index. cfm?id=21553).

The rare and distinctive, 5-foot-tall **whooping crane** spends winters at Aransas National Wildlife Refuge north of Corpus Christi, but you may also see roseate spoonbills, ibis, egrets, herons, Canada geese, and diving ducks. We came across dozens of **alligators** sunning themselves by the edges of the water. Indigenous armadillos and javelinas can also be seen there.

The whole Rio Grande River Valley is dotted with wildlife refuges that celebrate the unique bird, plant, and animal life here. **Bentsen–Rio Grande Valley State Park,** 2 miles south of Farm Market Road 2062, near Mission, is a good place to see **green jays, gold-fronted woodpeckers, white-winged doves, crested caracaras,** and the omnipresent **chachalacas.** It's open 8am to 5pm (© **800/792-1112;** www.tpwd.state. tx.us). At **Audubon Sabal Palm Sanctuary,** 5 miles east of Brownsville (take Farm Market Rd. 1419); you can walk through the last remaining grove of native Texas palm trees, *Sabal texana.* Take your binoculars (and insect repellent) on the nature-trail walk from the visitor center and maybe you'll glimpse a **green jay, black-bellied whistling duck,** or **hummingbirds.** Open 9am to 5pm (© **956/882-5050;** www. txaudubon.org/sabal).

On the Road

PADRE ISLAND NATIONAL SEASHORE

The only entrance to the paved road to the park is at North Padre Island outside Corpus Christi, and the paving ends in the parking lot of the Malaquite Visitor Center. The vast center of the island is accessible only to hikers and four-wheel-drive vehicles. No driving or camping is permitted on the sand dunes or in the sea grass.

South Padre Island, entered from Port Isabel in the Brownsville area, has 34 miles of broad sandy beaches, the southernmost 5 miles adjacent to low- and high-rise hotels, condominium towers, and restaurants. The road, Park 100, is paved for 15 miles, but the northern end is mostly undeveloped.

South Padre Island also has, according to local legend, some $62,000 worth of 19th-century gold coins and jewelry buried there by John Singer of the sewing machine family when the Civil War broke out. He and his wife, who lived in a driftwood house on the island about 25 miles north of the southern end, buried their valuables in the sand dunes, but when they came back after the war, the dunes had shifted, and the gold was never found. In spite of, or perhaps because of, these rumors (and others about gold-laden Spanish ships running aground and sinking off Padre Island), the use of metal detectors or any other treasure-hunting devices is banned.

Today, wildflowers cling to the dunes, sea grasses blow in the winds from the gulf, and collector-quality seashells sweep in with each tide—along with an assortment of litter from Gulf of Mexico shipping routes.

An automobile may be driven 5 miles past the end of the paved road in the park on the beach when conditions allow—**don't try this in your motor home**—and only four-wheel-drive vehicles are permitted past the MILEPOST 5 sign.

Warning: RVers without a tow vehicle would be wise to leave the rig in the parking lot and set out on foot. Stories abound of overambitious drivers mired down in the sand, and the park's newspaper cautions: "There are no services or means to contact anyone for help should you need it. The park service does not monitor CB radio, nor will it attempt to tow vehicles. Wreckers, when they can be induced to travel down island, cost hundreds of dollars."

No vehicles are permitted on the dunes, mud flats, or grasslands.

The seashore has an ongoing program to protect endangered sea turtle species found in the Gulf of Mexico—the Kemp's Ridley, loggerhead, hawksbill, leatherback, and green turtles. If you see a sea turtle alive or dead along the beach, notify a park ranger rather than approaching the turtle yourself.

Bird-watching is exceptionally good here, with more than 350 species of seasonal and year-round winged residents. **Portuguese man-of-war jellyfish** sometimes wash up on the beaches here. Give them a wide berth because their sting is extremely painful.

Call for **park information** (© **361/949-8068;** www.nps.gov/pais).

Campground Oases on Padre Island National Seashore

Padre Island National Seashore's Malaquite Beach Campground. With 50 paved parallel-parking or back-in sites along the beach, the campground has picnic tables, toilets, cold showers, and a sanitary dump. No hookups, no reservations, and a 14-day maximum stay. There are also weekend ranger programs and ranger-led beach walks. Ask about the weather conditions, which may vary from the mainland weather. Sites $8. It's ¾ mile south of the ranger station visitor center along the island's one road (✆ 361/949-8068; www.nps.gov/pais).

South Padre Island's Isla Blanca Park. Operated by Cameron County, the park is on a 1-mile white-sand beach on the Gulf of Mexico and has 396 full-hookup sites with 30-amp electric, flush toilets, showers, and a Laundromat. There are bike trails, a marina, a water park, a swimming pool, and a grocery store. *Note:* Do not take any kind of glass onto the beach. There is a heavy fine for doing so. Sites $10–$25. From Hwy. 100, drive east across the causeway, then south on Park Rd. 100 to the park (✆ 956/761-5493; www.co.cameron.tx.us/parks/isla_blanca.htm).

South Padre Island KOA. Located on a slim finger of land surrounded by the Gulf of Mexico and Laguna Madre Bay, the campground allows for all kinds of watersports, including boating and fishing. There's a pool, Wi-Fi, cable TV, and 209 full hookups with 30- and 50-amp electric. Sites $44–$67 (✆ 800/562-9724 or 956/761-5665; www.koa.com).

Long Island Village. This park in **Port Isabel** is a lavish, full-service RV resort where some 120 condo spaces (out of 898) are made available by their owners to overnighters. The big-rig sites have landscaping, cable TV, 30- and 50-amp electric, a pool, and a spa. Visitors enjoy boating activities. Rates are about twice what some local parks charge, but in this world, you get what you pay for. Sites $46–$69. On South Padre Island at 900 Garcia St. (✆ 956/943-6449; www.longislandvillage.com).

THE TEXAS RIVIERA

The balmy Gulf Coast likes to call itself "the Texas Riviera," but don't expect to find *Lifestyles of the Rich and Famous*. There's more Bubba-and-barbecue than Bardot-and-bouillabaisse.

Because of consistent moderate-to-high winds and expanses of open water, the Corpus Christi area has been named one of the world's 10 best windsurfing destinations. It's not a bad place to fly a kite, either. And Corpus Christi—locals call it Corpus—has become one of the top snowbird (or "winter Texan") winter resorts.

Jean Lafitte and his pirates hung around the area in the early 19th century, and General Zachary Taylor and his troops grouped here to invade Mexico in 1846. The oldest house, built in 1848, is called the Centennial House and has foundations made of shellcrete, cement made from oyster shells. Gutzon Borglum, who went on to create Mount Rushmore, built the city's sculptured 14-foot-high seawall after a 1919 hurricane. The handsome wall is broken up with stairs down to the beach, which allow for a view of the sea beyond.

Texas Talk

Blue norther: A fast-moving cold front in fall or winter, which can cause temperatures to drop 50°F in a half-hour.

Down island: The roadless part of Padre Island, where two-wheel-drive vehicles, especially RVs, can't go. If they try anyway, there are no tow trucks that will come to pull them out for less than $500 or so.

Dry whiskey: Peyote cactus, also called "mescal," which contains a variety of psychoactive alkaloids; it grows wild in Big Bend and is illegal to harvest or possess.

Maverick: An unbranded cow, named for Sam Maverick, who refused to brand his cattle so that he could claim any unbranded animal on the range.

Tejas: A group of Indian tribes for which Texas was named, and regarded as friendly by the Spanish invaders until the Spanish wore out their welcome.

Texas ironwood: The mesquite tree, its wood used for barbecuing and smoking meats or making furniture, its long bean pods used for animal feed, flour, beer, or wine.

Texas strawberries: Pickled jalapeño peppers held by the stem and eaten whole in one bite.

Texas turkeys: Armadillos, used for food during hard times like the Depression; also sometimes used in chili, but not legally unless the animal has died from natural causes or been hit by a car.

Tinajas: Rock cavities that trap rainwater, a good place to look for game after a rainstorm in Big Bend.

Whoopers: Short for whooping cranes, the endangered species that winters in Aransas National Wildlife Refuge.

Winter Texans: RVers from colder climates, many of whom spend winter in the Lower Rio Grande Valley.

If you take the **free ferry** over to Port Aransas on Mustang Island from Route 361 east of Aransas Pass, watch for the bottlenose dolphins that usually swim along with the boat.

Brownsville was the site of the last shots fired in the Civil War, a full month after Lee surrendered to Grant at Appomattox. But the city always had problems: It was taken over briefly in 1859 by Juan Cortina, either a Mexican bandit or a folk hero, depending on which side you were on; then occupied by the Confederates during the Civil War; after which it was taken by the Union, and then by the Confederates again.

Campground Oases on the Texas Riviera
Lake Corpus Christi/Mathis KOA Campground. The campground is open year-round by a lake near a 47-acre wildlife reserve, and it's not far from the King Ranch,

South Texas Campgrounds

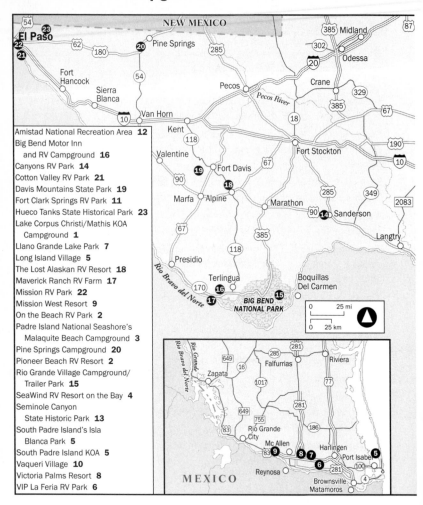

Amistad National Recreation Area **12**
Big Bend Motor Inn
  and RV Campground **16**
Canyons RV Park **14**
Cotton Valley RV Park **21**
Davis Mountains State Park **19**
Fort Clark Springs RV Park **11**
Hueco Tanks State Historical Park **23**
Lake Corpus Christi/Mathis KOA
  Campground **1**
Llano Grande Lake Park **7**
Long Island Village **5**
The Lost Alaskan RV Resort **18**
Maverick Ranch RV Farm **17**
Mission RV Park **22**
Mission West Resort **9**
On the Beach RV Park **2**
Padre Island National Seashore's
  Malaquite Beach Campground **3**
Pine Springs Campground **20**
Pioneer Beach RV Resort **2**
Rio Grande Village Campground/
  Trailer Park **15**
SeaWind RV Resort on the Bay **4**
Seminole Canyon
  State Historic Park **13**
South Padre Island's Isla
  Blanca Park **5**
South Padre Island KOA **5**
Vaqueri Village **10**
Victoria Palms Resort **8**
VIP La Feria RV Park **6**

by Texas standards. Of the 137 sites, 100 have full hookups with 30- and 50-amp electric. There are plenty of opportunities for fishing and boating. Sites $32–$37. It's on Rte. 3024. To get there from I-37, take exit 47 if southbound or exit 40 if northbound and follow the signs (© **800/KOA-8601** [562-8601] or 361/547-5201; www. koa.com).

Pioneer Beach RV Resort. Located in **Port Aransas,** the Pioneer resort is the top-rated campground on the coastal bend, with 14 acres of resort-style niceties, from a clubhouse with a kitchen to the fish-cleaning facilities. The 365 full-hookup sites have 30- and

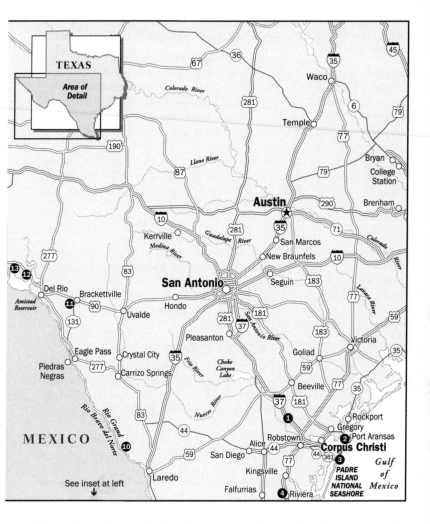

50-amp electric, big-rig pull-throughs, and easy beach access for fishing and swimming in the Gulf of Mexico. Sites $39–$45. It's south of Port Aransas on Rte. 361 (© **888/480-3246** or 361/749-6248; www.campingfriend.com/pioneerbeachresort).

On the Beach RV Park. Also in Port Aransas, On the Beach is not as highly rated as the Pioneer resort, but it is, as the name suggests, on the beach south of town. Some 34 of the 59 sites are full hookups and pull-throughs adequate for big rigs, and they have cable TV. Sites $36–$57. 907 Beach Access Rd. 1A (© **800/932-6337** or 361/749-4909; www.onthebeachrvpark.com).

The Comanche Moon

Old-timers on both sides of the Rio Grande call the first full moon of autumn the Comanche moon, because that was when bands of Comanches would go out on raids into northern Mexico. They rode through Big Bend on what came to be called the Comanche War Trail, burning, pillaging, and taking anything they could use or sell, including hostages. After receiving the inadvertent gift of horses from the Spanish, they became perhaps the greatest horsemen the world has ever seen.

The only way the U.S. Army could figure out how to get rid of the Comanches was to decimate the tribe's basic food supply, so they called in the buffalo hunters. One man could kill 1,000 or more buffaloes in 3 months. He was paid well for his skills. 🚐

SeaWind RV Resort on the Bay, Riviera. SeaWind is a comfortable resort with 160 full hookups, wide sites, 30- and 50-amp electric, patio pads, telephone hookups, and post office boxes. Unlike most RV resorts with these features, it is a public park and is in Kaufer-Hubert Memorial Park near the water at Riviera Beach. It has daily, weekly, and monthly rates. Sites $25. Rte. 77 at Riviera (© **361/297-5738;** http://home.granderiver.net/~seawind).

THE LOWER RIO GRANDE RIVER VALLEY

A rich river delta, the 100-mile strip along the river called "the Valley" has a 340-day growing season and a new crop to harvest every month. Citrus was planted more than a century ago, and breakfast eaters cherish the area's ruby red grapefruit. Whether it's for the grapefruit or the weather, so many visitors have flocked here lately that the valley has added a new area code.

The town of **McAllen,** center of the winter Texan activity, was founded by a canny Scot who built a hotel here, then donated land for a railroad depot so the train would stop near his property.

Laredo is where Antonio Zapata, military leader of the self-proclaimed Republic of the Rio Grande, was captured and beheaded after 283 days of revolution against the government of Mexico's General Santa Anna. His head was displayed on a pole, which ended the dissension. Historical artifacts of that period are on display in the town's **Museum of the Republic of Rio Grande,** 10003 Zaragoza St. Tuesday through Saturday 9am to 4pm; Sunday 1 to 4pm. Admission $5 (© **956/727-0977;** www.webbheritage.org/riograndehistory.htm).

At **Los Ebanos,** near Mission, you'll find the last remaining hand-drawn ferry crossing the Rio Grande.

The town of **Alice** lights up for the month of December, with more than 280,000 Christmas lights in a 2-block area in the middle of town.

Campground Oases in the Lower Rio Grande River Valley

Mission West Resort in **Mission** has 320 full hookups with 30-amp electric, a central modem and security, a pool, and a 9-hole golf course. Sites $35. It's off Expwy. 83 at Inspiration Rd., then just over 1 mile on Business 83 (🕾 **956/585-5551;** www. missionwestresort.com).

VIP La Feria RV Park. This park has 306 full hookups with 30-amp electric and fairly wide sites, two heated pools, cable TV, plus lots of planned activities. Sites $28. Monthly rates available. 600 Expwy. 63 in **La Feria** (🕾 **956/797-1401;** www.vipla feria.com).

Victoria Palms Resort, Donna. This huge RV resort has more than 1,000 sites geared toward retirees and winter Texans. There are usually 528 available with full hookups, 30- and 50-amp electric, 42 wide pull-throughs, city water, and satellite TV. Gilding the lily, there's an activities director, a computer club, a dance floor, heated therapy pools, a full-service restaurant, a post office, beauty and barber shops, free cable TV, a library, billiards rooms, live dance bands, a ceramics shop, an exercise room, and card rooms—and even motel suites if you're expecting visitors. Sites $35–$50. 602 N. Victoria Rd. (🕾 **800/551-5303** or 956/464-7801; www.victoria palms.com).

Llano Grande Lake Park. Adjacent to the Llano Grande Golf Course in Mercedes, the park offers many of the same enticements to retirees as Victoria Palms; however, it is slightly smaller with only 800 sites, 616 with full hookups with 30- and 50-amp electric, and 265 pull-throughs that are each 40X70 feet. Bingo, movies, square and ballroom dancing, a rock shop, exercise and Aquacize classes, and photo and art instruction can certainly fill the day. Sites $30–$50. Located at Mile 2 west in Mercedes. From Hwy. 83 W., exit at Mile 2 west; turn left at the light to the entrance (🕾 **800/656-2638** or 956/565-2638; www.llanogranderesort.com).

Vaqueri Village. Northwest of Laredo at Los Botines, the park has 14 paved pull-through sites with patios and full hookups with 30- and 50-amp electric. The office is modem-friendly. Sites $25–$35. Monthly rates $350–$450. It's off I-35 at U.S. 83, exit 18, then north 2½ miles on U.S. 83 (🕾 **956/417-4141**).

TRAVEL TIP: CROSSING THE BORDER

If you want to venture into any of the Mexican border towns along the Rio Grande, park your RV on the U.S. side and walk across to go shopping or dining. Don't forget your passport!

The Sounds of the Rio Grande

All along the Rio Grande, listen for the unique local music called variously *conjunto, norteño, tejano,* or Tex-Mex, an odd mix of eastern European accordion, Mexican 12-string guitar, string bass, and trap drums, with electric bass and guitar, keyboards, and alto saxophone sometimes laid in. The sound is influenced by the polka, Mexican ballads, country/western, and salsa. The border towns between Brownsville and Laredo are good places to hear it.

A bit up the Gulf Coast, you'll find zydeco alive and well in Corpus Christi, where the **Texas Jazz Festival** (℗ 361/688-1296; www.texasjazz-fest.org) takes place every year in October at Heritage Park. ▰▰▰

Campground Oases on the Road to West Texas

Fort Clark Springs RV Park. A private park near **Brackettville's** Alamo Village Movie Location and historic Fort Clark, this one has 85 full hookups, 30- and 50-amp electric, cable TV, flush toilets, showers, and a Laundromat. Sites $25. Just off U.S. 90 at Rte. 674 (℗ **800/937-1590** or 830/563-9340; www.fortclark.com).

Amistad National Recreation Area. At Amistad, a sprawling 85-mile-long man-made lake jointly owned by the United States and Mexico, there are **two park campgrounds** with a total of 47 sites suitable for RVs less than 28 feet. There are chemical toilets and cooking grills, but no piped water or hookups. Along with year-round fishing, some shotgun and bow-and-arrow hunting is permitted. Go scuba diving in the lake, with the best visibility in winter and early spring. Lake use $4. Sites $6–$8. It's west of Del Rio on U.S. 90 (℗ **830/775-7491;** www.nps.gov/amis).

Seminole Canyon State Historic Park. This park is home to many ancient Indian pictographs and paintings on canyon walls. The ones in Fate Bell Shelter are believed to have been painted 5,000 years ago; visitors can enter the area only with a ranger. Guided tours are led year-round (Wed–Sun 10am and 3pm). The hike is moderately strenuous. Some 23 campsites have water, 20- and 30-amp electrical hookups, and sanitary dumps, and there are hiking and biking trails. Reservations are advised, especially Mar–June; call at least 4 weeks in advance. Sites $20. Near **Comstock,** 30 miles northwest of Del Rio on U.S. 90, 8¾ miles west of the junction of Rte. 163 (℗ **800/792-1112** reservations or 432/292-4464; www.tpwd.state.tx.us).

Canyons RV Park. Canyons is the only game in town in **Sanderson,** Texas, so if you're looking for an overnight hookup between the Del Rio area and Big Bend, this is pretty much it. It has 25 full hookups with cable TV, long pull-throughs, and a salon (just the thing after a long, dusty day in West Texas). Sites $20–$23. It's right on Hwy. 90, 1½ miles east of the junction with Rte. 285, so you can't miss it (though anytime someone tells us that, we miss it). Call for reservations—or in case you miss it (℗ **432/345-2916**).

BIG BEND NATIONAL PARK

A huge, but lightly visited park because of the relatively inaccessible location, Big Bend (**www.nps.gov/bibe**) sprawls over 1,250 miles of varied terrain. Its mountains, desert, river flood plains, and rocky canyons are bisected by a sometimes-turbulent Rio Grande.

The local Indians say this is where the Great Spirit put all the leftover rocks after he created the earth. The **Big Bend pterodactyl,** with its 51-foot wingspan, the largest flying creature known, lived here 65 million years ago.

While the park is home to 1,100 plant species, 75 mammal species, 6 amphibian and reptile species, and 400 species of birds, you'll see mostly **roadrunners** and **jack-rabbits,** creosote bush, and ocotillos if you don't take a hike or spend time searching out the others. We photographed some exquisite beavertail cactus in vivid fuchsia bloom on a December visit. The dagger-tipped *lechaguilla* is a unique local plant that you'll see; it's a favored food for the **javelina,** or collared peccary, a wild pig found throughout the park. Endangered **peregrine falcons** are still found as well, protected during nesting season, when rafting through the canyons is forbidden.

Watch out for **scorpions** and **centipedes,** both nocturnal, that might be inside your shoes if you leave them outside overnight. **Rattlesnakes** and **copperheads** also inhabit the area; so wear high boots when hiking off the usual tourist trails. While **mountain lions** are rarely seen, there have been two attacks in recent years. If you encounter one, park rangers advise you to stay where you are, waving your arms, shouting, and throwing rocks. Never run.

There are two unusual industries that used to be in Big Bend—it was home to the second-largest cinnabar mine in the world, which produced liquid mercury until the

Teepees are roadside picnic spots in West Texas.

Big Bend Wildlife, or How to Avoid an Unpleasant Encounter

The signs and warnings are everywhere: THIS IS BEAR AND MOUNTAIN LION COUNTRY, and although one of the thrills of visiting Big Bend National Park is the opportunity to see wildlife, for the safety of both humans and animals, always keep your distance. Rangers say that since the 1950s there have been more than a thousand sightings of mountain lions in the park and numerous sightings of black bears.

Hikers, especially in the Chisos Mountains, should be especially careful to minimize the danger of an encounter. First, discuss your hiking plans with park rangers to see if any recent mountain lion sightings have taken place where you plan to hike. Don't hike alone, especially at dawn or dusk. Watch children carefully—never let them run ahead. If you do end up face-to-face with a mountain lion, rangers offer these tips: Don't run, but stand your ground, shout, wave your arms, and try to appear as large as possible. If you have children with you, pick them up. If the mountain lion acts aggressively, throw stones, and try to convince it that you are not prey, but actually dangerous. Then report the incident to a ranger as soon as possible.

The other animal you may see is one of the estimated 10 to 20 black bears that live in the Chisos Mountains. Bears are attracted to food, and the best way to avoid an unwanted encounter is to keep a clean camp. Park rangers recommend that you store all foodstuffs, cooking utensils, and toiletries in a hard-sided vehicle. Food storage lockers are available for hikers and campers, and you should always dispose of garbage properly in the receptacles provided. If you see a bear, keep a safe distance; do not approach or follow it and never attempt to feed a bear. Report any bear sightings to a ranger.

Bears and mountain lions aren't the only wild animals in the park. Many visitors see **javelinas** (officially known as collared peccaries), which look a bit like their rather distant relatives, pigs, and are very nearsighted. A group of 10 to 20 is often seen in and near the Rio Grande Village Campground. Some of them have learned to recognize the crinkling sound of potato chip bags and will run toward the sound in hopes of a snack. Although javelinas are not aggressive, they are easily frightened and could inflict some damage with the javelin-sharp tusks from which they get their name.

Also deserving of mention are the park's poisonous snakes, scorpions, spiders, and centipedes, which are most active during the warmer months. Rangers advise that you watch carefully where you put your feet and hands, and use flashlights at night. Hikers may want to consider wearing high boots or protective leggings. It's also a good idea to check your shoes and bedding before use. 🚐

Big Bend National Park

▲	Campground
⊼	Picnic area
▭▭	Primitive road (4-wheel drive only)
▮◆▮	Ranger Station
– –	Unpaved road

veins ran out before World War II; and the unique *candlelilla* plant, whose wax was used for candles, chewing gum, and phonograph records until 1950. It's now illegal to gather it in the park.

RVers headed for Big Bend National Park should fill up their gas tanks before leaving U.S. 90 at Marathon or Marfa. There is a service station in the park, but hours of operation are limited.

A breathtaking drive that should not be missed by travelers with smaller RVs is the route through the **Big Bend Ranch State Environmental Area** along Route 170 between Presidio and Study (pronounced *Stew*-dy) Butte. Some guidebooks discourage RVers from this route because of a 1-mile-long 15% grade between Lajitas and Redford, although we had no problem driving it in our 36-foot motor home. Along the way, roadside rest stops have individual teepee shelters with picnic tables and grills.

Primitive hiking and backpacking, rafting, and canoeing are enjoyed in the area. For information on sports facilities, or the occasional 10-hour bus tours through the park's outback, visit the **Barton Warnock Environmental Education Center.** The entrance fee is $3 for adults 13 and older. Open daily 8am to 4:30pm. It's 1 mile east of Lajitas on FM 170 (*©* **432/424-3327**; www.tpwd.state.tx.us/spdest/findadest/parks/barton_warnock).

Campground Oases Around Big Bend National Park

Rio Grande Village Campground. In Big Bend National Park, this campground is 20 miles southeast of the park's Panther Junction headquarters on the river. Adjacent to the 100 tree-shaded sites without hookups is a general store, along with a large parking lot with 25 full hookups with 30-amp electric, which is called **Rio Grande Village Store and Trailer Park.** Sites $29. Stay here if hookups are essential. Otherwise, the campground is a much nicer place, with sites laid out in a circle like pioneer wagons. Hiking trails set out from here, and there are flush toilets and pay showers, and also a sanitary dump station. Sites $14. The campgrounds are on Rte. 118, 20 miles east of Panther Junction. For reservations (required Nov 15–Apr 15), call *©* **877/444-6777** or visit www.recreation.gov.

Maverick Ranch RV Park is adjacent to the **Lajitas Resort and Spa.** The 25,000-acre resort is on FM 170, 1 mile past the State Park Information Station. There are 101 full hookups with 30- and 50-amp electric, and 60 are pull-throughs. RV patrons have use of the resort facilities at a discount. Sites $29 for full hookup, $165 per week (*©* **877/LAJITAS** [525-4827] or 432/424-5000; www.lajitas.com).

Big Bend Resort & Adventure Golf Resort. This **Terlingua** campground provides a big dollop of civilization among the back roads of West Texas, with 120 full hookups, 30- and 50-amp electric, satellite TV, a Laundromat, a grocery store, food service, and motel units. Guests enjoy horseback riding, river rafting, and bird-watching. Reserve well ahead for the chili cook-off weekend in early Nov. Sites $27–$30. Located at the junction of Rte. 118 and Farm Rd. 170 (*©* **800/848-BEND** [2363] or 432/371-2218; www.bigbendresort.com).

THE WILDS OF WEST TEXAS

"Not a stone, not a bit of rising ground, not a tree, not a shrub, nor anything to go by," Coronado is said to have sighed as he passed through West Texas en route to the seven cities of Cíbola, where he expected to find gold. He didn't realize what wonders he was missing.

CAMPGROUND TIP

Though the **Rio Grande Village Store and Trailer Park** in Big Bend has 25 paved, full-hookup spaces that are booked on a first-come, first-served basis inside the adjacent village store, it is basically a parking lot with electricity and plumbing. If you can go self-contained for a couple of days, consider staying instead at the nearby **Rio Grande Village Campground** (see above).

The interior of Judge Roy Bean's combination courtroom and bar in Langtry.

One of our favorite West Texas towns is **Marfa,** site of the famous "Marfa ghost lights" (see "Off-the-Wall Attractions," earlier in this chapter). It was also the primary location for the 1956 blockbuster film *Giant.* The El Paisano Hotel, listed on the National Register of Historic Places, has a photo display in the lobby with photographs of the film's lead actors: James Dean, Elizabeth Taylor, and Rock Hudson. The town was also the setting for the play and 1982 film *Come Back to the Five and Dime, Jimmy Dean, Jimmy Dean,* about the effect of the filming of *Giant* on the town. To complete the trio of trivia lore, Marfa also boasts the highest golf course in Texas, at a 4,882-foot elevation.

Another of our favorites is **Langtry,** perhaps the most famous of all the tumbleweed-tossed, one-horse Texas towns. Here, Judge Roy Bean ruled as "the law west of the Pecos" and indulged in his admiration of British actress Lillie Langtry by naming his combination saloon and courtroom *The Jersey Lilly* and claiming he had also named the town for her. Railroad records of the time show it was actually named for a construction foreman named Langtry, so the wily Bean probably cashed in on the coincidence.

Although she was often invited to visit by the judge, who knew her only from photographs in the popular press, the actress never got to Langtry until a few months after the judge's death in 1904, when she was welcomed effusively by his son and other locals. A nicely restored version of his Jersey Lilly saloon, where a defendant after a trial was ordered to buy a round of drinks for the judge and jury, tells the whole story. Also here is a museum with dioramas and recorded tales of the judge, a visitor center, and a short nature trail through a cactus garden, with area trees and plants labeled.

INSIDER TIP: MAKE SURE YOU'LL FIT!

In Big Bend National Park, the 7-mile, dead-end **Green Gulch Road** to Chisos Basin is limited to RVs under 24 feet or 20-foot travel trailers pulled by trucks or autos. The same is true for the **Ross Maxwell Scenic Drive** between the Sotol Overlook and Castolon. If you have questions about which roads may be inaccessible for your RV, ask the rangers at the **Panther Junction Visitor Center,** in the park at the junction of U.S. 385 and 118 (© **432/477-2251**). A road guide booklet sold at the center is also helpful.

There are two replicas of the Jersey Lilly, one in the **Whitehead Memorial Museum,** where the judge and his son are buried on the museum grounds, and the other in Pecos in the **West of the Pecos Museum. Whitehead** is open Tuesday to Saturday 9am to 4:30pm, Sunday 1 to 5pm. Admission $5 adults, $4 seniors, $3 youth 13 to 16, $2 children 6 to 12, free for children 5 and under. It's at 1301 S. Main St., Del Rio (© **830/774-7568;** www.whiteheadmuseum.org). **West of the Pecos** is open Monday to Saturday 9am to 5pm, Sunday 1 to 4pm (closed Memorial Day to Labor Day Sun–Mon). Admission $4 adults, $3 seniors, $1 children 6 to 18, free for children 5 and under; it's at 120 E. First St. and Cedar Street (© **432/445-5076;** www.westofthepecosmuseum.com).

Cary Grant slept in Van Horn, they say, at the old **El Capitan Hotel,** now the Van Horn State Bank. **Shafter,** a ghost of a town on U.S. 67 between Presidio and Marfa, was once the silver mining capital of Texas.

Presidio's original town name was Nuevo Real Presidio de Nuestra Señora de Betlena y Santiago de Las Amarillas de La Junta de Los Ríos Norte y Conchos. It is also known as the "Hottest Town in Texas" and the "Onion Capital of the World."

Camels were trained for combat at Fort Davis in the Davis Mountains after an idea introduced in the pre–Civil War days by Jefferson Davis, then secretary of war, for whom the fort was named. The camels worked out much better than mules in the desert terrain, except for an unfortunate tendency for the males to bite each other in the legs if left untended. When the Civil War started, the fort was abandoned, then taken over by the Confederates briefly before it was burned by the Mescalero Apaches. Although the U.S. Army rebuilt the fort after the war, it never followed up on the combat camel idea because Davis, having served as president of the Confederacy during the war, was considered a traitor.

Campground Oases in West Texas

Davis Mountains State Park, Fort Davis. The park has 27 full hookups, 61 with 30- and 50-amp electric and water. Spacious and well laid out, most sites are shaded by oak trees. There are flush toilets and showers, along with a sanitary dump station and a playground. You may be visited in late afternoon by a family of mule deer or see a resident longhorn herd. The weather is comfortable for camping year-round. The **Fort Davis National Historic Site** nearby has been beautifully restored and has a living history program in summer. Sites $19–$24. On Rte. 118 west of the town of Fort Davis. Call for campground **reservations** (✆ **512/389-8900**) or fort information (✆ **432/426-3337;** www.tpwd.state.tx.us).

The Lost Alaskan RV Resort. Mush, you huskies! The Lost Alaskan is in the West Texas town of **Alpine,** about 4,000 miles south of Alaska, but with plenty of year-round sunshine. With 93 full-hookup sites, 30- and 50-amp electric, lots of shade trees, cable TV, bird-watching, and a modem-friendly office, it has everything the average Alaska RV park has, except fishing. Sites $32–$35. It's at 2401 N. Hwy. 18, just past the junction of Hwy. 223 (✆ **800/837-3604;** www.lostalaskan.com).

GUADALUPE MOUNTAINS NATIONAL PARK

One of our least-known national parks, this dramatic mountain range contains **Guadalupe Peak,** at 8,749 feet, the highest mountain in Texas. The surrounding countryside is so wild that many of the peaks in the range are still unnamed (**www.nps.gov/gumo**).

Camping here is at Pine Springs Campground (see below), where the area is divided into tent camping sites in natural terrain with space for a tent and car parking, and RV camping sites in a paved area like a parking lot with double-size sites marked off and numbered. Some sites have a little dirt beside them and a chained-down picnic table, while others are just wide parking sites. Hikers are cautioned not to park in the numbered RV sites, but sometimes they do anyway. There are no hookups, and camping is $7 a night, half-price for seniors with national park passes.

From the camping areas, some 80 miles of trails set out into the backcountry, but the terrain should not be attempted by anyone except experienced backpackers. Permits are required for overnight trips; get them at the headquarters **visitor center,** 4200 Smith School Rd., Austin. There is also a short slide show about the park and its geological and human history. Other park sights include the ruins of a Butterfield Stage Station and the Frijoles Ranch and Museum, the latter concerned with man's encroachment into this area.

A Campground Oasis at Guadalupe Mountains National Park

Pine Springs Campground. There are paved pull-through sites in parking-lot style, with restrooms and hiking trails, but no hookups. Reservations are not accepted, and pets are not permitted. Sites $8. Located in Guadalupe Mountains National Park, 110 miles east of El Paso on Rte. 62/180. Call for information (✆ **915/828-3251;** www. nps.gov/gumo).

EL PASO

Originally named El Paso del Norte by Juan de Oñate, the rich grandson-in-law of Cortes, the pass here was the main route between Mexico and the missions in San Antonio and East Texas.

Five Ways to Enter Terlingua's International Chili Cook-Off

Terlingua, west of Big Bend National Park on Route 170, is the birthplace of the chili cook-off competition, founded in 1967 by humorists Wick Fowler and H. Allen Smith. A later rivalry split the ranks of chili-heads, and now there are two annual cook-offs in Terlingua, on the first Saturday of November, attracting more than 5,000 people. Here are a few ways to enter.

1. Enter a sanctioned **CASI** (Chili Appreciation Society International) cook-off and win one of the top three prizes. Contact Renee Moore, 214 El Camino Rd., Bastrop, 78602 (℃ **251/228-0807;** www.chili.org).

2. Accumulate points at these cook-offs during the chili year (Oct 1–Sept 30) for placing among the top 12 at each.

3. Show up in Terlingua on the first Saturday in November and see if one of the competing qualifying teams needs an extra helper at the CASI cook-off. On the Saturday before the cook-off, there is a "Beans, Wings, and Salsa" competition that anyone can enter.

4. Cook your chili anyhow. While the judges will ignore you, you might get some attention from the chili-heads. Remember, no beans are allowed!

5. Look for the rival Terlingua cook-off, labeled the Original and held the same weekend behind Arturo White's store on Hwy. 170. It claims to be the original version and has less rigid rules. Call for a nitty-gritty rundown (℃ **817/421-4888**).

In early February, Terlingua holds a Cookie Chill-Off—a competition for no-bake desserts—to raise funds for the Terlingua Foundation. 🚐

The local Tigua Indians, many converted to Christianity by the Spanish in the 17th century, settled at Ysleta when a mission was established there in 1680. Today, the town, completely surrounded by El Paso, is the oldest continuously occupied settlement in Texas.

El Paso del Norte was eventually divided into two border towns, which today are called Juarez and El Paso.

Together in one area, you'll find the 1910 **Paso del Norte Hotel,** now the Camino Real, with its Tiffany stained-glass dome, on Mills and El Paso; the **Plaza Theater** on West Mills Avenue, built in 1930, with a ceiling full of twinkling stars and a cloud machine; and the site of the old **Acme Saloon** on San Antonio, where John Wesley Hardin, considered the fastest gun in the West, was shot (some say in the back of the head) in 1895. Both Hardin and his killer, lawman John Selman, are buried in the city's **Concordia Cemetery,** just north of I-10 at the U.S. 54 interchange on Yandel Drive. Hardin's grave is in the Boot Hill section of the graveyard, near the gate to the walled Chinese section. He claimed to have shot 40 men. A newspaper of the time reported, "except for being dead, Hardin looked remarkably well."

The city's wild and woolly gunslinging era ran from around 1880 to 1916, with everyone from Texas Rangers to Mexican revolutionaries engaging in brawls and shootouts. Neither of its most famous marshals, Bat Masterson and Wyatt Earp, was able to tame El Paso. One marshal, Dallas Stoudenmire, saw four men gunned down in 5 seconds (he killed three of them), only a block from the spot where he would be shot dead a year later.

The **San Jacinto Plaza** in downtown El Paso was donated to the city in 1873 by a city parks commissioner. He stocked a small pond in the plaza with alligators, and some of these reptiles lived there until the 1960s.

The **El Paso Museum of History** is a good place to fill up on local history with exhibits and dioramas. The museum is located at 510 North Santa Fe at the corner of Missouri, downtown, just off I-10 (© **915/351-3588;** www.elpasotexas.gov/history).

The distinctive architecture of the **University of Texas at El Paso** was inspired by a *National Geographic* magazine photograph of a Bhutan lamasery, because the Himalayas in the background reminded the first dean's wife of El Paso's mountains.

Fort Bliss, we are reminded, is bigger than Rhode Island. It has three military-related museums: The **Museum of the Non-commissioned Officer,** in Building 11331 at Barksdale and 5th streets in Biggs Army Airfield; the **Air Defense Artillery Museum,** in Building 5000 on Pleasanton Road near Robert E. Lee Road; and the **Fort Bliss Museum,** on Pleasanton Road and Sheridan Drive. Free admission to all museums; call for information (© **915/568-3390;** www.bliss.army.mil). Call ahead to make sure the public is being admitted to the active military base, and make sure you bring along ID, which may be required for admittance.

El Paso is also home to a classic Spanish drama festival, an international rodeo, a balloon festival, and a holiday tour of lights. Call the **El Paso Convention and Visitors Bureau** (© **800/351-6024;** www.visitelpaso.com).

Campground Oases Around El Paso

Hueco Tanks State Historical Park. The park has 20 campsites with water and electrical hookups and a sanitary dump station on the premises, as well as flush toilets, showers,

INSIDER TIP: VISITING KING RANCH

Sign the King Ranch Visitor Center guest register and you too may get a Christmas card that reads: "The grass is short, the range is dry / Good prospects ain't a half inch high / The cows ain't fat, this verse ain't clever / But Merry Christmas, same as ever."

WALKING TO MEXICO FROM TEXAS

If you decide to walk across one of the bridges into a Mexican border town for a few hours, you'll still need to have proof of citizenship with you—a passport or a passport card. A driver's license is not considered adequate proof of citizenship.

a pond, and a playground. The *huecos,* or natural rock basins that trap water, have aided travelers in this arid terrain for centuries. Many of them, from prehistoric hunters and gatherers to '49ers on their way to the California gold rush, repaid the hospitality with primitive rock drawings and initials. Ruins from a stage stop of the old Butterfield Over-land Mail stagecoach have also been moved here. Rock climbing is a major activity, except during summer, when the rocks are too hot to handle. Entrance fee $5; campsites $14–$16. Located 32 miles east of El Paso on Rd. 2775 just north of U.S. 62/180. Call for reservations (© **915/857-1135;** www.tpwd.state.tx.us).

Mission RV Park. We'd like to be more enthusiastic about Mission RV Park in El Paso, since it is usually our first choice for staying overnight there, but it's just off I-10 and below the flight paths of El Paso International Airport. We've tried all the other local campgrounds—great in winter, hot in summer, and dust-blown on windy days—and Mission gets the nod for location if you want easy access to downtown, the Tigua Reservation, or Juarez. It has 188 sites with 80 full hookups with 30- and 50-amp electric, 75 pull-throughs, city water, satellite TV, and a modem-friendly office. Sites $35. It's at exit 34 off I-10, on the north side next door to the El Paso Museum of History (© **800/447-3795** or 915/859-1133; http://missionrvparklp. com).

Cotton Valley RV Park. If you're in El Paso to enjoy the steak dinners at Cattleman's Steakhouse (listed under "Five Special Splurges," earlier in this chapter), you'd do well to choose this place. It has 58 full hookups with 30- and 50-amp electric, and paved interior roads make it a good choice for big rigs, despite blowing sand on windy days. Sites $23. It's 10 min. away from Cattleman's in **Clint,** at I-10, exit 42 (© **915/ 851-2137**).

Six Special Side Trips

1. **Stop in at the King Ranch, Kingsville.** Southwest of Corpus Christi, the King Ranch covers more than 825,000 acres and is three times bigger than the state of Rhode Island. It developed the Santa Gertrudis cattle breed. The visitor cen-ter showcases a small museum and conducts bus tours around the ranch daily. Admission $8 adults, $4 children 5 to 12. Mon–Sat 10am–4pm; Sun 1–5pm. On the western edge of Kingsville off W. Hwy. 141 (© **361/592-8055;** www. king-ranch.com).

2. **See the whooping cranes at Aransas Wildlife Refuge.** The flock of endangered 5-foot-tall cranes that spend winters here has grown from 18 in 1937 to some 140 today. Local boats take you out from **Rockport Harbor** to see them, weather permitting. The season runs from Dec–Mar. Boat tours: $45 per person. Call for reservations for boat tours (© **877/892-4737** or 800/782-2473) or refuge information (© **361/286-3559;** www.fws.gov/southwest/refuges/texas/aransas).

3. **Visit the no-bars Gladys Porter Zoo in Brownsville.** Endangered species from all over the world make up the population. Ranked as one of America's top zoos, it's at Ringgold and Sixth streets, and it's wheelchair-accessible. Daily 9am–5pm. Admission $9.50 adults, $8 seniors, $6.50 children 2–13; 500 Ringgold St. (© **956/546-7187;** www.gpz.org).

4. **Visit John Wayne's Alamo.** It's not the original in San Antonio, but the one built near **Brackettville** for the 1960 movie of the same name. The kids will like the imitation better, because there are daily shootouts staged during summer. The village has 28 buildings, including a John Wayne Museum and a working ranch. Parts of the TV miniseries *Lonesome Dove* were also shot here. You'll find **Alamo Village** 7 miles north of town on Route 647. Daily 9am–6pm (closed Christmas week). Admission $11 adults, $5 children (© **830/563-2580;** www.alamovillage.com).

5. **Head 'em off at the canyon like the cavalry tried with the Apaches.** Fort Davis National Historic Site (**www.nps.gov/foda**) is a re-creation of a 19th-century fort in a spectacular box canyon setting. It was home of the U.S. Ninth Cavalry "Buffalo Soldiers," who were African-American troops called that by the Apaches for their courage and their dark curly hair. The fort presents a living history program in summer with costumed re-enactors, as well as Black History events in Feb. Most evocative of all, if you're standing on the empty parade ground, is the recording played at regular intervals, including bugle calls and the sound of cavalry troops with jingling spurs and hoofbeats. Daily 8am–5pm (closed national holidays). The fort has a museum and gift shop on the premises. In the Davis Mountains south of I-10 on Rte. 17. The **Fort Davis Chamber of Commerce** can answer questions about the area (© **800/524-3015** or 432/426-3015; www.fortdavis.com).

6. If you really think you must, **hop the border into Mexico.** Bridges off U.S. 281 along the Rio Grande btw. Brownsville and Hidalgo will take you into Mexico. Here are some tips courtesy of the *Big Bend Area Travel Guide:*

   • North Americans need a passport to go into (and come back from!) Mexico. See **http://travel.state.gov/passport** for details.

   • If you drive across an international bridge, your driver's insurance from home is good for only 15 miles into Mexico.

   • Time zones in Mexican border cities do not always match those across the Rio Grande in Texas.

- Never, ever, under any circumstances, carry a gun into Mexico no matter where you hide it in your vehicle; it is against Mexican law, and you will be jailed immediately with no questions asked.

- If you have any questions about what you can legally bring back from Mexico, contact **U.S. Customs & Border Protection** (© 432/229-3349; www.cbp.gov).

In the Heart of the Heartland: Iowa, Illinois & Indiana

FOR RESIDENTS OF BOTH COASTS, THE HEART OF AMERICA IS A mysterious checkered terrain seen from a plane window on a clear day, but for anyone who takes the time to visit, there's a wonderful world of surprises.

Iowa, Illinois, and **Indiana** are where pop-culture icons were born and popcorn grows, where corn on the cob (and in grain elevators) is a commodity, and the pork tenderloin sandwich is a food group.

Anyone who thinks **Iowa** isn't sexy hasn't seen *The Bridges of Madison County* (1995) or *Field of Dreams* (1989); hasn't heard of America's leading advice-to-the-lovelorn columnists, Ann Landers and Dear Abby, both Iowa-born; and perhaps doesn't realize Oscar winners John Wayne and Donna Reed and singer Andy Williams came from this state. Iowa is also designated the official birthplace of Captain James T. Kirk, of the Starship *Enterprise,* who will be born there in 2282.

We were properly respectful when entering **Illinois,** home of Abraham Lincoln, birthplace of Carl Sandburg and Ronald Reagan, and the beginning of historic Route 66; however, we dissolved into giggles upon learning it was also the birthplace of Popeye, Tarzan, and Dick Tracy, and the home of Superman.

Indiana makes us giddy with museums dedicated to the FBI and its search for the Most Wanted (John Dillinger Museum in the Welcome Center, Hammond); to the Wizard of Oz (the Yellow Brick Road in Chesterton); and to an almost-forgotten vice president (Dan Quayle Center and Museum, Huntington). It's where the Duncan yo-yo and cinnamon red-hot candies (mmm!) are made.

Indiana is where movie icon James Dean, pop-music icon John Mellencamp, and gangster John Dillinger were born; where Garfield the Cat and Raggedy Andy were created; where Johnny Appleseed retired; and where basketball great Larry Bird was born and has returned. It's where factories in a 20-mile radius turned out the only 481 Duesenberg cars ever made and where they produce today's best pickles and potato chips.

Indiana is where Bloomington-born Hoagy Carmichael first recorded "Stardust" in the Gennett Studios, a major recording center in the 1930s. It's where local boy Red Skelton made good when he ran away from his home in Vincennes to join the Hagenbeck Circus in Peru; and it's the birthplace of Colonel Harland Sanders of Kentucky Fried Chicken fame. And while Cole Porter never penned songs like "Gary, Indiana" (that was written by Iowa's Meredith Willson), he always kept in mind his hometown of Peru by ordering 9 pounds of chocolate fudge from Arnold's Candies—then having it shipped to wherever he was in the world each month of his adult life.

Illinois is where the name of a character created by Popeye cartoonist Elzie Segar—Eugene the Jeep—was given to the army's first all-terrain vehicle; where Orson Welles and Paul Newman made their theatrical debuts; and where a blacksmith named John Deere started making steel plows in 1837.

Musician Miles Davis was from the river town of Alton, feminist Betty Friedan and comedian Richard Pryor from Peoria, Carl Sandburg from Galesburg, and Ernest Hemingway from Oak Park. Walt Disney was born in Chicago, Ray Bradbury in Waukegan, and Charlton Heston in Evanston.

Tampico's Ronald Reagan remains the only Illinois-born U.S. president to date. William Jennings Bryan, who was born in the southern Illinois town of Salem and ran unsuccessfully for president in 1896, 1900, and 1904, was the only candidate who could have upstaged the actor-president as the first Illinois-born chief executive.

One Illinois city, Danville, claims at least five native sons who made good, and all of them came home in 1988 to be photographed together—Bobby Short, Donald O'Connor, Dick and Jerry Van Dyke, and Gene Hackman.

The 1854 Kathryn Beich candy factory in Bloomington is still turning out Bit-O-Honey and Laffy Taffy, and a fast food shrine to McDonald's in Des Plaines is now a museum. Bloomington/Normal's Shirk Products is the sole producer of Beer Nuts.

Iowa is where American icons John Wayne of *Red River (1948),* Andy Williams of "Moon River," and Glenn Miller of "Moonlight Serenade" were born; where Clint Eastwood wooed Meryl Streep on the covered bridges of Madison County, and where a chartered plane carrying Buddy Holly, Richie Valens, and J. P. Richardson, the Big Bopper, crashed in the snow, killing all three on "the day the music died."

The famous advice-to-the-lovelorn columnists, twins Ann Landers and "Dear Abby" Abigail Van Buren, were born in Sioux City; jazz great Bix Beiderbecke came from the opposite side of the state in Davenport; and the thriller *Twister* (1996) was filmed in an RV park in Eldora. (Just kidding; actually, an RV park was built and operated for a while on the location in 1998.)

The Heartland is where you go to tour RV plants, ride antique carousels, visit pioneer towns and historic farms, eat dinner at an earlier hour than you thought possible (some restaurants close at 8pm), and rediscover yourself in a friendly, easygoing atmosphere where life is simpler and richer.

RVing in the Heartland

This part of the Midwest is generally RV-friendly, in part because many of the biggest brand names—Winnebago, Jayco, Coachmen, Gulf Stream, Holiday Rambler, Newmar, Shasta, Damon, and Forest River—are manufactured here. Back roads are usually well marked with a fairly good surface, except in Iowa, where many of the county roads are still unpaved.

While we'd hesitate to call Midwestern drivers slow, some of them do move more deliberately, you might say, than East Coast and West Coast drivers. This does not refer to the drivers in greater Chicago, who, faced with heavy traffic on rough, often potholed highways (and these are the interstates!) sometimes indicate their displeasure at sharing their roadways with RVs.

Iowa Highlights

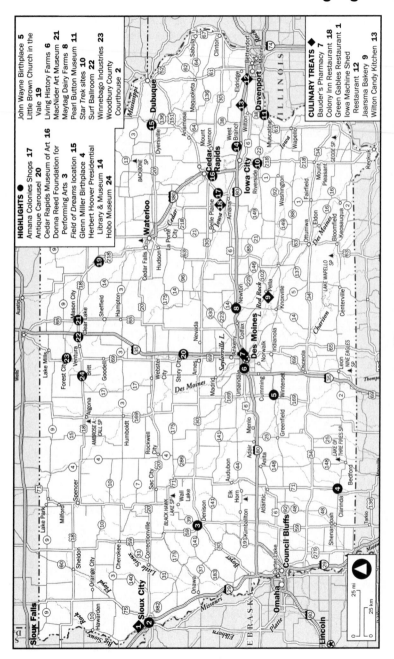

HIGHLIGHTS ●

Amana Colonies Shops **17**
Antique Carousel **20**
Cedar Rapids Museum of Art **16**
Donna Reed Foundation for Performing Arts **3**
Field of Dreams location **15**
Glenn Miller Birthplace **4**
Herbert Hoover Presidential Library & Museum **14**
Hobo Museum **24**
John Wayne Birthplace **5**
Little Brown Church in the Vale **19**
Living History Farms **6**
MacNider Art Museum **21**
Maytag Dairy Farms **8**
Pearl Button Museum **11**
Star Trek sites **10**
Surf Ballroom **22**
Winnebago Industries **23**
Woodbury County Courthouse **2**

CULINARY TREATS ◆

Bauder's Pharmacy **7**
Colony Inn Restaurant **18**
Green Gables Restaurant **1**
Iowa Machine Shed Restaurant **12**
Jaarsma Bakery **9**
Wilton Candy Kitchen **13**

Chicago makes a central starting point for this tour, especially if you plan to fly in and rent an RV locally, but you could also begin to the southeast in Indianapolis or to the west in Sioux City or Omaha.

HITTING THE HIGHLIGHTS

If you only have 2 weeks to explore this part of the Heartland, you'll have to choose between sticking to a leisurely pace through one or two of the states or making a quick drive through all three.

The latter allows for an overview, but you may miss some of the fascinating footnotes along the way. From Chicago, head west through Rockford and Galena to Dubuque and *Field of Dreams* country, then west to Waterloo and Cedar Falls and south to Des Moines and Madison County. From here, head east again through Iowa City and the Amana Colonies, then to the Quad Cities, where you reenter Illinois. Drop south to Peoria and Springfield, then east to Indianapolis. From here, it's a short drive to the Fort Wayne area, then north again to Chicago. You'll have covered a minimum of about 1,200 miles, plus added detours.

GOING FOR THE LONG HAUL

A tour of Iowa might begin in Sioux City, then follow the Missouri River south to Council Bluffs, then east to Madison County (home of the famous bridges), through Des Moines, and north to Story City and Clear Lake. From here, travel east to Mason City—setting for *The Music Man* (1962)—then south through Cedar Falls to the Dubuque area and the location for *Field of Dreams* (1989). After that, zag west through Anamosa and the Grant Wood country, to Iowa City and the Amana Colonies, then east to the Quad Cities of Davenport, Moline, Bettendorf, and Rock Island. You'll cover roughly 1,000 miles, more if you take some scenic detours.

From the Quad Cities, head east into Illinois, then south through Peoria to New Salem and Springfield's Lincoln Country. If you have time, detour west to Hannibal and the Great River Road along the Mississippi. South of St. Louis you'll find Chester, home of Popeye, and still farther south, at the bottom of the state, Metropolis, hometown of Superman. From Metropolis, head east to Shawneetown, on the Indiana border, then cross into southern Indiana at New Harmony. This Illinois itinerary covers about 750 miles.

From New Harmony, Indiana, drive northeast toward Indianapolis, pausing in Brown County at Nashville and nearby Columbus, then head northwest on I-74 from the capital to Crawfordsville. From here, drive north to Battle Ground, then east to Peru and then southeast to Fairmount. After paying your respects to James Dean, continue southeast to Muncie and Richmond. This Indiana itinerary covers some 500 miles.

Head north from Richmond to Fort Wayne, then detour to Grabill, St. Joe, and Auburn for special surprises. From Auburn, head for the Amish country at Shipshewana and the nearby RV country around Elkhart and South Bend. Follow the Indiana Turnpike with detours to Indiana Dunes, Chesterton, Valparaiso, and Hammond, and then drive on to Chicago, detouring over to Joliet to see the magnificent opera house. This rambling itinerary through northern Indiana covers less than 500 miles.

Illinois Highlights

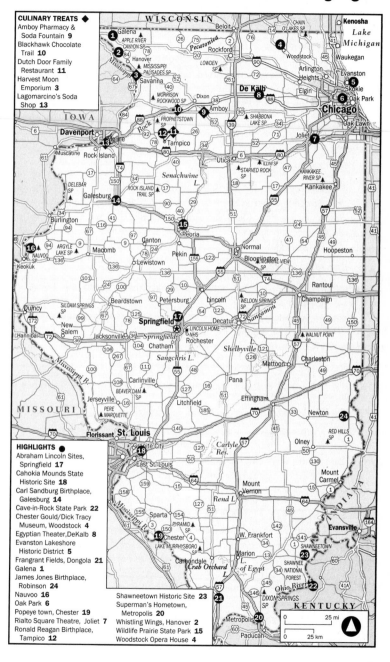

CULINARY TREATS ◆
Amboy Pharmacy &
  Soda Fountain **9**
Blackhawk Chocolate
  Trail **10**
Dutch Door Family
  Restaurant **11**
Harvest Moon
  Emporium **3**
Lagomarcino's Soda
  Shop **13**

HIGHLIGHTS ●
Abraham Lincoln Sites,
  Springfield **17**
Cahokia Mounds State
  Historic Site **18**
Carl Sandburg Birthplace,
  Galesburg **14**
Cave-in-Rock State Park **22**
Chester Gould/Dick Tracy
  Museum, Woodstock **4**
Egyptian Theater, DeKalb **8**
Evanston Lakeshore
  Historic District **5**
Frangrant Fields, Dongola **21**
Galena **1**
James Jones Birthplace,
  Robinson **24**
Nauvoo **16**
Oak Park **6**
Popeye town, Chester **19**
Rialto Square Theatre, Joliet **7**
Ronald Reagan Birthplace,
  Tampico **12**

Shawneetown Historic Site **23**
Superman's Hometown,
  Metropolis **20**
Whistling Wings, Hanover **2**
Wildlife Prairie State Park **15**
Woodstock Opera House **4**

Travel Essentials

WHEN TO GO

Summer is the prime season here, but that's also when the locals go driving, camping, and sightseeing. We've traveled the area in May, when there's a chance of rain on some days, but temperatures are mild, and in late September and October, which is practically perfect. We once had a lovely RV trip through northern Indiana and Illinois in early March, marred by a sudden snowstorm over northern Indiana. Freak weather conditions, called "the lake effect," can create unusual snow and ice storms, especially in autumn, in the lakeshore areas.

WHAT TO TAKE

If you've packed your RV properly with walking shoes, binoculars, a raincoat, and a camera, you should have everything you need for the Heartland. We have also flown into St. Louis and rented a Rialta camping van locally, then pulled into a bargain-priced variety store and bought inexpensive bedding, reusable plastic dishes, and a couple of pots and pans.

WHAT TO WEAR

Clean and decent is the rule for summer clothing. Modest shorts and T-shirts pass muster for the whole family on a hot day, but if you stop to go to a local church or a nice restaurant, you might want a light cotton dress and lightweight long pants. When the fashion police aren't around, the male half of this duo may don a lightweight, short-sleeved RV jumpsuit on driving days.

TRIMMING COSTS ON THE ROAD

Restaurant portions are generous, so when we pick up a meal to go, we often buy one to share between the two of us.

Gas prices vary from state to state, so it's a good idea to exchange price information with fellow RVers who have just driven through the state to which you're headed. We carry binoculars within reach to scan gas station price signs ahead, so we can get in the correct lane to turn if we find a cheap price.

Farmers' markets and roadside produce stands have great buys on local fruit and vegetables in season.

WHERE TO GET TRAVEL INFORMATION

Stop at state tourist information offices located on interstate highways near the state borders. A blue tourist information sign is usually posted shortly after the signs welcoming visitors to the state. You can pick up armloads of free brochures from open racks.

Iowa has an attractive **welcome center** outside the Quad Cities at **LeClaire,** exit 306 near the I-80 crossing for the Mississippi River. Styled like a riverboat captain's house overlooking the river, it showcases a museum of famous Iowans (John Wayne, Mamie Eisenhower, Herbert Hoover, and Buffalo Bill). In addition to the free maps, booklets, and brochures, you'll find gift shop items made in the state, including jellies

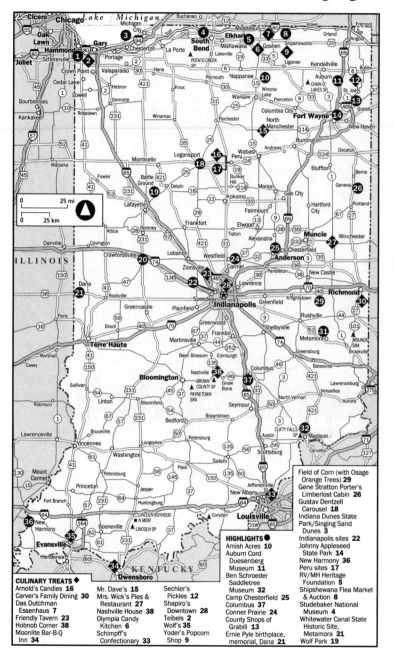

Indiana Highlights

HIGHLIGHTS ●
Amish Acres **10**
Auburn Cord Duesenberg Museum **11**
Ben Schroeder Saddletree Museum **32**
Camp Chesterfield **25**
Columbus **37**
Conner Prairie **24**
County Shops of Grabill **13**
Ernie Pyle birthplace, memorial, Dana **21**
Field of Corn (with Osage Orange Trees) **29**
Gene Stratton Porter's Limberlost Cabin **26**
Gustav Dentzell Carousel **18**
Indiana Dunes State Park/Singing Sand Dunes **3**
Indianapolis sites **22**
Johnny Appleseed State Park **14**
New Harmony **36**
Peru sites **17**
RV/MH Heritage Foundation **5**
Shipshewana Flea Market & Auction **8**
Studebaker National Museum **4**
Whitewater Canal State Historic Site, Metamora **31**
Wolf Park **19**

CULINARY TREATS ◆
Arnold's Candies **16**
Carver's Family Dining **30**
Das Dutchman Essenhaus **7**
Friendly Tavern **23**
Hobnob Corner **38**
Moonlite Bar-B-Q Inn **34**
Mr. Dave's **15**
Mrs. Wick's Pies & Restaurant **27**
Nashville House **38**
Olympia Candy Kitchen **6**
Schimpff's Confectionary **33**
Sechler's Pickles **12**
Shapiro's Downtown **28**
Teibels **2**
Wolf's **35**
Yoder's Popcorn Shop **9**

from the Amana Colonies and crunchy peanut brittle from Brittles Candy Company in Clinton.

If you want to amass material ahead of time so you can study it, contact the following state government tourist information offices:

- **Illinois Bureau of Tourism,** 500 E. Monroe St., Springfield, IL 62701 (© **800/226-6632** or 217/785-6276; www.enjoyillinois.com).

- **Indiana Department of Commerce, Tourism Development Division,** 1 N. Capitol Ave., Ste. 600, Indianapolis, IN 46204 (© **800/667-9800** or 317/232-8881; www.in.gov/visitindiana).

- **Iowa Division of Tourism,** 200 E. Grand Ave., Des Moines, IA 50309 (© **888/472-6035** or 515/725-3084; www.traveliowa.com).

DRIVING & CAMPING TIPS

Be cautious about weather. In tornado season, local TV stations usually run tornado warnings by county at the bottom of the screen, so look up the name of the county you're in and the counties nearby when you stop for the night. If an alarm sounds, leave your motor home and proceed to the campground's designated shelter and remain until the alert is over.

The first time we ran into this on a dark and windy spring night in Bowling Green, Kentucky, we were having a candlelight dinner and listening to CDs. We saw our fellow campers hurrying in singles and pairs toward the recreation center, and figured there was a bingo game or ice-cream social. Not until the next morning did we realize there had been a tornado warning.

You can also run into heavy driving **rain** so powerful that you should pull over (well off the roadway) at the first opportunity and wait it out.

On **secondary and rural roads,** particularly when they are narrow, **exercise caution** and drive slowly, because you may round a turn and find a large tractor, a horse-drawn Amish carriage, or even a herd of dairy cattle crossing from the pasture to the barn in front of you. These roads are also famous for making sudden left or right turns at a property boundary.

A random observation: There's nothing an Iowan loves better than laying down a good cloud of dust from a motor vehicle, be it a tractor, car, or pickup.

The Best Heartland Sights, Tastes & Experiences

OFF-THE-WALL ATTRACTIONS

James Dean's Hometown, Fairmount, Indiana. Not only a museum, but a shop in Fairmount, Indiana, is dedicated to the moody movie icon of the 1950s who died in an automobile crash in 1955 at age 24. Although he was born in nearby Marion, he spent all but 4 of his first 18 years in Fairmount.

At the **Fairmount Historical Museum** are high school papers of Dean's, as well as his favorite motorcycle, an address book, clothing, and film costumes. It also sells souvenirs; you can buy James Dean's mug on ashtrays, T-shirts, belt buckles, calendars, coffee cups, and place mats. Mar–Nov Mon–Sat 10am–5pm, Sun noon–5pm. Donation requested. 203 E. Washington St. For information, call the Fairmount Historical Museum (© **765/948-4555;** www.jamesdeanartifacts.com).

James Dean Gallery is a shop in Fairmount that has information about Dean and maps to the area. Fairmount is about halfway between Indianapolis and Fort Wayne; from I-69, take State Rte. 26 W. and drive 5 miles into Fairmount. At 425 Main St. (© **765/948-3326;** www.jamesdeangallery.com).

The Surf Ballroom, Clear Lake, Iowa. It's still a concert site as well as the historic location where rock stars Buddy Holly, Richie Valens, and J. P. Richardson (the Big Bopper) made their last appearances before dying in the crash of a chartered aircraft taking off from Clear Lake. Photographs and memorabilia of the musicians are displayed. Also playing in the concert that night of February 3, 1959, were Dion and the Belmonts, as well as Waylon Jennings, who let Richardson, sick with a cold, take his place on the ill-fated plane. Mon–Fri 9am–5pm (when the box office is open or a staff member is around, for a small fee). It's in downtown Clear Lake at 460 N. Shore Dr. on the lakefront. From I-35, take the U.S. 18 exit and drive west to Buddy Holly Place. The ballroom is just beyond it on the left (© **641/357-6151;** www. surfballroom.com).

John Dillinger Museum, Hammond, Indiana. Located in the Welcome Center just off I-80 at exit 3, Kennedy Avenue South, the interactive museum portrays a historical adventure illustrating the life and times of John Dillinger and other gangsters during the 1930s Depression era. Learn about the birth of the FBI as it chased Dillinger and his gang through the Midwest. Artifacts include a copy of the wooden gun he used in one of his prison escapes and the trousers he wore when he was shot down leaving the Biograph Theater in Chicago. Daily 10am–4pm. Admission $4 adults, $3 seniors, $2 children 6–12, free for children 5 and under. Indiana Welcome Center, 7770 Corinne Dr., Hammond (© **219/989-7979;** www.dillingermuseum.com).

Pearl Button Museum, Muscatine, Iowa. The world's only pearl button museum can be found in—where else?—the world's pearl button capital. In 1910, this Iowa town produced more than a third of the world's pearl buttons, cutting them from clamshells from the Mississippi River. The whole process is spelled out in the museum. Today the town has several plastic factories that turn out buttons. The Japanese came into the business in the 1920s, a curator told us, just about the time the river's clam supply was being depleted. Tues–Sat 10am–4pm. Free admission, but $5 donation appreciated ($1 for students). 117 W. 2nd St. (© **563/263-1052;** www.muscatine history.org).

Indiana's Singing Sand Dunes. At Indiana Dunes National Lakeshore, north of I-94 between Michigan City and Gary, you can walk on the sands and hear them sing. This is one of the rare beaches where this phenomenon occurs; the sand's sounds are caused by the wind whistling through quartz crystals, combined with moisture, pressure, and friction from walking feet. Visitor Center daily 8am–4:30pm. Look for access signs to

If you're a superfan, you can visit Superman's hometown: Metropolis!

the National Lakeshore from Rte. 12. $6 day fee, $15 campground. (© **219/926-7561;** www.nps.gov/indu).

The Bridges of Madison County, Winterset, Iowa. Five covered bridges more than a century old are within 15 miles of town, mostly on unpaved roads. The one featured most prominently in the Clint Eastwood/Meryl Streep film is Roseman; you may not recognize it with its coat of red paint, since it was artificially aged for the film. Get a map from the Winterset Chamber of Commerce at 73 W. Jefferson St. (© **515/462-1185;** www.madisoncounty.com).

Superman's Hometown, Metropolis, Illinois. In 1972, the only town in America named Metropolis decided to promote itself as Superman's Metropolis, and put a 9-foot bronze statue of the Man of Steel in the town square, then added a Super Museum (daily 9am–5pm), Superman billboards, and even a water tower honoring the superhero. An official Superman phone booth lets you talk to him when you lift the receiver, and you can pick up the local newspaper, which is called *The Daily Planet.* In the spring of 2001, the actor who portrays Superman for Metropolis donned his costume and married his fiancée by the statue in the square. Open 9am–5pm. Admission $5. For information, call the Chamber of Commerce, 517 Market St. (© **800/298-6119** or 618/524-5518 for museum; www.supermuseum.com).

Dances with Wolves at Wolf Park, Battle Ground, Indiana. You can have a howling good time every Saturday night as well as some other nights of the year by joining the wolves in a few choruses at 75-acre Wolf Park. Year-round Sat 7:30–9pm;

May–Nov Fri–Sat 7:30–9pm and Tues–Sun 1–5pm. Admission $7 adults, $5 children 6–13. The park is 2 miles north of Battle Ground; follow the signs (© **765/567-2265**; www.wolfpark.org).

John Wayne's Birthplace, Winterset, Iowa. The simple four-room house at 216 S. 2nd Ave. has been restored as it was in 1907, the year Wayne was born, and photos and memorabilia (including his eye patch from *True Grit,* 1969) trace his career. Daily 10am–4:30pm. Guided tours are $6 adults, $5 seniors, $2 children (© **515/462-1044**; www.johnwaynebirthplace.org).

SPECIAL SPLURGES: OFFBEAT SHOPPING OPS
The Country Shops of Grabill, Indiana. Well off the beaten track, this charming Amish town is also home to 30,000 square feet of antiques. Shops at 13756 State St.: Mon–Sat 9am–5pm; Sun noon–5pm. Call for shop information (© **260/627-6315**).

Shops of the Amana Colonies, Amana, Iowa. For beautiful country crafts such as quilts, hand-crafted wood furniture, woolen items, homemade jams, sweet fruit and berry wines, and handmade baskets, browse through the colorful stone houses–turned–shops in the seven villages of the Amana Colonies. Visitors Center, 622 46th Ave. (© **800/579-2294**; www.amanacolonies.com).

Shipshewana Auction & Flea Market, Shipshewana, Indiana. More than 1,000 vendors sell everything from quilts to copper kettles, while a dozen auctioneers simultaneously take bids on live horses and cows. While the auction takes place only on Wednesday, and the Flea Market on Tuesday, the town's shops, 345 S. Van Buren St., are open Monday to Saturday year-round. For information, call (© **260/768-4129**; www.tradingplaceamerica.com).

Blackhawk Chocolate Trail, Blackhawk Waterways area, Illinois. This toothsome trail takes you through four counties in northwestern Illinois: Carroll, Ogle, Lee, and Whiteside. Savor the hand-dipped chocolates from the **Harvest Moon Emporium** in Savanna and Little Chocolatier, Inc., in Rock Falls. Hot fudge sundaes are served at Amboy's old-fashioned soda fountain (see "Six Candy Kitchens, Soda Fountains & Ice-Cream Parlors," below), and Oreo flurries are a delight at Tampico's **Dutch Diner Family Restaurant**. Call for Chocolate Trail details (© **800/678-2108** or 815/946-2277; www.thechocolatetrail.com).

THREE FABULOUS FACTORY TOURS
1. **Winnebago Industries, Forest City, Iowa.** It was a tour through this factory's assembly line, plus a good experience with a leased RV, that convinced us to buy a motor home. The world's largest production plant has a catwalk that allows visitors to watch the manufacturing operation (no photos allowed). Tours: Apr–Oct daily 9am and 1pm (closed holidays and 1 week in July). The plant is at 1045 S. 4th St. From I-35, take the Hwy. 9 west exit and go west to Hwy. 69 and turn south. When you get into Forest City, turn right on 4th Street. Call ahead (© **641/585-3535**; www.winnebagoind.com).

2. **Sechler's Pickles, 5686 SR1, St. Joe, Indiana.** This tour starts out back, where huge vats of cucumbers are pickling in brine for anywhere from 10 weeks to 18 months, so you can see what a serious business it is. Then you go inside and watch the workers processing and packing the pickles; not every kind is produced every day. Afterward, visit the showroom, where you can sample and purchase any of the varieties Sechler's (pronounced *Seck*-lers) makes. Tours: Apr–Oct weekdays 9–11am (every half-hour) and 12:30–2pm. Call ahead for reservations (✆ **800/332-5461** or 260/337-5461; www.gourmet pickles.com).

3. **Maytag Dairy Farms, Newton, Iowa.** A member of the family that developed Maytag washing machines in 1907 gave his name to America's most famous blue cheese. Frederik Maytag founded the washing machine company, his son Elmer assembled a herd of Holstein cows in the 1920s, and Elmer's son Fred Maytag II built a cheese-making plant in 1941. The rich, full flavor of this exceptionally good cheese comes from a longer curing process. Maytag blue is cured in salt and aged for 1 month in a cave, then coated in wax and aged 5 months in a second cave. Free videos of the dairy operation: weekdays 9am–5pm, Sat 9am–1pm. There's also a shop where you can buy the cheese, or it can be shipped. Call to place orders or to get directions to the farm (✆ **800/247-2458** or 641/792-1133; www.maytagdairyfarms.com).

SEVEN TAKEOUT (OR EAT-IN) TREATS

1. **Green Gables Restaurant, Sioux City, Iowa.** The epitome of a town's "nice" restaurant, this eatery is run by family members. We got two delicious takeout lunches for $10 and change: stuffed peppers with mashed potatoes, and fried chicken. The Green Gables has been feeding Sioux City since 1929. Open Sun–Fri 11am–9pm, Sat 11am–10pm (closed Christmas). It's at 1800 Pierce St., at the corner of 18th St., a half-mile north of downtown (✆ **712/258-4246**).

2. **Jaarsma Bakery, Pella, Iowa.** Dutch letters are flaky pastries filled with marzi-pan (almond paste), shaped like letters of the alphabet, and sometimes sprinkled with sugar. We tasted them first at the Des Moines Farmers Market, but learned they were made in Pella, a town influenced by early Dutch settlers. The bakery, which began back in 1898, is at 727 Franklin St. on the south side of the town square, in a building with a brick facade that will remind you of Amsterdam. Open Mon–Sat 6am–6pm. While you're nibbling on a letter, you can see the *Klokkenspel* (glockenspiel) animated clock a half-block to the east. The figures perform daily at 11am and 1, 3, 5, and 9pm (✆ **641/628-2940;** www.jaarsma bakery.com).

3. **Shapiro's Downtown, Indianapolis, Indiana.** It may not look like your favor-ite neighborhood deli, but when you get inside this sprawling cafeteria/restau-rant, one sniff will correct any false impressions. At 808 S. Meridian St., this is

the place for early breakfasts, fresh baked rye bread and bagels, towering corned beef and pastrami sandwiches, pickled herring, and strawberry cheesecake. Year-round daily 6:30am–8pm (© **317/631-4041;** www.shapiros.com). Shapiro's also has two other area locations: in Carmel (just north of Indianapolis) and at the Indianapolis International Airport.

4. **The Iowa Machine Shed Restaurant, Davenport, Iowa.** A favorite Sunday lunch spot for locals, this sprawling eatery is decorated with carved pigs and tractors outside, and old farm implements, calendars, seed brochures, and sun-bonnets inside. Our takeout here scored some pluses (a baked potato soup with sour cream, chives, and grated yellow cheese; yummy fried chicken; and a giant apple dumpling) and one big minus (a breaded pork tenderloin sandwich that was made out of—ugh—chopped pork instead of a juicy, tender slice of pounded tenderloin). It's at 7250 Northwest Blvd., just off I-80 at exit 292. Open Mon–Sat 6am–10pm, Sun 7am–9pm (© **563/391-2427;** www. machineshed.com).

5. **Mrs. Wick's Pies & Restaurant, Winchester, Indiana.** Located at 217 Green-ville Ave., Mrs. Wick's shop sells fresh and frozen pies in 31 varieties, plus soups, sandwiches, and salads. Her sugar cream pie, called Indiana farm pie, is delicious and long-lasting when refrigerated. It costs $1.80 a slice, $5 and up for a pie. Mon–Thurs 6am–7pm, Fri 6am–8pm, Sat 6am–2pm (© **800/642-5880** or 765/584-3700; www.wickspies.com).

6. **Colony Inn Restaurant, the Amana Colonies, Amana, Iowa.** If you're really hungry, you'll love the cooking at the family-style restaurants around the Ama-nas; what it can lack in finesse, it makes up for in quantity. Since we never want seconds and we were tired from traveling all day, we wanted to get takeout food and relax over a bottle of wine in our motor home. Only the genial folks at the Colony Inn Restaurant, 741 47th Ave., the third place we tried, were kind enough to let us do that. We sampled bratwurst and sauerkraut, fried chicken, and strawberry-rhubarb pie, all of it well worth taking home. It's open for break-fast, lunch, and dinner (© **319/622-3030**).

7. **Teibels, Schererville, Indiana.** At the busy intersection of U.S. 30 and Hwy. 41, this sprawling restaurant covers an area the size of an airplane hangar, with banquet rooms and a coffee shop. There's plenty of room for RVs in the parking lot. On a midday Saturday, we joined a small cluster of people waiting for a table in the coffee shop, a room with all the charm of a dentist's office without the magazines, so we opted for takeout food. For less than $15, we carried away a quarter of a crunchy fried chicken, a heap of delicate boned and buttered lake perch, french fries, rice pilaf, coleslaw, hot rolls, melted butter, and tartar sauce for the fish. Mon–Thurs 11am–9pm, Fri–Sat 11am–10pm, Sun 11am–8pm (© **219/865-2000;** www.teibels.com).

SIX CANDY KITCHENS, SODA FOUNTAINS & ICE-CREAM PARLORS

1. **Olympia Candy Kitchen, Goshen, Indiana.** This Greek family business is busy all day, from breakfast coffee to luncheon olive burgers with homemade mayonnaise. Savor the hand-dipped chocolates, caramel turtles, chocolate-covered cherries, and handmade candy canes all day. Mon, Tues, Thurs, and Fri 7am–5pm; Sat 7am–3pm; Sun 9am–1pm; closed Wed. At 136 N. Main St. since 1912; Olympia Candy Kitchen will ship candies (℃ **574/533-5040;** www.olympiacandykitchen.com).

2. **Amboy Pharmacy & Soda Fountain, Amboy, Illinois.** Chocolate phosphates and hot fudge sundaes top the menu in this nostalgic soda fountain. Summer daily 6am–5pm; winter Mon–Sat 8am–5pm. Located at 202 E. Main St. (℃ **815/857-2323**).

3. **Schimpff's Confectionary, Jeffersonville, Indiana.** This 1891 family confectionary features the original tin ceiling, a soda fountain, antique memorabilia, and yummy candies like cinnamon red hots that they'll ship to you. Weekdays 10am–5pm, Sat 10am–3pm (closed major holidays). It's in the Historic Downtown Business District at 347 Spring St. (℃ **812/283-8367;** www.schimpffs.com).

4. **Lagomarcino's Soda Shop, Moline, Illinois.** This simple candy store and soda shop, founded in 1908 in a Victorian brick building at 1422 5th Ave., smells like heaven because of the homemade ice cream, hot fudge sauce, and handmade chocolates. Mon–Sat 9am–5:30pm (℃ **309/764-1814;** www.lagomarcinos.com). Lagomarcino's also has a second location in East Davenport, Iowa (℃ **563/324-6137**).

5. **Bauder's Pharmacy, Des Moines, Iowa.** Established in 1922, this is the place for homemade ice cream, turtle sundaes (with caramel, nuts, and chocolate), and cherry Cokes. Weekdays 8:30am–6pm, Sat 9am–3pm, Sun 10am–2pm. Located at 3802 Ingersoll Ave. (℃ **515/255-1124**).

6. **Wilton Candy Kitchen, Wilton, Iowa.** Set in an 1856 structure on the main street of town, this family-owned soda fountain, sandwich shop, and ice-cream parlor may be the oldest in the country. When we last visited, it was still operated by George Nopoulos, son of Gus Nopoulos, a Greek immigrant who bought the business in 1910. The family likes to say Gus invented the banana split when he had too many ripe bananas. It's a wonderfully evocative soda fountain that still makes malts, phosphates, cherry Cokes, exotic sundaes, and grilled ham-and-cheese sandwiches. Daily 7:30am–5pm. On 310 Cedar St. (℃ **563/732-2278;** www.wiltoncandykitchen.com).

WILDLIFE-WATCHING

Except for **birding,** the Midwest is light on wildlife viewing compared to some of the other destinations in this book. However, Council Bluffs, Iowa, has a lot of **black**

squirrels that are so popular, they're protected by a city ordinance that makes it illegal to annoy, worry, maim, injure, or kill one.

White squirrels are the mascots of Olney, Illinois, pink-eyed and bushy-tailed, most easily seen in the Olney City Park.

Every Fourth of July, the city of Roachdale, Indiana, schedules a **cockroach race** with contestants from around the world. Starters hold eager contestants at the gate with flypaper until an official calls out, "Gentlemen and ladies, start your cockroaches!"

America's largest concentration of **ring-billed gulls** visits Lake Erie's western basin each fall.

In Peoria, Illinois, the **Wildlife Prairie State Park** displays animals you might have seen in Illinois 200 years ago—**wolves, bison, black bears, elk, cougars, otters,** and **waterfowl.** The park is 10 miles west of downtown on Route 8 at 3826 N. Taylor Rd.; it can easily be reached from I-74, exit 82; signage is posted. It's open daily 9am to 6:30pm, except mid-December through February 9am to 4:30pm. Admission $7 adults, $5 children 4 to 12, free for children 3 and under. (© **309/676-0998;** www.wildlifeprairiestatepark.org).

On the Road

THE WILDS OF WEST IOWA

The state of **Iowa** is bisected by I-35 as it runs north-south from border to border, so we'll refer to all of the state west of I-35 as West Iowa. Sioux City on the Missouri River is one of those places where the West truly begins. If you come into town from the south or east, the **Sergeant Floyd Monument** looms from a hilltop, marking the final resting place of the only member of the Lewis and Clark Expedition to die on the journey. He fell ill suddenly and expired, probably from appendicitis, on August 20, 1804. In town, the richly ornamented and extraordinary **Woodbury County Courthouse,** designed in 1918 by three associates of Louis Sullivan in that Chicago master's style, signals the last vestige of the Midwest before the West begins.

About 80 miles east of Sioux City is the town of **Wall Lake,** where singer Andy Williams was born in a simple house with a sign out front to let you know this is the place. It's open in summer on Saturday and Sunday from 2 to 4pm, or by appointment at other times (© **712/664-2119**).

Oscar-winning Donna Reed (best supporting actress for *From Here to Eternity,* 1953) is remembered with a statelier monument in her hometown of **Denison,** 30 miles southwest of Wall Lake at the junction of U.S. 30 and U.S. 59. The **Donna Reed Foundation for the Performing Arts** displays her Oscar statue, awards scholarships in performing arts, and holds an annual 9-day festival in June, with acting workshops led by Hollywood professionals. The Donna Reed Theater, built as an opera house in 1914, was restored by the foundation named for the actress. Because she also starred in a perennial Christmas favorite with Jimmy Stewart, the city of Denison uses its title, *"It's A Wonderful Life,"* as a community slogan. A miniature model of the town of Bedford Falls is on display in the performing arts center, and a

FARM FACTS

As a renewable resource, a single Iowa farm produces enough food to feed 279 people. Iowa wouldn't be Iowa without its farm country. Walk through the state's history and chat with costumed interpreters from five different eras at **Living History Farms** in Urbandale, a suburb of Des Moines (May to early Sept daily 9am–5pm and early Sept to late Oct Wed–Sun noon–5pm). The collection of farms and villages includes a 1700 Ioway Indian village, an 1850 pioneer farm, an 1875 frontier town, and a 1900 farm. Admission $12 adults, $11 seniors, $7 children 4 to 12. Plan to spend the day. It's at 11121 Hickman Rd. (© **515/278-5286;** www.lhf.org).

turn-of-the-20th-century soda shop and candy store is part of the complex at 1305 Broadway (© **800/336-4692** or 712/263-3334; www.donnareed.org).

Some 30 miles south of Denison as the crow flies are the Danish villages of **Elk Horn** and **Kimballton.** The former has a Danish windmill, the latter a replica fountain of Copenhagen's Little Mermaid, and both are chockablock with folk dancers, Scandinavian gift shops, and bakeries.

The little town of **Adair** at exit 86 off I-80 displays a locomotive wheel and a plaque noting an 1873 landmark—the world's first robbery of a moving train, committed when Jesse James and his gang held up a train on this spot.

The **Winterset** area in Madison County, southwest of Des Moines where U.S. 169 intersects Iowa 92, has turned into the state's most visited area because of Robert Waller's book and Clint Eastwood's film *The Bridges of Madison County* (1995). Pick up a map to the six bridges from the **Chamber of Commerce** at 73 W. Jefferson St. in Winterset (© **800/298-6119** or 515/462-1185; www.madisoncounty.com).

John Wayne's birthplace, also open daily, is in downtown Winterset at 224 S. 2nd St. (See "Off-the-Wall Attractions," earlier in this chapter.)

If you're around **Des Moines** on a Saturday morning in summer, check out the **downtown farmers' market** on Court Street near 4th. In addition to Iowa corn and tomatoes, you'll find Asian specialty vegetables, freshly cooked samosas, and plenty of cut flowers. It runs May through October, 7am to noon, and parking is free in the vicinity (© **515/286-4928;** www.downtowndsm.com).

One of the rare Herschell-Spillman **antique carousels** that are still operating is less than 50 miles north of Des Moines in **Story City.** Take exit 124 from I-35 and drive 2 miles west. The carousel resides in the town's North Park, which will be on the right as you drive into town. The hand-carved animals include 20 horses, two chickens, two pigs, several dogs, and a "whirling lovers tub." At the top are painted canvas murals and carved gargoyles, and a 1936 Wurlitzer Military Band Organ provides the music. The carousel operates Monday and Tuesday noon to 6pm, Wednesday to Sunday noon to 8pm, and on May and September weekends only, noon to 8pm. $1 a ride (© **515/733-4214;** www.storycity.net/visiting/carousel).

"The Day the Music Died" was February 3, 1959, when Buddy Holly, Richie Valens, and J. D. Richardson (the Big Bopper) died in a plane crash just outside **Clear Lake, Iowa.** They had appeared that evening at the **Surf Ballroom,** still home to rock 'n' roll and big bands, and open during weekday office hours for fans who want to visit. (See "the Surf Ballroom" in "Off-the-Wall Attractions," earlier in this chapter.) A dedicated fan can pick up a map to the crash site at the ballroom or the **Clear Lake Chamber of Commerce,** 205 Main Ave. (© **800/285-5338;** www.clear lakeiowa.com).

If you really want to get "bummed" out, drive another 25 miles west of Clear Lake on U.S. 18 to **Britt,** home of the annual **National Hobo Convention** in early August. If younger readers wonder what a hobo is, the dictionary definition is "a tramp or vagrant," but a more romantic explanation might be "a man (or woman) who spends his life traveling from place to place without a ticket, most often by rail." This legendary gathering started in 1900, then picked up again in 1933 when the Great Depression caused many people to hit the road. The history of the convention and its annually elected kings and queens (Box Car Myrtle, Iowa Blackie, Ohio Ned, Blue Moon, and New York Maggie among them) are on display Monday to Friday from 10am to 4pm at the **Hobo Museum,** 51 Main Ave. S., Britt, admission $3 (© **641/ 843-9104;** www.hobo.com/museum.html).

About 15 miles northeast of Britt is another tribute to life on the road, albeit a more comfortable one. Forest City is the home of **Winnebago Industries,** the world's first assembly-line RV plant. The 60-acre facility also has a visitor center, and factory tours are available (see "Three Fabulous Factory Tours," earlier in this chapter).

Campground Oases in Western Iowa

Sioux City North KOA campground is across the river in **South Dakota,** but only a few miles from Sioux City, Iowa. The nicely landscaped park has level, shady pull-throughs, a store, and hot food service, as well as a computer connection for e-mail. Ice-cream socials take place here. Apr to mid-Oct. Sites $35–$45. It's just off I-29 at exit 2; the address is 601 Streeter St., North Sioux City (© **800/562-5439** or 605/232-4519 reservations; www.siouxcitykoa.com).

Lake Anita State Park, Anita. This large park has trees and grass at some sites, and fishing, swimming, and boating are permitted in the lake. There are 52 sites with 30-amp electrical hookups, 40 full hookups, and water, along with a dump and toilets with showers. No reservations. Sites $9–$19. Off I-80 at exit 70, then south on Iowa 148 for 4½ miles (© **877/427-2757;** www.iowadnr.gov/Destinations/State ParksRecAreas/IowasStateParks.aspx).

Des Moines West KOA, Adel. With a great location, this park is in the heart of corn country—there's an all-you-can-eat corn-on-the-cob festival in Adel every summer. It's near the Living History Farms and the bridges of Madison County. The park provides 67 pull-throughs and 67 full hookups with up to 50-amp electric. There's LP

Moonlight Serenade

Bandleader and arranger **Glenn Miller** was born March 1, 1904, in Clarinda, near the Missouri border in the southwestern corner of Iowa near the junction of U.S. 17 and Iowa 2. His hometown salutes him every June with a festival that usually features the Glenn Miller Orchestra, along with other military and dance bands, plus a parade. The museum is open Tuesday to Sunday 1 to 5pm. Admission: $6 adult, $5 seniors, 12 and under free. **Glenn Miller Birthplace Society,** 122 W. Clark St., P.O. Box 61, Clarinda, IA 51632 (© **712/542-2461;** www.glennmiller.org).

gas service and visitors enjoy free fishing. Open year-round. Sites $34–$38. It's 17 miles west of Des Moines on I-80, exit 106, at 3418 L Ave. in Adel; follow the signs (© **800/562-2181** or 515/834-2729; www.koa.com).

Clear Lake State Park, west of Clear Lake. This park has 30-amp electrical hookups on 168 sites, a dump, and pay showers, and visitors enjoy lake fishing. Sites $16. From I-35, take exit 193 and go west on Rte. 106 for 1 mile; then turn south on Rte. 107 and travel 2 miles to Rte. B-35. The park is a half-mile west (© **641/357-4212;** www.iowadnr.gov/Destinations/StateParksRecAreas/IowasStateParks.aspx).

Prairie Rose State Park in **Harlan** has 77 back-in sites with 20- to 30-amp electrical hookups, eight sites with full hookups, and a dump. It's also wheelchair accessible, and visitors enjoy freshwater swimming and boating. No reservations. Sites $9–$16. West of Elk Horn on Rte. M47 (© **712/773-2701** information; www.iowadnr.gov/Destinations/StateParksRecAreas/IowasStateParks.aspx).

A SENTIMENTAL JOURNEY THROUGH EASTERN IOWA

Eastern Iowa makes us think of wistful love songs like Rodgers and Hammerstein's Oscar-winning "It Might As Well Be Spring" from the film *State Fair* (1945) about a farm family's adventures at the Iowa state fair, and "Good Night My Someone" from Meredith Willson's *The Music Man* (1962). The latter is set in the fictional River City, based on Willson's hometown of Mason City. You'll find it in north-central Iowa, 8 miles east of Clear Lake on U.S. 18.

Willson's boyhood home at 314 S. Pennsylvania Ave. is open May to October on Friday through Sunday afternoons from 1 to 4pm. "The Music Man" footbridge across Willow Creek on 2nd Street SE was named in honor of the musical and its composer.

Remember TV's *Kukla, Fran and Ollie?* In another look back, you can visit the Bil Baird marionettes and puppets at Mason City's **Charles H. MacNider Art Museum,** next door to the footbridge at 303 2nd St. SE. It's open Tuesday, Wednesday, Friday, and Saturday 9am to 5pm, and Thursday 9am to 9pm; free admission (© **641/421-3666;** www.macniderart.org).

Iowa Campgrounds

Amana Colonies RV Park **6**
Clear Lake State Park **9**
Des Moines West KOA **4**
George Wyth Memorial State Park **8**
Lake Anita State Park **3**
Prairie Rose State Park **2**
Sioux City North KOA **1**
Squaw Creek Regional Park **7**
West Liberty KOA **5**

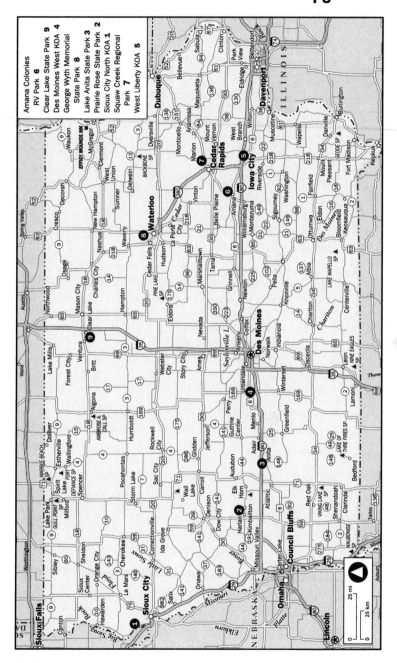

253

You can visit the *Field of Dreams* in Dyersville, Iowa.

Readers of a certain age may even remember the **Little Brown Church in the Vale,** immortalized in the hymn "The Church in the Wildwood." The song was written in 1857 by a young music teacher who came to Iowa to visit his fiancée and was entranced by a place on the Little Cedar River which he thought would be ideal for a church. In 1864, he came back to discover that a church had been built on that spot. Today, the Congregational church, which serves primarily as a wedding chapel, is open to the public daily from 7am to 7pm; take exit 220 off Avenue of the Saints Highway, then go 2 miles east of **Nashua** on Hwy. 346, to 2730 Cheyenne Ave. (✆ **641/435-2027;** www.littlebrownchurch.org).

Dyersville, the location for the Kevin Costner film *Field of Dreams* (1989), its farmhouse, cornfields, and baseball field intact, is 26 miles west of Dubuque. To get to the site, follow 3rd Avenue NE north from Dyersville (there are directional signs) to 28963 Lansing Rd. There, the only commercial aspects of the area, open from April to November, are two separate (and rival) souvenir stands selling baseball memorabilia and logo items like T-shirts. The baseball field itself overlaps two farm properties owned by two different families who have differing views on how (and whether to) develop the area further. The farmhouse used in the film is not open to the public (✆ **888/875-8404;** www.fieldofdreamsmoviesite.com).

On the way to or from the *Field of Dreams* site, stop by the **National Farm Toy Museum** at 1110 16th Ave. Court SE in Dyersville (it's on the right as you drive toward the baseball field) to look over some of the 30,000 farm toys that fill two huge floors of displays. Admission $5 adults, $4 seniors, $3 children 6 to 17, free for children 5 and under. Dyersville is a major manufacturing area for farm toys; ask about factory outlet stores in the area if you know any collectors. Open daily 8am to 6pm (✆ **563/875-2727;** www.nationalfarmtoymuseum.com).

Cedar Rapids has a colorful (and gentrified) 2-block **Czech Village** of bakeries, meat markets, gift shops, breweries, and restaurants, plus a new museum of Czech and Slovak Heritage. It's on 16th Avenue SW between C Street and Cedar River, just east of exit 18 off I-380. You can also get a good look at the famous Quaker Oats plant from I-380.

The much-visited **Amana Colonies** lie southwest of Cedar Rapids off U.S. 152, strung along Route 220. There are seven communal religious villages founded by German immigrants in the 1850s—**Amana, Middle Amana, High Amana, East Amana, West Amana, South Amana,** and **Homestead.** The society practiced the crafts of their old-world towns, handing down techniques from one generation to another. In 1932, the communities decided to separate church and state, and reorganized the Amana Society as a for-profit enterprise. The most famous product, the Amana refrigerator/freezer, is still crafted here, but the company now has outside ownership.

Today, visitors can shop in the woolen mill, furniture shop, cooper shop, broom and basket shop, bakeries, meat markets, and quilt shops. But most people spend their spare time eating the rib-sticking German cooking that is served family-style, dishes like *rouladen* (beef rolls stuffed with pickles, onions, and carrots), *sauerbraten* (vinegar-marinated roast beef), and locally made bratwurst with sauerkraut. Be prepared for big crowds in summer, especially on the weekends.

Forget about driving in the villages; just find a spot to park your RV (there's usually space around the Woolen Mill or you could check into the Amana Colonies RV Park) and take a walk. Streets are lined with lovely stone houses, the gardens are filled with flowers, and quilts and other crafts hang outdoors to entice shoppers. For more information, call the **Amana Colonies Welcome Center,** 622 46th St. (© **800/579-2294;** www.amanacolonies.com).

About 15 miles south of Iowa City, a mile west of U.S. 218 on Route 22, is the future birthplace of *Star Trek* leader Captain James T. Kirk. He's scheduled to be born in 2282, according to the plaque. It seems the town of **Riverside** was trying to come up with something to draw a few tourists, and somebody remembered reading an interview with *Star Trek* creator Gene Roddenberry in which he said Kirk "was born in a small town in Iowa." Armed with that offhand comment, city fathers approached Roddenberry with their idea, and he gave them permission to designate Kirk's future birthplace.

In the little park in the center of town is a 20-foot replica of the Starship *Enterprise* and the memorial plaque. We were even more amused by a big sign in the window at the Senior Citizens Meal Services, which read, COME IN AND SHARE A MEAL WITH THE ANCESTORS OF CAPTAIN KIRK. Call for more information on the town of Riverside (© **319/648-3501;** www.riversideiowa.org).

Some 25 miles due east of Riverside on Route 22 is the town of **Muscatine,** where the world's only pearl button museum is located. (See "Off-the-Wall Attractions," earlier in this chapter.) After seeing the museum, head to a fruit stand and buy one of the local cantaloupes or watermelons if they're in season.

About 10 miles east of Iowa City off I-80 at exit 254 is **West Branch,** where Herbert Hoover, the 31st president, was born in 1867. Historical exhibits, the presidential library, a museum, his birthplace, and a schoolhouse are all part of the complex, which is open daily 9am to 5pm. Admission $6 adults, $3 seniors, free for children 15 and under. For information, contact the **Presidential Library and Museum** at 210 Parkside Dr. (© **319/643-5301;** http://hoover.archives.gov); and the **National Historic Site** (© **319/643-2541;** www.nps.gov/heho).

The **Quad Cities—Davenport and Bettendorf, Iowa,** and **Moline and Rock Island, Illinois—**are river towns where fur trading was established in 1812. The first railroad bridge across the Mississippi was built in Davenport in 1856, and a young lawyer named Abraham Lincoln, representing the railroad, argued a subsequent lawsuit between river traders and the railroad.

Camping Oases in Eastern Iowa

George Wyth Memorial State Park lies between Cedar Falls and **Waterloo,** and is quite rustic for its location, with an expanse of grass and trees with back-in sites, and 46 sites with 30-amp electrical hookups. No reservations. Sites $16. Off I-380 at George Wyth Park exit (© **319/232-5505;** www.iowadnr.gov/Destinations/State ParksRecAreas/IowasStateParks.aspx).

Amana Colonies RV Park is a big grassy field and has 250 sites with water and 30- and 50-amp electric, plus 148 full-hookup sites and Wi-Fi. This RV park is in moderate walking distance of Amana, the main tourist center. It's a good idea to reserve ahead, since there are often groups in residence. It's closed in winter. Sites $24–$32. It's a half-mile south of **Amana** on S.R. 220. Call for reservations (© **800/471-7616** or 319/622-7616; www.amanarvpark.com).

Squaw Creek Regional Park, Marion, just outside Cedar Rapids in Marion, has big grassy sites spaced well apart, as well as 47 sites with 30- and 50-amp electrical hookups and a sanitary dump. It's closed in winter, and they don't take reservations.

YOUNG MAN WITH A HORN

Bix Beiderbecke, the influential jazz musician, was born in Davenport, Iowa, in 1903. Many readers may know the romanticized version of him as the "Young Man with a Horn" in a 1938 Dorothy Baker novel and later depicted by Kirk Douglas in the 1950 film. Harry James dubbed Bix's licks in that flick. Every year in late July or early August (call for dates), Davenport celebrates the **Bix Beiderbecke Memorial Jazz Festival,** competing with the State Fair as Iowa's most popular event. Call for information (© **888/BIX-LIVS** [249-5487] or 563/324-7170; www. bixsociety.org).

Classic Americana

Iowa artist Grant Wood created one of the most reproduced (and parodied) paintings since *Whistler's Mother* with his painting *American Gothic* in 1930, which portrays his sister Nan and his dentist, Dr. B. H. McKeeby, in front of a Gothic farmhouse with a pitchfork. The house is on American Gothic Street in the town of Eldon in southeastern Iowa, 16 miles southeast of Ottumwa on Route 16; visitors are permitted to photograph the outside of the building, but not go inside. Wood was born in **Anamosa,** 20 miles northeast of Cedar Rapids via U.S. 151, where the largest collection of American Gothic parodies and a film about Wood can be seen in the **Grant Wood Tourism Center and Gallery** (daily 1pm–4pm) at 124 E. Main St. (© **319/462-4267;** www. grantwoodartgallery.org).

The most complete collection of Wood's works is in the **Cedar Rapids Museum of Art,** 410 3rd Ave. SE (Tues, Wed, Fri, Sat noon–4pm; Thurs noon–8pm; Sun noon–4pm); admission $5 adults, $4 seniors and students, free for children 18 and under (© **319/366-7503;** www.crma.org). More Wood paintings including a self-portrait are in the **Figge Art Museum** at 225 W. 2nd St. in Davenport (Tues–Sun 10am–5pm); admission $7 adults, $6 seniors, $4 children (© **563/326-2045;** www.art-dma.org). 🚐

Sites $10–$15. To get there, take exit 24A from I-380 and go west on Rte. 100 to the junction with S.R. 13, then turn right to the marked entrance of the park (© **319/892-6450**).

West Liberty KOA is close to the Herbert Hoover National Historic Site, not far from the Amana Colonies and convenient to Riverside, Wilton, and the riverboat gambling across the river in Council Bluffs. It's open all year with 45 pull-throughs and full hookups with electrical connections up to 50 amps. Sites $27. 15 miles east of Iowa City off I-80 at exit 259 south. Call for reservations (© **800/562-7624** or 319/627-2676; www.koa.com).

NORTHERN ILLINOIS: U. S. GRANT TO RONALD REAGAN

Galena in the northwestern corner of Illinois is one of the prettiest historic hill towns anywhere, but it's not easy to maneuver a motor home through it; we suggest instead finding a parking space on the edge of town and taking a steep, challenging walk. **Ulysses S. Grant** is the big name in town. He worked here as a clerk before the Civil War and returned afterward to accept a splendid brick house as a gift from the town. He then stayed there during the summer and fall of 1868, when he was running for president. He returned in 1879 after his two-term presidency was clouded with scandal. But Galena won't hear any trash talk about Grant, even if he didn't spend a lot of his retirement in residence.

LONG BEFORE OK CORRAL

The peripatetic **Wyatt Earp** grew up in Pella, Iowa; his house is preserved at 507 Franklin St. He ran away to join the Union Army when he was 15, but was discovered and brought back. In 1864, the Earps and 40 other Iowans went by wagon train to California.

Just 20 miles south of Galena along U.S. 20, then south on Route 84, is **Hanover,** home of **Whistling Wings,** the largest mallard hatchery in the world. A gift shop at 113 Washington St., on the right as you drive south, sells frozen and smoked ducks, plus live ducks, duck eggs, and duck guano, as well as mallard sweatshirts and T-shirts. The cooked, smoked ducks are delicious. The shop will also ship some merchandise (© **815/591-3512**).

Across the top of the state is **Woodstock,** on U.S. 14 about 20 miles east of Rockford as the crow flies, with a lot of pop culture heritage for its modest size. The Bill Murray film *Groundhog Day* (1993) was filmed here, with the town standing in for Punxatawney, Pennsylvania. The restored 1890 **Woodstock Opera House** on the town square is where Orson Welles and Paul Newman, both of whom attended school here, made their theatrical debuts, and the **Chester Gould/Dick Tracy Museum** is in the Old Courthouse Arts Center. Although Gould was born in Oklahoma, his first major success was with Hearst's Chicago newspaper, *The American,* in 1921, and he created the square-jawed detective with the wristwatch telephone in 1931. For information, call the **Woodstock Recreation Dept.** (© **815/338-4363;** www.woodstock-il.com).

Southeast of Rockford in **DeKalb** is another impeccably restored period theater, an Egyptian Revival–style movie house called the **Egyptian,** on North 2nd Street near Lincoln Highway. If you're there in August for the Sweet Corn Festival, you'll sample free corn on the cob.

Heading west again to **Dixon, Ronald Reagan** admirers can see the **boyhood home** (a restored two-story white frame house in Dixon at 816 S. Hennepin Ave.) of the 40th president and film star, along with his **birthplace** (a six-room apt. above a bakery in nearby Tampico on Main St.).

Joliet, southwest of Chicago near where I-80 and I-55 intersect, has taken the 1926 **Rialto Square Theatre** and restored it to its grand days as a vaudeville movie palace. With interior details inspired by the Hall of Mirrors at Versailles, Paris's Arc de Triomphe, and Rome's Pantheon, the awesome building shows off a huge crystal chandelier with 250 lights in a block-long lobby, and it glitters with ornate gilded trim in the 2,000-seat auditorium. The original **Barton Grande Theatre Pipe Organ,** which accompanied silent films and vaudeville shows with music and sound effects, is still played.

When the Rialto reopened in 1981, flamboyant pianist Liberace, one of its first headliners, quipped, "At last! A theater to match my wardrobe!"

To the southwest lies the legendary city of **Peoria,** where the Rock Island Line used to chug into the depot by the river. When we last visited, the chugs were more like chug-a-lugs, because the restored station had been turned into a railroad-themed bar and restaurant complex. Now we hear that the place that saluted the golden days of dining cars has closed, yielding to a trendy new Italian restaurant. Maybe trains don't play in Peoria.

Everyone from Richard Nixon to native son Richard Pryor has asked, "Will it play in Peoria?" But the longest-running drama in the city's history was a strike against the local Caterpillar company.

Between Peoria and Galesburg, 50 miles northwest, lies **Spoon River,** the setting for Edgar Lee Masters's evocative poems that bring alive the people of Lewistown, Illinois. In his book *Spoon River Anthology,* he let them talk about life as if they were speaking from the grave. The only problem was that locals said Masters didn't disguise the local individuals well enough in their sad histories and worst traits. He was so disliked that the book, published in 1915, was banned from the local schools and public library for years.

Today, all is forgiven as the town celebrates his fame with an annual festival during which two dozen costumed residents read the poems at the Oak Hill Cemetery.

Joliet's Rialto Square Theatre has been beautifully restored.

Masters himself is buried in Oakland Cemetery in Petersburg, near New Salem State Historic Site. It's not far from the graves of Vachel Lindsay, who died in 1931, and of Ann Rutledge, Abraham Lincoln's fiancée in New Salem, who died in 1835 at the age of 19. Her tombstone was carved posthumously with a quote from a Masters poem: *I am Ann Rutledge who sleep beneath these weeds / Beloved in life of Abraham Lincoln / . . . Bloom forever, O Republic, from the dust of my bosom.*

Galesburg is a pretty town from another era, proud of its 19th-century architecture. The home at 331 E. 3rd St., where poet **Carl Sandburg** was born in 1878, is also his burial spot; his ashes are buried under Remembrance Rock (named for his only novel) in the park behind the house. Signs throughout town point to his birthplace, open daily year-round except holidays. Suggested donation $2 adults, $1 children (© **309/342-2361;** www.sandburg.org).

Over on the Mississippi River, on Route 96 along the Great River Road, the historic town of **Nauvoo** recalls the strife-filled story of the Mormons. Today, it's mostly a museum town staffed with costumed interpreters who tell the story of Mormon prophet Joseph Smith and his brother Hyrum, chased along with their followers first from New York and then from Missouri to this place on the Mississippi. By 1842, the town had a population of 15,000 Mormons, making it the largest town then in Illinois.

In 1844, after introducing the custom of polygamy into the faith, Smith announced that he would run for president. When a local newspaper criticized his leadership, he and Hyrum destroyed the presses. For this, the brothers were imprisoned in nearby Carthage, where a mob broke into the jail and shot them. After this, the Mormons, led by Brigham Young, migrated to Utah in 1846, leaving the town abandoned for several years until a French community called the Icarians arrived and set up an operation producing wine and cheese.

By 1856, the French too were gone, but a German group came in to continue the cheese tradition, and today you can sample delectable **Nauvoo Blue cheese** in local shops as you tour the town. The buildings are open year-round, and the **Tourist Reception Center at 1295 Mulholland St.** is open from April to November daily from 9am to 4:30pm, with maps and a self-guided cassette tape tour (© **217/453-6648;** www.beautifulnauvoo.com).

Campground Oases in Northern Illinois

Starved Rock State Park near **Utica** is a 2,630-acre preserve around a sandstone bluff where a band of Illiniwek Indians starved while besieged by their enemies below. The campground has 133 level back-in sites with 20- and 30-amp electric and water hookups. A sanitary dump, restrooms, and showers are also in the campground. Sites $30. To get there, take Rte. 178 off I-80, go south 4 miles, and then turn east on Rte. 71 for 2 miles. Call for information (© **815/667-4726;** http://dnr.state.il.us/lands/land mgt/parks/ilstate.htm).

Chicago Northwest KOA Campground in **Union** is not really near Chicago—no campground is—but it's in an attractive site, with its own false-front strip of antiques

Northern Illinois Campgrounds

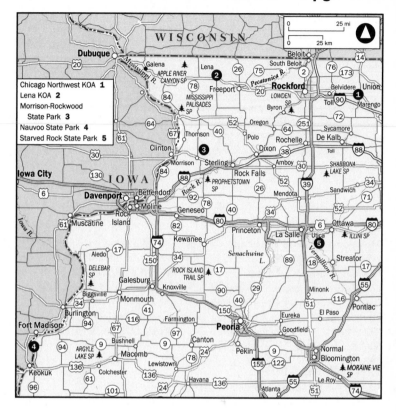

Chicago Northwest KOA **1**
Lena KOA **2**
Morrison-Rockwood
State Park **3**
Nauvoo State Park **4**
Starved Rock State Park **5**

shops next door and near the Illinois Railroad Museum. There are 88 sites with 30- and 50-amp electric and 32 full hookups. Sites $30–$50. From I-90, take the exit at Marengo-Hampshire west on Rte. 20 and drive 4½ miles to South Union Rd., where you'll turn right. Follow signs to Wild West Town. Call for reservations (*©* **800/562-2827** or 815/923-4206; www.koa.com).

Nauvoo State Park has both pull-through and back-in sites with 30-amp electrical hookups and a sanitary dump. No reservations. Sites $12–$20. South of the historic Mormon town on Rte. 96. Call for information (*©* **217/453-2512;** http://dnr.state. il.us/lands/landmgt/parks/r4/nauvoo.htm).

Lena KOA at Lena is 35 miles west of Galena. It's a good location for sightseeing in Lena and visiting Whistling Wings in Hanover and the Lena Cheese Factory Outlet Store on U.S. 20, 5 miles west of Lena. The campground has a swimming pool and double tube slide, 67 full hookups with up to 50-amp electricity and pull-throughs. Apr–Nov. Sites $25–$45. It's on U.S. 20 about ¼ mile east of the

SPRINGFIELD & RVS DON'T MIX!

Springfield is a city that doesn't seem to like RVs. The last time we were there, the parking lot at the Lincoln home was only big enough for cars, and for blocks around the historic sites, NO PARKING FOR VANS AND RVS signs were posted. If you're pulling a tow car, use that to visit the sites; if not, we'd suggest leaving your RV at the campground and taking a bus or cab into the historic district.

intersection with State Hwy. 73. Call for reservations (℃ **800/562-5361** or 815/369-2612; www.koa.com).

Morrison-Rockwood State Park is at the edge of **Morrison,** just across the Mississippi from Clinton, Iowa. Some 92 gravel sites, most shaded, have 30-amp electrical hookups, and there's a dump. There's food service, fishing, swimming, and boating here, but reservations are not accepted. It's easier to get here than it sounds; signage is good, so you shouldn't get lost. Sites $15. From U.S. 30 in Morrison, take S.R. 78 north 1 mile to Damien Rd., then go 1½ miles east to Crosby Rd., then a half-mile north to the park. Call for information (℃ **815/772-4708;** http://dnr.state.il.us/lands/landmgt/parks/r1/morrison.htm).

LINCOLNLAND

Kentucky-born Abraham Lincoln is linked forever with Illinois. The only home he ever owned is restored and open for visitors in **Springfield.** Some 17 miles northwest, the historically preserved village of **New Salem,** where Lincoln served as postmaster, merchant, surveyor, and captain of the town's militia, is a park open daily year-round, except on holidays and Tuesdays and Wednesdays in winter. As militia captain, Lincoln took his unit to participate in the Black Hawk War where, he liked to say, they fought only mosquitoes.

When he was 25, while still studying law, he won a seat in the Illinois legislature. Two years later, he was elected to a second term, and after passing the bar exam, he spent half of each year as a circuit-riding attorney and judge in the 11,000-square-mile Eighth Judicial Circuit.

The town of **Lincoln,** off I-55 at exit 133, was the first to be named for Abe, in 1853 when he was still riding the circuit. The townspeople called for him to christen it, and he picked up a ripe watermelon, broke it open, and sprinkled the juice on the site.

Perhaps the most famous of the courthouses where he practiced was in **Beardstown,** 46 miles northwest of Springfield via Route 125. Here, Lincoln defended a New Salem friend on a charge of murder. After a witness testified he saw the fatal fight

Lincolnland Campgrounds

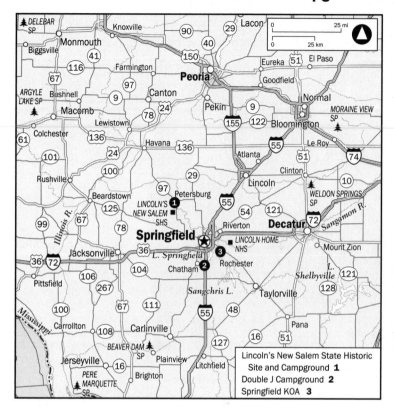

Lincoln's New Salem State Historic
Site and Campground **1**
Double J Campground **2**
Springfield KOA **3**

break out in the light of a high moon after a revival camp meeting, Lincoln produced an 1857 almanac showing that the moon had set before midnight that night. His client was acquitted.

Lincoln is buried in **Springfield's Oak Ridge Cemetery** beside Mary Todd, Tad, Eddie, and Willie Lincoln. His memory is also recalled at the family home at 8th and Jackson streets; at the law offices at 6th and Adams streets where he practiced from 1843 until he left for Washington; at the Old State Capitol in the Downtown Mall where he said, "A house divided against itself cannot stand"; at Bank One, 6th and Washington streets, where his Springfield Marine and Fire Insurance Company ledger is on display; and at the Lincoln Depot, 10th and Monroe streets, where he said goodbye to Springfield after being elected president.

Springfield's Vachel Lindsay could be called Lincoln's poet, and Galesburg's Carl Sandburg, also a poet, won the Pulitzer Prize for his six-volume biography of Lincoln, which provides valuable insight into the late president.

A statue commemorates Abraham Lincoln in the village of New Salem.

Campground Oases in Lincolnland

Double J Campground is 15 minutes south of Downtown **Springfield.** From I-72, take I-55 S. to exit 83 to 9683 Palm Rd. in Chatham. There are 135 sites, with 68 full hookups. Amenities include a large pool, minigolf, Wi-Fi, plus an RV Sales & Service Center on-site. Apr–Oct. Sites $35 (© **888/483-9998** or 217/483-9998; www.double jcampground.com).

Springfield KOA, Rochester, Illinois. It's in a quiet area with swimming, and golf and fishing are nearby. There are 86 sites with 30-amp electric, 52 with full hookups. Sites $28–$39. Take exit 94 off I-55, then travel east 5 miles on Stevenson Rd. and follow the KOA signs for 2 more miles (© **800/562-7212** or 217/498-7002; www. koa.com).

Lincoln's New Salem State Historic Site and Campground, Petersburg, Illinois. This simple campground is adjacent to the village where Lincoln lived for 6 years, and has 100 back-in sites with 30- and 50-amp electric, restrooms, and a dump. No reservations. Apr–Oct. Sites $10–$30. It's 2 miles south of Petersburg on Rte. 97. Call for information (© **217/632-4003**; www.petersburgil.com/p_newsalem.html).

SOUTHERN ILLINOIS: THE PIASA BIRD TO THE MAN OF STEEL

The **Great River Road** follows the Mississippi River along a meandering 2,350-mile journey from its birth in Lake Itasca, Minnesota, to New Orleans, Louisiana. Dramatically different from the farmlands of northern Illinois, the southern part of the state has forests and lakes, craggy sandstone formations and cypress swamps, ancient Indian mounds, and early European settlements that still carry the imprint of their founders.

Starting in **Kampsville** on the Illinois River, take Route 100 to **Grafton** where the Illinois meets the Mississippi. They don't merge here, but run side by side for several miles, the Illinois clear and the Mississippi muddy. At **Alton,** Route 100 becomes Route 3 and meanders south to **Cairo,** where the Mississippi and Ohio rivers converge with a similarly dramatic difference in color.

The old river towns carry their own distinctive ambience. **Elsah** is particularly charming with its parallel one-way streets and little limestone and clapboard cottages. The entire town is on the National Register of Historic Places. **Don't try to drive in here with a large motor home** (we found it touch-and-go in a Rialta van). Try to find a spot at the parking lot by the river at the entrance to town, or, if you're carrying your bicycles on your RV, park in Alton and take the 15-mile paved Senator Vadalabene Bike Trail back to Elsah. If you do visit Elsah, note little Principia College, where actor Robert Duvall is an alumnus.

The painting of the legendary fierce **Piasa** (pronounced *Pie*-a-saw) **Bird,** a birdlike monster said to devour men, was noted by French explorers Jacques Marquette and Louis Jolliet, who saw it high on the bluffs of the Mississippi River near Alton in 1673. A re-creation of that original painting, a local landmark, can be seen today on the bluff just north of Alton on the Great River Road. The town of Alton, however, makes one wonder what constitutes greatness. A life-size statue of Alton-born Robert Wadlow, whose height of almost 9 feet made him the world's tallest man, is on display, but nowhere could we find a tribute to native son Miles Davis, one of America's greatest jazz musicians. His family left Alton when Miles was 4 years old, and he grew up in East St. Louis, Illinois. Alton also provides easy access to St. Louis, across the river, if you want to explore that city.

On the Illinois side of greater St. Louis is one of the great archaeological sites of the Midwest, the **Cahokia Mounds** (http://cahokiamounds.org). They're believed to have been the site of the first and largest of the great towns constructed by the Native Americans of the Mississippi area, and the largest prehistoric city north of Mexico City. Some 100 earthen mounds were built here between A.D. 900 and 1250, and some 40 remain, though the site was abandoned by 1500.

An arrangement of wooden posts in the ground suggests a horizon calendar, and so the area has been dubbed **Woodhenge,** after England's Stonehenge. To get to Cahokia Mounds State Park from Hwy. 3, drive south to I-55/70 and take the interstate east to exit 6. Turn south and then, almost at once, turn east on Collinsville Road, Route 7850, to the park. There are directional signs. The outdoor park is open daily, except on major holidays.

Eat your spinach in the Popeye-loving town of Chester, Illinois.

Continue south on Route 3 to **Chester,** home of Elzie Segar, the cartoonist who created **Popeye,** his girlfriend Olive Oyl, Wimpy, Swee'pea, Bluto, and all those other characters after he took a $20 correspondence school course in cartooning. Less known is an earlier character called Eugene the Jeep, with a bright-red nose and a long tail, which kept moving over any kind of terrain. After Segar's death in 1938, the Army named its new all-terrain vehicle a Jeep, also called a G.P. for General Purpose Vehicle, after the cartoon character.

In Chester, you'll find antiques shops and statuary that depict Segar's characters, but the most famous **Popeye statue** is on the west side of town, in a park named for his creator on the road to the Chester Bridge that crosses the Mississippi. Since there are so many trees in the vicinity, look to the left for the statue if you're headed toward the Mississippi, to the right if you're headed away from it. Route 3 continues south along the Mississippi through some beautiful scenery. If you accidentally crossed the Mississippi into Missouri in your quest for the Popeye statue, try to turn around and come back to Chester to follow Route 3 south. The next bridge across the river isn't until Cape Girardeau, 41 miles south.

Fragrant Fields, an herb farm and tearoom in Dongola, at exit 24 off I-57, sells specialty herbs, geraniums, and other fragrant plants from its gardens and greenhouses, and an elegant afternoon tea is served. There's also a shop where you can buy potpourri in a dozen different fragrances. It's at 102 S. Garden St. (© **618/ 203-9106;** http://fragrantfields.com).

Superman's town of **Metropolis** is on the Mississippi at the southern tip of Illinois, at exit 37 off I-24. The whole town has been turned over to the Man of Steel. He welcomes you from a billboard when you drive into town, signals from the water tower that looms over the town, and comes into his own in the town square, where a 9-foot bronze statue poses heroically, a perfect spot for a Kodak moment. There's a phone booth where you can change clothes or pick up the receiver and listen to

Southern Illinois Campgrounds

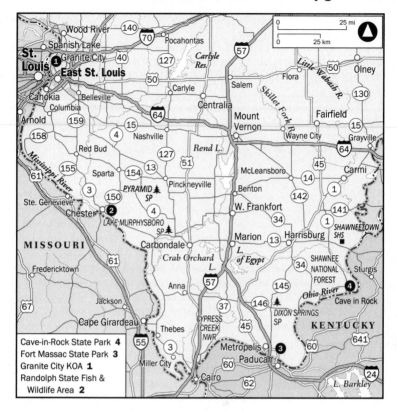

Cave-in-Rock State Park **4**
Fort Massac State Park **3**
Granite City KOA **1**
Randolph State Fish &
    Wildlife Area **2**

Superman. Across the street is the **Super Museum** with the planet's largest collection of Superman memorabilia, including the costume worn by George Reeve, TV's first superman; props from Superman films; rare toys; and comic books. It's at 517 Market St. Open daily 9am to 5pm; admission $5 adults, free for children 5 and under (© **618/524-5518;** www.supermuseum.com).

Some savvy city fathers back in 1972 realized they lived in the only incorporated city in the United States named Metropolis, so who's to say this isn't Superman's town? They even named the local paper *The Daily Planet,* and in the spring of 2001, the Metropolis actor who depicts Superman got married in his costume to his real-life sweetheart in the town square by the statue.

A jog north on Route 145 connects with Route 146, so you can follow along the scenic Ohio River. Just 2 miles south from the junction with Route 1 is **Cave-in-Rock State Park** (www.dnr.state.il.us/lands/landmgt/parks/r5/caverock.htm), named for a cave with a 55-foot-wide opening overlooking the Ohio River, where outlaws hid to rob and kill unsuspecting river travelers. The cave headquarters was used from 1797 to the mid-1800s.

A cutoff via Route 13 can take you to Old Shawneetown and the **Shawneetown Historic Site** (www.state.il.us/hpa/hs/shawneetown_bank.htm), today almost deserted. Once it was the gateway to the West for settlers traveling the Ohio River on their way to Manifest Destiny. The brick-and-sandstone First State Bank of Illinois was built in 1839; the John Marshall Bank and Home, built in 1818, served as the first bank in Illinois.

If you continue north on Route 1, you can make a convenient detour to **New Harmony, Indiana** (see "Back Home Again in Indiana: Southern Indiana," below) via Route 14.

Fans of Heath candy bars may want to continue north to **Robinson,** 3 miles west of Route 1 on Route 33. The crunchy, chocolate-covered toffee bar was developed here in 1915, and the factory is still here.

We're not sure the candy served as inspiration or writer fuel for **James Jones,** also born in Robinson 6 years later in 1921, but we're glad that it's here where he began writing his novel *From Here to Eternity.* Robinson's third claim to fame is the grave of the only woman ever hanged in Illinois. Elizabeth Betsey Reed was executed in 1845 after a jury found her guilty of poisoning her husband with arsenic-laced sassafras tea. While jailed in nearby Palestine, she tried to escape by setting the jail on fire; she was then moved to the Lawrence County Jail. They say some 20,000 people showed up to watch the hanging. She's buried next to her husband in Baker Cemetery near Heathsville on Route 33. For information on everything in Robinson, contact the **Chamber of Commerce** at 113 S. Court St. (© **618/546-1557;** www.robinson chamber.org).

Campground Oases in Southern Illinois

Cave-in-Rock State Park is in a town called **Cave in Rock.** There are 34 paved, back-in sites with 30-amp electrical connections, along with a dump station. Visitors have access to food service, swimming, and fishing. No reservations. Sites $10–$20. On Rte. 1, 2 miles south of its junction with Rte. 146; call for information (© **618/289-4325;** http://dnr.state.il.us/lands/landmgt/parks/ilstate.htm).

Randolph State Fish & Wildlife Area in **Chester** allows for camping without hookups, and there's a dump station, toilets, and food service. Some 95 narrow pull-through and back-in grass sites are available on a first-come, first-served basis. Sites $8–$15. To get there, go east 3 miles on Rte. 150 from its junction with Rte. 3 and follow the signs. 4301 S. Lake Dr., Chester (© **618/826-2706;** http://dnr.state.il.us/lands/landmgt/parks/r4/rand.htm).

Fort Massac State Park near **Metropolis** has 50 narrow back-in sites with 30- and 50-amp electrical hookups. Sites $20. Take exit 37 from I-24 and follow U.S. 45 for 2½ miles west toward town; the park is on the left at 1398 E. 5th St. Call for information (© **618/524-4712;** http://dnr.state.il.us/lands/landmgt/parks/ilstate.htm).

Granite City KOA. In **Granite City, Illinois,** across the river from St. Louis, it's convenient to Alton and the northern river towns, as well as the Cahokia Mounds.

The campground has 64 pull-throughs, a dataport for e-mail, and 76 full hookups with electrical connections up to 50 amps. Mid-Mar to Oct. Sites $35–$41. Take exit 3 off I-270 and drive south ¼ mile to Chain of Rocks Rd.; then turn east for a half-mile to 3157 W. Chain of Rocks Rd. Call for reservations (© **800/562-5861** or 618/931-5160; www.koa.com).

BACK HOME AGAIN IN INDIANA: SOUTHERN INDIANA

Some of our best friends are from Indiana—actors, writers, publishers, public relations executives—and they go home as often as possible. The state is near the top of our list for favorite RV destinations, because we can count on finding something weird or wonderful, often both, on our visits there.

Indiana is a treasure trove of home cooking, food festivals and food producers, offbeat museums, and some eccentric slices of Americana. For instance, take the **breaded tenderloin sandwich,** that uniquely Hoosier snack that's little known outside the state. Hoosier hogs are appreciated in a wide variety of guises, but nowhere more so than when they're turned into the breaded tenderloin sandwich, a hot, crunchy, Frisbee-sized circle of lean, juicy pork pounded paper-thin, then breaded and deep-fried. Finally, at its crispy peak, it's gently lifted out of the pan and nestled into a warm, supersize hamburger-style bun with garnishes such as lettuce, tomatoes, sliced raw onions, pickles, mustard, and mayonnaise.

New Harmony, at the junction of state highways 66 and 69, and 7 miles due south of exit 4 off I-64, is a good place to start a tour of southern Indiana, especially if you're going to or coming from southern Illinois. The first settlers in what they called Harmonie were a German communal group called Harmonists or Rappites (after their leader, George Rapp), who arrived in 1814 with followers from Pennsylvania to settle along the Wabash River. Their aim was to practice perfectionism and celibacy in anticipation of the Second Coming of Christ. The community was one of the first planned towns in America, and for 10 years it flourished in farming, manufacturing, and commerce. Although the followers were abstemious, they made beer and whiskey to sell as far away as New Orleans. Their best-known export was a fine-quality flannel marked with a golden rose, as were all the New Harmony goods.

But the settlers were troubled by malaria, a nationwide depression that reduced the demand for their goods, and the nonappearance of Christ, so they moved back to Pennsylvania and founded a new town named Economy.

In 1825, a Welsh textile magnate named Robert Owen bought New Harmony from Rapp and brought his family, along with a group of Scottish scientists and intellectuals, to establish a Utopian community. It failed in 2 years, but Owen's sons stayed on to continue their father's ideas—free public schools, public libraries, equal education for boys and girls, and kindergarten for young children—and wound up establishing the Smithsonian Institution.

Today, the town is a photogenic community of unpainted wood houses from the early 1800s, picket fences, a row of handsome brick and sandstone buildings along Main Street filled with charming shops and boutiques, a modern "roofless" church designed by Philip Johnson, and the postmodern Atheneum designed by Richard Meier in 1979. You can wander around on your own, if you like, or start at the **Atheneum**/Visitor's Center with a short film, a museum display of town models, and a guided tour. It's open daily 9:30 to 5pm, except major holidays. Walking tours cost $10 adults, $9 seniors, $5 children 7 to 17, free for children 6 and under, $25 for a family (✆ **800/231-2168;** www.usi.edu/hnh).

The prettiest town along the Ohio River is **Madison** in southeastern Indiana. In the 19th century, it was a major river port and meatpacking center; by midcentury, it was the state's largest city. But in 1847, when it became the terminus of the first railroad in Indiana, other towns began siphoning off its business, and Madison declined into a sleepy town with gracious houses designed by architect Francis Costigan. The **Shrewsbury House,** 301 W. 1st St., is a good example of his Greek Revival structures, with its three-story freestanding spiral staircase. The **Ben Schroeder Saddletree Factory Museum** is housed in the original 19th-century factory at 106 Milton St.; "Saddletrees" were the wooden frames for saddles, and early ones were just crosses of wood. Open mid-April through October on Saturday and Sunday 1 to 4:30pm and Monday 10am to 4:30pm. Tours are held on the hour. Admission $3. **Historic Madison,** at 500 W. St., can provide information on the museum and self-guided tours of the town (✆ **812/265-2967;** www.historicmadisoninc.com).

North of Madison about 50 miles as the crow flies is **Metamora,** site of the other **Whitewater Scandal.** In 1836, the Indiana legislature decided to build a 76-mile canal between Hagerstown and Lawrenceburg, with 56 locks and seven dams, plus an aqueduct that would carry the canal 16 feet above Duck Creek, a waterway that flowed through Metamora. The canal was a washout, literally, from frequent floods. The railroad arrived before its construction was completed, which cinched the expensive failure and drove the state into bankruptcy. A harried legislature passed regulations that would prohibit the state of Indiana from ever contracting debt again, and those regulations still exist.

After World War II, restoration began on the Metamora lock, an old gristmill from 1845, and the Duck Creek Aqueduct, believed to be the only one of its kind left. By the 1960s, gentrification added craft shops, antiques stores, galleries, and a sightseeing boat along the canal (cost $4). Today, visitors can take a canal cruise on a horse-drawn boat, wander the streets of the town, and explore some 100 shops and cafes in 19th-century wooden buildings. For information, call the **Whitewater Canal State Historic Site** (✆ **765/647-6512;** www.indianamuseum.org/sites/whit.html).

Brown County in south-central Indiana is a favorite weekend getaway for Hoosiers to see dogwood and redbud in spring and gorgeous foliage in the fall, and to shop for antiques and taste treats in a trio of towns around the junction of state routes 46 and 135. Parking for large motor homes is scarce on summer Sundays, but we found a spot in the high-school parking lot and walked into Nashville. Potters, painters, and quilt makers share storefronts with fudge and cookie makers, country stores, and antiques shops. The most famous eatery is in the **Nashville House** at the corner of Main and Van Buren, which earned its renown by deep-frying biscuits and serving them with baked apple butter.

A horse-drawn barge along the Whitewater Canal in Metamora, Indiana.

The hamlet of **Gnaw Bone,** 6 miles east of Nashville on Route 46, makes sorghum, a sort of molasses, at the Brown County Sorghum Mill every September through November.

Nearby **Bean Blossom,** 5 miles north of Nashville on Route 135, is home of the annual **Bill Monroe Bluegrass Festival** (www.beanblossom.us), along with a museum devoted to the music. For information, call the **Brown County Convention and Visitors Bureau** (© **800/753-3255;** www.browncounty.com).

Southern Indiana has plenty of appealing towns on the "country-cute" side like Metamora and Bean Blossom, Gnaw Bone, and Nashville. However, the class act is **Columbus,** a blend of award-winning architecture and small-town charm. South of Indianapolis off I-35 at exit 68, this town of 34,000 seems an unlikely location for a major collection of public and commercial buildings by the leading contemporary architects of the world.

The city's architectural legacy began back in 1942 when controversial Finnish architect Eliel Saarinen was commissioned to design the First Christian Church. It was one of the first modern churches built in the United States and is said to have influenced American church design ever since.

In 1957, the town's leading industry, Cummins Engine Company (the people who put the diesel into diesel pushers), made an offer to pay architectural fees for a new school of building designs if the school used an architect from a list of major international designers. Later, it established a foundation to establish the same policy for all public buildings in town.

ON THE BARBECUE TRAIL

You can follow the Ohio River around Indiana's southern border, perhaps pausing in Evansville to pick up some barbecue at **Wolf's**, 6600 1st Ave. Daily 10am to 9pm (© **812/424-8891**; www.wolfsbrbq.com). You could even detour south across the Kentucky border to Owensboro's **Moonlite Bar-B-Q Inn** for barbecued mutton (delicious!) and Kentucky burgoo (a thick, tomato-based stew). The location, 2840 W. Parrish Ave., is also U.S. 56. Monday through Thursday 9am to 9pm; Friday and Saturday 9am to 9:30pm; Sunday 9am to 3pm (© **800/322-8989** or 270/684-8143; www.moonlite.com).

Whose work can you see? **I. M. Pei** designed the town library with its Henry Moore sculpture in front; **Eero Saarinen,** Eliel's equally famous son, designed the Irwin Union Bank and Trust Company; **Edward Larrabee Barnes** and **Richard Meier** each designed an elementary school; and **Robert Venturi** designed a firehouse. Allow 2½ to 5½ hours to cover the city's more than 50 sites; see "Architecture Watch," later in this chapter, for information.

Campground Oases in Southern Indiana

Harmonie State Park. There are 200 pull-through and back-in sites, all fairly narrow, with 20- and 30-amp electrical hookups, along with a sanitation dump and restrooms with showers. No reservations. Sites $11–$39. It's 4 miles south of **New Harmony** on State Hwy. 69 and then 1 mile west on S.R. 269. Call for information (© **812/682-4821;** www.in.gov/dnr/parklake/2981.htm).

Brookville Lake has 562 paved sites and 62 full hookups with 20-amp electric. There are restrooms and a dump station, and Brookville lake for fishing, boating, and swimming. There is a 14-day maximum stay. Sites $11–$39. Brookville, Indiana, is 7½ miles north of Hwy. 52 on Hwy. 101 (© **765/647-2657;** www.in.gov/dnr/parklake/2961.htm).

Bill Monroe Memorial Music Park & Campground has 300 back-in sites, 30-amp electrical hookups, restrooms, showers, and a dump. Sites $27–$35. On S.R. 135 in **Bean Blossom** north of **Nashville, Indiana.** Call for reservations (© **812/988-6422;** www.beanblossom.us).

Brown County State Park has 401 narrow back-in sites with 30-amp electrical hookups, restrooms, showers, and a dump. Sites $28. It's 2 miles southwest of town on S.R. 46 W. in **Nashville, Indiana.** Call for information (© **812/988-6406;** www.in.gov/dnr/parklake/2988.htm).

Southern Indiana Campgrounds

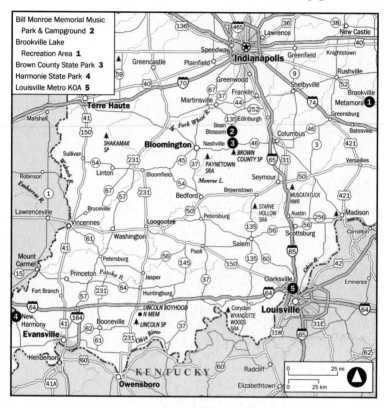

Bill Monroe Memorial Music
   Park & Campground **2**
Brookville Lake
   Recreation Area **1**
Brown County State Park **3**
Harmonie State Park **4**
Louisville Metro KOA **5**

Louisville Metro KOA is open year-round with 78 full hookups and electrical connections up to 50 amps. The campground also has dataports for collecting e-mail, sells LP gas, and has cable TV and Wi-Fi. Visitors enjoy miniature golf, food service, and fishing. Sites $30–$44. Across the Ohio River from Louisville in **Clarksville, Indiana.** Call for reservations (© **800/562-4771** or 812/282-4474; www.koa.com).

NORTHERN/CENTRAL INDIANA: BEN HUR'S CHARIOT, THE INDY 500 & THE '47 STUDEBAKER

Revered by auto racing fans as the home of the Indianapolis Motor Speedway, Indianapolis is also remembered as the home of folksy poet James Whitcomb Riley (although probably not by the same folks). Riley spent the last 23 years of his life with longtime friends Major and Mrs. Charles Holstein at 528 Lockerbie St. (of which he wrote, "Such a dear little street it is"); ironically, his benefactors have been forgotten, and the majestic brick home is called the **James Whitcomb Riley house.**

The **Indianapolis 500** in May for Indy cars, dating from 1911, and the **Brickyard 400** in August for stock cars, pack the town with racing fans. The rest of the year, you can visit a museum with racing cars from the 1920s and other racing memorabilia, or take a bus ride around the oval track at a slow-pokey 35 miles an hour.

Our own favorite sight in Indianapolis is the ornate 1901 Beaux Arts **Soldiers' and Sailors' Monument** in Monument Circle, in the heart of the city. Alexander Ralston, an assistant of Pierre Charles L'Enfant, who created the street layout in Washington, D.C., designed the hub-and-spoke street pattern in the downtown area. The Indiana Statehouse and the Circle Theatre are worth a visit, as is the Art Deco **Madame Walker Theatre Center,** 617 Indiana Ave. (© **317/236-2099;** www.walkertheatre.com), honoring the first female self-made millionaire in America. Madame Walker manufactured beauty products for African-American women. Call for general information on Indianapolis (© **800/238-INDY** [4639] or 317/464-2222; www.indychamber.com).

Northeast of the city is **Conner Prairie,** a living history museum that re-creates an 1836 village with costumed guides who demonstrate life in the early years of Indiana. It's open May through October from Tuesday to Saturday 10am to 5pm; Sunday 11am to 5pm. Admission $14 adults, $13 seniors, $9 children 2 to 12. Located at 13400 Allisonville Rd., 4 miles south of Noblesville off Route 19 (© **317/776-6000;** www.connerprairie.org).

Iowa isn't the only state famous for **covered bridges.** Indiana's **Parke County,** west of Indianapolis almost to the Illinois border, boasts 32 of them, some said to be haunted. An annual October **Covered Bridge Festival** funds bridge upkeep. Call for information and a site map (© **765/569-5226;** www.coveredbridges.com).

A state historical site dedicated to a beloved World War II figure, war correspondent **Ernie Pyle,** is just west of Parke County in Vermillion County. It's 1 mile north of U.S. Hwy. 36 on Indiana State Road 71, at 120 W. Briarwood Ave., in his hometown of **Dana,** near the Illinois border. A Quonset hut **visitor center** displays memorabilia; admission is $3.50 adults, $3 seniors, $2 children 4 to 11, free for children 3 and under. After closing for over a year due to state budget cuts, it's now open again on weekends: Saturday 10am to 4pm; Sunday 1 to 4pm (© **765/665-3633**).

Northeast of Dana in **Crawfordsville,** another Indiana writer is remembered with more pomp and ceremony—General Lew Wallace, author of *Ben-Hur,* who wrote the first part of the book in Indiana, then finished it when he was territorial governor in New Mexico. The popular book has never been out of print since it appeared in 1880. **The General Lew Wallace Study & Museum** is at 200 Wallace Ave., and annual chariot races are staged here in October. It's just 2 miles south of exit 34 off I-74. Tours are led from Wednesday to Saturday 10am to 5pm and Sunday 1 to 5pm (by appointment Mon–Tues). Admission is $5 adults, $1 students, free for children 6 and under (© **765/362-5769;** www.ben-hur.com). For other information, call the **Crawfordsville Convention & Visitors Bureau,** 1141 Meridian Plaza (© **800/866-3973;** www.crawfordsville.org).

Anderson, 25 miles northeast of Indianapolis, is home to the spectacular **Paramount Theatre Centre & Ballroom,** a rare "atmospheric" theater with a rose-and-blue sky and Moorish balconies, which re-creates a midsummer evening in Spain. Besides special evening performances and concerts, the theater is open for guided tours

Tender Tenderloins

Mr. Dave's in North Manchester, 40 miles west of Fort Wayne on State Route 114, serves an award-winning classic tenderloin sandwich, crisp but modest in size, and served with pickles only; it also sells frozen ready-to-fry breaded tenderloins to take home. 102 Main St., Monday through Saturday noon to 8pm (✆ **260/982-4769**).

Das Dutchman Essenhaus, Middlebury, east of Elkhart on U.S. 20, an Amish-style restaurant complex the size of an airplane hangar, serves all-you-can-eat fried chicken dinners, large tenderloin sandwiches, and 27 varieties of pie. Monday through Saturday 6am to 8pm (✆ **800/455-9471**; www. essenhaus.com).

Hobnob Corner, Nashville, Indiana. Past a detour into southern Indiana, this popular Brown County eatery serves tenderloin sandwiches along with strawberry sodas and a variety of soups and sandwiches. A former dry goods store located at 17 W. Main St., this inexpensive spot has wooden booths and plank floors. Monday and Tuesday 8am to 3pm; Wednesday through Sunday 8am to 8pm (✆ **812/988-4114**).

The **Friendly Tavern, Zionsville,** at 290 Main St., just outside Indianapolis, is a longtime Hoosier favorite for tenderloin sandwiches. Monday through Saturday 11am to 10pm (✆ **317/873-5772**).

Mrs. Wick's Pies & Restaurant, at 100 Cherry St. in Winchester, east of Muncie, is famous for pies, but also turns out two versions of a tenderloin sandwich, breaded or grilled. Weekdays 6am to 7pm; Saturday 6am to 2pm (✆ **765/584-7437**; www.wickspies.com).

Carver's Family Dining, Richmond, Indiana, has breakfast, lunch, and dinner specials, plus popular pork tenderloin sandwiches. It's at 2270 Chester Blvd. Daily 5am to 10pm (✆ **765/966-8565**). 🚐

Tuesday through Friday from noon to 5pm; cost is $3 (✆ **800/523-4658**; reservations: 765/642-1234, ext. 11; www.andersonparamount.org).

Séances and evoked ectoplasm are everyday occurrences at **Camp Chesterfield,** a spiritualist compound in Chesterfield, off I-69 at Hwy. 32 near Anderson. This is one of several centers for spiritualism in the United States; others are Lily Dale, New York, and Cassadega, Florida. Open to the public daily from 9am to 5pm, the camp has lodgings, a cafeteria, an art gallery, a bookstore, and a museum. Consultations by appointment can be scheduled with the mediums of Chesterfield, who are said to go into trances, cause spirits to materialize, and predict the future (✆ **765/378-0235**; www.campchesterfield.net).

Another once-popular author from Indiana is **Gene Stratton-Porter,** who wrote *A Girl of the Limberlost* and other sentimental novels with nature lore about Loblolly Marsh near her hometown of Geneva. Also a naturalist and photographer, she lived at

An old circus wagon at the Peru Circus City Festival Museum.

200 E. 6th St., 1 block east of U.S. 27, in a rustic, 14-room log home, the Limberlost Cabin. As a state historic site, it's open to visitors; her moth collection is on display inside (© **260/368-7428;** www.genestrattonporter.net). Geneva is 35 miles south of Fort Wayne at the junction of U.S. 27 and Hwy. 116.

Peru, Indiana, is the birthplace of **Cole Porter.** His home on East 3rd Street and gravesite in Mount Hope Cemetery can be visited, as well as the **Miami County Museum,** 51 N. Broadway, where his black 1955 Cadillac is on display. The car, which appeared in *The Godfather* (1972), was shipped back and forth six times from New York to the French Riviera, where the composer used to spend his summers. Open Tuesday to Saturday 9am to 5pm; free admission. For information, call the **Miami County Museum** (© **765/473-9183;** www.miamicountymuseum.com).

Every month, Cole Porter had a standing order for 9 pounds of chocolate fudge to be shipped to him by **Arnold's Candies.** The confectionary, now located at 288 E. Main St., still uses the same recipe.

The **Circus City Festival Museum,** at 154 N. Broadway, commemorates with artifacts and historical photographs the days when Peru was winter headquarters for many world-famous circuses. Open daily 9am to 1pm and 2 to 5pm. Donations accepted (© **765/472-3918;** www.perucircus.com/museum.htm).

From the Circus Museum, it's 14 miles west to **Logansport,** where one of only three working models of a **Gustav Dentzell carousel** still operates between Memorial Day and Labor Day, on summer weekends and weekday evenings for 75¢ a ride. Climb aboard one of the 29 hand-carved wooden horses or a wooden goat, reindeer, giraffe, lion, or tiger in the town's Riverside Park on Riverside Drive. The carousel is open in summer on weekdays 6 to 9pm, Saturday and Sunday 1 to 9pm. Call the **Cass County Carousel** (© 574/753-8725).

The grave of John Chapman, also known as Johnny Appleseed, can be found in Fort Wayne's **Johnny Appleseed Park** at Coliseum Boulevard and Parnell Avenue off I-69 at exit 111.

Anyone who likes antique cars, especially highly polished, expensive ones, should not miss the **Auburn Cord Duesenberg Museum** in **Auburn,** 17 miles north of Fort Wayne and 2 miles off I-69 at exit 129, in town at 1600 S. Wayne St. The museum displays more than 100 classic automobiles manufactured in Indiana between 1900 and 1937. The moderately priced Auburn, later the stylish Cord, and the legendary Duesenberg, the most expensive car on the market in the 1930s, were produced here. The phrase "it's a doozy," meaning something extraordinary, may well originally have been "it's a Deusy," according to the museum curators. Open daily 9am to 5pm. Admission $10 adults, $6 students, $25 family (© 260/925-1444; www.acdmuseum. org).

Northern Indiana's Amish country, the nation's third-largest Amish settlement, lies east of Elkhart; the towns of **Shipshewana** and **Middlebury** are particularly colorful. Amish farmers drive horse-drawn black buggies along country lanes and, to a lesser extent, highways, so watch your speed; and Amish restaurants serve mind-boggling amounts of food family-style, so watch your diet. Handmade copper utensils, horses and cows, quilts, home-baked bread, and exotic popcorns are all for sale. The *Deutsch Kase House* (German Cheese House), with an Amish staff, has samples of the cheeses it makes, including baby Swiss, Colby, and hot pepper cheese at modest prices.

The **Shipshewana Auction & Flea Market** is world-famous with its 1,000 vendors, livestock auctions, and Amish-Mennonite foods. The Flea Market, 345 S. Van Buren St., is open Tuesday and Wednesday 8am to 5pm; the auction is held on Wednesday from 9am to 1pm (© 260/768-4129; www.tradingplaceamerica.com).

In **Elkhart,** you can visit vintage RVs at the **RV/MH Heritage Foundation** at 21565 Executive Pkwy., Monday to Saturday 9am to 4pm. Admission $8 adults, $6 seniors, $3 children (© 574/293-2344; www.rvmhhalloffame.org). If you want to take a **factory tour** and see how some brands are manufactured, you'll find **Coachmen, Jayco,** and **Shasta Industries** in Middlebury; **Carriage** in Millerburg, **Damon and Forest City** in Elkhart; **Holiday Rambler** in Wakarusa; and **Newmar** in Nappanee.

The farm home at **Amish Acres** in **Nappanee,** 15 miles south of Elkhart on Hwy. 19, 1 mile west of the junction with U.S. 6, is on the National Register of Historic Places. The **Restaurant Barn** serves up the award-winning Threshers Dinner of ham, beef, chicken, and turkey, plus countless side dishes and desserts, plus a summer-only Bountiful Breakfast Buffet. 1600 W. Market St. It's open Monday to Saturday 11am to 7pm, Sunday 11am to 6pm (© 800/800-4942 or 574/773-4188). In the **Round Barn Theatre,** the Amish musical *Plain and Fancy,* a Broadway hit in the 1950s, is presented during summer. Call **Elkhart County Visitors Center** (© 800/262-8161; www.amishcountry.org).

Many in Indiana's Amish community still use horse-drawn buggies.

Nearby **South Bend,** about 15 miles west of Elkhart, is home to Notre Dame of "Win this one for the Gipper" fame, one of Ronald Reagan's cinematic golden moments. The Golden Dome atop the university's main building is the symbol for this whole area, discovered by French explorer LaSalle in 1681 and again by Norwegian athlete Knute Rockne in 1918 when the alumnus and star player became football coach.

The **Studebaker National Museum** is engrossing, even for non-motorheads. It's a collection of machinery dating from Henry Studebaker's wooden wheelbarrow, which he sold in vast quantities to miners in the California gold rush. Henry was one of five Studebaker brothers, and the $8,000 he brought back from California set the family up in a blacksmith shop. They made supply wagons for the Union Army in the Civil War, then went into carriages (one of them took Abraham Lincoln to Ford's Theater the night he was assassinated), and then into horseless carriages. Perhaps their most famous was the 1947 Studebaker, designed by Raymond Loewy, a packaging expert, with a front and rear end that were exactly the same shape. A favorite joke at the time was that you couldn't tell whether it was coming or going.

An interesting prototype was the Packard Prediction, built for the 1956 Chicago World's Fair, which forecast tail fins, sliding glass car roofs, and many other details. The only one ever built is in the Studebaker National Museum, at 201 Chapin St. Open daily 10am to 5pm. Admission is $8 adults, $6.50 seniors, $5 children (© **574/ 235-9714;** www.studebakermuseum.org). For more information about Notre Dame and South Bend, contact the **South Bend Visitors Bureau,** 401 E. Colfax Ave. (© **800/519-0577;** www.ci.south-bend.in.us).

Chesterton, 4 miles north of I-80/90, the Indiana Turnpike, at exit 31, ranks as a first-rate discovery for trivia nuts, film fans, Americana buffs, and literary detectives. It was in this pretty town that L. Frank Baum and family spent their summers while he was working on *The Wizard of Oz.* He was writing for a magazine for interior decorators in Chicago, and the Indiana dunes town was close enough for a getaway. His son founded the International Wizard of Oz Club in this area, and today the town salutes the Wizard and all denizens of Oz, particularly the few surviving Munchkins who are feted at celebrity parties and gala dinners every September. The Yellow Brick Road shop–cum–museum sells memorabilia from the film. **Indiana Dunes State Park,** inside the national lakeshore of the same name, is north of here on State Route 49. For information, call the **Porter County Visitor Information Center** (© **800/283-8687** or 219/926-2255).

Campground Oases in Northern/Central Indiana

Johnny Appleseed Campground, Fort Wayne. In Johnny Appleseed Park (see above), this grassy, tree-shaded campground has 36 sites with 30-amp electric and some haphazardly arranged water connections that may require a long hose. There's also a dump station. The campground is closed during the annual mid-September Johnny Appleseed Festival. No reservations. Sites $17–$21. Call for information (© **260/427-6720;** www.fortwayneparks.org).

Crawfordsville KOA, Crawfordsville. This campground is adjacent to a commercial strip of restaurants, motels, and malls. It has 53 large pull-through sites with up to 50-amp electrical hookups, 30 full hookups, cable TV, and dataports for retrieving and sending e-mail. Sites $34–$43. On U.S. 231, 1 mile south of I-74 at exit 34. Call for reservations (© **800/562-4191** or 765/362-4190; www.koa.com).

Turkey Run State Park, Marshall. This scenic recreation area in the middle of Parke County's covered-bridge country is excellent for hiking, canoeing, and horseback riding on rental horses. The campground has 213 large back-in and pull-through sites with 30-amp electrical hookups and wheelchair access. Sites $17–$32. Just 1 hour west of Indianapolis and convenient to both the Ernie Pyle and Lew Wallace historic sites, the park is on State Rd. 47, 2 miles east of its junction with U.S. 41 (© **765/597-2635;** www.in.gov/dnr/parklake/2964.htm).

A Box of Popcorn

According to the U.S. Popcorn Board, the average American eats about 68 quarts of popcorn a year. The oldest ears of popcorn ever found were 5,600 years old and were discovered in a bat cave in New Mexico in 1948. Columbus and his crew were offered popcorn as trade goods when they first arrived in the West Indies.

Popcorn was the first "puffed cereal" in America; colonial housewives served it with sugar and cream for breakfast.

The American love affair with popcorn got a major boost during World War II when sugar was sent overseas for U.S. troops, reducing the amount of candy available, so per capita consumption of popcorn tripled.

Many Americans buy microwave ovens just so they can make popcorn at home, but few realize popcorn was instrumental in the invention of the microwave. Percy Spencer discovered in 1945 that popcorn would pop when placed under microwave energy. He then experimented with other foods, which led to the invention of the microwave oven.

Valaparaiso, Indiana, honors Orville Redenbacher with a popcorn festival every Labor Day weekend on Saturday downtown (© **219/464-8332;** www.popcornfest.org). **Yoder's Popcorn Shop,** 4 miles south of Shipshewana, Indiana, on Route 200 S., sells a variety of popcorn, including black jewel. Open 9am to 5pm. Call for information and orders (© **800/892-2170;** www.yoderpopcorn.com).

The best place to admire popcorn as a work of art is outside **Dublin, Indiana,** where artist Malcolm Cochran's *Field of Corn (with Osage Orange Trees)* symbolizes the town's farming history and memorializes rural landscape that is being consumed by development. The outdoor artwork displays 109 white concrete ears of corn rising 5 to 6 feet out of the ground with a background of Osage orange trees, which once provided natural fencing for farmers. *Field of Corn* is located in Sam and Eulalia Frantz Park at the corner of Frantz and Rings roads. From I-70, take exit 17A, drive east on State Route 161 to Frantz Road, turn right, and continue another 2 miles. The city of Dublin has also commissioned other distinctive public artworks, including *Chief Leatherlips Monument* and *Watch House.* For information, call the **Dublin Convention & Visitors Bureau** (© **800/828-8414**).

South Bend Elkhart North KOA, Granger. Handy for RV tours and South Bend sightseeing, this campground has 46 full hookups with up to 50-amp electric, along with dataports, cable TV, and miniature golf. Sites $52–$57. Take exit 83 from I-80/90 and go north 2 miles on State Rd. 23; turn left onto Princess Way at Burger King (© **800/562-2470** or 574/277-1335; www.koa.com).

Northern/Central Indiana Campgrounds

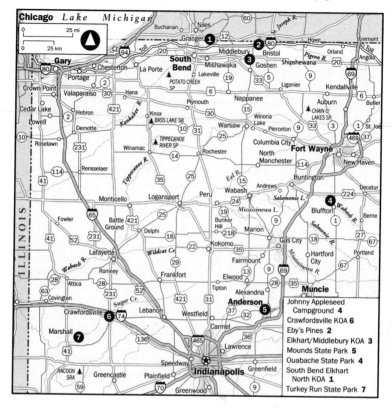

Mounds State Park. The park has 75 narrow campsites that are pull-throughs and back-ins with 30-amp electrical hookups. Sites $28. Closed in winter. East of **Anderson** 2½ miles on Rte. 232 (℃ **765/642-6627;** www.in.gov/dnr/parklake/2977.htm).

Elkhart/Middlebury KOA, Middlebury. In the heart of Amish country, this campground has a heated pool, a petting zoo, up to 50-amp electrical connections, and dataports. Amish country tours depart from the campground. Sites $33–$50. It's 4 miles north of Middlebury on State Rd. 13, and from I-80/90, 1½ miles south via exit 107 (℃ **800/562-5892** or 574/825-5932; www.koa.com).

Eby's Pines, Bristol. Also convenient to Amish country, this family campground lined with pine trees used to be open year-round; we stayed here comfortably in the snow. Now, however, it's open from mid-April through mid-October only. There are 200 pull-through and back-in sites with 30-amp electric in mostly side-by-side hookups, with only 29 full hookups. There are a lot of activities, plus a store with limited supplies. Sites $33–$40. Take the Bristol exit 101 from I-80/90; go south on Rte. 15

for about a mile, then east 3 miles on State Rd. 120 (*©* **574/848-4583;** www. ebyspines.com).

Ouabache State Park in **Bluffton** is pronounced "Wabash" the Indian name for the river that flows nearby. There are 77 sites with 30-amp electric, no full hookups, and no pull-throughs. Sites are narrow but long (15x45). A lake for fishing and boating has rental equipment. Travel east 2 mi. on Hwy. 124 to Hwy. 201, then south .75 mi. to SH-316, and southeast .5 mi. to park. $28. (*©* **260/824-0962;** www.in.gov/dnr/parklake/2975.htm).

ARCHITECTURE WATCH

The American Institute of Architects ranks **Columbus, Indiana,** sixth in the United States for architectural innovation and quality of design in public and private buildings. From Eliel Saarinen's First Christian Church of 1942 to the 1994 Pritzger Award–winning remodeling of an 1864 Victorian house into the city's new visitor center, the city is chockablock with fine architecture. Information for guided tour tickets and do-it-yourself driving tours is available at the **visitor center** at 506 5th St. (*©* **812/378-2622;** http://columbus.in.us).

In **Sioux City, Iowa,** the elaborately decorated **Woodman County Courthouse** is a strikingly original work of art created by three students of Chicago architect Louis Sullivan and is worth a detour for avid photographers. William Steele with Purcell & Elmslie created the structure, which was finished in 1918. The courthouse, downtown at 7th and Douglas streets, is still in use and open to the public during normal business hours.

Galena, Illinois, is a dictionary of 19th-century architectural styles from Federal, Greek Revival, Steamboat Gothic, and Italianate to Second Empire, Gothic Revival, Romanesque Revival, and Queen Anne. You can pick up a walking tour map at the Historical Society on Bench Street; more than 90% of the town's buildings are on the National Register of Historic Places.

Springfield, Illinois, is home to Frank Lloyd Wright's **Dana-Thomas house,** built in 1904, but still fresh and contemporary-looking today. It's been described as Wright's first "blank check" commission. Wright designed all the furniture, windows, and lighting fixtures, and pieces of pottery and sculpture still sit exactly where Wright specified they should go. In the library, Wright designed art-glass doors on all the cabinets so that the books, with their irregular shapes and colors, wouldn't clutter up his design. His client, socialite Susan Lawrence Dana, paid the architect a then-grand sum of $60,000. At 301 E. Lawrence Ave., the house is open for tours Wednesday through Sunday 9am to 4pm. Suggested donation $5 adults, $3 children, $13 family (*©* **217/782-6776;** www.dana-thomas.org).

In Evanston's **Lakeshore Historic District,** the lovely Sheridan Road drive goes past mansions built between the 1880s and the 1920s, a mélange of styles including French châteaux, Tudors, Victorians, Prairie Style, and Arts and Crafts. The magnificent **Baha'i House of Worship** at 100 Linden Ave. in Wilmette and an early Frank Lloyd Wright design, 850 Sheridan in Glencoe, are both along the route. (Edgar Rice Burroughs lived at 700 Linden Ave. when he published *Tarzan of the Apes.*)

Frank Lloyd Wright's Dana-Thomas House in Springfield, Illinois.

Oak Park is the site of many of Wright's best works in the Prairie Style, with 20 houses that can be seen on a neighborhood walking tour with an audiotape guide. The designer's home and studio can also be toured, $15 adults, $13 seniors and youth ages 4 to 17. For information, call the **Frank Lloyd Wright Preservation Trust (© 312/ 994-4000;** www.gowright.org).

The Florida Keys (with Side Trips to the Everglades & Orlando)

KEY WEST IS "THE LAST RESORT," THE T-SHIRT CAPITAL OF THE world, the place Tennessee Williams called Cocalooney Key. A sign at the end of the dock says 90 MILES TO CUBA, and a local mayor once water-skied the distance.

It's where fashion icon Calvin Klein bought a million-dollar bird cage, where "tea dancing" doesn't call for white gloves, and where the former presidents Truman, Kennedy, Nixon, and Bush all lodged at the same upscale fishing lodge—Cheeca Lodge—though not at the same time.

The Keys are where the famous 1948 film noir *Key Largo* with Humphrey Bogart and Lauren Bacall was not filmed, although the Key Largo tourist office implies it was. The 1955 movie *The Rose Tattoo* with Burt Lancaster and Anna Magnani was filmed here, much of it in author Tennessee Williams's own house, a fact hardly (if ever) mentioned in Key West.

It's the home of swashbuckling buccaneers, where Harry S. Truman played poker, where ice from the frozen lakes of Maine was delivered by ship until well into the 20th century, where Anna Pavlova danced with the Russian Ballet, and Truman Capote danced with Tennessee Williams.

RVing the Keys

The first overland transportation to Key West was an extension of Henry M. Flagler's railroad, called "Flagler's Folly" or "the railroad that went to sea," which covered 25 miles of the distance on land, 75 miles over water.

The aging tycoon's railway began in 1896 when Flagler, content in north Florida's St. Augustine until the freeze of 1894–95 destroyed all the citrus and vegetables north of Palm Beach, decided to move south to get warm. The indomitable Julia Tuttle, a dowager bent on bringing attention to south Florida, sent a bouquet of fresh orange blossoms to Flagler from her farm, along with an offer to share the land owned by the Tuttles and their neighbors, in exchange for Flagler extending his railway to their village on the banks of the Miami River. He did, she did, and the rest is history.

From 1905 to 1912, Flagler took his rail line even farther south along the Florida Keys, despite the naysayers, running 150 miles of track that connected the Florida mainland with the southern islands. He died shortly after it was finished, secure in the fact that his biggest accomplishment, the famous Seven Mile Bridge, would also be his lasting monument. Although many of the railroad tracks were uprooted by a hurricane in 1935, the bridge remained.

Engineers used the old railroad pilings to support the 43 bridges of the Overseas Highway, which opened in 1938. While the original bridges and road have been widened or replaced, you can still see some of them, including the first Seven Mile Bridge. In April, the annual Seven Mile Bridge Run sets out from Marathon with runners from all over the world.

For RVers, even those towing 40-foot travel trailers, these long, flat, overwater roads are good, free of curves and hills.

The drive from Miami to Key West is 3 to 4 hours each way if you don't stop—but if you don't stop, you have little reason to drive down.

HITTING THE HIGHLIGHTS

For most RVers, it's an easy matter to drive the Keys from Miami and back in 1 day, but that would defeat the best reasons for coming—a little sightseeing, a little fishing, a little beach camping, and fresh seafood (maybe some you caught yourself) for dinner.

Allow a half-day for snorkeling at one of the national or state parks. Take a detour into **Everglades National Park** via Route 9336 from Homestead and walk the board-walk trails with binoculars to catch sight of **herons, egrets, white ibis,** and **alligators** (see "Two Great Side Trips," later in this chapter). Bicycle around Key West for a day and catch the highlights.

Who knows? You still might have time left over to take the kids to Disney World on the way back home (see "Two Great Side Trips," later in this chapter).

GOING FOR THE LONG HAUL

If you wanted to hang around Key West for the season—and a lot of people do—you could spend some time creatively by signing up for adult courses in Spanish, bird-watching, or swamp ecology at the **Florida Keys Community College** in **Key West** (© **305/296-9081**), which has satellite campuses in **Key Largo** (© **305/852-8007**) and **Marathon** (© **305/743-2133**); all three campuses share the same website (www.fkcc.edu). Other classes that are sometimes offered include quilting, watercolor painting, and puppet theater.

Travel Essentials

WHEN TO GO

The weather is warm year-round, but the winter months have the most comfortable temperatures for bicycling around Key West. Late spring brings bright blooms to Key West's streets—bougainvillea, jacaranda, and oleander. Summer's muggy temperatures often combine with ferocious but brief thunderstorms; more rainfall comes down during fall and winter, but rarely enough to bother your sightseeing. Hurricane season is early fall. Spring break can fill the streets of Key West with party-hearty college students—consider yourself forewarned. And year-round cruise-ship arrivals jam Mallory Square with day-trippers.

Florida Keys Highlights

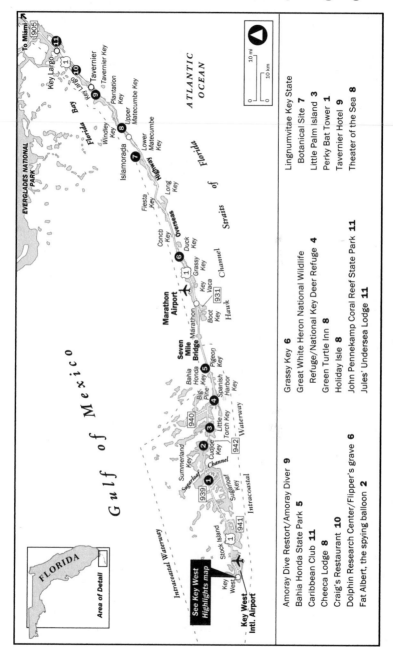

Amoray Dive Restort/Amoray Diver **9**
Bahia Honda State Park **5**
Caribbean Club **11**
Cheeca Lodge **8**
Craig's Restaurant **10**
Dolphin Research Center/Flipper's grave **6**
Fat Albert, the spying balloon **2**

Grassy Key **6**
Great White Heron National Wildlife
 Refuge/National Key Deer Refuge **4**
Green Turtle Inn **8**
Holiday Isle **8**
John Pennekamp Coral Reef State Park **11**
Jules' Undersea Lodge **11**

Lingnumvitae Key State
 Botanical Site **7**
Little Palm Island **3**
Perky Bat Tower **1**
Tavernier Hotel **9**
Theater of the Sea **8**

WHAT TO TAKE

Bring binoculars, a camera, powerful insect repellent to combat champion mosquitoes, a sun hat, and good strong sunblock. If you've forgotten your sunblock or are running low, pick up some of the excellent, locally produced **Key West Aloe Sunblock** (www.keywestaloe.com) at its shop/factory on Front Street.

WHAT TO WEAR

Shorts and flip-flops with a tank top or T-shirt is the most common outfit on the streets of Key West on a hot day, but something a little more conservative is appreciated in upscale restaurants and hotels. If you splurge on a meal or stay overnight at Little Palm Island (see "Eight Special Splurges," below), take some casually elegant resort-type sportswear. Carry a sweater or jacket for rainy days or cool evenings in winter. If you forget anything, you can find plenty of well-made, moderately priced sportswear manufactured locally.

TRIMMING COSTS ON THE ROAD

The most expensive item for RVers in the Florida Keys is a hookup site at a private campground, so if money is tight, head instead for the state parks and Everglades National Park for an overnight or two. It's easiest to get a site if you arrive early in the morning on a weekday when public schools are in session.

Restaurant portions are generous all over south Florida, so if you're not starving, plan to split some servings, especially the main dish. This is easiest to do tactfully if you order it as takeout. Or pick up a walk-around lunch or snack from the Cuban sandwich or conch fritter vendors.

While Key West has some options for entertainment, we find some of the attractions overpriced. The Hemingway House is almost as interesting from the outside as it is inside, and cheaper. Unless you're a real Hemingway fan or a six-toed cat freak, we suggest you take a picture, and then walk on by.

The Conch Train and Trolley tours are cute, and ideal for day-trippers off the cruise ships, but you can cover the same territory by bicycle (rentals are easy to find if you're not carrying your own) or even on foot. Pick up the **free walking-tour brochures** from the **tourist information office** in **Mallory Square.** Since the open-air trolleys use amplified narration, you could tag along behind one on your bike and hear the same information and corny jokes for which the day-trippers pay $20.

WHERE TO GET TRAVEL INFORMATION

Call © **800/771-KEYS** [5397] only within the Florida Keys area for a live multilingual operator who provides assistance with problem-solving. The number is staffed 24 hours a day, 7 days a week. Call **Florida Keys Information** (© **800/FLA-KEYS** [352-5397]; www.fla-keys.com) to get a video and brochure. Call **Florida State Parks** for a free state parks guidebook (© **850/245-2157;** www.floridastateparks.org). **Florida RV Parks and Campgrounds** supplies Florida campground info and will, upon request, send a free directory of more than 300 listings, with maps and 30 campground brochures (© **850/562-7151;** www.floridacamping.com).

DRIVING & CAMPING TIPS

- **"MM" means mile marker.** The letters MM, which you'll see throughout this chapter and on material about the Keys, stand for Mile Marker, the most commonly used address. The markers are green-and-white signs on the right shoulder of the road. Miles are measured from Key West (MM 0) to the mainland (MM 126).

- **Don't mess with the coral.** The pieces of coral and coral souvenirs you'll see for sale in the Keys come from the Philippines. The taking of any Florida coral is illegal, and snorkelers and divers who harm it or the other protected species are subject to fines and punishment.

- **Don't mess with the manchineel tree, either.** The pretty little manchineel tree growing on the beach with its green and yellow leaves makes an inviting canopy in a rain shower. But watch out—it literally drips a burning, acidlike poison from its leaves as the rain runs down them. Never touch its tiny applelike fruit, its thick milky sap, or its smooth gray trunk. Everything about it is poisonous.

- **Keep on your toes to get a campsite.** Privately owned RV parks in the Keys, particularly those that are so-called "condo parks" (meaning they sell memberships or timeshares), can be pricey, especially at high season, when the entire population of Canada and the upper Midwest seems to be in residence. Expect to be charged $40 or much more for an overnight hookup. Multiple-night stays will trim the price, as will opting for just water and electric. Even the state parks are expensive compared to those in other states. They make half their sites available for advance booking, but only within 60 days of your anticipated arrival. For first-come, first-served sites in the state parks, go in the morning and get your name on a waiting list if the park is full, then come back in midafternoon to see if you've scored a space.

- **Call ahead about pets.** Many Florida recreation areas and state parks, as well as some private RV parks, have a hotly debated "no pets" rule. Be sure to call ahead if you're traveling with furry friends.

The Best Sights, Tastes & Experiences of the Keys

OFF-THE-WALL ATTRACTIONS

Coral Castle, in Homestead. Located off U.S. 1 at SW 157th Avenue on your way to the Keys, Coral Castle is a living testimony to "the magic and power of love." It seems a heartsick Latvian named Ed Leedskalnin was jilted by a 16-year-old girl and made his way to south Florida. There, he spent the next 25 years carving 1,100 tons of coral into pieces of furniture and other unwieldy artifacts, including a table shaped like the state of Florida, all in memory of her. What he did for love, or rather how he did it, is still a mystery, since he weighed only 97 pounds and did not use any heavy machinery to move the blocks of coral. (One lunatic-fringe tome suggests he had the help of aliens in flying saucers.) When the neighbors came around to look, he stopped working until they left. He died of starvation, it's said, in 1951, with thousands of dollars hidden around the coral house. There's a Psychic Fair held on the grounds on the first Saturday of every month, but if some folks know what happened, they'll never tell. Sun–Thurs 8am–6pm; Fri–Sat 8am–8pm. Admission $9.75 adults, $6.50 seniors, $5 children 7–12, free for children 6 and under. The museum is at 28655 S. Dixie Hwy. (© **305/248-6345;** www.coralcastle.com).

Duval Street, Key West. Key West conchs jokingly claim that Duval is the longest street in the world because it stretches from the Gulf of Mexico to the Atlantic Ocean (a distance of about 1½ miles). Late at night, the pub-lined street is also the setting for "the Duval crawl."

Fat Albert, the spying balloon, Cudjoe Key. Fat Albert bobs around 2,000 feet above Cudjoe Key (when he isn't blown off his tether), watching for drug dealers in small planes and boats heading across the Florida straits. His avoirdupois is made up of millions of bucks of electronic surveillance gear.

Flipper's grave, Grassy Key. Yes, *that* Flipper, whose real name was Mitzi. A 30-foot-high monument to a mother and baby dolphin is also on the site, on U.S. 1 at MM 59 on Grassy Key, as is the Dolphin Research Center (see "Eight Watery Wonders," later in this chapter; © **305/289-1121;** www.dolphins.org).

Gatorland, Kissimmee. Tupperware World Headquarters and Gatorland are near each other on Route 441 between Orlando and Kissimmee. Since Tupperware no longer gives tours, though, we now head for Gatorland with its alligators and crocodiles. You walk into the jaws of a plaster alligator, then watch live alligators leap out of the water to snag a mouthful of chicken dangling overhead in the Gator Jumparoo show. Old-time gator wrestling, an alligator breeding marsh, even a smokehouse offering tidbits of smoked gator ribs and deep-fried gator nuggets are highlights of one of the few old Florida roadside attractions remaining amid the Disney/Universal virtual world. Daily 9am–5pm. Admission $23 adults, $15 children 3–12, free for children 2 and under. Discounts for online purchase. Gatorland is at 14501 S. Orange Blossom Trail. Call for details (© **800/393-JAWS** [5297]; www.gatorland.com).

Goofy graves, Key West. At the Key West Cemetery, seek out especially the stones of B. P. Roberts (1929–79), engraved "I Told You I Was Sick" (at the end of Seventh St.); another gravestone that says, "A Devoted Fan of Singer Julio Iglesias"; the grave of Joseph "Sloppy Joe" Russell, Hemingway's favorite bartender, who died on a 1941 fishing trip with the author; and the famous "bound woman" on the grave of Archibald John Sheldon Yates (at the intersection of Angela and Grinnell). Most are stone vaults raised above the impenetrable coral base and the high water table. The cemetery is open dawn to dusk.

Lots of people, lots of beer, lots of fish. If you like to hang out in crowds with people who swap fishing stories and drink beer, **Holiday Isle** at MM 84 on appropriately named

Windley Key is mobbed on winter weekends. If you don't like such crowds, consider yourself forewarned (℃ **800/327-7070** or 305/664-2321; www.holidayisle.com).

The Perky Bat Tower, Sugarloaf Key. This tower is not a celebration of energetic nocturnal flying mammals, but rather an effort to lure some to devour the mosquitoes that were the scourge of the area. Built on Sugarloaf Key in 1929 by a real estate promoter named R. C. Perky, the tower was supposed to bring in bats so Perky's resort would be bug-free. Perky, his casino, cabins, and fishing resort are long gone, but the bat tower still stands—and the mosquitoes are still flying. Located on U.S. 1 near MM 17 on the Gulf side.

Sunset at Key West's Mallory Square. A nightly happening, with fire-eaters, jugglers, mimes, contortionists, T-shirt sellers, fortunetellers, and unicyclists. Thousands attend, starting about 2 hours before sunset (**www.sunsetcelebration.org**).

Trails of Margaritaville. Jimmy Buffett fans will enjoy this 90-minute walking tour through Key West, which points out the many haunts of Buffett (lots of bars) plus numerous tales (true or not) of Key West. The tour starts from Captain Tony's Saloon at 428 Greene St. at 4pm for $20 per person. Call ahead and **make reservations** since the number of participants is limited (℃ **305/292-2040**).

EIGHT SPECIAL SPLURGES

1. **Book a stay on Little Palm Island.** Book a day or two at the most laid-back and romantic, not to mention expensive, resort in the Keys, reached by launch from Little Torch Key at MM 28.5 for guests whose reservations are in the computer. Snorkeling, bonefishing, sunset sailing, and fine dining are some of the popular activities. At night, you snuggle down in one of 30 South Pacific– style ersatz grass huts that miraculously conceal a Jacuzzi tub, a minibar, and a queen-size bed. Nonresident guests may reserve for lunch or dinner (℃ **800/343-8567**; www.littlepalmisland.com).

2. **Have lunch at Louie's Backyard.** In Key West's varied dining scene, most visitors regard Louie's as the obligatory spot for dinner out; however, we prefer lunch, sitting at outdoor tables with a view of sailboats gliding past. A warm fried-chicken salad (spears of chicken atop greens) is a house special, and fresh grilled fish is accompanied by Cuban black beans, fried plantains, and lime wedges. Reserve well ahead at this eatery, at 700 Waddell Ave. Musician Jimmy Buffett used to eat here when he lived in the big white house next door (℃ **305/294-1061**; www.louiesbackyard.com).

3. **Shell out for a lazy open-air tour of Key West.** The colorful Conch Train and the Old Town Trolley (operated by two different firms) leave from Mallory Square and provide 90 minutes of corny, good-natured jokes aimed at the over-50 cruise-ship day-trippers. You'll get good views of 60 or so must-see spots around town. Tickets for each tour are $29 adults, $20 students, children 4–12 free. **Conch Train:** ℃ **888/916-8687**; www.conchtourtrain.com. **Old Town Trolley:** ℃ **888/910-8687**; www.trolleytours.com/key-west).

4. **Expand your imagination with a Ghost Tour of Key West.** It leaves nightly from 423 Fleming St. You'll be led on a lantern evening stroll down Key West's shadowy lanes and discover the ghosts and legends of this haunted paradise. Tours depart nightly at 8 and 9pm year-round, but space is limited, and reservations are required. Tickets are $15 adults, $10 children 4–12, free for children 3 and under (© **305/294-9255;** www.hauntedtours.com).

5. **Take a cat to see the coral.** The *Amoray Diver,* a motorized catamaran from Key Largo's Amoray Dive Resort, can take 49 snorkelers or 34 scuba divers out to the Key Largo National Marine Sanctuary for some coral-reef viewing. Cost is $80 per person, per trip. Reservations are requested (© **800/4-AMORAY** [426-6729] or 305/451-3595; www.amoray.com).

6. **Parasail 600 feet above Key West** from a catamaran. Anyone can do it, say the people at Fury Catamarans, promising dry takeoffs and landings from the boat and tandem rides. Cost is $40. Hey, enjoy; we'll be watching from the Hilton with a cold drink in our hands. Departures are from the Hilton Marina; reservations are required (© **877/994-8898** or 305/294-8899; www.furycat.com).

7. **Drop by Cheeca Lodge for seafood.** If you want to splurge on a politically correct seafood meal, this Islamorada hotel restaurant is your kind of place. The ever eco-aware lodge took all conch dishes off its menu several years ago because taking the mollusks in U.S. waters is illegal; therefore, all conch is imported from the Bahamas and is "neither indigenous nor fresh," says chef Dawn Seiber, a native of the Keys. She serves Jamaican seafood soup instead of conch chowder and buys much of her fish and shellfish from seafood farms. Polish off a piece of passion-fruit pie for dessert. Located on U.S. 1 at MM 82. Call for reservations (© **800/327-2888** or 305/664-4651; http://cheeca.com).

8. **Take a seaplane to Fort Jefferson.** Head to the Dry Tortugas, 68 miles west of Key West, to see the remains of this 19th-century brick fort. It was the Civil War prison for Dr. Samuel Mudd, who set John Wilkes Booth's leg, broken on his jump to the stage of Fords Theater after he assassinated Abraham Lincoln. Mudd was accused of conspiring in the crime, although it is generally believed he was innocent of any knowledge of it. He was released in 1867 after a heroic stint taking care of 270 men who came down with yellow fever. While the visit itself is $5, getting there costs around $199 per adult, $149 per child for a half-day trip. You can look down into the clear water from the plane and see numerous shipwrecks below, as well as sharks and rays. The fort itself is as eerie and haunted a place as you'll ever see under a hard blue sky and dazzling sunlight. Call **Seaplanes of Key West** (© **305/294-4014;** http://keywestseaplanes.com).

GREAT TAKEOUT (OR EAT-IN) TREATS

The cheeseburgers at Jimmy Buffett's Margaritaville, Key West. The ones at Jimmy's restaurant are almost as famous as the song of the same name; most customers order margaritas as well. It's at 500 Duval St. (© **305/292-1435;** http://margaritaville keywest.com).

Talkin' Conch: A Keys Glossary

Conch (Konk): A native of the Keys; named for a chewy gastropod that inhabits local waters.

Eyebrow house: A house where the second-story roof overhangs the windows.

Fretsaw: Gingerbread trim on houses, much of it applied by ships' carpenters from termite-resistant hardwood.

Hardwood hammock: Not a bed slung between two posts, but a dense grove of small hardwood trees growing on a limestone reef in a marshy area at a slightly higher elevation, so they form humps.

Mangroves: Small, broadleaf, evergreen tropical trees growing in marshes or tidal shores with much of their root systems exposed.

Shotgun house: A long hall through which you could shoot a bullet, and which runs from front to back through a house.

Square grouper: What local fishers call bales of marijuana bobbing in the water, thrown overboard by drug smugglers when the Coast Guard is near.

Stranger: Everybody on the Keys who's not a conch.

Tourist tree: The gumbo-limbo, whose peeling red-orange bark looks like the result of a bad sunburn.

The Key lime pie at Key West Key Lime Pie Company, Key West. If the urge for Key lime pie overwhelms you, head for the Key West Key Lime Pie Company for a sublime takeout wedge of pie in a plastic container with a fork. Some eaters were so overcome by its taste that they ate it standing up right in the shop. Other, more discreet nibblers like us waited until we got outside. It's delectable. 200 Elizabeth St. (© 800/376-0806 or 305/296-0806; www.keylimeshop.com).

Seafood at the Half-Shell Raw Bar, Key West. A longtime local favorite, with paper plates, plastic forks, and a big turnover of tables around mealtime. It sells shrimp from the local fleet, as well as clams and oysters on the half-shell and a tasty conch chowder. The cracked conch—breaded and fried conch steak—is yummy. 231 Margaret St. (© 305/294-7496; www.halfshellrawbar.com).

The Sloppy Joes at Sloppy Joe's, Key West. The sandwich may or may not have originated here, but it's a good story. It serves the Original Sloppy Joe as well as the Sloppy Joe Quesadilla. The bar is hard to miss; just follow the cruise-ship day-trippers to 201 Duval St. (© 305/294-5717; www.sloppyjoes.com).

Weekly Thanksgiving dinner at Pepe's, Key West. Pepe's is a resoundingly local Key West eatery, there since 1909 and noted for huge breakfasts and haphazard decor that includes everything from Christmas lights to nude paintings. Every Thursday night, a Thanksgiving dinner is served, along with oysters from Apalachicola Bay (safest to eat cooked). It's at 806 Caroline St. (© **305/294-7192;** www.pepescafe.net).

Cuban sandwiches at the Five Brothers Grocery, Key West. Get them to take out. Alternatively, try the hot, deep-fried cornmeal *bollitos* (fritters) with *a buchi,* a single shot of sweet Cuban espresso. At the corner of Southard and Grinnell sts. (© **305/ 296-5205;** 5brothersgrocerytripod.com).

Street food, Key West. Key West street vendors proffer conch fritters, Cuban coffee, hot dogs, piña coladas, and dolphin sandwiches (no, not Flipper, but the fish Hawaiians call mahimahi).

Turtle steak, and so on, at the Green Turtle Inn, Islamorada. Years ago, the Green Turtle Inn was the first (and last) place where we ever knowingly ate alligator, and, yes, it does taste sort of like chicken. These days, it serves farm-raised turtle steaks and chowders, as well as its own canned conch chowder, politically correct turtle soup (they use north Florida river turtles), and Key lime pie filling to go if you want to stock up the RV. It's old-fashioned, good-natured, eclectic, and eccentric, as well as usually crowded, with only a faint whiff of tourist trap. At MM 81 in Oceanside (© **305/664-2006;** www.greenturtlekeys.com).

"The world's best fish sandwiches" at Craig's Restaurant, Tavernier. The best is grouper, but sometimes they're out of it and substitute catfish or dolphin (mahimahi). Messy to eat, the sandwich is on grilled whole wheat bread with cheese, tomato, lettuce, and tartar sauce. Good if you're looking for a quick and casual lunch. At MM 90.5 (© **305/852-9424;** http://craigsrestaurant.com).

The fresh grilled seafood at Kelly's, Key West. Its full name is Kelly's Caribbean Bar, Grill and Brewery. The grilled seafood is topped off with a boutique brew. Daily noon–10pm. 301 Whitehead St. at the corner of Caroline St., just off Duval (© **305/293-8484;** www.kellyskeywest.com).

Traditional Native American dishes at the Miccosukee Restaurant, near Shark Valley. Miccosukee serves traditional dishes like fried catfish, pumpkin bread, and Indian fry bread (crunchy deep-fried bread dough), which can be topped with ground beef and garnishes to make an Indian taco. Daily 9am–3pm. On Tamiami Trail (U.S. 41), MM 70, near Shark Valley (© **305/552-8365;** www.miccosukee.com).

EIGHT WATERY WONDERS

1. **John Pennekamp Coral Reef State Park.** Near **Key Largo** and part of the Florida Keys National Marine Sanctuary, this is a 78-square-mile underwater park made up of reefs like those that formed the Keys. The living coral colonies are endlessly fascinating for divers and snorkelers; there are underwater observation rooms and glass-bottomed boats for those who want to keep their heads above water. The reef has more than 50 forms of coral and 500 species of tropical fish, and is the only living coral reef in the continental United States. It's at MM 102.5 (© **305/451-6300;** www.floridastateparks.org/pennekamp).

2. **Islamorada.** Islamorada is a popular fishing resort area on **Upper Matecumbe Key** with the Theater of the Sea and its dolphin and sea-lion shows, plus a shark pool and aquarium. **Lignumvitae Key State Botanical Site,** MM 78.5 (© **305/664-2540;** www.floridastateparks.org/lignumvitaekey) displays rare *Lignum vitae* trees, a dense wood that can outlast steel. **Indian Key** is a formerly settled key where John James Audubon visited in 1832. The latter two are uninhabited islands that can be toured with park rangers, but you have to get there by kayak or canoe (© **305/664-9814;** www.floridastateparks.org/indiankey).

3. **Grassy Key.** Located near Marathon Shores, Grassy Key is the location of the **Dolphin Research Center** at MM 59, where visitors can learn about the activities and the intelligence of bottlenose dolphins and California sea lions. Daily 9am to 4:30pm (closed holidays). Admission $20 adults, $17 seniors 55 and over, $15 children 4–12, free for children 3 and under. 58901 Overseas Hwy. Call for information (© **305/289-1121**) and reservations (© **305/289-0002;** www.dolphins.org).

4. **Jules' Undersea Lodge.** Ever want to spend the night underwater? Then make a reservation at Jules' Undersea Lodge, the world's first underwater hotel, with two bedrooms below the surface and a price starting around $400 a night per person, including meals. Beginning divers and snorkelers are welcome. It's at 51 Shoreland Dr., MM 103.2, in **Key Largo.** Call for information (© **305/451-2353;** www.jul.com). No alcohol is permitted unless you're on your honeymoon, in which case champagne is permissible. But we wonder: How can they tell if you're really on your honeymoon?

5. **Biscayne National Park.** Biscayne National Park is an aquatic park with 181,500 acres of islands and reefs. Several concessionaires offer boat tours from the park itself. Two shallow-draft, glass-bottomed Reef Rovers set out from the park's Convoy Point headquarters daily and skim lightly over the reefs. Afternoon snorkel and scuba trips (with rental equipment available) last 4 hours and depart at 1:30pm, while morning reef sightseeing tours start at 10am. Headquarters are 9 miles east of **Homestead** at 9700 SW 328th St. Reservations required (© **305/230-7275;** www.nps.gov/bisc).

6. **July Underwater Music Festival, Big Pine Key.** Divers listen to an underwater symphony at Looe Key National Marine Sanctuary, one Saturday in July 10am–4pm. 31020 Overseas Hwy., MM 31. Call for details (© **305/872-2411;** www.lowerkeyschamber.com).

7. **Bahia Honda State Park, Bahia Honda Key.** The park has one of the best sandy beaches in the Keys, allowing you the luxury of wading out into the water on sand instead of—ouch—coral. It's 12 miles south of Marathon, MM 37 (© **305/872-3210;** www.floridastateparks.org/bahiahonda).

8. **Dog Beach, Key West.** Dog Beach, near Louie's Backyard, is the only beach in Key West where owners and dogs can swim together. The so-called nude canals in an abandoned real estate development on Sugarloaf Key's Sugarloaf Boulevard are where clothing-optional sunbathers gather to catch some rays between dips.

WILDLIFE-WATCHING

There are several **wildlife refuges** in the Keys, each named for the species that inhabits it. The **Crocodile Lake National Wildlife Refuge** (www.fws.gov/refuges/profiles/index.cfm?id=41581) on North Key Largo has the single largest population of **alligators** in the United States, with as many as 500 in residence. The refuge is closed to the public, due to its small size and the sensitivity of the habitats and wildlife to human disturbance. It's difficult to see crocodiles from the roads bordering the refuge, but they can be seen nearby at Everglades National Park.

Less frequently seen are the state's numerous nonpoisonous **snakes,** and the three poisonous ones. Most deadly is the dainty, pretty orange-and-black-banded **coral snake,** but as an old swamper told us once, "He's gonna have to chew on you a long time before you die." Keep your eye out for cottonmouth moccasins sunning on a stretch of boardwalk in a swampy area, or diamondback rattlesnakes in a palmetto patch or hammock.

The shyest of Florida's indigenous fauna is the **manatee,** a 1-ton, plant-eating sea mammal that is also called a "sea cow." As legend has it, early sailors thought these were mermaids, but anybody who made a mistake like that must have been away from women a long, long time. The biggest threat to the dwindling manatee population is the south Florida boats with whirring propellers that tear into the mammal's tender flesh.

The best place to see the manatee up close is at **Homosassa Springs Wildlife State Park,** where a number of them are in residence, either lazily floating around in the water or scarfing down lettuce from their underwater "salad bar." You'll also see Florida alligators and crocodiles and learn the difference between the two during one of the park's excellent Animal Encounters programs. The park is about 90 miles west of Orlando on the Gulf of Mexico off U.S. 19, at 4150 S. Suncoast Blvd. Open daily 9am to 5:30pm. Admission $13 adults, $5 children 6 to 12, free for children 5 and under (© 352/628-5343; www.floridastateparks.org/homosassasprings).

You'll have easier sightings of **osprey,** which usually nest atop utility poles (their nests are big and klutzy-looking), and white egrets, which stalk haughtily in marshes and ponds, especially in spring. We spotted several from the walkways in **Everglades National Park.** Check in at the **Royal Palm Visitor Center,** 3 miles past the park entrance; a campground without hookups is nearby. A number of walking trails, most of them over boardwalk, take you into the swamp.

At **Big Pine Key,** delicate little 30-inch **Key deer,** like miniature white-tailed deer, roam in the **National Key Deer Refuge;** go early in the morning or just before dusk for the best chance of sighting them. There are fewer than 300 left in existence. Stop off at the visitor center at **Pine Key Shopping Center** (with the Winn-Dixie), near MM 30.5 off U.S. 1. They'll give you a brochure and map of the area. Or call the Ranger's Office of the **National Key Deer Refuge,** 179 Key Deer Blvd., Big Pine Key Plaza (© 305/872-2239; www.fws.gov/nationalkeydeer).

Also on this key is the **Great White Heron National Wildlife Refuge** (www.fws.gov/nationalkeydeer/greatwhiteheron). These big, graceful birds are among the most beautiful of all seabirds. Freshwater ponds on the key have led some geologists to suggest the herons might have been part of the Appalachian Mountain range. The refuge is located at MM 28 through 31. For information, call the National Key Deer Refuge (see above).

On the Road

KEY LARGO

Key Largo, the classic 1948 Humphrey Bogart and Lauren Bacall film, was shot almost entirely on a Hollywood soundstage. However, that didn't stop the town of Rock Harbor from taking the name Key Largo after clearing it with the U.S. Postal Service in 1952, then building a cottage industry around the film's stars, none of whom were in town during the filming. A boat that might have been used in *The African Queen* (1951) is on display at the Holiday Inn Key Largo, and, according to local tourist handouts, is "a nostalgic addition to Key Largo's unique old film atmosphere." In addition, you can also see the *Thayer IV* from *On Golden Pond* (1981), which was shot in New Hampshire.

Ironically, the only location in town where some second-unit footage for *Key Largo* was actually shot was the funky Caribbean Club Bar at MM 104, and that was at the original club that burned down in the 1950s and was replaced with the present one.

The old **Tavernier Hotel** in the downtown district claims to be the first hotel in the Keys, and managed to survive the great, unnamed Labor Day hurricane of 1935. Back then, weathermen didn't do cute stand-ups in front of cameras, so tropical storms didn't need names.

Seven Mile Bridge takes you through the Florida Keys.

Old hands say the upper Keys have the best fishing, especially around Marathon and Islamorada, the latter usually billed as the Sportfishing Capital of the World. However, visitors with visions of Hemingway dancing in their heads keep driving south to Key West before booking a boat.

Bonefish inhabit the shallow waters of mangrove islets on the Gulf of Mexico side (but are not as easy to catch as they look), while **marlin** and **sailfish** are deepwater dwellers, so you'll require a captain and crew to take you out into the Atlantic. Charter boats and guides can be found at **Garrison Bight Marina** on Palm Avenue in Key West or at one of the charter fishing fleet companies on U.S. 1 just south on Palm Avenue.

KEY WEST
Part One: Cayo Hueso Becomes Key West

The 8-square-mile coral island used to be called *Cayo Hueso* (meaning "bone key"), the name derived from piles of human bones found by early visitors. No one is quite sure where the bones came from, but they were already in place when the first non-Indians, a bunch of buccaneers, hit town. Ponce de León had probably discovered the Keys in 1513 as he worked his way north looking for the Fountain of Youth, which he found in St. Augustine.

In 1815, Cayo Hueso belonged to Juan Pablo Salas of St. Augustine under a Spanish land grant, but when Florida became part of the United States in 1821, he sold it to John Simonton, an American businessman, for $2,000. Simonton called in the U.S. Navy's Anti-Pirate Squadron, drove out the pirates, and put the place under military control. From that day forward until 1974, there was always a navy base on Key West.

By the 1830s, the island, now anglicized into Key West, was inhabited primarily by "wreckers" who made their livings from what was euphemistically known in the 1800s as the "wrecking trade." It involved salvaging sunken ships—even perhaps, as some historians suggest, luring those same ships to wreck onto the shoals and then salvaging them. In a good season, more than one ship a week would run aground. The best wreckers, it's said, lived aboard their ships so they could get to a wreck even more quickly.

KEY LIME PIE

Key limes, which in this country grow only in the Florida Keys, are not green, but yellow fruits the size of a golf ball, with green speckles. Ergo, the filling in a genuine Key lime pie is also yellow, not green. The first Key lime pie is thought to have been whipped up in the kitchen of the Curry Mansion in Key West, now a popular Caroline Street bed-and-breakfast.

You can visit the Audobon House in Key West.

Most were cockneys from the Bahamas, along with Loyalists to the British Crown after the Americans won the Revolutionary War, plus a polyglot assortment of Cubans, seafarers from New England, and, later, émigrés from the Civil War.

But both the buccaneers and the wreckers missed the greatest haul of loot ever recovered by American salvage hunters: **Mel Fisher's** treasure trove from the sunken Spanish galleons *Atocha* and *Santa Margarita,* millions of dollars worth of gold bars, silver coins, and emeralds. The ships sank off Key West in 1622 on their way back to Spain, laden with the riches of the New World. Some key pieces of the indescribably valuable finds are on display in **Mel Fisher's Maritime Heritage Museum** (see "Things to Do in Key West for Around 10 Bucks," below) at 200 Greene St. in **Key West.** (On our first visit, Fisher's mother sold us the tickets and showed us around with visible maternal pride.)

At the turn of the 20th century, the city, already the richest settlement in Florida, was the cigar-producing capital of the world. Many of the 6,000 cigar makers were Cubans who flocked here to find work.

The wrecking industry bottomed out in 1921—"The navy put channel markers and buoys to warn the ships about the reef," locals said—and the cigar industry burned out when investors in Ybor City, near Tampa, lured the cigar manufacturers away with promises of fewer labor problems.

By the late 1920s, Key West had become a backwater and one of the poorest places in the United States. In 1934, with 80% of the population unemployed, the city declared bankruptcy, and the federal government sent in a New Deal administrator called Julius Stone who decided to turn the island into a tropical tourist paradise. He put people to work painting and cleaning up the town and the beaches, training young women to be hotel maids, even suggesting that all the local men wear shorts to appear picturesque.

The plan was a huge success in the winter of 1934–35, but the Labor Day hurricane of 1935 swept away the railway tracks and with them all the hopes and dreams. Tourism increased again after World War II, spurred by sailors who had been stationed here.

Part Two: A Bird in the Bush

Writers and artists have always been fascinated with Key West. One of the first was John James Audubon, who arrived in 1832 aboard the cutter *Marion*. A crack shot, the Haitian-born painter, naturalist, and egoist had worked his way through the American South as a tutor and dancing master, often biting the hand that fed him. His modus operandi was to kill as many birds from a species as he could because he enjoyed shooting. Then he mounted one or two of them and arranged them in a habitat, often tree branches. While Audubon usually drew the birds himself, a young assistant—one or another always traveled with him—filled in the backgrounds. In Key West, Audubon produced two bird drawings, one of them a white-crowned pigeon perched on a branch of an orange-blossomed Geiger tree.

This type of tree was introduced from the West Indies by Captain John Geiger, who also built the house now called the Audubon House, although Audubon's connection with it is tenuous.

Part Three: The Further Adventures of Key Weird

Its detractors may sometimes refer to Key West as "Key Weird," but it's certainly a town that knows how to party.

April's Conch Republic Days celebrate the time not long ago (Apr 1982) when the Border Patrol put up roadblocks on Route 1 to look for drugs and illegal aliens. Tourists took one look and turned back, and the town's income fell off considerably. So Key West proclaimed itself the Conch Republic and seceded from the United States, then applied for foreign aid. This weeklong celebration usually involves silliness such as a bed race and a lot of drinking.

Tennessee Williams's birthday, March 25, is often an occasion for celebrating, as is the weekly Doris Day Night at a local gay bar, and, of course, every day at sunset, when there's a lot of drinking.

We're fond of the Laundromat at the corner of Margaret and Truman streets, named, logically enough, the Margaret-Truman Drop-off Launderette.

The big brick building down by the dock was designed in 1890 as a government office building (or so a Conch tour guide told us), and the engineer had almost completed it when he died. A second engineer was sent in from up north and made them start all over again, digging a huge basement for oil-fired heating equipment, adding chimneys, and making the roofs steep enough "so the snow could slide off."

Florida Keys Campgrounds

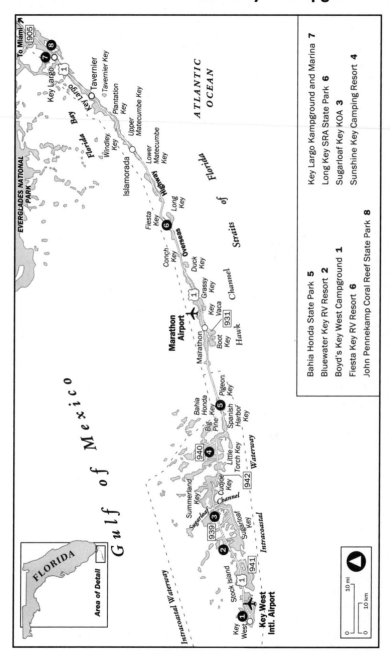

Bahia Honda State Park **5**

Bluewater Key RV Resort **2**

Boyd's Key West Campground **1**

Fiesta Key RV Resort **6**

John Pennekamp Coral Reef State Park **8**

Key Largo Kampground and Marina **7**

Long Key SRA State Park **6**

Sugarloaf Key KOA **3**

Sunshine Key Camping Resort **4**

HEMINGWAY'S CATS

The six-toed cats all over the grounds of the Hemingway House are said to be descended from Hemingway's own cat. While far short of the 70 kept by the author at his Cuban farm, the Key West team numbered 42 at our last visit and cost $700 a month to feed.

Kelly's Caribbean Bar, Grill and Brewery (© 305/293-8484; www.kellyskey west.com) at 301 Whitehead St. near Caroline Street, once owned by actress Kelly McGillis, is in the old Pan American Airways building. Before that, it was the Pigeon House, used to raise homing pigeons sent out with boats so if the crew got into trouble, the captain could release a bird, and help could be sent.

The city's sizable gay population has done the most to restore the old Conch houses, setting up a flourishing bed-and-breakfast community, and glamorizing the mainstream in this laid-back, peaceable community.

But some of the high hilarity of the 1980s softened somewhat around the millennium, in some cases to the detriment of the lounge scene. **La Te Da** (local nickname of the La Terraza de Marti, 1125 Duval St.; © 877/528-3320 or 305/296-6706; www.lateda.com) and its Sunday afternoon tea dances have toned down the campiness, with no more owner-and-dog look-alike contests like the one described by Joy Williams in her guidebook *The Florida Keys:* "The Look-Alike trophy went to Frank Cicalese and his Chihuahua Sam. They appeared as identical, perfectly pink Easter bunnies in identical bunny suits, slippers, and hats, carrying matching Easter baskets. Both wore sunglasses."

Getting Around Key West

Rent a **bicycle** or **moped** from one of the shops along Truman Avenue, especially if you're traveling in a motor home without a tow vehicle (that way, you can leave the rig plugged in). If you don't want to do the pedaling yourself, hail a **pedicab** and let one of the well-tanned and shapely young things pedal you around. That's how they stay well tanned and shapely.

You can also hop aboard an **Old Town Trolley** or **Conch Tour Train** (tickets are sold in Mallory Sq. or aboard the vehicles). These open-air trams zigzag across town for 90 minutes while a friendly driver fills you in with yarns, anecdotes, and a collection of corny jokes.

Three Key West Sights

The Ernest Hemingway Home and Museum. This home where the author lived with his second wife, Pauline, from 1931 to 1940, is a National Historic Landmark. Self-guided or escorted tours are available through the house and gardens, where a number

HIGHLIGHTS

Captain Tony's Saloon **3**

Conch Tour Trains/
  Old Town Trolley **1**

Dog Beach **14**

Ernest Hemingway Home
  and Museum **18**

Five Brothers Grocery **11**

Half-Shell Raw Bar **10**

Jimmy Buffet's
  Margaritaville **7**

Kelly's **4**

Key West Aquarium **3**

Key West Cemetery **12**

Key West Key
  Lime Pie Co. **15**

Key West Lighthouse
  Museum **17**

La Te Da
  (La Terraza de Marti) **16**

Little White House **8**

Louie's Backyard **14**

Mallory Square **1**

Margaret Truman Drop-Off
  Launderette **13**

Mel Fisher's Maritime
  Heritage Museum **2**

Pepe's **9**

Sloppy Joe's **5**

Turtle Kraals **10**

Oldest House &
  Museum **6**

of feral six-toed cats wander at will. Daily 9am–5pm. Admission $12 adults, $6 children, free for children 5 and under. 907 Whitehead St. (𝒞 **305/294-1136;** www.hemingwayhome.com).

The Key West Aquarium. You can hand-feed sharks, pet a barracuda, or reach into a touch tank to feel sea creatures. The ticket is good for several days if you want to return. Feeding times: 11am and 1, 3, and 4:30pm. Daily 10am–6pm. Admission $12 adults, $5 children. 1 Whitehead St. (𝒞 **800/868-7482** or 305/296-2051; www.keywestaquarium.com).

Six-toed cats still prowl the premises of the Ernest Hemingway Home and Museum.

The Little White House. This is where Harry and Bess Truman vacationed in winter 11 times during his presidency, beginning in 1946. Recently restored to the 1940s period with original furniture, the museum provides a guided tour and a video. Daily 9am–4:30pm (last tour). Admission $16 adults, $14 seniors, $5 children 5–12, free for children 4 and under. 111 Front St. (✆ **305/294-9911;** www.trumanlittlewhite house.com).

Things to Do in Key West for Around 10 Bucks

1. **Visit the Mel Fisher Maritime Heritage Museum.** Heft a solid gold bar and see silver bars, emeralds, and golden chalices from 17th-century Spanish galleons, all discovered by the late treasure hunter Mel Fisher. Weekdays 8:30am– 5pm, Sat–Sun 9:30am–5pm. Admission $13 adults, $11 students, $6.25 children. 200 Greene St. (✆ **305/294-2633;** www.melfisher.org).

2. **Touch turtles at the old Turtle Kraals.** *Kraals* is a South African term for corrals. These *kraals* once held turtles along the shore until they went to the cannery and became turtle steaks and turtle soup. Today, the *kraals* are the home of the Florida Marine Conservancy. Sick and injured sea turtles and birds are tended here, and there's a touch tank for kids. Daily 11am–midnight. Free admission. 1 Land's End Village at Land's End Marina at the **Turtle Kraals Restaurant & Bar** (✆ **305/294-2640;** www.turtlekraals.com).

3. **Visit the Oldest House Museum,** formerly the Wrecker's Museum. It's where a sea captain and his nine daughters once lived. The 1829 house displays memorabilia of the wrecking business; there's also an elaborately furnished period dollhouse. Mon–Sat 10am–4pm. Free admission. 322 Duval St. (℮ **305/294-9501;** www.oirf.org/museum.htm).

4. **Climb the stairs at the Key West Lighthouse Museum.** A spiral staircase inside leads up to a panoramic view of the island from this 1847 lighthouse, which was the recipient of an award-winning restoration in 1987. Exhibits tell the history of the town and the Keys. Daily 9:30am–4:30pm (closed Christmas). Admission $10 adults, $9 seniors, $5 children, free for children 5 and under. 938 Whitehead St. (℮ **305/295-6616;** www.kwahs.com/lighthouse. htm).

Key West at Night

The Keys' theme song is about wasting away in **Margaritaville,** easy enough to do at singer Jimmy Buffett's popular eatery and nightspot of the same name, where you'll hear you-know-what played frequently if not incessantly. It's at 500 Duval St. (℮ **305/292-1435;** http://margaritavillekeywest.com). If you want something more down-to-earth, check out the **Caribbean Club** at MM 104.5 in Key Largo, the only local location used for the eponymous movie. But don't expect Bogart/Bacall types; it's more of a redneck-and-biker bar (℮ **305/451-4466**).

Hemingway's favorite bar in Key West, as everybody knows, was called **Sloppy Joe's,** and you can't miss the large bar with neon signs screaming the name at 201 Duval St. (℮ **305/294-5717;** www.sloppyjoes.com). When Hemingway drank there, however, Sloppy Joe's was down the street at the present site of **Captain Tony's Saloon,** 428 Greene St. (℮ **305/294-1838;** www.capttonyssaloon.com), which used to be owned by Tony Tarracino, a former Key West mayoral candidate. Late one night back in 1937, Sloppy Joe Russell and his barflies moved the bar furniture from the old building over to the new building to protest a $1 raise in the rent on the former.

Then there's the famous "Duval crawl," an evening spent prowling mile-long Duval Street, checking out the bars and restaurants, the attire of the natives, and the general wackiness. Once upon a time, six different taverns along this street were named Bucket of Blood.

Campground Oases in the Keys

John Pennekamp Coral Reef State Park. This park on **Key Largo** has 47 gravel sites that are shady, with water and 30- and 50-amp electrical hookups, flush toilets, showers, and a sanitary dump. Visitors enjoy swimming, fishing, and boat rentals. The reef lies several miles offshore, so you can just jump out of the RV and dive into the Gulf. No pets. Sites $36. Located at MM 102 (℮ **305/451-1202**); call for Florida Parks central reservations (℮ **800/326-3521;** www.floridastateparks.org/pennekamp).

And Then I Wrote . . .

Key West claims eight Pulitzer Prize winners among its residents, and, according to a knowledgeable local, more than 100 published authors live there at present.

Writer John dos Passos passed through in the 1920s, looked around, and recommended it to fellow writer Ernest Hemingway, who arrived in 1928, finished off *A Farewell to Arms* in a rented house on Summer Street in 1929, then bought a fine house on Whitehead Street in 1931.

To Have and Have Not, published in 1937, is what Hemingway called his Key West novel. One of the "have-nots" was Harry Morgan, a local fishing charter-boat operator reduced to rum running and smuggling Chinese immigrants into the United States. The author, however, was clearly one of the "haves," with a wealthy wife, a limestone mansion, the first swimming pool in Key West, and a 40-foot boat named *Pilar*.

Somewhere in the mid-1930s, while still married to his second wife, Pauline, Hemingway spotted journalist Martha Gelhorn at Sloppy Joe's. She would become his third wife in a short and tumultuous marriage after he divorced Pauline in 1940 and left Key West for good.

"You'll like Key West," Papa is reported to have written to a friend 2 decades later. "It's the St-Tropez of the poor."

Key Largo Kampground & Marina. From the juncture of U.S. 1 and Samson Road (MM 101), go east ¼ mile on Samson. Of the 171 sites, 17 are pull-throughs and 39 are full hookups with 30- and 50-amp electric. Enjoy the ocean, saltwater fishing, boating, a heated pool, and activities. Sites $60–$75 (✆ **305/451-1431;** www.keylargo kampground.com).

Fiesta Key RV Resort, Layton. The campground has 333 sites with full or partial hookups, 30- and 50-amp electric, flush toilets, and showers. There's a sanitary dump, a Laundromat, a grocery store, a heated pool and spa, an adult recreation room, a boat ramp, and a dock. Boat rentals are available to registered campers. Pets are permitted, but rates are high at $69–$129 a night. MM 70 on **Long Key** (✆ **305/664-4922;** www.fiestakeyrvresort.com).

Long Key SRA State Park, Layton. Long Key SRA has 60 sites with water and 30/50-amp electrical hookups, flush toilets, and showers. It has an oceanfront setting, and visitors enjoy fishing and boat rentals. Most sites are shaded. There's a well-labeled nature walk and some good bird-watching on the flats. No pets. Sites $20. MM 67 (✆ **305/664-4815;** www.floridastateparks.org/longkey).

Bahia Honda State Park. Bahia Honda has a 48-site campground with water and 20- and 30-amp electrical hookups, flush toilets, and showers. Some of the sites have shade and there's a sanitary dump. Visitors enjoy fishing, swimming, boating, and a marina. The beach is good, and there are wading birds and a small nature trail. No pets and no slide-outs. Sites $26. MM 37 (© **800/326-3521** or 305/872-3210; http://floridastateparks.org/bahiahonda).

Sunshine Key Camping Resort. Sunshine Key, on **Big Pine Key,** has 362 sites with water and 30- and 50-amp electric, all with full hookups. The park permits pets, which must abide by a long list of rules. There's also a private beach, a marina, a clubhouse, a pool, and waterfront sites, as well as nature trails and a bird sanctuary. Rates depend on the season and site location. Sites $65–$130. MM 39 (© **800/852-0348** or 305/872-2217).

Sugarloaf Key KOA. This private RV park has 212 sites, half of them grassy and half gravel. With full hookups in 150 sites, the park has 30- and 50-amp electric, cable TV, flush toilets, showers, a Laundromat, and a grocery store. Some sites are shaded. Visitors enjoy fishing and a swimming pool. Pets are allowed. Sites $80–$119. North of Key West at MM 20 (© **800/562-7731** or 305/745-3549; www.koa.com).

Bluewater Key RV Resort. The resort has 81 sites, 68 with full hookups, including 30- and 50-amp electric. There's a heated pool, modem and phone hookups, a dog-walking area, cable TV, and city water. Visitors enjoy ocean swimming. Sites $55–$140. On the ocean side at MM 14.5 outside of **Key West** (© **800/237-2266** or 305/745-2494; www.bluewaterkey.com).

Boyd's Key West Campground. Boyd's promises 24-hour security and local bus service at its location. It has 203 full hookups with 30- and 50-amp electric, city water,

Bahia Honda State Park offers a beautiful beach and campsite.

and cable TV, and it's modem-friendly. Some sites are on the water, and the swimming pool is resort-size, with plenty of lounging space. Visitors enjoy ocean swimming and saltwater fishing. There are some pet restrictions. Sites $60–$120. 6401 Maloney Ave. (© **305/294-1465;** www.boydscampground.com).

Two Great Side Trips

EVERGLADES NATIONAL PARK

Everglades National Park (www.nps.gov/ever) is not only the world's largest freshwater marsh, but also the third-largest national park in the lower 48 states, exceeded in size only by Yellowstone and Death Valley.

It is also, unfortunately, our most endangered national park because of encroaching housing developments, agricultural runoff, and several disastrous fires during the past several years.

The **Everglades** has had a human population for some 3,000 to 5,000 years. The Calusa Indians, hunters and gatherers who sometimes grew to 7 feet tall and lived off shellfish, left behind 20-foot mounds of shells, the tallest landmarks in the Everglades. Then came the Spanish with their weapons and European diseases, followed by the Creeks from Georgia and Alabama who fled south. They were called Seminoles by non–Native Americans, who ordered them to move to Oklahoma.

But the Seminoles declared war on the United States Army and fought sporadically from the early 1830s to 1859. Today, Native Americans in the Everglades are descendants of the survivors and call themselves Miccosukee.

Visitors here can go **sportfishing** in Florida Bay, where no commercial fishing is allowed; hike and walk on trails and on boardwalks above the marsh; rent boats, canoes, and bicycles; or take boat cruises into Florida Bay from the **Flamingo Marina Store.** The park's entrance is south of Homestead off the Florida Turnpike, also known as Route 1 or the Dixie Highway. Turn off onto Route 9336. The turns to the park are well marked. In the 38 miles from the entrance to the **Flamingo Visitor Center** at the southern end of the park, you pass through six different ecosystems, but the changes are so subtle that you'll have to watch for them.

A second Everglades **visitor center** is at Shark Valley on the Tamiami Trail, U.S. 41, with wildlife tram tours into the sawgrass prairie. Call for information about the park (© **305/242-7700;** www.nps.gov/ever).

Campground Oases in the Everglades

Long Pine Key Campground. In **Everglades National Park,** the campground has 108 paved sites, toilets, a sanitary dump, and bass fishing on Long Pine Key Lake. No hookups, no reservations. Some sites are shaded. Wooden overlooks and boardwalks in the park allow for good bird-watching. Sites $16; 14-night limit. It's 10 miles south of the junction of U.S. 1 and Rte. 9336 (© **305/242-7873;** www.nps.gov/ever).

Flamingo Campground. Also in **Everglades National Park,** Flamingo Campground has 234 paved back-in sites, with hookups available at 41 sites. Sites $16 ($30 for sites with hookups); 14-night limit. It's 38 miles southwest of the park entrance on the

Everglades National Park Campgrounds

Boardwalk RV Resort **2**

Flamingo Campground **5**

Long Pine Key Campground **4**

Miami Everglades Campground **1**

Southern Comfort RV Resort **3**

park road, a continuation of Rte. 9336 (for reservations call ✆ **877/444-6777;** or reserve online at www.recreation.gov).

Southern Comfort RV Resort. Located in **Florida City,** Southern Comfort is adjacent to the entrance to Everglades National Park. It has 350 full hookups, 30- and 50-amp electric, and optional phone hookups. Visitors enjoy planned activities (including exercise classes), special dinners, tournament shuffleboard courts, and 24-hour security. Rates are refreshingly lower than in the Keys, but there are pet restrictions. Sites $43. 345 E. Palm Dr. (✆ **888/477-6909** or 305/248-6909; www.socorv.com).

Boardwalk RV Resort. This new park in Homestead has 144 full-hookup sites with 30-amp electric. It boasts a designer clubhouse, nearby championship golf courses, a 24-hour security gate, a dance floor, and an air-conditioned exercise facility. Sites $45–$75. 100 NE 6th Ave. (✆ **800/410-5182** or 305/248-2487; http://boardwalkrv. com).

Miami Everglades Campground. Near Monkey Jungle and the Miccosukee Indian Casino, the park has a security gate, satellite TV, shade from fruit trees, and wide pull-through sites. We spent the month of February there, and found it comfortable and convenient, despite a long rush-hour commute into Miami. (The solution? Don't go.) What we really liked was the park's paved 1-mile walking trail around the perimeter, and the neighboring wholesale plant nurseries and strawberry fields. Some 300 sites have water and 20- and 30-amp electric, and 252 are full hookups. Sites $39–$59. It's 6 miles west of the junction of U.S. 1 and SW 186th St. (✆ **800/917-4923** or 305/233-5300; www.miamicamp.com).

Yacht Haven Park and Marina. This is a good choice if you're hitting **Fort Lauderdale** before or after your Everglades visit. There are 250 full hookups with 30- and 50-amp electric, and most are paved with patios, with some back-ins. The sites are narrow but deep, with alternating front and back sites that make them seem wider than they are. Reserve in advance in the winter, since half of Quebec comes here to escape the Canadian winter. Occasionally, there will be an opening for an overnight stay. There are some pet restrictions. Visitors enjoy Internet access, along with fishing and boating from the Marina. Rates are $45–$71, less by the week. Off I-95 at exit 27 (✆ **800/581-2322** or 954/583-2322; www.yachthavenpark.com).

ORLANDO

The Orlando area has a dizzying array of diverting, tacky, educational, glitzy, environmentally sensitive, and generally expensive attractions, which you'll be able to find on your own. So we offer our perspective from the point of view of vacationers traveling by recreational vehicle.

Summer is the busiest season in Orlando, with more than 100,000 admissions a day at the various attractions, but it has some of the worst weather, hot and muggy much of the time. If you can possibly visit during any other season, do so.

If not, start out as early in the morning as possible—some attractions open at 7am—and budget your midday time so you can return to the RV and its air-conditioning or hit the water parks with a splash.

Entertainment venues are spread out all over the greater Orlando area, including the Walt Disney World complex at Lake Buena Vista and Universal Studios between Bay Hill and the turnpike. The colorful Church Street Station, in downtown Orlando at 129 W. Church St., is a fanciful collection of shops, restaurants, and music halls created from Orlando's railway station and filled with antiques and oddments. Kissimmee, the world headquarters for Tupperware, is where most of the RV parks are located.

Orlando/Disney Area Campgrounds

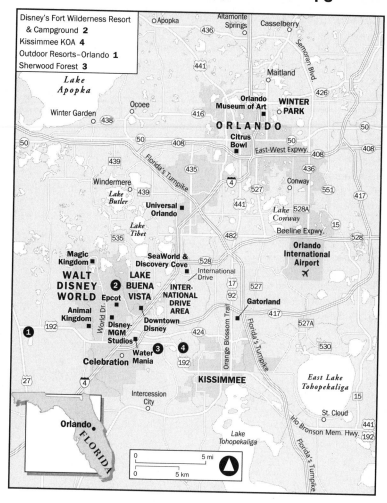

Disney's Fort Wilderness Resort
  & Campground **2**
Kissimmee KOA **4**
Outdoor Resorts–Orlando **1**
Sherwood Forest **3**

It's also where you'll find **Gatorland** (℡ **800/393-5297;** www.gatorland.com), open daily 9am to 5pm ($23 adults/children 13 and up, $15 children 3–12, free for children 2 and under), and located on U.S. 441 next to the Tupperware plant; and the **Medieval Times Dinner Tournament,** 4510 U.S. 92 (℡ **407/396-1518;** www. medievaltimes.com), with shows nightly at 8pm ($60 adults, $36 children).

If you're traveling by motor home, you'll find it easier to have a tow car along or to rent a car in the area.

Campground Oases in Orlando

Disney's Fort Wilderness Resort & Campground, in Lake Buena Vista. Disney's own campground at the Disney complex combines Walt Disney World attractions with RV camping—and you don't even need an RV to do it, since it has rental RVs on the premises. There's a free shuttle to all the Disney attractions (although in summer at peak hours, it can be jampacked) and a full restaurant and lounge on the premises. Some 799 of the paved sites are full hookups with 20-, 30-, and 50-amp electric, city water, and cable TV. There's also Wi-Fi and a modem-friendly office. Sites $57–$116. Drive ¾ mile from exit 25B off I-4 to the marked entrance (© **407/ 939-2267;** http://disneyworld.disney.go.com).

Kissimmee KOA. This KOA is within driving distance of the major Orlando attractions, and also provides free transportation to certain attractions, on-site car rental, and discount ticket sales. With 95 full hookups, most of the sites are paved, some are shaded, and all are 30 feet wide. Sites $50–$99. 2644 Happy Camper Place (© **800/562-7791** or 407/396-2400; www.koa.com).

Sherwood Forest. Sherwood Forest is just down the road from the KOA in Kissimmee, with 337 full-hookup grassy sites, most of them wide pull-throughs with 30- and 50-amp electric. It even has park models (a sort of mobile home) for rent if you don't have an RV or have friends coming to visit. Sites $39–$60. 5300 Irlo Bronson Hwy. (© **800/548-9981** or 407/396-7431; www.rvonthego.com/Sherwood-Forest-RV-Resort.html).

Outdoor Resorts–Orlando. This excellent condo park chain offers both RV sites and RVs for rent, so it's a good place for wannabe RV owners to try out different models. About 40 of the 980 sites are available for overnighters and all have full hookups, with 30- and 50-amp electric. Stay 6 nights and get the 7th night free. Expect to pay around $39 per night for a site, more for a rental. It's 5 min. west of Walt Disney World on U.S. 192 in Clermont (© **800/531-3033** or 863/424-1259; www.oro-orlando.com).

The Blue Ridge Parkway & Skyline Drive

VIRGINIA IS WHERE EIGHT U.S. PRESIDENTS WERE BORN, WHERE 60% of the Civil War's battles were fought, and where "Taps" was composed, *Dirty Dancing* (1987) was filmed, and ChapStick was invented. It's where George Marshall wrote his Plan, where Jerry Falwell launched the Moral Majority, and where Disney lost the Third Battle of Manassas when the company proposed to build a Civil War theme park next to the battlefield, which caused such a storm of protest that the Mouse had to back off.

Country singing legend Patsy Cline, who died in a plane crash here at the age of 30, was born and buried in Winchester; the Statler Brothers were born and continue to live in Staunton; and Bela Bartok dropped by Hot Springs long enough to compose his *Piano Concerto No. 3*.

It's where John-Boy said goodnight to the rest of the Walton family, where Cyrus McCormick invented the first mechanical reaping machine, where a local doctor named Charles Kenneth Pepper gave his name to a soft drink, and where Rudolph Valentino's 1925 Rolls-Royce came to rest in the Historic Car and Carriage Caravan at Luray Caverns.

At the Old Fiddlers Convention in Galax, Virginia, some RVing musicians get together.

Ronald Reagan filmed *Brother Rat* (1938) in the cadet barracks at Virginia Military Institute (VMI), the same school where Stonewall Jackson's horse Little Sorrel was stuffed for the VMI Museum. Despite being somewhat moth-eaten, Little Sorrel is its most popular exhibit. The horse fared better than the general, who was accidentally shot by his own troops at Chancellorsville in 1863 and died a week later. The raincoat he was wearing with the bullet hole in evidence is in the same museum. Jackson is buried in two places: his arm in Wilderness Battlefield and the rest of him in Stonewall Jackson Memorial Cemetery in Lexington.

Western Virginia is where Henry Ford couldn't cash a check—he was on one of his famous camping trips with Thomas Edison and Harvey Firestone (see "RV History: The Tin Can Tourists" in chapter 1, "Life on the Road: A Personal & Public History of RVing"). It's where John D. Rockefeller used to throw dimes into the pool by the first tee at the Homestead's Cascades golf course to watch the caddies scramble; and where the late multimillionaire treasure-hunter Mel Fisher came up from Key West to search for the Beale Treasure, now worth about $23 million (see "Off-the-Wall Attractions," later in this chapter).

In the Blue Ridge Mountains of North Carolina, Tom Dula (better known as Tom Dooley of "Hang Down Your Head" fame) was imprisoned in Wilkes County Jail in Wilkesboro after killing his sweetheart. Frankie Silver, heroine of an even bigger ballad, became the first woman to be hanged in the state when she was tried and put to death in Morganton for murdering her two-timing lover Johnny, who "done her wrong."

The Blue Ridge Parkway provides some of most beautiful scenery around.

Virginia Highlights

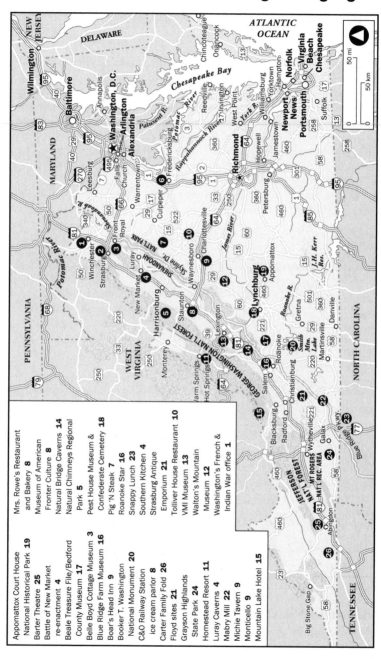

Appomattox Court House National Historical Park **19**
Barter Theatre **25**
Battle of New Market re-enactment **4**
Beale Treasure File/Bedford County Museum **17**
Belle Boyd Cottage Museum **3**
Blue Ridge Farm Museum **16**
Boar's Head Inn **9**
Booker T. Washington National Monument **20**
C&O Railway Station ice cream parlor **8**
Carter Family Fold **26**
Floyd sites **21**
Grayson Highlands State Park **24**
Homestead Resort **11**
Luray Caverns **4**
Mabry Mill **22**
Michie Tavern **9**
Monticello **9**
Mountain Lake Hotel **15**

Mrs. Rowe's Restaurant and Bakery **8**
Museum of American Fronter Culture **8**
Natural Bridge Caverns **14**
Natural Chimneys Regional Park **5**
Pest House Museum & Confederate Cemetery **18**
Pig 'N Steak **7**
Roanoke Star **16**
Snappy Lunch **23**
Southern Kitchen **4**
Strasburg Antique Emporium **2**
Tolliver House Restaurant **10**
VMI Museum **13**
Walton's Mountain Museum **12**
Washington's French & Indian War office **1**

RVing the Blue Ridge Parkway & Skyline Drive

The combined mileage of the Blue Ridge Parkway and Skyline Drive is 575 miles, plus any side trips you'll want to add along the route.

If you're going from north to south, Skyline Drive begins at Front Royal, Virginia, and the two-lane road snakes its way 105 miles through Shenandoah National Park, then joins up with the Blue Ridge Parkway at Rockfish Gap near Waynesboro, Virginia. The mileposts are numbered from 0.6 at Front Royal's fee entrance station to 105 at Rockfish Gap and the entrance to the Blue Ridge Parkway, which starts again at Milepost 0. While there are frequent turnouts, not all of them are long enough for a big rig.

The maximum speed limit along the parkway is 45 mph, but don't expect to maintain that with the curving road and sightseeing traffic.

HITTING THE HIGHLIGHTS

If you diligently drive the route from Washington, D.C., to the Great Smoky Mountains, you could cover it in less than a week by cutting down on the side trips.

While the ridge routes along Skyline Drive and the Blue Ridge Parkway are beautiful drives, you should also plan to take parallel routes through country towns and farm communities from time to time to get a better sense of the people who live there.

Plan ahead selectively to cover some of the many battlefields, living history exhibits, and historic homes throughout the Appalachians.

GOING FOR THE LONG HAUL

If you're a craftsman or collector of antiques, you could happily and perhaps profitably spend a season or two ensconced in the Appalachians, where people are friendly and prices are modest. There are crafts courses open to the public and countless antiques shops and rural flea markets. One of the biggest and most famous is the Hillsville Flea Market every Labor Day weekend, with more than 2,000 vendors on hand. It's about 8 miles north of the Blue Ridge Parkway, near Mile 200, via old Route 52 or I-77.

If you're a Civil War buff, Virginia will be endlessly fascinating, since more than half of the battles were fought there and the subject is taken seriously at battlefields and museums.

Travel Essentials

WHEN TO GO

Early spring through late fall is best. Dogwood and wildflowers begin to bloom in April. Peak time for the showiest blooms is mid-May to mid-June for flame azalea and mountain laurel, with June the best month for the vivid purple Catawba rhododendron. Craggy Gardens around Mile 365 is a particularly good place to see the latter. Autumn foliage creates another peak season as the trees turn color and begin to drop their leaves. Expect long and slow-moving lines of traffic sometimes during spring blossom, late summer, and autumn foliage seasons. Many of the facilities along the route are closed in winter. Plan early morning starts, when the air is usually clearest, and then stop in early afternoon to camp.

WHAT TO TAKE

Bring binoculars, cameras, hiking boots, sunscreen, mosquito repellent, detailed area maps, and fishing tackle if you want to go fishing. Carry a sweater or jacket even in midsummer, because evenings are cool.

WHAT TO WEAR

Casual but smart sportswear is best if you plan to visit resorts or restaurants, especially in fashionable northern Virginia. Along the Blue Ridge Parkway and in North Carolina, things are a bit more casual, so your usual RV garb will pass muster almost everywhere.

TRIMMING COSTS ON THE ROAD

Shop at **local fruit stands** for fresh produce; you'll find fresh-from-the-farm seasonal fruit and vegetables at prices far below what supermarkets charge.

Steer clear of commercial theme parks and heavily touted roadside attractions such as Natural Bridge and Luray Caverns. Besides charging admission fees, they are surrounded by other attractions that seem particularly alluring to children. Instead, take a free hike to a nearby waterfall or scenic overlook.

You'll save money, too, if you can **stay self-contained** with overnight stops rather than hooking up at a private campground adjacent to the parkway.

WHERE TO GET TRAVEL INFORMATION

Call for a packet of Virginia information, 901 E. Byrd St., Richmond, VA 23219 (© **800/VISIT-VA** [847-4882]; www.virginia.org). Our experience was that it was delivered more promptly than any other state's information.

For **Shenandoah National Park** information, write 3655 Hwy. 21 E., Luray, VA 22835. $10 entrance fee (© **540/999-3500;** www.nps.gov/shen).

For information about the **Blue Ridge Parkway,** write 199 Hemphill Knob Rd., Asheville, NC 28803 (© **828/271-4779;** www.nps.gov/blri).

For details about state parks, contact **Virginia State Parks Department of Conservation and Recreation,** 203 Governor St., Ste. 302, Richmond, VA 23219 (© **804/786-1712;** www.dcr.virginia.gov).

Call for reservations in a **state park campground** (© **800/933-PARK** [7275]; www.dcr.virginia.gov).

North Carolina Tourism is at 301 N. Wilmington St., Raleigh, NC 27699 (© **800/VISIT-NC** [847-4862] or 919/733-4171; www.visitnc.com).

Tennessee Tourism is at 312 N. Rosa L. Parks Ave., Nashville, TN 37243 (© **800/TENN-200** [836-6200] or 615/741-2159; www.tnvacation.com).

Call for information on **Great Smoky Mountains National Park** (© **865/436-1220;** www.nps.gov/grsm).

You'll find costumed reenactors at the Museum of American Frontier Culture.

DRIVING TIPS

- **Check the weather.** Winter is often mild, but periods of fog or rain may make it difficult to drive larger RVs along the ridge route. In summer, unfortunately, increased pollution and haze along Skyline Drive have greatly reduced visibility.

- **Don't be a road hog.** Because the two-lane roadways are heavily traveled, RVers should remember to pull out into the frequent overlooks and turnouts to let traffic behind them go past.

- **BYOB.** Southern states have local liquor-control laws governed by the city, county, or community. If you are accustomed to having wine with dinner, it's a good idea to inquire about the restaurant's policy before you go. Some permit diners to bring their own.

The Best Blue Ridge Sights, Tastes & Experiences

10 TERRIFIC SPOTS WHERE HISTORY COMES ALIVE

1. **Museum of American Frontier Culture, Staunton, Virginia.** It shows us where many 18th- and 19th-century settlers originated—neat, small farms in England, Northern Ireland, and the German Rhineland—and the influence of

all three is seen in a typical Shenandoah Valley farm. Costumed interpreters carry out daily and seasonal tasks, from plowing to planting, spinning to gardening. Admission $10 adults, $9.50 seniors, $9 students, $6 children 6–12, free for children 5 and under. Summer daily 9am–5pm; winter daily 10am–4pm. From I-81, take exit 222, and then follow the signs on Rte. 250 W. to 1290 Richmond Ave. (© **540/332-7850;** www.frontiermuseum.org).

2. **Appomattox Court House National Historical Park, outside Lynchburg, Virginia.** The park comprises many original historic structures along with several reconstructed buildings, so that the entire village is re-created as it was when General Robert E. Lee surrendered to General Ulysses S. Grant here in 1865, signaling the end of 4 years of Civil War. Living history exhibits in summer animate Meeks Store, Woodson Law Office, and Clover Hill Tavern, and there's a museum as well. Admission $4 adults in summer, $3 adults in winter, free for children 15 and under. Daily 8:30am–5pm (closed major winter holidays). It's 20 miles east of Lynchburg via Rte. 460 to Rte. 24 (© **434/352-8987,** ext. 40; www.nps.gov/apco).

3. **VMI Museum, Lexington, Virginia.** Located at the Virginia Military Institute, 415 Letcher Ave. in Lexington, this museum chronicles the story of the nation's first state-sponsored military college. It has reopened following a $3.5-million expansion and renovation of Jackson Memorial Hall, which exhibits the heritage of VMI in the collection of 15,000 artifacts. These include the uniform worn by Stonewall Jackson when he was mortally wounded; the shiny helmet worn by General George Patton in World War II; the mounted hide of "Little Sorrel," Jackson's war horse; plus the Henry Steward Antique Firearms Collection. Daily 9am–5pm (© **540/464-7334;** www.vmi.edu/museum).

4. **Battle of New Market reenactment, New Market, Virginia.** A reenactment of the 1864 Battle of New Market takes place every year on May 15, re-creating the battle when 247 young cadets, the entire student body of Virginia Military Institute, fought alongside Confederate soldiers against the Union Army. Ten cadets died, including a descendant of Thomas Jefferson, and 47 others lay wounded. The Hall of Valor in the New Market Battlefield Park commemorates the battle. New Market is in the Shenandoah County of Virginia, near the intersection of I-81 and Rte. 211. For information, contact the **New Market Chamber of Commerce** (© **540/740-3212;** www.newmarketcoc.net).

5. **The Blue Ridge Farm Museum, Ferrum, Virginia.** The Farm Museum displays an 1800 German-American farm and the daily life of settlers who came here, with heirloom vegetables, vintage livestock breeds, and costumed interpreters. Admission $4 adults, $3 seniors and children. Apr–Oct Sat 10am–5pm, Sun 1–5pm. From Roanoke, take U.S. 220 south to Rte. 40. Ferrum is about 12 miles southwest off Rte. 40 W. (© **540/365-4416;** www.blueridgeinstitute.org/farm.htm).

6. **Mabry Mill, near Meadows of Dan, Virginia.** Mabry Mill is animated with craftsmen and musicians during the summer and fall. Besides the water-powered

gristmill and a shop selling its stone-ground flours and meal, there's a coffee shop serving pancakes and country ham. Prepare for a queue on weekends when the locals go. Daily May–Oct. Mile 176 of the Blue Ridge Pkwy. (**restaurant: ✆ 276/952-2947**).

7. **Booker T. Washington National Monument.** Located where the great educator and inventor was born in 1856, the monument features demonstrations of 19th-century farming methods. The house where Washington, his mother, and two other children slept on a dirt floor has been reconstructed on the site. Daily 9am–5pm. It's at 12130 Booker T. Washington Hwy. in Hardy, Virginia, 20 miles southeast of Roanoke via Rte. 116 south, then Rte. 122 north, near Smith Mountain Lake. Free admission. Open 9am–5pm (**✆ 540/721-2094;** www. nps.gov/bowa).

8. **The Mast General Store, near Boone, North Carolina.** The Mast General Store was built in 1883 and is a living example of a 19th-century country store with its potbellied stove and old advertising posters. With merchandise "from cradles to caskets" and the family's 1812 log cabin and 1885 farmhouse (now an inn) nearby, it is a good example of a mountain farm complex. It's also great fun to browse through the packed shelves of this rambling store, listed on the National Register of Historic Places. (There are seven other branches of Mast throughout the Carolinas, and in Knoxville, TN.) Mon–Sat 10am–6pm, Sun 1–6pm. In **Valle Crucis,** 7 miles south of Boone on Rte. 194 (**✆ 828/963-6511;** www.mastgeneralstore.com).

Mabry Mill on the Blue Ridge Parkway.

Blue Ridge Highlights & Campgrounds

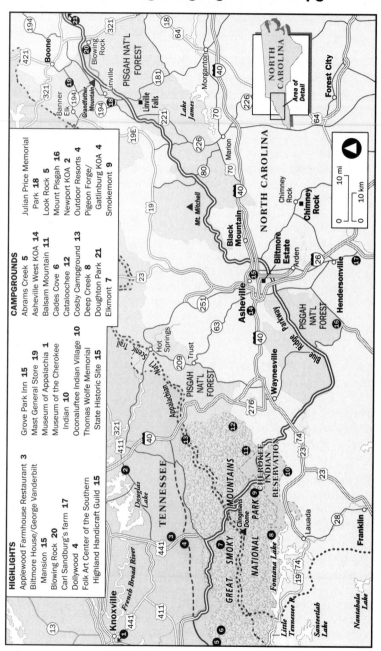

HIGHLIGHTS

Applewood Farmhouse Restaurant **3**
Biltmore House/George Vanderbilt
   Mansion **15**
Blowing Rock **20**
Carl Sandburg's farm **17**
Dollywood **4**
Folk Art Center of the Southern
   Highland Handicraft Guild **15**
Grove Park Inn **15**
Mast General Store **19**
Museum of Appalachia **1**
Museum of the Cherokee
   Indian **10**
Oconaluftee Indian Village **10**
Thomas Wolfe Memorial
   State Historic Site **15**

CAMPGROUNDS

Abrams Creek **5**
Asheville West KOA **14**
Balsam Mountain **11**
Cades Cove **6**
Cataloochee **2**
Cosby Campground **13**
Deep Creek **8**
Doughton Park **21**
Elkmont **7**
Julian Price Memorial
   Park **18**
Look Rock **5**
Mount Pisgah **16**
Newport KOA **2**
Outdoor Resorts **4**
Pigeon Forge/
   Gatlinburg KOA **4**
Smokemont **9**

9. **The Museum of Appalachia, Clinton, Tennessee.** Though it's a bit off the basic route, for anyone going or coming from the Midwest or West it could be on the way. This living village preserves the lifestyle of the southern Appalachians as its costumed interpreters split shingles, plow fields, play fiddles, and cook meals in dirt-floor cabins. A museum displays 250,000 regional artifacts, including a Roy Acuff fiddle and Sergeant Alvin York's World War I Army jacket. Admission $15 adults, $12 seniors, $5 children 6–12, free for children 5 and under. Daily 9am–5pm. Located 16 miles north of Knoxville at exit 122 from I-75, at 2819 Andersonville Hwy. (© **865/494-7680;** www.museumof appalachia.org).

10. **Oconaluftee Indian Village, Cherokee, North Carolina.** This is a re-created Cherokee village from 225 years ago, before many of the tribe were taken to Oklahoma on a forced relocation, still remembered as the Trail of Tears. One-fourth of the Cherokees died on the 1,000-mile journey. Descendants of the 1,200 tribal members who escaped and fled into the Great Smoky Mountains in 1838 make up an 8,000-member reservation today. Costumed animators make pottery, weave baskets, sew beadwork, and build canoes in traditional fashion. The **Museum of the Cherokee Indian** on Rte. 441 (follow signs from the hwy.) is a remarkable exhibit of Cherokee history. Museum daily 9am–5pm (closed major holidays). Village mid-May to late Oct. Admission $10 adults, $6 children 6–13. For information, contact the visitor center (© **800/438-1601;** www.cherokee-nc.com).

OFF-THE-WALL ATTRACTIONS

The world's largest man-made illuminated star, Roanoke, Virginia. The star is more than 88 ft. high and it shines nightly until midnight from a mountain above Roanoke. Like a fluorescent tube, the 50-year-old-plus monument usually glows in a ghostly blue-white and hums to itself, but turns red, white, and blue on patriotic holidays and turns just plain red when there's a traffic fatality in the area. Newscaster Lowell Thomas and actor John Payne, Roanoke-born, dedicated it in 1949.

The haunted caves of Natural Bridge Caverns. A moaning female ghost lives inside the limestone formations and pipes up periodically, scaring the wits out of guides and tourists. The sound has been heard for more than a century at the caverns, on U.S. 11 near the Natural Bridge. If the ghost disappoints, there's a wax museum on the premises (© **800/533-1410** or 540/291-2121; www.naturalbridgeva.com).

The Whitetop Mountain Ramp Festival, Whitetop, Virginia. Not dedicated to freeway entrances, but to a strong-smelling wild onion of the same name. At the annual festival in mid-May, you get the chance to sample ramps cooked with bear meat, with trout, in soups, and in salads. It's held at Mount Rogers Fire Hall in Whitetop, southwestern Virginia (off U.S. 58 near the VA/TN/NC borders), with bluegrass music, a crafts fair, and a quilting display (© **276/388-3332;** www.blue ridgemusic.org).

The Pest House Medical Museum in the Old City Cemetery, Lynchburg, Virginia. The museum with the irresistible name attracts the morbid and medical-minded to Lynchburg's Old City Cemetery at 4th and Taylor streets. In the 19th century, patients ill with smallpox or measles were quarantined in the Pest House, and then, when they died, were buried in the cemetery next door. The museum, viewed through the windows, has curiosities such as an 1860s hypodermic needle and an early chloroform mask. Daily dawn–dusk. 401 Taylor St. (© 434/847-1465).

The Belle Boyd cottage museum, Front Royal, Virginia. This is the former residence of a teenage girl who doubled as a Confederate spy. She gathered information on the Union Army by eavesdropping, then hopped on a horse and rode 15 miles in the middle of the night to take the information to Stonewall Jackson—and the Confederates defeated the Yankees at the Battle of Front Royal in 1862. Admission $3. The cottage, at 101 Chester St., is open variable hours, so call ahead (© **540/636-1446;** www.warrenheritagesociety.org/belleboyd.php).

The mysterious Beale Treasure, Bedford, Virginia. The legend of the Beale Treasure is based on three pages of cryptically coded information in a strongbox left with a Lynchburg hotel owner in 1822. Only one of the pages has been decoded; it claims there are 2,981 pounds of gold and 5,092 pounds of silver buried in the Bedford area, worth millions today. There's a significant amount of literature and theories about the treasure, and one website gives a good overview (www.roanokeva.com/stories/beale. html). The late Key West treasure hunter Mel Fisher took a crack at it without any luck. The **Bedford City/County Museum** houses the file; Mar–Dec Mon–Fri 10am–5pm. Located at 201 E. Main St. (© **540/586-4520;** www.bedfordvamuseum.org).

Blowing Rock, North Carolina. A strong updraft at a rock ledge hanging over the Johns River Gorge usually returns items tossed over the edge. An Indian legend says a maiden prayed to the god of the winds for the return of her warrior, who had fallen over; the wind blew him back. About 50 miles south, as the crow flies, Dr. Elisha Mitchell, a college professor taking measurements on a mountain later named for him, had no such luck. He fell to his death over a ledge by a waterfall in 1857. On Rte. 321, South Blowing Rock. Call the **Blowing Rock Chamber of Commerce** (© **877/750-INFO** [4636] or 828/295-4636; www.blowingrock.com).

SOME SPECIAL SPLURGES

1. **Visit the Grove Park Inn.** Plan a meal or even an overnight in Asheville's baronial Grove Park Inn, built in 1913 by a tycoon from Tennessee. Author F. Scott Fitzgerald frequently stayed here when visiting his wife, Zelda, who spent the latter part of her life in a local mental hospital. He usually stayed in room no. 441, which is still decorated as it was during his visits. Check out the elevators by the huge stone fireplaces; they actually run up the chimney shafts. To get there from Greenville, South Carolina, take Hwy. 25 north about 55 miles. To get there from Winston-Salem, North Carolina, take I-40 west about 140 miles to 290 Macon Ave. (© **800/438-5800** reservations or 828/252-2711 information; www.groveparkinn.com).

2. **Go shopping for authentic mountain handicrafts.** With an RV, you can probably find space for some split-willow baskets, a handmade broom, wooden toys, or even a hand-stitched heirloom quilt. They're all for sale at the **Folk Art Center of the Southern Highland Handicraft Guild** on the North Carolina end of the parkway at Mile 382, in Asheville. Daily 9am–5pm (closed holidays; ℂ **828/298-7928;** www.southernhighlandguild.org).

3. **Have tea or a meal at the Homestead Resort.** Don your smartest outfits and hit the Homestead Resort at mealtime (call ahead for reservations) for a sumptuous lunch or dinner in the grand old resort tradition. Teatime with violins is also a classic pleasure here in this redbrick, Colonial-style building dating from 1892. A hotel has been on the site for 230 years because of the healing springs. At one time, the waters were promised to cure such maladies as gum-boot poisoning, clergyman's throat, and a surfeit of freckles. There's a parking lot large enough for RVs halfway down the hill to the hotel, but the doorman may eye your rig nervously if you drive right down to the *porte-cochere.* It's at 7696 Sam Snead Hwy. in Hot Springs, Virginia, on U.S. 220 near the West Virginia border (ℂ **866/354-4653** reservations or 540/839-1766 information; www. thehomestead.com).

4. **Visit America's largest private home.** The 250-room George Vanderbilt mansion on the **Biltmore Estate** in Asheville (see "Asheville," later in this chapter) is open for public viewing. There's also a raft of other moneymaking ventures there, from gift shops to a winery, as well as seasonal and evening events. Admission (depending on date) $44–$60 adults, $24–$30 children 10–16, free for children 9 and under. Estate daily 11am–6pm. Biltmore House daily 9am–3:30pm, Fri–Sun 9am–4:30pm. From the Blue Ridge Parkway, the Biltmore Estate is 4 miles from the Hwy. 25 north exit. From I-40 West, the entrance is north of exit 50B on Hwy. 25. From I-40 East, the entrance is north of exit 50 on Hwy. 25 (ℂ **800/411-3812** or 828/225-1333; www.biltmore.com).

5. **Go antiques-hunting in the 100-shop Strasburg Antique Emporium.** The emporium has 60,000 sq. ft. of display space, with dealers selling everything from Civil War–era buttons to *Jetsons* lunchboxes. Daily 10am–5pm. Located at 160 N. Massanutten St. in the northern Virginia town of Strasburg, near Front Royal and the beginning of Skyline Dr. (ℂ **540/465-3711;** www.strasburg emporium.com).

6. **Cash in a chicken or ham for theater tickets at Virginia's state theater in Abingdon (not really…).** During the Depression, farmers paid for their tickets to the **Barter Theatre** with produce. (These days, you have to pay with cash or a credit card!) Gregory Peck, Patricia Neal, Hume Cronyn, and George C. Scott all worked here early in their careers. The theater once paid royalties to Irish playwright and noted vegetarian George Bernard Shaw by sending him a country ham, which he returned with a note requesting spinach instead. From Hwy. 81, take exit 17. Follow signs to the theater, which is

at 127 W. Main St. (box office and administration: © **276/628-3991;** www. bartertheatre.com).

7. **Take a hot-air balloon ride.** Float over some of the Shenandoah Valley's landmarks from the lavish grounds of the **Boar's Head Inn.** It's also a top-seeded tennis resort, ranking among *Tennis Magazine*'s top 50, and scene of a Merrie Olde England Christmas banquet starring a you-know-what on a silver platter. The inn is at 220 Ednam Dr., in Charlottesville (© **800/476-1988** or 434/296-2181; www.boarsheadinn.com).

8. **Find a mountain lodge that takes you back 30 years.** At least that's what the producers of *Dirty Dancing* (1987) thought when they used **Mountain Lake Hotel** to stand in for a Poconos resort in the '60s. May–Oct. To find it, leave I-81 at exit 118B and follow Rte. 460 west, bypassing Blacksburg, to Rte. 700, then drive 7 miles up a winding road to Mountain Lake (© **800/346-3334** or 540/626-7121; www.mtnlakehotel.com).

GREAT TAKEOUT (OR EAT-IN) TREATS

Carl's Frozen Custard, Fredericksburg, Virginia. Carl's turns out 120 gal. of this classic dessert (in vanilla, chocolate, and strawberry) daily in a 1940s ice-cream machine. Look for the stand at 2200 Princess Anne St. (on the corner of Princess Anne and Hunter sts.). Open daily 11am–11pm. (© **540/372-4457**).

C&O railway station ice-cream parlor, Staunton, Virginia. An authentic Victorian-era ice-cream parlor on Middlebrook Ave. in the center of Staunton dishes up sodas and sundaes in the restored C&O railway station. For more railway comestibles, try the crab croquettes at Charlottesville's **C&O Restaurant,** 515 E. Water St., across from the train station. Sun–Thurs 5–10pm; Fri–Sat 5–11pm (© **434/971-7044;** www.candorestaurant.com).

Toliver House Restaurant, Gordonsville, Virginia. Toliver House serves up old-fashioned fried chicken. Fri–Sun 11:30am–2:30pm; Tues–Sat 5:30–9pm. At the junction of U.S. 15, 33, and State Rd. 231 at 209 N. Main St. in the town of Gordonsville, northeast of Charlottesville (© **540/832-0000**).

> *"The South is that part of America where no soft drink is ever called a soda."*
> —Reynolds Price

Snappy Lunch, Mount Airy, North Carolina. Mount Airy is the hometown of Shirley Slater, coauthor of this book, and TV star Andy Griffith, as well as the **Andy Griffith Museum,** 213 Rockford St. Admission $3. Open Mon–Fri 9am–5pm, Sat 11am–4pm, Sun 1:30–4:30pm (© **336/786-7998;** www.andygriffithmuseum.com). Sheriff Andy often referred to the Snappy Lunch, which is an actual eatery notable for its pork-chop sandwiches. A boneless pork chop is flattened and tenderized, dipped

Visit America's largest private home, the Biltmore Estate.

into batter, sizzled in hot oil, and served in a hamburger bun, dressed "all the way," with tomatoes, onion, mayonnaise, mustard, coleslaw, and chile sauce. Great (but messy) to go, and have it with a sweet tea! Mon–Sat 5:45am–1pm. It's off the Blue Ridge Pkwy. near the Virginia/North Carolina border off I-77, exit 102, at 125 N. Main St. (© **336/786-4931**).

The Southern Kitchen, New Market, Virginia. This nonfancy place is famous for peanut soup (which we've always been fond of), along with a dish called Lloyd's Fried Chicken. Sun–Thurs 7am–9pm; Fri–Sat 7am–10pm. On U.S. 11, a half-mile south of the I-81 interchange at 9567 S. Congress Ave. (© **540/740-3514**).

Mrs. Rowe's Restaurant & Bakery, Staunton, Virginia. Rowe's is a longtime sanctuary for Virginia home cooking—and coincidentally where the Statler Brothers often eat. Have the fried chicken, real mashed potatoes, hot biscuits, and homemade rolls, and for dessert, traditional banana pudding. Mon–Sat 7am–8pm; Sun 7am–7pm. 74 Rowe Rd. Take exit 222 off I-81 (© **540/886-1833;** www.mrsrowes.com).

The Pig 'N Steak, Madison, Virginia. The Pig 'N Steak is one of Virginia's top barbecue places, but also where the fictional Jason Walton from the TV series used to play the piano at the "Dew Drop Inn." Hickory pit–smoked ribs are the draw here. Mon–Thurs 11am–9pm; Fri–Sat 11am–9:30pm; Sun 11am–7:30pm. The restaurant is north of Charlottesville at 313 Washington St. in Madison, at the stoplight (© **540/ 948-3130;** www.pigandsteak.com).

Applewood Farmhouse Restaurant, Sevierville/Pigeon Forge, Tennessee. The hot fried apple pies at Applewood are prepared while you watch through a glass window. Look for Dolly Parton chocolate lollipops in the candy shop at the farm's complex of food preparation centers. Daily 8am–9pm. Located at 230 Apple Valley Rd. off U.S. 441 (shop: © **800/421-4606;** restaurant: © **865/428-1222;** www.applewood farmhouserestaurant.com).

EVERYTHING YOU EVER WANTED TO KNOW ABOUT COUNTRY HAM

Yankees may invest fortunes in mail-order Smithfield hams, but the fine cured ham you'll encounter in restaurants and roadside stands throughout this drive is correctly called "country ham."

The Smithfield ham began in the 17th century when local farmers let their hogs run loose in the peanut fields after harvest to eat up the leftovers. They soon found they had an excellent-tasting ham with yellow fat that kept the meat from drying out, an export in great demand back in England. These hams are smoked and coated with black pepper. Only hams produced by peanut-fed hogs in the peanut belt and processed in Smithfield, a small town in Tidewater, Virginia, near Norfolk, can be called Smithfield hams.

Country ham, on the other hand, is a product of the Appalachians that can be either smoked or dry-cured without smoke. The fresh ham is rubbed down with a dry mix of salt, sugar, and perhaps saltpeter, and then covered for 4 to 6 weeks in a bed of salt. Then it is washed and trimmed, usually hung by the hock in a smokehouse where it sweats in hickory smoke through the summer. A total of 9 to 12 months is the minimum curing period. Some processors skip the smoking stage, saying the smoke makes little flavor difference. And some processors label their hams "sugar cured," although the sugar has no part in the curing.

The finished ham is a salty, densely textured, and intensely flavored meat that can be sliced raw and fried, or boiled whole and then baked. If you buy a country ham to take home, it will keep for a long time, up to a year, if stored in a cool, dark place. A cooked ham also keeps well under refrigeration, and a small bit of it sliced or diced can add flavor to any number of dishes.

To prepare a country ham, you need to soak it for 24 hours in a pot of cold water, then drain it, scrub off the spices and any mold from the surface, and put it in a fresh kettle of cold water to cover. Cook it at a simmer for 20 minutes per pound or until the flat bone at the butt end is loose enough to move back and forth, usually from 4 to 5 hours. When it's cool enough to handle, cut off the skin and excess fat, but leave a half-inch layer of fat to cover. Remove the loose, flat bone. Put liquid in the pan (water, wine, ginger ale, or sherry) to cover the pork by an inch and bake in a slow oven for an hour, covered with foil. Then remove the foil, score the fat, and cover it with any paste or glaze you wish (a mix of brown sugar, cornmeal, and a little prepared

Southern Accents: A Glossary

Bald: A treeless area at about 4,000 feet covered with shrubs or grass, perhaps part of earlier Indian agricultural clearing or the product of lightning fires.

Holler: A yell of communication between farms in the days before telephones; also, a valley or "hollow."

Moonshining: Making illegal corn liquor in "dry" areas of the South; most rural areas have a few moonshiners, but you're not likely to encounter any unless you know the locals very well.

Pop: A soft drink.

Put up: To can or preserve foods for winter. 🚐

or dry mustard is good). Return it to the oven for a half-hour, basting frequently. Then cool and slice it in very thin slices. It's delectable with hot biscuits.

OUTDOOR ACTIVITIES

Hikers will find plenty of **trails,** from 10-minute leg-stretchers to longer, more demanding walks along the way. In **Shenandoah National Park,** more than 500 miles of side trails set out from the ridge road (www.nps.gov/shen).

One of the most famous walking trails in America, the **Appalachian Trail,** stretches from Maine to Georgia across the crest of the mountains. Some of the prettiest of the trail's 500 miles in Virginia are those in Shenandoah National Park between Front Royal and Rockfish Gap. The trail also parallels the Blue Ridge Parkway for 103 miles between Rockfish Gap and Mile 103.

Canoe trips along the **Shenandoah River** for novices or experienced canoeists can be booked with **Downriver Canoe Company** at 884 Indian Hollow Rd. in **Bentonville,** Virginia, from April to late October (© **800/338-1963;** www.downriver.com). If you want to paddle your own canoe, it can provide a shuttle service. **Front Royal Canoe Company** in **Front Royal** (© **800/270-8808** or 540/635-5440; www.front royalcanoe.com) can take you along the Shenandoah between mid-March and mid-November. **Shenandoah River Outfitters** in **Luray** is open year-round for rentals, overnight trips, and all-you-can-eat steak dinners on the trail (© **800/6CANOE-2** [622-8832] or 540/743-4159; www.shenandoahriver.com).

Horseback riding along mountain trails is popular in the fall, and a good alternative to driving when traffic on the roadways may be bumper-to-bumper. Guided rides from **Skyland Lodge Stables** in Shenandoah National Park leave several times a day. Call a day in advance for reservations (© **800/778-2871** or 540/999-2210; www. visitshenandoah.com).

WILDLIFE-WATCHING

The **Blue Ridge Mountains** are the stomping ground for all manner of birds and mammals, from **whitetail deer** and **black bears,** on display at the privately owned **Grandfather Mountain Park,** to **wild turkeys,** which we've glimpsed several times from the roadway. Seldom seen but indisputably present are **bobcats,** sometimes glimpsed at night. Most commonly sighted along the roadways are **woodchucks** (groundhogs), **chipmunks,** and **squirrels** in the daytime; **skunks, raccoons, opossums,** and **foxes** at night. More than 100 bird species may be seen during spring migrations.

Some 300 or more **wild ponies** wander in **Grayson Highlands State Park** (www. dcr.virginia.gov/state_parks/gra.shtml), off U.S. 58 near the point where Virginia, North Carolina, and Tennessee meet; a few of them are rounded up each fall to be auctioned off in the park during the last week of September.

On the Road

THE SHENANDOAH VALLEY

Nobody knows for sure what *Shenandoah* means. It has been translated variously as "sprucy stream," "land of the big mountains," even "daughter of the stars." One etymologist says it is the Iroquois word for "deer," animals that are still plentiful in the valley.

The fragrance of apples perfumes the valley, from the pink-and-white blossoms in spring through the harvest of the fruit in autumn, and the sweet-sour tang of apple cider in winter in the apple sheds.

History is deeply etched in the towns along the Shenandoah River, once America's western frontier. During the Civil War, the northern Virginia town of Winchester changed hands 72 times—and 13 times on one particularly memorable day. Pick up a walking tour map at the city's welcome center (1360 S. Pleasant Rd.) and see the modest log-and-limestone cabin on Braddock Street, which was **George Washington's office** during the French and Indian War. It's now a museum at 32 W. Cork St.; admission $5. It's open April through October, Monday to Saturday 10am to 4pm, Sunday noon to 4pm (© **540/662-4412**). A brick house down the street was Stonewall Jackson's headquarters during the Civil War. Call the **Winchester Chamber of Commerce** (© **540/662-4118**; www.winchesterva.org).

Virginia's Museum of American Frontier Culture in Staunton is a re-created village of cottages, barns, and farms. It shows the farmsteads the settlers left in the Old World, as well as the way they reinterpreted them in the New World. (See "10 Terrific Spots Where History Comes Alive," earlier in this chapter.)

Thomas Jefferson is still very much alive in the countryside around Charlottesville, where people speak of "Mr. Jefferson" as they would a respected neighbor. **Monticello,** the dream home he designed and built, is magnificent, but not overwhelming, because it is built on a human scale. Meriwether Lewis and William Clark brought the moose and deer antlers in the entry hall back to Jefferson from their explorations in the West. Monticello is in the Virginia Piedmont about 2 miles southeast of Charlottesville.

To get there, take I-64, exit 121 (if traveling westbound) or exit 121A (if traveling eastbound), make a right at the first light for the Monticello Visitor Center, or make a left at the first light for Monticello itself (© **434/984-9822**; www.monticello.org).

Jefferson was hospitable to guests, spending freely to entertain, even though he died $100,000 in debt, the equivalent of $1 million today. Dinner began at 4pm and

Celebrating Patsy Cline

Die-hard country music fans know Winchester native Virginia Hensley became singer Patsy Cline. She sang "Walkin' After Midnight" on the nationally televised *Arthur Godfrey's Talent Scouts* in 1957 and the record sold a million copies. Other tunes like "Leavin' on Your Mind," "Imagine That," and "Crazy" (written by Willie Nelson) will forever be linked to Patsy Cline.

She was only 30 years old when she, Hawkshaw Hawkins, Cowboy Copas, and her manager Randy Hughes died in a plane crash in March 1963. Her body was brought home and buried in Shenandoah Memorial Park, 3 miles south of town on U.S. 522.

The **Patsy Cline Historic House,** 608 S. Kent St., where she lived with her mother, Hilda Hensley, from 1943 to 1953, is now a museum dedicated to her life. It has some of her personal items and a gift shop selling mementos. Guided tours take about 40 minutes. Admission is $6 for adults, $5 for seniors, $4 for children 11 to 18, and free for kids 9 and under and active-duty military. The house is open from April to October, Tuesday to Saturday 10am to 4pm and Sunday noon to 4pm, and from November to the first week of December, Friday to Saturday 10am to 4pm and Sunday 1 to 4pm. The first week in December celebrates Patsy Cline Christmas with special events evoking her life. It's closed January to March.

The **Winchester/Frederick County Visitors Center (www.visit winchesterva.com)** distributes directions to Gaunt's Drug Store at Loudoun and Gerrard streets, where Cline worked; Handley High School at 425 Handley Blvd., where she studied; the house at 720 S. Kent St., where she married second husband Charlie Dick; and her grave.

For more information about the house and other facets of Cline's life, contact **Celebrating Patsy Cline, Inc.** (© **540/622-5555;** www.celebrating patsycline.org). 🚐

often continued until dark, and the president had fine wines shipped from France to accompany the vegetables from his gardens. Dishes were prepared by one of his servants, who had trained in Paris.

Jefferson tried to establish a vineyard at Monticello, so he would be pleased to note that today the Charlottesville area is the **wine capital of Virginia,** with 10 local wineries producing table vintages. Get a free wine country guide from the **Virginia Wine Marketing Program,** 1001 E. Broad St., Ste. 140, Richmond, VA 23219 (© **800/828-4637** or 804/344-8200; www.virginiawine.org).

Campground Oases in the Shenandoah Valley

Lake Fairfax Park. A Corps of Engineers Public Park in **Reston, Virginia,** Lake Fairfax Park is 50 miles east of Front Royal (not actually in the Shenandoah Valley) and within commuting distance of Washington, D.C. It has 136 sites, 54 of them

You'll enjoy the natural wonders of the Blue Ridge Mountains and Shenandoah Valley.

with 15- and 30-amp electrical hookups. Toilets, showers, and a sanitary dump are provided, and there is a 14-day limit. Open year-round. Sites $29–$45. From the junction of I-495 and Rte. 7, head west 6½ miles on Rte. 7 to Rte. 606, then south just over 1 mile to 1400 Lake Fairfax Dr. Turn left into the entrance (© **703/471-5415**; www.fairfaxcounty.gov/parks/lakefairfax).

The Front Royal Campground. This KOA campground has a big swimming pool and 350-ft. water slide (there's a fee for the latter), a hot tub, miniature golf, and a stocked fishing pond. The 96 sites and 42 full hookups, though not large, are terraced and landscaped, some of them paved and some of them gravel, and the hilltop locations allow for cooling breezes in summer. For sightseers who don't want to drive their RVs into Washington, D.C., the park offers a daily shuttle tour by advance reservation. Mid-Mar to late Nov. Sites $38–$43. Located just outside Front Royal. Take Rte. 81 to Rte. 66 E.; take exit 6 onto Rte. 340 S. Drive through town past Shenandoah National Park on the left. The entrance is 4½ miles past the national park, also on the left (© **540/635-2741**; www.frontroyalrvcampground.com).

Mathews Arm. The Mathews Arm in **Shenandoah National Park** has several tree-shaded loops with 180 gravel back-in sites, not all of them large enough for big RVs. There are toilets and a sewage disposal dump, but no hookups, showers, or Laundromat. Ranger campfire programs are presented several times a day on summer weekends, less often during the week. Camping is on a first-come, first-served basis.

Designated campsites are available for travelers with disabilities. Late May–Oct. Sites $16. On Skyline Dr. at Mile 22 south of the Front Royal entrance (© **540/999-3500** or 877/444-6777; www.recreation.gov).

Big Meadows Campground. Also in **Shenandoah National Park,** Big Meadows provides 177 RV sites in a designated area separate from tent campsites. Hot showers are available for a small fee, and there's a sanitary dump, a Laundromat, and firewood for sale, but no hookups. Ranger campfire programs are scheduled daily in summer (© **540/999-3231**). Most sites are paved and can be reserved in advance. Sites $20. On Skyline Dr. at Mile 51.2 (© **877/444-6777;** www.recreation.gov).

Lewis Mountain Campground. In **Shenandoah National Park,** Lewis Mountain Campground has 31 sites, half of them tent sites and 3 of them pull-throughs, which in this park means a sort of curved driveway off the main road. There are no hookups and no sanitary dump, and sites are available on a first-come, first-served basis. Sites $16. Off Skyline Dr. at Mile 57.5 (© **540/999-3500;** www.nps.gov/shen).

Loft Mountain. Loft Mountain is our favorite of the four sites in **Shenandoah National Park.** It has 219 paved sites, most of them shaded, and 140 pull-throughs, and some are long enough for big rigs. Sites are available on a first-come, first-served basis, and there is a sanitary dump, but no hookups. Ranger campfire programs are provided daily in summer, except on Wed. Sites $15. Off Skyline Dr. at Mile 79.5 (© **877/444-6777** or 540/999-3500; www.nps.gov/shen).

THE BLUE RIDGE PARKWAY

Construction began in 1935, and the final leg of the 469-mile road was finally completed in 1987 with the spectacularly engineered Linn Cove Viaduct, which seems to float lightly around venerable Grandfather Mountain as though suspended in midair.

Skyline Drive and the **Blue Ridge Parkway** were among President Franklin D. Roosevelt's projects for the Civilian Conservation Corps (CCC) during the Depression in the 1930s. The intention was to provide drivers with a variety of untrammeled rural scenes, with the road following the landscape for scenery rather than speed, which is limited to 45 mph. The park area along the two roads averages about 1,000 feet wide, including the roadbed.

Split-rail fences, small log cabins, water-operated mills, barns, and farm fields may be glimpsed along the roadsides, as well as brilliant pink and lavender stands of wild rhododendron and mountain laurel and vivid orange splashes of flame azaleas in late spring and early summer. Arched stone bridges ornament the roads that cross over or under the parkway.

Along the route are nine visitor centers and 11 campgrounds, none with hookups, but all accessible to any but the largest RVs. It passes through four national forests and the Cherokee Indian Reservation at its southern end, where it connects with Newfound Gap Road and the Great Smoky Mountains National Park.

The Appalachian Mountains were once the western frontier, and the isolated homesteads that remain—such as the **Puckett Cabin** at Mile 189, where "Aunt

Virginia Campgrounds

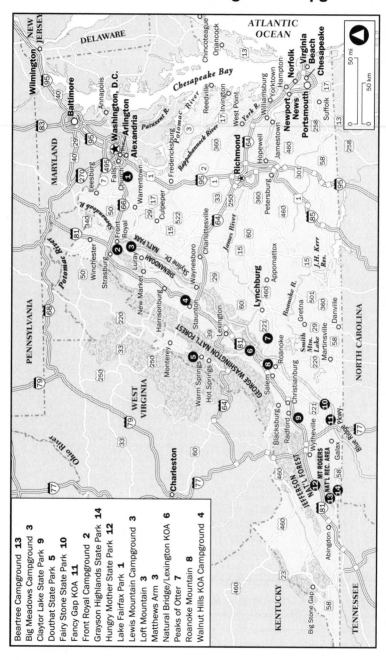

Beartree Campground **13**
Big Meadows Campground **3**
Claytor Lake State Park **9**
Douthat State Park **5**
Fairy Stone State Park **10**
Fancy Gap KOA **11**
Front Royal Campground **2**
Grayson Highlands State Park **14**
Hungry Mother State Park **12**
Lake Fairfax Park **1**
Lewis Mountain Campground **3**
Loft Mountain **3**
Matthews Arm **3**
Natural Bridge/Lexington KOA **6**
Peaks of Otter **7**
Roanoke Mountain **8**
Walnut Hills KOA Campground **4**

Orlean" Puckett gave birth to 24 children, none of whom lived past infancy; and the **Brinegar Cabin** at Mile 238, where weavers show how mountain women made fabrics—give a clearer picture than any history book of the hard and often lonely life of these fiercely independent people.

Our own favorite stop along the parkway is **Mabry Mill,** where volunteer musicians and craftspeople may hold an impromptu dulcimer concert or tell tall tales to a group of wide-eyed children. Someone is usually weaving split-willow baskets or whittling or blacksmithing, and the miller is almost always there, turning out white stoneground cornmeal for sale by the bag. You can sample cornmeal and buckwheat pancakes at the restaurant next door, along with slabs of country ham and hot homemade biscuits. (See "10 Terrific Spots Where History Comes Alive," earlier in this chapter.)

NINE BLUE RIDGE THINGS TO DO

1. **Head down into Luray Caverns.** Luray is the biggest among a number of cave complexes that lie like honeycombs beneath the Shenandoah Valley. It's big enough for those who are claustrophobic to go inside to see and hear the world's only "stalacpipe" organ: tuned stalactites that are tapped with rubber-tipped hammers to make music. (How do you tune a stalactite? By grinding it down slightly.) Trivia lovers will like discovering the petrified fried eggs on one canyon wall and the blind albino shrimp in the underground river. But check out the times for the frequent carillon concerts, played out of the bell tower near the entrance. You don't want to be standing too near. Admission $23 adults, $21 seniors, $11 children 6–12, free for children 5 and under. 970 U.S. Hwy. 211 W. Daily 9am–6pm, depending on season. Call for time of last tour (© 540/743-6551; www.luraycaverns.com).

2. **Visit Thomas Jefferson's vegetable gardens at Monticello.** The gardens are a re-creation of his original plantings, which he painstakingly documented in 1807. Some rare and exotic vegetables no longer produced anywhere else share space with familiar favorites such as asparagus and artichokes, as well as 15 different varieties of English peas. Jefferson is the gardener who introduced eggplant to the United States. Daily 8am–5pm. Tours $22 adults, $8 seniors and children (© 434/984-9822; www.monticello.org).

3. **Drink a Dr Pepper in rustic Rural Retreat, Virginia.** Tilt a cool one back in memory of the soda's inventor, a lovesick pharmacist's assistant who fell head over heels for his boss's daughter, was forbidden to woo her, and finally moved to Waco, Texas. There, he patented and bottled his soft drink, named for his former boss and sweetheart's father, Dr. Charles Pepper. At exit 60 from I-81 (© 276/686-4221; www.townofruralretreat.com).

4. **Check out far-out Floyd, Virginia.** Six miles off the Blue Ridge Parkway near Mile 165, Floyd is where New Age/neohippie handicrafts gallery New Mountain Mercantile coexists with a 75-year-old general store that holds free hoedowns every Fri. Just down the road at 113 E. Main St. is **Blue Ridge Restaurant,** with home cooking and real mashed potatoes. Daily 6am–8pm

Country Music's Crooked Road

Southwestern Virginia has been central to the evolution of country music since the first European settlers arrived in these hills and valleys with few possessions other than their mandolins and fiddles. Some of the great country artists hail from here—the Carter Family, Ralph Stanley, the Stonemans—and numerous music festivals, such as the famous Old Fiddler's Convention in Galax, are part of the weekend fun.

The area's music heritage is formally recognized by the **Crooked Road: Virginia's Heritage Music Trail** (© 276/492-2085; www.thecrookedroad. org). This official route follows U.S. 23, U.S. 421, U.S. 58, U.S. 221, Va. 8, and Va. 40 for more than 200 miles from Breaks in the west to Rocky Mount in the east. Along the way it passes such country music shrines as the **Ralph Stanley Museum & Traditional Music Center** in Clintwood; the **Carter Family Fold** in Hiltons; the **Birthplace of Country Music Museum** in Bristol; the **Blue Ridge Music Center** on the Blue Ridge Parkway; the **Rex Theater** in Galax; the **Floyd Country Store** in Floyd; and the **Blue Ridge Music Institute** in Ferrum.

(© 540/745-2147). Then there's **Country Sales,** 117-A Main St. (© 540/745-2001), featuring the biggest collection of bluegrass music in the world, they say. Finally, just when you think you're getting a fix on Floyd, you run into **Château Morrisette Winery** (© 540/593-2865) with its jazz concerts, wine tastings, and French restaurant. At Mile 165, take State Route 8 north for 5 miles into Floyd. Contact the **Floyd County Chamber of Commerce,** 201 E. Main St., for more information (© 540/745-4407; www.visitfloyd.org).

5. **Lunch at Charlottesville's historic Michie Tavern.** Pronounced "*Mick-ey,*" the Michie Tavern serves traditional Southern dishes, from fried chicken and biscuits to black-eyed peas, stewed tomatoes, and cornbread (all for about $12), plus Virginia wines. Daily 11:30am–3pm. Located at 683 Thomas Jefferson Pkwy. on Rte. 53 southeast of the city (© 434/977-1234; www.michietavern.com).

6. **Follow the sound of fiddles to Bristol, Virginia.** The birthplace of country music has a mural commemorating Mother Maybelle Carter, matriarch of the legendary Carter Family, on State Street at Volunteer Parkway (on the side of the Lark Amusement Bldg., facing east). Every Sat at 7:30pm, there's a live bluegrass show ($10 admission fee) at the **Carter Family Fold** in Hiltons, Virginia. It's off U.S. 58, 5 miles east of Kingsport, Tennessee (take Rte. 58—off exit 1 from Rte. 81—about 20 miles into Hilton; signs will show the directions to the house). Arrive early so you can browse through the displays of 78-rpm recordings, photographs, and instruments in the **A. P. Carter Museum,** which is open on Sat from 6–7:30pm (© 276/386-6054; www.carterfamily fold.org).

7. **Head for the Galax Moose Lodge #733 Old Fiddlers' Convention in Galax, Virginia.** Located just off the Blue Ridge Pkwy. via Rte. 97 W., Galax hosts the world's oldest and largest old-time fiddlers' contest during the second week in Aug. It draws musicians who play as much for their own pleasure and each other as for the audience of thousands for this 60-year-old tradition. Many musicians arrive and stay in their own RVs, so other RVers should feel right at home. $70 per site. Call for complete information (📞 **276/236-8541**; www.oldfiddlers convention.com).

8. **Visit the annual Natural Chimneys Jousting Contest.** The oldest continuously operated sporting event in the country is set against a backdrop of castlelike rock towers. The Aug tournament has been going on since 1821 at this site near Mount Solon, southwest of Harrisonburg on Rte. 607. **Natural Chimneys Regional Park** and its 156 RV hookup sites (only four full hookups) are nearby (📞 **888/430-2267** or 540/350-2510; www.co.augusta.va.us/Index. aspx?page=616).

9. **Run over and say "hidy" to John-Boy and his family.** The Waltons Mountain Museum in **Schuyler, Virginia,** on Rte. 617, commemorates the hometown of Earl Hamner, Jr., creator of *The Waltons* TV series, and includes video interviews

Literary Lights

Poet and Lincoln biographer **Carl Sandburg**, whose name is linked forever with Chicago, spent the last 22 years of his life on his farm at Flat Rock, near Hendersonville, North Carolina. Now a National Historic Site, the farm that Sandburg called **Connemara** is where the two-time Pulitzer Prize winner wrote a novel, poems, a screenplay (for *The Greatest Story Ever Told*), and his autobiography, in between playing his guitar and singing folk songs. His wife, Paula Steichen, sister of photographer Edward Steichen, raised prize goats; there's still a herd of them around. The farm is on Little River Road off Route 25, 3 miles south of Hendersonville, and is open daily 9am to 5pm. Free admission; tours $5 adults, $3 children (📞 **828/693-4178**).

Old Kentucky Home, the boardinghouse at 48 Spruce St. in Asheville where author **Thomas Wolfe** spent his childhood and which he immortalized as Dixieland in his autobiographical novel *Look Homeward, Angel,* has served in recent years as the Thomas Wolfe Memorial State Historic Site, but was damaged by fire and had to undergo reconstruction. It is now restored and open Tuesday through Saturday 9am to 5pm, Sunday 1 to 5pm; admission $1 adults, 50¢ children. Located at 52 North Market St. (📞 **828/253-8304;** www.wolfememorial.com). The angel of the book title was a funeral monument sold by Wolfe's father and can be seen in Hendersonville's Oakdale Cemetery ornamenting the grave of Margaret E. Johnson. 🚐

Musician at the Old Fiddlers' Convention in Galax, Virginia.

and episodes from the show, as well as re-creations of the Hollywood sets for the series. (The "real" Waltons Mountain can be found at Frazier Park near Gorman in Southern California, where location filming for the series often took place; one of this book's authors appeared occasionally on the show.) The museum is right on Rte. 617 at the top of a hill. Early Mar to early Dec daily 10am–3:40pm (closed major holidays). Admission $7 adults and children 6 and over, free for children 5 and under. 6484 Rockfish River Rd. (© **434/831-2000;** www.waltonmuseum.org).

Campground Oases Along the Blue Ridge Parkway

Walnut Hills KOA Campground. Near **Staunton, Virginia,** Walnut Hills is a good base for visiting the notable Civil War sites in the area, as well as the Frontier Culture Museum. Most of the 112 modem-friendly sites are wide and shaded, with 30- and 50-amp electrical hookups, 60 full hookups, and satellite TV. Open year-round. Sites $32–$55. Take exit 217 from I-81 and drive west on 654 to Rte. 11, then south to Rte. 655 and follow the signs (© **800/699-2568** or 540/337-3920; www.walnuthills campground.com).

Natural Bridge/Lexington KOA. This KOA has 54 sites with 31 full hookups and pull-throughs. There are flush toilets, showers, a sanitary dump, a Laundromat, a grocery store, LP gas, and dinner nightly. Open year-round. Sites $32–$79. Off I-81, exit 180 (© **800/KOA-8514** [562-8514] or 540/291-2770; www.koa.com).

Peaks of Otter. Peaks of Otter, on the Blue Ridge Pkwy., has 141 paved sites, some with shade, and 25 pull-throughs. There are flush toilets, piped water, and a sanitary dump. No hookups. Each site has a table and fireplace. No reservations. May–Oct. Sites $16. At Milepost 86 near **Bedford, Virginia** (© **540/586-7321;** www.nps.gov/ blri/peaks.htm).

Douthat State Park. Listed on the National Register of Historic Places for the role it played in the development of parks around the United States, Douthat State Park has been a family tradition in Virginia for more than a half-century. The Whiteoak campground has 31 gravel sites with 30-amp electrical hookups, toilets, showers, and a sanitary dump station. The area also has lodges, cabins, a restaurant, and bathhouses. Visitors enjoy boating and fishing in a lake stocked with trout. Sites $24–$25. Take exit 27 off I-64 to Rte. 629; then turn north for 7 miles, in **Clifton Forge** (© **800/933-PARK** [7275] or 540/862-8100; www.dcr.virginia.gov/state_parks/dou.shtml).

Roanoke Mountain. Roanoke Mountain, near **Vinton** at Mile 120 of the Blue Ridge Pkwy., has 31 campsites, some shaded and all paved. There are flush toilets, piped water, and a sanitary dump station. No hookups, no reservations; 14-day camping limit. Towed vehicles are not permitted on the Roanoke Mountain scenic loop drive. May–Oct. Sites $16. To get to the campground from Vinton, go east 2 miles on State Rd. 24 to Blue Ridge Pkwy., then south 8 miles and it's on the right side (© **540/982-9242**).

Claytor Lake State Park. Claytor Lake State Park, near **Dublin, Virginia,** has 40 sites, with water and 30-amp electrical hookups. Visitors enjoy bass fishing, swimming, fishing, boating, and boat docks at the lake. Some sites are shaded, some are pull-throughs. The historic Howe House features exhibits about the life of the early settlers in this region. Spring–autumn. Sites $25. Located on State Rd. 660, 2 miles south of I-81 at exit 101 (© **800/933-PARK** [7275] or 540/643-2500; www.dcr. virginia.gov/state_parks/cla.shtml).

Fairy Stone State Park. Fairy Stone State Park is named for the little brown crossshaped stones found in the area, which legend says are the tears shed by elves and fairies when Christ was crucified. While hunting for them is permitted, don't worry if you can't find one on the ground; gift shops in the area will be glad to sell you one. There are 51 sites with water and 30-amp electrical hookups, flush toilets, showers, and a sanitary dump station. There is a 31-ft. limit. Visitors enjoy bass fishing and swimming, and there's a boat ramp and rentals. Spring–summer. Sites $26. On Rte. 57 btw. **Stuart and Bassett, Virginia** (© **800/933-7275** reservations or 276/ 930-2424; www.dcr.virginia.gov/state_parks/fai.shtml).

Fancy Gap KOA Campground. Some of the campground's 84 sites are shaded, and there are 15 pull-throughs; 84 are full hookups with 30-amp electric. Year-round. Sites $35–$39. It's ¼ mile down Rte. 683 off the Blue Ridge Pkwy. in **Fancy Gap, Virginia,** at Mile 199.5 (© **800/562-1876** or 276/728-7776; www.koa.com).

Hungry Mother State Park. Located near **Marion, Virginia,** Hungry Mother has 75 sites with 15-, 30-, and 50-amp electric and water hookups, 22 full hookups, and a sanitary dump. Since some of the sites are quite narrow, it does not permit slide-outs, but a lake allows for freshwater fishing, swimming, and boating. Year-round. Sites $20–$28. Take exit 47 off I-81 and follow Rte. 11 to State Rd. 16; then drive north 4 miles (📞 **276/781-7400;** www.dcr.virginia.gov/state_parks/hun.shtml).

Beartree Campground. Mount Rogers National Recreation Area, near **Marion,** is tucked into the corner of southwestern Virginia, not far from where its border touches both North Carolina and Tennessee. Beartree Campground has 74 gravel sites with flush toilets and showers, and a sanitary dump station. Visitors enjoy trout fishing and swimming. No hookups, no slide-outs. Spring–autumn. Sites $19–$38. It's 7 miles east of Damascus on U.S. 58 (📞 **276/388-3642;** www.fs.fed.us/outernet/r8/gwj/mr/index.shtml).

Grayson Highlands State Park. Located near **Mouth of Wilson, Virginia,** Grayson Highlands Park has 64 sites with electrical hookups and a sanitary dump station. The town name comes from its position at the head of Wilson Creek, famous for its trout fishing, and the campground provides good fishing access to the stream. Year-round. Sites $26. From I-81, take exit 45 and go south on State Rd. 16 to Rte. 58, then west 8 miles (📞 **276/579-7092;** www.dcr.virginia.gov/state_parks/gra.shtml).

Doughton Park, Laurel Springs, North Carolina. Doughton Park has 26 paved sites, flush toilets, a sanitary dump, and a planned activities schedule. No hookups, no reservations, no slide-outs. This is an especially good place to spot deer at dawn and dusk. Mid-May to Oct. Sites $20. On the **Blue Ridge Pkwy.** at Mile 238.5 (📞 **336/372-8568**).

Julian Price Memorial Park, North Carolina. Julian Price Memorial Park has 68 paved sites, flush toilets, and a sanitary dump. Visitors enjoy fishing and boating. No hookups, no reservations. Most sites are shaded; 30 are pull-throughs; 14-day maximum stay. May–Nov. Sites $16. On the **Blue Ridge Pkwy.** near Mile 297 (📞 **828/963-5911**).

ASHEVILLE

The pretty mountain city of Asheville will be forever mingled with the memory of native son **Thomas Wolfe** to many readers. His thinly fictionalized story of "Altamont" and Eliza Gant's "Dixieland" boardinghouse in his novel *Look Homeward, Angel* apparently embarrassed everyone in town, including his mother, the model for the boardinghouse keeper. His books were banned by the local public library until 1935, when F. Scott Fitzgerald, shocked that the local author was not represented, bought two copies of *Look Homeward, Angel* and donated them to the library.

Later, after Wolfe's death (he died before his 38th birthday), all was forgiven, and **Old Kentucky Home,** that boardinghouse at 52 N. Market St., is today the **Thomas Wolfe Memorial State Historic Site** (**www.wolfememorial.com**).

Another Blue Ridge author, Greensboro-born short story writer **O. Henry** (William Sydney Porter), is buried in Asheville's Riverside Cemetery, on Birch Street, not far from Thomas Wolfe's grave.

In years past, a lot of wealthy Americans liked the city's cool summer climate and clear mountain air enough to set up seasonal residences. They included Henry Ford, Thomas Edison, John D. Rockefeller, Grover Cleveland, and Theodore Roosevelt. In the 1890s, George Washington Vanderbilt, grandson of the fabulously wealthy Commodore Vanderbilt, constructed **Biltmore House,** a 250-room French Renaissance mansion at the edge of Asheville. It's open daily for fairly pricey house tours (see "Some Special Splurges," earlier in this chapter, for hours and prices), as well as rose garden tours and wine-tasting from the Vanderbilt vineyard. If the mansion looks familiar, it was the location for the Peter Sellers film *Being There* (1979), as well as the home of Macaulay Culkin's title character in the film *Richie Rich* (1994). From the Blue Ridge Parkway, Biltmore is about 4 miles from the Hwy. 25 north exit. From I-40 W., the entrance is north of exit 50B on Hwy. 25. From I-40 E., the entrance is north of exit 50 on Hwy. 25 (© **800/411-3812** or 828/225-1333; www.biltmore.com).

Besides its evocative turn-of-the-20th-century resort buildings (see Grove Park Inn under "Some Special Splurges," earlier in this chapter), Asheville also is a treasure trove of Art Deco architecture, with a city hall and First Baptist Church (5 Oak St.) from the 1920s, as well as the handsome S&W Cafeteria on Patton Avenue.

Campground Oases near Asheville

Mount Pisgah, Wayneville, North Carolina. Mount Pisgah has 67 paved campsites with patios, some with shade, along with flush toilets, a sanitary dump station, and a grocery store. No hookups or reservations. 14-day camping limit. May–Nov. Sites $16. On the Blue Ridge Pkwy. near Mile 408 (© **828/298-0398**).

Asheville West KOA, Candler, North Carolina. This pleasant wooded campground has big, level pull-throughs with cable TV, free Wi-Fi, and 30- and 50-amp electric, plus 42 full hookups. Visitors enjoy fishing and some hiking trails. Sites $32–$45. 309 Wiggins Rd. It's 12 miles west of town, reached by making a loop from exit 37 off I-40 and going under the interstate, following the signs, and then going back under the interstate again (© **800/562-9015** or 828/665-7015; www.koa.com).

GREAT SMOKY MOUNTAINS NATIONAL PARK

The most visited national park in the system, **Great Smoky Mountains in Tennessee and North Carolina** gets some eight million people a year passing through its rather garish portals: the commercial strip in **Cherokee** on the east side with its "Indian chiefs" standing by Plains Indian teepees, holding tom-toms, and wearing feathered war bonnets that Cherokees never used; and gaudy **Gatlinburg,** which has turned shopping, sleeping, and eating into big business.

The only place tackier than either one is nearby **Pigeon Forge** with its flashy **Dollywood** (© **800/365-5996** or 865/428-9488; www.dollywood.com) theme park and

Dolly Parton invites visitors to Dollywood, in Pigeon Forge, Tennessee.

bumper-to-bumper traffic inching its way past wall-to-wall motels and fast-food joints. Country singer/movie star Dolly Parton, keeping abreast (so to speak) of the trend, has turned this formerly bucolic pottery-making village near her birthplace into a tourist town gripped with gridlock. If we didn't know better, we'd think she built it to get even with some brats who snubbed her in grammar school. Open hours and dates vary widely; call first. Admission: $57 adults and children 12 and over, $54 seniors, $46 children 4 to 11, free for children 3 and under.

You can get away from it all if you try, however. Pay heed to any of the "Quiet Walkways" signs within the national park to take an easy and enchanting streamside or woodland stroll. Exploring the side roads leads to special pleasures. A detour to **Clingmans Dome** winds past the Indian Gap Trailhead with its ruts well worn from the countless horse-drawn vehicles that labored along this former toll road in the 19th century. Hiking trails, except in the most popular months of June, July, and October, are often uncrowded, since many of the visitors are making a beeline for Gatlinburg or Pigeon Forge.

The park is an international Biosphere Reserve and a World Heritage Site, and bear sightings are fairly common, with some 850 of the furry fellows in residence. Peregrine falcons and river otters have also been seen there.

Campground Oases in Great Smoky Mountains National Park

There are 10 developed campgrounds in the park, none with showers or hookups. The summer camping limit is 7 days, with 14 days permitted at campgrounds open in winter.

Advance reservations for summer and fall camping may be made at **Cades Cove, Elkmont,** and **Smokemont** campgrounds (© 877/444-6777; www.recreation.gov).

Great Smoky Mountains RV Safety Tips

A traffic sign just inside the park from the Gatlinburg entrance to Great Smoky Mountains National Park cautions that tunnels ahead on the highway have a clearance of only 12 feet, 2 inches, a close call for many modern, basement-model motor homes with roof air conditioners, TV antennae, and satellite dishes.

"I wish they had consulted with me before they put that up," said a ranger on duty at Sugarlands Visitor Center. "The 12-foot measurement is on the extreme sides of an arched tunnel that measures 17 feet in the center, and almost all the RVs get through without scraping."

When in doubt, inch toward the center when entering the tunnel, and you should clear it without a problem.

The same ranger cautioned that motor homes and vehicles pulling trailers should avoid traveling the dirt and gravel scenic drives in the park, but that the popular Cades Cove Loop is accessible to all.

About the campground limits specified in the park newspaper and listed above, he said RVs slightly larger than the limit may be able to access some sites in the campgrounds if the driver is adept.

An **Auto Touring Map** ($1) is available at the park visitor centers, mapping most of the 270 miles of roadway in the Great Smoky Mountains. Check at **Sugarlands Visitor Center** at the Gatlinburg, Tennessee, entrance; **Oconaluftee Visitor Center** at the Cherokee, North Carolina, entrance; and **Cades Cove Visitor Center** on Cades Cove Road, 2 miles south of Townsend, Tennessee. In addition, a knowledgeable ranger can recommend which routes to take and which to avoid, depending on your RV's dimensions.

Except during the winter, there are sewage dump stations at **Smokemont, Cades Cove, Deep Creek,** and **Cosby** campgrounds, and across from the Sugarlands Visitor Center at the Gatlinburg entrance. These campgrounds are on a first-come, first-served basis. Get information at the rangers' offices.

Abrams Creek. Not accessible to any other park areas, Abrams Creek has 16 sites. No RVs over 12 ft. Mid-Mar to early Nov. Sites $20. Reached by Happy Valley Rd. from Chilhowee, Tennessee, at the extreme western end of the park (© **865/436-1200;** www.nps.gov/grsm).

Balsam Mountain. Do not attempt to drive beyond the campground along the one-way gravel Balsam Mountain Rd., because motor homes and vehicles pulling trailers are prohibited. There are 46 sites, accommodating RVs up to 30 ft. Late May to late Sept. Sites $14. Balsam Mountain is accessed by the Blue Ridge Pkwy. from Mile 458.2 and 12 miles along the paved, but narrow, steep, and winding Heintooga Ridge Rd. spur (© **865/436-1200;** www.nps.gov/grsm).

Cades Cove. Cades Cove has 159 sites and allows RVs up to 35 ft. Year-round. Sites $20. Reached by the loop road from Sugarlands Visitor Center outside Gatlinburg or from the Townsend Visitor Center entrance on Tennessee's Rte. 73. Reservations required (℡ **877/444-6777**; www.nps.gov/grsm).

Cataloochee. Cataloochee has 27 sites, accommodating RVs up to 31 ft. Mid-Mar to early Nov. Sites $20. Reached from I-40 at exit 20 along Cove Creek Rd. (much of it unpaved) in North Carolina (℡ **865/436-1200**; www.nps.gov/grsm).

Cosby Campground. Outside the bustling little town of Cosby, Tennessee, the Cosby Campground has 165 sites accommodating RVs up to 25 ft. Mid-Mar to early Nov. Sites $14. On Rte. 32 off U.S. 321 (or via the Foothills Pkwy. turnoff, exit 443 from I-40; ℡ **865/436-1200**; www.nps.gov/grsm).

Deep Creek. Deep Creek has 92 sites that take RVs up to 26 ft. Early Apr to early Nov. Sites $17. On Deep Creek Rd., just inside the park boundary from Bryson City, North Carolina (℡ **865/436-1200**; www.nps.gov/grsm).

Elkmont. Elkmont has 220 sites accommodating RVs up to 35 ft. Mid-Mar to late Nov. Sites $17–$23. Just off Cades Cove Rd., not far from Sugarlands Visitor Center at Gatlinburg (℡ **865/436-1200**; www.nps.gov/grsm).

Look Rock. Look Rock has 68 sites for RVs up to 35 ft. Late May to early Nov. Sites $14. At the edge of the park's northwest boundaries off Foothill Pkwy., 10 miles northeast of Chilhowee (℡ **865/436-1200**; www.nps.gov/grsm).

Smokemont. Smokemont has 142 sites accommodating RVs up to 40 ft. Year-round. Sites $20. Along Newfound Gap Rd., a few miles north of Oconaluftee Visitor Center on the North Carolina side of the park (℡ **865/436-1200**; www.nps.gov/grsm).

Campground Oases on the Tennessee Side of the Smokies

Pigeon Forge/Gatlinburg KOA. This has a great location for families who want to visit Dollywood and revel in the tourist traps of Pigeon Forge—it's only a few blocks off the main street and has trolley shuttle service to town and to Dollywood. The 189 hookup sites have 30-amp electric, and 106 are full hookups; they're spacious and mostly gravel-surfaced, with some paved or grassy sites. Visitors enjoy cable TV, shuffleboard, a heated pool, and a hot tub. Year-round. Sites $38–$82. From the junction of U.S. 411 and Wears Valley Rd. (U.S. 321 S.), go south 2¼ miles on U.S. 411 to Dollywood Lane, east ⅓ mile to Cedar Top Lane, then north 1,000 ft., then follow the signs. Call well in advance for summer and fall (℡ **800/KOA-7703** [562-7703] or 865/453-7903; www.koa.com). If Pigeon Forge is full, try **Newport KOA.** Year-round. Sites $32–$38. On Rte. 27W-70. 1⅔ miles west of I-40, exit 432B, a half-hour from the Great Smoky Mountains National Park entrance, Pigeon Forge, Dollywood, or Gatlinburg (℡ **800/KOA-9016** [562-9016] or 423/623-9004; www.koa.com).

Outdoor Resorts. Like its sister resorts in Palm Springs, Outdoor Resorts, in Gatlinburg's Cobbly Nob resort area, is a "condo park," meaning the sites are owned and occupied, except for 70 full hookups (in this park) available to transient visitors. These spacious, clean, beautifully landscaped parks are a cut above most private RV parks, and, if you're fussy about your surroundings, they're worth the price. Sites $35–$45 (about $10 a night higher than some neighboring parks). Located on Hwy. 321 N. out of Gatlinburg (© **800/677-5861** or 865/436-5862; www.outdoor-resorts.com/gatlinburg).

The Lobster Coast: New England & the Canadian Maritimes

AS THE MAN WHO LED A LOBSTER ON A LEASH THROUGH THE gardens of the Palais Royal in Paris explained, "I have a liking for lobsters. They are peaceful, serious creatures. They know the secrets of the sea."

Lobsters were served at the first Thanksgiving dinner, and were so plentiful that until the 20th century they were used for fertilizer, bait, and jail food. The largest lobster ever recorded was 48 pounds with a length of 3½ feet. They are nocturnal and generally eat fish and shellfish.

Our Lobster Land drive covers New England and Canada's Maritime provinces of New Brunswick, Prince Edward Island, and Nova Scotia.

It was along this North Atlantic coast that Alexander Graham Bell invented the telephone and Guglielmo Marconi sent out the first radio message to cross the Atlantic from North America. It's where Ruth Wakefield baked the first Toll House cookies, and where Sicily-born Benedetto Capalbo floated the first submarine sandwich. So popular were submarine sandwiches during World War II that Capalbo supplied 500 a day to the submarine base in New London, Connecticut—which is how the sandwich he called a "grinder" got its new name.

New England is the birthplace of the graham cracker and the Parker House roll, where Lydia Pinkham's Vegetable Compound "for periodic female weakness" was produced, and where the birth control pill was invented. It's where Lizzie Borden took an ax and the Brink's burglars took a powder, where Earl Tupper sealed up Tupperware, Clarence Birdseye flash-froze food, and the first snowmobile cranked up back in 1913.

The first Frisbees came from fun-loving Bridgeport, Connecticut, where Robert Mitchum was born and P. T. Barnum lived. Originally spelled "Frisbies," they were actually pie tins from a local bakery with the name stamped on the bottom, and in the '20s, tossing them around was a fad for Yale students.

Newport, Rhode Island, boasts the first traffic ordinance (1687) and the first automobile arrest—for speeding at 15 mph (1904).

Saint John, New Brunswick, is where Donald Sutherland was born, MGM's Louis B. Mayer grew up, Captain Kidd pillaged, and the King of Siam's Anna Leonowens retired to found an arts academy. Benedict Arnold was burned in effigy and driven out of town—not for being a traitor (he was a hero to the Loyalists) but for nefarious business dealings.

Prince Edward Island (PEI) is where a red-haired, pigtailed orphan named Anne of Green Gables, from a book by Lucy Maud Montgomery back in 1908, is a cottage industry; where "supper" is usually preceded by "lobster"; and potatoes have their own museum. If Malpeque oysters and seaweed pie are on the menu and Seaman's soft drinks (birch beer, ginger brew, root beer, lime rickey) are close at hand, you can be sure you're on PEI.

Nova Scotia is where ice hockey was born (in Windsor around 1830), Alexander Graham Bell and the schooner *Bluenose* retired (Bell in Baddeck, the *Bluenose* in Lunenberg), and most of the victims of the *Titanic* were buried (in Halifax), since it was the closest landfall to the sinking.

RVing in New England & the Maritimes

The Lobster Coast route heads north along the edge of Connecticut and Rhode Island, jogs over to Cape Cod, then back up the shore to Boston, Salem, and Gloucester, the 18-mile coastline of New Hampshire, and the 3,500-mile coastline of Maine. After that, it carries on through New Brunswick's Loyalist and Acadian country to Nova Scotia. Prince Edward Island, which also has fine lobsters, was once accessible only by plane or ferry, inconvenient but not impossible for RVers, but now you can easily get there using the 7.9-mile Confederation Bridge from New Brunswick. The whole route one-way is approximately 1,200 miles, more if you dip into all Maine's picturesque coves and make a loop around Nova Scotia, and explore inland.

Canada's Maritimes allow good driving in most areas for freewheelers, but maneuvering an RV through New England is not always easy. Roads are narrow and often crowded with traffic, especially in summer around Cape Cod or Kennebunkport, and there are not a lot of pullover spots spacious enough for a big rig. The best way to explore most of the towns and villages along the Lobster Coast is to park your RV and set out on foot.

HITTING THE HIGHLIGHTS

If 2 weeks is the maximum time you have for a Lobster Land vacation, you'll be able to make the coastal drive to Nova Scotia and back from a New York or Connecticut starting point, including the journey around Cape Cod; however, you might have to miss islands like Nantucket, Martha's Vineyard, and Prince Edward Island. Allow the first week for New England and the second week for Canada's Maritimes. June is less crowded than July and August and the autumn months, but some of the campgrounds and attractions may not be open.

GOING FOR THE LONG HAUL

If you want to spend more than 2 or 3 weeks on the Lobster Coast, you'd better make your plans and arrangements well in advance for July and August. And don't expect to get reduced rates for a long stay in a private campground during the summer; one New Hampshire operator charged us double for the Fourth of July weekend, even though we were in residence for a month, because that's his peak season. As a Cape

Highlights of the New England Coast

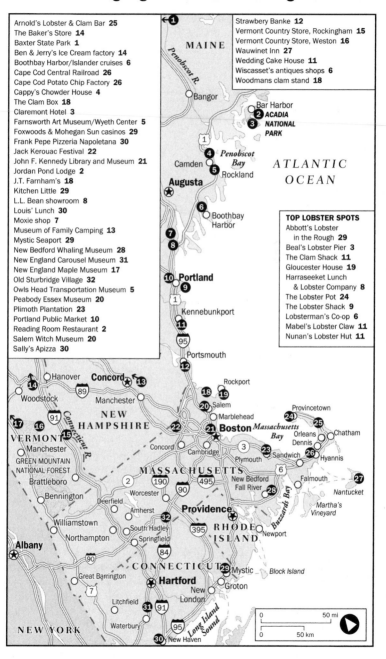

Arnold's Lobster & Clam Bar **25**
The Baker's Store **14**
Baxter State Park **1**
Ben & Jerry's Ice Cream factory **14**
Boothbay Harbor/Islander cruises **6**
Cape Cod Central Railroad **26**
Cape Cod Potato Chip Factory **26**
Cappy's Chowder House **4**
The Clam Box **18**
Claremont Hotel **3**
Farnsworth Art Museum/Wyeth Center **5**
Foxwoods & Mohegan Sun casinos **29**
Frank Pepe Pizzeria Napoletana **30**
Jack Kerouac Festival **22**
John F. Kennedy Library and Museum **21**
Jordan Pond Lodge **2**
J.T. Farnham's **18**
Kitchen Little **29**
L.L. Bean showroom **8**
Louis' Lunch **30**
Moxie shop **7**
Museum of Family Camping **13**
Mystic Seaport **29**
New Bedford Whaling Museum **28**
New England Carousel Museum **31**
New England Maple Museum **17**
Old Sturbridge Village **32**
Owls Head Transportation Museum **5**
Peabody Essex Museum **20**
Plimoth Plantation **23**
Portland Public Market **10**
Reading Room Restaurant **2**
Salem Witch Museum **20**
Sally's Apizza **30**

Strawbery Banke **12**
Vermont Country Store, Rockingham **15**
Vermont Country Store, Weston **16**
Wauwinet Inn **27**
Wedding Cake House **11**
Wiscasset's antiques shops **6**
Woodmans clam stand **18**

TOP LOBSTER SPOTS
Abbott's Lobster
  in the Rough **29**
Beal's Lobster Pier **3**
The Clam Shack **11**
Gloucester House **19**
Harraseeket Lunch
  & Lobster Company **8**
The Lobster Pot **24**
The Lobster Shack **9**
Lobsterman's Co-op **6**
Mabel's Lobster Claw **11**
Nunan's Lobster Hut **11**

MAINE

Penobscot R.

Bangor

Bar Harbor
ACADIA
NATIONAL
PARK

Penobscot
Bay

Camden
Rockland
Augusta

ATLANTIC
OCEAN

Boothbay
Harbor

Portland

Kennebunkport

Portsmouth

Hanover   Concord
Woodstock   Manchester   NEW   Rockport
HAMPSHIRE   Salem
VERMONT   Marblehead   Provincetown
Manchester   Boston   Massachusetts Bay   Orleans   Chatham
GREEN MOUNTAIN   Concord   Cambridge   Plymouth   Sandwich   Dennis
NATIONAL FOREST   MASSACHUSETTS   Hyannis
Brattleboro   Worcester   New Bedford   Falmouth
Bennington   Deerfield   Fall River   Nantucket
Williamstown   Amherst   Providence   Martha's Vineyard
Albany   Northampton   South Hadley   RHODE   Newport
Springfield   ISLAND
Great Barrington   CONNECTICUT   Mystic   Block Island
Hartford   New
Litchfield   London   Groton
Waterbury   Long Island Sound
NEW YORK   New Haven

0   50 mi
0   50 km

347

Cod friend reminded us, they have to make their profits for the whole year in only a few short months.

The only time more popular than July and August in New England is the autumn foliage season when "leaf peepers" arrive by the car and busload. It's the prettiest time of year, so take refuge in some off-the-beaten-track towns and villages or head north to Canada to wait out the invasion. New Brunswick is filled with great discoveries and is uncrowded year-round; you could spend a month exploring there. While Nova Scotia and Prince Edward Island tend to be busier in summer, you can still find some space.

Travel Essentials

WHEN TO GO

Summer and fall are the prime lobster seasons, and also when the weather is best. That's also when everyone goes to New England and the Maritimes. If you go too early in June, you'll encounter bugs: the mosquitoes, black flies, and "no-see-ums." Autumn is crowded with leaf peepers, who go for the fall foliage. They travel in groups, often by tour bus.

WHAT TO TAKE

Bring binoculars, a camera, rain gear, hiking boots, a sun hat, sunscreen, and insect repellent. To enter Canada, a passport will be needed. A driver's license alone is not acceptable.

WHAT TO WEAR

If you want to mingle at the posher purlieus of New England, like Bar Harbor, Nantucket, and Martha's Vineyard, you can wear anything from the L.L.Bean, J. Crew, or Land's End catalogs, Topsiders without socks, plaid or khaki Bermuda shorts, Oxford cloth shirts, and pastel sweaters tied around your neck. Otherwise, don your usual RV garb, and you'll fit in almost everywhere.

Always have a sweater or jacket handy. The Maine coastal weather on a summer day is described by Frances FitzGerald as "Baked Alaska"—a simultaneous sensation of hot sun and cool breeze. And Nova Scotia residents were nicknamed "Bluenoses" for bearing up under the cold winters.

TRIMMING COSTS ON THE ROAD

First of all, never eat your lobster in a restaurant. You can pick it up either live or cooked at a lobster pound. Take a live lobster back to the RV and cook it or refrigerate it until later (see "Looking for Lobster in All the Right Places," later in this chapter). A hot cooked lobster can be brought back to the RV or eaten on the spot at a picnic table, thoughtfully provided by the lobster pound (a lobster shack or a holding tank for lobsters) or by the town. At many pounds, you'll be able to pick up side dishes and beverages, even beer or wine, to go with your steaming crustacean.

Make the most of admission to living history parks by planning to spend the day, either taking a lunch or buying one (prices are reasonable) in the on-site restaurants.

If you have children along, they'll experience new dishes and utensils so interesting that they'll forget they never liked such-and-so.

Plan your beach visits for state parks or national parks like Cape Cod or Acadia; many of the beaches in the northeast are private.

WHERE TO GET TRAVEL INFORMATION

It's easy to find out what's going on in New England and the Maritimes. Stop at any tourist information spot, particularly those on main highways at the entrance to a state or province; and you can pick up campground information, times and prices for attractions, maps, and leaflets on everything from local farmers' markets to self-guided drives or walks—all free. If you want to get information and maps ahead of time, contact the following tourism offices:

- **Connecticut Commission on Culture and Tourism,** 1 Constitution Plaza, Hartford CT 06103 (℃ **888/CT-VISIT** [288-4748]; www.ctvisit.com).

- **Maine Office of Tourism,** 189 State St., State House Station 59, Augusta, ME 04333 (℃ **888/624-6345;** www.visitmaine.com).

- **Massachusetts Office of Travel & Tourism,** 10 Park Plaza, Boston, MA 02116 (℃ **800/227-6277** or 617/973-8500; www.massvacation.com).

- **New Hampshire Office of Travel and Tourism,** P.O. Box 1856, 176 Pembrooke Rd., Concord, NH 03302 (℃ **800/FUN-IN-NH** [386-4664], ext. 169 or 603/271-2665; www.visitnh.gov).

- **New Brunswick Tourism,** Dept. 243, P.O. Box 12345, Campbellton, NB, Canada E3N 3T6 (℃ **800/561-0123** in the U.S. and Canada outside New Brunswick; www.tourismnewbrunswick.ca publishes a *New Brunswick Travel Guide*).

- **Nova Scotia Tourism,** P.O. Box 456, Halifax, NS, Canada B3J 2R5. They can also make reservations at hotels or campgrounds (℃ **800/565-0000;** http://explore.novascotia.com or www.novascotia.com).

- **Rhode Island Tourism Division,** 315 Iron Horse Way, Ste. 101, Providence, RI 02905 (℃ **800/250-7384;** www.visitrhodeisland.com).

- **Tourism Prince Edward Island,** Marketing Council Visitor Services, P.O. Box 2000, Charlottetown, PEI, Canada C1A 7N8 (℃ **800/463-4PEI** [4734] or 902/368-444; www.tourism.com).

DRIVING & CAMPING TIPS

- **Watch for low and narrow passes.** On New England and Canada's old side roads, be a stickler for reading underpass and tunnel clearance signs, gauging overhead branches, and eyeballing narrow roads before you start your turn.

- **Beware of small-scale campgrounds.** Many of the RV parks and campgrounds in this region were built a few decades ago to accommodate mostly tent campers and small trailers or folding camping trailers. Today's large motor homes with extra-wide bodies and slide-outs—as well as basement storage that means more

Canadian Maritimes Highlights

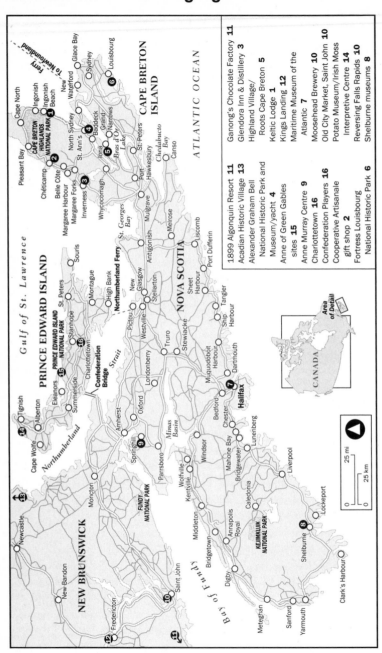

Ganong's Chocolate Factory **11**
Glendora Inn & Distillery **3**
Highland Village/
  Roots Cape Breton **5**
Keltic Lodge **1**
Kings Landing **12**
Maritime Museum of the
  Atlantic **7**
Moosehead Brewery **10**
Old City Market, Saint John **10**
Potato Museum/Irish Moss
  Interpretive Centre **14**
Reversing Falls Rapids **10**
Shelburne museums **8**

1899 Algonquin Resort **11**
Acadian Historic Village **13**
Alexander Graham Bell
  National Historic Park and
  Museum/yacht **4**
Anne of Green Gables
  sites **15**
Anne Murray Centre **9**
Charlottetown **16**
Confederation Players **16**
Cooperative Artisanale
  gift shop **2**
Fortress Louisbourg
  National Historic Park **6**

height on top, satellite dishes, and rooftop air conditioners—may face a tight squeeze in some New England campgrounds.

- **Check ahead about power requirements.** Many older campgrounds have not added 50-amp electric, although most (not all) have 30-amp. Particularly in New England and Canadian state and provincial parks, the hookups may offer 15- or 20-amp electric only. We found it a good idea to phone ahead and emphasize our size and amperage requirements, then reiterate it when we checked in so we weren't assigned a spot that wouldn't fit.

- **Expect fog.** You'll probably encounter some foggy or misty patches of road along the coast, especially in the mornings, with drizzle that might go on all day.

Best Sights, Tastes & Experiences of the Lobster Coast (& Inland)

OFF-THE-WALL ATTRACTIONS

The New England Carousel Museum, Bristol, Connecticut. Here is everything you need to know about carousels and carved wooden horses. You can watch antique wooden horses being reconstructed, learn the distinctive characteristics of the different types, and see some of the band organs that cranked out the music for the carousels. Mar–Dec Mon–Sat 10am–5pm, Sun noon–5pm. Closed Jan–Feb. Admission $5 adults, $4.50 seniors, $2.50 children 4–14, free for children 3 and under. The museum is at 95 Riverside Ave., Rte. 72 (© **860/585-5411;** www.thecarouselmuseum.org).

The New England Maple Museum, Rutland, Vermont. You'll meet an animatronic New England maple-syrup maker, see some dioramas that show sugaring in the early 1900s, admire some maple syrup–inspired folk art, and take a maple-syrup tasting (don't knock it if you haven't tried it) that reveals the subtle flavor differences btw. the grades. An extensively stocked gift shop sells everything you can imagine that's maple syrupy, and then some. May 23–Oct 31 daily 8:30am–5:30pm; Nov 1–Dec 23 and mid-Mar to May 22 daily 10am–4pm. Closed Jan–Feb. Admission $2.50 adults, $2 seniors, 75¢ children 6–12. North of Pittsford, on Rte. 7 (© **802/483-9414;** www.maplemuseum.com).

Vermont Country Store, Rockingham and Weston. Want to pick up some Bag Balm to keep your hands soft and supple? How about some almost-forgotten candies like Walnetos or Valomilk bars? Or want to pick up and pull up some elastic-free, all-cotton Buster Brown socks? Head for the Vermont Country Store. It has two locations, but we like the Rockingham branch with its bargain attic, really a ground-level side building full of steeply discounted items that are so weird, they might not sell even at 75% off. You can also taste and buy Vermont farmhouse cheeses, including a wonderful Crowley Colby–type cheese "made just down the road," along with Vermont common crackers baked on the premises. Rockingham store: daily 9am–5:30pm. Off exit 6 from I-91 to Rte. 103 to 1292 Rockingham Rd. (© **802/463-2224;**

www.vermontcountrystore.com). The main store is a few miles northwest in Weston, on Rte. 100 at 367 Main St. (© **802/824-3184**). It's open daily 8:30am–6pm.

Ben & Jerry's Ice Cream Factory Tours, Waterbury, Vermont. We learned the hard way not to arrive on a holiday weekend at Ben & Jerry's; every sport utility vehicle in the Northeast was unloading, and the wait for a tour time was more than an hour. Fortunately, the parking lot has an area for RVs, or we would probably have turned around and left. They suggest you arrive before noon. When ice cream is not being produced (Sun and holidays), you see a video, but still get free samples. A gift shop sells all sorts of cow logos; a scoop shop dips out your favorite flavor. Tours leave every 10 min., year-round except on major holidays. Daily 9am–8pm in summer; daily 10am–6pm in winter. Sign-ups are on a first-come, first-served basis. Admission $3 adults, $2 seniors, free for children 12 and under. It's on Rte. 100 north of exit 10 from I-89 (© **802/846-1240,** ext. 2264; www.benjerry.com).

The Baker's Store, Norwich, Vermont. For anyone who loves to cook, this store stocks everything that's in the King Arthur Flour catalog, and it's as enthralling as a museum. Pans, cutters, yeasts, flours, mixes for everything from pizza dough to scones, dried herbs and spices, whisks, Bundt cake pans—everything imaginable lines the well-stocked shelves. To gild the brioche, there's an on-premises bakery selling breads and pastries from the adjoining King Arthur kitchens. Mon–Fri 7:30am–6pm; Sat 8:30am–6pm; Sun 8:30am–4pm. On Rte. 5, just off exit 13 from I-91 (© **800/827-6836**; www.kingarthurflour.com).

Cape Cod Potato Chip Factory, near Hyannis, Massachusetts. Watch the chips being kettle-cooked one batch at a time at Breed's Hill Road in Independence Park near Hyannis, where 200,000 bags of the crunchy darlings are turned out every day. They'll give you a free bag as you leave. Self-guided tours are permitted year-round Mon–Fri 9am–5pm. Closed weekends. From Rte. 6, turn onto Rte. 132; on Rte. 132, take a left at the 6th traffic light onto Independence Dr.; go to the 2nd stop sign, and take a right onto Breed's Hill Rd. The chip factory is on the left (© **888/881-CHIP** [2447] or 508/775-7253; www.capecodchips.com).

The Salem Witch Museum. In a former church by Salem Common, the museum re-creates the hysteria of the 17th-century witch hunts with satanic symbols, taped music, mimed hangings in silhouette, and other spooky silliness performed with more enthusiasm than expertise. The audience loves it. Daily 10am–5pm. Admission $8.50 adults, $7 seniors, $5.50 children 6–14. It's in downtown Salem, on Rte. 1A diagonally across from the Commons (© **978/744-1692;** www.salemwitchmuseum.com).

Peabody Essex Museum, Salem, Massachusetts. Also in Salem, this classy museum on East India Square displays an astonishing collection of the curiosities that local sea captains brought back home from the exotic East—shrunken heads, stuffed penguins, giant sea clams, ship models, Chinese export porcelain, Polynesian barkcloth, Japanese warrior costumes, and a huge moon bed carved from a single piece of teak. Year-round Tues–Sun 10am–5pm. Admission $15 adults, $13 seniors, $11 students, free for children 16 and under. Take Rte. 128 N. to exit 25A. Follow Rte. 114 E. into Salem. Follow the signs to 161 Essex St. (© **866/745-1876** or 978/745-9500; www.pem. org).

The Wedding Cake House, Kennebunk, Maine. Located at 104 Summer St., Rte. 35 in Kennebunk, this gorgeous 19th-century house was built, it is said, by a sea captain for his new bride because he went to sea without having a taste of his wedding cake. It's a drive-by site not open to the public.

Owls Head Transportation Museum, Owls Head, Maine. Watch the Red Baron's Fokker triplane from World War I soar into the sky or listen to the hiss of a Stanley Steamer. On summer weekends, you not only see antique motorcycles, biplanes, automobiles, and farm machinery, but hear them and smell them—these antique machines are all in working order and cranked up regularly. Visitors may even be offered a ride in a Model T Ford or a ride in a biplane ($200 for 20 min.). Call ahead to see which machines are running and when. Daily 10am–5pm (closed holidays). Admission $10 adults, $8 seniors, free for children 17 and under. The museum is 2 miles south of Rockland on Rte. 73 at 117 Museum St. (© **207/594-4418;** www. ohtm.org).

Claremont Hotel, Southwest Harbor, Maine. The nine-wicket croquet tournaments held the first week in Aug at the Claremont Hotel, on the Claremont Rd. in Southwest Harbor, draw international attention from the croquet circuit; you can watch the action from the big front porch. Take the Maine Turnpike to Augusta, and exit to Rte. 3. Then take Rte. 3 through Ellsworth to the Trenton Bridge and Mount Desert Island. Once over the bridge, take Rte. 102 to 22 Claremont Rd. in Southwest Harbor. Call for dates (© **207/244-5036;** www.theclaremonthotel.com).

The Reversing Falls Rapids, Saint John, New Brunswick. The reversing rapids are produced by a phenomenon called a tidal bore. It happens twice a day when high tides in the Bay of Fundy cause the Saint John River to turn back on itself and flow upstream until the bay again drops below the river level and the river reverses flow. Since the tides here are the highest in the world and the river bed has an underwater ledge, the boiling and surging of the water are dramatic. The best way to watch is from Fallsview Park, near the Reversing Falls Information Center (15 Market Sq., Saint John, New Brunswick). The highest tides are when the moon is full. Sea kayaking in the bay is the latest thrill around Saint John. For information, call **Tourism Saint John** (© **866/GOFUNDY** [463-8639] or 506/658-2990; www.cityofsaintjohn.com or www.tourismsaintjohn.com).

Glendora Inn & Distillery, Cape Breton Island, Nova Scotia. For a real Scottish moment, head for this distillery, in operation since 1990, where the only single-malt Scotch whiskey in North America is produced. You can take a tour every hour on the hour. May–Oct daily 9am–5pm. Tours C$7 per person. 13727 Hwy. 19, btw. Mabou and Inverness (© **902/258-2662;** www.glenoradistillery.com).

Anne Murray Centre, Springhill, Nova Scotia. This is the most popular tourist attraction in town, dedicated to the pop singer whose recording of "Snowbird" might well be the theme song for all winter-escaping RVers. You should be able to find a copy in the gift shop, if you want to spring for the admission fee. Mid-May to Oct daily 9am–5pm. Admission C$6 adults, C$5 seniors, C$5 children 6–18, free for children 5 and under, $18 family. It's at 36 Main St., Springhill, Nova Scotia (© **902/597-8614**; www.annemurray.com).

The Potato Museum, O'Leary, and Irish Moss Interpretive Centre, Miminegash, Prince Edward Island. In these two museums, you'll learn about two important agricultural products. The Potato Museum is just off Rte. 142 in the town of O'Leary. Potatoes, the economic mainstay, are lauded in pictures, videos, and exhibits (see the giant sculpted potato, visit the Amazing Potato, and taste the cooked potatoes in the kitchen). Irish moss, a seaweed better known as carrageenan, is gathered when storms loosen it, and the whole town goes down to the shore with scoops. The economically valuable carrageenan is a starchy substance that has no calories or flavor and is used to thicken dairy products, toothpaste, shampoo, cough syrup, and other products. A cafe at the Interpretive Centre serves seaweed pie. **Potato Museum** (© **800/565-3475** or 902/859-2039; www.peipotatomuseum.com): mid-May to mid-Oct Mon–Sat 9am–5pm, Sun 1–5pm. Admission C$6 per person, C$14 family. **Irish Moss Interpretive Centre** (© **902/882-4313**): mid-June to Sept daily 10am–7pm. Free admission. Cafe: Mon–Sat 11am–7pm; Sun noon–8pm. On Rte. 14 (Lady Slipper Dr.) in Miminegash.

FIVE THOUGHT-PROVOKING PLACES

The John F. Kennedy Library and Museum, Boston, Massachusetts. Exhibits, films, tapes, and slides trace JFK's career and that of his brother Robert. A half-hour biographical film runs regularly. The striking building design is by I. M. Pei. Daily 9am–5pm (closed major holidays). Admission $12 adults, $10 seniors, $9 children 13–17. Located by the sea; follow directional signs from I-93 to Columbia Point (© **866/535-1960** or 617/514-1600; www.jfklibrary.org).

Baxter State Park. Maine's 200,000-acre Baxter State Park is rugged, primitive, and guaranteed to stay pristine forever. In the 1920s, Governor Percival Proctor Baxter suggested the legislature acquire Mount Katahdin and its surroundings for a park, but the legislators balked at the expense. So Baxter spent the next 30 years buying up parcels of land himself and donating them as a park "to be maintained primarily as Wilderness . . . [and] be Forever Wild." Roads are gravel or dirt and usually narrow and winding. **RVs over 22 ft., motorcycles, and pets are not permitted in the park;** all overnight camping is by reservation only. Backpackers and hikers will find 175 miles of wilderness trails. Even if you take a 4X4 and drive through the park, you'll have to get out and walk down a trail to see the most spectacular scenery; it's designed that way. Both access roads require a permit and fee. Admission $14 for out-of-state residents; free for Maine residents. The park can be found northwest of Millinocket off Rte. 11/157 via a paved private road to the park entrance or via Rte. 163 E. from

Adesque Isle to Ashland, then by private unpaved road into the park. Call the phone number or visit the website for reservation forms that can be printed out and must be mailed in (© **207/723-5140;** www.baxterstateparkauthority.com).

The Maritime Museum of the Atlantic, Halifax, Nova Scotia. A deck chair and other artifacts from the *Titanic* are among the displays. As the closest port to the disaster, Halifax hosted hundreds of funerals for more than 10 days. Today, the unclaimed bodies of some 150 victims are buried in three different Halifax cemeteries. Only 5 years later, the city faced its own disaster, the Halifax Explosion, when two ships, one of them carrying a half-million pounds of TNT plus other explosives, collided in the harbor, killing 2,000 people instantly and destroying much of the city. Mon–Sat 9:30am–5:30pm (and some evenings); Sun 1–5:30pm. Admission C$9 adults, C$8 seniors, C$5 children, free for children 5 and under, C$23 family. Located at 1675 Lower Water St., in Halifax, Nova Scotia (© **902/424-7490;** http:// museum.gov.ns.ca/mma).

New Bedford Whaling Museum, New Bedford, Massachusetts. The cobblestone streets of old New Bedford's harbor have been turned into a Whaling National Historic Park with this fine museum at its heart. Dominating the lobby is a 66-ft. skeleton of a blue whale. The world's largest ship model, of the whaling ship *Lagoda,* half its real size, allows visitors to walk around the deck; while an adjacent exhibit of a whaleship fo'c'sle (forecastle) provides a realistic picture of life at sea on these voyages that lasted many months. Across the street is the Seaman's Bethel, the site of the sermon in Herman Melville's *Moby Dick.* A self-guided "Moby-Dick Trail" takes you around sites mentioned in the book. Daily 9am–5pm, except major holidays. Admission $14 adults, $12 seniors, $6 children 6–14. The museum is at 18 Johnny Cake Hill at the corner with William St. in the historic waterfront area of New Bedford (© **508/997-0046;** www.whalingmuseum.org).

Farnsworth Art Museum/Wyeth Center, Rockland, Maine. A thrifty New England spinster named Lucy Farnsworth, the last remaining member of her family, died at 97 in 1935, leaving $1 million–plus to preserve the family home and create a library and art museum in her father's memory. Today, the 50-year-old museum is a complex of five buildings, four in Rockland and the fifth in nearby Cushing. A six-level art museum preserves the work of native Maine artists and artists who did significant works in Maine, such as the Wyeths, Winslow Homer, John Marin, George Bellows, Edward Hopper, and Rockwell Kent. The austere Wyeth Center, located in a former church adjacent to the Farnsworth home and museum, displays works by N. C. Wyeth, his son Andrew Wyeth, and Andrew's son James (Jamie) Wyeth. But most evocative of all for Andrew Wyeth fans is the Olson House, the gray farmhouse near Cushing that is seen in many of his paintings, notably *Christina's World.* Unfurnished, the house displays copies of Wyeth's works in the rooms where they were painted. **Main museum:** May 15–Nov 1 Mon–Tues and Thurs–Sun 10am–5pm, Wed 10am–8pm; Nov 2–May 14 Wed–Sun 10am–5pm. **Farnsworth Victorian Homestead:** May 15–Nov 1 daily 10am–5pm; Dec Sat–Sun 10am–5pm. **Olson House:** May

22–Oct 12 daily 11am–4pm. (All closed Thanksgiving, Christmas Day, and New Year's Day.) Farnsworth Victorian Homestead and Olson House admission $17 adults, $15 seniors and students 17 and over, free for children 16 and under. Olson House admission $10. The complex is at 16 Museum St. in Rockland (℃ **207/596-6459**), where you can also get a map and directions to the Olson House (℃ **207/354-0102;** www.farnsworthmuseum.org).

LIVING HISTORY SITES

New England and Canada's Maritimes have a plethora of "animated" villages that re-create life in earlier times. Costumed actors, also called interpreters or animators, usually portray a real person who lived in the village. Some villages are fixed permanently in a given year, and day-to-day life goes on exactly as it would have then. No one seems to mind if you come into the kitchen while a meal is being prepared, poke your head into the barn, or talk to someone tending a garden or feeding the animals. They are happy to pose for pictures as well.

Mystic Seaport. Connecticut's Mystic Seaport is a restored 19th-century village with whaling ships, costumed craftsmen to chat with, and maritime artifacts. The construction of a replica of the *Amistad,* the early-19th-century schooner depicted in Steven Spielberg's film (1997) of the same name, docks at Mystic Seaport during the winter. You can visit the "floating classroom" along with many other hands-on and educational activities and exhibits. Plan to spend a full day at this engrossing place. Apr–Oct daily 9am–5pm. Admission $24 adults, $22 seniors, $15 children 6–17, free for children 5 and under. Located at exit 90 off I-95 (℃ **888/9-SEAPORT** [973-2767] or 860/572-5339; www.mysticseaport.org).

Plimoth Plantation. At Plimoth Plantation, near **Plymouth, Massachusetts,** you can talk with Pilgrims who are still living in the year 1627, tending their crops and remembering their long, cramped sea journey on the *Mayflower.* You'll hear 17 different dialects in the village, reflecting the regions from which the Pilgrims came. Even the livestock is authentic, "back-bred" to re-create the Pilgrims' stock. You can watch handcrafted items being made, which are for sale. Apr–Nov daily 9am–5pm. A combination ticket, including the 1-hr. *Mayflower* cruise, is $30 adults, $27 seniors, $19 children 6–14. Accessible only from southbound Rte. 3. Take exit 4 to the Plimoth Plantation Hwy. and follow the signs to 137 Warren St. (℃ **508/746-1622;** www.plimoth.org).

Old Sturbridge Village. Old Sturbridge Village has re-created rural New England life in 1830, with costumed interpreters, craftsmen, farm animals, and the beginnings of industry with shoemakers, coopers, tanners, and blacksmiths. Daily 9:30am–5pm (closed Mon in winter). Admission $20 adults, $18 seniors, $7 children 3–17. Tickets good for 2 days. Located on Rte. 20 at 1 Old Sturbridge Rd. in **Sturbridge, Massachusetts,** at the intersections of I-84 and I-90 (℃ **800/733-1830** or 508/347-3362; www.osv.org).

Strawbery Banke. This 10-acre historic community has 42 buildings, 7 of which illustrate different time periods in the area's history, plus 17th-century herb and vegetable gardens, furnished houses, and crafts shops for weavers, coopers, cabinetmakers, potters, and boat builders. Entrance tickets are good for 2 days; you may need that to see it all. May–Oct daily 10am–5pm. Admission $15 adults, $10 children, free for children 5 and under, $40 family. Located in **Portsmouth,** along **New Hampshire**'s 18 miles of coastline; take I-95 to exit 7, and follow signs from the exit to a 10-acre site near the waterfront (© **603/433-1100;** www.strawberybanke.org).

Shelburne, Nova Scotia. Once the fourth-largest city in North America, Shelburne is now a sleepy little town with a magical historical complex. In 1783, 10,000 Loyalists from the United States, protesting the American Revolution and remaining loyal to the British Crown, arrived in ships from New York City. In the historic district is a re-creation of the oldest store in the Americas, a dory-making shop that still produces the working boats in traditional fashion, and the only remaining privately owned cooperage (barrel-making shop) in North America. The Shelburne waterfront along Dock Street was also the location for the 1994 film *The Scarlet Letter.* Some attractions are open seasonally. June to mid-Oct daily 9:30am–5:30pm; **Shelburne Museum** open off season Tues–Sat 2–5pm. Admission for four museums C$8, single museum C$3. The four museums are: the **Muir-Cox Shipyard/Interpretive Centre,** 7 St. George St. (© **902/875-2483**); the **Ross-Thomson House & Store Museum,** Charlotte Lane (© **902/875-4141;** http://museum.gov.ns.ca/rth); **Shelburne County Museum,** 20 Dock St. (© **902/875-3219;** www.historicshelburne.com/scm); and **Dory Shop Museum,** 20 Dock St. (© **902/875-3219;** http://museum.gov.ns.ca/dory). On the southeast tip of Nova Scotia on Rte. 103, 60 miles southwest of Liverpool.

Fortress Louisbourg National Historic Park. One of North America's largest historical reconstructions, Fortress Louisbourg, near **Sydney, Nova Scotia,** is for us the most fascinating and realistic of all. Here, it's always the summer of 1744, and the fortress is staffed with scruffy, unruly soldiers (who would be mutineers 6 months later) and French aristocrats in exquisite houses. Inns with pewter mugs and earthenware dishes serve 18th-century food to visitors. "A moment in time" is portrayed in remarkable detail by a cast of more than 100 in and around the 50 or so buildings. Spend at least a half-day; try to arrive first thing in the morning. Buy a loaf of soldiers' bread from the bakery and some farm cheese from the Destouches House to take along on the road (but bring your own plastic bags to take them back to the RV—there was no plastic in 1744). Also, bring a jacket and an umbrella, as the weather can change suddenly along this coast. Daily 9:30am–5pm. Admission C$18 adults, C$15 seniors, C$9 children 6–16, free for children 5 and under, C$44 family. Located south of Sydney, Nova Scotia, on Rte. 22 just beyond the modern town of Louisbourg. Take exit 8 near Sydney (© **902/733-2280;** www.pc.gc.ca/ihn-nhs/ns/louisbourg/index).

Kings Landing. This re-creation of a Loyalist settlement of the early 1800s has more than 100 costumed animators and 60 buildings—farmhouses, mills, churches, and inns. You may see Scottish dancing or caber tossing. Early June to mid-Oct daily

Highland Village offers a glimpse of life in 19th century Cape Breton.

10am–5pm. Admission C$16 adults, C$14 seniors, C$13 students, C$11 children 6–16, free for children 5 and under, C$37 family. Located on the Trans-Canada Hwy. near **Fredericton, New Brunswick,** about 60 miles north of Saint John (℃ **506/363-4999;** www.kingslanding.nb.ca).

Acadian Historic Village. You'll have a window into the lives of Acadians btw. 1780 and 1890, watching costumed residents from fur trappers to blacksmiths at work. A cafeteria and restaurant in the village serve traditional Acadian dishes, which bear no resemblance whatsoever to the food their Cajun cousins cook in Louisiana. June to late Sept daily 10am–6pm. Admission C$16 adults, C$14 seniors, C$11 children, free for children 5 and under, C$38 family. West of **Caraquet** on Rte. 11 near Chaleur Bay on the banks of the Riviere-du-Nord, about 160 miles north of Moncton (℃ **506/726-2600;** www.villagehistoriqueacadien.com).

Highland Village. Scottish Americans looking for their roots should visit the Highland Village on Rte. 223 in Iona, on the south shore of **Cape Breton Island, Nova Scotia** at 4119 Hwy. 223, which commemorates the settlement of the area by the Highland Scots. The village has 10 historic structures dating from 1810 through the early 20th century, which have been moved here and staffed with costumed interpreters doing traditional crafts and farming. June to mid-Oct daily 9:30am–5:30pm. Admission C$9 adults, C$7 seniors, C$4 children 6–17, free for children 5 and under, C$22 family. It's in **Iona** by the Bras d'Or Lake in the heart of Cape Breton Island (℃ **902/725-2272;** http://museum.gov.ns.ca/hv). Also on the premises is **Roots Cape Breton,** a computerized genealogical research center with data collected from census, cemetery, birth, death, and marriage records.

Confederation Players, Charlottetown, Prince Edward Island. Costumed interpreters conduct walking tours and perform daily vignettes from 1864 when the Fathers of the Confederation met here to form a union of the colonies. These strolling players are happy to pose for your cameras as well as reenact history. Various package tours: July–Aug daily 10am–5pm (© **800/955-1864;** www.tourism charlottetown.ca).

10 SPLURGES

1. **Spend a weekend at the Wauwinet on Nantucket.** Wauwinet, at 120 Wauwinet Rd., is an elegantly understated, gray-shingled, white-trimmed seaside inn on a remote, sandy neck of land btw. Nantucket Harbor and the Atlantic. The whole place looks as though it were decorated by Ralph Lauren, with Martha Stewart arranging the flowers; it has sailboats, clay tennis courts, bicycles, a 21-ft. launch available for picnics and bay cruises, and an elegant dining room called **Toppers.** Nantucket is accessible by ferry from Hyannis, Massachusetts. Call for reservations (© **800/426-8718;** www.wauwinet.com).

2. **Go shopping in Nantucket.** Pick up a classic Nantucket Lightship Basket purse, considered an heirloom that increases in value; prices start at around $350. You can also visit the **Nantucket Lightship Basket Museum** at 49 Union St. ($5 admission) and take a weaving workshop (© **508-228-1177;** www.nantucketlightshipbasketmuseum.org). Or you could choose some delectable chocolate almond buttercreams in pretty hand-painted tins at **Sweet Inspirations** at 26 Centre St. (© **508/228-5814;** www.nantucketchocolate. com). For some of us, that's a splurge.

3. **Take a scenic cruise aboard the *Argo.*** From Boothbay Harbor, the boat takes you to a clambake at Cabbage Island, where each person feasts on fish chowder, two lobsters, steamed clams, corn on the cob, Maine potatoes, and blueberry cake ($60 per person; late June to mid-Sept). There's also a full-service bar. Call for information and reservations (© **207/633-7200**).

4. **Check out the treasures in Wiscasset's antiques shops.** There are more than 20 shops within walking distance of each other, featuring everything from early American furniture to 19th-century paintings. Wiscasset is about 15 miles east of Bath on U.S. 1.

5. **Take a summer whale-watching cruise.** Boats leave from Hyannis and Provincetown on Cape Cod, and from Gloucester. Take a camera, binoculars, a jacket, a securely fitting hat, and sunscreen. **From Provincetown:** Dolphin Fleet (© **800/826-9300;** www.whalewatch.com), $42 adults, $39 seniors, $34 children. **From Hyannis:** Hyannis Whale Watcher Cruises (© **800/287-0374;** www.whales.net), $47 adults, $40 seniors, $28 children. **From Gloucester:** Yankee Whale Watch (© **800/WHALING** [942-5464]; www.yankeefleet. com), $45 adults, $38 seniors, $29 children; Cape Ann Whale Watch (© **800/877-5110;** www.caww.com), $45 adults, $41 seniors, $30 children;

and Seven Seas Whale Watch (© **888/283-1776;** www.7seas-whalewatch. com), $45 adults, $39 seniors, $29 children. The last cruise leaves from Rose's Wharf, Gloucester, from exit 10 off Rte. 128, and there's plenty of parking—RVs are welcome.

6. **Alexander Graham Bell's Yacht, Baddeck, Nova Scotia.** Learn to sail aboard Alexander Graham Bell's 59-ft. yacht *Elsie,* which has been cruising the Bras d'Or from Baddeck, Nova Scotia, for 80 years. You can book lessons, as well as day cruises, overnights, and cruises of up to 2 weeks btw. mid-June and the end of Oct. Day cruises have a maximum of 10 people, a minimum of 4; C$99 per person or C$750 to charter the boat. Call Captain Patterson (© **902/ 295-7245**).

7. **Book a dinner train ride on the vintage Cape Cod Central Railroad.** Enjoy a five-course meal on a 2-hour twilight ride through 42 miles of the Cape. $70, adults only. There are also day trips at 11am and 2pm; $42 adults, $30 children 3–11. Located at 252 Main St., Hyannis, Massachusetts (© **508/771-3800;** www.capetrain.com).

8. **Go antiques shopping along Old King's Highway on Cape Cod.** Also known as Rte. 6A, Old King's Highway is lined with countless antiques shops. Glass collectors must not miss the **Sandwich Glass Museum** in Sandwich, showcasing glassware made here btw. 1825 and 1888 with sand imported from New Jersey (Cape Cod sand has iron oxides that discolor the glass). At 129 Main St. at the junction of Main St. and Rte. 130. Apr–Dec daily 9:30am–5pm; Feb and Mar Wed–Sun 9:30–5pm. Admission $5 adults, $1.25 children (© **508/888- 0251;** www.sandwichglassmuseum.org).

9. **Take a day sail aboard a Maine windjammer out of Camden.** The *Appledore,* a windjammer that has sailed around the world, will take you out among the rocky islands of Penobscot Bay where seals sun on the rocks and porpoises play in the water. Come to the dock at Bayview Landing by the Town Landing and sign up or call ahead; $40. Mid-June to mid-Oct (© **207/236-8353;** www. appledore2.com).

10. **Stop off for lunch or tea at a 19th-century resort.** Relive the golden days of summer-long vacations in old-fashioned resort hotels by visiting the half-timbered **1899 Algonquin,** 184 Adolphus St. in St. Andrews-by-the-Sea, New Brunswick, surrounded by manicured lawns, lush gardens, and a century-old golf course (© **866/540-4403** or 506/529-8823; www.fairmont.com/ algonquin); or **Keltic Lodge** (built in 1940, but looking much older) near Ingonish Beach on Nova Scotia's Cape Breton Island (© **800/565-0444;** www. signatureresorts.com). In **Bar Harbor, Maine,** the Bar Harbor Inn's **Reading Room Restaurant** opened its doors in 1887. Now the re-created inn serves sumptuous (if expensive) lobster rolls and more pedestrian fare such as fish and chips and hamburgers. It's on the waterfront by the Municipal Pier (© **800/248- 3351** or 207/288-3351; www.barharborinn.com).

LOOKING FOR LOBSTER IN ALL THE RIGHT PLACES

Where to Find 'Em

A single-minded lobster lover along the Maine coast can cheerfully overlook Bar Harbor day-trippers and T-shirt vendors, fudge fairs, and ye olde gift shoppes to search out a lobster pound or an "early bird lobster dinner." Before 5:30 or 6pm, you can dine on a whole fresh lobster weighing around 1¼ pounds, at that day's price. You might even hit a two-for-one special, two 1-pounders on the same plate and enough for two people. This is best done as takeout, since the thrifty New England proprietors usually won't allow two people to share. With a little concentration, you can hit a couple of these spots before prices go up for the evening and they have to get ready for dinner.

How to Eat 'Em

The peerless *Homarus americanus northern,* or American lobster, has meaty front claws that his warm-water cousins lack. We also think he is much more succulent.

Only when driven to desperation (or boredom) should you order lobster prepared any way other than steamed or boiled, except on a cold day, when a lobster stew goes down well, and perhaps at lunchtime, when a lobster roll fills the bill. For the uninitiated, a lobster roll is a top-sliced hot dog bun filled with chunks of cold lobster moistened with mayonnaise or melted butter or both, and sometimes with the added crunch of chopped celery.

Buying 'Em Live

When buying a live lobster, look for the liveliest, with a good greenish-brown color. Avoid any lobsters that have turned blue. Pick a feisty one, just as you would a puppy at the pound, and look for long antennae. That means it's been at the pound less time than the ones with short antennae, which get bitten off. Lobsters can last up to 2 days out of seawater if you refrigerate them in your RV in a heavy brown paper bag with a few strands of seaweed or several layers of newspapers. Never close a lobster up in a plastic bag, where it will suffocate, or store it in a pot of cold tap water, where it will drown.

How to Cook 'Em

To cook a lobster, put several inches of water—preferably seawater—in a pot, bring it to a boil, and drop the lobster in, holding it by the underside of the body to keep it from splattering the water, then cover the pot quickly. Listen for the water to boil again, then reduce the heat to keep it from boiling over. The lobster is cooked when all of its shell has turned red, usually in as little as 10 minutes for a small lobster to 20 minutes for a large one. The happy medium seems to be 13 or 14 minutes for a 1¼-pounder, adding 3 minutes for each additional quarter-pound. Softshell lobsters, if you're lucky enough to find some, take less time. Another expert suggests that when the lobster turns bright red and floats, cook for 3 or 4 minutes longer.

The British Society for the Prevention of Cruelty to Animals suggests the most humane way to cook a lobster is to lower it into the pot head first, starting with cold water, which will put the lobster to sleep as it warms.

TOP LOBSTER SPOTS

Nunan's Lobster Hut, Cape Porpoise, Maine. At Nunan's, the crustaceans are steamed to order in a little water rather than boiled in a lot. A bag of potato chips and a hard roll with butter fill out the dinner tray. Finish off with a slice of homemade apple or blueberry pie. No reservations or credit cards. Daily 5–9pm. 9 Mills Rd. (© 207/967-4362; www.nunanslobsterhut.com).

Beal's Lobster Pier, Southwest Harbor, Maine. Beal's serves softshell lobster, steamer clams, corn on the cob, and onion rings. You sit at picnic tables at the end of the pier and feast. Memorial Day to Oct daily 7am–5pm. Located at 182 Clark Point Rd., at the end of the road (© 207/244-7178; www.bealslobster.com).

Lobsterman's Co-Op, Boothbay Harbor, Maine. Here, you'll find a wooden pier with outdoor picnic tables and a choice of hardshell or softshell lobsters (defined on a hand-printed sign as soft shell = less meat, sweeter taste). To that definition, we can add "easier to crack open." While fat gulls perched on the rail look on, you can devour lobsters with melted butter, a bag of potato chips, corn on the cob, onion rings, steamed or fried clams, and jug wine by the glass or pitcher. Memorial Day to Columbus Day daily 11:30am–9pm. At 97 Atlantic Ave., near the aquarium (© 207/633-4900; www.boothbaylobsterwharf.com).

Abbott's Lobster in the Rough is a classic lobster pound.

Lobster Trivia Quiz

The Maine Lobster Promotion Council put out a trivia quiz to test your lobster IQ. Here are some of the questions. You'll find the answers following the quiz.

1. The lobster's nervous system most closely resembles the nervous system of what insect?

2. How long have lobsters been harvested in Maine?

3. What do lobsters eat?

4. What is the tomalley, the light green substance found in the lobster's carapace?

5. Why do lobsters turn red when they are cooked?

6. How fast can a lobster swim?

ANSWERS: (1) The grasshopper. (2) The first report of caught lobsters was in 1605 when early explorers caught them in a net. Commercial lobstering began in the mid-1800s. (3) Crabs, clams, mussels, starfish, sea urchins, and other lobsters. (4) The liver and pancreas of the lobster, which can contain contaminants; consumers are urged not to eat the tomalley, although some lobster aficionados relish it. The red coral eggs found inside the female lobster, on the other hand, are treasured by gourmets and used in sauces or cooking. (5) The lobster shell carries different color pigment chromatophores; when cooked, all but the red pigment called astaxanthin are masked. No matter what color the lobster shell when raw, it will turn red when cooked. (6) By flipping its tail and swimming backward, a lobster can cover 25 feet in just under a second.

The Gloucester House, Gloucester, Massachusetts. At the Gloucester House, waitresses call you "dearie" and serve an inexpensive assembly-line clambake with lobster, clam chowder, corn on the cob, and watermelon at long wooden tables out back. Winter daily 11:30am–8pm; summer daily 11:30am–9pm. Located at 63 Rogers St. (© 898/283-1812; www.thegloucesterhouse.com).

Harraseeket Lunch & Lobster Company, South Freeport, Maine. Harraseeket is at a pier on the harbor, and the town won't let RVs access the quarter-mile residential street down to the pier. If you really want a lobster, park along South Freeport Rd. and send one member of the party to walk to the lobster company, while the other stays with the RV in case you need to move. Go around back at the lobster company, place your order, and take a number. About 20 min. later, you'll have your freshly cooked crustaceans. If you have a legal parking space, you can both walk down and eat on the premises if you can find a seat. Pound open daily 7am–7pm. Located at the Town Landing at 36 Main St. (© 207/865-3535; www.harraseeketlunchandlobster.com).

The Story Behind PEI's Lobster Suppers

Lobster suppers have a long history on Prince Edward Island, beginning decades ago as community suppers. The opening of lobster season was celebrated in community halls, church basements, or even outdoors.

Local fishermen donated the lobster, farmers the potatoes and milk for chowder. Someone's cold cellar would provide cabbage and carrots for coleslaw. Strawberries were the first fruit of the season. Biscuits, bread, pies, and squares came from local housewives, along with their own pickles. Everyone pitched in.

Soon word spread. Townfolk wanted to go, as did savvy tourists. In 1963, Father Denis Gallant, pastor at St. Ann's Church in Hope River, started serving lobster dinners in the basement of the church to help pay off the mortgage. At the time, they charged C$1.50 for a full dinner. St. Ann's continues to operate lobster suppers and boasts they are the "original." As a nonprofit organization, they support charities close to the heart of the community, as well as the church.

St. Ann's Church Lobster Suppers (*©* **902/621-0635**; www.lobster suppers.com) is just off Route 224. It's open mid-June to late September, Monday through Saturday from 4 to 8:30pm daily, except Sunday. Cost is C$33–47 lobster dinner; C$30–C$40 for alternates: chicken, salmon, scallops, shrimp, haddock, steak, or surf and turf. Credit cards are accepted and a children's menu is available.

New Glasgow Lobster Suppers began in 1958 when the Junior Farmers Organization held a fundraiser. The Nicholson and MacRae families of the original founders continue operating New Glasgow Lobster Suppers to this day. Meals include unlimited chowder, mussels, bread, desserts, and beverages. Both suppers are important to their communities, providing employment in a region where jobs have been scarce. Many students have put themselves through school on their supper earnings.

The food set out at those original gatherings set the tone for the more authentic of today's lobster suppers. Begin your feast with chowder, mussels, and salads. Be careful you don't fill up on the delicious homemade rolls. Lobster is served at its best, fresh cooked, with a touch of the sea to keep it honest (hot or cold, your choice). The size of lobster you order will determine the price. They crack it for you and provide the tools to help you get every morsel. Finish off your meal with home-style desserts. Credit cards are accepted. Expect to pay up to C$40 each, plus your liquor.

New Glasgow Lobster Suppers (*©* **902/964-2870**; www.peilobster suppers.com) is on Route 258 (just off Rte. 13), open daily from June through mid-October, 4 to 8:30pm. Lobster suppers range from C$30 to C$65 per person, depending on the size of the lobster. Less expensive alternatives are scallops, roast beef, ham, salmon, chicken, or a vegetarian option. There's a good kids' menu, and credit cards are accepted. 🚐

Abbott's Lobster in the Rough, Noank, Connecticut. Abbott's serves fresh boiled lobster with coleslaw and its own label potato chips at outdoor picnic tables by the water. You can get clams on the half-shell or in chowder, or a lobster roll, if you'd prefer. Weekdays are less crowded, and there is adequate RV parking. Early May and early Sept to mid-Oct Fri–Sun noon–7pm; late May to early Sept daily noon–9pm. Located at 117 Pearl St. in Noank, just south of Mystic on Rte. 217 (© **860/536-7719;** www.abbotts-lobster.com).

The Old City Market, Saint John, New Brunswick. The Old City Market sells live or cooked lobsters to take out or ship home, as well as lobster rolls and cooked lobster tails. Everywhere, you see paper bags of dark-red flaky leaves, called dulse, dried seaweed that is a favored local snack and very much an acquired taste. The market dates from 1876 and is built to resemble the inverted keel of a ship. There's a glass-walled solarium next door if you want to eat your lobster here. Daily 8am–6pm. 49–51 Charlotte St. Or head for **Billy's Seafood Company** (daily 11am–10pm) in the north corner if you favor a sit-down meal (© **888/033-FISH** [3471] or 506/672-FISH [3474]; www.billysseafood.com).

The Lobster Shack, Cape Elizabeth, Maine. The Lobster Shack occupies an incomparable setting by the sea at the end of Two Lights Rd., by the lighthouse in Cape Elizabeth. A local landmark, it encourages you to "come as you are" and offers "eat in or takeout" service. You can also choose btw. eating indoors or by the seaside at picnic tables above the rocks. Apr to mid-Oct daily 11am–8pm. 225 Two Lights Rd. (© **207/799-1677;** www.lobstershacktwolights.com).

Mabel's Lobster Claw, Kennebunkport, Maine. Mabel's, where George and Barbara Bush indulge in the peanut butter ice-cream pie, has softshell lobster in season (July–Sept) and lovely lobster rolls that you can eat there or as takeout. Apr–Nov daily 11:30am–3pm and 5–9pm. 124 Ocean Ave. (© **207/967-2562;** www.mabelslobster.com).

The Clam Shack, Kennebunkport, Maine. The Clam Shack is on Dock St. on the bridge. There's no place nearby big enough for an RV to park, but if a passenger hops out to get the food while the driver goes into town and parks for a while (there's often a wait), you can get fantastic lobster rolls to go or serious baskets of fried clams. May–Oct daily 11am–9pm (© **207/967-2560** takeout, 207/967-3321 market; www.theclamshack.net).

The Lobster Pot, Provincetown, Cape Cod. This funky but pricey restaurant in a two-story clapboard house serves classic clam chowder along with local clambake dinners, and has takeout chowder and lobster. You can sit inside or on an open deck on the upper level, called Top of the Pot, but you can't drive or park an RV in P-town. Apr–Nov daily 11am–10pm. Located at 321 Commercial St. (© **508/487-0842;** www.ptownlobsterpot.com).

Prince Edward Island's Famous Lobster Suppers, Prince Edward Island. All summer long, the island holds lobster suppers as fundraisers, special events, or daily occurrences. Watch for the signs as you walk, bike, or drive around. **St. Ann's Church in Hope River,** 5km (3 miles) from Stanley Bridge off Rte. 224, for instance, has served them every summer for nearly 50 years; Mon–Sat 4–8:30pm; 1 lb. lobster C$32, 2 lb. C$45 (**©** **902/621-0635;** www.lobstersuppers.com). **New Glasgow Lobster Suppers** serves from its own pound at 604 Rte. 258, 10km (6 miles) southeast of Cavendish; daily 4–8:30pm; C$31–C$85 for lobster dinner (**©** **902/964-2870;** www.peilobstersuppers.com).

TAKEOUT (OR EAT-IN) NON-LOBSTER TREATS

Kitchen Little, Mystic Seaport, Connecticut. Kitchen Little is a tiny restaurant that serves breakfast and lunch, both memorable meals, especially when taken in the back garden by the water. We opted for an early lunch to miss the breakfast rush and ate a cup (served in a coffee mug) of light and unique clam chowder in a thin, clear broth redolent of fresh clam, followed by a fried scallop roll and a lobster roll. The late breakfasters around us were feasting on huge omelets, pancakes with fresh strawberries, and eggs with cheese and jalapeño peppers. Daily 6:30am–2pm. On Rte. 27, 2 blocks east of the Mystic Seaport entrance, at 135 Greenmanville Ave., near the Mystic Seaport Museum (**©** **860/536-2122;** www.kitchenlittle.org).

Woodmans clam stand, Essex, Massachusetts. The first clam was fried and served at Woodmans back in 1916, so they say, and today you can get clams as takeout or eat them there, after standing at a counter and watching them fry. This style of service is called "in the rough," but the delectable clams and their companion onion rings are silky inside, crunchy outside. The clam fritters aren't bad, either. In fact, we defy you to drive out of the parking lot past the giant plaster clam without succumbing to the irresistible urge to taste at least one. We've been there a number of times and the long queue to get in has defeated us only twice (during Memorial Day weekend one year, Labor Day weekend another). Daily 11am–10pm. It's at 121 Main St. (**©** **800/649-1773** or 978/768-6057; www.woodmans.com).

J. T. Farnham's, Essex, Massachusetts. To continue our tale from Woodmans (see above), we drove down Eastern Ave. (Rte. 133) toward Gloucester, and on the edge of Essex we found Farnham's, a smaller, less crowded restaurant. As at Woodmans, diners order from the counter, then take a seat in the restaurant or wait until the takeout is ready. The fried clams are crunchy, crisp, and luscious; the fish and chips light and delicious; and the clam chowder as rich and thin as any model's dream. In a moment of weakness, we also ordered the fried onion rings (the servings are enormous), and reheated both potatoes and onion rings the next day without any loss of quality. Mar–Nov daily 11am–9pm. You can call ahead for takeout; 88 Eastern Ave. (**©** **978/768-6643**).

The Clam Box. Another fried clam standby awaits aficionados just north of Essex in **Ipswich,** the center for great clam digging. The Clam Box, at 246 High St. (Rte. 133) on the north end of town, looks a little like a takeout box itself (be prepared for a wait). Mar–Dec Mon and Wed–Thurs 11am–8pm, Fri–Sat 11am–8:30pm (**©** **978/ 356-9707;** www.ipswichma.com/clambox).

The tidy little Clam Box in Ipswich looks like a takeout box itself.

Arnold's Lobster & Clam Bar, Eastham on Cape Cod, Massachusetts. The onion rings at Arnold's are extra-special, and the steamed lobster, fried clams, steamers, and mussels aren't bad, either. Prices are modest, and there's little decor, but the patio and picnic tables among the pines are always filled with happy eaters. Beer and wine are available. May–Sept daily 11:30am–8pm. At 3580 State Hwy., Rte. 6 (© **508/255-2575**; www.arnoldsrestaurant.com).

Frank Pepe Pizzeria Napoletana, New Haven, Connecticut. Frank Pepe's claims to have baked America's first pizza in 1925. It still uses the original brick ovens to turn out the famous white clam pie, a tomato-free pizza. Mon–Sat 11:30am–10pm; Sun noon–10pm. Pepe's is at 157 Wooster St. (© **203/865-5762**; www.pepepizzeria). Its pizza-making neighbor 1 block down the street is **Sally's Apizza.** Sally's was a favorite of Bill Clinton in his Yale days, and it makes a fresh tomato pie in summer and a broccoli-cheese pie year-round. Wooster St., where the pizzerias are located, is in a residential area on the east edge of town (watch for signs) with adequate street parking for RVs early in the evening, but not later. Tues–Sat 5–10:30pm; Sun 5–10pm. 237 Wooster St. (© **203/624-5271**; www.sallysapizza.com).

Louis' Lunch, New Haven, Connecticut. It was in New Haven that Louis Lassen made the first hamburgers (so they say) in 1900, and four generations later, Louis' Lunch on Crown St. is still serving them plain on toasted bread, with no hamburger buns, ketchup, mayo, mustard, or special sauce allowed. Tues–Wed 11am–4pm; Thurs–Sat noon–2am. Closed Sun–Mon and Aug. Located at 261–263 Crown St., downtown btw. Temple and College sts. (© **203/562-5507**; www.louislunch.com).

Harraseeket Lunch & Lobster, Freeport, Maine. Harraseeket serves the famous whoopie pie, a pair of big, cakelike chocolate cookies sandwiched together with fluffy marshmallow cream. It's an old Maine treat, usually homemade and always wrapped and ready to go on the cafe counter. May to mid-June and Labor Day to Columbus Day daily 11am–7:45pm; mid-June to Labor Day daily 11am–8:45pm. It's on Main St. in South Freeport (for instructions about getting there, see "Top Lobster Spots," above; ✆ 207/865-3535).

Moxie, the first carbonated soft drink, Lisbon Falls, Maine. Sample the descendant of the first carbonated soft drink, Moxie, in its tiny Maine headquarters in Lisbon Falls, btw. Brunswick and Lewiston. Developed in 1876 as Beverage Moxie Nerve Food, it predated Coca-Cola by a decade, and lent its name to the slang vocabulary of the '20s, when *moxie* meant "a lot of nerve." Today the company sells memorabilia and soft drinks from the store. You can also have it shipped by the case. Mon–Sat 9am–5pm; Sun 9am–4pm. 2 Main St. at the junction of Rte. 196 (✆ 207/353-8173). Check out the **Moxie Festival** in early June (**www.moxiefestival.com**).

Jordan Pond Lodge, Acadia National Park, Maine. Afternoon tea at Jordan Pond Lodge begins at 11:30am and features popovers and strawberry jam in an old-fashioned garden filled with dahlias, sweet peas, and delphiniums. The island is called Mount Desert, but usually pronounced "Des-*ert.*" Think sweet thoughts, and call ahead. On the Park Loop Rd. (✆ 207/276-3316; http://thejordanpondhouse.com).

Cappy's Chowder House, Camden, Maine. Cappy's ladles up clam chowder by the cup or bowl to eat there or as takeout, and it also serves bar drinks in Mason jars. This is the town where *Peyton Place* was set. Poet Edna St. Vincent Millay worked as a waitress at the nearby Whitehall Inn during the summer of 1912. Daily 11am–11pm. It's at 1 Main St. in Camden (✆ 207/236-2254; www.cappyschowder.com).

The Portland Public Market, Portland, Maine. This indoor market also has snack bars and takeout food, counters heaped with fresh seafood, farmhouse cheeses, and butter made in Maine. Greengrocers carry more than one variety of Maine-grown potatoes. Mon–Sat 8am–7pm; Sun 10am–5pm. Located at 28 Monument Sq. on the corner of Cumberland (✆ 207/228-2056; www.publicmarkethouse.com).

Ganong's Chocolate Factory, St. Stephen, New Brunswick. Just across the border from Maine, Ganong's is where the candy bar was invented when the owner wrapped some slabs of chocolate in waxed paper to take on a fishing trip. Among its unique sweets are "chicken bones," crunchy, white-striped, cinnamon-flavored logs with a bittersweet chocolate center (✆ 888/270-8222 or 508/485-5600; shop online at www.ganong.com). In early Aug., the town celebrates a 6-day chocolate festival.

Moosehead Brewery, Saint John, New Brunswick. In summer, drop by the **Moosehead Country Store** on Main St. for a Moosehead cap or T-shirt. The brewery is at 89 Main St. W. (✆ 506/635-7000; http://moosehead.ca). Store: daily 9am–5pm (✆ 506/635-7020).

Malpeque oysters. Look for briny Malpeque oysters, a Prince Edward Island specialty, on menus throughout Canada's Maritime Provinces in season; and search out the fundraiser lobster suppers around Prince Edward Island at churches and other community centers. You'll not only dine copiously and well, but you'll find the natives are friendly on their own turf.

WILDLIFE-WATCHING

It always comes as a surprise to New England visitors when they learn there are still plenty of **moose** in the woods, although the only people that seem to run into them do it literally. Throughout New Hampshire, road signs tally the number of moose hit by cars during the year.

White-tailed deer are plentiful throughout New England and the Maritimes, as are **beavers, raccoons, porcupines,** and **skunks. Black bear** are occasionally spotted. The **red fox** is common in Maine's Acadia National Park, but rarely seen by visitors.

With all that ocean, you'll find an abundance of marine life, especially **whales.** Humpbacks, fin whales, and occasionally rare right whales (rare because they were the "right" whale for whalers and therefore virtually decimated) may be spotted, most easily aboard a whale-watching boat. You'll also usually see **seals, porpoises,** and **dolphins.** We've seen more humpback whales off Boston than in the Arctic, Antarctic, or anywhere else.

Day cruises go out from Connecticut's Waterford; Maine's Bangor, Boothbay, Lubec, Northeast Harbor, and Portland; Massachusetts's Barnstable, Boston, Gloucester, Plymouth, Provincetown, and Rockport; New Hampshire's Rye Harbor; Nova Scotia's Cheticamp, Big Bras d'Or, and Westport; and New Brunswick's Grand Manan Island, near Campobello.

Pelagic seabirds, those that return to land only for breeding and raising their young, are frequently sighted along the coastline. Look for storm petrels, shearwaters, gannets, guillemots, razorbills, and puffins.

The National Audubon Society and the Canadian Wildlife Service have been working on a project since 1971 to return the **puffins** to Seal Island off Rockland, Maine. The once-thriving colony of birds was almost wiped out around the turn of the 20th century by hunters.

On the Road

CAPE COD

The Pilgrims landed at the tip of Cape Cod, where Provincetown is located, before they reached Plymouth Rock, on November 11, 1620. They stayed for 36 days before crossing Cape Cod Bay to Plymouth.

The famous rock, what's left of it, is shielded under a Grecian colonnade, and a replica *Mayflower* is staffed by costumed personnel.

Things are a bit more crowded these days. Try to avoid arriving on a summer weekend—or during the months of July and August—if you want easy driving and a place to park within walking distance of kitschy little Provincetown. Autumn is a beautiful season on the Cape, and you can have the beaches to yourself.

Traffic on Route 28, the southernmost highway across the cape, is very slow because the area is built up like a quaint megalopolis. A far better route for RVers is smooth-running Route 6. Route 6A is the one to take if you like a slow-moving drive through villages with antiques shops and country inns.

For 30 miles of protected and beautiful **beaches,** but no camping, head for Cape Cod National Seashore. Unfortunately, it has only six parking lots, which fill up by midmorning in summer. Those at Nauset Light Beach and Wellfleet's Marconi Beach have steep stairways leading down to the beach. **Hiking trails** set out from Salt Pond Visitor Center in Eastham, where there's spacious parking for RVs, and Head of the Meadow Trailhead in Truro, both off Route 6. **Bicycle trails** run along both sides of the Cape Cod Canal, with parking available in the Sandwich Marina area, adjacent to the National Seashore from Eastham North.

Bayside beaches have warmer water and less turbulent surf than oceanside beaches. Low tide is best for beach hiking, because the sand is packed; at high tide, you'll be struggling through looser, deeper sand.

For information, contact the **Cape Cod Chamber of Commerce,** 737 Main St., Hyannis, MA 02601 (© **888/CAPE-COD** [227-3263] or 508/771-1224; www.capecodchamber.org).

NANTUCKET

Leave your RV on the mainland and take a day trip on the ferry to the island of Nantucket from Hyannis at 220 Ocean St., via **Hy-Line Cruises** (© **800/492-8082** or 508/778-2600; www.hylinecruises.com), daily year-round. Traditional ferry: $45 adults, children 12 and under free; high-speed ferry: $77 adults, $51 children. Then, rent a bicycle to see the island. Along with the island's free public beaches and good seafood restaurants, there are bright flowers blooming in front yards everywhere, which makes it one of New England's prettiest places; plus, there's a **Whaling Museum** and 11 other equally appealing little museums (**www.nha.org/sites**).

Nothing built after the 1920s gets any notice from the local guides. Walking tours meander through the main part of town, past the shingled houses graying in the weather, the brick houses built by whaling barons, and the newer Federal and Victorian houses. In the early summer, lupine, iris, and lemon lilies grow along the walkways, while old-fashioned hollyhocks, alyssum, geraniums, hydrangeas, and nasturtiums bloom in pint-size gardens. *Rosa rugosa*, with its big red rose hips, thrives in hedges everywhere.

Tour guides like to point out one house occupied by a writer who traveled around the world twice before deciding that Nantucket was the best place; he nailed two pairs of shoes by the door to show his traveling days were over.

Thomas Mayhew purchased Nantucket Island for £40 in 1659 from Lord Sterling, who had been granted it by Charles I. After holding onto the island for 18 years, Mayhew sold it for only £30 and two beaver hats.

New England Coast Campgrounds

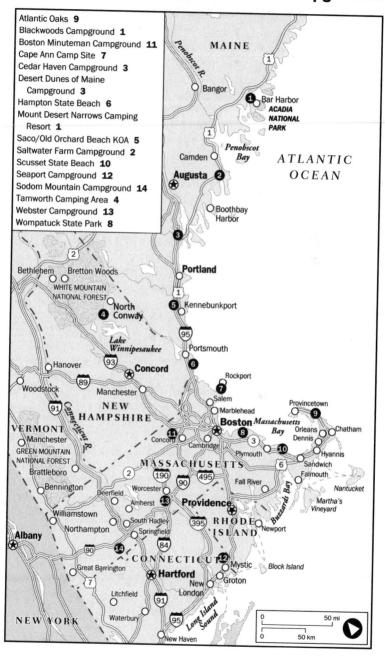

Atlantic Oaks **9**
Blackwoods Campground **1**
Boston Minuteman Campground **11**
Cape Ann Camp Site **7**
Cedar Haven Campground **3**
Desert Dunes of Maine
  Campground **3**
Hampton State Beach **6**
Mount Desert Narrows Camping
  Resort **1**
Saco/Old Orchard Beach KOA **5**
Saltwater Farm Campground **2**
Scusset State Beach **10**
Seaport Campground **12**
Sodom Mountain Campground **14**
Tamworth Camping Area **4**
Webster Campground **13**
Wompatuck State Park **8**

MAINE

Penobscot R.

Bangor

Bar Harbor
ACADIA
NATIONAL
PARK

Camden

Penobscot Bay

ATLANTIC
OCEAN

Augusta **2**

Boothbay
Harbor

3

Portland

Bethlehem   Bretton Woods
WHITE MOUNTAIN
NATIONAL FOREST
North
Conway **4**

5 Kennebunkport

95

Portsmouth

Lake
Winnipesaukee

Hanover
93
Concord

6

Rockport

7

Salem

Woodstock

Manchester

NEW
HAMPSHIRE

91

Marblehead

Boston *Massachusetts Bay*

Provincetown

9

VERMONT
Manchester
GREEN MOUNTAIN
NATIONAL FOREST
Brattleboro

Concord **11**

Cambridge

8

3

Orleans
Dennis

Chatham

Plymouth

10

Hyannis

Bennington

2

Deerfield

MASSACHUSETTS

190 **90** **495**

Fall River

Sandwich

6

Falmouth

Worcester
13

Providence

Nantucket

Martha's
Vineyard

Williamstown

Amherst
South Hadley
Springfield

RHODE
ISLAND

Buzzards Bay

Albany

Northampton

395

Newport

90 **14**

CONNECTICUT **12** Mystic

Block Island

Great Barrington

Hartford

New
London

Groton

Litchfield

7

84

NEW YORK

91

Waterbury

95

Long Island
Sound

New Haven

0   50 mi
0   50 km

Investing with the Mashantucket Pequots & Mohegans

Foxwoods Casino Resort, one of the biggest and most profitable casinos in the United States, is in Ledyard, Connecticut, about 6 miles north of I-95's exit 92 or I-395's exit 79A near Mystic Seaport on the Mashantucket Pequot Indian Reservation. The Pequots were decimated in the 17th century by settlers and militia, but since the casino opened, their numbers, once down to one surviving resident on the reservation, have been increasing (© **800/FOX-WOOD** [369-9663]; www.foxwoods.com).

Practically next door, you can see where the profits went, and make your own investment in the $193-million, 100,000-square-foot **Mashantucket Pequot Museum.** This awesome museum recreates a glacial crevasse, a computer-animated caribou kill from 11,000 years ago, and a full-size 16th-century village of Eastern woodland Indian life that the visitor can see, hear, and smell. Your tickets—$15 adults, $13 seniors, $10 children 6 to 15—can be applied toward a membership (starting at $40) that allows free entrance in the future, plus special events and discounts at the museum shop. The museum is open Wednesday to Saturday 10am to 4pm (© **800/411-9671;** www.pequotmuseum.org).

Foxwoods and nearby **Mohegan Sun** are rival tribal casinos, and are constantly adding additions to outdo each other: You'll find new hotels, a changing variety of restaurants (both budget and high-end), many free activities, ranging from fireworks to farmers' markets, and entertainers within and outside the casinos. (Mohegan also owns a professional basketball team, the WNBA's Connecticut Sun.) Big-name entertainment stars play the showrooms and auditoriums in both casinos, and both also provide plenty of free entertainment.

Mohegan Sun is also off I-395 at exit 79A, then east 1 mile on Route 2A (© **888/226-7711** information, 888/777-7922 reservations; www.mohegansun.com).

Mohegan Sun welcomes RVs in its Turtle parking lot, but you'll need to fill out a permit, which can be downloaded here: **www.mohegansun.com/getting-here/parking.html**. Foxwoods also offers RV parking in Lot A. You'll need to call ahead (© **860/312-3333**) to let them know you're coming, and a staffer will take your information when you arrive. 🚐

The early Nantucket sailing ships always carried a crew of four young boys of ages 13 or 14 in each whale boat, along with a master and a harpooner. The boys did not necessarily choose to go whaling, but in Nantucket, they were not acceptable suitors for a bride until they had been around Cape Horn and had taken a whale.

Rules like this probably contributed to the sheer "islandness" that Nantucketers display, a quirky and cantankerous quality that dictates the island's idiosyncrasies.

Here, the world is divided into two simple camps—"on island," which is Nantucket, and "off island," which is everywhere else.

And that's where everybody else comes from, swelling the population to as many as 50,000 in summer, thronging the streets and filling the restaurants at lunchtime. So locals often partake of a midmorning meal, then splurge on a late dinner after the last of the day-trippers have taken the ferry back to the mainland.

Nantucketers claim all the young people and rock stars go to trendier Martha's Vineyard. "We're happy in Nantucket that they're happy over there," one resident told us.

For more information about Nantucket, contact **Nantucket Island Chamber of Commerce,** Zero Main St., Nantucket, MA 02554 (© **508/228-1700;** www.nantucketchamber.com).

Campground Oases in Connecticut, Massachusetts & New Hampshire

Seaport Campground, Old Mystic, Connecticut. Located 3 miles from Mystic Seaport, the campground has 130 sites. Sites are fairly well spaced, with water and electrical hookups, a sanitary dump, hot showers, flush toilets, a Laundromat, and a playground. Visitors enjoy fishing. High season (June 26–Sept 6) sites $45–$47; off season (Apr 15–June 25 and Sept 7–Oct 31) sites $36–$38. To get there, take exit 90 from I-95 to Rte. 184, at Old Mystic, Connecticut (© **866/617/8464;** www.seaport campground.com).

Scusset State Beach, Sagamore, Massachusetts. The campground has 98 RV sites with 30-amp electric, water hookups, and a sanitary dump for registered guests only. There's a fishing pier, showers, flush toilets, and piped water. No reservations. Year-round. Sites $20–$22. Located at Sagamore on the Cape Cod Canal near the junction of routes 3 and 6 (© **508/888-0859;** www.mass.gov/dcr/parks/southeast/scus.htm).

JACK KEROUAC FESTIVAL

Every year at the end of September, Jack Kerouac's birthplace of Lowell, Massachusetts, celebrates the birthday of the author of *On the Road* (1957) and what he called his "spontaneous prose" about life on the highways of America (**www.lowell celebrateskerouac.org**). Kerouac himself hated that his fame cost him a lack of privacy and fretted that he'd lost the gift of high-speed writing during the 1960s in California. He and his wife returned to Lowell to live with his mother for several years; then he took his family to St. Petersburg, Florida, where he died in 1969 at the age of 47. He's buried in Lowell's Edson Cemetery on Gorham Street.

Atlantic Oaks, Eastham, Massachusetts. Atlantic Oaks has 75 full hookup sites with 30-amp electric, a dump station, and cable TV. Sites are wide for New England. There are some pet restrictions. It's within walking distance of Arnold's Lobster & Clam Bar. High season (June 25–Sept 5) sites $63; off season (May 1–June 24 and Sept 6–Nov 1) sites $53. It's a half-mile north of the entrance to Cape Cod National Seashore on U.S. 6 (© 800/332-2267 or 508/255-1437; www.capecamping.com).

Wompatuck State Park. Southeast of Boston at Hingham, Wompatuck has 260 grassy and shady sites, 138 of them with 20-amp electrical hookups. We stayed there early in the season with few neighbors, but in July and Aug it can get crowded, especially on weekends. Prices are modest, and there are restrooms and showers, a sanitary dump station, and a 14-day camping limit. Sites $14. 1¾ miles on State Rd. 228 to Free St., then 1 mile east to Union St., then south 1½ miles on the marked turnoff (© 781/749-7160; www.mass.gov/dcr/parks/southeast/womp.htm).

Boston Minuteman Campground, Littleton, Massachusetts. This is a good choice if you're towing a car and want a base for jaunts into the surrounding area. You will be close to Concord and Lexington, Salem, Gloucester, Lowell, and Boston. Trust us, you do not want to take a motor home into downtown Boston. There are 83 gravel sites, mostly shaded, with 19 pull-throughs, 30- and 50-amp electric, 52 full hookups, and Internet access. Sites $36–$51. From exit 30 on I-495, go west on Rte. 2A for 2½ miles to the campground (© 877/677-0042; www.minutemancampground.com).

Cape Ann Camp Site. Listed under **Gloucester,** but actually on the Cape Ann Peninsula, the Cape Ann Camp has 100 sites, some with great views of the water. Water and 30- and 50-amp electric are available in all sites, but only 45 also have sewer hookups. There is a dump station. We recommend that anyone with a large motor home or towing a long trailer or fifth-wheel not drive up to the office at the top of the hill, but call and let them send someone to meet you at the entrance, where some of the larger sites are located. Sites $44–$52. Off exit 13 from Rte. 128, take Concord St. for 1 mile; then go right to 80 Atlantic St. (© 978/283-8683; http://capeanncampsite.net).

The Museum of Family Camping

Visit the **Museum of Family Camping** at Bear Brook State Park in Allenstown, New Hampshire, to walk through a free exhibit of the evolution of family camping, from tents and bedrolls to today's modern RVs. The museum is set indoors and out around a pine grove. It's open Memorial Day to Columbus Day daily 10am to 4pm. Free admission, but donations accepted. Allenstown is in Merrimack County on Route 28 between Epsom and Suncook, about 15 minutes from Concord. From the junction of routes 4 and 28 at the Epsom Traffic Circle, drive south 5½ miles on Route 28 to the park entrance, then northeast 1½ miles on Bear Brook State Park Road to the museum (© 603/485-3782; www.ucampnh.com/museum).

Webster Campground. There are 104 sites, 29 of them pull-throughs, with a lot of shade. You'll find 35 30-amp electrical hookups, five full hookups, cable TV, and a modem-friendly office. Apr–Oct. Sites $32–$36. Near Old Sturbridge Village in the Worcester area off exit 10 from the Massachusetts Turnpike, at 106 Douglas Rd., Rt.16. (© **866/562-1896** or 508/943-1895; www.webstercamp.com).

Sodom Mountain Campground. Located in **Southwick, Massachusetts,** Sodom Mountain has 105 spacious, shaded sites with water and electric, and 65 have full hookups. There are also a few teepees with floors where campers can unroll sleeping bags. Early May to mid-Oct. Sites $42–$45. It's located near Springfield, 3 miles west of Rte. 57 from the junction of 57 and routes 10 and 202 (© **413/569-3930;** www.sodommountain.com).

Hampton State Beach. The state of New Hampshire likes RV campers, so you can find a state park right by the ocean in **Hampton**—which not only has 28 sites with full hookups with 20- and 30-amp electric, but also imposes a 3-day minimum stay. There are some pet restrictions. May–Oct. Sites $50. From the junction of I-95 and Rte. 101 (exit 2), go east 3 miles on Rte. 101 to Rte. 1A, then south 2 miles. The entrance is on the left. Call for **information** (© **603/926-3748;** www.nhparks.state. nh.us); or for **reservations** only, call 7 days in advance (© **877/NHPARKS** [647-2757]; www.nhstateparks.org/explore/state-parks/hampton-beach-state-park.aspx).

Tamworth Camping Area. On the edge of Tamworth, New Hampshire, this is a sprawling campground on a family farm, complete with barn and farm animals. Some 100 spaces have secluded, tent-size sites by the Swift River and big-rig sites in an open field. There are 58 sites with water and 15- and 30-amp electrical hookups, and 10 full hookups. Tamworth is a quiet New England village not far from bustling Conway and its factory outlet shopping. Mid-May to mid-Oct. Sites $30–$43. From the junction of highways 25 W. and 16, go north a half-mile on Hwy. 16 to Depot Rd., then west 3 miles. The entrance is on the left (© **800/274-8031** or 603/323-8031; www.tamworthcamping.com).

MOUNT DESERT ISLAND

Maine's Mount Desert Island (pronounced Des-*ert* by some, *Des*-ert by others) is home to most of the serene and scenic Acadia National Park, as well as the overcrowded summer streets of Bar Harbor. Even in August, the climate is fresh and cool.

Landscape painters from the group called the Hudson River School came here in 1844 to paint. They sold the pictures to wealthy Northeast urbanites who traveled to see the places depicted, then in typical robber baron fashion, ended up buying the real estate in their canvases to build elaborate 30-room summer "cottages" patterned after Tudor hunting lodges and Scottish castles.

Most of the grandiose cottages are gone now, victims of a 5-day fire that swept through Bar Harbor in 1947, changing the town's image considerably.

Summer residents of the island, many of them millionaires, were responsible for preserving the 35,000 acres of land in Acadia National Park and handing them over to the government in 1916. John D. Rockefeller, who disliked automobiles and

The Beans of Freeport, Maine (& More)

Freeport, formerly famous as the home of L.L.Bean, has turned into the factory outlet capital of New England, with about 100 shops, including a vast L.L.Bean emporium open 24 hours a day, 365 days a year. There are several RV campgrounds with hookups in the vicinity if you've shopped till it's time to drop (see "Campground Oases in Maine," above). Call for a free visitor guide (© **800/865-1994;** www.freeportusa.com). The main L.L.Bean showroom is on Main Street, and a smaller factory outlet store, adjacent to the town's RV parking lot, is open during regular business hours. 🚐

preferred driving through the parklands in a horse-drawn carriage, commissioned over 50 miles of gravel carriage roads. Today, hikers, bicyclists, and bird-watchers are more in evidence than carriages in summer, and cross-country skiers use the roads in winter. The 27-mile **Park Loop Road** for automobiles is accessible for RVs. Entrance fee $20.

Call **Acadia National Park** for more information about camping and hiking (© **207/288-3338;** www.nps.gov/acad).

Campground Oases in Maine

Saco Old Orchard Beach. This comfortable, centrally located RV park has big wooded sites and a large, heated swimming pool. Belgian waffle and blueberry pancake breakfasts are served on summer weekends, and nightly desserts include blueberry pie. Enjoy a lobster cruise along the coast, along with lots of scenery and nearby shopping. There are 83 sites in a wooded park, more than half of them pull-throughs, with city water and 20- and 30-amp electric, and 50 full hookups. May–Oct. Sites $39–$62. It's off exit 5 from the Maine Turnpike, then exit 2B from I-195 and north 1½ miles (© **800/KOA-1886** [562-1886] or 207/282-0502; www.koa.com).

Saltwater Farm Campground, Cushing. This is an excellent stop for visits to both the Olson House at Cushing and the Farnsworth Art Museum in Rockland. There are 45 sites with 30- and 50-amp electrical hookups, and 35 with full hookups. Visitors enjoy the pool and a dataport for laptops. Mid-May to mid-Oct. Sites $35–$45. From U.S. 1 in Thomaston by the Maine State Prison Craft Store, turn south on Wadsworth St. and travel 1½ miles to the campground on the left (© **207/354-6735;** www. saltwaterfarmcampground.com).

Cedar Haven Campground. In **Freeport** and a tad closer to the shopping, Cedar Haven purports to be the closest campground to L.L.Bean, only 2 miles away. It's also modem-friendly, with 54 30-amp electrical hookups and big-rig capability, 19 full hookups, cable TV, a camp store, and a sanitary dump station. May–Oct. Sites $28–$32. Located at 39 Baker Rd. (© **207/869-5026;** www.cedarhavenfamily campground.com).

Desert Dunes of Maine Campground. Also in **Freeport,** you'll find this campground, with a free shuttle into town (it's 2½ miles from L.L.Bean) so that some family members can go shopping while others hike around the sand dunes. There are 40 sites with water and 20- and 30-amp electrical hookups, 14 full hookups, a sanitary dump, a pool, a store, and a Laundromat. May–Oct. Sites $35–$39. From the junction of I-95 and Desert Rd. (exit 19), go west 2 miles on Desert Rd. The entrance is on the left. Call for reservations (© **207/865-6962;** www.desertofmaine.com).

Mount Desert Narrows Camping Resort. This is a resort-style park on the ocean with some grassy, tree-shaded, fairly spacious sites. There are 189 sites with full and partial hookups. There's a swimming pool, a video-game room, a playground, and a Laundromat, along with hot showers. Maine lobsters are even sold here in July and Aug. Sites $33–$45 May 15–June 14 and early Sept to late Oct; $43–$80 mid-June to Labor Day. On Rte. 3 (Bar Harbor Rd.) in **Bar Harbor** (© **866/917-4300** or 207/288-4782; www.barharborcampingresorts.com).

Blackwoods Campground. This campground has toilets, a sanitary dump, no hookups, and a 14-day maximum stay. Seawall, the park's other campground, is on a first-come, first-served basis. Blackwoods requires advance reservations for its 45 RV sites (no slide-outs). June 15–Sept 15. Sites $20. Located in **Maine's Acadia National Park** (© **207/288-3338;** www.nps.gov/acad).

NOVA SCOTIA'S CAPE BRETON ISLAND

Cape Breton Highlands National Park in the wild and rocky Cape Breton Islands is the northernmost thrust of Nova Scotia into the Atlantic. The poetic headlands are dashed by the surf and softened by morning mists.

A Dollar Is a Dollar

At press time, the Canadian dollar and U.S. dollar were trading at approximately a 1-to-1 value, although that rate will fluctuate. Go to **www.oanda. com** for updates to the currency exchange rate. ▄▆▅

A **184-mile loop** begins at Baddeck, a tranquil seaside village that was the long-time summer home of Alexander Graham Bell, who is buried here. The **Alexander Graham Bell National Historic Park and Museum,** 559 Chebucto St., reveals the inventor's energetic and creative mind, which ranged far beyond the telephone to working with the deaf, early aircraft, and the conversion of seawater to fresh water. Daily 8:30am to 6pm. Admission C$8 adults, C$6.55 seniors, C$3.95 children, C$20 family (© **902/295-2069;** www.capebretonisland.com/agbell.htm).

Take the **Cabot Trail,** Canada Route 105, north of Baddeck in a clockwise direction for easier driving, especially if you begin in the morning, to the cluster of towns named after it along the Margaree River.

Follow the river to the coast and you'll encounter a series of French Acadian villages—**Belle Cote, Terre Noire, St. Joseph du Moine, Grand-Etang**—whose residents still speak the 18th-century French of their Norman ancestors. The Cape Breton Acadians show off their regional cooking and handicrafts at the **Cooperative Artisanale gift shop,** 15067 Main St., Cheticamp. It's open early May to the end of October from 8am to 9pm (© **902/224-2170**). In the restaurant, local women serve chicken *fricot* (Acadian stew), potato pancakes, fish chowder, homemade pies, and gingerbread with syrup. In the crafts shop upstairs, you can browse among the hooked rugs, woodcarvings, hand-knit sweaters, and quilts.

From **Cheticamp,** you enter the park itself with its dazzling vistas of beaches and stark cliffs sculpted by the wind and sea. Except for occasional campgrounds and picnic areas, you'll encounter no habitation until Pleasant Bay. Then, the road turns inland to the sweeping grandeur of the highlands and distant vistas of the churning sea, interspersed with wooded valleys.

Note **Neils Harbour,** bright with colorful, painted houses and fishing boats, lobster pots, and fishnets. Thrifty fishermen usually daub the cottages with whatever paint is left over from the boats.

A few miles south at **Ingonish Beach,** a side road leads to the splendid **Keltic Lodge** (see "10 Splurges," earlier in this chapter; © **800/565-0444;** http://keltic lodge.ca). Moody, mist-clouded **Cape Smoky** lies south of Ingonish Beach, along with Wreck Cove, Skir Dhu (Gaelic for "Black Rock"), and North Shore. From there, you can sometimes see the Bird Islands, a protected nesting area for cormorants, puffins, petrals, and terns. The park's Bog Trail is suitable for wheelchairs.

For more information, contact **Destination Cape Breton,** P.O. Box 1448, Sydney, NS, Canada B1P 6R7 (© **902/563-4636;** www.cbisland.com).

Canadian Maritimes Campgrounds

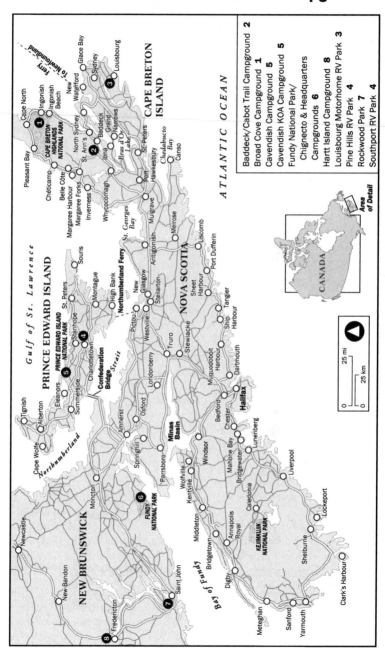

Baddeck/Cabot Trail Campground **2**
Broad Cove Campground **1**
Cavendish Campground **5**
Cavendish KOA Campground **5**
Fundy National Park/
Chignecto & Headquarters
Campgrounds **6**
Hartt Island Campground **8**
Louisbourg Motorhome RV Park **3**
Pine Hills RV Park **4**
Rockwood Park **7**
Southport RV Park **4**

ATLANTIC OCEAN

Area of Detail

CANADA

25 mi

25 km

CAPE BRETON ISLAND

NOVA SCOTIA

PRINCE EDWARD ISLAND

Gulf of St. Lawrence

NEW BRUNSWICK

Bay of Fundy

Fishing boats at White Bay, Cape Breton.

Campground Oases in Canada's Maritimes

Rockwood Park. This 2,200-acre park in the city of **Saint John, New Brunswick,** welcomes RVers with 19 pull-through sites, 180 with water and 30-amp electrical hookups, and 57 full hookups. There's a dump station, flush toilets, showers, picnic tables, and fireplaces. The park, just 5 minutes from central Saint John, makes a good stopover for travelers who enjoy fishing, swimming, a golf course, and a zoo. No reservations. Sites C\$31. Take exit 113 from Hwy. 1 westbound or exit 111 and Rte. 100 eastbound (✆ **506/652-4050;** www.rockwoodpark.ca).

Fundy National Park. Located near Alma, New Brunswick, this park has two campgrounds with hookups and kitchen shelters. **Chignecto Campground** has 127 sites with water and 30- and 50-amp electrical hookups; **Headquarters Campground** has 29 full-hookup sites with 30-amp electric. Sites C\$36. To get to Headquarters, follow Rte. 114 for a half-mile northwest; to get to Chignecto, continue on another 2 miles. Call for **information** (✆ **506/887-6000**) or for **reservations** (✆ **877/RESERVE** [737-3783]; www.pc.gc.ca/pn-np/nb/fundy/index.aspx).

Broad Cove Campground, Ingonish Beach, Nova Scotia. Cape Breton Highlands National Park's Broad Cove Campground has 83 full-hookup sites with 15- and 30-amp electric, along with flush toilets and showers. Visitors enjoy fishing, swimming, and a playground. There's also a fine 18-hole golf course called Highland Golf Links inside the park. No campground reservations. Sites C\$23–C\$34. Located 7 miles north of the East Park entrance on Cabot Trail (© **902/285-2691**; www.pc.gc.ca/pn-np/ns/cbreton/activ/activ.aspx).

Louisbourg Motorhome RV Park. Located in the town of **Louisbourg, Nova Scotia,** near the national historic park, the RV park has 36 full hookups with 15- and 30-amp electric. The park is modem-friendly and has flush toilets, showers, and a sanitary dump. Guests enjoy fishing and the oceanside setting. Mid-May to Oct. Sites C$23–C$30. From the junction of Hwy. 22 and Harbour Front Crescent (in the town center), go northeast 61m (200 ft.) on Harbour Front Crescent. The entrance is on your left. Call for reservations (© **866/733-3631**; www.louisbourg.com/motorhomepark).

The Baddeck/Cabot Trail Campground. At this Good Sam campground, you can leave your RV in camp and take off to drive the Cabot Trail with your car, truck, or a rental vehicle. There are 123 sites with water and 30-amp electric, and 64 full hookups. The campground also allows free fishing on a watery arm of the Bras d'Or Lake, along with access to a major 18-hole golf course. Guests enjoy guided tours of the Cabot Trail. Sites C$30–C$37. Located off Trans-Canada Hwy. 105 at exit 8 or 9 (© **902/295-2288** or 866/404-4199 reservations; www.baddeckcabottrail campground.com).

The Loyalists & the Acadians

By the end of the American Revolution, 40,000 Americans loyal to the British Crown had fled north to Canada. Some 14,000 arrived in what is now New Brunswick, with land grants along the Saint John River given to them by the Crown. In 1785, they incorporated their settlements into the city of Saint John.

Meanwhile, to the south in the pretty village of St. Andrews-by-the-Sea, across the Passamoquody Bay from Maine, other Loyalists put their houses on rafts and towed them over the water to Canada. Kings Landing near Fredericton re-creates a Loyalist community from the early 1800s with costumed interpreters. (See "Living History Sites," earlier in this chapter.)

The Canadian Acadians, in an area of Nova Scotia, New Brunswick, and Maine once called Acadia, are cousins of the Louisiana Cajuns. Descended from French peasant families who were the first European settlers in Canada, the Acadians in 1755 refused to swear allegiance to the British Crown and so were ordered deported. Some fled to other parts of the North Atlantic coast, others south to French-speaking Louisiana. Henry Wadsworth Longfellow dramatized the story in his poem "Evangeline."

Today, the Acadians remaining in Canada continue to speak French and to protect their cultural inheritance. The Acadian Historical Village near Caraquet re-creates their early settlements.

Lighthouse on Campobello Island, New Brunswick.

Hartt Island Campground. The Hartt Island Campground provides 85 campsites with water and 50-amp electrical hookups, and 58 full hookups. Sites C$39. You can go freshwater fishing in the Saint John River or visit King's Landing Historical Settlement. Near the New Brunswick capital of **Fredericton** on Rte. TCH 2 (*©* **866/462-9400** or 506/462-9400; www.harttisland.com).

Cavendish Campground. The **Prince Edward Island National Park** was established to protect sand dunes, beaches, sandstone cliffs, saltwater marshes, freshwater ponds, and cultural and architectural treasures such as the Green Gables farm site and Dalvay-by-the-Sea Hotel. Its newest acquisition is the Greenwich Sand Dune System. Cavendish Campground provides 78 full-hookup sites with 15- and 30-amp electric. Both the park and the campground require a national park personal use permit. Late June to early Sept. Sites C$25–C$33. Off Rte. 6 on Gulf Shore Pkwy. Call for information on permits and camping reservations (*©* **800/213-PARK** or 902/672-6350; www.pc.gc.ca/pn-np/pe/pei-ipe/activ/activ2.aspx).

Cavendish KOA Campground. This KOA has a good central location for Prince Edward Island sightseeing and—good news for big-rig drivers—some 50-amp electrical hookups, as well as a heated swimming pool. There are 215 grassy sites, all with water and 30- and 50-amp electric, and 113 full hookups. Sites C$28–C$45. Located on Rte. 6, near Green Gables, Cavendish Beach, and Rainbow Valley (*©* **800/KOA-1879** [562-1879] or 902/963-2079; www.koa.com).

Anne of Green Gables Sites

Anne of Green Gables, the heroine of a series of books, movies, and television shows, is a cottage industry on Prince Edward Island (PEI), because PEI has taken the unique step of trademarking the name. All summer, *Anne of Green Gables—The Musical* (seats C$35–C$75) is performed in the Mainstage Theatre at the Charlottetown Festival, usually for matinees and evening shows, but occasionally alternating with other shows (box office ✆ **800/565-0278;** http://charlottetownfestival.com).

The Lucy Maud Montgomery Birthplace, New London. This house and antiques shop at the junction of routes 6 and 20 houses Montgomery's wedding dress and other personal mementos; open early May to mid-October. Admission is C$3 adults, C$1 children. Call for information (✆ **902/963-2231**).

Green Gables Post Office and the site of **Lucy Maud Montgomery's home, Cavendish.** The site of the farmhouse where the author was brought up by her strict grandparents is east of the junction of routes 6 and 13. Parking is at the Green Gables Post Office or down the gravel side road at the bookstore. A short walking trail leads to the site from both the post office and the bookstore. (For information, visit www.peisland.com/lmm.)

The Anne of Green Gables Museum at **Silver Bush, Park Corner.** Her aunt and uncle's big white house at the old Campbell homestead is filled with many artifacts. Also at Park Corner on Route 20 is the **Lucy Maud Montgomery Heritage Museum,** displaying family artifacts and items written about in her books. Admission C$5 adults, $1 children. Both museums are open from June to October. Call for information (✆ **800/665-2663** or 902/886-2884; www.annemuseum.com).

Green Gables House, Cavendish. Her cousins' home, which Montgomery used as the setting for her novel, has been extensively restored, with Lovers' Lane and Haunted Wood nearby; off Route 6 just west of Route 13. It's open from mid-May to October. Admission C$8 adults, C$7 seniors, C$4 children, C$20 family. Call for information (✆ **902/672-6350**; www.gov.pe.ca/greengables).

Avonlea, Cavendish. A commercial version of Anne's village of Avonlea (which was based on Cavendish) is populated with costumed characters. Enjoy pony rides, cow milking, fiddling, storytelling, and free tastings of Anne of Green Gables chocolates and raspberry cordials throughout the summer season. Admission C$20 adults, C$18 seniors, C$16 children (✆ **902/963-3050**; www.avonleavillage.com). 🚐

Pine Hills RV Park. Pine Hills has 134 full-hookup sites with 30- and 50-amp electric. There are free daily hayrides and movies, along with a swimming pool and a playground. May–Sept. Sites C$30–C$38. Located btw. **Charlottetown** and Cavendish in Harrington on Rte. 15 (✆ **877/226-2267** or 902/672-2081; www.pinehillsrvpark.com).

Southport RV Park, Stratford, Prince Edward Island. Closest to **Charlottetown,** on the beach, this park overlooks the Hillsborough River and has 41 full hookup sites with 30- and 50-amp electric. Apr–Nov. Sites C$33–C$42. 20 Stratford Rd. (*©* **902/ 569-2287**).

Five Side Trips

1. **Visit Newport, Rhode Island.** Take a detour off I-95 in Rhode Island to U.S. 1 along the coast, then across Rte. 138 and over the spectacular Newport Toll Bridge into the city of Newport. This is where Jackie and Jack Kennedy got married, where Claus von Bulow's trial took place, and where various Vander- bilts, Astors, and Belmonts built 70-room "cottages," many of which are restored and open to the public. (Extra-wide and extra-long RVs and travel trailers should skip the trip into Newport since the streets can be narrow and congested, with limited parking.) Contact the **Newport County Convention and Visitors Bureau,** 22 America's Cup Ave. (*©* **401/849-8048;** www.newport ri.com). From here, it's an easy dash up to **Fall River, Massachusetts,** where Lizzie Borden may or may not have dispatched her parents with an ax. The relics from the trial, including the alleged murder hatchet, are on display at the **Fall River Historical Society** at 451 Rock St. Apr to mid-Nov Tues–Fri 9am– 4:30pm; Sat–Sun 1–5pm (*©* **508/679-1071;** www.lizzieborden.org). Lizzie was acquitted and lived in Fall River until her death in 1927; her home is now a B&B.

2. **Follow the painters through Maine.** Maine's pristine beauty has drawn many artists over the years, including Andrew Wyeth. His famous *Christina's World* was painted at the Olson farm in Cushing, near Rockland. Winslow Homer painted at Prouts Neck, south of Portland, and Edward Hopper's Maine was captured in his lighthouse paintings at Two Lights in Cape Elizabeth. Hopper also painted with fellow artists George Bellows and Rockwell Kent at Monhegan Island; they followed their former teacher Robert Henri there. Boat service to the island is provided by **Hardy Boat Cruises** in **New Harbor;** the round-trip costs $32 adults, $18 children (*©* **800/2-PUFFIN** [278-3346]; www.hardy boat.com). Bear in mind that the trip can be rough. It's said that Winslow Homer got so seasick on the way over that he never got off the boat at Monhe- gan Island, but just turned around and went home. Motor vehicles are prohib- ited on the island.

3. **Visit an FDR summer home.** Take the short detour from Whiting, Maine, up Rte. 89 and across the bridge at Lubec to Campobello Island in Canada, the summer home of Franklin D. Roosevelt. He was vacationing here in 1921 when he was stricken with polio. The garden is magnificent, the house evocative, even poignant, with FDR's austere bedroom. The surrounding countryside has a number of wooded and beachfront walking trails where there's a chance of spotting deer, osprey, eagles, and, below the rocky ledges by the beach, seals.

Herring Cove Provincial Park, with 98 campsites, is on the island; 40 of the sites have 30-amp electrical hookups. Sites $25 (© **506/752-7010**). Take an umbrella if you go walking. Contact **Campobello Park** (© **506/752-2922; www.nps.gov/roca**).

4. **Visit the Acadian shore around northern New Brunswick.** Drive north from Moncton to Shediac, self-proclaimed "Lobster Capital of the World," where you can pick up a crustacean at a stall on the wharf and cook it yourself, or pop into popular **Fisherman's Paradise** for table service. The town's annual lobster festival is in early July. Acadian towns in this region and the **Acadian Historical Museum** restaurants serve unique ethnic dishes like *fricots* (stews) based on potatoes and various kinds of meat. A *poulet fricot* is a chicken stew; *rapure* is a pie with pork and a potato crust. Look for children selling blueberries by the roadsides in summer. Contact **Tourism New Brunswick** (© **800/561-0123; www.tourismnewbrunswick.ca**).

5. **Take the ferry from Hyannis to Martha's Vineyard.** The ferry takes walk-on passengers and their bicycles to Martha's Vineyard, where summer weekends can see as many as 80,000 visitors, with traffic and parking nightmares. Chic shopping and fashionable restaurants give the impression of gentrification, but institutions like the **Black Dog Tavern** by the ferry landing, with its sought-after T-shirts, are still around (© **800/626-1991; www.theblackdog.com**). Bear in mind a couple of Vineyard peculiarities—beaches are privately owned down to the low-tide mark, and Martha's Vineyard is dry except for drinks served at restaurants in Edgartown and Oak Bluffs (you can take your own wine or beer when you're going out to dinner). The traditional ferry round-trip cost is $45 adults, children 5–12 free; the high-speed ferry costs $71 adults, $48 children 5–12 (© **800/492-8082; www.hylinecruises.com**).

Harry & Shirley's RV Buying & Renting Guide

Just as with permanent homes, some people are RV buyers and some are RV renters. This section will provide the information you need for whichever profile you fit.

13 RV Types & Terms

14 To Rent or Buy?

RV Types & Terms

AT THE BEGINNING, WE TOOK SOLEMN OATHS NOT TO REFER TO our motor home as a "rig" (although we're not above calling her "Winnie" for Winnebago—but only in private). We also swore we'd never (a) wear visored caps (although they are handy for keeping sun out of the driver's eyes); (b) display a carved wooden nameplate saying, "Hi, we're Harry and Shirley from L.A."; or (c) refer to ourselves as "pilot" and "copilot," terms we considered unbelievably coy the first time we heard them.

However, like some New Year's resolutions, these proclamations have undergone a bit of change. "Rig" has become "vehicle" (sometimes), and "copilot" is now "navigator." But we still haven't carved out the nameplate.

Just as we had to learn certain technical terms to work as film actors, then pick up a new set of terms as professional travelers, so we've had to adopt certain accepted terms from the RV world in order to correctly describe the vehicles. This chapter gives a few of the terms you'll need to know to get along. More glossary words will turn up in chapter 14, "To Rent or Buy?" as they become necessary. Don't worry about memorizing them yet. All will be revealed, as we say when we're stuck 5 hours in the Beijing airport, or the ship for which we're waiting in Ibiza never arrives, or we're questioned by the Tunisian police, who suspect we're spies because we're carrying cameras.

In the section after the glossary are definitions and descriptions of the major varieties of RVs: **type A motor homes, type B van campers,** and **type C mini–motor homes** (previously called Class A, B, and C), **truck campers, folding camping trailers, travel trailers,** and **fifth-wheel travel trailers.**

The ABCs of RVs: A Glossary of Common RV Terms

Airbag: In RV terms, a sort of shock absorber positioned at the forward and rear axles of a motor home.

Arctic Pack: Also spelled Arctic Pac and Arctic Pak, an optional kit to insulate RVs for winter camping.

Auxiliary battery: Extra battery to run 12-volt equipment.

Basement model: An RV that uses large storage areas under a raised chassis.

Bunkhouse: An RV area containing bunk beds instead of regular beds.

Cab-over: Part of a type C mini–motor home overlapping the top of the vehicle's cab, usually containing a sleeping area, storage, or entertainment center.

Camper shell: Removable unit to fit in the bed of a pickup truck.

Cassette toilet: Toilet with a small holding tank that can be removed from outside the vehicle in order to empty it.

CCC (Cargo Carrying Capacity): The maximum permissible weight of all pets, personal belongings, food, tools, and other supplies you can carry in your motor home. This is the GVWR minus the UVW (see below).

Cockpit: The front of a motorized RV where the pilot (driver) and copilot (navigator) sit.

Coupler: The part of the trailer that hooks to the hitch ball.

Crosswise: A piece of furniture arranged across the RV from side to side rather than front to rear.

Curbside: The side of the RV that would be at the curb when parked.

Curb weight: The weight of an RV unit without water in the holding tanks, but with automotive fluids such as fuel, oil, and radiator coolant.

Diesel pusher: A motor home with a rear diesel engine.

Dry weight or unloaded weight: Manufacturer's weight estimate with no passengers, fuel, water, or supplies.

Entry level: A price deemed attractive for first-time RV buyers.

Garden tub: A bathtub angled into the bathroom so plants can be put on the wide edges against the corner walls.

Gaucho: Sofa/dinette bench that converts into a sleeping unit; a term used less now than formerly.

GAWR (Gross Axle Weight Rating): The maximum permissible weight that can be carried by an axle with weight evenly distributed through the vehicle.

GCWR (Gross Combination Weight Rating): The maximum allowable weight for the combination of vehicle, tow vehicle, passengers, cargo, and all fluids (water, fuel, propane, and so on).

Generator: Small engine fueled by gasoline or propane that produces 110-volt electricity, built into many RVs, but also available as a portable option.

Gooseneck: A colloquial name for fifth-wheel travel trailers.

GTWR (Gross Trailer Weight Rating): The maximum allowable weight of a fully loaded tow vehicle.

GVW (Gross Vehicle Weight): Total weight of a fully equipped and loaded RV with passengers, gas, oil, water, and baggage; must not be greater than the vehicle's GVWR.

GVWR (Gross Vehicle Weight Rating): The amount of total loaded weight a vehicle can support; determined by the manufacturer, this amount must not be exceeded.

> *"Look, Dad, it's got a TV and everything so the driver can watch television!"*
>
> —Child's comment on seeing a van camper at the L.A. RV Show

Hard-sided: RV walls made of aluminum or other hard surface.

High profile: A fifth-wheel trailer with a higher-than-normal front to allow more than 6 feet of standing room inside the raised area.

Hitch: The fastening unit that joins a movable vehicle to the vehicle that pulls it.

Hitch ratings: The maximum amount of weight the hitch can handle—Class I up to 2,000 pounds, Class II up to 3,500 pounds, Class III up to 7,500 pounds, Class IV up to 10,000 pounds, and Class V up to 14,000 pounds. A fifth-wheel hitch can handle up to 25,000 pounds.

Holding tanks: Tanks that retain wastewater when the RV unit is not connected to a sewer. The gray-water tank holds wastewater from the sinks and shower; the black-water tank holds sewage from the toilet.

Inverter: A unit that changes 12-volt direct current to 110-volt alternating current to allow operation of computers, TV sets, and such when an RV is not hooked up to electricity.

Island queen: Not Hawaii's Queen Liliuokalani, but a queen-size bed with walking space on both sides.

Leveling: Positioning the RV in camp so it will be level, using ramps (also called levelers) under the wheels, built-in scissors jacks, or power leveling jacks.

Pop-up: Foldout or raised additions to an RV that add height for standing room.

Porta Potti: Brand name for a portable plastic toilet frequently used in folding camping trailers without facilities.

Self-contained: An RV that needs no external connections to provide short-term cooking, bathing, and heating, and could park overnight anywhere.

Shore cord: The external electrical cord that connects the vehicle to a campground electrical hookup.

Slide-out: A unit that slides open when the RV is parked to expand the living area.

Soft-sides: Telescoping side panels on an RV can be raised or lowered, usually constructed of canvas or vinyl and mesh netting.

Solar panels: Battery chargers that convert sunlight to direct current electricity.

Street side: The part of the vehicle on the street side when parked.

Tail swing: The rear motion of a motor home built on a short chassis with a long rear overhang when the vehicle turns sharply; in simpler terms, the reason we knocked down that road sign when we came out of the driveway.

RV 'RITHMETIC

In addition to the verbiage in this section, you've got to learn a few numbers to talk the RV talk, since most (but not all) RV manufacturers use as model numbers an abbreviated code that can give you basic information about the vehicle—**28 RQ,** for instance, will often mean a 28-foot vehicle with a rear queen bed, and **34 D** may mean a 34-foot diesel pusher.

Folding camping trailer ready for the road.

Telescoping: Compacting from front to back and/or top to bottom to make the living unit smaller for towing and storage.

Three-way refrigerators: Refrigerators that can operate on a 12-volt battery, propane, or 110-volt electrical power.

Tow car: A car towed by an RV to be used as transportation when the RV is parked in a campground; also called a dinghy.

Turning radius: The distance across the diameter of an arc in which a vehicle can turn.

UVW (Unloaded Vehicle Weight): The weight with full fuel, water, LPG (liquid propane gas), driver, and passenger weights.

Wide body: Designs that stretch RVs from the traditional 96-inch width to 100 or 102 inches.

Winterize: To prepare the RV for winter use or storage.

Types of RVs

There are two basic types of recreational vehicles based on locomotion—towable vehicles and motorized vehicles.

Towables, such as folding camping trailers, travel trailers, and fifth-wheel travel trailers, are living units that can stand alone in camp, but are hitched to motor vehicles to travel. Truck campers, compact living units that travel atop the bed and cab of a pickup truck, are also part of the towable team.

Motorized vehicles include motor homes and van campers, both of which are self-contained units built on a truck or van chassis with living, sleeping, cooking, and bathroom facilities accessible from the driver's area without leaving the vehicle. More and more, the dividing line is blurred between van camper and mini–motor home as more compact units fitted with all the necessities for self-contained camping appear on the market. At the present time, however, the type A motor home, the type B van camper, and the type C mini–motor home are still considered three different vehicle categories.

In most models and price ranges, the buyer can choose interior colors and fabrics from samples if the models on the lot are not to his liking.

Gas prices may add to the vacation cost estimates that follow, depending on how much you drive each day and what states you are visiting. Check **www.gasbuddy.com** or another site/app for the cheapest current prices across the country.

TOWABLE RVS
Folding Camping Trailers

Think of it as a modern-day covered wagon, with your own team of oxen or horses already in your garage.

Affordable, open and airy, easy to store and tow, these lightweight units are the closest thing to tent camping, will fit into a carport or garage, and can usually be towed even by compact cars. From a traveling configuration that resembles a small U-Haul trailer, the RV unfolds to standing-room height with collapsible side walls to form two screened, covered wings, each containing a double bed area.

The center section has a solid floor that supports cooking, dining, and lounging areas, some converting to provide even more sleeping space, as well as optional toilet and shower facilities. Some models are equipped with heating and air-conditioning options, and most have a gas cookstove that can be used inside the unit or plugged into outside connections.

Generally the least expensive of the RVs, folding camping trailers are priced from $5,000 to $18,000, and may sleep as many as eight. The average price is around $7,600. Whereas the original units had canvas and/or screen sides, newer models also have the choice of vinyl or even lightweight aluminum hard siding.

Budget-minded families with small children, tent campers who seek a bit more luxury without giving up the canvas-and-campfire ambience, and even veteran RVers seeking a simpler travel lifestyle enjoy these vehicles.

Average Cost of Using a Folding Camping Trailer

The Go Camping America Committee made a study of the costs of a 10-day vacation for a family of four, traveling from Phoenix, Arizona, to Napa, California, in their personal automobile and towing a folding camping trailer. By staying at campgrounds (local average rate of $33 per night) and preparing the majority of their meals, they would save 52% or $2,379 over the same trip taken by car, with hotel stays (averaging $122 per night) and restaurant meals.

Folding Camping Trailers: The Plus Side

- **Ease of towing, with good gas mileage and lower wind resistance.** Even a compact car can handle most, and they can go anywhere the family car can go and can be left behind in camp while the family sets out to explore the area by car.

Erecting a folding camping trailer, Des Moines KOA campground.

- **Economical to purchase and operate.** These units offer many options found in more expensive RVs, such as air-conditioning, heating, bathroom facilities, three-way refrigerators, awnings, and roof racks that can carry boats or bicycles atop the folded unit. Naturally, the more options added, the more expensive the unit is.

- **Easy to store.** Garage or carport storage capability of these small units eliminates the potential problems created by larger RVs. Folded, they measure from 5 to 19 feet long and are usually less than 5 feet high.

Folding Camping Trailers: The Minus Side
- **Not always convenient.** Most folding camping trailers use a hand-cranked system for raising and lowering, simple enough when the operator is fit and the weather nice, but not always pleasant in the rain when you're trying to keep the wing mattresses dry.

- **Limited on-road access to stored items.** The unit is not usable when underway unless you crank it open at rest stops. Some models have front storage units that are accessible when the unit is folded if you want to get to picnic items, toys, or bicycles. Access to kitchen and toilet facilities is available only when the rig is set up.

- **May mildew if left wet.** If a canvas unit is closed when wet, it has to be unfolded at home and dried out completely before storing or it can mildew. Vinyl units can simply be wiped dry.

• **Limited toilet facilities.** Some models do not have toilet or shower facilities or offer them only as an option. Most have a storage area for a portable toilet that must be emptied manually. When you're camping in areas that have public toilets and showers, it won't be a problem, but self-contained camping is not feasible.

Truck Campers

For people who own a pickup truck, the easiest and least expensive RV addition might be a truck camper—a unit that slides onto the bed of a pickup, sometimes overhanging the cab or the rear of the vehicle. Most models sleep two to six people and cost between $4,000 and $26,000, with the average price around $14,490. Since the unit is slid on and off, the truck continues to be useful as a hauling and transportation vehicle without the camper.

Sportsmen particularly like the rugged outdoorsy capability of truck campers because they can remove the camper and set it up in camp, then use the truck to go to and from the ski area, fishing hole, or trail head. It is also possible to tow a boat, snowmobile, horse trailer, or jet skis behind a truck camper, something not permitted with other towables.

Low-profile pop-up models are available, as well as units that have optional electrical systems to load and unload the camper from the truck bed. They are often equipped with a bathroom and kitchen.

Units range from 7 to 18 feet long, with a cab-over bed extending over the pickup's cab. Sofa or dinette built-ins may convert to form a second sleeping area, but

Truck camper.

these are usually fairly short beds. A step leads from the lower floor area up to the cab-over bed.

Buyers of truck campers should plan to spend extra time matching camper to pickup. Some dealers may not be conversant with the details that make the combination work, so it is essential to be sure the camper's weight is compatible with the truck carrying it. If an additional vehicle is being towed, the GCWR (Gross Combination Weight Rating) must also be considered.

Average Cost of Using a Truck Camper

On a cost comparison survey, a family of four with a light-duty truck and truck camper on a 10-day tour, who stay in campgrounds and prepare most of their meals at campsites, will save $2,054 over a family traveling by car, staying in hotels, and eating in restaurants.

Truck Campers: The Plus Side

- **Economical.** Cheaper to buy, maintain, and operate than most other towables, with better gas mileage.

- **Versatile.** The camper unit can be removed and stored at home or set in place at the campground, and the truck kept separately. With a self-contained camper and a 4WD truck, you can go almost anywhere.

- **Durable.** Most models are made to endure tougher road conditions than other towables.

- **Passenger convenience.** In most states (except Maine, Mississippi, New Hampshire, New Mexico, North Dakota, Pennsylvania, and Wisconsin), passengers are permitted to ride inside a truck camper. California permits passengers to ride inside only if there is communication possible with the driver and if the door can be opened from inside and outside. Several areas in Canada (Newfoundland/Labrador, Nova Scotia, Saskatchewan, and the Yukon) do not permit passengers to ride inside a truck camper.

Truck Campers: The Minus Side

- **Floor space is limited inside.** There's inadequate room for two adults to move around freely at the same time. However, some newer models have slide-outs to expand the living area.

- **Hard to handle.** Weight distribution and a higher center of gravity often mean more difficulty in handling these units on the road.

Travel Trailers

Vans, autos, or pickup trucks can tow these soft- or hard-sided RVs, depending on their weight. They sleep from two to eight people and usually contain full bathroom and kitchen facilities. They range from 10 to 40 feet long.

Models come in a traditional box shape, an aerodynamic or teardrop shape, and as a hard-sided telescoping travel trailer that can be lowered for towing and storage and

Exterior of a travel trailer.

raised for campground living. Prices range from $8,000 to $76,000, with an average cost of around $15,700.

"Slide-outs" that are expanded at the campsite to add more walking-around room have greatly enhanced the comfort of travel trailers and fifth-wheels. Some models may have as many as four slide-outs. There are, however, some campgrounds that prohibit RVs using slide-outs.

Travel trailers often have two doors with a sofa and dinette slide-out area, which could be made into a second sleeping area. Sometimes the bathroom is split into two sides, and both linoleum and carpet are used on the floors, the former in the kitchen and bathroom, the latter in the bedroom and living room.

Average Cost of Using a Travel Trailer

A family of four traveling on a 3-day getaway, in their car or light truck, towing a travel trailer and staying in campgrounds where they prepare most of their meals, will save $323 or 31% over the same trip via car.

Travel Trailers: The Plus Side

- **Easy to unhitch.** Travel trailers can be unhitched at the campsite, releasing the tow vehicle for local errands and touring.

- **Large selection of interiors.** Travel trailers come in a wide variety of floor plans, with homelike furniture, full kitchens, and bathrooms. Many models have two doors, and some have a forward bedroom and rear bunkhouse design to sleep the whole family without converting other furniture into beds.

- **Can be pulled by most vehicles.** Today's travel trailers take a greater variety of towing options, including 4X4s, light trucks, full and midsize cars, station wagons, and minivans.

Travel Trailers: The Minus Side

- **Can be hard to handle.** Some drivers find handling a travel trailer, especially when backing up, takes extra skill right from the beginning.

- **Not always convenient and economical.** Wind resistance is greater with travel trailers, and hitching or unhitching can be a nuisance in bad weather.

- **Will cost you more in tolls.** For both travel trailers and fifth-wheels, road tolls based on axles will be higher.

Fifth-Wheel Travel Trailers

These are the most luxurious of the towables, popular with full-timers and snowbirds who cite the ease of maneuvering and towing, the generous storage areas, large living space, and homelike design. The raised forward section that fits over the truck bed allows a split-level design. This area is usually a bedroom and bathroom, but is sometimes a living room or kitchen/dining area instead. By the time basement storage and slide-outs are added, a fifth-wheel is comparable in comfort to a condo or a home in the suburbs.

There are numerous bedroom options, as well as living, dining, and bathroom choices, in a 36-foot fifth-wheel. The slide-out contains a sofa and dining-room

Interior of a travel trailer.

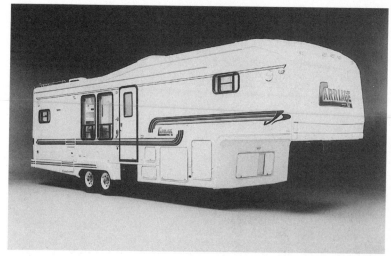

Exterior of a fifth-wheel.

furniture, while a second optional slide-out in the bedroom area can add more room there. There's often space for a washer/dryer, bedroom TV, entertainment center, and large sitting area.

Fifth-wheels sell from $13,000 to $102,000 and up, with an average cost of around $35,500. They are from 22 to 40 feet long.

Average Cost of Using a Fifth-Wheel

For average expenditures on vacations, see "Travel Trailers," above.

Fifth-Wheels: The Plus Side

- **Maneuverability and towability.** These are major assets; fifth-wheels are easier to handle than a travel trailer because the hitch is in the bed of the truck, with less vehicle trailing behind. This also creates a shorter turning radius.

- **Easy to unhitch.** Like the other towables, the fifth-wheel can be unhitched and left at the campsite while the truck is available for touring or shopping in the area.

- **Allows storage in your pickup.** The truck bed can still be used for storage with the addition of a pickup bed cover.

Fifth-Wheels: The Minus Side

- **Can't carry passengers on the road.** Because a truck is the obligatory tow vehicle and passengers are not permitted to ride in the fifth-wheel in 29 states and eight Canadian provinces, large families might find them inconvenient for long trips.

Interior of a fifth-wheel.

- **Limited headroom.** In many forward bedroom models, except those labeled "high profile," there is not quite enough headroom for anyone over 6 feet tall to stand up straight.

- **No entry from towing vehicle.** As with all towables, you have to exit the towing vehicle and go outdoors to enter the RV, an inconvenience in bad weather.

MOTORIZED RVS
Type B Van Campers

Also called type B motor homes, these conversions are built within the framework of a van, but with raised roofs or lowered floor sections to allow passengers to stand upright, at least in the center of the vehicle. Galleys, freshwater hookups, sleeping and dining areas that convert to beds, even toilets and showers are readily available in these versatile vehicles.

Ranging from 18 to 22 feet in length, van campers sell from $42,000 to $74,000 (on the upper end comparable in price to an entry-level motor home), with an average cost of around $58,500. Most sleep two to four people, but also can carry four to six adults as a weekday commuter vehicle. They typically sleep four people, two in the overhead bunk and two on the convertible sofa. A drop-in table fits in front of the sofa for dining.

One enterprising man we met at the Los Angeles RV show was buying a camper van with four swivel passenger seats to use on weekend family trips, but hoped to pay for it by carrying weekday commuters who appreciate having a toilet, microwave, and TV set on the daily run.

Custom van conversions are available from a number of manufacturers at an average price of about $28,500. For a list of manufacturers that make van conversions, contact **RVIA,** P.O. Box 2999, Reston, VA 22090 (© **703/620-6003;** www.rvia.org).

Average Cost of Using a Van Camper

A family of four using their own van camper or van conversion, staying in campgrounds, and preparing all their meals in camp, spends an average of $615 for 3 days; $1,350 for 7 days; and $2,837 for 14 days.

Van Campers: The Plus Side

- **Multipurpose use.** These RVs double as a second car to use around town or for carpooling.

- **Easy to drive, with good gas mileage.** Van campers can go anywhere a passenger car can, including areas in national parks where larger RVs may be restricted.

- **Cozy (the good kind).** Self-contained van campers mean there's no need to leave the vehicle to use any of the facilities.

- **Easy to park.** Unlike other motorized or towable RVs, the camping van can fit into almost any spot left in a campground, so it's good for TGIF getaways and late arrivals.

Van Campers: The Minus Side

- **Cozy (the bad kind).** While most van campers can sleep four people, they'd have to be very good friends or, more likely, a couple with one or two small

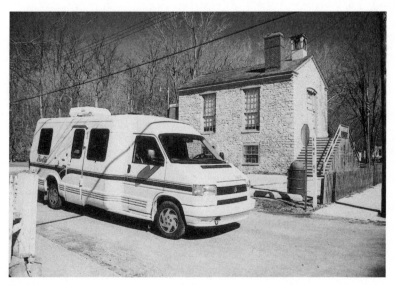

Rialta van camper.

Exterior of mini–motor home.

children. The living area is extremely compact for a family spending a rainy day inside.

• **Susceptible to wear and tear.** Because a van camper doubles as a second car, the greater mileage accrued by the time you want to sell it could make it harder to sell or trade than a larger motor home.

• **Not always easy to set up.** Making up some of the optional beds in these vans could knock your back out—even before you lie down.

• **Limited storage space.** You'll have to carry fewer clothes and supplies than in other RVs, meaning more frequent laundry and grocery stops. Also, the mini-fridge may not have a freezer.

Type C Mini–Motor Homes

Familiar, convenient, and affordable, the type C (think cab-over bed) motor home packs a lot of living in a compact space. Also called mini–motor homes, the units are built on a truck or van chassis, and usually range in length from 19 to 31 feet. Wide-body designs up to 8½ feet across and diesel engine options are available, as well as low-profile models that can be telescoped for travel and storage to less than 8 feet high. Type Cs are priced from $48,000 to $140,000 or more, with the average price around $63,000. Some models offer slide-outs that increase the usable living space.

Normally, a cab-over bed is above the driver's seat, while a sofa provides additional sleeping space. A dinette, rear galley, and bathroom complete the interior. In some models, the cab-over may be turned into an entertainment center with a double bed in back and dining on a drop-in table by the sofa.

INSIDER TIP

Despite its generally smaller size, in our experience, the type C gets no better gas mileage than a small type A, except in the models constructed of extra-lightweight materials.

Average Cost of Using a Type C Mini–Motor Home

A family of four people traveling on a 10-day journey in their own motor home, staying in campgrounds and preparing most of their meals in camp, will save $1,704 or 37% over a similar trip in a car, staying in hotels and eating in restaurants.

Mini–Motor Homes: The Plus Side

- **Easy to drive.** Type Cs are more maneuverable for beginning RV drivers than most type A motor homes.

- **Comfortable and compact.** Mini–motor homes are as livable as larger motor homes, but take up less parking and campground space.

Mini–Motor Homes: The Minus Side

- **So-so sleeping accommodations.** The cab-over bed is not appealing for claustrophobic adults, but kids love it. In general terms, the sleeping accommodations,

Interior of mini–motor home with entertainment area replacing cab-over bed.

except where there is a rear bedroom, are less private than in the type A motor homes when more than two people are traveling together.

- **Limited driving visibility.** Because of the overhang from the "cab-over" bed, visibility is limited to a normal-size windshield, while most type A motor homes provide larger windshields.

Type A Motor Homes

A self-propelled motor vehicle chassis with a living unit built on it, the type A motor home offers the widest range of choices in the RV fleet—from small, 22-foot, fully equipped entry-level vehicles to enormous, 45-foot, buslike wide-body coaches with slide-outs, ice makers, washer/dryers, beautiful furnishings, and marble bathrooms. They're priced from $58,000 up to $1,400,000 for the most deluxe models, with the average around $190,000.

Decor can vary from the old-fashioned but tough velour fabrics in slate blue or green in the lower-priced vehicles to Bluebird Wanderlodge's cushy white leather furniture, with brass trim, parquet floors, and sculpted area rugs.

A standard entry-level 28-foot model will contain cockpit seats that swivel; the choice of a sofa with drop-in tables or a dinette, either of which can be made into a bed; a bathroom; and a rear island queen-size bed with an option of twin beds.

Average Cost of Using a Type A Motor Home

A family of four using their own motorhome, staying in campgrounds and preparing all their meals in camp, spends an average of $1,512 for 3 days; $3,490 for 7 days; and $7,038 for 14 days.

Exterior of type A motor home.

Interior of a type A motor home.

Type A Motor Homes: The Plus Side

- **Always accessible from the front seats without going outside.** The type A motor home lets you pull over to fix lunch, use the bathroom, or take a quick nap by the side of the road or in a parking lot.

- **Bigger windshield and windows than type C.** You'll have greater visibility when traveling and better vantage points for photographs.

- **Livability.** A big, open sense of space and luxury makes the type A the most livable of the motorized RVs for most people.

- **No setup required.** In most type As, all the living areas are ready for two people, without any additional conversion. (For sleeping more than two, however, a sofa or dinette usually has to be made up.)

Type A Motor Homes: The Minus Side

- **It's your only wheels.** Unless you're towing a car, a type A has to be unplugged and moved anytime you need to go out shopping or sightseeing away from the campground.

- **Tough to maneuver.** The larger type A motor homes can present maneuvering problems in narrow city streets with heavy traffic, as well as parking problems almost everywhere, except mall and supermarket parking lots. When street parking is feasible, remember that you'll have to feed 2 or even 3 meters instead of one. Height and width limitations prohibit entering most parking garages and can present problems in clearing low overhanging roofs and narrow tunnels or bridges.

- **Low mileage.** Gas mileage is quite low, usually under 10 miles to the gallon.

- **Sometimes too big for parks and campgrounds.** Choosing a size to match your travel style is critical, since larger units cannot be accommodated in some campgrounds and are not permitted to enter certain narrow or winding roadways in national parks such as Glacier, Big Bend, and Zion.

10 QUESTIONS TO ASK YOURSELF WHEN SELECTING AN RV

1. **How often will I use the vehicle?** Some RV owners in cold climates have to winterize and store the RV, while others use it year-round. If you think you may use it only once a year for a 2-week family vacation, it might be cheaper to rent rather than buy.

2. **Where will I store the vehicle?** City dwellers have to rent storage space because there's nowhere to store their motor home on their property. But even suburbanites may face parking regulations that preclude keeping an RV in the driveway or on the street. Owners with a large garage might consider folding camping trailers, truck campers, or telescoping travel trailers that are compact enough to store inside. Some travelers who like to visit the same park or campground year after year might want to store the vehicle permanently at the vacation location.

3. **Do I already have part of an RV unit?** If you have a pickup, for example, depending on its size, you're already capable of handling a towable, such as a travel trailer, truck camper, or fifth-wheel. Most family cars can pull a small travel trailer or folding camping trailer.

4. **How much money can I spend?** Those on a budget and young families often begin by buying an entry-level RV in whichever category they want. With sticker shock a strong factor these days, more and more manufacturers are offering lower-priced models in all categories. Previous RV owners often, but not always, look to buy a larger, newer, more expensive model. A few choose to downgrade for a simpler travel lifestyle. In many cases, interest paid on your loan to purchase an RV is tax-deductible since the RV is considered a second home.

5. **How many people does the RV need to accommodate on a routine trip?** There's a big difference between a salesman's estimate of how many people a vehicle can sleep and the reality of the number it can comfortably accommodate. Some people dislike the idea of making a bed out of a sofa or dinette night after night during a vacation. Others don't want someone climbing over them in the middle of the night to go to the bathroom. A major consideration is how many seat belts are in the vehicle if it's a motorized RV. All states but New Hampshire now require that all passengers in the vehicle be secured by seat belts, and will not authorize more passengers than there are seat belts provided.

6. **How will I be using the vehicle?** People who like to stay in one place, such as a private campground with swimming pools and putting greens, will want a more luxurious vehicle than campers who want to go out in the woods in a national park or forest, build a campfire, and cook outdoors. Travelers who want to stop at a different campground every night need to give priority to the ease of setting up camp and fuel efficiency. Snowbirds who want to stay cheaply all winter on BLM desert lands or other self-contained camping should look for vehicles with greater capacity in water storage and holding tanks.

7. **Which is more important, generous living space in the vehicle or more flexible handling, parking, and roadway options?** In making a decision on vehicle size, 1 foot in length or 4 inches in width can make a tremendous difference. Spend a lot of time mentally moving around in the floor plan, or even physically moving around in the vehicle at the dealer's or the RV show, to assess its livability. Know your size requirements before setting out to look at vehicles, especially if you're considering a motor home; you'll save a lot of time on the lot.

8. **How important is personal privacy?** Some types of RVs have more solid-door privacy areas than others. In particular, the shower and toilet facilities in folding camping trailers or camping vans, when they are provided at all, may allow minimum privacy. Travel trailers, fifth-wheels, motor homes, and some truck campers provide facilities in a completely closed-off area. Sleeping facilities, as well, may be open or shielded with curtains rather than doors, as in many folding camping trailers, truck campers, and even type C mini–motor homes.

9. **What kind of fuel do I want the vehicle to burn, gasoline or diesel?** The consensus is that diesel engines cost more on initial purchase, but less in the long run to operate. One disgruntled RVer, however, has gone on record complaining about the high cost of oil and filters for diesel engines. Diesel engines usually seem quieter in the cockpit than gasoline engines, because they are positioned in the rear of the vehicle.

10. **Will I be happy with a standard "off-the-rack" model RV, or do I want some special features and options?** Manufacturers are coming up with new "toys" and gimmicks for today's younger market. Hi-tech elements such as computer stations, satellite dishes, and electronic navigational systems have joined the rearview cameras and slide-outs as common optional equipment. Other design elements include slide-out patios, retractable sunroofs, roof patios, beds stored under the floor that can pop up at bedtime, voice-controlled lighting, and eye-controlled outside mirrors that can be adjusted just by looking at them.

14

To Rent or Buy?

FOR A FIRST-TIME RV TRAVELER, RENTING A UNIT OF THE SAME type that you're considering buying can be an invaluable help in making up your mind. Just be sure to allow enough time—1 week is the minimum, 2 weeks is better—to get comfortable with the day-to-day logistics of handling it on the road and hooking it up.

Our first RV experience was a 6-week lease on a 27-foot motor home needed for a book assignment that required us to visit more than 100 remote ski areas. If we'd been renting it for only a few days, we'd probably have turned it back in and said RVing was not for us. (See chapter 1, "Life on the Road: A Personal & Public History of RVing.")

When they heard about our plans, well-meaning friends regaled us with their experiences. A West Los Angeles bookstore owner took her family out for a month, but they used the RV only for travel and sleeping. "We never cooked a single meal inside," she said. "It seemed too complicated."

A couple from San Diego had tried a rented motor home for 2 days, then, frustrated by slow road speeds, turned it back in and set out in their Mercedes 300 SL instead.

But even that's a record compared to a short-tempered lawyer and his wife, who rented an RV for a weekend and gave it up less than an hour into the trip.

Note that none of these users gave the vehicle the old college try.

Two Ways to Check Out Campground Life Without an RV

1. **Check into a Kamping Kabin or Kamping Kottage at a nearby KOA (Kampgrounds of America) campground.** Kamping Kabins, one- and two-room rustic log cabins and small lodges with porches and double beds plus bunk beds, can sleep from two to six people at $45 to $150 a night. Kamping Kottages provide a kitchenette, dining area, bathroom with shower, and sleeping quarters for four, with a porch swing and sometimes fireplaces and air conditioners. It's a good introduction to camping, especially for families with kids. The fee includes use of the campground's toilet and shower facilities, pool, playground, Laundromat, and store. The Kabins do not have bathrooms, but an

INSIDER TIP: PLAN AHEAD

Reserve a rental RV *at least* a month in advance, 3 months during peak vacation time. If planning to rent in Alaska, reserve 6 to 12 months ahead.

outdoor grill and picnic table are provided. You need to bring your own bedding, lantern, and cooking utensils. Get a full list of locations from KOA, free at any KOA campground or by sending $6 (for S&H) to KOA Directory, P.O. Box 30558, Billings, MT 59114. You can also call the administrative offices (© **888/562-0000;** http://koa.com/lodges-cabins-cottages).

2. **Call around to the campgrounds in your area or the area you'd like to visit and ask if they have any rental RV units.** Sometimes a popular area may offer RVs already in place, hooked up and available for rent by the night. See "The Best Campground Directories," in chapter 3, "Where to Sleep: Campgrounds & RV Parks," for a listing of campground guides.

Renting

WHEN TO RENT RATHER THAN BUY

- **When setting out on your very first RV journey.**
- **When considering replacing your current RV with a different type.**
- **When your family can only take a 2-week vacation once a year, but wants to do it in an RV.** That way, you can test-drive different models, and if/when you decide to buy, you'll have plenty of experience.
- **When you want to travel several weeks far from home**—say, in a distant part of the United States—or take a camping trip in Europe. Popular fly-and-drive packages are available from many companies.
- **When you want to drive the Alaska Highway** (see chapter 6, "Driving the Alaska Highway") in one direction only and/or without subjecting your own vehicle to inescapable wear and tear.

WHERE & HOW TO RENT

A great many rental RVs are booked by European and Australian visitors to the United States who want to see our national parks or drive along the coast of California.

The most common unit available for rental is the **motor home,** either the larger type A or the type C mini–motor home, which accounts for 90% of all rentals. Prices begin at around $975 a week.

Use of the generator is not usually included in the fee. You would need it only for operating the ceiling air-conditioning, microwave, and TV in a place without electrical hookups. The dealer will know how much time you've logged by reading the generator counter, usually located by the on/off switch.

When you find a company that rents travel trailers, you'll find they usually require that you furnish your own tow vehicle, hitch, and electrical hookups on the tow vehicle.

Some companies offer a furnishings package with bedding, towels, dishes, cooking pots, and utensils for a flat price of around $100 for kitchen needs and $50 for bedding per trip. Other add-on kits are those containing power cords and hoses, plastic trash bags, toilet chemicals, and a troubleshooting guide.

Be sure you're provided with a full set of instruction booklets and emergency phone numbers in case of a breakdown. The best thing to have is a 24-hour emergency toll-free number in case of a problem.

When in doubt, ask fellow RVers what to do. They're always glad to help, but sometimes hesitant to offer for fear of offending. No matter how much you bustle around like you know what you're doing, the veterans in the campground can spot a goof-up a mile away.

Before setting out, be sure the dealer demonstrates all the components and systems of your unit. Take careful notes and, just as with rental cars, check for dents and damage from prior use before leaving the lot.

To find information about RV rental companies all over the United States and Canada, check out the website of **Recreation Vehicle Rental Association (RVRA;** ℂ **888/467-8464** or 703/591-7130; www.rvra.org). You'll find a directory with addresses, phone numbers, and prices for European, Canadian, and U.S. companies listed by city and state or province. There is also a companion page, **Rental Ventures,** with additional helpful information. Write to RVRA, 3930 University Dr., Fairfax, VA 22030-2525.

Cruise America, the largest rental company in the U.S., with more than 120 outlets, has added budget items such as camping vans, fully equipped travel trailers, and fold-out truck campers with compact pickups to tow them. It answers the requests from European campers in America, who are responsible for one-half to two-thirds of the company's rentals. Rentals will range from $800 to $6,350 a week. 11 West Hampton Ave., Mesa, AZ 85250 (ℂ **800/671-8042** or 480/464-7300; www.cruiseamerica.com).

INSIDER TIP: KNOWING WHAT TO BRING

Get a detailed list of what furnishings are included in your rental so you'll know what necessary items you have to supply. It may be easier to bring things from home than to spend vacation time searching for them on the road.

Adventure Rentals in Ontario, California, claims to have the largest trailer rental department in the United States, offering folding camping trailers from $520 a week and travel trailers from $775 a week. No rentals are made to anyone under 25. Renters supply a tow vehicle, hitch and electrical connections, bedding, and utensils. A cleaning deposit of $45 is required and forfeited if the vehicle is not returned clean; the company has its own dump stations for holding tanks. 1200 W. Mission Blvd., Ontario, CA 91762 (✆ **909/983-2567;** www.adventurerentals.net).

Altman's Winnebago in Carson, California, has type A and type C new motor homes for rent. A typical rental charge for a small type C motor home would be around $1,000 to $1,500 a week. Rental of a type A motor home would run around $1,988 a week. Additional charges would be $15 a day for insurance, with optional charges for a kitchen kit (pots, dishes, glasses; $99 per trip) and a bedroom kit (bedding and towels; $26 per person per trip; 22002 Recreation Rd.; ✆ **888/820-0800** or 310/518-6182; www.altmans.com).

Many rental companies offer **free airport pickup and return,** if you notify them ahead of time of your flight number and estimated arrival time.

Finally, if you fall in love with your rental vehicle (as we did our first one), you might be able to negotiate a purchase price that would subtract your rental fee from the total. If the vehicle is a couple of years old, the price should be even lower, since most dealers get rid of vehicles after 2 or 3 years.

One source for **low-priced used RVs** is **Cruise America's RV Depots,** lots that sell previously rented units at discounted prices, along with a 12-month, 12,000-mile warranty and free emergency road assistance for a year. Call and ask for national fleet sales (✆ **800/327-7799**).

FIVE MONEY-SAVING RENTAL TIPS

1. **Check prices with several companies before making a decision.** Establish exactly what the lowest-price rental will include, such as free miles, amenities like dishes and linens, and breakdown service.

2. **Try to plan your trip for shoulder seasons or off season.** This may vary seasonally, depending on the rental area, but if you're not on the road when everyone else is, you should see a drop in the weekly rental price.

3. **Check in advance to see if your own automobile insurance agent will cover your rental insurance.** They can usually do it more cheaply than the rental company.

INSIDER TIP: ENSURE YOU'RE INSURED

Normally, **insurance on a rental RV** is not covered on your personal automobile insurance, so ask your agent for a binder that extends your coverage to the RV for the full rental period. Many dealers require the binder before renting you a vehicle.

INSIDER TIP: BE PREPARED

Read through your instruction sheets and checklists at least once before setting out, then daily before hooking up and unhooking until you know the whole routine. Otherwise, you may—as we did that first time—drive miles out of your way to an RV dealer to find out why your generator doesn't work, only to learn it never works when your gas level drops below one-quarter of a tank.

4. **Try to plan a loop trip from the area where the rental unit is based to avoid drop-off charges.** An exception is on long, major journeys such as Alaska or Baja California, when you might want to pay the drop-off charge and fly back, rather than repeat the arduous drive back to the beginning.

5. **Negotiate based on selection.** The more units a company has, the wider your choice, but if you're flexible about what sort of rig you rent, you may be able to negotiate a better price if the selection is limited.

NINE BIG RENTAL COMPANIES

1. **Cruise America,** 4,000 units nationwide (© **800/327-7799;** www.cruise america.com).

2. **El Monte RV Center,** 950 units nationwide (© **888/337-2214;** www.elmonte rv.com).

3. **Adventure Rentals,** 26 units in Ontario, California (© **909/983-2567;** www. adventurerentals.net).

4. **Moturis, Inc.,** 300 units in Hawthorne, California, near LAX; 400 units in San Francisco and other cities in the United States (© **866/688-8772;** www. moturis.com).

5. **Road Bear Intl.,** 100 units in Agoura Hills, California; also in San Francisco, Las Vegas, Denver, and New York City (© **866/491-9853;** www.roadbearrv.com).

6. **Nolan's RV Center,** 120 units in Denver, Colorado (© **800/232-8989;** www. nolans.com).

7. **Western Motor Coach,** 95 units in Lynnwood, Washington (© **866/794-4540;** www.westernrv.com).

8. **Altman's Winnebago,** 45 units in Carson, California, near LAX (© **888/820-0800** or 310/518-6182; www.altmans.com).

9. **Vintage Surfari Wagons,** fleet of seven classic Volkswagen camper buses for touring the western United States, $106 per day, $725 per week, in Costa Mesa, California (© **949/716-3135;** www.vwsurfari.com).

INSIDER TIP

Just as with car rentals, be sure to establish how many free miles you get and what the cost per mile is beyond that limit.

Buying

SHOPPING AT RV SHOWS

Dozens of national and regional RV shows are held annually, most during the winter months. They make especially safe hunting grounds for three types of people: looky-loos who have no idea what they want, but are not about to succumb to the first smooth-talking salesman they encounter; well-researched potential buyers who know exactly what they want and are ready to make a deal; and RV owners who want to see the latest technical and design innovations, but are basically happy with their existing rigs.

The action gets hot and heavy during the last day or two of a show, when it's possible to stumble across an offer you can't refuse. On the other hand, if you're susceptible to super salesmen, tread carefully or you may be driving a brand-new rig home from the show.

Besides acres of new RVs to explore, a show usually presents seminars on how to "full-time" or where to travel, along with a bazaar of esoteric gadgets from no-snore pillows to salad-makers (as well as a lot of helpful and practical items), and entertainment from Dixieland or country music musicians to a walk-through virtual-reality module.

For a free listing of RV shows, contact the **Recreation Vehicle Industry Association (RVIA),** 1896 Preston White Dr., Reston, VA 20195 (© **703/620-6003;** www. gorving.com or www.rvia.org), or watch your local newspapers for a show in your area.

SHOPPING AT RV DEALERS

Start visiting local RV dealers and spend an afternoon walking the lot looking at types of vehicles and mentally moving into them. The dealer can give you a brochure to take home and study, with specific details about all the vehicle's features, along with floor plans.

Every dealer has a number of previously owned vehicles taken in as trade-ins, or RVs it is brokering for the owners. You can figure that the used vehicle could be one-third to half the price of a new model. Purchasing from a reputable dealer increases the chance that the RV will be in good condition and gives you someplace to return if there's a problem.

Don't worry about taking up time if you're not ready to buy yet. Sooner or later you will be, and dealers are accustomed to the allure of a new and unfamiliar RV both to wannabe and veteran owners.

Expect the best buys in December and January, when dealers want to get the previous year's models off the lot to make room for the new year's models. Get on their mailing list for any sales they may have in the future.

WHERE *NOT* TO SHOP FOR AN RV

Avoid parking-lot and campground "distress" sellers who give you a spiel about bad luck and a desperate need for cash. A nationwide group of con artists who call themselves "Travelers" make a big profit selling cheaply made travel trailers, which also serve as living quarters and office headquarters for numerous other scams.

Be extremely careful buying from any private party unless you know a great deal about the RV you're considering and can make a clear-eyed evaluation of it before signing the deal. If it looks beat up and shows wear inside and out, walk away. Chances are, if the owner has treated the superficial areas badly, the systems you can't see are also flawed. Remember, with motorized vehicles, you're buying both a used car and a used house.

RV PRICES

Prices (entry, midrange, upscale, and luxury) vary according to the type of RV. Motor homes range from $58,000 at entry level to $1,000,000 and up for luxury. Type C mini–motor homes range from $48,000 to $140,000; fifth-wheels $13,000 to $102,000; travel trailers $8,000 to $76,000; van campers $42,000 to $74,000; truck campers $4,000 to $26,000; and folding camping trailers $5,000 to $18,000.

FINANCING

Because RV buyers are generally considered more reliable for a loan than car buyers (only 1.4% of all RV loans are delinquent), loans are easier to get. Check with banks, savings and loan associations, finance companies, credit unions, or the RV dealer. Loans for big new RVs typically range from 10 to 12 years, even 15, with many asking a 20% down payment or less. A few lenders may require a 25% down payment. Financing packages for used RVs are usually for up to 8 years. Interest on the loan is

---

INSIDER TIP: SEAL OF APPROVAL

RVs that carry the **RVIA Seal** affixed to the vehicle in the vicinity of the doorway are certified by the manufacturer to comply with 500 specifications for fire and safety, plumbing and electrical systems, and LP gas systems established by the American National Standards Institute. The Recreation Vehicle Industry Association, representing builders of more than 95% of all RVs sold in the United States, makes periodic unannounced plant inspections to ensure members maintain an acceptable level of compliance.

INSIDER TIP

Renting your RV to others to help defray costs of ownership may appeal to you. If you decide to try it, check the costs of upgrading your insurance policy to cover any liability, and see if a local dealer might add it to his rental fleet for a share of the profits.

deductible as second-home mortgage interest, if the unit contains basic cooking, sleeping, and toilet accommodations. Call or go online to get free **IRS publications** detailing interest information (𝄞 **800/829-3676**) and request Publication 936, "Home Interest Deduction," (www.irs.gov/publications/p936/index.html), and Publication 523, "Selling Your Home" (www.irs.gov/publications/p523/koi.html).

BEFORE BUYING A USED RV

1. **Take a long test drive.** Watch gauges closely, and check all systems personally from toilet flush to water pump and heater. Look for dry rot in any areas with wood, or water stains that may be signs of leaks.

2. **Ask questions.** Ask the owner very direct and specific questions about all systems in the vehicle.

3. **Have the RV inspected.** Ask a knowledgeable friend, or better still, hire an RV mechanic to look at the vehicle.

4. **Check the book value of the rig.** Find out the current value in a Kelley Blue Book or NADA (National Automobile Dealers Association) Guide; your bank loan officer should have current copies.

5. **Shop around.** Check comparable models and prices at another dealer's lot to have a price comparison.

PUBLICATIONS FOR CAMPERS & RV OWNERS

Camping Today, FCRV, 4804 Transit Rd., Bldg. 2, Depew, NY 14043. Membership dues to Family Campers & RVers: $25 per year (𝄞 **716/668-6242**; www.fcrv.org/Camptoday/campingtoday.php).

Escapees, Inc., 100 Rainbow Dr., Livingston, TX 77351. Dues for new members: $70 per year (𝄞 **888/757-2582**; www.escapees.com).

Family Motor Coaching, 8291 Clough Pike, Cincinnati, OH 45224. $50 per year (𝄞 **513/474-3622**; www.fmca.com).

Highways, TL Enterprises, 2575 Vista Del Mar Dr., Ventura, CA 93001. $6 per year (𝄞 **805/667-4100**; www.goodsamclub.com/highways).

Useful RV Websites

www.fmca.com: Family Motor Coach Association's online guide to that organization's events.

www.funoutdoors.com: American Recreation Coalition's site includes outdoor activities, recreation information sources, research, and statistics.

www.funroads.com: Offers personalized RV trip planning and maps and other information.

www.gocampingamerica.com: From National Association of RV Parks and Campgrounds, camping information for more than 3,100 member properties.

www.goodsamclub.com: Membership club with campground discounts and other RV goods and services.

www.gorp.com: Dedicated to outdoor recreation and scenic drives, a guide to campgrounds and lists of information sources.

www.gorving.com: A comprehensive source of RV information by the Go RVing Coalition, a nonprofit organization.

www.koa.com: Kampgrounds of America list of its member parks and information about facilities.

www.motorhomemagazine.com: *MotorHome* magazine's site.

www.rvadvice.com: Created and maintained by an RV service technician featuring basic maintenance and repair information.

www.rvamerica.com: An RV sales and industry information site sponsored by *RV News* magazine.

www.rvclub.com: An Internet gathering place for RV enthusiasts.

www.rvda.org and **www.rvra.org**: How to buy and rent RVs.

www.rvdoctor.com: A source of technical information on RV maintenance.

www.rvhome.com: An independent referral service representing about 50 rental companies.

www.rvia.org: A variety of information about manufacturers, retail shows, and clubs.

www.rvusa.com: Lists RV dealers, manufacturers, parts and accessory sources, rentals, and campgrounds.

www.trailerlife.com: From *Trailer Life* magazine.

www.woodalls.com: From Woodalls Publications, a useful site providing information about RV and tent camping, from manufacturers to destinations.

www.workamper.com: A site dedicated to helping RVers find full- or part-time jobs.

Midwest Outdoors, 111 Shore Dr., Burr Ridge, IL 60527. $15 per year (℃ **630/887-7722;** www.midwestoutdoors.com).

MotorHome, TL Enterprises, 2575 Vista Del Mar Dr., Ventura, CA 93001. $20 per year (℃ **800/678-1201;** www.motorhomemagazine.com).

Pop Up Times, 301 W. 12th St., The Dalles, OR 97058. $12 for four issues (℃ **760/595-8939;** www.popuptimes.com).

RV West, 100 7th Ave. S., Ste. 100, Cranbrook, BC, V1C 2J4. $14 per year (℃ **250/426-7253;** www.rvwest.com).

Trailblazer, Thousand Trails/NACO, 2325 Hwy. 90, Gautier, MS 39553. $14 per year (℃ **800/388-7788;** www.1000trails.com).

Trailer Life, TL Enterprises, 2575 Vista Del Mar Dr., Ventura, CA 93001. $22 per year (℃ **805/667-4100;** www.trailerlife.com).

Workamper News, 709 W. Searcy St., Heber Springs, AR 72543. $25 per year (℃ **800/446-5627** or 501/362-2637; www.workamper.com).

Index

Abbey, Edward, 126
Abbott's Lobster in the
  Rough (CT), 365
Abrams Creek (TN), 342
Acadia National Park (ME),
  375–376
Acadian Historic Village
  (NB), 358
Acme Saloon (TX), 230
Action Jackson's Bar
  (AK), 145
Adair (IA), 250
Adventure Rentals, 412, 413
Aerial Tramway (CA), 69
Agua Caliente Casino
  (CA), 75
Air filter, 28
Akta Lakota Museum
  (SD), 179
Alabama Hills Loop (CA),
  86–87
Alamo Village (TX), 233
Alaska, 135–164
Alaska Highway, 135,
  138–140
Alaska Hotel Café & Dew
  Drop Inn, 152
Alaskan Brewing Company
  (AK), 148
Alaska Riverboat *Discovery,*
  157
Alaska Salmon Bake, 157
Alaska State Council on the
  Arts, 146
Alaska Wild Berry chocolates
  (AK), 147

Alexander Graham Bell
  National Historic Park
  and Museum (NS), 378
Alexander Graham Bell's
  Yacht (NS), 360
Alice (TX), 220
Alpine (TX), 209
Al's Oasis (SD), 178
Altman's Winnebago,
  412, 413
Alyeska (AK), 164
Amana (IA), 245
Amana Colonies (IA), 255
Amana Colonies RV Park
  (IA), 256
Amargosa Opera House
  (CA), 61
Amboy Pharmacy & Soda
  Fountain (IL), 248
Amish Acres (IN), 277
Amistad National Recreation
  Area (TX), 222
Amoray Diver (FL), 292
Anasazi State Park Museum
  (UT), 132
Anchorage (AK), 161–162
Anchorage Museum of
  History and Art
  (AK), 161
Andy Griffith Museum
  (VA), 325
Anne Murray Centre
  (NS), 354
The Anne of Green Gables
  Museum (PEI), 383
Anne of Green Gables sites
  (PEI), 383

Antelope Island State Park
  (UT), 129
Antelope Valley California
  Poppy Reserve (CA), 86
Antelope Valley Indian
  Museum (CA), 61
Antennas, 30
Anza Borrego State Park
  (CA), 66–68
Appalachian Trail (VA), 328
Appledore (ME), 360
Applewood Farmhouse
  Restaurant (TN), 327
Appomattox Court House
  (VA), 319
Aransas Pass (TX), 207
Aransas Wildlife Refuge
  (TX), 233
Arches National Park (UT),
  102, 103, 128
Argo (ME), 359
Arnold's Lobster & Clam Bar
  (MA), 367
Artists Palette Road (CA), 80
Asheville (NC), 339–340
Asheville West KOA
  (NC), 340
Atlantic Oaks (MA), 374
Atlin Road (Yukon/
  BC 7), 163
Auburn Cord Duesenberg
  Museum (IN), 277
Audubon, John James, 300
Audubon Sabal Palm
  Sanctuary (TX), 214
Avonlea (PEI), 383

419

Backing-up directions, giving, 7

The Baddeck/Cabot Trail Campground (NS), 381

Badlands, 166

The Badlands (SD), 182–183

Badlands National Park (SD), 198–199

The Bagdad Cafe (CA), 61

Baha'i House of Worship (IL), 282

Bahia Honda State Park (FL), 295, 306–307

The Baker's Store (VT), 352

Balloon Above the Desert (CA), 69

Balsam Mountain (NC), 342

Barkerville (BC), 163

Barstow Station (CA), 61, 88

Barstow Triangle (CA), 88

Barter Theatre (VA), 324–325

Barton Grande Theatre Pipe Organ (IL), 258–259

Battle of New Market reenactment (VA), 319

Bauder's Pharmacy (IA), 248

Bauers Canyon Ranch RV Park (UT), 114–115

Baxter State Park (ME), 354–355

Beale Treasure (VA), 323

Beal's Lobster Pier (ME), 362

Bean Blossom (IN), 271

Beardstown (IL), 262–263

Bear Lake KOA (UT), 129

Beartree Campground (VA), 339

Beaver KOA (UT), 115

Behunin Cabin (UT), 122

Bellagio (NV), 82

Belle Boyd cottage museum (VA), 323

Bell's Farm to Market (TX), 213

Ben & Jerry's Ice Cream Factory Tours (VT), 352

Ben Schroeder Saddletree Factory Museum (IN), 270

Bentsen-Rio Grande Valley State Park (TX), 214

Bicentennial Highway (UT), 97, 132

Big Bend National Park (TX), 210, 223–228

Big Bend Ranch State Environmental Area (TX), 225

Big Bend Resort & Adventure Golf Resort (TX), 226

Big Meadows Campground (VA), 332

Big Pine Campground (SD), 190

Big Pine Key (FL), 296

Big Rock Candy Mountain (UT), 99

Big Spring Canyon Overlook (UT), 124

Bill Monroe Bluegrass Festival (IN), 271

Bill Monroe Memorial Music Park & Campground (IN), 272

Biltmore Estate (NC), 324

Biltmore House (NC), 340

Binoculars, 14–15, 26–28

The Bird House Bar (AK), 145

Biscayne National Park (FL), 295

Blackhawk Chocolate Trail (IL), 245

Black Hills (SD), 166, 170, 176

Black Hills Central Railroad (SD), 176

The Black Hills National Forest Campgrounds (SD), 188, 190

Black Hills Playhouse (SD), 190

Black Hills Wild Horse Sanctuary (SD), 199

Black Rock Campground (CA), 78

Blackstone RV Park (NV), 86

Blackwoods Campground (ME), 377

Blowing Rock (NC), 323

Blue Bell ice cream (TX), 211

The Blue Ridge Farm Museum (VA), 319

Blue Ridge Parkway (VA), 316, 319, 332, 334–339

Bluewater Key RV Resort (FL), 307

Boardwalk RV Resort (FL), 310

Boar's Head Inn (VA), 325

Bodie (CA), 87

Bodie State Historic Park (CA), 87

The Bonanza Gold Motel and RV Park (YT), 156

Bonanza Meat Company (AK), 148

Booker T. Washington National Monument (VA), 320

Boot Hill (Mount Moriah Cemetery; SD), 172

Borrego Palm Canyon Campground (CA), 67

Boston Minuteman Campground (MA), 374

Boulder Creek RV Resort (CA), 82

Boyd's Key West Campground (FL), 307–308

Brackettville (TX), 233

The Braeburn Lodge (AK), 148

Brian Head (UT), 132

The Bridges of Madison County (IA), 244, 250

Brighton (UT), 129

Brinegar Cabin (VA), 334
Bristlecone Loop trail (UT), 118
Bristlecone pine forest (CA), 87
Bristol (VA), 335
British Columbia, northern, 150, 152–156
Britt (IA), 251
Broad Cove Campground (NB), 380–381
Brookville Lake (IN), 272
Brown County (IN), 270
Brown County State Park (IN), 272
Brownsville (TX), 208–209
Bryce Canyon KOA (UT), 118
Bryce Canyon Lodge (UT), 118
Bryce Canyon National Park (UT), 96–97, 105, 106, 116, 118
Bubble wrap, 18
Buffalo, 174, 178–179, 181
Bullfrog Basin loop (UT), 133
Bullfrog Campground (UT), 124
Bumbleberry Inn (UT), 107
Burner igniters, 15
Butch Cassidy, 100, 102
Butch Cassidy Campground (UT), 120
Buying an RV, 414–416

Cabazon (CA), 63
Cable TV connections, 49
Cabot Trail (NS), 378
Cades Cove (TN), 341–343
Caesars Palace (NV), 83
Café Central (TX), 211
Cahokia Mounds (IL), 265
Calf Creek Recreation Area (UT), 122, 132
Calico (CA), 76
Calico Ghost Town (CA), 78

California desert region, 55–80
California poppy trail, 86
Camp Chesterfield (IN), 275
Campground Services RV Park (Watson Lake, YT), 152, 154–155
Camping, 37–48
Campobello Island (NB), 384–385
C&O railway station ice-cream parlor (VA), 325
Canoeing, North Dakota, 181
Canyonlands National Park (UT), 122, 124–126
Canyons RV Park (TX), 222
Cape Ann Camp Site (MA), 374
Cape Cod (MA), 369–370
Cape Cod Central Railroad (MA), 360
Cape Cod Potato Chip Factory (MA), 352
Capitol Reef Inn & Cafe (UT), 107–108
Capitol Reef National Park (UT), 97, 121–122
Cappy's Chowder House (ME), 368
Captain Tony's Saloon (FL), 305
Caravans, 31–32
Caribbean Club (FL), 305
Carl's Frozen Custard (VA), 325
Caro's (TX), 212
Carter Family Fold (VA), 335
The Carvers Cafe at Mount Rushmore (SD), 172
Carver's Family Dining (IN), 275
Cassiar Highway (BC 37), 163
Castle Creek Winery (UT), 106
Cataloochee (NC), 343
Cattleman's Steakhouse (TX), 211

Cave-in-Rock State Park (IL), 267, 268
Cavendish Campground (PEI), 382
Cavendish KOA Campground (PEI), 382
Cedar Breaks National Monument (UT), 119, 121, 132
Cedar City (UT), 119–121
Cedar Haven Campground (ME), 377
Cedar Pass Campground (SD), 188
Cedar Rapids (IA), 255
Cedar Rapids Museum of Art (IA), 257
Celebrity Tour (CA), 74
Cellphones, 30
Century Mobile Home & RV Park (UT), 130
Chairs, outdoor, 15
Charles H. MacNider Art Museum (IA), 252
Chase Lake National Wildlife Refuge (ND), 182
Château Morrisette Winery (VA), 335
Checklists for packing, 14
Cheeca Lodge (FL), 292
Cherry Hill (UT), 130
Chester (IL), 266
Chester Gould/Dick Tracy Museum (IL), 258
Chesterton (IN), 279
Cheticamp (NS), 378
Chetwynd (AK), 145
Cheyenne Crossing Café, Lodge & Store (SD), 177
Cheyenne River Sioux Tribe (SD), 179
Chicago Northwest KOA Campground (IL), 260–261
Chilkoot Charlie's Rustic Alaskan Bar, 161
Chinatown Cafe (SD), 177
The Chuckwagon Patio (ND), 177

Circleville (UT), 100
Circleville RV Park and
  Country Store (UT), 121
Circus Circus (NV), 83
Circus Circus KOA (NV), 85
Circus City Festival Museum
  (IN), 276
City Center (NV), 83
The Clam Box (MA), 366
The Clam Shack (ME), 365
Claremont Hotel (ME), 353
Claybanks RV Park
  (BC), 153
Claytor Lake State Park
  (VA), 338
Clear Lake (IA), 251, 252
Clingmans Dome (TN/
  NC), 341
Coachella Music Festival
  (CA), 74
Coachella Valley Preserve
  (CA), 61, 67
Colony Inn Restaurant
  (IA), 247
Colorado River, 97, 98
Columbus (IN), 271, 282
Concordia Cemetery (TX),
  230–231
Confederation Players
  (PEI), 359
Connemara (NC), 336
Conner Prairie (IN), 274
Cooperative Artisanale gift
  shop (NS), 378
Coral Castle (FL), 289–290
Corn Palace (SD), 170–171
Cosby Campground
  (TN), 343
The Cosmopolitan (NV), 83
Cotton Valley RV Park
  (TX), 232
Cottonwood Campground
  (ND), 196
Cottonwood House
  (BC), 163
Cottonwood Visitor Center
  (CA), 77–78
Cotulla Style Pit Bar-B-Q
  (TX), 212

Country Sales (VA), 335
Covered Bridge Festival
  (IN), 274
Cowboy's Smoke House
  (UT), 108
Craig's Restaurant (FL), 294
Crawfordsville (IN), 274
Crawfordsville KOA
  (IN), 279
The Crazy Cajun (TX), 212
Crazy Horse Memorial (SD),
  171, 187
Crocodile Lake National
  Wildlife Refuge (FL), 296
Crooked Road: Virginia's
  Heritage Music Trail, 335
Crow Creek Sioux Tribe
  (SD), 179
Cruise America, 411–413
Crystal City (TX), 206
Custer State Park (SD),
  178–179, 181–182, 190

The Dakotas, 165–200
Dakota Sioux Casino
  (SD), 176
Dalton Highway (AK), 162
Dana (IN), 274
Dana-Thomas house
  (IL), 282
Dances with Wolves
  (film), 179
Dances with Wolves at Wolf
  Park (IN), 244–245
Das Dutchman Essenhaus
  (IN), 275
Dates (CA), 65
Davis Mountains State Park
  (TX), 228–229
Dawson City (YT), 156
Dawson Creek (BC), 152
Dawson Peaks Resort & RV
  Park (YT), 148, 155
Dead Horse Point State Park
  (UT), 127, 133
Deadwood (SD), 172,
  175, 192
Deadwood KOA (SD), 191
Dean, James, 242–243

Death Valley National Park
  (CA), 62, 63, 66, 67,
  80, 82
Deep Creek (NC), 343
Delicate Arch (UT),
  103, 128
Dempster Highway
  (Canada), 162–163
Denali National Park (AK),
  158–160
Denali Park Resorts
  (AK), 160
Denison (IA), 249
Desert Adventures (CA), 72
Desert Dunes of Maine
  Campground, 377
Desert Memorial Cemetery
  (CA), 74
Desert Sun Resort (CA), 62
Desert Tortoise Natural Area
  (CA), 87
Desert View Tower (CA), 88
Des Moines (IA), 250
Des Moines West KOA (IA),
  251–252
Desolation Canyon
  (UT), 105
Devil's Garden Campground
  (UT), 128
Devil's Gulch (SD), 173
Devil's Tower KOA
  (WY), 198
Devil's Tower National
  Monument (WY), 198
Diamond Tooth Gertie's
  (AK), 145
Diamond Tooth Gertie's
  Casino (YT), 156
Dinosaur Park (SD), 168
Disney's Fort Wilderness
  Resort & Campground
  (FL), 312
Dodge City (UT), 104
Dog Beach (FL), 295
Dollywood (TN), 340–341
Dolphin Cove Oyster Bar
  (TX), 212
Dolphin Research Center
  (FL), 295

Donna Reed Foundation for the Performing Arts (IA), 249–250
Dos Passos, John, 306
Double J Campground (IL), 264
Double Musky Inn Restaurant (AK), 148
Doughton Park (NC), 339
Douthat State Park (VA), 338
Downtown RV Park (Watson Lake, YT), 154
Driving schools, 13
Driving tips, 26–27
Dry Weight, 14
Dusting and debugging, 50
Duval Street (FL), 290
Dyersville (IA), 254

Earthquake Park (AK), 161
East Mojave National Scenic Area (CA), 89
East Shore RV Park (CA), 79
Eby's Pines (IN), 281–282
Eddie McStiff's (UT), 108
The Egyptian (IL), 258
El Capitan Hotel (TX), 228
Elkhart (IN), 277
Elkhart/Middlebury KOA (IN), 281
Elk Horn (IA), 250
Elkmont (TN), 341–343
Elk Mountain National Park (SD), 191
El Mirage (CA), 64
El Monte RV Center, 413
El Paso (TX), 229–232
El Paso Chili Company (TX), 213
El Paso Museum of History (TX), 231
El Paso Saddleblanket Trading Post (TX), 208
Elsah (IL), 265
Emerald Pools trail (UT), 114
Enroute Camping (CA), 44

The Ernest Hemingway Home and Museum (FL), 302–303
Escapees RV Club, 32
Ethel M Chocolates (NV), 85
Everglades National Park (FL), 296, 308–310

Fabulous Palm Springs Follies (CA), 74
Fairbanks (AK), 157–158
Fairmount (IN), 242–243
Fairy Stone State Park (VA), 338
Fall River (MA), 384
Fancy Gap KOA Campground (VA), 338
Farm Island Recreation Area (SD), 198
Farnsworth Art Museum/Wyeth Center (ME), 355–356
Fat Albert (FL), 290
Fat Tire Festival (UT), 127
Field of Dreams (film), 254
Fiery Furnace (UT), 128
Fiesta Key RV Resort (FL), 306
Fifth-wheel travel trailers, 398–400
Financing, 415–416
Firearms, 29–30
Firehouse Brewing Company (SD), 177
Fires, campground, 46
Fisher Towers (UT), 102–103
Five Brothers Grocery (FL), 294
Flamingo Campground (FL), 308–309
Flipper's grave (FL), 290
The Florida Keys, 285–308
Floyd (VA), 334
Flying J Real Value Club, 32
Folding trailers, 393–395
Food, 16–26

Fort Bliss (TX), 231
Fort Clark Springs RV Park (TX), 222
Fort Davis National Historic Site (TX), 209, 229, 233
Fort Jefferson (FL), 292
Fort Massac State Park (IL), 268
Fort Nelson (BC), 152
Fort Ransom State Park (ND), 181, 195
Fortress Louisbourg National Historic Park (NS), 357
Fort St. John (BC), 154
Fort Stockton (TX), 206
Fountain of Youth Spa Campground (CA), 68
4 Bears RV Park (ND), 196
Foxwoods Casino Resort (CT), 372
Fragrant Fields (IL), 266
Frantic Follies (AK), 147
Freeport (ME), 376, 377
Fremont Indian State Park (UT), 121
Friendly Tavern (IN), 275
Front Royal Campground (VA), 331
Fruita (UT), 122
Fuel, saving money on, 27–28
Fundy National Park (NB), 380
Furnace Creek Campground (CA), 80, 82

Galax Moose Lodge #733 Old Fiddlers' Convention (VA), 336
Galena (IL), 257, 282
Galesburg (IL), 260
Game Lodge Campground (SD), 190
Ganong's Chocolate Factory (NB), 368
Gateway to the Narrows trail (UT), 114
Gatorland (FL), 290, 311

General Lew Wallace Study & Museum (IN), 274
General Patton Memorial Museum (CA), 78
George Wyth Memorial State Park (IA), 256
Gladys Porter Zoo (TX), 233
Glen Canyon National Recreation Area (UT), 97, 133
Glendora Inn & Distillery (NS), 353
The Gloucester House (MA), 363
Gnaw Bone (IN), 271
Golden Nugget Camper Park (AK), 161
Goldfields Bakery (AK), 148
Gold Rush Campground (YT), 156
Good Sam Club, 32, 42, 45
Goulding's Monument Valley Campground & RV Park (UT), 104
Grabill (IN), 245
Grafton (UT), 102
Grand Forks (ND), 177, 178
Grand Staircase–Escalante National Monument (UT), 96
Granite City KOA (IL), 268–269
Grassy Key (FL), 295
Gray Canyon (UT), 105
Grayson Highlands State Park (VA), 329, 339
Great River Road (IL), 265
Great Smoky Mountains National Park (TN/NC), 340–343
Green Gables House (PEI), 383
Green Gables Post Office (PEI), 383
Green Gables Restaurant (IA), 246
Green Gulch Road (TX), 228
Green Turtle Inn (FL), 294

Grove Park Inn (NC), 323
Guadalupe Mountains National Park (TX), 229
Gustav Dentzell carousel (IN), 276–277

Hadley Orchard (CA), 65
Half-Shell Raw Bar (FL), 293
Hallie's Hall of Fame Museum (TX), 206
Halls Crossing Campground (UT), 124
Hampton State Beach (NH), 375
Happy Traveler RV Park (CA), 76
Harmonie State Park (IN), 272
Harraseeket Lunch & Lobster Company (ME), 363, 368
Harrison Country Club (BC), 153
Hartt Island Campground (NB), 382
Headlights, 28
The Heartland (Iowa, Illinois, and Indiana), 235–283
Hemingway, Ernest, 302–303, 306
Herring Cove Provincial Park (NB), 385
Hickman Bridge (UT), 121
Hidalgo (TX), 206
Highland Village (NS), 358
Hitchin' Post RV Park (NV), 86
Hobnob Corner (IN), 275
Hobo Museum (IA), 251
Holding tanks, 51
Hole N" The Rock Home (UT), 100
Holiday Isle (FL), 290–291
Homestake Gold Mine (SD), 199–200
Homestead Resort (VA), 324
Homestead RV Park (AK), 160
Homosassa Springs Wildlife State Park (FL), 296

Horsethief Lake Campground (SD), 188
Hosts, campground, 48
Hotel Fantasy Springs Resort Casino (CA), 75
Hotel Limpia (TX), 213
Hotel Nipton (CA), 77
Hueco Tanks State Historical Park (TX), 231–232
Hungry Mother State Park (VA), 339
Hyder (AK), 145
Hy-Line Cruises (MA), 370

Illinois, 235, 236, 239, 242, 257–269
Imperial Sand Dunes Recreation Area (CA), 88
Indiana, 235, 242, 269–283
Indiana Dunes National Lakeshore, 243–244, 279
Indio Date Festival (CA), 74
Ingalls Family Homestead (SD), 199
Ingonish Beach (NS), 378
Insurance, 31, 412
International Chili Cook-Off (TX), 230
International Vinegar Museum (SD), 173
Internet access, 33
Inyo National Forest (CA), 87
Iowa, 235–238, 240, 242, 249–257
The Iowa Machine Shed Restaurant (IA), 247
Irish Moss Interpretive Centre (PEI), 354
Isla Blanca Park (TX), 216
Islamorada (FL), 295
Island in the Sky area of Canyonlands (UT), 126

Jaarsma Bakery (IA), 246
James Dean Gallery (IN), 243
Jamestown Campground (ND), 196

James Whitcomb Riley house (IN), 273
Jewel Cave National Monument (SD), 200
Jiberto's Taco Shop (CA), 66
John Dillinger Museum (IN), 243
John F. Kennedy Library and Museum (MA), 354
Johnny Appleseed Campground (IN), 279
Johnny Appleseed Park (IN), 277
John Pennekamp Coral Reef State Park (FL), 294, 305
Joliet (IL), 258
Jordan Pond Lodge (ME), 368
Joshua Tree National Park (CA), 76, 77
J. T. Farnham's (MA), 366
Jules' Undersea Lodge (FL), 295
Julian Price Memorial Park (NC), 339
Julio's Café Corona (TX), 213
July Underwater Music Festival (FL), 295
Jumbo Rocks Campground (CA), 78
Juniper Campground (ND), 196

Kamloops RV Park (BC), 153
Kantishna Roadhouse (AK), 145
Kelly's (FL), 294
Kelly's Caribbean Bar, Grill and Brewery (FL), 302
Kenmare (ND), 182
Kerouac, Jack, 373
Key deer (FL), 296
Key Largo (FL), 297–298, 306
Key West (FL), 290–295, 298–308

Key West Aquarium (FL), 303
Key West Cemetery (FL), 290
Key West Lighthouse Museum (FL), 305
Kimballton (IA), 250
King Ranch (TX), 232
Kings Landing (NB), 357–358
Kissimmee KOA (FL), 312
Kitchen Little (CT), 366
Knotts Soak City (CA), 69
KOA campgrounds, 40, 42, 409–410
Kodachrome Basin State Park (UT), 119, 132
Kolob Canyons (UT), 130

La Borde House (TX), 211
Lagomarcino's Soda Shop (IL), 248
Laguna Atascosa National Wildlife Refuge (TX), 214
Lake Anita State Park (IA), 251
Lake Corpus Christi/Mathis KOA Campground (TX), 217–218
Lake Fairfax Park (VA), 330–331
Lake Mitchell Campground (SD), 191–192
Lake Powell (UT), 97, 105–106
Lakeshore Historic District (IL), 282
Lakota people (SD), 179
Landry's Seafood (TX), 207–208
Langtry (TX), 227
Laredo (TX), 206–207, 220
Las Vegas (NV), 82–86
Las Vegas Museum of Organized Crime and Law Enforcement (NV), 85
Las Vegas Springs Preserve (NV), 85
Latchstring Village (SD), 179

La Te Da (FL), 302
Laughlin (NV), 86
Lawrence Welk homestead (ND), 174
Lazy J RV Park and Campground (SD), 188
Legion Lake Campground (SD), 190
LEGOland California, 68
Lena KOA (IL), 261
Lewis and Clark trail (SD), 198
Lewis Mountain Campground (VA), 332
Liard River Hot Springs Provincial Park (BC), 154
Lincoln (IL), 262
Lincoln, Abraham, 262–264
Lincoln's New Salem State Historic Site and Campground (IL), 264
Little Bighorn Battlefield National Monument (MT), 183–185
Little Brown Church in the Vale (IA), 254
Little Diner (TX), 213
Little Palm Island (FL), 291
Little Spearfish Canyon (SD), 179
Living Desert (CA), 67
Llano Grande Lake Park (TX), 221
Lobsterman's Co-Op (ME), 362
The Lobster Pot (MA), 365
The Lobster Shack (ME), 365
Loft Mountain (VA), 332
Logansport (IN), 276
Long Island Village (TX), 216
Long Key SRA State Park (FL), 306
Long Pine Key Campground (FL), 308
Look Rock (TN), 343
Los Ebanos (TX), 220
The Lost Alaskan RV Resort (TX), 229

Louie's Backyard (FL), 291
Louisbourg Motorhome RV
  Park (NS), 381
Louis' Lunch (CT), 367
Louisville Metro KOA
  (IN), 273
Lower Emerald Pool trail
  (UT), 114
Lower Rio Grande River
  Valley (TX), 220–221
Lucy Maud Montgomery
  Birthplace (PEI), 383
Lucy Maud Montgomery
  Heritage Museum
  (PEI), 383
Lucy Maud Montgomery's
  home (PEI), 383
Lung Duck Tong Restaurant
  (AK), 149
Luray Caverns (VA), 334
Luxor (NV), 83

Mabel's Lobster Claw
  (ME), 365
Mabry Mill (VA),
  319–320, 334
McAllen (TX), 220
McCallum Theatre for the
  Performing Arts (CA), 75
MacDonald Campground
  (BC), 154
McKinley, Mount (AK), 147
Mac's Pit Barbecue
  (TX), 213
Madame Walker Theatre
  Center (IN), 274
The Mad Greek's (CA), 65
Madison (IN), 270
Madison (SD), 200
Malaquite Beach Camp-
  ground (TX), 216
Malibu Beach RV Park
  (CA), 79
Mallory Square (FL), 291
Mammoth Site (SD), 199
Marathon (TX), 210–211
Marfa (TX), 207, 227
Margaritaville (FL),
  292, 305

The Maritime Museum of
  the Atlantic (NS), 355
Martha's Vineyard
  (MA), 385
Mashantucket Pequot
  Museum (CT), 372
The Mast General Store
  (VA), 320
Mathews Arm (VA),
  331–332
Maverick Ranch RV Park
  (TX), 226
Maytag Dairy Farms
  (IA), 246
The Maze (UT), 124
Medieval Times Dinner
  Tournament (FL), 311
Medora (ND), 177–178,
  194, 196, 200
Medora Musical (ND),
  177, 194
Mel Fisher Maritime
  Heritage Museum
  (FL), 304
Metamora (IN), 270
Metropolis (IL), 244,
  266–267
Mexico, 233–234
MGM Grand (NV), 84
Miami County Museum
  (IN), 276
Miami Everglades Camp-
  ground (FL), 310
Miccosukee Restaurant
  (FL), 294
Michie Tavern (VA), 335
Middlebury (IN), 277
The *MILEPOST*, 143
Mile 0 RV Park and Camp-
  ground (BC), 153
Minot KOA (ND), 195
Mirage (NV), 83
Mission RV Park (TX), 232
Mission West Resort
  (TX), 221
Missouri River (ND), 181
Moab (UT), 103, 127
Moab Brewery (UT), 127
Moab KOA (UT), 127

Moab Slickrock Bicycle Trail
  (UT), 127
Mohegan Sun (CT), 372
Mojave Desert (CA), 76–79
Monticello (VA),
  329–330, 334
Monument Valley Navajo
  Tribal Park (UT), 103–104
Moon Lake State Recreation
  Site (AK), 157
Moosehead Brewery
  (NB), 368
Mormons, 94–95, 122, 260
Morongo Casino (CA), 75
Morrison-Rockwood State
  Park (IL), 262
Motorized RVs, 392–393,
  400–406
Moturis, 413
Mounds State Park (IN), 281
Mountain Lake Hotel
  (VA), 325
Mount Desert Island (ME),
  375–376
Mount Desert Narrows
  Camping Resort (ME), 377
Mount McKinley (AK), 147
Mount Moriah Cemetery
  (SD), 172
Mount Pisgah (NC), 340
Mount Rushmore (SD), 166,
  172, 176, 185–186
Mount Rushmore/Hill City
  KOA (SD), 188
Moxie (ME), 368
Mr. and Mrs. Claus at Santa
  Claus House (AK), 145
Mrs. Rowe's Restaurant &
  Bakery (VA), 326
Mrs. Wick's Pies &
  Restaurant (IN),
  247, 275
Muncho Lake Provincial
  Park (BC), 154
Murph's Gaslight (CA), 65
Muscatine (IA), 255
Museum of American
  Frontier Culture
  (VA), 318

Museum of Appalachia (Tennessee), 322

Museum of Family Camping (NH), 10, 374

Museum of Geology (SD), 168

Museum of the Cherokee Indian (NC), 322

Museum of the Republic of Rio Grande (TX), 220

Mystery Mountain Resort (SD), 188

Mystic Seaport (CT), 356

Nantucket (MA), 359, 370–373

Nashville House (IN), 270

National Buffalo Museum (ND), 174

National Farm Toy Museum (IA), 254

National Historic Site (IA), 256

National Hobo Convention (IA), 251

National Key Deer Refuge (FL), 296

Native Americans, the Dakotas, 176, 179–180

Natural Bridge Caverns (VA), 322

Natural Bridge/Lexington KOA (VA), 337

Natural Bridges National Monument (UT), 97, 132

Natural Chimneys Jousting Contest (VA), 336

Nauvoo (IL), 260, 261

Navajo Loop Trail (UT), 118

The Needles (UT), 124, 126

Needles KOA Kampground (NV), 86

Neils Harbour (NS), 378

Nenana (AK), 145

New Bedford Whaling Museum (MA), 355

New England and the Canadian Maritimes, 345–385

New England Carousel Museum (CT), 351

New England Maple Museum (VT), 351

New Glasgow Lobster Suppers (PEI), 364, 366

New Harmony (IN), 269–270

Newport (RI), 384

Newport KOA (TN), 343

New Salem (IL), 262

Newspaper Rock State Historic Park (UT), 101

New York, New York (NV), 84

Niña, Pinta, and *Santa María* replicas (TX), 206

Nipton (CA), 77

Nolan's RV Center, 413

Non-Resident Violators Compact, 28

The Noriega Hotel (CA), 66

North Campground (UT), 118–119

Northern Lights RV Park Ltd. (BC), 153–154

Nunan's Lobster Hut (ME), 362

Oak Ridge Cemetery (IL), 263

Oasis RV Park (NV), 86

Oconaluftee Indian Village (NC), 322

Ocotillo Wells State Vehicular Recreation Area (CA), 68

Oglala Sioux Tribe (SD), 180

Old City Market (NB), 365

Oldest House Museum (FL), 305

Old Kentucky Home (NC), 336, 339

Old Sturbridge Village (MA), 356

Old Time Saloon Number 10 (SD), 172

Olympia Candy Kitchen (IN), 248

On the Beach RV Park (TX), 219

Orange Grove RV Park (CA), 79

Orlando (FL), 310–312

Ouabache State Park (IN), 282

Outdoor Resorts (TN), 344

Outdoor Resorts of America (CA), 76

Outdoor Resorts–Orlando (FL), 312

Owls Head Transportation Museum (ME), 353

Packing tips, 18

Padre Island National Seashore (TX), 215–216

Painted Canyon (ND), 194

Palm Canyon Resort and RV Park (CA), 68

Palm Springs (CA), 55, 62, 63, 68–76

Paramount Theatre Centre & Ballroom (IN), 274–275

Paris (NV), 84

Parke County (IN), 274

Paso del Norte Hotel (TX), 211, 230

Patsy Cline Historic House (VA), 330

Peabody Essex Museum (MA), 352–353

Peacock Alley Bar & Grill (ND), 177

Peaks of Otter (VA), 338

Pearl Button Museum (IA), 243

Pechanga RV Resort (CA), 76

Peggy Sue's 50's Diner (CA), 66

Peoria (IL), 259

Pepe's (FL), 293–294

Perky Bat Tower (FL), 291

Peru (IN), 276

Pest House Medical Museum in the Old City Cemetery (VA), 323
Petrified Forest State Park (UT), 132
Pets, camping with, 44–46
Pheasant, world's largest (SD), 173, 174
Piasa Bird, 265
Pigeon Forge/Gatlinburg KOA (TN), 343
Pig 'N Steak (VA), 326–327
Pine Hills RV Park (PEI), 383
Pine Springs Campground (TX), 229
Pioneer Beach RV Resort (TX), 218–219
Pioneer Park (AK), 157
Pipestem Creek (ND), 177
Pitchfork Steak Fondue (ND), 177–178
Plat system (UT), 99
Plaza Theater (TX), 230
Plimoth Plantation (MA), 356
Point Supreme Campground (UT), 121
Popeye statue (IL), 266
Portage Glacier (AK), 164
Portland Public Market (ME), 368
Potato Bowl USA (ND), 177
Potato Museum (PEI), 354
Prairie Dog Town (SD), 199
Prairie Edge Trading Co. & Galleries (SD), 176
Prairie Rose Carousel (ND), 174
Prairie Rose State Park (IA), 252
Prairie Village (SD), 200
Prehistoric Museum of the College of Eastern Utah, 100
Presidential Library and Museum (IA), 256
Presidio (TX), 228

Price City Cemetery (UT), 101
Prince Edward Island's Famous Lobster Suppers, 365–366
Publications, 416, 418
Puckett Cabin (VA), 332, 334
Pump House Restaurant (AK), 147

Qiviut (AK), 147
Quad Cities, 238, 256
Queens Garden Trail (UT), 118

Rafter J Bar Ranch Campground (SD), 190
Randolph State Fish & Wildlife Area (IL), 268
Randsburg (CA), 87
Rapid City (SD), 166, 168
Rapid City KOA (SD), 191
Raspberries, Utah, 106–107
Reagan, Ronald, 258
Recipes, 18–24
Recreation Vehicle Industry Association (RVIA), 11–12, 414
Recreation Vehicle Rental Association (RVRA), 411
Red Canyon RV Park (UT), 119
Red Rock Canyon State Park (CA), 79, 88
Red Trail Campground (ND), 196
Rental Ventures, 411
Renting RVs, 409–418
Republic of the Rio Grande Museum (TX), 206–207
Restaurant Barn (IN), 277
The Reversing Falls Rapids (NB), 353
Rialto Square Theatre (IL), 258
Riley Creek Campground (AK), 160
Rio Grande (TX), 209

Rio Grande Village Campground (TX), 226
Rio Grande Village Store and Trailer Park (TX), 226
Rivers Edge RV Park (AK), 158
Riverside (IA), 255
Riverside Resort RV Park (NV), 86
The Riverway (Rte. 128; UT), 133
Roadrunner, world's largest (TX), 206
Roanoke Mountain (VA), 338
Roberts Prairie Dog Town (SD), 183
Robinson (IL), 268
Rockwood Park (NB), 380
Ross H. Maclean Rotary RV Park (BC), 154
Ross Maxwell Scenic Drive (TX), 228
The Rough Riders Hotel (ND), 178
Ruby's Inn (UT), 118
Ruddy's 1930s General Store Museum (CA), 69
Rural Retreat (VA), 334
Rushmore, Mount, 166, 176, 185–186
Rushmore Plaza Civic Center (SD), 168
RV Driving School (TX), 13
RVIA Seal, 415
RV/MH Heritage Foundation (IN), 277
RVs
fifth-wheel travel trailers, 398–400
glossary of common terms, 389–392
motorized RVs, 392–393, 400–406
questions to ask yourself when selecting, 406–407
renting vs. buying, 409–418

towable, 392–400
travel trailers, 396–400
truck campers, 395–396
types of, 392–393

Saco Old Orchard Beach
(ME), 376
Saddleback Butte State Park
(CA), 79
Saddles and saddle blankets
(TX), 208
St. Ann's Church Lobster
Suppers (PEI), 364, 366
St. Joseph Indian School
(SD), 179
The Salem Witch Museum
(MA), 352
Sally's Apizza (CT), 367
Salt Lake City (UT),
129–130
Salt Lake City KOA
(UT), 130
Salton Sea (CA), 87
Saltwater Farm Campground
(ME), 377
Sammy's Woodfired Pizza
(CA), 65
San Andreas Fault (CA), 72
Sandburg, Carl, 260, 336
San Diego Zoo Safari
Park (CA), 68
Sandwich Glass Museum
(MA), 360
San Jacinto Plaza
(TX), 231
San Rafael Swell (UT), 96
Santa Ana National Wildlife
Refuge (TX), 214
Sasquatch Provincial Park
(BC), 153
Satellite dishes, 49
Sauropod Track Site
(UT), 101
Scenic Byway Route 12
(UT), 130
Schimpff's Confectionary
(IN), 248
Scotty's Castle (CA), 63

Scusset State Beach
(MA), 373
Seaport Campground
(CT), 373
Seasons, 38
SeaWind RV Resort on the
Bay (TX), 220
Sechler's Pickles (IN), 246
Seminole Canyon State
Historic Park (TX), 222
Seniors, 42
Sergeant Floyd Monument
(IA), 249
Shady Acres RV Park
(UT), 128
Shafter (TX), 228
Shapiro's Downtown (IN),
246–247
Shawneetown Historic Site
(IL), 268
Shelburne (NS), 357
Shenandoah National Park
(VA), 328, 331–332
Shenandoah Valley (VA),
329–332
Sherman's Deli and Bakery
(CA), 65
Sherwood Forest (FL), 312
Shields Date Gardens (CA),
65–66
Ship Creek Landings
Downtown RV Park
(AK), 161–162
Shipshewana (IN), 277
Shipshewana Auction & Flea
Market (IN), 245, 277
Shrewsbury House (IN), 270
The Sign Post Forest
(AK), 144
Sikanni River RV Park
(BC), 154
Silver Creek RV Park
(NV), 86
Silver View RV Resort
(NV), 86
Simon & Seafort's Saloon &
Grill (AK), 147
Sioux City (IA), 282

Sioux City North KOA
(IA), 251
Siouxland Buffalo (ND), 178
Sioux Pottery and Crafts
(SD), 176
Sioux tribes (the Dakotas),
179–180
Skyline Drive (VA), 319, 332
Sleeping by the side of the
road, 36
Slickrock, 107
Slickrock Trail (UT), 105
Sloppy Joe's (FL), 293, 305
Smokemont (NC), 341–343
Snappy Lunch (VA),
325–326
Snow Canyon State Park
(UT), 104, 115
Sodom Mountain Camp-
ground (MA), 375
Soldiers' and Sailors'
Monument (IN), 274
Solitude (UT), 129
Sonny Bono Salton Sea
National Wildlife Refuge
(CA), 87
Sourdough Campground
(AK), 157
Sourdough pancakes
(AK), 149
South Bend (IN), 278
South Bend Elkhart North
KOA (IN), 280
South Campground (UT),
115–116
South Dakota. See The
Dakotas
Southern Comfort RV Resort
(FL), 309
The Southern Kitchen
(VA), 326
South Padre Island (TX),
215–216
South Padre Island KOA
(TX), 216
Southport RV Park (PEI), 384
Spanish Trail RV Park and
Campground (UT), 128

Spa Resort Casino (CA), 68–69, 75

Spearfish Canyon National Scenic Byway (SD), 199

Spectra Point Trail (UT), 120

Speed limits, 28

Spoon River (IL), 259–260

Spotlight 29 (CA), 75

Springfield (IL), 262, 282

Springfield KOA (IL), 264

Springs RV Resort (BC), 153

Squaw Creek Regional Park (IA), 256–257

Squaw Flat (UT), 126

Star, largest man-made illuminated (VA), 322

Starved Rock State Park (IL), 260

State Game Lodge, Custer State Park Resort (SD), 178

Steen, Charlie, 100–101

Stockade Lake Campground (SD), 190

Story City (IA), 250–251

Stovepipe Wells (CA), 80

Strasburg Antique Emporium (VA), 324

Stratosphere Tower (NV), 84

Stratton-Porter, Gene, 275–276

Strawberry Flats Campground (BC), 154

Strawbery Banke (NH), 356–357

Studebaker National Museum (IN), 278–279

Sugarloaf Key KOA (FL), 307

Sully's Hill National Game Preserve (ND), 182

Sul Ross State University (TX), 209

Sunset Campground (CA), 80

Sunset Campground (UT), 118–119

Sunshine Key Camping Resort (FL), 307

Superman's Hometown (IL), 244

Super Museum (IL), 267

The Surf Ballroom (IA), 243, 251

Taku Smokeries Market Place (AK), 149

Tamworth Camping Area (NH), 375

Tavernier Hotel (FL), 297

Taylor Highway (AK), 162

Teibels (IN), 247

Temple Square (UT), 129

Terlingua (TX), 230

The "Teslin taxi" (AK), 144

Texas, 201–234

Texas Cowboy Poetry Gathering, 210–211

Texas International Fishing Tournament (TIFT), 209

Texas Jazz Festival, 222

"Texas Riviera," 216–220

Texas State Aquarium, 208

Theodore Roosevelt National Park (ND), 166, 192–194, 196, 200

Thermometer, world's tallest (CA), 63

This Is the Place State Park (UT), 129

Thomas Wolfe Memorial State Historic Site (NC), 339

Thousand Trails, 43

Three Affiliated Tribes Museum (ND), 200

Tigua Indian Reservation (TX), 213–214

Toad River Lodge (AK), 144

Toliver House Restaurant (VA), 325

Top of the World Highway (Yukon Rte. 9), 162

Tortilla Factory (TX), 213

Towable RVs, 392–400

Trailer Life, 39

Trailer Life Campground, RV Park and Services Directory, 40

Travel trailers, 396–400

Treasure Island (NV), 84

The Trial of Jack McCall (SD), 172

Triple G Hideaway (BC), 154

Triple R Dude Ranch (SD), 176

Truck campers, 395–396

Tuacahn Amphitheatre (UT), 114

Turkey Run State Park (IN), 279

Turnagain Arm (AK), 161, 164

Turtle Kraals (FL), 304

Turtle River State Park (ND), 195

Turtles, giant (ND), 174

Type A motor homes, 404–406

Type B van campers, 400–401

Type C mini-motor homes, 402–404

United Tribes International Powwow (ND), 180

University of Texas at El Paso, 231

Upheaval Dome (UT), 124

Uprising Adventures (CA), 64

U.S. Army Corps of Engineers, 40

U.S. Forest Service, 41

Utah, 91–133

Utah Shakespearean Festival, 120

UVW (Unloaded Vehicle Weight), 14

Vagabundos del Mar, 33

Valencia Travel Village (CA), 79

Valentine (TX), 206

Val Verde Winery (TX), 207
Van campers, 400–402
Vaqueri Village (TX), 221
Vegas Extreme Skydiving (CA), 64
The Venetian (NV), 84
Vermont Country Store, 351–352
Vernal (UT), 99–100
VF Factory Outlet (TX), 208
Victoria Palms Resort (TX), 221
VillageFest (CA), 74–75
Vintage Surfari Wagons, 413
VIP La Feria RV Park (TX), 221
Virginia, 313–344
Virginia's Museum of American Frontier Culture (VA), 329
VMI Museum (VA), 319
Volunteering as a host, 42

Wahweap Campground (UT), 124
Wall Drug Store (SD), 170, 178
Wall Lake (IA), 249
Walnut Hills KOA Campground (VA), 337
Waltons Mountain Museum (VA), 336–337
Washing your RV, 50
Watchman Campground (UT), 115–116
Water, drinking, 24–25
  in Alaska, 144
Water heater, 25
Waterloo (IA), 256
Waterpocket Fold (UT), 121
Water purifier, 25
Watson Lake (BC), 152
Wauwinet (MA), 359
Waxing your RV, 50–51
Wayne, John, birthplace (IA), 245, 250
Websites, 417
Webster Campground (MA), 375

The Wedding Cake House (ME), 353
Weeping Rocks trail (UT), 114
West Branch (IA), 256
Western Motor Coach, 413
West Liberty KOA (IA), 257
Westmark RV Park, Beaver Creek (YT), 157
West of the Pecos (TX), 228
West of the Pecos Museum (TX), 228
West Rim trail (UT), 114
Whaling Museum (MA), 370
Wheelers RV Resort & Campground Directory, 41
Whistling Wings (IL), 258
Whitehead Memorial Museum (TX), 228
Whitehorse (YT), 156
White Pass and Yukon Route Railroad (AK), 147
Whitetop Mountain Ramp Festival (VA), 322
Whitewater Scandal (IN), 270
Widman's Candy Store (ND), 178
Wildflower Festival (UT), 119
Wildflower viewing, California, 67
Wildlife Loop Road in Custer State Park (SD), 199
Wildlife Prairie State Park (IL), 249
Williams, Tennessee, 300
Willow Flat (UT), 126
Willow Springs International Raceway (CA), 63–64
Wilton Candy Kitchen (IA), 248
Winchester/Frederick County Visitors Center (VA), 330
Wind Cave National Park (SD), 191, 199
Wind Farm Tours (CA), 69, 72
Winnebago Industries (IA), 11, 245, 251

Winter camping, 45–47
Winterset (IA), 250
Wiscasset (ME), 359
Wolfe, Thomas, 336, 339
Wolfe Ranch (UT), 102
Wolf Park (IN), 244–245
Wompatuck State Park (MA), 374
Wood, Grant, 257
Woodall's Campground Directory, 41
Woodbury County Courthouse (IA), 249
Woodhenge (IL), 265
Woodman County Courthouse (IA), 282
Woodmans clam stand (MA), 366
Woodstock (IL), 258
Wounded Knee Massacre site (SD), 184
Wrangell-St. Elias National Park and Preserve (AK), 163
Wyeth, Andrew, 384
Wynn (NV), 84

Yacht Haven Park and Marina (FL), 310
Yermo (CA), 78
Yogi Bear's Jellystone Park Campground Directory, 41
Yukon Rte. 9 (Top of the World Highway), 162
Yukon Territory (Canada), 156
Yuma (CA), 88

Zion Canyon Campground (UT), 116
Zion Canyon Drive (UT), 110
Zion Canyon Giant Screen Theatre (UT), 100
Zion Narrows trail (UT), 114
Zion National Park (UT), 96–97, 108–116
Zzyzx (CA), 77

Photo Credits